# Written at the Pitch of Battle . . .

These selections communicate to the reader the sensibility of the Sixties with a vividness that hindsight inhibits. And in the process of re-experiencing (or experiencing for the first time) . . . medium of these writ- . . . dge how much of the . . . applicable and relevant

. . . ed in the selection and . . . pieces in this anthol-

. . . e what seem to be the . . . Sixties:

The Politicization of Culture
Some New Sensibilities
The Exploding Arts
Messages from the Media

—FROM THE INTRODUCTION

# THE SIXTIES

### EDITED BY
## GERALD HOWARD

# WASHINGTON SQUARE PRESS
#### PUBLISHED BY POCKET BOOKS NEW YORK

A Washington Square Press Publication of
POCKET BOOKS, a Simon & Schuster division of
GULF & WESTERN CORPORATION
1230 Avenue of the Americas, New York, N.Y. 10020

ISBN: 0-671-42389-4

First Washington Square Press printing January, 1982

10 9 8 7 6 5 4 3 2 1

WASHINGTON SQUARE PRESS, WSP and colophon are
trademarks of Simon & Schuster.

Printed in the U.S.A.

# ACKNOWLEDGMENTS

"The New Mood in Politics" by Arthur Schlesinger, Jr. is reprinted from *Esquire*, January 1960. Copyright © 1960 by Arthur Schlesinger, Jr. Reprinted by permission of the author.

"Patriotism" by Paul Goodman is reprinted from *Growing Up Absurd*. Copyright © 1960 by Paul Goodman. Reprinted by permission of Random House, Inc.

"Culture and Politics" by C. Wright Mills is reprinted from *Power, Politics and People: The Collected Essays of C. Wright Mills*, edited by Irving Louis Horowitz. Copyright © 1963 by the Estate of C. Wright Mills. Reprinted by permission of the Oxford University Press, Inc.

"The Conquest of the Unhappy Consciousness: Repressive Desublimation" by Herbert Marcuse is reprinted from *One-Dimensional Man*. Copyright © 1964 by Herbert Marcuse. Reprinted by permission of Beacon Press.

"The Two Nations" by Michael Harrington is reprinted from *The Other America*. Copyright © 1962 by Michael Harrington. Reprinted by permission of Macmillan Publishing Co, Inc.

"The Fire Next Time" by James Baldwin is excerpted from "Down at the Cross: Letter from a Region of My Mind" in the book *The Fire Next Time*. Copyright © 1963 by James Baldwin. Reprinted by permission of The Dial Press.

"Domestic Law and International Order" by Eldridge Cleaver is reprinted from *Soul on Ice*. Copyright © 1968 by Eldridge Cleaver. Reprinted by permission of the McGraw-Hill Book Company.

"Superman Comes to the Supermarket" by Norman Mailer is reprinted from *The Presidential Papers*. Copyright © 1960, 1961, 1962, 1963 by Norman Mailer. Reprinted by permission of G. P. Putnam's Sons.

"The Girl of the Year" by Tom Wolfe is reprinted from *The Kandy-Kolored Tangerine-Flake Streamline Baby*. Copyright © 1964 by the New York Herald Tribune, Inc. Reprinted by permission of Farrar, Straus and Giroux, Inc.

"Apocalypse: The Place of Mystery in the Life of the Mind" by Norman O. Brown is reprinted from *Harper's Magazine*, May 1961. Copyright © 1961 by Norman O. Brown. Reprinted by permission of the author.

"Transcendental Experience" by R. D. Laing is reprinted from *The Politics of Experience*. Copyright © 1967 by R. D. Laing. Reprinted by permission of Penguin Books, Limited, London, England.

With love to my parents, of course, who lived through my living through all this. Many thanks to my friends Peter Kaldheim, Susan Weinstein, Terry Trucco and Harry Trumbore, who shared generously of their minds, their encouragement and their bookshelves. Thanks also to the New York Public Library, without which this project would not have been possible, financially or temporally. And my deepest gratitude to my editor, John Thornton—a teacher, a friend and an editor's editor.

O pleasant exercise of hope and joy!
For mighty were the auxiliars which then stood
Upon our side, us who were strong in love!
Bliss was it in that dawn to be alive,
But to be young was very heaven! O times,
In which the meagre, stale, forbidding ways
Of custom, law, and statute, took at once
The attraction of a country in romance! . . .

•  •  •

Now was it that *both* found, the meek and lofty
Did both find, helpers to their hearts' desire,
And stuff at hand, plastic as they could wish,
Were called upon to exercise their skill,
Not in Utopia—subterranean fields—
Or some secreted island, Heaven knows where!
But in the very world, which is the world
Of all of us—the place where, in the end,
We find our happiness, or not at all!

—WILLIAM WORDSWORTH, from *The Prelude*,
BOOK XI, FRANCE, lines 105–12, 136–44

What am I now that I was then?
May memory restore again and again
The smallest color of the smallest day:
Time is the school in which we learn,
Time is the fire in which we burn.

—DELMORE SCHWARTZ, "For Rhoda"

# Contents

## II.  SOME NEW SENSIBILITIES

## III.  THE EXPLODING ARTS

## IV.  MESSAGES FROM THE MEDIA

## V.   CODA

# Introduction

### Looking Backward:
### The Sixties Seen from the Eighties

I spent ten years living through the Sixties, from ages ten to twenty. I spent the next ten years trying to figure out what happened, what went right and what went wrong. I spent six months editing this anthology, up to my ears in every variety of cultural expression from the Sixties, and retrospective memoirs, studies and histories. Yet I still sometimes find it difficult to gain a secure mental purchase on this incredible episode in American life. I mean this in the literal sense of "not credible." Time and again I have come across passages, images, statements that repel belief, the way the undrawn sections of a lithographic stone repel the printer's ink.

For example, in 1969 Jerry Rubin published a book called *Do It!* ("READ THIS BOOK STONED!" is the advice on the copyright page.) Rubin, along with Abbie Hoffman, was of course one of the Katzenjammer Kids of the revolutionary media theater of the Sixties, responsible for such inspired Yippie/Dada gestures as appearing before the House Committee on Un-American Activities in a Revolutionary War get-up, and temporarily bringing to a halt the activities of the New York Stock Exchange with a shower of money tossed from the visitors' gallery. The experience of reading *Do It!* today is almost archaeological; the book is also, to put it mildly, quotable:

> Puritanism leads us to Vietnam. Sexual insecurity results in a supermasculinity trip called imperialism. American foreign policy, especially in Vietnam, makes no sense except sexually. America has a frustrated penis trying to drive itself in Vietnam's tiny slit to prove it is the man.

• • •

> The Youth International revolution will begin with mass breakdown of authority, mass rebellion, total anarchy in every institution in the Western world. Tribes of longhairs, blacks, armed women, workers, peasants and students will take over. . . . The White House will become one big commune with free food and housing, everything shared. . . . The Pentagon will be replaced by an LSD experimental farm. . . . People will farm in the morning, make music in the afternoon, and fuck wherever and whenever they want to. The United States will become a tiny Yippie island in a vast sea of Yippieland love.

• • •

> Money is shit. Burning money, looting, and shoplifting can get you high.

• • •

> The money economy is immoral, based totally on power and manipulation, offending the natural exchange between human beings: an exchange based on common need. Looting is a natural expression of the money system. Capitalism is stealing. . . . All money represents theft. To steal from the rich is a sacred and religious act.

This last snippet of late-Sixties baroque is given a special edge if you've read Rubin's convincing imitation of Whittaker Chambers on the Op-Ed page of *The New York Times* (July 30, 1980). There, discussing the apparent contradiction of his radical past with his new position as a handsomely paid securities analyst "investigating new companies of the future, including those producing solar and other alternative-energy sources," he tells us that he is still concerned about the common good, "but I know I can be more effective today wearing a suit and tie and working on Wall Street than I can be dancing outside the walls of power." (From *Do It!*: "We found ourselves in front of the stock market at high noon. The strangest creeps you ever saw are walking around us: people with short hair, long ties, business suits, and brief-cases.") What the country needs now, Rubin tells us, is a good dose of entrepreneurial capitalism and individual eco-nomic initiative to get us out of the doldrums, and he just wants to help. (From *Do It!*: "A hip capitalist is a pig capitalist.")

Hanging Rubin with his own inconsistencies and hypocri-sies is effortless sport. Is there any point, then, in devoting mental time and energy to the meaning of Jerry Rubin? I think so, actually.

The first mistake to avoid, though, in beginning to think about *Do It!* and its author is to take them completely seriously. The put-on, after all, was one of the central forms of cultural expression in the Sixties, and Rubin's persona and rhetoric had more to do with Mike Fink or Paul Bunyan and the traditions of American comic braggadocio than with any remotely conceivable political reality.

The second mistake to avoid is not to think at all about *Do It!* and its author and the whole complex of attitudes and developments behind them. Apocalyptic rhetoric and bour-geois baiting were favorite cultural pastimes by the time *Do It!* reached print; Rubin's rantings differed hardly at all from much of the received wisdom of the time. To cite another example more or less selected at random, here is Richard Gilman in *The Confusion of Realms* describing an uproarious evening circa 1968 at a panel discussion on the Living Theatre, entitled "Theater or Therapy," before an audience of New York literary notables:

. . . the heckling suddenly breaks out much more vio-lently. All over the auditorium people leap to their feet hollering or run shouting and gesticulating through the aisles. They are immediately identifiable as members of the Living Theatre, some twenty or twenty-five of them dressed in hippy outfits of various kinds or "colorful" costumes. They keep up their screaming, the import of what they are saying being that the proceedings are foolish. "Go home, go home!" one of them keeps screaming. "Don't listen to this bullshit!" . . . Now the meeting house is a scene of near chaos. The Living Theatre members, scrambling down from the balcony, racing through the aisles, scream imprecations at the audience. "Fuck you, liberals!" one yells over and over, while another grabs a woman's purse, runs in front of the podium and empties the contents of the purse over the auditorium floor. The learned and talented audience is registering shock, dismay, or anger; shouting matches take place everywhere.

This episode actually happened; incredulity is the natural but inadequate response.

Neither will irony suffice. In her review of *Bonnie and Clyde* Pauline Kael observes, "We tend to find the past funny and the recent past campy-funny." Consider the case at hand. In the space of eleven years Rubin's prose has come to sound to our ears like some quaintly weird linguistic artifact, on the order of "Hubba! hubba!" or "Beat me, daddy, eight to the bar." A recent *New Yorker* cartoon shows a neatly groomed woman executive explaining to a colleague about a photograph on her desk: "Oh, that was me on the ashram." Over the past couple of years Abbie Hoffman, Mark Rudd, Bernadine Dohrn and Cathlyn Wilkerson have finally surfaced from the underground—and they seem as strange to us as those Japanese soldiers who would occasionally be flushed from the jungles of Pacific atolls a decade or more after the armistice. In San Francisco a specialty shop sells "butcher-block" tables made from the dance floor of the original Fillmore Auditorium (or "Fillmore West"), for now prosperous ex-hippies presumably a piece of the True Cross for their kitchens.

From one point of view this sort of distancing effect is nothing more than the same mechanism in American popular culture that the makers of *Bonnie and Clyde* exploited so knowingly in handling their Depression-era material. But we also laugh at what makes us uneasy, to take the curse off it. I'd like to suggest that beyond the usual American tendency to turn everything into a joke, behind our present reaction to the Sixties there lies a good deal of ambivalence and unassuaged guilt over the boundless expectations and the crushing failures, a personal sense of loss and responsibility. Also, a certain sadness that either the widely anticipated apocalypse never came or that it came and went, leaving us with lives still to live and moral complexities still to sort out.

What I'm trying to describe is a species of disaffection shared by a generation of now not-so-young Americans, a disaffection more widespread, I suspect, than is immediately apparent. By any yardstick these are cheesy times we live in. But if you happened to grow up in a time when paradise on earth seemed close enough to touch, when identity and society took on an extraordinary and exhilarating fluidity, when our social ills were earnestly believed to be curable with enough money and good will, then real contemporary American life is likely to seem particularly inadequate. If you wore a "Give a Damn" button in the Sixties—and maybe even *did*—or if you are black, headlines like "City's Poor Blacks Say That Their Hopes of the '60s Have Withered" and "Watts, on 15th Anniversary of the Riots, Is a Worse Hovel Than It Was" should make you cringe.

Up to a certain point the waning of the Sixties' influence in American culture almost (it sometimes seems) to the vanishing point makes sense. The drastic turning inward of the Seventies that can be seen in such diverse phenomena as the jogging craze, the therapy boom, nutritional fetishism, disco and est, while hardly a sign of cultural health, can perhaps be explained and partially excused as a natural counterreaction to the body blows administered to the national psyche in the nightmarish years of the late Sixties—a kind of hangover treatment. (Some of these developments, we should also note, have their roots in the experimentation of the Sixties with radical alterations of consciousness and the self.)

This is a familiar cultural dialectic. Malcolm Cowley, in his memoir —*And I Worked at the Writer's Trade,* discusses the processes whereby literary generations succeed one another and proposes a systolic/diastolic or contractive/expansive model. Thus, in American literature the Fifties can be seen as an archetypal systolic period, characterized by the carefully composed dramas of alienation and despair of such writers as Salinger, McCullers and the early Updike and Malamud, and the restrictive emphasis on form of the reigning New Critics. Reacting against this privatization and formalization of literature, the characteristic writers of the diastolic Sixties— Kesey, Mailer, Pynchon, Vonnegut, Barth, Heller, Barthelme and others—achieved dazzling end-runs around the strictures of psychological realism to open up the forms of the novel, short story and memoir. History, fantasy, myth, science, madness and every level of culture from highest mandarin to crassest pop became grist for these writers' sensibilities. In this the writers of the Sixties were acutely attuned to the experimental spirit of the decade.

Cowley does not take his analysis much past the Sixties, but, extending his categories, we can clearly see the Seventies as the systolic or contractive period we would expect. As we enter the Eighties, are we now at the start of another diastolic period? And if so, how will the products of the cultural revolution of the Sixties, who in so many ways had the whip hand earlier than any generation within memory, and who are now just beginning to enter positions of genuine power and influence, shape and respond to it?

The expected return outward of our cultural focus does indeed appear to be taking place—but with a decidedly nasty edge to it. Americans *have* taken fresh and panicky notice of the realities surrounding them, particularly economic realities. Inflation, recession, the energy crisis and the deterioration of our competitive edge over international rivals have rudely shaken our complacent expectation of endless prosperity. Clearly the quest for inner peace needs to be tabled for the more urgent business of taking care of business.

The last time our economic situation looked this glum, in the Depression, adversity acted as a kind of social glue, a spur to sharing and sacrifice. Now, however, the sudden shrinking of the economic pie has given everyone, it seems, the go-ahead to turn ruthlessly territorial about his slice. We can see this all too clearly in the crazy-quilt of single-issue and special-interest groups that influence our politics, in real estate fever and in the domination of the nonfiction bestseller lists by titles on getting and spending. The current totemization of the free market and the vilification of "big government" by a wide spectrum of conservatives from neo- to Neanderthal (complete with a decorative set of curves "proving" that tax cuts needn't result in cutbacks of government services) is really a species of callous individualism. A sense of compassion and cohesive community is conspicuously absent from our public life.

This unedifying spectacle is mirrored in the private and personal realms. Careerism is rampant in American education; liberal arts courses go begging for enrollments if they don't "pay off" in jobs or higher salaries, while business, law and medicine are experiencing a glut. This same kind of calculation obtains after graduation, as each new crop of M.B.A.'s vocally declares its intention to keep careers and incomes on a rigidly defined schedule. Office politicking is widely prescribed as a necessary job skill. (This whole ethos is defined for me in an obnoxious advertisement for Sperry Topsiders: "Could you imagine climbing to the top of the corporate ladder faking it?" We now locate our authenticity in our deck shoes.)

Where, in the midst of all these dispiriting developments, is the voice of the generation once hailed on the front pages of the newsmagazines as "the most idealistic in history"? The generation that took Norman O. Brown as one of its heroes and his *Life Against Death* as a sacred text, and thus know, from reading the "Filthy Lucre" section, the unsavory scatological psychology of money grubbing? In that *annus mirabilis* 1968, William Burroughs wrote in *Esquire* from the Democratic Convention in Chicago, "The youth rebellion is a worldwide phenomenon that has not been seen before in history. I do not believe they will calm down and be ad execs at thirty as the Establishment would like us to believe." The echo of these words, and a good many words of their own, must haunt the minds of many of my contemporaries as they in fact settle into an uneasy or wholehearted truce with safe, straight life. (Who among us, as we turn thirty, does not blush inwardly as we remember the famous dictum about our untrustworthiness?)

This is certainly not leading up to an exhortation to break out the love beads and tie-dyed T-shirts for a rerun of Woodstock, or the gas masks for another March on the Pentagon. My hope is to make it possible to think about the Sixties seriously, without recourse to nostalgia. But there are ironies in the current counterreaction against the politics and culture of the Sixties, their disavowal by many of the same people who created, embodied and lived them, that need serious exploration.

Sometimes one wonders whether we aren't witnessing, in a milder form, a replay of the mass recantation in the Fifties of the American radicals of the Thirties and Forties in the wake of Stalinism and the Cold War. In many ways Norman Podhoretz's political memoir of the ideological "terror" (his phrase) of the Sixties, *Breaking Ranks,* reads like a contemporary version of *The God That Failed*—the "God" in this

case being the radical humanism whose voice first sounded
strongly in the magazine *Commentary* that Podhoretz edits.
Jerry Rubin's apostasy and his embrace of capitalism have
already been noted. And here is Susan Sontag, arch aestheti-
cian of the Sixties sensibility and uncompromising scourge of
America's violent, genocidal tendencies, speaking today:

> While the justice of the protests [against the war] were
> undeniable, there were also illusions and misconceptions
> about what was possible in the rest of the world. It was
> not so clear to many of us as we talked of American
> imperialism how few options many of these countries
> had except for Soviet imperialism, which was maybe
> worse. When I was in Cuba and North Vietnam, it was
> not clear to me that they would become Soviet satellites,
> but history has been very cruel and the options available
> to those countries were fewer than we had hoped. It's
> become a lot more complicated. (*The New York Times*,
> Nov. 11, 1980)

Norman Mailer, the protean, Faustian, emblematic figure
of the Sixties, who taught so many of the Sixties generation
the rewards and pitfalls of pushing oneself to the edge of
every experience, wrote something in the winter of 1951–52 in
the famous *Partisan Review* symposium, "Our Country and
Our Culture," that seems very germane. Standing aside from
the rush of leftish intellectuals in a hurry to reconcile
themselves with postwar America, Mailer declared sardoni-
cally, "This period smacks of healthy manifestoes. Everywhere the American writer is being dunned to become
healthy, to grow up, to accept the American reality, to
integrate himself, to eschew disease, to revalue institutions. Is
there nothing to remind us that the writer does not need to be
integrated into his society, and often works best in opposition
to it? I would propose that the artist feels most alienated
when he loses his sharp sense of what he is alienated from."
The Eighties are not the Fifties; few of the people reading this
are likely to be artists; but at a time when "adjustment" to the
rules of the manipulative American ethos seems so universal
and either transparently cynical or resigned, the alienation
Mailer prescribes—the alienation so spectacularly vindicated

by Mailer himself through his splendid achievements in the decade that was to come—sounds very good for our spiritual health.

## Did the Sixties Really Happen? Notes Toward an Answer

The preceding pages set forth and explore some of the questions that I had as I began to put together this anthology. With certain exceptions—I discuss three very important ones in the last part of this introduction—I was not satisfied with the way the Sixties had been treated in either fiction, drama or nonfiction. Some writers took easy advantage of the built-in and by now tired symbolism and imagery of the decade—moon shots, assassinations, be-ins, protests, rock concerts, etc.—in the process lending a prefab cast to works of the imagination. Others took the decade so personally that any sense of its larger progress was lost in the welter of bewildering transformations ("changes," remember?) so many people experienced. I felt that an anthology of selections from the decade itself, carefully chosen and thematically arranged, would be one way of avoiding these pitfalls. The selections, written at the pitch of battle, would communicate to the reader the sensibility of the Sixties with a vividness that hindsight inhibits. And in the process of re-experiencing (or, for some, experiencing for the first time) the Sixties through the medium of these writings, the reader could at the same time judge for himself how much of the Sixties seem valuable, applicable and relevant to the current state of affairs.

This is what I have tried to accomplish in my selection and organization of the pieces in this anthology. In almost all cases the pieces were written during the Sixties by Americans, exceptions being the selections by Tomkins, Dickstein, Berman, Lois and Vassi, which were written in the Seventies, and the piece by Laing, an Englishman. My preference has been for forceful pieces that were widely read at the time of their publication and whose influence radiated outward, in many cases, with electrifying force—the selections by Wolfe, Goodman, Baldwin, McLuhan, Brown and Sontag, for example—over more sedate and interpretive writing. I also exercised a preference for elegant or powerful writing over the strident or sloppy, which preference accounts for the absence of some of the more extreme statements of the time and the relative maturity (during the Sixties) of the roster of contributors.

In organizing the selections into the four thematic sections and placing them within those sections, I have tried to construct, albeit in a rough way, an intellectual history of the decade. The four sections isolate what seem to me to be the dominant themes of the Sixties: "The Politicization of Culture" explores the extraordinary activism of the Sixties, so much of it adversary in nature, and the politicization of spheres of experience not usually associated with politics; "Some New Sensibilities" presents statements characteristic of the utopian, millenarian and apocalyptic passions that animated so much of the culture of the decade, the eager transvaluation of all values; "The Exploding Arts" shows how similar energizing forces animated a period of amazing creativity and experimental breakthroughs in literature and the various arts, and how the realms of high and popular culture entered a period of cross-fertilization; and "Messages from the Media" highlights aspects of a conundrum that first struck with particular force in the Sixties: the question of how much reality survives the *images* of reality we are bombarded with, and how that bombardment alters our ways of apprehending the world. Within each section I have arranged the pieces in a compromise between the thematic and chronological, the aim being to give a coherent sense of the decade's progress; each section is constructed as a sort of mini-history of that particular area of cultural endeavor in the Sixties.

There are a number of caveats and apologies I would like to register in advance about the editing of this book. In the first place, the organizational scheme inevitably has an arbitrary element to it, especially when applied to a period like the Sixties, one of whose hallmarks was, in Richard Gilman's phrase, "the confusion of realms." The categories in this book leak, as they did in real life, which is one of the reasons, in fact, that the Sixties make such a fascinating subject for study: The connections emerge in the most unlikely places.

I am also acutely aware of how much of the Sixties is *not* represented in the pages that follow. This anthology could be double its present size without undue redundancy. Because of limitations of space and economics, however, my final editorial principle has been to include not what I would simply like to have in the book, but what I feel I cannot leave out. I particularly regret that for reasons of space I was unable to include certain pieces which could have amplified a theme, offered thoughtful dissents or expanded a perspective. The portrait of the Sixties presented here is slightly less rounded and three-dimensional than I might have wished. Any collection of this sort is a compromise between the encyclopedic and the practical; I apologize here to whoever may feel miffed at the absence of a movement, intellectual issue, artwork or whatever from these pages.

Related to this principle is my stress on statements from the left and the cultural vanguard. I don't mean to suggest that the critical, the radical, the revolutionary and the avant-garde were the only modes of expression. But they *were* the most characteristic of their time, and it is the characteristic, the indigenous, that I wanted to concentrate on. Expressed within these selections are the animating ideas of the decade, placed in such a way, I hope, as to yield a kind of intellectual mosaic.

It was ideas, above all, that I wanted to isolate. This anthology does not have any documentary intention as such. Events such as the King and Kennedy assassinations, for instance, or the 1968 Chicago Democratic convention receive only glancing mention in the course of this book. But the shattering impact of these events reverberates, nevertheless, through many of the pieces. Each piece in this book was selected, ultimately, to shed light on an aspect of that most elusive quality, the sensibility of an age of astounding vitality and energy.

Finally, the opinions of the contributors to this anthology do not necessarily reflect the opinions of the editor. But a good many of them do. This book grew out of an urgent, almost obsessional curiosity about the Sixties, and a related distaste for the present state of affairs. Where did all this hope, energy, idealism, optimism and invention come from? Why have so many of the promises of the Sixties gone unfulfilled? So soured us, in fact, as to spawn the noxious reaction I've tried to describe? These are questions worthy of obsession.

In January 1960 Arthur Schlesinger, Jr., could write with astonishing prescience in "The New Mood in Politics": "Thus, the Sixties will probably be spirited, articulate, inventive, incoherent, turbulent, with energy shooting off wildly in all directions. Above all, there will be a sense of motion, of leadership, and of hope." But by 1976 Joan Didion, with her unerring sense of spiritual vacancy and drift, could write, "This sense that the world can be reinvented smells of the Sixties in this country, those years when no one at all seemed to have any memory or mooring." These two radically divergent perspectives combine imperfectly in most of us to form a fractured, Cubist image of the Sixties. This anthology has been assembled to help place the Sixties in a more balanced perspective.

What will the reader find, then, in the pages that follow? To start with, this chorus of voices from the Sixties amounts, I think, to a clarion call to the strenuous life. Hindsight has made the considerable achievements of the Sixties in the way of political reform, personal transfiguration and artistic breakthrough seem somehow easy or inevitable. They were neither. Many of these pieces, especially from the earlier part of the decade, have a palpable quality of courage and daring, contain or are in search of, in Mailer's phrase, "the ineluctable ore of the authentic" that was for the Sixties a kind of Holy Grail. To encounter Paul Goodman on society, James Baldwin on race relations, Norman Mailer on Kennedy, George Dennison on libertarian education, Norman O. Brown on scholarship, R. D. Laing on madness, Michael Harrington on our invisible poor, Susan Sontag on the new aesthetics, Herbert Marcuse on the mechanisms of repression or Pauline Kael on the commercial film was to subject one's received ideas to the most explosive reexamination. These and many other insights, breakthroughs and revolutions in consciousness were achieved by daring and passionate application of intelligence and will, and they seemed to demand a response in kind from their readers.

This kind of willingness to experiment, rethink, reimagine, redefine and rebel is one of the deepest and certainly the most inspiring tendencies of American culture. We have always, at least until recently, felt that we owned and lived in the future. In this sense the widespread attempt in the Sixties to throw off the dead hand of the past was quintessentially in the American grain. Here Goodman's *Growing Up Absurd* is as relevant to the American dilemma in 1982 as it was in 1960. In his introduction to that book, Goodman decried the strange passivity of the population in the face of the urgent and universally acknowledged need for change, wondering whether "people are so bemused by the way that business and politics are carried on at present, with all their intricate relationships, that they have ceased to be able to imagine alternatives. We seem to have lost our genius for inventing changes to satisfy crying needs." As so many of the pieces in this book demonstrate, the Sixties was in fact *the* decade of "imagined alternatives." Some were salutary, some were effective, some were misguided, some were silly or overblown. But that so many *were* imagined in such a short space of time is cause for wonder and reflection.

It remains to be pointed out how naive and exploitable much of this revolutionary fervor was. Certainly the *least* inspiring tendency of American culture is its ability to make anything and everything turn a buck. There was enough fraudulence, ego-tripping and cold commercial calculation underlying much of the self-righteous rhetoric of the Sixties to give us pause. Norman Podhoretz can now write shrilly, but not without justification, of the hypocritical aspects of the Sixties:

> I doubt if this kind of hypocrisy had ever before reached the brazen and comical heights it did in the sixties, when a whole new breed of hustlers (rock stars, publishing tycoons, drug dealers, and other enterprising entrepreneurs) amassed huge fortunes by preaching against "the rat race," "materialism," "consumerism," and "middle-class values" in general, while providing entertainment and other services to a new mass market defined precisely by its repudiation of such values, but still prosperous enough, thanks to parental allowances and grandparental trust funds, to enrich those catering to its particular tastes. *(Breaking Ranks)*

That's one way of looking at it. Who could deny, for example, that there is a great satirical novel to be written about Hollywood's discovery of the youth market in the late Sixties and the subsequent greening of Beverly Hills? Certain of the pieces in this book—Tom Wolfe's "Girl of the Year," Warren Hinckle's "A Social History of the Hippies," Marco Vassi's "Relaxation, Awareness, and Breathing" and Leslie Epstein's "Walking Wounded, Living Dead"—touch on or suggest the moral smugness and self-aggrandizement that Podhoretz rails against.

But there is a larger, more interesting and more crucial question here that Podhoretz misses. What really happens when a whole culture goes avant-garde, or tries to? Can such subterranean, intensely in-group cultural revolutions as the psychedelic experiments of Ken Kesey and the Merry Pranksters or the new frontiers of boredom and perversity explored by Andy Warhol and his gang of merry deviates survive with anything like their original integrity of vision and their intensity intact when millions take them up?

Obviously not. But what do you get instead? A terrifically confused, interesting and anxious culture. Alan Kaprow, the chief theoretician of "Happenings," astutely analyzed them as the artists' last ditch attempt to outwit and keep ahead of an art public desperately eager to absorb every new advance. This anxiety to stay ever abreast of the avant-garde and the hip became epidemic in the Sixties and resulted in a dizzying succession of new styles, sounds, fashions and attitudes. "Now" was never more "now" than then. The flip side of the ineluctable ore of the authentic was the inexpressible aura of the ephemeral.

Fueled by an economic boom and a postwar demographic bulge of the under-thirty population—the major consumers and creators of our cultural styles—the Sixties produced more and better ephemera than ever before. Do you remember . . . the twist, the hully gully, the mashed potato, James Bond movies, mini-skirts, protest songs, Pop Art, Op Art, be-ins, underground movies, the British Invasion, Laugh-In, put-ons, Screaming Yellow Zonkers, the Mersey Beat, sick comics, Jean Shrimpton, surf music, folk rock, Motown, "The Man from U.N.C.L.E.," the Rat Pack, mods, rockers, Murray the K and submarine-race watching, the Smothers Brothers, "Telstar" (the song), "The Twilight Zone," "The Untouchables," Carole Doda, the topless bathing suit, Swinging London, Volkswagen ads, the Crystals, the Ronettes, Little Eva, Phil Spector and his "wall of sound" and so on and so on and so on.

Tom Wolfe, the bardic poet of all this great new stuff, invented a brand-new kind of prose to celebrate it, featuring breathless apostrophes full of creative punctuation and peculiar pet words and phrases ("Santa Barranza!" "great smokin' blue gumballs god almighty dog," "creeps and kooks and nutballs with dermatitic skin and ratty hair and corroded thoracic boxes," "flaming little buds"), punctuated by mock-

serious sociological analyses of the form of disorientation at
hand. Why did Americans go nuts in this way? Wolfe traced
the existence of such diverse phenomena as Las Vegas
architecture, stock-car racing, custom cars, "Girl of the Year"
Baby Jane Holzer and "the first Tycoon of Teen" Phil Spector
to the profusion of money and leisure time now enjoyed by
such groups as teenagers and "lumpen proles," who could
now afford to indulge their tastes. And all of a sudden it *was*
the lower orders who were creating the new styles and setting
the fashion, society and art worlds on their heads—a new
democracy of culture. The Scene was born, a zappy new kind
of bohemia. The distinctions between high and low culture,
the *haute monde* and the *hoi polloi,* became impossibly
blurred, to everybody's evident delight.

Especially blurred were the distinctions between fine art
and popular art, and between art and life itself. Some of the
ephemera delighted simply because it *was* ephemera. I can't
resist quoting this Proustian remembrance of the summer of
1963 from Andy Warhol's eidetic memory:

> The girls that summer in Brooklyn looked really great. It
> was the summer of the Liz-Taylor-in-Cleopatra look—
> long, straight, dark, shiny hair with bangs and Egyptian-
> looking eye makeup. . . . This was the summer before
> the Motown sound got really big and it was also the last
> summer before the English Invasion. The show at the
> Fox had the Ronettes, the Shangri-Las, the Kinks, and
> Little Stevie Wonder. . . . It was a great summer. The
> folk-singer look was in—the young girls with the bangs
> were wearing shifts and sandals and burlapy things; but
> looking back I can see that maybe by way of the
> Cleopatra look, folk evolved into something slick and
> fashionable that would eventually become the geometric
> look. *(POPism)*

This is a fair sample of the time-machine quality of
Warhol's Sixties memoir and the kind of pleasure a complete
concentration on surfaces can give. ("It is only the shallow
people who do not judge by appearances."—Oscar Wilde, as
quoted by Susan Sontag in the epigraph to her essay "Against
Interpretation.") The lure of the surface, the temporary, the
throwaway was the essence of the Pop Art created by Warhol,
James Rosenquist, Claes Oldenburg, Jim Dine, Tom Wessel-

mann and others—they transformed the ephemeral into art. Sometimes art *aspired* to be ephemeral, as with "happenings." Sometimes erstwhile ephemera became so wonderful that it turned into a new kind of populist art—the music of the Beatles, the Doors, Bob Dylan, Aretha Franklin, Otis Redding and vintage Motown groups being the most obvious examples.

"Is it art?" is a subtextual question underlying a great deal of Sixties culture, but, in the wake of the mass merchandising of hip, only the hopelessly straight were so gauche as to ask it out loud. In as fluid a situation as this, avoiding a fixed position and "going with the flow" was the best strategy. The real difficulty in the Sixties was getting a straight answer—and not just from the artists. Were we being lied to about the Vietnam war all along? Was the Warren Commission a snow job? Was there really such a thing as the "new Nixon"? Was media oracle Marshall McLuhan for real? Serious? *Right?*

So questions of sincerity and authenticity arose in the realm of art and communications as well as in the personal and the political. What threads connected the put-on and the pragmatic, cool, knowing, antisentimental attitude that *Esquire* dubbed "The New Sentimentality" to the widespread urge to touch existential and spiritual bottom? The coolly ironic mood characteristic of so much of Sixties art seems to contradict the heated idealism, political activism and self-exploration so equally characteristic of the Sixties. Jacob Brackman, in an article entitled "My Generation" (*Esquire*, October 1968), suggested that the mockery and japes hid a deeper core of authentic hurt: "Our disappointment ran so deep we goofed all over them" (i.e., the media men and their anxious inquiries as to Youth's feelings about assassinations, sex, drugs, Nehru jackets, revolution, Eugene McCarthy). Mocking the doomed glamor and romanticism of F. Scott Fitzgerald's generation of flaming youth, Brackman adopted the wounded but tough voice of the prematurely experienced: "We are setting off where you broke down, Fitzboomski; a sensibility delicate as tears, you took too long to realize how lost you were. We arrive precociously at consciousness, with nothing to live up to." The put-ons, the Bogart toughness, the pervasive irony were the masks, then, to camouflage desperation.

In this, as in so many other ways, the Sixties was a cultural funhouse, a mirror maze. In Marcuse's terminology, apparent freedoms were proffered in place of *real* ones. The confusions between the authentic and the ephemeral, the genuinely revolutionary and the merely self-indulgent, the hard-won insight and the borrowed attitude, *were* shrewdly exploited for profit. More than any other single factor I think this accounts for the cultural implosion of the Seventies. The young in particular were fed, and eagerly consumed, inflated fantasies of instant political and cultural transformation. Their subsequent rude encounters with reality in the form of the endless Vietnam war, economic recession, the Nixon administration, the intransigence of racial discrimination and poverty and the existence of evil and disorder in the very heart of the counterculture were therefore many times multiplied in their shattering effect. It was the reality principle that perhaps suffered the greatest subversion of all in the Sixties.

The Sixties, finally, do not seem susceptible to any kind of neat summary; such confusions and contradictions as I've mentioned could be multiplied. But a metaphor may help where capsulization fails: the Sixties as a cultural chain reaction that got out of control.

In nuclear physics the energy given off by an atomic pile depends on the statistical frequency of the collisions of stable atoms with particles from unstable ones. The higher the rate of collision, the more energy given off, which rate in turn depends on the mass and density of the radioactive material. The amount of radioactive material needed to create a self-sustaining chain reaction is known as the critical mass. Atomic-energy plants utilize carefully controlled chain reactions in their cores; nuclear explosions, in contrast, are chain reactions gone wild, liberating unthinkable amounts of energy in a split second.

A dynamic culture works, in many ways, like a chain reaction. It maintains a critical (but balanced) cultural mass in which the constant collisions sustain a steady release of energy. The Sixties, however, were a time when an extraordinary number of cultural forces collided, loosening bonds and setting off fresh collisions in their wake, and this liberated energy coursed throughout our society. The country was riding the crest of economic expansion unprecedented in history. The largest number and percentage of young people ever were struggling to maturity, lending an adolescent excitement and confusion to the culture at large. A system of mass communication of unheard-of extent and efficiency was at last in place, creating a kind of tribal simultaneity in the way a huge population could communicate with itself. Allied with this was a massive new marketing apparatus exquisitely synchronized with shifts in the national psyche.

And that psyche underwent increasingly accelerated changes. The paradoxes and limits and dangers underlying the postwar Pax Americana were becoming disturbingly manifest. The heroic Black civil rights revolt galvanized the American conscience and served as a model for new means of political action. A new president was elected who seemed preternaturally attuned to the spirit of the times—young, energetic, charismatic, media-handsome. Mass education and communication had conquered various forms of repression and provincialism in the country, and America felt itself as powerful and autonomous culturally as it was militarily and economically. The struggle for mere sustenance won, a kind of ontological hunger seized the nation. Rock 'n' roll, a raw and powerful new form of music, crystallized all the youthfulness, dynamism and hypersexuality on the loose—the Pied Piper's tune of the new freedoms.

These and dozens of other developments, discoveries and trends converged in a period of amazing cultural density. At the beginning of the decade these collisions yielded many healthy syntheses—the Peace Corps, for instance, which allied our international anxieties with our innate idealism. But too much happened too quickly. As these collisions multiplied and accelerated, the syntheses began to be outnumbered by the confused mismatings: drugs with rock music with radical politics, for example. The energies liberated became anarchic, formless and destructive. The classic definition of fanaticism—redoubling one's efforts when one's aim is lost—fits this feverish activity. Developments throughout the culture reinforced each other almost randomly until a pitch of entropic frenzy was reached. An implosion was inevitable. To use a related metaphor from astrophysics, dying stars reach their peak of brilliance as novas immediately before they collapse into dead dwarf stars.

What we were left with, then, was a large number of unfinished revolutions. In *Growing Up Absurd* Goodman speaks with frightening cogency of the costs of the missed and compromised revolutions of modern times in the areas of economics, politics, education, childrearing, popular culture and others. The promise of the Sixties was that the culmination of those revolutions was at last within reach. And because of our keen sense that this was so, the failure of this promise has left us confused, resentful and disarmed before the worst forces in American life, unable to imagine or forcefully present real alternatives.

Because the need for those alternatives is no less urgent in 1980 than it was in 1960, coming to terms with the Sixties, with our past and our former selves, is a crucial piece of cultural business. Also, in all likelihood, as they recede in time the Sixties will ultimately be studied as one of the handful of archetypal moments in cultural history—the American Twenties, the postwar Weimar period in Germany, Vienna at the turn of the century being others—when the modern world revealed and realized its true inner logic and illogic. There are three writers in particular who I believe have anticipated the avenues of inquiry most useful to these tasks. I'd like to devote the rest of this introduction to synopses of their points of view.

### Taking the Sixties Seriously: Three Exemplary Approaches

The three works that I have found most suggestive in their conceptualizing of the Sixties, and most successful in redeeming them for serious consideration, are Morris Dickstein's *Gates of Eden: American Culture in the Sixties,* Harris Wofford's *Of Kennedys and Kings: Making Sense of the Sixties* and Marshall Berman's long essay in the January 1974 *American Review,* "Sympathy for the Devil: Faust, the '60s, and the Tragedy of Development." These works intersect with each other in various ways that I will point out. But what I find most interesting is that their authors each came to the Sixties with their sensibilities already well formed in the Fifties and thus experienced the Sixties with a fresh astonishment, intensity and delight, which those who started out in the Sixties and could take them for granted may not have had. Knowing who they were, Dickstein, Wofford and Berman took greater pleasure in the liberating process of discovering what they, their country and their culture could become. With their finely tuned moral sensibilities from the Fifties, they combine acute and sometimes contradictory senses of losses and gains, connections and disconnections, in revealing ways.

Morris Dickstein's *Gates of Eden* is, as far as I know, the first full-dress critical study of American culture in the Sixties to reach print. (His discussion of black humor in the Sixties begins on p. 272.) A literary critic educated at Columbia, Yale and Oxford whose deepest intellectual debt is to his teacher and mentor, Lionel Trilling, Dickstein focuses on, in Trilling's phrase, "the bloody crossroads" where literature and politics meet—in the Sixties a crowded intersection indeed. Dickstein shows in fascinating detail just how broad the continuum was between cultural and political expression in the Sixties, and how behind them both lay the animating force of those millenarian passions that recur again and again in American history. As he writes, "The sixties gave impetus to both revolution and reform, and tried to combine the quest for social justice with the search for personal authenticity. The civil rights movement and the 'human potential' movement were agreed on one thing: man's right to happiness in the here-and-now."

"Only connect" was E. M. Forster's prescribed remedy for alienation and atomization; in the Sixties that Dickstein re-creates for us, the impulse to connect *everything*—sometimes in counterproductive ways—becomes manifest. His critical method is appealingly congruent with his message, mixing as it does critical discussions of texts with political commentaries with personal reminiscences with cultural history. He shows, for instance, that the radical innovations in literary form and feeling carried on by writers as diverse as Barthelme, Pynchon, Vonnegut, Roth, Reed and Heller emerged from the pressure of these writers' individual visions—the same pressures that caused in other venues radical innovations in politics, the visual arts and sexual and social arrangements. He re-creates with particular poignance for this reader how on a radicalized campus like Columbia's the political excitement and urgency could electrify the classroom in unexpected ways. Of teaching a Great Books seminar at Columbia circa 1967, he writes, "There was something phantasmagorical about studying Thucydides during the Vietnam war. His account of the moral and military decline of Athens and especially the doomed Sicilian expedition had just the exemplary meaning he intended; the parallel to America's overseas adventure was overwhelming and inescapable." He ranges far outside the usual province of the literary critic to discuss with complete seriousness the musical careers of Dylan, the Beatles, the Rolling Stones and other artists, making surprisingly fruitful perceptual leaps. ("Dylan went electric at almost the very moment that Lyndon Johnson began bombing North Vietnam and escalating the war in the South. The increasing violence and intensity of Dylan's work mirrored the expanding violence in the country.")

The ability to see a culture whole, to perceive the inescapable connections between forms of expression and broad cultural forces, is essential to understanding it. Dickstein gives us a culture animated in its every part with an acceleration toward the Blakean "Gates of Eden."

Harris Wofford's fine and haunting book *Of Kennedys and Kings* mixes fascinating historical detail with seasoned reflection to give us a fresh view of three central political figures of the Sixties: John F. Kennedy, Robert F. Kennedy and Martin Luther King, Jr. A close associate of King's from the mid-Fifties until his assassination, the civil rights coordinator on the Kennedy presidential campaign staff, then his Special Assistant for Civil Rights, and later the Associate Director of the Peace Corps, Wofford enjoyed an extraordinary view of the most inspiriting and the most horrifying developments of the decade. A public man through and through, Wofford succeeds in recovering for us "'the public happiness' (as John Adams puts it)" of the early Sixties, "an era of unprecedented convergence of popular initiative and public power [that] saw a surge in the spirit of national service, with people in surprising numbers really interested in what they could do for their country." Wofford avoids both the breathless tones of Camelot-worship and the cynicism of latter-day disillusionment. In his insider's account of the heady atmosphere of the Kennedy years, the heroism and moral courage and successes of the King-led civil rights movement, the romantic idealism and sheer political creativity that attended the creation of the Peace Corps and the mobilization of the resources of the federal government against poverty and racial injustice in the first years of the Johnson administration, Wofford's evocation of "public happiness" rings true. This is an invaluable gift of restoration in our present political disarray.

And a crucial one. As Wofford writes, "Making sense of

the sixties is important unfinished business because the widespread misreading of that curious and critical decade is one of the reasons it is so hard for anyone . . . to succeed as President." Against the vigor of these initiatives Wofford juxtaposes the darker, ambiguous, seamy and tragic aspects of the Kennedy and Johnson years: the vicious campaign of spying and subversion the FBI waged against King; the preference for what was perceived as the pragmatic over the moral in the Kennedy administration, and the disastrous faith placed in the efficacy of the military and intelligence; the sinister web of assassination plots woven by the CIA against Castro, some involving the Mafia, and the hideous possibility that they may have resulted in the President's assassination; and of course Johnson's obsession with our Vietnam adventure, so fatal to his domestic program.

The disjuncture of these two realms suggests a tragic flaw of arrogance in the high purpose of Sixties politics, and Wofford adopts the language of Greek epic, comedy and tragedy in discussing his principals. He sees King and John and Robert Kennedy as both comic and tragic heroes: great men, but also greatly flawed. King, for instance, was referred to ironically by many of his younger associates as "De Lawd" for his messiah complex, while John Kennedy's pride and worldliness were surely too extensive for his, and the country's, good. He describes the moral growth of Robert Kennedy in the wake of his brother's murder; his brooding and his transformation from a somewhat callow hardnose; his study of the Greeks and his anguished impromptu address to black citizens in Indianapolis on the night of King's death in which he quoted "my favorite poet, Aeschylus" verbatim; and Stewart Udall's ominous feeling in the wake of RFK's decision to run for the presidency "that it was like a Greek tragedy in the sense that events themselves had been determined by fates setting the stage, and that there was really little choice left." In JFK's character Wofford discerns the same tension that Stringfellow Barr ascribes to the Greeks in *The Will of Zeus*—a book Wofford gave to Kennedy— between Achilles' leonine courage, which yet proved inadequate to the problems of the Greeks, and Odysseus' wise, crafty problem solving; in a covering note Wofford wrote that the book made him think of Kennedy's task of "moving America toward the spirit of Odysseus."

Tragedy, comedy and epic are literature's most profound

ways of giving form and meaning to the otherwise meaning-less facts of time, hope, human enterprise, disaster and folly. Wofford is largely successful in redeeming our own recent experience for the dignity of these categories.

Finally, Marshall Berman's astonishing essay "Sympathy for the Devil" (the last section of this piece has been chosen as the "Coda" for this book; see p. 495) combines Dickstein's pan-cultural scope of reference with Wofford's vocabulary of tragedy to achieve what is the most satisfying meditation on the Sixties I have read. In it Berman succeeds in the unlikely and considerable feat of reading Goethe's *Faust* as a symbolic text for the tragic overreaching of the Sixties, our whole culture's flirtation with the darker powers of this earth.

Berman first introduces himself as he was the day before the 1967 March on the Pentagon, the high-water mark of the Sixties—a newly minted young college professor, a Fifties person at heart but "wonderfully drunk on the spirit of the times," with his wide, bright red tie, newly long hair, in the throes of personal transformation. In a chance encounter an old professor (not named, but recognizably Lionel Trilling) gently chides Berman for his "Exorcise the Pentagon" button, asking whether he hasn't abdicated his intellectual responsi-bility for the politics of superstition. Berman parries the charge with a reference to Goethe's Faust, who entraps Mephistopheles in a pentagram, and characterizes the coming march as a thoroughly Faustian, hence humanist, enterprise. Still, the encounter unlocks Berman's ambivalences toward "the flying leaps of faith" he saw his students taking into esoteric religiosity, and about wearing "a button that pro-claimed the politics of demonology and sorcery." He soothes his uneasiness, though, with the thought that only by appro-priating the language and sensibility of belief could the protestors confront the vastly evil reality of the Pentagon, the darkest side of their own country.

However, the themes of diabolic power and Faustian ambition multiply the next day in Washington as Berman, confronted by the huge Pentagon building, realizes that the powers commanded by *its* inhabitants make them no less Faustian than the demonstrators chanting the exorcism ritual outside. To the chanters the rite takes on something "irresisti-bly real," and as night falls they come to feel that the demonstration, so far joyful and hopeful, has instead turned into a phantasmagorical trip to the underworld. The symbol had turned into the reality, and the protestors were to find out how feeble their magic was in the face of demonic forces, much the same knowledge Faust himself gains when he has a brief, fearful encounter with the dread Earth Spirit. Along with Norman Mailer in *The Armies of the Night,* Berman sees the March on the Pentagon as pivotal and emblematic: "Our day and night at the Pentagon, like Faust's encounter with the Earth Spirit, marked a deepening of thought and desire, a new awareness of ominous, fearful powers that had to be dealt with before our dreams of freedom and self-fulfillment could be made real."

This loss of innocence, this darkening cast of the late Sixties, found its archetypal expression in the Rolling Stones' demonic song "Sympathy for the Devil." Mick Jagger, assuming the persona of Lucifer, mocks his listeners as the spirit of disorder presiding over the disasters of history: the crucifixion, the French and Russian revolutions, the Nazi blitzkrieg, the Kennedy assassinations. Over and over Jagger arrogantly demands "What's my name?"; by 1968, Berman writes, the young, the radical, the committed were very well able to recognize Lucifer and, no longer innocent of their own dark places, to extend him their sympathy. (I am playing the song while I write this; I must have heard it thousands of times, but still the hairs bristle at the back of my neck.) This was the song the Stones were playing at the disastrous Altamont concert in 1969 when a black man waving a gun was murdered by the Hell's Angels; Jagger, for once shaken by the violent disorder he mimes and teases and draws from his audience, asked from the stage, "Why is there always trouble when we sing this song?"

More trouble followed. The subsequent nightmarish cultural descent into the maelstrom in the late Sixties and early Seventies was marked by such hideous events as the Manson murders, the rampages of the fanatic Weatherpeople, the fatal explosion of a radical bomb factory in Greenwich Village, the shootings at Kent State and Jackson State, the deaths of rock stars Jimi Hendrix, Janis Joplin and Jim Morrison. The Sixties ended finally with many people dead, many more wasted, and everybody badly shaken. Berman writes, "If . . . life in the '60s was a collective journey to the underworld, it is terrifying to notice how many of us have failed to come back. And even those of us who have made it back find ourselves too shaky, too precarious to think about any new voyages for a while."

From this brilliant statement of the theme of the demonic in the Sixties, Berman launches into extended analysis of Goethe's Faust as "the patron saint of all contemporary overreachers," the liberator of human energies, the reshaper of the world, whose vast heroic ambitions "generate unforeseen disaster and hurl him into implosions of despair." Faust's intimacy with the devil has given him the power to realize his ambitions, but at an unrealized tragic cost. Citing Marx's characterization of Faust as the perfect symbol for bourgeois man no longer able to control the forces he has unleashed, Berman then proceeds to an inspired and intricate reading, through the eyes of a Sixties survivor, of Goethe's *Faust* "as the first, and so far still the best *tragedy of development.*"

This reading is too detailed to summarize here, but he traces Faust's metamorphosis from a bookish intellectual to the archetype of the Developer—that destroyer of the repressive yet humanly scaled old order in the name of progress and modernity. "But as much as Faust has developed both himself and his society," Berman concludes, "his self-awareness and his moral imagination are still a wasteland. Indeed, his great heroic work of development has helped to lay his soul to waste. This is the way the tragedy of development works."

Berman shows us just how right Mailer was when he characterized the Sixties as a Faustian age, and how economic visionaries like Bernie Cornfeld, liberal technocrats like Clark Kerr, Robert McNamara and Walt Rostow, psychedelic entrepreneurs like Ken Kesey and Timothy Leary, ego monsters like Mailer himself and our own Sixties Ahab, LBJ, all shared in the prevailing blindness and hubris that went hand in glove with the boundless, thoughtless sense of infinite expectations. "So many new sources of liberty and happiness and so few dues to pay!"

Berman ends his wonderful essay with a dying fall: the Faustian Sixties succeeded by the banal Seventies. But while admitting "the terrible force of all the pain we saw and felt—and sometimes caused" in the Sixties, he concludes that cynicism and passivity are no substitute at all for the heroic striving, so deeply characteristic of the great modern spirits, that gives tragedy meaning—"This is what tragic heroism, and authentic radicalism, and sympathy for the devil are all about."

To conclude: From these three writers we can extract insights that seem to me absolutely crucial to any reexamination of our recent past. We can see American culture in the Sixties as a continuum of politics, literature, music and personal expression all drawing from the same reservoir of utopian energy. We can regain our sense of public heroism and of a happy, hopeful political estate, tempered by hindsight and a tragic understanding of human limitations. And ultimately our sense of unity and our sense of tragedy can coalesce into a meditation on the Sixties in America as illustrating on the broadest canvas imaginable the Faustian drama of modern Western man. We can achieve that "tragic sense of life" so typical of Fifties intellectualism, but deepened and broadened by experience. Seen this way—and this is the way I have to see it—coming to a serious understanding of and rapprochement with that amazing period of our history takes on urgent importance for us all—the Sixties survivors and those who come after us. At bottom, that's what this anthology is all about.

# I

# The Politicization
of Culture

There is a call to life a little sterner,
And braver for the earner, learner, yearner.
Less criticism of the field and court
And more preoccupation with the sport.
It makes the prophet in us presage
The glory of a next Augustan age
Of a power leading from its strength and pride,
Of young ambition eager to be tried,
Firm in our free beliefs without dismay,
In any game the nations want to play.
A golden age of poetry and power
of which this noonday's the beginning hour.

—ROBERT FROST, "For John F. Kennedy His Inauguration"


Moloch! Moloch! Robot apartments! invisible suburbs!
skeleton treasuries! blind capitals! demonic industries!
spectral nations! invincible madhouses! granite cocks!
monstrous bombs!

—ALLEN GINSBERG, *Howl*


We had fed the heart on fantasies,
The heart's grown brutal from the fare;
More substance in our enmities
than in our love . . .

—W. B. YEATS, "Meditations in Time of Civil War"

This anthology on the American Sixties begins, fittingly enough, with an article that appeared precisely at the chronological start of the decade. Reading Arthur Schlesinger, Jr.'s January 1960 *Esquire* piece, "The New Mood in Politics," today, one wonders just what Professor Schlesinger *knew* to provide such a strikingly accurate foretaste of the New Frontier of the Kennedy Administration eight months before the nomination. It's as if Schlesinger were conjuring Kennedy out of thin air with stirring rhetoric—a rhetoric that would sound over and over throughout Kennedy's thousand days in office.

What Schlesinger articulated in this article, of course, was a mood of dissatisfaction and anticipation widely shared by activist-minded liberal intellectuals at the start of the decade. Echoing Schlesinger's dim view of the Fifties, Eric Goldman (later to become Lyndon Johnson's favored intellectual-at-large in the same way Schlesinger served Kennedy) wrote in the January 1960 issue of *Harper's Magazine* in "Good-By to the 'Fifties—and Good Riddance," "We've grown unbelievably prosperous and we maunder along in a stupor of fat. We are badly scared by the Communists, so scared that we are leery of anybody who so much as twits our ideas, our customs, our leaders. We live in a heavy, humorless, sanctimonious, stultifying atmosphere, singularly lacking in the self-mockery that is self-criticism. Probably the climate of the late Fifties was the dullest and dreariest in our history." And the managerial guru Peter Drucker ended his three-part article, "Politics for a New Generation," in the August 1960 issue of the same magazine this way: "We are, I suspect, ready for effective leadership from the next President. We know by now that we have to be both a 'superpower' to survive and 'the last best hope on earth' to prevail. The whole moral and intellectual climate of the country may change overnight, if only we get, next January, a President who takes a big view of his function, who takes pride rather than fright from the challenges that lie ahead —a President who demands much from us." (Presumably this piece was written two or three months before its publication date, well before Drucker could have known for certain that Kennedy would be the Democratic nominee.)

These statements by Goldman and Drucker, the Schlesinger piece and Norman Mailer's panegyric to JFK as the first hipster presidential candidate that opens the next section all reveal how badly our intellectuals needed to feel that the White House was again in the hands of a politician in their own image. The call was for a Rooseveltian president (TR *and* FDR) who could harness private energies to great public concerns. William James's phrase "the moral equivalent of war" was much in vogue as the country felt itself beginning to tackle the agenda of unfinished national business listed by Schlesinger: the achievement of racial justice, the care of the disadvantaged, the elevation of popular culture, the reanimation of the national spirit. There was a widespread sense as Kennedy took office that many of our most intractable national problems were finally on the road to being solved. With a dangerous arrogance we felt much the same way about the problems of the world as well; here are some further lines from Frost's inauguration poem that more than a few world leaders took umbrage at:

> We see how seriously the races swarm
> In their attempts at sovereignty and form.
> They are our wards we think to some extent

> For the time being and with their consent,
> To teach them how Democracy is meant.

This is the same tone of voice that Woodrow Wilson used forty-five years earlier when, driven to distraction by the revolutionary upheavals south of the border in Mexico, he exclaimed, "We'll teach them to elect good men!"

So, fired by visions of "a golden age of poetry and power," moved equally by idealism and ambition, the best and the brightest flocked to Washington in a spirit reminiscent of the New Deal. It was the Peace Corps that best embodied and exemplified the sometimes inspired political creativity of the New Frontier. Kennedy had floated the idea of an overseas volunteer service in a speech at the University of Michigan in the last weeks of his campaign, and the vaguely formed notion caused a sort of spontaneous combustion. Students at the university, galvanized by the idea, collected petitions and wrote letters—a development covered in award-winning fashion by the then editor-in-chief of the *Michigan Daily,* Tom Hayden—and enthusiasm snowballed until Kennedy found his campaign rhetoric transformed into a *fait accompli.* (As President-elect he received more mail on the Peace Corps than on any other subject.) Sargent Shriver, Kennedy's brother-in-law and the man chosen to be the first director of the Peace Corps, which was established by executive order on March 1, 1961, later characterized the distance here between the actual political intentions and aroused public expectations as "a creative spark-gap" of the kind that moves American history. In this the creation of the Peace Corps had much in common with various actions taken by the Kennedy Administration in the civil rights struggle. The Administration was often forced into reluctant action by initiatives on the part of activists that they (the activists) might not have taken had they not felt—feelings based more on faith than concrete evidence—that the Administration was irrevocably committed to their movement.

While it was a fresh, successful response to a reawakened sense in the country of America's international mission and destiny, enthusiasm for the Peace Corps would surely never have reached the fever pitch it did had not the notion of a global struggle with communism still gripped the national imagination. The strongest *idée fixe* of Schlesinger's piece is just that struggle, and the conjunction of a call for high moral purpose with an erasure of the missile gap, jarringly contradictory to our ears today, characterizes perfectly the New Frontier's world view.

There was a deeper vein of radical disaffection with American life and with just this kind of thinking that would become progressively more widespread and bitter as the decade wore on and the "creative spark-gap" between expectations and fulfillment widened to an unbridgeable gulf. The remaining selections in this section capture various aspects of this disaffection, which was to politicize every aspect of our cultural life to an unprecedented degree.

The next three selections introduce three of the elder statesmen and patron saints of radicalized youth: Paul Goodman, C. Wright Mills and Herbert Marcuse. By 1960 these men were fully mature intellectual mavericks who had already formulated their radical criticisms of the American way of life and forcefully stated them during the Fifties. But it was really only in the Sixties that their message found its true, widespread audience among the young, who could summon the idealism and moral stamina that paying heed to these criticisms required.

Paul Goodman was the most influential of the three. A poet, novelist, psychological therapist and utopian anarchist of the most uncompromising sort (he once picketed his publisher, Random House, during a strike for peace), and, although married, a homosexual given to incautious displays in public of sexual ardor, Goodman had the genius to perceive how much his own inevitable alienation had in common with "the problems of youth in the organized system." As diagnosed so thoroughly in his immensely popular classic, *Growing Up Absurd* (1960), the greatest problem for youth is how to grow up at all in a culture in which transparent dishonesty and cynicism blight their ingenuous faith in nobility, community and honest, "manly" work. When several years later Bob Dylan was to complain, "I've got nothin', Ma, to live up to," he was singing Goodman's song.

As Goodman analyzed it, when the only game in "the apparently closed room" of society is the rat race, the young have a limited range of choices. Most join the rat race with little illusion about their motives and find their natural talents blunted and their ideals blighted. Others, the Beats, see the sell of modern American life for what it is and become "the Early Resigned," dropping down and out into a marginal Bohemia to practice picturesque disaffiliation with "artistic" trappings. A third group, the juvenile delinquents, or "the Early Fatalistic," see how slim their chances are for even a spot in the rat race and form their own communities in the guise of gangs, with a perverse but nonetheless potent value system or code of behavior.

Goodman's book was greeted by many, especially the young, as a door suddenly opening in the apparently closed room: here seemed to be an alternative. In the "Patriotism" chapter reprinted here, the faithful hewing of Goodman to common sense and to almost classical standards of political justice and community values shows how he became a hero to that considerable segment of youth who indeed felt that there was little in mid-twentieth century America to feel patriotic about. The radicalism of the Sixties grew not so much out of ideology, economics or specific issues as from a disgust at being used, lied to and ignored, and from a refusal to enter a society that appeared to offer nothing worthy of emulation. Goodman gave powerful expression to this inchoate sense of yearning. Reading him, we see how the subsequent political crisis was, at its roots, a cultural crisis as well. (For a distinctly Goodmanesque look at the ends and means of education, see the George Dennison piece on libertarian education in the succeeding section.)

C. Wright Mills, a sociologist and author of such works of social criticism as *White Collar* (1951), *The Power Elite* (1956), *The Causes of World War III* (1958) and *Listen, Yankee* (1960), a chorus of voices from the Cuban revolution, never achieved the visibility of Goodman. (He died in 1962.) But he was a particular hero of the more cerebral branch of the New Left for his biting polemical style, for his restoration of explicit political content to the supposedly purely empirical and value-free discipline of sociology and for his indifference to so many of its higher trivialities. In the intellectual atmosphere of the late Fifties, which celebrated the "end of ideology," a feeling that political questions previously discussed in terms of liberalism and socialism could now be reduced to questions of economic and social technique, Mills persisted in raising hard questions: Who holds power? What constitutes rationality? Where can morality be learned? Mills felt that the celebration of the end of ideology masked the ascendance of *another* ideology so pervasive that few people could transcend its categories of thought. This new ideology, which he felt gripped both the United States and Russia, combined the imperatives of the Warfare State with those of the Welfare State—a permanent war economy linked with a system of meaningless but frenzied production and consumption. Citizens were reduced to the status of "technological idiots," "cheerful robots" structurally incapable of escaping the system of thought that held them captive.

As with Goodman, in Mills's way of thinking politics becomes less a matter of issues than a cultural struggle, in the broadest sense, to open up the structure of society to critical inquiry. The Mills essay reprinted here, "Culture and Politics," is a cogent formulation of this theme, of "the rationality without reason" that governs the modern state and the critical need to bring history back into human control. And in this struggle it is the left intelligentsia, not the proletariat working class, as in classical Marxism, that becomes the genuine agent of historical change, since the struggle of the left is not so much for control of the means of production as to reveal the irrationality of the status quo. In another well-known essay, "The New Left," Mills explicitly anointed the student rebels in Britain, the United States, Cuba, Korea and elsewhere as the special carriers of the historical mission of the left: "Who is it that is thinking and acting in radical ways? All over the world—in the [Soviet] bloc, outside the bloc, and in between —the answer's the same: it is the young intelligentsia." For statements such as this Mills became a posthumous saint of the new generation of leftists.

Although they arrived at their positions from differing intellectual routes, the message of the sociologist Mills and the philosopher and radical Freudian Herbert Marcuse were strikingly congruent. Both decried the ways in which the modern state blunted the capacities of its citizens for critical independent thought, creating instead, in Marcuse's phrase, "the happy consciousness." But Marcuse's analysis of this process was more thoroughgoing, and also more recondite; of all the writers and thinkers represented in this book, Marcuse is certainly the most difficult to comprehend (with the possible exception of Marshall McLuhan, whose dodge-'em-car style of intellection and exposition is part of his charm).

But it was as a prophet of instinctual liberation in a world where the sublimation necessary for survival has been rendered unnecessary by technological progress that Marcuse gained his widest following, not just among young leftists, but also among a broader segment of youth carrying the banners of sexual freedom as well. In his most famous work, *Eros and Civilization* (1954), Marcuse provided a utopian vision of a world freed from the "surplus repression" at present visited by society on its members, a civilization finally without discontents.

There are comic aspects to Marcuse's totemization in the Sixties for which Marcuse himself cannot really be blamed. Marcuse's work is at times numbingly difficult, and how much of *Eros and Civilization* and *One-Dimensional Man* was even partially understood by the hippies who so eagerly preached and practiced a vulgarized version of "polymorphous perversity" is open to question. There was in the late Sixties a funny piece in *Playboy*—an ironic location, actually, since Hugh Hefnerism was one of Marcuse's prime targets—that described the clash of cultures that occurred when Marcuse first arrived on a California campus to take up a new academic post. The hip kids on campus (which at that point probably meant everybody) were clearly expecting a kind of elderly satyr figure, tooting on a panpipe and pinching coeds. What in fact they got was a dour, severe, intellectual emigré whose style and character had been formed in the distinctly un-Dionysiac groves of German academe. It was a bummer from which the students had difficulty recovering.

It was in Marcuse's *One-Dimensional Man* that he and Mills converged most strikingly. There he argues that the modern technological state, with its apparently endless capacity to "deliver the goods" to its citizens, offers, in fact, a new form of totalitarianism in which opposition *seems* nonsensical. The constellation of increased productivity and increased consumption "reduces the use value of freedom; there is no reason to insist on self-determination if the administrated life is the comfortable and even the 'good' life."

How this paradoxical method of increasing apparent freedom as a means of decreasing real freedom works in the realms of culture and sexuality is examined in the excerpt reprinted here from the chapter entitled "The Conquest of the Unhappy Consciousness: Repressive Desublimation." In the first part of this chapter Marcuse offers a somewhat nostalgic lament for European high culture—the works of Goethe, Beethoven, Flaubert, Baudelaire, Ibsen, Rimbaud and Dostoevsky, for example, which embody a transcendent, conscious alienation that Marcuse terms "the Great Refusal." By trivializing and banalizing these supreme achievements of European culture, modern technological society neutralizes their subversive content. In much the same way, Marcuse argues, by degrading libido into delimited sexuality, which is then treated as simply another item of commodity fetishism, technological society extends an apparent sexual freedom that defuses the absolute demands of the Pleasure Principle—the demands that keep the need for real liberation alive in our consciousness.

From the highly abstract formulations of Marcuse we move to the heartbreakingly concrete insights into the nature and reality of poverty in this country to be found in Michael Harrington's *The Other America*. In political terms one of the most influential books of the decade, Harrington's book, two decades later, can still bring angry tears to its readers' eyes; it is a classic account of dispossession on the order of *The Grapes of Wrath* or *Let Us Now Praise Famous Men*. It contradicted in the most forceful terms the blithe liberal notions that prosperity was just around a corner for all Americans in our abundant society. (Cf. Schlesinger's remark in "The New Mood in Politics" that "There are still pools of poverty which have to be mopped up; but the central problem will be increasingly that of fighting for individual dignity, identity, and fulfillment in an affluent mass society"; or J. K. Galbraith's statement in *The Affluent Society* that poverty in this society was "no longer a mass affliction, [but] more nearly an afterthought.") Ironically, *The Other America* almost suffered the fate of its subject—invisibility—until a long, laudatory review by Dwight Macdonald in *The New Yorker* brought it to the attention of its proper audience. That audience included President Kennedy and his economic advisers; Harrington's book can properly be said to be one of the prime moving forces in the subsequent War on Poverty.

The "other America" of Harrington's title numbered some forty million citizens who were living below the poverty line, as defined by the federal government—blacks, Hispanics, the rural poor and the aged. They existed virtually unnoticed in the midst of the greatest prosperity in our—in any country's —history. Poverty being a relative concept, this put a special edge on the suffering. In the cities they lived in the projects, ghettoes and cheap hotels far away from the prosperous business centers and residential neighborhoods and suburbs. The aged lived lonely, hidden lives in their homes and apartments, struggling to cope on a fixed income with the inevitable medical problems and their attendant increase in costs. The verdant valleys and mountains of Appalachia masked the most desperately disadvantaged white Americans, many technologically dispossessed, thrown from their semiskilled occupations by the same automation that brought greater abundance elsewhere. The invisible poor lived in a culture of poverty in which the difficulties of simply getting by fed on each other, breeding disease, apathy, mental breakdown—a new kind of helplessness and hopelessness radically different from the difficulties faced by the earlier generation of the disadvantaged, the immigrant groups. To this country's credit, Harrington's act of social imagination in discovering the existence and the plight of the poor decisively affected our social conscience. In the excerpt reprinted in this anthology we hear the true voice of the Great Society, in much the way Schlesinger's piece gives voice to the New Frontier.

The pieces by Goodman, Mills, Marcuse and Harrington provide a fair sampling of the positions and the intellectual underpinnings of the extraordinary resurgence of radicalism in the Sixties, the New Left—for all intents and purposes a term synonymous with the student revolt. Yet, as previously noted, particular positions and issues were scarcely at the heart of this revolt. Rather it was existential and romantic at its core. Student revolutionaries discovered their positions in the process of acting on them. As Carl Oglesby approvingly wrote, in the introduction to his *New Left Reader*, of Students for a Democratic Society (SDS) and the Student Non-Violent Coordinating Committee (SNCC), "Both groups shared a pathological distrust for what they sneeringly called ideology. . . . They wanted to go south and get their hands and their heads—their lives—into the dangerous, the moral, and therefore the authentic. The instinct from the beginning was to discover the streets. . . ." There was more of Mailer than Marx in this attitude. And there was not a great deal of the intellectual in the radicalization of this new generation of leftists, according to Oglesby: "The new activists acquired their radical anti-authoritarianism at the end of the police sticks that are swinging from one end of the earth to the other. . . . The policeman's riot club functions like a magic wand under whose caress the banal soul grows vivid and the nameless recover their authority—a bestower, this wand, of the lost charisma of the modern self: I bleed, therefore I am." Here, in Marshall Berman's phrase, was a full-blown "politics of authenticity," unthinkable apart from the larger cultural upheavals taking place.

Despite this paean to existential politics, Oglesby's reader, in both its introduction and selections, displayed a certain spiky, dour, European-influenced intellectualism. Selections included pieces by Fanon, Marcuse, Mills, Regis Debray, the French student revolutionary Daniel Cohn-Bendit and the German Rudi Dutschke, while the introduction was studded with references to advanced Marxist thinkers. Only a student, or recent student, would approach American politics in this fashion. Which brings up the observation of how utterly anomalous the student revolt of the Sixties was in the larger context of American campus quiescence. Student revolts in Europe and the Third World have historically constituted the most deadly serious form of political action; both Mao and Ho Chi Minh were student firebrands, for instance. But only in the Sixties did students in this country participate in, and for a time take the lead in, the worldwide youth rebellion. Perhaps the absence of a tradition of effective student adversary politics was in part responsible for the final failure of the student revolt; American students were not used to winning, or even trying to win.

In any case, there was no dearth of issues for student rebels to address themselves to. But whether the issue was civil rights, the war in Vietnam, student power, free speech on campus or any other, the malaise, the alienation, the sense of powerlessness, the hunger for the real preceded the activist impulse.

How durable and effective this form of politics could be was of great concern to the older generation of radicals. Their first impulse was to welcome warmly this upsurge of social concern and passionate commitment. Yet the student counterreaction to the staunch anti-communism that the democratic left was forced to adopt in the Fifties, in part out of genuine revulsion (the largest part, certainly), but also in part as a defensive measure to avoid being hounded to death by McCarthyism, reopened some of the deepest wounds of the left. And the later hardening of the New Left's political outlook into ideological rigidity—the irony, considering the existential beginnings!—as the country became dangerously polarized, disturbed thoughtful leftists like Irving Howe, who wished to keep the lines of communication and consensus open. Howe addressed himself to the shortcomings of a rebellion based on the imperatives of the self, expressed as much in style as in thought, in an article entitled "New Styles in Leftism," which stirred up a hornets' nest of controversy. He acutely pinpointed the way in which radicals had removed themselves from the possibility of genuine political change with their rhetorical, ideological and tactical excesses—and he paid the price with the resulting vituperation.

Just underneath the surface of Howe's dissent was the Oedipal drama of radical fathers and sons; the relation was symbolic and also, in many cases, biological. One of the things that gives a special edge to the second great failure of the left in this century to alter the realities of economic and political power in this country is how predictably the mistakes were repeated. From a spontaneous, warm-spirited movement spawned in the struggle for civil rights, openly romantic and anarchistic (in the best sense), and later able to command genuine demographic clout as the escalating Vietnam war bred opposition, the left turned dogmatic, authoritarian and blindly self-righteous. The similarities with the earlier break-up of the American left in the late Thirties, its inability to build any bridge to the larger American public and its collapse into vindictive dogmatism, are dispiriting in the extreme. From this perspective the longevity and stubborn allegiance to the reality principle of Howe, Harrington and other democratic socialists look sensible *and* heroic.

The word "revolution" was tossed about in the Sixties in every conceivable context, so much so that it eventually lost any genuine meaning. The one domestic area in which the word largely retained its applicability, however, was the Black revolution in consciousness, which expressed itself in pride, anger and, finally, frustrated violence. The only wonder about this revolution was that it took as long as it did to take place.

The early heroic years of the civil rights movement in the South were absolutely crucial in forming the tactics and style for subsequent adversary action, Black and white. Such manifestations of Black impatience as the spontaneous rash of lunch-counter sit-ins throughout the South in the dawn of the Sixties signaled the final demise of the white-approved Black leadership and the politics of delay. In their place arose a style of grass-roots, nonviolent, persistent political action that offered the inspiring spectacle of a long-suffering, oppressed group declaring in the most visible manner that they would no longer stand for it. Suddenly the least powerful members of our society seemed to become the special custodians of the American conscience. The initiatives of the civil rights movement in the South were crucial in mobilizing the federal government to combat blatant discrimination and segregation, while a generation of student radicals, Black and white, learned crucial lessons on voting drives.

Yet from a certain point of view, without for a second minimizing its sacrifices and accomplishments in the South, the movement's struggle could be seen as an especially arduous form of "mopping up"—bringing a legally backward area of the country into line with twentieth-century standards of fairness and justice. Events in the South and the glaringly clear injustices gave northern liberals multiple opportunities for lecturing and self-congratulation. But it came as a rude shock when the Black revolt spread northwards and westwards to the seething city ghettoes, where the problems of economic inequality and *de facto* segregation were so much more difficult to solve, if no less urgent.

The eloquent messenger to the white world of this growing Black rage was James Baldwin. In his 1958 report on school desegregation in the South, "A Fly in the Buttermilk," Baldwin, a northerner, had written that "our troubles were the same troubles, and unless we were very swift and honest, what is happening in the South will be happening in the North tomorrow." *(Nobody Knows My Name)* We were not swift and honest, and as the bills due for white hypocrisy and inaction mounted, it was Baldwin's voice that informed us of the cost.

What was unique about Baldwin's jeremiads, however, was that his most disturbing insights concerned not just the plight of Blacks, but also the spiritual price white Americans paid for their dishonesty and willful ignorance. The last lines of Baldwin's great essay "Fifth Avenue, Uptown" read, "It is a terrible and inexorable law that one cannot deny the humanity of another without diminishing one's own in the face of one's victim. One sees oneself. Walk through the streets of Harlem and see what we, this nation, have become." The most revealing word in this passage is the pronoun "we." Baldwin was a writer rooted in the Fifties, in the problems of self—in his case the dilemma of being at once a Black, an American, an artist and a homosexual. Situated uneasily between the ghetto and the Black church of his youth and the white literary world, Baldwin mined his ambivalences for a handful of disturbing, powerful essays of lasting art.

None was more electrifying than Baldwin's long 1963 meditation on race relations and report on the Black Muslims in *The New Yorker*, "Down at the Cross: Letter from a Region in My Mind," the conclusion of which is reprinted here. The existence of the separatist Muslims, with their uncompromising enmity to the white world and the Christian religion, came as a shock to white Americans, who had entertained the illusion that Blacks were satisfied with the tepid gradualism they were being offered. Most shocking was the sudden realization that Blacks were quite capable of the hatred the white world had richly earned. (In his *Autobiography*, Malcolm X compared the reaction to the 1959 television documentary "The Hate That Hate Produced," which unveiled the Muslims to the country at large, to the panic caused by Orson Welles's radio broadcast of *War of the Worlds*.) It knocked into a cocked hat the comfortable notions that Blacks dearly wanted to be integrated, to become just like whites, and were grateful for whatever justice was granted them.

It was a rude enough awakening to hear the absolute contrary from the firebrand oratory of Malcolm X. But for educated whites, to be told by Baldwin, a Black writer of elegant style and impeccable literary credentials, that Blacks had every reason to despise whites and that the country was poised on the edge of a racial conflagration was doubly shocking. Baldwin's stature imparted a particular urgency to the message.

He was not crying wolf, as the subsequent riots in the Black ghettoes of Los Angeles, Newark, Detroit, Plainfield, Cleveland and other cities proved. Summers became long, hot seasons of tension as the nation watched anxiously for the next outbreak of frustrated violence. Shaken to its foundations, the country entered into a period of intense introspection about the roots of violence and racial hatred in the American experience.

One of the most impressive products of this introspection was the *Report of the National Advisory Commission on Civil Disorders,* a massive (650-odd pages in paperback) summation of the findings of the presidential commission convened after the violent summer of 1967. Rereading the famous opening pages today, one is struck and impressed by the Baldwin-like urgency of tone:

> Our nation is moving toward two societies, one black, one white—separate but unequal. . . . To pursue our present course will involve the continuing polarization of the American community and, ultimately, the destruction of basic democratic values. . . . The alternative will require a commitment to national action—compassionate, massive, and sustained, backed by the resources of the most powerful and richest nation on this earth. From every American it will require new attitudes, new understanding, new will.

The Kerner Commission report was the result of the best impulses that moderate Americans could call forth. But almost simultaneously with the report another book was published that signalled the alarming drift of the Black consciousness toward a revolutionary consciousness: Eldridge Cleaver's *Soul on Ice.* Cleaver, like Malcolm X, became a convert to the Black Muslims while in prison, and it was a powerfully transfiguring experience. (A high proportion of Black Muslims were, in fact, prison converts; as Malcolm X explained, "The reason is that among all Negroes the black convict is the most perfectly preconditioned to hear the words 'The white man is a devil.'") Like the *Autobiography*—a classic not simply of Black literature, but of American literature—and the works of Frantz Fanon, *Soul on Ice* looked deeply and unflinchingly into the roots of Black identity and Black rage, and the pathologies underlying Black–white relations. Much was questionable about this. Cleaver, for instance, took Baldwin viciously to task for his homosexuality, claiming that it was the expression of Baldwin's self-hatred as a Black and that it made it impossible for him to comprehend the priapic basis of Black–white encounters. Cleaver also made an attempt to define Black rape of white women as a political act. Here was the whirlwind Baldwin had warned that white America would reap. The selection that ends this section, "Domestic Law and International Disorder," is the clearest, most frightening expression in this book of the apocalyptic expectations nourished by the tragic failures and polarization of American society in the late Sixties. That the shooting war Cleaver so clearly expected never came about in the way he expected is slight comfort, given the persisting problems of race in this society more than a decade later.

# The New Mood in Politics

## Arthur Schlesinger, Jr.

At periodic moments in our history, our country has paused on the threshold of a new epoch in our national life, unable for a moment to open the door, but aware that it must advance if it is to preserve its national vitality and identity. One feels that we are approaching such a moment now—that the mood which has dominated the nation for a decade is beginning to seem thin and irrelevant; that it no longer interprets our desires and needs as a people; that new forces, new energies, new values are straining for expression and for release. The Eisenhower epoch—the present period of passivity and acquiescence in our national life—is drawing to a natural end.

As yet, the feeling is inchoate and elusive. But it is beginning to manifest itself in a multitude of ways: in freshening attitudes in politics; in a new acerbity in criticism; in stirrings, often tinged with desperation, among the youth; in a spreading contempt everywhere for reigning clichés. There is evident a widening restlessness, dangerous tendencies toward satire and idealism, a mounting dissatisfaction with the official priorities, a deepening concern with our character and objectives as a nation.

Reprinted from *Esquire*, January 1960.

Let me list some expressions of the discontent, the desire for reappraisal, the groping for something better:

The rise of the Beat Generation is plainly in part the result of the failure of our present society to provide ideals capable of inspiring the youth of the nation.

The revival in the last two or three years of satire (not altogether to be dismissed by the appellation "sick humor") is another expression, as in the Twenties, of contempt for the way things currently are going.

The religious boom (Billy Graham, etc.) suggests the widespread yearning for spiritual purpose of some sort in life.

The top book on the fiction best-seller list for many months was Pasternak's *Doctor Zhivago*—again a symptom of the felt need for some kind of spiritual affirmation.

A book like J. K. Galbraith's *The Affluent Society* sells fifty thousand copies in hard cover; David Riesman's *The Lonely Crowd* and W. H. Whyte's *The Organization Man* sell hundreds of thousands in paperback—all this means that our intellectuals are beginning to draw the new portrait of America out of which new political initiatives will in due course come, and that people are responding to their portrayal.

Somehow the wind is beginning to change. People—not everyone by a long way, but enough to disturb the prevailing mood—seem to seek a renewal of conviction, a new sense of national purpose. More and more of us, I think, are looking for a feeling of dedication, for a faith that what we are doing is deeply worthwhile—the kind of inspiration and lift we had for a while in the Thirties and again during World War II.

The threats of communism and nuclear catastrophe ought perhaps to be enough to give us this sense of purpose, but they don't seem to. Certainly the goal of adding to our material comforts and our leisure time has not filled our lives. Are we not beginning to yearn for something beyond ourselves? We are uncertain but expectant, dismayed but hopeful, troubled but sanguine. It is an odd and baffled moment in our history—a moment of doubt and suspense and anticipation. It is as if increasing numbers of Americans were waiting for a trumpet to sound.

At bottom, perhaps, we are seeking a new articulation of our national values in the belief that this will bring about a new effectiveness in our national action. For national purpose is not something that is enshrined in monuments or preserved in historic documents. It acquires meaning as part of an ongoing process; its certification lies, not in rhetoric, but in performance. The values of the Fifties have been, to a great degree, self-indulgent values. People have been largely absorbed in themselves—in their own careers, their own lives, their own interests. We tend to cover up our self-absorption by saying that what is good for our own interests is good for the country; but this is a gesture of piety. In fact, we start from our own concerns and work outward, rather than start from the national needs and work inward.

The badge of our self-indulgence has been the contemporary orgy of consumer goods. The chairman of the President's Council of Economic Advisers, Dr. Raymond J. Saulnier, recently stated his concept of the role of the American economy: "Its ultimate purpose is to produce more consumer goods. This is the goal. This is the object of everything that we are working at; to produce things for consumers." Not to produce better people or better schools or better health or better national defense or better opportunities for cultural and spiritual fulfillment—but to produce more gadgets and gimmicks to overwhelm our bodies and distract our minds. As against what we self-righteously condemn as the godless materialism of the Communists we seem to have dedicated ourselves to a godly materialism of our own.

But materialism—the belief that the needs of life can be fulfilled by material opulence—is not enough. It will not truly achieve for our own citizens what Herbert Croly used to call the promise of American life, for that is a moral and spiritual promise. And it will not offer an effective counterfaith—or even an effective counterbalance—against communism. Under the spell of materialism, our nation has allocated its abundance to private satisfaction rather than to public need, with the result that the wealthiest nation in the world suddenly seems to be falling behind in education, falling behind in science, falling behind in technology, falling behind in weapons, falling behind in our capacity to stir the minds and hearts of men. Russia, a much poorer nation, more than makes up for its smaller annual output by its harder sense of national purpose.

Our situation would be troubling enough if there were no world civil war. But the existence of the world civil war trebles every bet. We are coming to realize that we need a new conviction of national purpose not only as a matter of taste but as a matter of desperate necessity. And so the time is drawing near for a revision of our national priorities, a revaluation of our national values, a renewal of our national purpose. This process of reorientation will be the mainspring of the politics of the Sixties. As we commit ourselves to this vast challenge, we will cross the threshold into what promises to be one of the exciting and creative epochs in our history.

Now there is little to be gained in denouncing the values of the Fifties as meager and mean. It is important rather to understand why we have dallied with such values—why our nation, in a time of danger, should have lowered its sights, renounced older concepts of high national purpose and elevated private consumer satisfaction into a controlling national ethic. There is, I believe, no insoluble mystery here. Nor can we properly shift the blame for our condition from ourselves to our leaders. Certainly our leadership has failed in this decade to develop our potentialities of national power and to meet the onward rush of national needs. But it has just as certainly succeeded in expressing the moods and wishes of the electorate.

What accounted for the torpor of the Fifties? The answer, I think, is plain enough. The basic cause was the state of national exhaustion produced by the two preceding decades of continuous crisis. During the Thirties, Forties and into the Fifties the American people went through the worst Depression of their history, the worst hot war of their history, the worst cold war of their history, the most aggravating limited war of their history. During these decades, two aggressive Presidents kept demanding from us a lively interest in public policy and kept confronting us with tough problems of national decision. But no nation can live in tension indefinitely. By the early Fifties, the American people had had it. We were weary and drained. We were tired of subordinating the reality of our daily lives to remote and abstract national objectives. We wanted a vacation from public responsibilities. We wanted to take up the private strands of existence, to bury ourselves in family, home, career.

The politics of the Fifties were, in consequence, the politics of fatigue. Twenty years of intense public activity, first at home, then abroad, had left the nation in a state of moral and emotional exhaustion. Lull was the natural and predictable result. President Eisenhower was the perfect man for the new mood. Where his predecessors had roused the people, he soothed them; where they had defined issues sharply, he blurred them over; where they had called for effort and action, he counseled patience and hoped things would work themselves out. Perhaps his particular contribution to the art of politics was to make politics boring at a time when the people wanted any excuse to forget public affairs. The nation needed an interval of repose in order to restore its physiological balance, and repose was what President Eisenhower gave them.

In so doing, he was playing his part in the larger rhythm of our politics. For the national life has always alternated between epochs of advance and epochs of consolidation, between times of action and times of passivity. We began the twentieth century with two decades of active and insistent leadership under the dominating Presidents—Theodore Roosevelt and Woodrow Wilson. These Presidents raised the national sights. They stood for a crusading fervor in politics, directed first to reform at home and then to carrying the gospel of democracy of the world. After two decades of this, the people could stand it no longer: 1920 was like 1952. They wanted "normalcy," and that is what they got from Warren G. Harding and his successors.

And so the Twenties was the decade of "normalcy." The politics of purpose gave way to the politics of lassitude. The nation swung from affirmative government to negative government. But, after a time, negative government began to seem insufficient. As the national energies began to be replenished, people started to tire of the official mood of aimlessness and complacency. Moreover, new problems, nurtured by the years of indifference, began to emerge— problems which required direction and vigor in their solution. The Wall Street crash and its aftermath provided dramatic evidence that drift was not enough as a national policy. The time had come for the reconquest of purpose.

And so the cyclical rhythm has continued. In the Thirties and Forties we had decades of purpose until we were tired again; in the Fifties, quiescence and respite until problems heaped up and batteries began to be recharged. If this rhythm continues according to schedule, the Sixties and Seventies should be decades of affirmation until we fall back into drift in the Eighties. The pattern of American politics has been an alternation between periods of furious performance which accomplish a lot of things but finally wear the people out to periods of stagnation which go on until new issues accumulate, flagging national energies revive and forward motion can be resumed. There is no reason to suppose now that this pendular motion has suddenly come to a full stop.

The question remains whether the nation could afford that holiday from responsibility in the Fifties which its every nerve demanded—whether it was wise to choose this point to rest on its oars. No doubt the condition of national weariness made it hard to exercise vigorous leadership in any case; but this scarcely excuses our leaders from not having tried harder. When America "took five," so to speak, in the Eighteen Eighties or the Nineteen Twenties, it didn't much matter. But the Nineteen Fifties were fatal years for us to relax on the sidelines. The grim and unending contest with communism was the central international fact of the decade, and the Communists took no time out to flop in the hammock. We did, and we have paid a cruel price for it.

In our decade of inertia, we squandered, for example, a commanding weapons lead until our Secretary of Defense now frankly concedes that by the early Sixties the Soviet Union, a nation supposedly far behind our own in economic and technological sophistication, will have a three-to-one superiority in the intercontinental ballistic missile, the weapon which may well be decisive in future wars. In this same decade, we came up with no new ideas in foreign policy (or, rather, with no new *good* ideas—our new ideas have either been busts, like the Baghdad Pact and the Eisenhower Doctrine, or else were, fortunately, never carried out, like unleashing Chiang Kai-shek and massive retaliation). This period of sterility in our conduct of foreign affairs stands in particular contrast to the astonishing decade of creativity which preceded it, from the Atlantic Charter to NATO and from Lend-Lease to Point Four.

The policy of drift not only lost us essential margins of power in the competition of coexistence. It also got us into trouble at home—and in so doing further damaged our power position relative to the Communist world. For most of this decade, for example, our national economic growth slowed down dangerously. Between 1947 and 1953 our gross national product increased at an average annual rate of 4.6 percent; between 1953 and 1958 the average annual rate of increase was only about 1.6 percent. (We are doing much better, of course, in 1959, but, even adding this in, the average annual rate of increase recently has been only about 2.5 percent.) The Soviet economy, according to the Central Intelligence Agency, continues to roar along at an average annual rate of 9.5 percent.

These have been years of enormous population growth in the United States. By 1960 we will have nearly 30,000,000 more people than in 1950—an increase of almost 3,000,000 a year. The annual appearance of millions of new boys and girls automatically creates needs for new hospitals, new houses, new schools, new communities; the relentless expansion is straining our facilities to the utmost. And these new boys and girls constitute our most valuable natural resource. Our future will depend on their knowledge, their education, their health, their strength, on the opportunities open to them to develop their abilities. From the viewpoint not only of humanity and equity, but of national power, these people should be a major object of national investment.

And it is precisely these new boys and girls who have been most forgotten during the consumer goods infatuation. We have chosen in this decade to invest, not in people, but in things. We have chosen to allocate our resources to undertakings which bring short-run profits to individuals rather than to those which bring long-run profits to the nation. "A nation that spends more per capita upon advertising than upon education," Barbara Ward has written, "has somewhere lost the path to the future." While our population billows, our national leadership has made only the most feeble efforts to enlarge our community services and facilities—schools, medical care, housing, urban and suburban planning, social security, roads, recreation, water, resources and energy development—to assure decent opportunities for these new children.

The result is the weird and intolerable suggestion that the United States, the richest country in the history of the world, can't "afford" an educational system worthy of its children, can't "afford" as many ICBM's as the less affluent Soviet Union, can't "afford" a proper resources policy, can't even, heaven help us, "afford" a decent postal system. Does anyone really suppose that we don't have the money to do

these things? Of course we have. It isn't that we can't afford
it; it is that we choose to expend our resources elsewhere.
Under a system where the production and consumption of
consumer goods is regarded as the be-all and end-all of
existence, where everyone's making a fast buck is supposed to
insure the common good, where private interests take priority
over the public interests, the public sector—everything from
schools to missiles—is systematically starved. If something
does not pay its way in the market place, it is felt to be hardly
worth doing at all. Is our land really dedicated to the notion
that only things which pay their way deserve to survive? If so,
we are doomed, because very little of genuine importance—
from education to defense—pays its own way in the market.

Our trouble is not that our capabilities are inadequate. It is
that our priorities—which means our *values*—are wrong.
While consumer goods heap up in our attics and basements,
while our advertising system knocks itself out trying to create
new wants which will require the manufacture of new consumer goods, while more and more of our resources are
absorbed in this mad business of chasing our own tail, the
public framework of society, on which everything else rests, is
overstrained by population growth and undercut by neglect.
Our communities grow more chaotic, our schools more
crowded, our teachers more overworked and underpaid, our
roads more dangerous, our national parks more unkempt,
our weapons development and foreign aid more catastrophi-
cally inadequate. While we overstuff ourselves as individuals,
we let the national plant run down. And it is the national
plant—above all, it is our national investment in people
(education, health, welfare, equal opportunity)—on which
our future depends. We are heading for the classical condition
of private opulence and public squalor. Let no one forget that
through history this condition has led to the fall of empires.

I suppose there might be an argument for the consumer-
goods ethos if it produced a happy society. Certainly the
consumer-goods age has made possible for the first time the
democratization of human comfort. No one in his senses
would wish to abolish the benefits of mass production and
mass distribution. But consumer goods as the underpinning of
life are one thing; as the main object of life, another. When
the production of consumer goods occupies the top priority in
society, it sets in motion a process which can only be
described as the institutionalization of the situation described

in *Macbeth: Nought's had, all's spent,/Where our desire is got without content.* The consumer-goods economy depends on a system of calculated and organized obsolescence.

In the Twenties, another consumer-goods era, people became progressively disturbed by the official notion that material abundance was the answer to everything. As the decade wore on, dissatisfaction mounted. Then with the Depression the rejection of drift and the reinstatement of national purpose became not only a preference but a necessity. Similarly today we are entering the phase of psychological restlessness and spiritual discontent.

Concrete issues already exist around us in abundance. What is needed is vision to unite these issues and to endow them with a broader meaning. These include such questions as:

• The revitalization of our community life (better planning of cities and suburbs, slum clearance, decent housing, urban renewal, area development).
• The reconstruction of our educational system.
• The improvement of medical care and of care for the aged.
• The assurance of equal rights for minorities.
• The freedoms of speech, expression and conscience.
• The development of our natural resources.
• The control of inflation.
• The improvement of social security.
• The refinement of our mass media and the elevation of our popular culture.
• The provision of adequate foreign aid.
• The prosecution of our weapons effort.

And, though we do not confront a Depression, the competition of the Communist world serves the same purpose of converting a preference into an imperative.

This is the challenge of the Sixties: the reorganization of American values. If we are going to hold our own against communism in the world, if we are going to build a satisfying life at home for ourselves and our children, the production of consumer goods will have to be made subordinate to some larger national purpose. As more and more people perceive the nature of our dilemma, they will demand the revival of public leadership, until in time the gathering discontent will find a national voice, like Theodore Roosevelt in 1901 and Franklin Roosevelt in 1933, and there will be a breakthrough into a new political epoch.

The hallmark of the Fifties has been the belief that what is good for one's own private interest is good for all. Charles E. Wilson gave this idea its classic formulation when he suggested that what was good for General Motors was good for the country. And many critics of Wilson have seemed to object less to the principle of Wilson's law than to his choice of beneficiary. Too many tend to assume that what is good for what we care about is good for the country; if we don't like business, then we suppose, if government would only cater to labor or to the farmers, everything would be all right.

But people can't fool themselves indefinitely into supposing that the national interest is only the extension of whatever serves their own power and pocketbook. I believe that millions already feel that the road to national salvation no longer lies in pushing their own claims to the uttermost. Farmers dislike the excesses of the farm program. Workers begin to wonder whether higher wages are the answer to everything. Businessmen know that everything else in society cannot be sacrificed to their own profits.

If the hallmark of the Fifties has been the belief in the sanctity of private interests, the hallmark of the Sixties, I suggest, may well be the revival of a sense of the supremacy of the public interest—along with the realization that private interests and the public interest often come into harsh conflict. Theodore Roosevelt once said, "Every man holds his property subject to the general right of the community to regulate its use to whatever degree the public welfare may require." If unlimited private indulgence means that there are not enough resources left for national defense or for education or medical care or decent housing or intelligent community planning, then in a sane society private indulgence can no longer be unlimited.

The new attitude toward the public interest will bring in its wake a host of changes. There will be a change, for example, in the attitude toward government. One of the singular developments of the last decade was the rise of the notion that government was somehow the enemy. This was not George Washington's attitude toward government, nor Alexander Hamilton's, nor Andrew Jackson's, nor Abraham Lincoln's. The great American statesmen have all seen government as one means by which a free people achieves its purposes. But in the Fifties we tended to suppose that a man engaged in making money for himself was in nobler work than a man serving the community (and that the more money he made, the greater his wisdom and virtue). That attitude will diminish in the Sixties. Young men will go into public service with devotion and hope as they did in the days of T.R., Wilson and F.D.R. Government will gain strength and vitality from these fresh people and new ideas.

Of course, affirmative government *per se* can no more be a sufficient end for a good society than consumer goods *per se*. The object of strengthening government is to give force to the idea of the public interest and to make possible the allocation of resources to necessary public purposes. There is no other way to meet the competition of communism. There is no other way to bring about a higher quality of life and opportunity for ordinary men and women.

This point—the quality of life—suggests the great difference between the politics of the Sixties and the politics of the Thirties. The New Deal arose in response to economic breakdown. It had to meet immediate problems of subsistence and survival. Its emphasis was essentially quantitative—an emphasis inevitable in an age of scarcity. But the Sixties will confront an economy of abundance. There are still pools of poverty which have to be mopped up; but the central problem will be increasingly that of fighting for individual dignity, identity and fulfillment in an affluent mass society. The issues of the new period will not be those involved with refueling the economic machine, putting floors under wages and farm prices, establishing systems of social security. The new issues will be rather those of education, health, equal opportunity, community planning—the issues which make the difference between defeat and opportunity, between frustration and fulfillment, in the everyday lives of average persons. These issues will determine the quality of civilization to which our nation aspires in an age of ever-increasing wealth and leisure. A guiding aim, I believe, will be the insistence that every American boy and girl have access to the career proportionate to his or her talents and characters, regardless of birth, fortune, creed or color.

The beginning of a new political epoch is like the breaking of a dam. Problems which have collected in the years of indifference, values which have suffered neglect, energies which have been denied full employment—all suddenly tumble as in a hopeless, swirling flood onto an arid plain. The chaos of the breakthrough offends those who like everything neatly ordered and controlled; but it is likely to be a creative confusion, bringing a ferment of ideas and innovations into the national life. Thus the Sixties will probably be spirited, articulate, inventive, incoherent, turbulent, with energy shooting off wildly in all directions. Above all, there will be a sense of motion, of leadership and of hope.

When this happens, America will be herself again. She will deal affirmatively and imaginatively with her problems at home. More than that, she will justify once again her claim to leadership of free peoples—a claim which cannot be founded on wealth and power alone, but only on wealth and power held within a framework of purpose and ideals.

Very little in history is inevitable. The cyclical rhythm we have identified in our national affairs offers no guarantee of national salvation. It will work only as men and women rise to a towering challenge. But very little is stronger than the aspiration of a free people. If the energy now bottled up in American society can win its release in the decade ahead, we will reverse the downward curve of American power and charge the promise of American life with new meaning. From the vantage point of the Sixties, the Fifties, instead of marking a stage in the decline and fall of the American republic, will seem simply a listless interlude, quickly forgotten, in which the American people collected itself for greater exertions and higher splendors in the future.

# Patriotism

## Paul Goodman

### 1

In 1783 Washington sent a circular letter to the States, describing the situation of the new nation as he saw it. "We have equal occasion to felicitate ourselves," he said, "on the lot which Providence has assigned to us, whether we view it in a natural, a political, or moral point of light." He pointed to the natural resources of the new nation, its independence and freedom, the Age of Reason during which it had come of age, an age of "the free cultivation of letters, the unbounded extension of commerce, the progressive refinement of manners, the growing liberality of sentiment, and above all the pure and benign light of Revelation. . . . If these citizens," he concluded, "should not be completely free and happy, the fault will be certainly their own. Such is our situation and such are our prospects."

It is hard to read these sentences without agitation and tears, for they are simply true and simply patriotic.

In the next generations, almost to our own times, patriotic rhetoric did not cease to sound, more pompously and falsely, but never without a core of truth. There was always something special in the American destiny to be proud of. In 1825 it was the broad democracy. In 1850 it was the magnificent spread and settlement from coast to coast. In 1875, the

From *Growing Up Absurd* (Random House, 1960).

material progress, the cable and the Pacific railroad, the building of modern industrialism. In 1900, America was the melting pot, the asylum of the poor and the oppressed.

In our century, the patriotic rhetoric began to be unbelievable—not by accident, for foreign wars (1898 and 1917) are incompatible with reasonable rhetoric. In recent decades there has been almost a surcease of such speech. Even references to the American Way, free enterprise, high production, and the economy of abundance have finally died out, because they call up the idea of tail fins and TV commercials. Highbrow journalists mention the American Way with scorn.

Our case is astounding. For the first time in recorded history, the mention of country, community, place has lost its power to animate. Nobody but a scoundrel even tries it. Our rejection of false patriotism is, of course, itself a badge of honor. But the positive loss is tragic and I cannot resign myself to it. A man has only one life and if during it he has no great environment, no community, he has been irreparably robbed of a human right. This loss is damaging especially in growing up, for it deprives outgoing growth, which begins with weaning from Mother and walking out of the house, of the chance of entering upon a great and honorable scene to develop in.

Culture is, first of all, city and patriotic culture. I shall try to show that patriotism is the culture of childhood and adolescence. Without this first culture, we come with a fatal emptiness to the humane culture of science, art, humanity and God; and this emptiness results in the best people *not* turning back, like Plato's philosopher who has emerged from the cave, to serve their country. Many of the best Americans have a strong philanthropic and local-community zeal, yet it would seem odd for somebody nowadays to put himself to a big and hard task just to serve his country, to make her better, and be proud of that. Young people aspire mightily to appearances on television and other kinds of notoriety, but I doubt that many now think of being honored by a statue in the park and winning "immortal" fame, the fame of big culture.

Let me make the same point by analyzing a remarkable proposition of Otto Jespersen, the grammarian. He shows that, contrary to expectation, a child does not learn his mother tongue at home from his mother and immediate family, he does not pick up their accent. The accent, vocabulary, syntax, and style that form his speech are learned from his first peer groups, outside the home. Jespersen does not explain it, but the psychology seems evident. Speech occurs at the stage of the developing of the "I," it is a forming of the image of the self, it is a self-appointment to one's ideal and putting on its uniform. Changes occur as we appoint ourselves to one peer group after another. At a certain stage a lad appoints himself or commits himself to a band of friends and puts on its jargon, jacket, tattoo, and masculine ring on the fourth finger of the left hand. If he is insecure and disturbed, this conformity is a cowering protection and the band is a delinquent gang, but in every case it is also, we see by the blazon, an achievement. And one way in which the Governor of New York does not take the juveniles seriously, when he speaks of giving them a sense of belonging, is that he does not offer an ideal that promises equal manliness. He has none to offer.

It is tragic when there is no great adult peer group to meet growth. Consider the case of an artist, my own case. To have simple and sounding language, rather than merely the lovely colloquialism of Sherwood Anderson or William Carlos Williams, it is necessary to believe in the great national culture of one's people. Our popular culture does not warrant the belief, even to make the sacrifice that Virgil made when he sadly gave up his best vision because strife-torn Rome needed a national poet. True, an artist can then jump to the international and universal, for mankind and God do not let him down (mankind is the fellow on one's own block), but this is at the loss of pomp and glitter, of the glancing present. Without a patriotic peer group, it is impossible to have the brilliance of Handel, the material grandeur of Venice. With us the style of the big bright sensation belongs to cheap musical dramas on Broadway.

## 2

The area of patriotism is intermediate between childhood and adulthood. We must delimit it carefully or we play into the hands of fools and rogues who have done our country plenty of damage.

To what can we correctly attach the adjective "American"? There is no "American" animal, sexual, or primary family life. The idea of American child-rearing or American medicine is idiotic, and the thought of an "American family" is abominable. At the further extreme, there is no "American" university, "American" science, religion, or peace. In only an equivocal sense is there an "American" art: the subject matter may be American, but the art is international and the aim is universal.

In between, however, there *is* an American landscape, an American primary and secondary education, an American classlessness, an American Constitution, an Anglo-American language, and an American kind of enterprising. That is, just where a child ventures from home and grows up through adolescence, the great environment becomes his scene, and this is American, a characteristic geography and history, place and community. It is just in growing up, which is the subject of this book, that a patriotic opportunity is essential. It is just this opportunity that, for ingenuous youth, is corrupted. And so it is hard to grow up.

Let us be quite clear what this American landscape and community is. I quote from a recent issue of *Life:*

[Teen-agers] own 10 million phonographs, over a million TV sets, 13 million cameras. Counting only what is spent to satisfy their special teen-age demands, the youngsters and their parents will shell out about $10 billion this year, a billion more than the total sales of GM. Until recently businessmen have largely ignored the teen-age market. But now they are spending millions on advertising and razzle-dazzle promotional stunts. If parents have any idea of organized revolt, it is already too late. Teen-age spending is so important that such action would send quivers through the entire national economy.

This is a description of the landscape, and the prose of *Life* is part of the landscape.

3

Equal to our businessmen, our government and public spokesmen have a knack for debasing the noble and making the excellent trivial. The current disease is to make Cold War capital out of everything, no matter what. We cannot dedicate a building of Frank Lloyd Wright's in New York without our Ambassador to the United Nations pointing out that such an architect could not have flourished in Russia. This is tasteless; the matter becomes serious when our freedoms are involved.

Not long ago there was a great to-do about the Russian censorship of Pasternak's *Dr. Zhivago*. The editorials and the rhetoric of organized friends of culture kept repeating freedom of speech, freedom of culture. (You would think that we did not have our own means of censoring, by commercial selection and by swamping.) But the outcry about Pasternak was not sincere, it was propaganda in the Cold War. In the same year, for instance, the Archbishop of Dublin effectually banned the spring theater festival because of plays of O'Casey and Joyce. (He refused to say the festival Mass if those plays were to be given. The director then canceled the plays. But the actors manfully struck and would not play at all, and this resulted in an important loss of tourist revenue. Such admirable behavior is inconceivable in my country.) On this theme, *The New York Times* ran no editorials, no, nor the New York *Herald Tribune*. For we are not at cold war with the Catholic hierarchy. (I wrote a letter to the *Times* asking that this and *Zhivago* be coupled for mention, but no one was interested.) But such behavior is patriotically disastrous; it teaches that our spokesmen are not earnest; they pick and choose when to stand up for freedom of thought. How then can a boy be proud? (But to be sure, we have little such freedom, compared with the British, for our *mass* media are not, like theirs, open to fundamental controversy. It is not surprising, therefore, that for English Angry Young Men an important topic is their outraged patriotism, whereas our Beats do not care about that.)

## 4

Consider the behavior of our professors and universities during the Dies, McCarthy and Feinberg Law investigations. It is hard to say which set the worse example to the students during those hearings: the Communist professors fearful for their jobs, or the colleges that—with magnificent exceptions, like Harvard—supinely received the investigators. A monumental blunder was being made—which did us desperate damage among thoughtful Europeans—and our professors shivered in their boots and our "radicals" hid like roaches. The important thing is not which group betrays the ideal in any particular case, but that young people become cynical about political action and resigned about the possibility of making a change. Following a party line, Communist teachers, e.g., at New York's City College, denied their membership. This was a disastrous betrayal of the students. Not that it is wrong to avoid insolent force with fraud, but that young students can grow only by politically affirming themselves. With the young, honor is more important than tactics or even than prudence. Leaders of youth must be knightly—a grisly identity, but there it is.

We have now passed through a decade in which the students in our colleges showed a political apathy probably unexampled in student history. Several causes have conspired to it. First, simple shell shock: the war and the atom bomb aroused such deep anxiety that the only defense against it was conventionality. (I remember lecturing on Kafka in 1948 to a hall of collegians consisting largely of veterans on the G.I. bill, and they frantically protested that Kafka was psychotic and should be paid no attention, he had no relation to reality—they who had lived through some of the Trial and were even then roaming under the Castle!)

Secondly, the students have been seduced by business firms, which tempt and reward them for conformity; but as W. H. Whyte, Jr. points out, they are eager to conform even before they are paid. Correspondingly, in its appeal to lower-class boys, the Army has found it wise to accept the stirring slogan, "Retire at 37." If you question a boy draftee who has reenlisted, he will explain that it is a "good deal." That is, the Army has become the IBM of the poor boy.

But finally, is there any doubt that an important cause of the present political apathy of the young is the dishonorable radical leadership that they had in the Thirties and Forties? They now believe that *all* political thinking is a sell—just as those bright Catholic lads who stop believing the superstitions of scholasticism now believe that all philosophy is an intricate fraud, including the truths of scholasticism.

This hipster skepticism is pervasive. It is partly, of course, resignation that a revolution has failed and the way is too thorny; but students are usually more resilient. I think that a more important factor is disgust that the radicals were not bona fide; the students were had. But also, I fear, it is cynical superiority, an identification with either the fraudulent or the powerful.

I referred above to the similarity between some of the Communists and young Organization Men today, in their lust for control apart from any objective good and, more deeply, in their use of an organized power-system in order to make the ingenuous and worthy not exist. In the Thirties it came about that Communists had high status in Hollywood and somewhat in publishing, so the two kinds of organized systems worked in the same offices—nor do I doubt that many of the refinements of present-day organization life were learned during this cohabitation. But it has remained for our own decade to enjoy the brutal comedy of McCarthy and the FBI investigating the Communists in Hollywood, so we had on one stage the three most cynical tribes in the country.

But let us go back to more simple ignobility.

## 5

Certainly the most thrilling and romantic happening of these years is the adventure in space, surpassing in promise the voyages of the fifteenth and sixteenth centuries. This adventure makes life worth the trouble again. When the Russians beat us out, we are miffed but we can be proud that these exploits have been performed by men and man is great; Copernicus was a Pole, Galileo an Italian, Kepler a German, Newton an Englishman—and the rockets were Chinese; and we hope that we shall win the next round, for it belongs to America to achieve first in this kind of enterprise. The experiments are expensive, but it seems mean-spirited to question the appropriations and few have done so. So far, grand. But now we have corrupted even the exploration of space into the Cold War. Against an agreement of the International Geophysical Year, we, like the Russians, withheld the wave length of a satellite for strategic reasons. (I was ashamed and again I wrote dutifully to *The New York Times*, but they again had no space for such an odd way of viewing the news.) Next, we carried out a secret nuclear experiment in the ionosphere, and this one was kept secret not from the Russians for military reasons, but from the American people, because of possible objections to the fallout. The *Times* kept the secret till the Russians were about to publish it, explaining (March 19, 1959), that "it had learned of the plans for Project

Argus last summer, some weeks before it took place. Nevertheless, scientists associated with the government said they feared that prior announcement of the experiment might lead to protests that would force its cancellation." A. J. Muste, an editor of *Liberation* magazine, asked them for an apology for this unexampled betrayal of journalistic responsibility, and got the astounding reply:

> It seems to me that you are suggesting that the *Times* enter the propaganda field and, in effect, set its judgment above that of military men and scientists as to what can be published. . . . After all, the *Times* is a responsible newspaper. [!!] [Robert Garst, Assistant Managing Editor. In *Liberation,* May, 1959.]

But what is the effect on our people when we are told that our chief newspaper does not print the news? Constitutionally, for instance, *how in a democracy do they then deserve their mailing privileges, to circulate their official press releases and advertisements for department stores?* [The purpose of second-class mail is to circulate information.] When Muste wrote a letter for publication about the *Times'* handling of the story, the *Times* found no space for that letter.

But to my mind, even more important is the effect of cutting people off from the adventure of science, no matter what the risks. What an illiberal and dishonorable policy to pursue! Our government cannot see that noble things must not be made base, romance must not be turned into disillusion, or what will become of the young people? Take another example. This glorious enterprise of space! And now we have chosen seven astronauts for special training. But the nemesis of the organized system haunts us. All prove to be white Protestant, in their early or middle thirties, married, with small children, and coming from small towns—in brief, models of salesmen or junior executives for International Business Machines. And these seven have now made a solemn pact, reported in the press, that whichever one goes aloft will split evenly with the others his take from syndicated stories and TV appearances. Concerning them, Dr. George Ruff, the Air Force psychiatrist who tested them, has explained, "Knowing the qualities that made them this way, and working hard at applying those qualities in your daily life, can help you [too] to come closer to achieving what they have become: comfortable, mature, and well-integrated individuals. It's a worthwhile goal."

Of course, by this writing (June 1960), it is commonly accepted that our new Midas satellite has the *function* of espionage. But it has remained for a proper scientist to hit the bottom: the professor who has advised us *not* to reply to any signals we might receive from outer space, because the astral beings are likely to be technically more advanced than we and they will come down and eat us up. This projection of the Cold War into the starry vault was favorably reported by the science editor of the *Herald Tribune*.

## 6

In the time of Washington, the public men—Adams, Jefferson, Madison, Marshall, Henry, Franklin, Hamilton, Jay—were a fair sampling of the good spirits in the country, humane, literate, brave, not self-seeking. (There is a remarkable letter of Jefferson's to David Rittenhouse, urging him to waste no more time in mere politics, for the world needed him more in his capacity as a scientist.) By and large, it could not be said of our presidents and governors at present, the symbols of the country, that they are a fair sampling of the best of us. It would not be difficult to make a list of a hundred, or two hundred, who are superior to them in every relevant way, in whom a boy could feel pride and trust.

Of course this is not a new trouble among us. Just as the European writers of the eighteenth century idolized our statesmen as if they were demigods, so in the nineteenth they spoke of their inferiority. This is the consequence of another missed revolution, the democratic revolution. A man of sense obviously cannot waste his life learning to sue to an ignorant electorate and coming up through political ranks in which disinterestedness and pure convictions are not the most handy virtues. Yet the fault is not with democracy, but that we have failed to have enough of it. For instance, if our emphasis had been on perfecting the town meeting and the neighborhood commune, there would not be ignorant electors and they would choose great officers. If people had the opportunity to initiate community actions, they would be political; they would know that finally the way to accomplish something great is to get together with the like-minded and directly do it.

But the men in power do not think politically either. For instance, this year we have had the usual spectacle of politicians going about the country looking for nominators for the Presidency, presumably (why else?) because they have important new programs to offer. But as soon as it becomes clear that the county leaders of the party do not want them, they retire from the race and rally to elect whomever. What becomes of the programs? Since this is what political responsibility means to a politician, why should the electorate respect politics, and how could an honest boy be inspired to enter on such a career?

In a recent essay, the historian Henry Steele Commager asks how it is possible that we have an absolute dearth of statesmen at present in America (he cannot think of one). Characteristically, we have an immense amount of formal training in flourishing institutes for public administration at Harvard, Princeton, Syracuse, Tufts, etc., as if we could get the thing by learning the role. Commager sensibly concludes that that training does not begin early enough and it lacks the content of actual experience. The environment does not encourage public service, it does not esteem public goods. Few fathers give much thought to the distant generations of posterity, and children do not take fire in reading about the great men of history and thinking "Why not I?" as a plausible purpose. And finally, says Commager, the narrow chauvinism and energetic hostility to subversive ideas that are now the test of our politicians are precisely disastrous to patriotism, for that must be spacious, disinterested, and broad-based, otherwise it is intolerable foolishness. Let me quote a fine passage:

> The men who won our independence and laid the foundations of the American nation were devoted patriots but they were, too, men of the world. They were children of the enlightenment. Reason taught them that all men were brothers, that purely national distinctions were artificial, that there existed a great community of arts and letters and philosophy and science cutting across and transcending mere national boundaries. . . . The nationalism of the eighteenth century did not rest on a narrow base but on a broad one. It did not find nourishment in fear and suspicion but in faith and confidence.

Perhaps one reason for the decline in statesmanship is that we have hemmed our potential statesmen in, we have denied them tolerant and spacious ideas.

As it is, what must be the effect on a boy when he comes to realize that the public spokesman up there is not even speaking his own words, but repeating, like a performer, something written for him by a staff from Madison Avenue? The boy must learn to shout, "Shame! make your own speech at least!"

Our present President (Mr. Eisenhower) is an unusually uncultivated man. It is said that he has invited no real writer, no artist, no philosopher to the White House. Presumably he has no intellectual friends; that is his privilege. But recently he invited the chief of the Russian government to a banquet and musicale. And the formal music of that musicale was provided by a Fred Waring band playing "Oh, What a Beautiful Morning" and such other numbers. This is disgraceful.

### 7

The American landscape has been badly corrupted. European writers no longer even notice the natural wonder of it, they are so put off by the ugliness and conformity of the towns. But worse than the ugliness and conformity is the neglect that baffles pride of place. Our poets try to move themselves by nostalgically repeating the names of towns: "Biloxi and Natchez, Pascagoula and Opelousas"—but beware of paying a visit.

The Americans disesteem public goods, and improving the landscape is a big expense. Historically, the neglect of appearance and plan of our scores of thousands of villages and small towns, especially in the Middle West and South—the diner, the Woolworth's, and two filling stations—can be analogized to the neglect of the present-day poor. In the tide of expansion, appearance was disregarded as not essential; later, the matter would be mopped up. But the neglect rigidifies, it is a hard core not easy to change.

Instead, the present tendency is to impose on the countryside a new corporation style altogether, in the form of shopping centers (=national chain supermarkets) on the highway. This works out disastrously for the communities, for these "centers" are not centers of villages, and there cease to be villages at all, simply scattered family houses. This is the end of a long process of disruption, for in any case the industry is gone, the men work in plants thirty miles away. It is possible to travel many miles even in New England and not see a single activity a man could make a living at, except automobile agencies and filling stations; not even a food store. The schools too are large and centralized. The families tend to move away frequently, but even while they are put, they are driving around. This does not make much community to grow up in.

In more primitive societies, a chief community activity is working together, thatching a roof, net fishing. But with us, precisely this co-operative labor, for instance the work in a factory, is removed from its community setting and emptied, by the relations of production, of any community spirit.

Places that have no shape have no face-to-face functioning, for the shape *is* the functioning community. The loveliness of so many hamlets in Europe is that they have shape and are built of local materials by local craft. Perhaps the people had to cluster to attend early masses. In Ireland, where they farm out the back door, the rows of thatched houses line both sides of a little street. In France, where men go off to their farms, there may be a square. In our own early New England villages, where congregational and political spirit was strong, there was a common green with public buildings, though the families lived scattered on the farms they worked. There was the shape of a community, with its economy, its crafts, and its ideas. The advantage of growing up in such a community in one's early years is evident. It is not family supervision, on which the physicians of juvenile delinquency are now laying such stress; quite the contrary! it is that the family does *not* have to bear the burden of teaching the culture. In a community, everybody knows the child face to face. There is an easy grading of overlapping ages, right up to the adults who are going about their business in a going concern, and not paying too much attention to children. A good city neighborhood works in the same way.

From this point of view, the swarm of kids in a city housing project form a better community than present-day country boys or the kids on Park Avenue. *Therefore* they have more local patriotism. The bother with this community chain, however, is that it terminates abruptly before it reaches the adults, who belong to a different world; so the kids are a gang and the local community spirit turns into loyalty to a Code; it does not eventuate in anything socially cohesive and culturally worth while. And such a gang is prone to be delinquent because, as we shall see, in such conditions it is the forbidden that best cements loyalty.

Politically, a delinquent gang is not lawless and not in the state of nature. Balked in its growth, the local loyalty turns on itself and simply reinvents the feud-code of Alfred the Great, marking out safe territories and making provision for special classes of revenge. On this view, if one teen-age gang, pursuing its vendetta, falls on another and murders a kid, it would not be our business to interfere in the law of that differently constituted society. Also, like Danes or Vikings of Alfred's time, they regard our larger society merely as a field of sport and plunder; they have not yet reinvented International Law. But we, of course, cannot view it so, for we live in an advanced state of politics and law: they are members of our community. We are not children but more experienced and somewhat wiser, and therefore responsible, so we cannot simply annihilate them like pirates (they are small in size, few in numbers, and armed with primitive weapons); and we cannot let them hurt themselves.

(I think it is wise sometimes to regard disaffected groups as if there *were* plausibly these two viewpoints, rival patriotisms. It is better humanity and it might make better law. The advantage is that it takes the disaffected seriously as disaffected, rather than merely pathological; it keeps in the foreground the question of allegiance. We must *deserve* allegiance.)

8

But they are children. Let us consider rather the peculiar patriotic problem of an older disaffected group, the Beat young men, for then we can see that it *is* a patriotic problem.

Here too, I think, there has often been a strong community influence of growing up together. For instance, fellows who went to Black Mountain College, which was oriented to community and creative arts—a powerful, and powerfully disaffecting, combination—are pillars of Beat society. Other fellows were buddies in the armed services. However it was, as Beat their community spirit is strong. They barge in to sleep, they share property, they share a culture. Now think of this community, disaffected from America, as engaged in a pathetic quest for some other big patriotism, an adult peer group.

We saw how, appointing themselves outcast, they affirm the accidental symbols of other outcast groups: Negro, Puerto Rican, and criminal. But this is pretty thin gruel for intellectual young men, many of whom have been to college. On the other hand, they are unable to make the jump to the great international humanist community because, simply, they don't know anything, neither literature nor politics. (I once taught at Black Mountain College, and to my astonishment I found that the students had never read the Bible, Milton, Dryden, Gibbon, etc., etc., nor did they feel—as a lack—that such things existed. But they knew odd facts about Mayan hieroglyphics which their teacher had been interested in.)

What then? Since it is necessary for grown fellows to have some major allegiance or other, they have latched on to the dead Japanese masters of Zen Buddhism. (This is a late effect of the early-century discovery of Japan by Fenollosa, Frank Lloyd Wright, the Misses Lowell and Ayscough, and Ezra Pound, suddenly reinforced by the postwar occupation under General MacArthur.) Now, as we shall see, Zen is *not* irrelevant to these young men's needs, for it is a theology and style of immediate experience. But the pathos is that Zen was the flower of an intensely loyal feudal system that fed, protected, and honored its masters, and to which the Zen masters in turn had fealty. For example, it is said that the haiku was invented by a poet as a public service when he was suicidally despondent because his Emperor had died. But Zen without farmers and servants is an airy business; and the young men, as we have seen, are betrayed into dubious devices to keep body and soul together, nor do they have a flag to salute.

## 9

I have tried broadly to paint some of the background conditions that discourage patriotism: the lack of bona fides about our liberties, the dishonorable politics in the universities, the irresponsible press, the disillusioning handling of the adventure in space, the inferior and place-seeking high officers of the State, the shameful neglect of our landscape and the disregard of community; later I shall speak of our trivial leisure which has no community meaning. But besides these not usually mentioned background conditions, there are of course the persistent immediate uglinesses that everybody talks about and every child sees: the cases of graft, social injustice, stupid law, and injustice to persons. Yet in an important sense, these scandals do not discourage patriotism, so long as there is the feeling of a persistent effort against them. My guess is that more pride of country is engendered by one good decision, or even a good powerful dissenting opinion, of the at least traditional Supreme Court, than by billions of repetitions of the pledge of allegiance.

Racial segregation and prejudice destroy community by definition, and we need not discuss them. Here again the revolution commenced in Jefferson's time and recommenced by the abolitionists, went unfinished; and we have inherited the consequences.

But it is perhaps useful to point out again that, when there is prejudice, the community of the dominant class is equally destroyed. The whites in the South, for instance, used to talk a blatant patriotism and a specious regionalism grounded in nothing but keeping the blacks under. The result is that flag and cross have become contemptible in their own eyes. (Real regionalism, that finds its culture and satisfaction in its own geography and economy and can withstand the temptations of the national cash-nexus, has long ago succumbed to Madison Avenue, Hollywood, and Wall Street.) Now that law and religion side against them, the Southerners are maniac with wounded conceit and sexual fear; their behavior on integration should be referred not to the Attorney General but to the Public Health Service. All this has come banging down on the children as the battleground. Yet, paradoxically, among all young people it is perhaps just the young people in the South, whites and Negroes both, who most find life worth living these days, because something real is happening. During the Montgomery bus boycott against Jim Crow, there was little delinquency among the Negro boys.

(In Northern cities and towns, also, the children are thrown into a central position in the community crisis of exclusion and prejudice, but sometimes as peacemakers. Let me give an interesting architectural example. It has become common to use the new centralized school building as the community building for meetings and recreation. One reason is economy. But another reason that is given is that the school is the one community function that brings together the otherwise discordant elements in the neighborhood, so maybe the adults can get together in the school. It is a curious situation when the grownups have to rely on the children to make sense for them, and when the school building is the chief community building. But it is better than nothing.)

## 10

Deep in the organized system itself there has been an important new effort toward community. The postwar boom in young marriages and the sensational rise in the urban birth rate that for the first time promises to surpass the rural birth rate, have been accompanied by the moving of affluent workmen to suburban projects and of the middle status to ranch houses. These new settlements devote time and energy to common interests. Do they do anything for local patriotism?

They are communities for small children, one to five, and for women as the mothers of small children. These are the groups in society unequivocally benefited by high production, full employment, and the high standard of living. They thrive on animal security. Labor-saving devices make the world of the infants much pleasanter. Morally and vocationally, there is no question that having and caring for the children is justified work for the mothers, necessary, honored, and using good human capacities. Nearly forty years ago, H. L. Mencken pointed out in his book on women that women had real jobs, whereas men were likely to be certified public accountants or politicians. Today, when so many work in the Rat Race, few would deny that he was right. So now men too try earnestly to devote themselves to the small ones as a secondary but real career. This is called the New Fatherhood.

The child world, in the suburbs and surrounding country, and somewhat less in the city, is the best that small children have had in modern times. The new psychology of belonging is feeble stuff, but the new psychology of infant care has been radical: no toilet training, permissive thumb sucking and pregenital sexuality, free crying and movement, exposure to the grownups' nakedness, honest answers to questions. The new medicine gets them quickly over the usual diseases (though there is debate about the later consequences). The school system as a whole is poor, but the nursery schools are often first-rate, progressive, and have intelligent and dedicated young teachers. It is said that children's toys and games are excellent, practical and imaginative, up to the age of six, when the commercial criteria of the eleven-billion-dollar market begin to operate.

For the adults, the improvement of this child's world results in genuine community participation, committee meetings and lectures on psychology, concern for traffic and zoning, and even extension courses in cultural subjects to create the proper atmosphere for growing up. It seems astonishing, given so much active participation, that these community activities have not much developed into other important political and social action. But courage gives out at the political issues relevant to age six. The sponsorship and control of the organized system are everywhere apparent.

(For instance, in a recent agitation that has prevented Negroes from moving into Deerfield, a suburb of Chicago —average income $9,000–10,000—an "attractive young married couple" explained that most of their friends had most of their money tied up in their houses: "We don't expect to live in them very long. Some of the junior execs expect to become seniors and move to the real North Shore, and a lot of us will be transferred all over the United States. When this happens, we want to be sure our houses have resale value." [Reported in *The New York Times*, April 17, 1960.] The spiritedness of this speaks for itself.)

Unfortunately, when the adults devote themselves thus to the child's world, there isn't much world for the child to grow up into in the next stage. For Father to guide his growing son, it is necessary for him to have a community of his own and be more of a man. In the circumstances this is difficult. But if there is no big environment, there are no grounds for patriotism.

The corporations, however, have now entered into this arena too, to organize the next stage of growing up. This is the meaning, surely, of the publicity that has been trumped up for the Little League, the baseball teams of subteen-agers sponsored and underwritten by various business firms. What value the Little League has as play, I don't know, I haven't watched games. The high-pressure advertising has been violently denounced by the older sports writers as giving kids an unsportsmanlike taste for publicity. As a school of rule making, responsibility, and impersonality, the Little League certainly cannot compare with the free games of the street, but we saw that these have been passing away. Economically, however, the function of the Little League is clear-cut: it is child labor, analogous to ten-year-olds picking hemp in the factory a century ago: it keeps idle hands out of mischief; it is not profitable as production, but it provides valuable training in attitude and work habits.

Viewed so, the suburban and exurban trends are the formation of a new proletariat, producers of offspring.

## 11

Naturally the Public Relations have been unable to restrain themselves from invading the public schools. The classes are flooded with pamphlets and documentary films on electronics and the introduction of cows into New Zealand, put out by Consolidated Edison, Ford, Shell, Westinghouse, the National Dairy Council, Union Carbide, Bell, etc., and even Merrill Lynch. These proclaim their sponsorship with more or less discreet plugs.

In the ninth grade, however, at a New York City school I know well, they have spent class time with an item called *The Educational ABC's of Industry*, a collection of advertisements interlarded with reading matter; and the class was actually required, by a teacher distracted by overwork, to copy out jingles in which *C* stands for Orange-*Crush*, "taste it and see," and *F* for the *Ford* Motor Company, "where the first car grew." I would gladly share this literature with the reader, but its publisher has not given me permission.

# Culture and Politics

## C. Wright Mills

We are at the ending of what is called The Modern Age. Just as Antiquity was followed by several centuries of Oriental ascendancy which Westerners provincially call The Dark Ages, so now The Modern Age is being succeeded by a post-modern period. Perhaps we may call it: The Fourth Epoch.

The ending of one epoch and the beginning of another is, to be sure, a matter of definition. But definitions, like everything social, are historically specific. And now our basic definitions of society and of self are being overtaken by new realities. I do not mean merely that we *feel* we are in an epochal kind of transition. I mean that too many of our explanations are derived from the great historical transition from the Medieval to the Modern Age; and that when they are generalized for use today, they become unwieldy, irrelevant, not convincing. And I mean also that our major orientations—liberalism and socialism—have virtually collapsed as adequate explanations of the world and of ourselves.

From *Power, Politics and People: The Collected Essays of C. Wright Mills*, ed. by Irving Louis Horowitz (Oxford University Press, 1963).

I

These two ideologies came out of The Enlightenment, and they have had in common many assumptions and two major values: in both, freedom and reason are supposed to coincide: increased rationality is held to be the prime condition of increased freedom. Those thinkers who have done the most to shape our ways of thinking have proceeded under this assumption; these values lie under every movement and nuance of the work of Freud: to be free, the individual must become more rationally aware; therapy is an aid to giving reason its chance to work freely in the course of an individual's life. These values underpin the main line of Marxist work: men, caught in the irrational anarchy of production, must become rationally aware of their position in society; they must become "class conscious"—the Marxian meaning of which is as rationalistic as any term set forth by Bentham.

Liberalism has been concerned with freedom and reason as supreme facts about the individual; Marxism as supreme facts about man's role in the political making of history. But what has been happening in the world makes evident, I believe, why the ideas of freedom and of reason now so often seem so ambiguous in both the capitalist and the communist societies of our time: why Marxism has so often become a dreary rhetoric of bureaucratic defense and political abuse; and liberalism, a trivial and irrelevant way of masking social reality. The major developments of our time can be adequately understood in terms of neither the liberal nor the Marxian interpretation of politics and culture. These ways of thought, after all, arose as guidelines to reflection about types of society which do not now exist. John Stuart Mill never examined the kinds of political economy now arising in the capitalist world. Karl Marx never analyzed the kinds of society now arising in the Communist bloc. And neither of them ever thought through the problems of the so-called underdeveloped countries in which seven out of ten men are trying to exist today.

The ideological mark of The Fourth Epoch—that which sets it off from The Modern Age—is that the ideas of freedom and of reason have become moot; that increased rationality may not be assumed to make for increased freedom.

## II

The underlying trends are well known. Great and rational organizations—in brief, bureaucracies—have indeed increased, but the substantive reason of the individual at large has not. Caught in the limited milieux of their everyday lives, ordinary men often cannot reason about the great structures—rational and irrational—of which their milieux are subordinate parts. Accordingly, they often carry out series of apparently rational actions without any ideas of the ends they serve, and there is the increasing suspicion that those at the top as well—like Tolstoy's generals—only pretend they know. That the techniques and the rationality of science are given a central place in a society does not mean that men live reasonably and without myth, fraud and superstition. Science, it turns out, is not a technological Second Coming. Universal education may lead to technological idiocy and nationalist provinciality, rather than to the informed and independent intelligence. Rationally organized social arrangements are not necessarily a means of increased freedom—for the individual or for the society. In fact, often they are a means of tyranny and manipulation, a means of expropriating the very chance to reason, the very capacity to act as a free man.

The atrocities of The Fourth Epoch are committed by men as "functions" of a rational social machinery—men possessed by an abstracted view that hides from them the humanity of their victims and as well their own humanity. The moral insensibility of our times was made dramatic by the Nazis, but is not the same lack of human morality revealed by the atomic bombing of the peoples of Hiroshima and Nagasaki? And did it not prevail, too, among fighter pilots in Korea, with their petroleum-jelly broiling of children and women and men? Auschwitz and Hiroshima—are they not equally features of the highly rational moral-insensibility of The Fourth Epoch? And is not this lack of moral sensibility raised to a higher and technically more adequate level among the brisk generals and gentle scientists who are now rationally—and absurdly—planning the weapons and the strategy of the third world war? These actions are not necessarily sadistic; they are merely businesslike; they are not emotional at all; they are efficient, rational, technically clean-cut. They are inhuman acts because they are impersonal.

### III

In the meantime, ideology and sensibility quite apart, the compromises and exploitations by which the nineteenth-century world was balanced have collapsed. In this sixth decade of the twentieth century the structure of a new world is indeed coming into view.

The ascendancy of the USA, along with that of the USSR, has relegated the scatter of European nations to subsidiary status. The world of The Fourth Epoch is divided. On either side, a superpower now spends its most massive and coordinated effort in the highly scientific preparation of a third world war.

Yet, for the first time in history, the very idea of victory in war has become idiotic. As war becomes total, it becomes absurd. Yet in both the superstates, virtually all policies and actions fall within the perspective of war; in both, elites and spokesmen—in particular, I must say, those of the United States—are possessed by the military metaphysic, according to which all world reality is defined in military terms. By both, the most decisive features of reality are held to be the state of violence and the balance of fright.

Back of this struggle there is the world-encounter of two types of political economy, and in this encounter capitalism is losing. Some higher capitalists of the USA are becoming aware of this, and they are very much frightened. They fear, with good justification, that they are going to become an isolated and a second-rate power. They represent utopian capitalism in a world largely composed of people whose experiences with real capitalism, if any, have been mostly brutal. They profess "democracy" in a nation where it is more a formal outline than an actuality, and in a world in which the great majority of people have never experienced the bourgeois revolutions, in a world in which the values deposited by the Renaissance and the Reformation do not restrain the often brutal thrust to industrialize.

United States foreign policy and lack of foreign policy is firmly a part of the absurdity of this world scene, and it is foremost among the many defaults of the Western societies. During the last few years, confronting the brinks, I have often suspected that the world is not at the third world war largely because of the calculation and the forbearance of the Soviet elite.

## IV

What kind of a society is the USA turning out to be in the middle of the twentieth century? Perhaps it is possible to characterize it as a prototype of at least "The West." To locate it within its world context in The Fourth Epoch, perhaps we may call it The Overdeveloped Society.

The *Underdeveloped Country* as you know, is one in which the focus of life is necessarily upon economic subsistence; its industrial equipment is not sufficient to meet Western standards of minimum comfort. Its style of life and its system of power are dominated by the struggle to accumulate the primary means of industrial production.

In a *Properly Developing Society,* one might suppose that deliberately cultivated styles of life would be central; decisions about standards of living would be made in terms of debated choices among such styles; the industrial equipment of such a society would be maintained as an instrument to increase the range of choice among styles of life.

But in *The Overdeveloped Nation,* the standard of living dominates the style of life; its inhabitants are possessed, as it were, by its industrial and commercial apparatus: collectively, by the maintenance of conspicuous production; individually, by the frenzied pursuit and maintenance of commodities. Around these fetishes, life, labor and leisure are increasingly organized. Focused upon these, the struggle for status supplements the struggle for survival; a panic for status replaces the proddings of poverty.

In underdeveloped countries, industrialization, however harsh, may be seen as man conquering nature and so freeing himself from want. But in the overdeveloped nation, as industrialization proceeds, the economic emphasis moves from production to merchandizing, and the economic system which makes a fetish of efficiency becomes highly inefficient and systematically wasteful. The pivotal decade for this shift in the United States was the twenties, but it is since the ending of the second world war that the overdeveloped economy has truly come to flourish.

Surely there is no need to elaborate this theme in detail; since Thorstein Veblen formulated it, it has been several times "affluently" rediscovered. Society in brief has become a great salesroom—and a network of rackets: the gimmick of success becomes the yearly change of model, as in the mass-society fashion becomes universal. The marketing apparatus transforms the human being into the ultimately-saturated man—the cheerful robot—and makes "anxious obsolescence" the American way of life.

## V

But all this—although enormously important to the quality of life—is, I suppose, merely the obvious surface. Beneath it there are institutions which in the United States today are as far removed from the images of Tocqueville as is Russia today from the classic expectations of Marx.

The power structure of this society is based upon a privately incorporated economy that is also a permanent war economy. Its most important relations with the state now rest upon the coincidence of military and corporate interests—as defined by generals and businessmen, and accepted by politicians and publics. It is an economy dominated by a few hundred corporations, economically and politically interrelated, which together hold the keys to economic decision. These dominating corporation-hierarchies probably represent the highest concentration of the greatest economic power in human history, including that of the Soviet Union. They are firmly knit to political and military institutions, but they are dogmatic—even maniacal—in their fetish of the "freedom" of their private and irresponsible power.

I should like to put this matter in terms of certain parallel developments in the USA and the USSR. The very terms of their world antagonism are furthering their similarities. Geographically and ethnically both are supersocieties; unlike the nations of Europe, each has amalgamated on a continental domain great varieties of peoples and cultures. The power of both is based upon technological development. In both, this development is made into a cultural and a social fetish, rather than an instrument under continual public appraisal and control. In neither is there significant craftsmanship in work or significant leisure in the nonworking life. In both, men at leisure and at work are subjected to impersonal bureaucracies. In neither do workers control the process of production or consumers truly shape the process of consumption. Workers' control is as far removed from both as is consumers' sovereignty.

In both the United States and the Soviet Union, as the political order is enlarged and centralized, it becomes less political and more bureaucratic; less the locale of a struggle than an object to be managed. In neither are there nationally responsible parties which debate openly and clearly the issues which these nations, and indeed the world, now so rigidly confront. Under some conditions, must we not recognize that the two-party state can be as irresponsible as is a one-party state?

In neither the USA nor the USSR is there a senior civil service firmly linked to the world of knowledge and sensibility and composed of skilled men who, in their careers and in their aspirations, are truly independent—in the USA of corporation interests, in the USSR of party dictation.

In neither of these superpowers are there, as central facts of power, voluntary associations linking individuals, smaller communities and publics, on the one hand, with the state, the military establishment, the economic apparatus on the other. Accordingly, in neither are there readily available vehicles for reasoned opinions and instruments for the national exertion of public will. Such voluntary associations are no longer a dominant feature of the political structure of the overdeveloped society.

The classic conditions of democracy, in summary, do not exactly flourish in the overdeveloped society; democratic formations are not now ascendant in the power structure of the United States or of the Soviet Union. Within both, history-making decisions and lack of decisions are virtually monopolized by elites who have access to the material and cultural means by which history is now powerfully being made.

## VI

I stress these parallels, and perhaps exaggerate them, because of the great nationalist emphasis upon the differences between the two world antagonists. The parallels are, of course, due in each case to entirely different sources; and so are the great differences. In the capitalist societies the development of the means of power has occurred gradually, and many cultural traditions have restrained and shaped them. In most of the Communist societies they have happened rapidly and brutally and from the beginning under tightly centralized authority; and without the cultural revolutions which in the West so greatly strengthened and gave political focus to the idea of human freedom.

You may say that all this is an immoderate and biased view of America, that America also contains many good features. Indeed that is so. But you must not expect me to provide A Balanced View. I am not a sociological bookkeeper. Moreover, "balanced views" are now usually surface views which rest upon the homogeneous absence of imagination and the passive avoidance of reflection. A balanced view is usually, in the phrase of Royden Harrison, merely a vague point of equilibrium between platitudes.

I feel no need for, and perhaps am incapable of arranging for you, a lyric upsurge, a cheerful little pat on the moral back. Yet perhaps, by returning to my point of beginning, I can remind you of the kinds of problems you might want to confront. I must make two points only: one about fate and the making of history; the other about the roles many intellectuals are now enacting.

Fate has to do with events in history that are the summary and unintended results of innumerable decisions of innumerable men. Each of their decisions is minute in consequence and subject to cancellation or reinforcement by other such decisions. There is no link between any one man's intention and the summary result of the innumerable decisions. Events are beyond human decisions: history is made behind men's backs.

So conceived, fate is not a universal fact; it is not inherent in the nature of history or in the nature of man. In a society in which the ultimate weapon is the rifle; in which the typical economic unit is the family farm and shop; in which the national-state does not yet exist or is merely a distant framework; and in which communication is by word of mouth, handbill, pulpit—in *such* a society, history is indeed fate.

But consider now the major clue to our condition, to the shape of the overdeveloped society in The Fourth Epoch. In modern industrial society the means of economic production are developed and centralized, as peasants and artisans are replaced by private corporations and government industries. In the modern nation-state the means of violence and of administration undergo similar developments, as kings control nobles and self-equipped knights are replaced by standing armies and now by fearful military machines. The *postmodern* climax of all three developments—in economics, in politics, and in violence—is now occurring most dramatically in the USA and the USSR. In the polarized world of our time, international as well as national means of history-making are being centralized. Is it not thus clear that the scope and the chance for conscious human agency in history-making are just now uniquely available? Elites of power in charge of these means do now make history—to be sure, "under circumstances not of their own choosing"—but compared to other men and other epochs, these circumstances themselves certainly do not appear to be overwhelming.

And surely here is the paradox of our immediate situation: the facts about the newer means of history-making are a signal that men are not necessarily in the grip of fate, that men *can* now make history. But this fact stands ironically alongside the further fact that just now those ideologies which offer men the hope of making history have declined and are collapsing in the overdeveloped nation of the United States. That collapse is also the collapse of the expectations of the Enlightenment, that reason and freedom would come to prevail as paramount forces in human history. It also involves the abdication of many Western intellectuals.

## VII

In the overdeveloped society, where is the intelligentsia that is carrying on the big discourse of the Western world *and* whose work as intellectuals is influential among parties and publics and relevant to the great decisions of our time? Where are the mass media open to such men? Who among those in charge of the two-party state and its ferocious military machines are alert to what goes on in the world of knowledge and reason and sensibility? Why is the free intellect so divorced from decisions of power? Why does there now prevail among men of power such a higher and irresponsible ignorance?

In The Fourth Epoch, must we not face the possibility that the human mind as a social fact might be deteriorating in quality and cultural level, and yet not many would notice it because of the overwhelming accumulation of technological gadgets? Is not that the meaning of rationality without reason? Of human alienation? Of the absence of any role for reason in human affairs? The accumulation of gadgets hides these meanings: those who use them do not understand them; those who invent and maintain them do not understand much else. That is why we may not, without great ambiguity, use technological abundance as the index of human quality and cultural progress.

## VIII

To formulate any problem requires that we state the values involved and the threat to these values. For it is the felt threat to cherished values—such as those of freedom and reason— that is the necessary moral substance of all significant problems of social inquiry, and as well of all public issues and private troubles.

The values involved in the cultural problem of freedom and individuality are conveniently embodied in all that is suggested by the ideal of The Renaissance Man. The threat to that ideal is the ascendancy among us of The Cheerful Robot, of the man with rationality but without reason. The values involved in the political problem of history-making are embodied in the Promethean ideal of its human making. The threat to that ideal is twofold: On the one hand, history-making may well go by default, men may continue to abdicate its willful making, and so merely drift. On the other hand, history may indeed be made—but by narrow elite circles without effective responsibility to those who must try to survive the consequences of their decisions and of their defaults.

I do not know the answer to the question of political

irresponsibility in our time or to the cultural and political question of The Cheerful Robot; but is it not clear that no answers will be found unless these problems are at least confronted? Is it not obvious that the ones to confront them, above all others, are the intellectuals, the scholars, the ministers, the scientists of the rich societies? That many of them do not now do so, with moral passion, with intellectual energy, is surely the greatest human default being committed by privileged men in our times.

# The Conquest of the Unhappy Consciousness: Repressive Desublimation

## Herbert Marcuse

Invalidating the cherished images of transcendence by incorporating them into its omnipresent daily reality, this society testifies to the extent to which insoluble conflicts are becoming manageable—to which tragedy and romance, archetypal dreams and anxieties are being made susceptible to technical solution and dissolution. The psychiatrist takes care of the Don Juans, Romeos, Hamlets, Fausts, as he takes care of Oedipus—he cures them. The rulers of the world are losing their metaphysical features. Their appearance on television, at press conferences, in parliament, and at public hearings is hardly suitable for drama beyond that of the advertisement,[1] while the consequences of their actions surpass the scope of the drama.

The prescriptions for inhumanity and injustice are being administered by a rationally organized bureaucracy, which is, however, invisible at its vital center. The soul contains few secrets and longings which cannot be sensibly discussed, analyzed, and polled. Solitude, the very condition which sustained the individual against and beyond his society, has become technically impossible. Logical and linguistic analysis

---

[1] The legendary revolutionary hero still exists who can defy even television and the press—his world is that of the "underdeveloped" countries.

From Chapter 3, "The Conquest of the Unhappy Consciousness: Repressive Desublimation," in *One-Dimensional Man* (Beacon Press, 1964).

demonstrate that the old metaphysical problems are illusory problems; the quest for the "meaning" of things can be reformulated as the quest for the meaning of words, and the established universe of discourse and behavior can provide perfectly adequate criteria for the answer.

It is a rational universe which, by the mere weight and capabilities of its apparatus, blocks all escape. In its relation to the reality of daily life, the high culture of the past was many things—opposition and adornment, outcry and resignation. But it was also the appearance of the realm of freedom: the refusal to behave. Such refusal cannot be blocked without a compensation which seems more satisfying than the refusal. The conquest and unification of opposites, which finds its ideological glory in the transformation of higher into popular culture, takes place on a material ground of increased satisfaction. This is also the ground which allows a sweeping *desublimation*.

Artistic alienation is sublimation. It creates the images of conditions which are irreconcilable with the established Reality Principle but which, as cultural images, become tolerable, even edifying and useful. Now this imagery is invalidated. Its incorporation into the kitchen, the office, the shop; its commercial release for business and fun is, in a sense, desublimation—replacing mediated by immediate gratification. But it is desublimation practiced from a "position of strength" on the part of society, which can afford to grant more than before because its interests have become the innermost drives of its citizens, and because the joys which it grants promote social cohesion and contentment.

The Pleasure Principle absorbs the Reality Principle; sexuality is liberated (or rather liberalized) in socially constructive forms. This notion implies that there are repressive modes of desublimation,[2] compared with which the sublimated drives and objectives contain more deviation, more freedom, and more refusal to heed the social taboos. It appears that such repressive desublimation is indeed operative in the sexual sphere, and here, as in the desublimation of higher culture, operates as the by-product of the social controls of technological reality, which extend liberty while intensifying domination. The link between desublimation and technological

---

[2] See my book *Eros and Civilization* (Boston: Beacon Press, 1954), esp. Chapter X.

society can perhaps best be illuminated by discussing the change in the social use of instinctual energy.

In this society, not all the time spent on and with mechanisms is labor time (i.e., unpleasurable but necessary toil), and not all the energy saved by the machine is labor power. Mechanization has also "saved" libido, the energy of the Life Instincts—that is, has barred it from previous modes of realization. This is the kernel of truth in the romantic contrast between the modern traveler and the wandering poet or artisan, between assembly line and handicraft, town and city, factory-produced bread and the homemade loaf, the sailboat and the outboard motor, etc. True, this romantic pre-technical world was permeated with misery, toil, and filth, and these in turn were the background of all pleasure and joy. Still, there was a "landscape," a medium of libidinal experience which no longer exists.

With its disappearance (itself a historical prerequisite of progress), a whole dimension of human activity and passivity has been de-eroticized. The environment from which the individual could obtain pleasure—which he could cathect as gratifying almost as an extended zone of the body—has been rigidly reduced. Consequently, the "universe" of libidinous cathexis is likewise reduced. The effect is a localization and contraction of libido, the reduction of erotic to sexual experience and satisfaction.[3]

For example, compare lovemaking in a meadow and in an automobile, on a lovers' walk outside the town walls and on a Manhattan street. In the former cases, the environment partakes of and invites libidinal cathexis and tends to be eroticized. Libido transcends beyond the immediate erotogenic zones—a process of nonrepressive sublimation. In contrast, a mechanized environment seems to block such self-transcendence of libido. Impelled in the striving to extend the field of erotic gratification, libido becomes less "polymorphous," less capable of eroticism beyond localized sexuality, and the *latter* is intensified.

Thus diminishing erotic and intensifying sexual energy, the technological reality *limits the scope of sublimation*. It also reduces the *need* for sublimation. In the mental apparatus, the tension between that which is desired and that which is

---

[3] In accordance with the terminology used in the later works of Freud: sexuality as "specialized" partial drive; Eros as that of the entire organism.

permitted seems considerably lowered, and the Reality Principle no longer seems to require a sweeping and painful
transformation of instinctual needs. The individual must
adapt himself to a world which does not seem to demand the
denial of his innermost needs—a world which is not essentially hostile.

The organism is thus being preconditioned for the spontaneous acceptance of what is offered. Inasmuch as the greater
liberty involves a contraction rather than extension and
development of instinctual needs, it works *for* rather than
*against* the status quo of general repression—one might speak
of "institutionalized desublimation." The latter appears to be
a vital factor in the making of the authoritarian personality of
our time.

It has often been noted that advanced industrial civilization
operates with a greater degree of sexual freedom—
"operates" in the sense that the latter becomes a market
value and a factor of social mores. Without ceasing to be an
instrument of labor, the body is allowed to exhibit its sexual
features in the everyday work world and in work relations.
This is one of the unique achievements of industrial society—
rendered possible by the reduction of dirty and heavy physical labor; by the availability of cheap, attractive clothing,
beauty culture, and physical hygiene; by the requirements of
the advertising industry, etc. The sexy office and sales girls,
the handsome, virile junior executive and floor walker are
highly marketable commodities, and the possession of suitable mistresses—once the prerogative of kings, princes, and
lords—facilitates the career of even the less exalted ranks in
the business community.

Functionalism, going artistic, promotes this trend. Shops
and offices open themselves through huge glass windows and
expose their personnel; inside, high counters and nontrans-
parent partitions are coming down. The corrosion of privacy
in massive apartment houses and suburban homes breaks the
barrier which formerly separated the individual from the
public existence and exposes more easily the attractive qualities of other wives and other husbands.

This socialization is not contradictory but complementary
to the de-erotization of the environment. Sex is integrated
into work and public relations and is thus made more
susceptible to (controlled) satisfaction. Technical progress

and more comfortable living permit the systematic inclusion of libidinal components into the realm of commodity production and exchange. But no matter how controlled the mobilization of instinctual energy may be (it sometimes amounts to a scientific management of libido), no matter how much it may serve as a prop for the status quo—it is also gratifying to the managed individuals, just as racing the outboard motor, pushing the power lawn mower, and speeding the automobile are fun.

This mobilization and administration of libido may account for much of the voluntary compliance, the absence of terror, the preestablished harmony between individual needs and socially-required desires, goals, and aspirations. The technological and political conquest of the transcending factors in human existence, so characteristic of advanced industrial civilization, here asserts itself in the instinctual sphere: satisfaction in a way which generates submission and weakens the rationality of protest.

The range of socially permissible and desirable satisfaction is greatly enlarged, but through this satisfaction, the Pleasure Principle is reduced—deprived of the claims which are irreconcilable with the established society. Pleasure, thus adjusted, generates submission.

In contrast to the pleasures of adjusted desublimation, sublimation preserves the consciousness of the renunciations which the repressive society inflicts upon the individual, and thereby preserves the need for liberation. To be sure, all sublimation is enforced by the power of society, but the unhappy consciousness of this power already breaks through alienation. To be sure, all sublimation accepts the social barrier to instinctual gratification, but it also transgresses this barrier.

The Superego, in censoring the unconscious and in implanting conscience, also censors the censor because the developed conscience registers the forbidden evil act not only in the individual but also in his society. Conversely, loss of conscience due to the satisfactory liberties granted by an unfree society makes for a *happy consciousness* which facilitates acceptance of the misdeeds of this society. It is the token of declining autonomy and comprehension. Sublimation demands a high degree of autonomy and comprehension; it is mediation between the conscious and the unconscious, between the primary and secondary processes, between the intellect and instinct, renunciation and rebellion. In its most accomplished modes, such as in the artistic *oeuvre*, sublimation becomes the cognitive power which defeats suppression while bowing to it.

In the light of the cognitive function of this mode of sublimation, the desublimation rampant in advanced industrial society reveals its truly conformist function. This liberation of sexuality (and of aggressiveness) frees the instinctual drives from much of the unhappiness and discontent that elucidate the repressive power of the established universe of satisfaction. To be sure, there is pervasive unhappiness, and the happy consciousness is shaky enough—a thin surface over fear, frustration, and disgust. This unhappiness lends itself easily to political mobilization; without room for conscious development, it may become the instinctual reservoir for a new fascist way of life and death. But there are many ways in which the unhappiness beneath the happy consciousness may be turned into a source of strength and cohesion for the social order. The conflicts of the unhappy individual now seem far more amenable to cure than those which made for Freud's "discontent in civilization," and they seem more adequately defined in terms of the "neurotic personality of our time" than in terms of the eternal struggle between Eros and Thanatos.

The way in which controlled desublimation may weaken the instinctual revolt against the established Reality Principle may be illuminated by the contrast between the representation of sexuality in classical and romantic literature and in our contemporary literature. If one selects, from among the works which are, in their very substance and inner form, determined by the erotic commitment, such essentially different examples as Racine's *Phèdre*, Goethe's *Wahlverwandtschaften*, Baudelaire's *Les Fleurs du Mal*, Tolstoy's *Anna Karenina*, sexuality consistently appears in a highly sublimated, "mediated," reflective form—but in this form, it is absolute, uncompromising, unconditional. The dominion of Eros is, from the beginning, also that of Thanatos. Fulfillment is destruction, not in a moral or sociological but in an ontological sense. It is beyond good and evil, beyond social morality, and thus it remains beyond the reaches of the established Reality Principle, which this Eros refuses and explodes.

In contrast, desublimated sexuality is rampant in O'Neill's alcoholics and Faulkner's savages, in the *Streetcar Named Desire* and under the *Hot Tin Roof*, in *Lolita*, in all the stories of Hollywood and New York orgies, and the adventures of suburban housewives. This is infinitely more realistic, daring, uninhibited. It is part and parcel of the society in which it happens, but nowhere its negation. What happens is surely wild and obscene, virile and tasty, quite immoral—and, precisely because of that, perfectly harmless.

Freed from the sublimated form which was the very token of its irreconcilable dreams—a form which is the style, the language in which the story is told—sexuality turns into a vehicle for the bestsellers of oppression. It could not be said of any of the sexy women in contemporary literature what Balzac says of the whore Esther: that hers was the tenderness which blossoms only in infinity. This society turns everything it touches into a potential source of progress *and* of exploitation, of drudgery *and* satisfaction, of freedom *and* of oppression. Sexuality is no exception.

The concept of controlled desublimation would imply the possibility of a simultaneous release of repressed sexuality *and* aggressiveness, a possibility which seems incompatible with Freud's notion of the fixed quantum of instinctual energy available for distribution between the two primary drives. According to Freud, strenghtening of sexuality (libido) would necessarily involve weakening of aggressiveness, and vice versa. However, if the socially permitted and encouraged release of libido would be that of partial and localized sexuality, it would be tantamount to an actual compression of erotic energy, and this desublimation would be compatible with the growth of unsublimated as well as sublimated forms of aggressiveness. The latter is rampant throughout contemporary industrial society.

Has it attained a degree of normalization where the individuals are getting used to the risk of their own dissolution and disintegration in the course of normal national preparedness? Or is this acquiescence entirely due to their impotence to do much about it? In any case, the risk of avoidable, man-made destruction has become normal equipment in the mental as well as material household of the people, so that it can no longer serve to indict or refute the established social system. Moreover, as part of their daily household, it may even tie them to this system. The economic and political connection between the absolute enemy and the high standard of living (and the desired level of employment!) is transparent enough, but also rational enough to be accepted.

Assuming that the Destruction Instinct (in the last analysis: the Death Instinct) is a large component of the energy which feeds the technical conquest of man and nature, it seems that society's growing capacity to manipulate technical progress also increases its *capacity to manipulate and control this instinct*, i.e., to satisfy it "productively." Then social cohesion would be strengthened at the deepest instinctual roots. The supreme risk, and even the fact of war would meet, not only with helpless acceptance, but also with instinctual approval on the part of the victims. Here too, we would have controlled desublimation.

Institutionalized desublimation thus appears to be an aspect of the "conquest of transcendence" achieved by the one-dimensional society. Just as this society tends to reduce, and even absorb opposition (the qualitative difference!) in the realm of politics and higher culture, so it does in the instinctual sphere. The result is the atrophy of the mental organs for grasping the contradictions and the alternatives and, in the one remaining dimension of technological rationality, the *Happy Consciousness* comes to prevail.

It reflects the belief that the real is rational, and that the established system, in spite of everything, delivers the goods. The people are led to find in the productive apparatus the effective agent of thought and action to which their personal thought and action can and must be surrendered. And in this transfer, the apparatus also assumes the role of a moral agent. Conscience is absolved by reification, by the general necessity of things.

In this general necessity, guilt has no place. One man can give the signal that liquidates hundreds and thousands of people, then declare himself free from all pangs of conscience, and live happily ever after. The antifascist powers who beat fascism on the battlefields reap the benefits of the Nazi scientists, generals, and engineers; they have the historical advantage of the late-comer. What begins as the horror of the concentration camps turns into the practice of training people for abnormal conditions—a subterranean human existence and the daily intake of radioactive nourishment. A

Christian minister declares that it does not contradict Christian principles to prevent with all available means your neighbor from entering your bomb shelter. Another Christian minister contradicts his colleague and says it does. Who is right? Again, the neutrality of technological rationality shows forth over and above politics, and again it shows forth as spurious, for in both cases, it serves the politics of domination.

> "The world of the concentration camps . . . was not an exceptionally monstrous society. What we saw there was the image, and in a sense the quintessence, of the infernal society into which we are plunged every day."[4]

It seems that even the most hideous transgressions can be repressed in such a manner that, for all practical purposes, they have ceased to be a danger for society. Or, if their eruption leads to functional disturbances in the individual (as in the case of one Hiroshima pilot), it does not disturb the functioning of society. A mental hospital manages the disturbance.

The Happy Consciousness has no limits—it arranges games with death and disfiguration in which fun, team work, and strategic importance mix in rewarding social harmony. The Rand Corporation, which unites scholarship, research, the military, the climate, and the good life, reports such games in a style of absolving cuteness, in its "RANDom News," volume 9, number 1, under the heading BETTER SAFE THAN SORRY. The rockets are rattling, the H-bomb is waiting, and the space-flights are flying, and the problem is "how to guard the nation and the free world." In all this, the military planners are worried, for "the cost of taking chances, of experimenting and making a mistake, may be fearfully high." But here RAND comes in; RAND relieves, and "devices like RAND'S SAFE come into the picture." The picture into which they come is unclassified. It is a picture in

---

[4] E. Ionesco, in *Nouvelle Revue Française*, July 1956, as quoted in *London Times Literary Supplement*, March 4, 1960. Herman Kahn suggests in a 1959 RAND study (RM-2206-RC) that "a study should be made of the survival of populations in environments similar to overcrowded shelters (concentration camps, Russian and German use of crowded freight cars, troopships, crowded prisons . . . etc.). Some useful guiding principles might be found and adapted to the shelter program."

which "the world becomes a map, missiles merely symbols [long live the soothing power of symbolism!], and wars just [just] plans and calculations written down on paper . . ." In this picture, RAND has transfigured the world into an interesting technological game, and one can relax—the "military planners can gain valuable 'synthetic' experience without risk."

## PLAYING THE GAME

To understand the game one should participate, for understanding is "in the experience."

Because SAFE players have come from almost every department at RAND as well as the Air Force, we might find a physicist, an engineer, and an economist on the Blue team. The Red team will represent a similar cross-section.

The first day is taken up by a joint briefing on what the game is all about and a study of the rules. When the teams are finally seated around the maps in their respective rooms the game begins. Each team receives its policy statement from the Game Director. These statements, usually prepared by a member of the Control Group, give an estimate of the world situation at the time of playing, some information on the policy of the opposing team, the objectives to be met by the team, and the team's budget. (The policies are changed for each game to explore a wide range of strategic possibilities.)

In our hypothetical game, Blue's objective is to maintain a deterrent capability throughout the game—that is, maintain a force that is capable of striking back at Red so Red will be unwilling to risk an attack. (Blue also receives some information on the Red policy.)

Red's policy is to achieve force superiority over Blue.

The budgets of Blue and Red compare with actual defense budgets . . .

It is comforting to hear that the game has been played since 1961 at RAND, "down in our labyrinthine basement— somewhere under the Snack Bar," and that "Menus on the walls of the Red and Blue rooms list available weapons and hardware that the teams buy . . . About seventy items in all." There is a "Game Director" who interprets game rules, for although "the rule book complete with diagrams and illustrations is 66 pages," problems inevitably arise during the play. The Game Director also has another important function: "without previously notifying the players," he "introduces war to get a measure of the effectiveness of the military forces in being." But then, the caption announces "Coffee, Cake, and Ideas." Relax! The "game continues through the remaining periods—to 1972 when it ends. Then the Blue and Red teams bury the missiles and sit down together for coffee and cake at the 'post mortem' session." But don't relax too much: there is "one real-world situation that can't be transposed effectively to SAFE," and that is—"negotiation." We are grateful for it: the one hope that is left in the real world situation is beyond the reaches of RAND.

Obviously, in the realm of the Happy Consciousness, guilt feeling has no place, and the calculus takes care of conscience. When the whole is at stake, there is no crime except that of rejecting the whole, or not defending it. Crime, guilt, and guilt feeling become a private affair. Freud revealed in the psyche of the individual the crimes of mankind, in the individual case history the history of the whole. This fatal link is successfully suppressed. Those who identify themselves with the whole, who are installed as the leaders and defenders of the whole can make mistakes, but they cannot do wrong— they are not guilty. They may become guilty again when this identification no longer holds, when they are gone.

# The Two Nations

## Michael Harrington

The United States in the sixties contains an affluent society within its borders. Millions and tens of millions enjoy the highest standard of life the world has ever known. This blessing is mixed. It is built upon a peculiarly distorted economy, one that often proliferates pseudo-needs rather than satisfying human needs. For some, it has resulted in a sense of spiritual emptiness, of alienation. Yet a man would be a fool to prefer hunger to satiety, and the material gains at least open up the possibility of a rich and full existence.

At the same time, the United States contains an underdeveloped nation, a culture of poverty. Its inhabitants do not suffer the extreme privation of the peasants of Asia or the tribesmen of Africa, yet the mechanism of the misery is similar. They are beyond history, beyond progress, sunk in a paralyzing, maiming routine.

The new nations, however, have one advantage: poverty is so general and so extreme that it is the passion of the entire society to obliterate it. Every resource, every policy, is measured by its effect on the lowest and most impoverished. There is a gigantic mobilization of the spirit of the society: aspiration becomes a national purpose that penetrates to every village and motivates a historic transformation.

From *The Other America* (The Macmillan Company, 1962).

But this country seems to be caught in a paradox. Because its poverty is not so deadly, because so many are enjoying a decent standard of life, there are indifference and blindness to the plight of the poor. There are even those who deny that the culture of poverty exists. It is as if Disraeli's famous remark about the two nations of the rich and the poor had come true in a fantastic fashion. At precisely that moment in history where for the first time a people have the material ability to end poverty, they lack the will to do so. They cannot see; they cannot act. The consciences of the well-off are the victims of affluence; the lives of the poor are the victims of a physical and spiritual misery.

The problem, then, is to a great extent one of vision. The nation of the well-off must be able to see through the wall of affluence and recognize the alien citizens on the other side. And there must be vision in the sense of purpose, of aspiration: if the word does not grate upon the ears of a gentile America, there must be a passion to end poverty, for nothing less than that will do.

In this summary chapter, I hope I can supply at least some of the material for such a vision. Let us try to understand the other America as a whole, to see its perspective for the future if it is left alone, to realize the responsibility and the potential for ending this nation in our midst.

But, when all is said and done, the decisive moment occurs after all the sociology and the description is in. There is really no such thing as "the material for a vision." After one reads the facts, either there are anger and shame, or there are not. And, as usual, the fate of the poor hangs upon the decision of the better-off. If this anger and shame are not forthcoming, someone can write a book about the other America a generation from now and it will be the same, or worse.

I

Perhaps the most important analytic point to have emerged in this description of the other America is the fact that poverty in America forms a culture, a way of life and feeling, that it makes a whole. It is crucial to generalize this idea, for it profoundly affects how one moves to destroy poverty.

The most obvious aspect of this interrelatedness is in the way in which the various subcultures of the other America feed into one another. This is clearest with the aged. There the poverty of the declining years is, for some millions of human beings, a function of the poverty of the earlier years. If there were adequate medical care for everyone in the United States, there would be less misery for old people. It is as simple as that. Or there is the relation between the poor farmers and the unskilled workers. When a man is driven off the land because of the impoverishment worked by technological progress, he leaves one part of the culture of poverty and joins another. If something were done about the low-income farmer, that would immediately tell in the statistics of urban unemployment and the economic underworld. The same is true of the Negroes. Any gain for America's minorities will immediately be translated into an advance for all the unskilled workers. One cannot raise the bottom of a society without benefiting everyone above.

Indeed, there is a curious advantage in the wholeness of poverty. Since the other America forms a distinct system within the United States, effective action at any one decisive point will have a "multiplier" effect; it will ramify through the entire culture of misery and ultimately through the entire society.

Then, poverty is a culture in the sense that the mechanism of impoverishment is fundamentally the same in every part of the system. The vicious circle is a basic pattern. It takes different forms for the unskilled workers, for the aged, for the Negroes, for the agricultural workers, but in each case the principle is the same. There are people in the affluent society who are poor because they are poor; and who stay poor because they are poor.

To realize this is to see that there are some tens of millions of Americans who are beyond the welfare state. Some of them are simply not covered by social legislation: they are omitted from Social Security and from minimum wage. Others are covered, but since they are so poor they do not know how to take advantage of the opportunities, or else their coverage is so inadequate as not to make a difference.

The welfare state was designed during that great burst of social creativity that took place in the 1930's. As previously noted its structure corresponds to the needs of those who played the most important role in building it: the middle third, the organized workers, the forces of urban liberalism, and so on. At the worst, there is "socialism for the rich and free enterprise for the poor," as when the huge corporation farms are the main beneficiaries of the farm program while the poor farmers get practically nothing; or when public funds are directed to aid in the construction of luxury housing while the slums are left to themselves (or become more dense as space is created for the well-off).

So there is the fundamental paradox of the welfare state: that it is not built for the desperate, but for those who are already capable of helping themselves. As long as the illusion persists that the poor are merrily freeloading on the public dole, so long will the other America continue unthreatened. The truth, it must be understood, is the exact opposite. The poor get less out of the welfare state than any group in America.

This is, of course, related to the most distinguishing mark of the other America: its common sense of hopelessness. For even when there are programs designed to help the other Americans, the poor are held back by their own pessimism.

On one level this fact has been described in this book as a matter of "aspiration." Like the Asian peasant, the impoverished American tends to see life as a fate, an endless cycle from which there is no deliverance. Lacking hope (and he is realistic to feel this way in many cases), that famous solution to all problems—let us educate the poor—becomes less and less meaningful. A person has to feel that education will do something for him if he is to gain from it. Placing a magnificent school with a fine faculty in the middle of a slum is, I suppose, better than having a run-down building staffed by incompetents. But it will not really make a difference so long as the environment of the tenement, the family, and the street counsels the children to leave as soon as they can and to disregard schooling.

On another level, the emotions of the other America are even more profoundly disturbed. Here it is not lack of aspiration and of hope; it is a matter of personal chaos. The drunkenness, the unstable marriages, the violence of the other America are not simply facts about individuals. They are the description of an entire group in the society who react this way because of the conditions under which they live.

In short, being poor is not one aspect of a person's life in this country; it is his life. Taken as a whole, poverty is a culture. Taken on the family level, it has the same quality. These are people who lack education and skill, who have bad health, poor housing, low levels of aspiration and high levels of mental distress. They are, in the language of sociology, "multiproblem" families. Each disability is the more intense because it exists within a web of disabilities. And if one problem is solved, and the others are left constant, there is little gain.

One might translate these facts into the moralistic language so dear to those who would condemn the poor for their faults. The other Americans are those who live at a level of life beneath moral choice, who are so submerged in their poverty that one cannot begin to talk about free choice. The point is not to make them wards of the state. Rather, society must help them before they can help themselves.

## II

There is another view about the culture of poverty in America: that by the end of the seventies it will have been halved.

It is important to deal in some detail with this theory. To begin with, it is not offered by reactionaries. The real die-hards in the United States do not even know the poor exist. As soon as someone begins to talk on the subject, that stamps him as a humanitarian. And this is indeed the case with those who look to a relatively automatic improvement in the lot of the other America during the next twenty years or so.

The second reason why this view deserves careful consideration is that it rests, to a considerable extent, upon the projection of inevitable and automatic change. Its proponents are for social legislation and for speeding up and deepening this process. But their very arguments could be used to justify a comfortable, complacent inaction.

So, does poverty have a future in the United States?

One of the most reasonable and sincere statements of the theme that poverty is coming to an end in America is made by Robert Lampman in the Joint Committee Study Paper "The Low-Income Population and Economic Growth." Lampman estimates that around twenty percent of the nation, some 32,000,000 people, are poor. (My disagreements with his count are stated in the Appendix.) And he writes, "By 1977–87 we would expect about ten percent of the population to have low income status as compared to about twenty percent now."

The main point in Lampman's relatively optimistic argument is that poverty will decline naturally with a continuing rate of economic growth. As the sixties begin, however, this assumption is not a simple one. In the postwar period, growth increased until about the mid-fifties. Then a falling off occurred. In each of the postwar recessions, the recovery left a larger reservoir of "normal" prosperity unemployment. Also, long-term unemployment became more and more of a factor among the jobless. There were more people out of work, and they stayed out of work longer.

In the first period of the Kennedy Administration, various economists presented figures as to what kind of Government action was necessary so as really to attack the problem of depressed areas and low-income occupations. There were differences, of course, but the significant fact is that the legislation finally proposed was usually only a percentage of the need as described by the Administration itself. There is no point now in becoming an economic prophet. Suffice it to say that serious and responsible economists feel that the response of the society has been inadequate.

This has led to a paradoxical situation, one that became quite obvious when economic recovery from the recession began in the spring of 1961. The business indicators were all pointing upward: production and productivity were on the increase. Yet the human indexes of recession showed a tenacity despite the industrial gain. Unemployment remained at high levels. An extreme form of the "class unemployment" described earlier seemed to be built into the economy.

At any rate, one can say that if this problem is not solved the other America will not only persist; it will grow. Thus, the first point of the optimistic thesis strikes me as somewhat ambiguous, for it too quickly assumes that the society will make the needed response.

But even if one makes the assumption that there will be steady economic growth, that will not necessarily lead to the automatic elimination of poverty in the United States. J. K. Galbraith, it will be remembered, has argued that the "new" poverty demonstrates a certain immunity to progress. In making his projection of the abolition of half of the culture of poverty within the next generation, Lampman deals with this point, and it is important to follow his argument.

Lampman rejects the idea that insular (or depressed-areas) poverty will really drag the poor down in the long run. As an example of this point, he cites the fact that the number of rural farm families with incomes of under $2,000 fell during the 1947–1957 period from 3.3 million to 2.4 million because of a movement off the farm.

This point illustrates the problem of dealing with simple statistics. A movement from the farm to the city, that is, from rural poverty to urban poverty, will show an upward movement in money income. This is true, among other reasons because the money income of the urban poor is higher than that of the country poor. But this same change does not necessarily mean that a human being has actually improved his status, that he has escaped from the culture of poverty. As was noted in the chapter on the agricultural poor, these people who are literally driven off the land are utterly unprepared for city life. They come to the metropolis in a time of rising skill requirements and relatively high levels of unemployment. They will often enter the economic under world. Statistically, they can be recorded as a gain, because they have more money. Socially, they have simply transferred from one part of the culture of poverty to another.

At the same time, it should be noted that although there has been this tremendous exodus of the rural poor, the proportion of impoverished farms in America's agriculture has remained roughly the same.

Then Lampman deals with Galbraith's theory of "case poverty," of those who have certain disabilities that keep them down in the culture of poverty. Here it should be noted again that Galbraith himself is somewhat optimistic about case poverty. He tends to regard the bad health of the poor, physical as well as mental, as being facts about them that are individual and personal. If this book is right, particularly in the discussion of the twisted spirit within the culture of poverty, that is not the case. The personal ills of the poor are a social consequence, not a bit of biography about them. They will continue as long as the environment of poverty persists.

But Lampman's optimism goes beyond that of Galbraith. He believes that disabilities of case poverty ("mental deficiency, bad health, inability to adapt to the discipline of modern economic life, excessive procreation, alcohol, insufficient education") are "moderated over time." And he takes as his main case in point education. "For example, average educational attainment levels will rise in future years simply because younger people presently have better education than older people. Hence, as the current generation of old people pass from the scene, the percent of persons with low educational attainment will fall."

This is true, yet it is misleading if it is not placed in the context of the changes in the society as a whole. It is much more possible today to be poor with a couple of years of high school than it was a generation ago. As I have pointed out earlier, the skill level of the economy has been changing, and educational deficiency, if anything, becomes an even greater burden as a result. In this case, saying that people will have more education is not saying that they will escape the culture of poverty. It could have a much more ironic meaning: that America will have the most literate poor the world has even known.

Lampman himself concedes that the aged are "immune" to economic growth. If this is the case, and in the absence of ranging and comprehensive social programs, the increase in the number and percentage of the poor within the next generation will actually increase the size of the other America. Lampman also concedes that families with female heads are immune to a general prosperity, and this is another point of resistance for the culture of poverty.

Finally, Lampman is much more optimistic about "nonwhite" progress than the discussion in this book would justify. I will not repeat the argument that has already been given. Let me simply state the point baldly: the present rate of economic progress among the minorities is agonizing slow, and one cannot look for dramatic gains from this direction.

Thus, I would agree with Galbraith that poverty in the sixties has qualities that give it a hardiness in the face of affluence heretofore unknown. As documented and described in this book, there are many special factors keeping the unskilled workers, the minorities, the agricultural poor, and the aged in the culture of poverty. If there is to be a way out, it will come from human action, from political change, not from automatic processes.

But finally, let us suppose that Lampman is correct on every point. In that case a generation of economic growth coupled with some social legislation would find America in 1987 with "only" ten percent of the nation impoverished. If, on the other hand, a vast and comprehensive program attacking the culture of poverty could speed up this whole development, and perhaps even abolish poverty within a generation, what is the reason for holding back? This suffer ing is such an abomination in a society where it is needless that anything that can be done should be done.

In all this, I do not want to depict Robert Lampman as an enemy of the poor. In all seriousness, the very fact that h writes about the subject does him credit: he has social eyes which is more than one can say for quite a few people in th society. And second, Lampman puts forward "A Program t Hasten the Reduction of Poverty" because of his genuin concern for the poor. My argument with him is not ove motive or dedication. It is only that I believe that his theor makes the reduction of poverty too easy a thing, that he ha not properly appreciated how deeply and strongly entrenche the other America is.

In any case, and from any point of view, the mora obligation is plain: there must be a crusade against thi poverty in our midst.

## III

If this research makes it clear that a basic attack upon povert is necessary, it also suggests the kind of program the natio needs.

First and foremost, any attempt to abolish poverty in th United States must seek to destroy the pessimism and fatalisn that flourish in the other America. In part, this can be don by offering real opportunities to these people, by changin; the social reality that gives rise to their sense of hopelessness But beyond that (these fears of the poor have a life of thei own and are not simply rooted in analyses of employmen chances), there should be a spirit, an élan, that communicate itself to the entire society.

If the nation comes into the other America grudgingly with the mentality of an administrator, and says, "All right we'll help you people," then there will be gains, but they wil be kept to the minimum; a dollar spent will return a dollar But if there is an attitude that society is gaining by eradicatin; poverty, if there is a positive attempt to bring these million of the poor to the point where they can make their contribu tion to the United States, that will make a huge difference The spirit of a campaign against poverty does not cost a singl cent. It is a matter of vision, of sensitivity.

Let me give an example to make this point palpable

During the Montgomery bus boycott, there was only one aim in the Negro community of that city: to integrate the buses. There were no speeches on crime or juvenile delinquency. And yet it is reported that the crime rate among Negroes in Montgomery declined. Thousands of people had been given a sense of purpose, of their own worth and dignity. On their own, and without any special urging, they began to change their personal lives; they became a different people. If the same élan could invade the other America, there would be similar results.

Second, this book is based upon the proposition that poverty forms a culture, an interdependent system. In case after case, it has been documented that one cannot deal with the various components of poverty in isolation, changing this or that condition but leaving the basic structure intact. Consequently, a campaign against the misery of the poor should be comprehensive. It should think, not in terms of this or that aspect of poverty, but along the lines of establishing new communities, of substituting a human environment for the inhuman one that now exists.

Here, housing is probably the basic point of departure. If there were the funds and imagination for a campaign to end slums in the United States, most of the other steps needed to deal with poverty could be integrated with it. The vision should be the one described in the previous chapter: the political, economic, and social integration of the poor with the rest of the society. The second nation in our midst, the other America, must be brought into the Union.

In order to do this, there is a need for planning. It is literally incredible that this nation knows so much about poverty, that it has made so many inventories of misery, and that it has done so little. The material for a comprehensive program is already available. It exists in congressional reports and the statistics of Government agencies. What is needed is that the society make use of its knowledge in a rational and systematic way. As this book is being written, there are proposals for a Department of Urban Affairs in the Cabinet (and it will probably be a reality by the time these words are published). Such an agency could be the coordinating center for a crusade against the other America. In any case, if there is not planning, any attempt to deal with the problem of poverty will fail, at least in part.

Then there are some relatively simple things that could be

done, involving the expansion of existing institutions and programs. Every American should be brought under the coverage of social security, and the payments should be enough to support a dignified old age. The principle already exists. Now it must be extended to those who need help the most. The same is true with minimum wage. The spectacle of excluding the most desperate from coverage must come to an end. If it did, there would be a giant step toward the elimination of poverty itself.

In every subculture of the other America, sickness and disease are the most important agencies of continuing misery. The New York *Times* publishes a list of the "neediest cases" each Christmas. In 1960 the descriptions of personal tragedy that ran along with this appeal involved in the majority of cases the want of those who had been struck down by illness. If there were adequate medical care, this charity would be unnecessary.

Today the debate on medical care centers on the aged. And indeed, these are the people who are in the most desperate straits. Yet it would be an error of the first magnitude to think that society's responsibility begins with those sixty-five years of age. As has been pointed out several times, the ills of the elderly are often the inheritance of the earlier years. A comprehensive medical program, guaranteeing decent care to every American, would actually reduce the cost of caring for the aged. That, of course, is only the hardheaded argument for such an approach. More importantly, such a program would make possible a human kind of existence for everyone in the society.

And finally, it must be remembered that none of these objectives can be accomplished if racial prejudice is to continue in the United States. Negroes and other minorities constitute only twenty-five percent of the poor, yet their degradation is an important element in maintaining the entire culture of poverty. As long as there is a reservoir of cheap Negro labor, there is a means of keeping the poor whites down. In this sense, civil-rights legislation is an absolutely essential component in any campaign to end poverty in the United States.

In short, the welfare provisions of American society that now help the upper two-thirds must be extended to the poor. This can be done if the other Americans are motivated to take advantage of the opportunities before them, if they are invited into the society. It can be done if there is a comprehensive program that attacks the culture of poverty at every one of its strong points.

But who will carry out this campaign?

There is only one institution in the society capable of acting to abolish poverty. That is the federal government. In saying this, I do not rejoice, for centralization can lead to an impersonal and bureaucratic program, one that will be lacking in the very human quality so essential in an approach to the poor. In saying this, I am only recording the facts of political and social life in the United States.

The cities are not now capable of dealing with poverty, and each day they become even less capable. As the middle class flees the central urban area, as various industries decentralize, the tax base of the American metropolis shrinks. At the same time, the social and economic problems with which the city must deal are on the rise. Thus, there is not a major city in the United States that is today capable of attacking poverty on its own. On the contrary, the high cost of poverty is dragging the cities down.

The state governments in this country have a political peculiarity that renders them incapable of dealing with the problem of poverty. They are, for the most part, dominated by conservative rural elements. In every state with a big industrial population, the gerrymander has given the forces of rural conservatism two or three votes per person. So it is that the state legislatures usually take more money out of the problem areas than they put back into them. So it is that state governments are notoriously weighted in the direction of caution, pinchpenny economics, and indifference to the plight of the urban millions.

The various private agencies of the society simply do not have the funds to deal with the other America. And even the "fringe benefits" negotiated by unions do not really get to the heart of the problem. In the first place, they extend to organized workers in a strong bargaining position, not to the poor. And second, they are inadequate even to the needs of those who are covered.

It is a noble sentiment to argue that private moral responsibility expressing itself through charitable contributions should be the main instrument of attacking poverty. The only problem is that such an approach does not work.

So, by process of elimination, there is no place to look

except toward the federal government. And indeed, even if there were alternate choices, Washington would have to play an important role, if only because of the need for a comprehensive program and for national planning. But in any case there is no argument, for there is only one realistic possibility: only the federal government has the power to abolish poverty.

In saying this, it is not necessary to advocate complete central control of such a campaign. Far from it. Washington is essential in a double sense: as a source of the considerable funds needed to mount a campaign against the other America, and as a place for coordination, for planning, and the establishment of national standards. The actual implementation of a program to abolish poverty can be carried out through myriad institutions, and the closer they are to the specific local area, the better the results. There are, as has been pointed out already, housing administrators, welfare workers, and city planners with dedication and vision. They are working on the local level, and their main frustration is the lack of funds. They could be trusted actually to carry through on a national program. What they lack now is money and the support of the American people.

There is no point in attempting to blueprint or detail the mechanisms and institutions of a war on poverty in the United States. There is information enough for action. All that is lacking is political will.

Thus the difficult, hardheaded question about poverty that one must answer is this: Where is the political will coming from? The other America is systematically underrepresented in the government of the United States. It cannot really speak for itself. The poor, even in politics, must always be the object of charity (with the major exception of the Negroes, who, in recent times, have made tremendous strides forward in organization).

As a result of this situation, there is no realistic hope for the abolition of poverty in the United States until there is a vast social movement, a new period of political creativity. In times of slow change or of stalemate, it is always the poor who are expendable in the halls of Congress. In 1961, for instance, the laundry workers were dropped out of the minimum wage as part of a deal with the conservatives. Precisely because they are so poor and cruelly exploited, no one had to fear their political wrath. They, and others from the culture of poverty, will achieve the protection of the welfare state when there is a movement in this land so dynamic and irresistible that it need not make concessions.

For that matter, it is much easier to catalogue the enemies of the poor than it is to recite their friends.

All the forces of conservatism in this society are ranged against the needs of the other America. The ideologues are opposed to helping the poor because this can be accomplished only through an expansion of the welfare state. The small businessmen have an immediate self-interest in maintaining the economic underworld. The powerful agencies of the corporate farms want a continuation of an agricultural program that aids the rich and does nothing for the poor.

And now the South is becoming increasingly against the poor. In the days of the New Deal, the Southern Democrats tended to vote for various kinds of social legislation. One of the most outspoken champions of public housing, Burnet Maybank, was a senator from South Carolina. For one thing, there is a Southern tradition of being against Wall Street and big business; it is part of the farmers' hostility to the railroads and the Babylons of the big city. For another, the New Deal legislation did not constitute a challenge to the system of racial segregation in the South.

But in the postwar period, this situation began to change. As industrialization came to the South, there was a growing political opposition to laws like minimum wage, to unions, and to other aspects of social change. The leaders of this area saw their depressed condition as an advantage. They could lure business with the promise of cheap, unorganized labor. They were interested in exploiting their backwardness.

The result was the strengthening of the coalition of Southern Democrats and conservative Northern Republicans. The Northern conservatives went along with opposition to Civil Rights legislation. The Southerners threw their votes into the struggle against social advance. It was this powerful coalition that exacted such a price in the first period of the Kennedy Administration. Many of the proposals that would have benefited the poor were omitted from bills in the first place, and other concessions were made in the course of the legislative battle. Thus poverty in the United States is supported by forces with great political and economic power.

On the other side, the friends of the poor are to be found in the American labor movement and among the middle-class liberals. The unions in the postwar period lost much of the élan that had characterized them in the thirties. Yet on questions of social legislation they remained the most powerful mass force committed to change in general, and to bettering the lot of the poor in particular. On issues like housing, medical care, minimum wage, and social security, the labor movement provided the strongest voice stating the cause of the poor.

Yet labor and the liberals were caught in the irrationalities of the American party system, and this was an enormous disadvantage to the other America. The unionists and their liberal allies are united in the Democratic party with the Southern conservatives. A Democratic victory was usually achieved by appealing to those who were concerned for social change. But at the same time it brought the forces of conservatism powerful positions on the standing committees of the Congress.

Indeed, part of the invisibility of poverty in American life is a result of this party structure. Since each major party contained differences within itself greater than the differences between it and the other party, politics in the fifties and early sixties tended to have an issueless character. And where issues were not discussed, the poor did not have a chance. They could benefit only if elections were designed to bring new information to the people, to wake up the nation, to challenge, and to call to action.

In all probability there will not be a real attack on the culture of poverty so long as this situation persists. For the other America cannot be abolished through concessions and compromises that are almost inevitably made at the expense of the poor. The spirit, the vision that are required if the nation is to penetrate the wall of pessimism and despair that surrounds the impoverished millions cannot be produced under such circumstances.

What is needed if poverty is to be abolished is a return of political debate, a restructuring of the party system so that there can be clear choices, a new mood of social idealism.

These, then, are the strangest poor in the history of mankind.

They exist within the most powerful and rich society the world has ever known. Their misery has continued while the majority of the nation talked of itself as being "affluent" and worried about neuroses in the suburbs. In this way tens of millions of human beings became invisible. They dropped out of sight and out of mind; they were without their own political voice.

Yet this need not be. The means are at hand to fulfill the age-old dream: poverty can now be abolished. How long shall we ignore this underdeveloped nation in our midst? How long shall we look the other way while our fellow human beings suffer? How long?

# The Fire Next Time

## James Baldwin

No one seems to know where the Nation of Islam gets its money. A vast amount, of course, is contributed by Negroes, but there are rumors to the effect that people like Birchites and certain Texas oil millionaires look with favor on the movement. I had no way of knowing whether there is any truth to the rumors, though since these people make such a point of keeping the races separate, I wouldn't be surprised if for this smoke there was some fire. In any case, during a recent Muslim rally, George Lincoln Rockwell, the chief of the American Nazi party, made a point of contributing about twenty dollars to the cause, and he and Malcolm X decided that, racially speaking, anyway, they were in complete agreement. The glorification of one race and the consequent debasement of another—or others—always has been and always will be a recipe for murder. There is no way around this. If one is permitted to treat any group of people with special disfavor because of their race or the color of their skin, there is no limit to what one will force them to endure, and, since the entire race has been mysteriously indicted, no reason not to attempt to destroy it root and branch. This is precisely what the Nazis attempted. Their only originality lay

From "Down at the Cross: Letter From a Region in My Mind" in The Fire Next Time (Dial Press, 1963).

in the means they used. It is scarcely worthwhile to attempt remembering how many times the sun has looked down on the slaughter of the innocents. I am very much concerned that American Negroes achieve their freedom here in the United States. But I am also concerned for their dignity, for the health of their souls, and must oppose any attempt that Negroes may make to do to others what has been done to them. I think I know—we see it around us every day—the spiritual wasteland to which that road leads. It is so simple a fact and one that is so hard, apparently, to grasp: *Whoever debases others is debasing himself.* That is not a mystical statement but a most realistic one, which is proved by the eyes of any Alabama sheriff—and I would not like to see Negroes ever arrive at so wretched a condition.

Now, it is extremely unlikely that Negroes will ever rise to power in the United States, because they are only approximately a ninth of this nation. They are not in the position of the Africans, who are attempting to reclaim their land and break the colonial yoke and recover from the colonial experience. The Negro situation is dangerous in a different way, both for the Negro *qua* Negro and for the country of which he forms so troubled and troubling a part. The American Negro is a unique creation; he has no counterpart anywhere, and no predecessors. The Muslims react to this fact by referring to the Negro as "the so-called American Negro" and substituting for the names inherited from slavery the letter "X." It is a fact that every American Negro bears a name that originally belonged to the white man whose chattel he was. I am called Baldwin because I was either sold by my African tribe or kidnapped out of it into the hands of a white Christian named Baldwin, who forced me to kneel at the foot of the cross. I am, then, both visibly and legally the descendant of slaves in a white, Protestant country, and this is what it means to be an American Negro, this is who he is—a kidnapped pagan, who was sold like an animal and treated like one, who was once defined by the American Constitution as "three-fifths" of a man, and who, according to the Dred Scott decision, had no rights that a white man was bound to respect. And today, a hundred years after his technical emancipation, he remains—with the possible exception of the American Indian—the most despised creature in his country. Now, there is simply no possibility of a real change in the Negro's situation without the most radical and far-reaching changes in the American political and social structure. And it is clear that white Americans are not simply unwilling to effect these changes; they are, in the main, so slothful have they become, unable even to envision them. It must be added that the Negro himself no longer believes in the good faith of white Americans—if, indeed, he ever could have. What the Negro *has* discovered, and on an international level, is that power to intimidate which he has always had privately but hitherto could manipulate only privately—for private ends often, for limited ends always. And therefore when the country speaks of a "new" Negro, which it has been doing every hour on the hour for decades, it is not really referring to a change in the Negro, which, in any case, it is quite incapable of assessing, but only to a new difficulty in keeping him in his place, to the fact that it encounters him (again! again!) barring yet another door to its spiritual and social ease. This is probably, hard and odd as it may sound, the most important thing that one human being can do for another—it is certainly *one* of the most important things; hence the torment and necessity of love—and this is the enormous contribution that the Negro has made to this otherwise shapeless and undiscovered country. Consequently, white Americans are in nothing more deluded than in supposing that Negroes could ever have imagined that white people would "give" them anything. It is rare indeed that people give. Most people guard and keep; they suppose that it is they themselves and what they identify with themselves that they are guarding and keeping, whereas what they are actually guarding and keeping is their system of reality and what they assume themselves to be. One can give nothing whatever without giving oneself—that is to say, risking oneself. If one cannot risk oneself, then one is simply incapable of giving. And, after all, one can give freedom only by setting someone free. This, in the case of the Negro, the American republic has never become sufficiently mature to do. White Americans have contented themselves with gestures that are now described as "tokenism." For hard example, white Americans congratulate themselves on the 1954 Supreme Court decision outlawing segregation in the schools; they suppose, in spite of the mountain of evidence that has since accumulated to the contrary, that this was proof of a change of heart—or, as they like to say, progress. Perhaps. It all depends on how one reads the word "progress." Most of the Negroes I know do not believe that this immense concession would ever have been made if it had not been for the competition of the Cold War, and the fact that Africa was clearly liberating herself and therefore had, for political reasons, to be wooed by the descendants of her former masters. Had it been a matter of love or justice, the 1954 decision would surely have occurred sooner; were it not for the realities of power in this difficult era, it might very well not have occurred yet. This seems an extremely harsh way of stating the case—ungrateful, as it were—but the evidence that supports this way of stating it is not easily refuted. I myself do not think that it can be refuted at all. In any event, the sloppy and fatuous nature of American good will can never be relied upon to deal with hard problems. These have been dealt with, when they have been dealt with at all, out of necessity—and in political terms, anyway, necessity means concessions made in order to stay on top. I think this is a fact, which it serves no purpose to deny, *but, whether it is a fact or not, this is what the black population of the world, including black Americans, really believe.* The word "independence" in Africa and the word "integration" here are almost equally meaningless; that is, Europe has not yet left Africa, and black men here are not yet free. And both of these last statements are undeniable facts, related facts, containing the gravest implications for us all. The Negroes of this country may never be able to rise to power, but they are very well placed indeed to precipitate chaos and ring down the curtain on the American dream.

This has everything to do, of course, with the nature of that dream and with the fact that we Americans, of whatever color, do not dare examine it and are far from having made it a reality. There are too many things we do not wish to know about ourselves. People are not, for example, terribly anxious to be equal (equal, after all, to what and to whom?) but they love the idea of being superior. And this human truth has an especially grinding force here, where identity is almost impossible to achieve and people are perpetually attempting to find their feet on the shifting sands of status. (Consider the history of labor in a country in which, spiritually speaking, there are no workers, only candidates for the hand of the boss's daughter.) Furthermore, I have met only a very few people— and most of these were not Americans—who had any real desire to be free. Freedom is hard to bear. It can be objected that I am speaking of political freedom in spiritual terms, but

the political institutions of any nation are always menaced
and are ultimately controlled by the spiritual state of that
nation. We are controlled here by our confusion, far more
than we know, and the American dream has therefore
become something much more closely resembling a nightmare, on the private, domestic, and international levels.
Privately, we cannot stand our lives and dare not examine
them; domestically, we take no responsibility for (and no
pride in) what goes on in our country; and, internationally,
for many millions of people, we are an unmitigated disaster.
Whoever doubts this last statement has only to open his ears,
his heart, his mind, to the testimony of—for example—any
Cuban peasant or any Spanish poet, and ask himself what *he*
would feel about us if *he* were the victim of our performance
in pre-Castro Cuba or in Spain. We defend our curious role in
Spain by referring to the Russian menace and the necessity of
protecting the free world. It has not occurred to us that we
have simply been mesmerized by Russia, and that the only
real advantage Russia has in what we think of as a struggle
between the East and the West is the moral history of the
Western World. Russia's secret weapon is the bewilderment
and despair and hunger of millions of people of whose
existence we are scarcely aware. The Russian Communists
are not in the least concerned about these people. But our
ignorance and indecision have had the effect, if not of
delivering them into Russian hands, of plunging them very
deeply in the Russian shadow, for which effect—and it is hard
to blame them—the most articulate among them, and the
most oppressed as well, distrust us all the more. Our power
and our fear of change help bind these people to their misery
and bewilderment, and insofar as they find this state intolerable we are intolerably menaced. For if they find their state
intolerable, but are too heavily oppressed to change it, they
are simply pawns in the hands of larger powers, which, in
such a context, are always unscrupulous, and when, eventually, they do change their situation—as in Cuba—we are
menaced more than ever, by the vacuum that succeeds all
violent upheavals. We should certainly know by now that it is
one thing to overthrow a dictator or repel an invader and
quite another thing really to achieve a revolution. Time and
time and time again, the people discover that they have
merely betrayed themselves into the hands of yet another
Pharaoh, who, since he was necessary to put the broken

country together, will not let them go. Perhaps, people being the conundrums that they are, and having so little desire to shoulder the burden of their lives, this is what will always happen. But at the bottom of my heart I do not believe this. I think that people can be better than that, and I know that people can be better than they are. We are capable of bearing a great burden, once we discover that the burden is reality and arrive where reality is. Anyway, the point here is that we are living in an age of revolution, whether we will or no, and that America is the only Western nation with both the power and, as I hope to suggest, the experience that may help to make these revolutions real and minimize the human damage. Any attempt we make to oppose these outbursts of energy is tantamount to signing our death warrant.

Behind what we think of as the Russian menace lies what we do not wish to face, and what white Americans do not face when they regard a Negro: reality—the fact that life is tragic. Life is tragic simply because the earth turns and the sun inexorably rises and sets, and one day, for each of us, the sun will go down for the last, last time. Perhaps the whole root of our trouble, the human trouble, is that we will sacrifice all the beauty of our lives, will imprison ourselves in totems, taboos, crosses, blood sacrifices, steeples, mosques, races, armies, flags, nations, in order to deny the fact of death, which is the only fact we have. It seems to me that one ought to rejoice in the *fact* of death—ought to decide, indeed, to *earn* one's death by confronting with passion the conundrum of life. One is responsible to life: It is the small beacon in that terrifying darkness from which we come and to which we shall return. One must negotiate this passage as nobly as possible, for the sake of those who are coming after us. But white Americans do not believe in death, and this is why the darkness of my skin so intimidates them. And this is also why the presence of the Negro in this country can bring about its destruction. It is the responsibility of free men to trust and to celebrate what is constant—birth, struggle, and death are constant, and so is love, though we may not always think so—and to apprehend the nature of change, to be able and willing to change. I speak of change not on the surface but in the depths—change in the sense of renewal. But renewal becomes impossible if one supposes things to be constant that are not—safety, for example, or money, or power. One clings then to chimeras, by which one can only be betrayed, and the entire hope—the entire possibility—of freedom disappears. And by destruction I mean precisely the abdication by Americans of any effort really to be free. The Negro can precipitate this abdication because white Americans have never, in all their long history, been able to look on him as a man like themselves. This point need not be labored; it is proved over and over again by the Negro's continuing position here, and his indescribable struggle to defeat the strategems that white Americans have used, and use, to deny him his humanity. America could have used in other ways the energy that both groups have expended in this conflict. America, of all the Western nations, has been best placed to prove the uselessness and the obsolescence of the concept of color. But it has not dared to accept this opportunity, or even to conceive of it as an opportunity. White Americans have thought of it as their shame, and have envied the more civilized and elegant European nations that were untroubled by the presence of black men on their shores. This is because white Americans have supposed "Europe" and "civilization" to be synonyms —which they are not—and have been distrustful of other standards and other sources of vitality, especially those produced in America itself, and have attempted to behave in all matters as though what was east for Europe was also east for them. What it comes to is that if we, who can scarcely be considered a white nation, persist in thinking of ourselves as one, we condemn ourselves, with the truly white nations, to sterility and decay, whereas if we could accept ourselves *as we are*, we might bring new life to the Western achievements, and transform them. The price of this transformation is the unconditional freedom of the Negro; it is not too much to say that he, who has been so long rejected, must now be embraced, and at no matter what psychic or social risk. He is *the* key figure in his country, and the American future is precisely as bright or as dark as his. And the Negro recognizes this, in a negative way. Hence the question: Do I really *want* to be integrated into a burning house?

White Americans find it as difficult as white people elsewhere do to divest themselves of the notion that they are in possession of some intrinsic value that black people need, or want. And this assumption—which, for example, makes the solution to the Negro problem depend on the speed with which Negroes accept and adopt white standards—is revealed in all kinds of striking ways, from Bobby Kennedy's assurance that a Negro can become President in forty years to the unfortunate tone of warm congratulation with which so many liberals address their Negro equals. It is the Negro, of course, who is presumed to have become equal—an achievement that not only proves the comforting fact that perseverance has no color but also overwhelmingly corroborates the white man's sense of his own value. Alas, this value can scarcely be corroborated in any other way; there is certainly little enough in the white man's public or private life that one should desire to imitate. White men, at the bottom of their hearts, know this. Therefore, a vast amount of the energy that goes into what we call the Negro problem is produced by the white man's profound desire not to be judged by those who are not white, not to be seen as he is, and at the same time a vast amount of the white anguish is rooted in the white man's equally profound need to be seen as he is, to be released from the tyranny of his mirror. All of us know, whether or not we are able to admit it, that mirrors can only lie, that death by drowning is all that awaits one there. It is for this reason that love is so desperately sought and so cunningly avoided. Love takes off the masks that we fear we cannot live without and know we cannot live within. I use the word "love" here not merely in the personal sense but as a state of being, or a state of grace—not in the infantile American sense of being made happy but in the tough and universal sense of quest and daring and growth. And I submit, then, that the racial tensions that menace Americans today have little to do with real antipathy—on the contrary, indeed—and are involved only symbolically with color. These tensions are rooted in the very same depths as those from which love springs, or murder. The white man's unadmitted—and apparently, to him, unspeakable—private fears and longings are projected on to the Negro. The only way he can be released from the Negro's tyrannical power over him is to consent, in effect, to become black himself, to become a part of that suffering and dancing country that he now watches wistfully from the heights of his lonely power and, armed with spiritual traveler's checks, visits surreptitiously after dark. How can one respect, let alone adopt, the values of a people who do not, on any level whatever, live the way they say they do, or the way they say they should? I cannot accept the proposition that the four-hundred-year travail of the American Negro should result merely in his attainment of the present level of the

American civilization. I am far from convinced that being
released from the African witch doctor was worthwhile if I
am now—in order to support the moral contradictions and
the spiritual aridity of my life—expected to become dependent on the American psychiatrist. It is a bargain I refuse.
The only thing white people have that black people need, or
should want, is power—and no one holds power forever.
White people cannot, in the generality, be taken as models of
how to live. Rather, the white man is himself in sore need of
new standards, which will release him from his confusion and
place him once again in fruitful communion with the depths
of his own being. And I repeat: The price of the liberation of
the white people is the liberation of the blacks—the total
liberation, in the cities, in the towns, before the law, and in
the mind. Why, for example—especially knowing the family
as I do—I should *want* to marry your sister is a great mystery
to me. But your sister and I have every right to marry if we
wish to, and no one has the right to stop us. If she cannot raise
me to her level, perhaps I can raise her to mine.

In short, we, the black and the white, deeply need each
other here if we are really to become a nation—if we are
really, that is, to achieve our identity, our maturity, as men
and women. To create one nation has proved to be a
hideously difficult task; there is certainly no need now to
create two, one black and one white. But white men with far
more political power than that possessed by the Nation of
Islam movement have been advocating exactly this, in effect,
for generations. If this sentiment is honored when it falls from
the lips of Senator Byrd, then there is no reason it should not
be honored when it falls from the lips of Malcolm X. And any
Congressional committee wishing to investigate the latter
must also be willing to investigate the former. They are
expressing exactly the same sentiments and represent exactly
the same danger. There is absolutely no reason to suppose
that white people are better equipped to frame the laws by
which I am to be governed than I am. It is entirely unacceptable that I should have no voice in the political affairs of my
own country, for I am not a ward of America; I am one of the
first Americans to arrive on these shores.

This past, the Negro's past, of rope, fire, torture, castra-
tion, infanticide, rape; death and humiliation; fear by day and
night, fear as deep as the marrow of the bone; doubt that he
was worthy of life, since everyone around him denied it;

sorrow for his women, for his kinfolk, for his children, who needed his protection, and whom he could not protect; rage, hatred, and murder, hatred for white men so deep that it often turned against him and his own, and made all love, all trust, all joy impossible—this past, this endless struggle to achieve and reveal and confirm a human identity, human authority, yet contains, for all its horror, something very beautiful. I do not mean to be sentimental about suffering—enough is certainly as good as a feast—but people who cannot suffer can never grow up, can never discover who they are. That man who is forced each day to snatch his manhood, his identity, out of the fire of human cruelty that rages to destroy it knows, if he survives his effort, and even if he does not survive it, something about himself and human life that no school on earth—and, indeed, no church—can teach. He achieves his own authority, and that is unshakable. This is because, in order to save his life, he is forced to look beneath appearances, to take nothing for granted, to hear the meaning behind the words. If one is continually surviving the worst that life can bring, one eventually ceases to be controlled by a fear of what life can bring; whatever it brings must be borne. And at this level of experience one's bitterness begins to be palatable, and hatred becomes too heavy a sack to carry. The apprehension of life here so briefly and inadequately sketched has been the experience of generations of Negroes, and it helps to explain how they have endured and how they have been able to produce children of kindergarten age who can walk through mobs to get to school. It demands great force and great cunning continually to assault the mighty and indifferent fortress of white supremacy, as Negroes in this country have done so long. It demands great spiritual resilience not to hate the hater whose foot is on your neck, and an even greater miracle of perception and charity not to teach your child to hate. The Negro boys and girls who are facing mobs today come out of a long line of improbable aristocrats —the only genuine aristocrats this country has produced. I say "this country" because their frame of reference was totally American. They were hewing out of the mountain of white supremacy the stone of their individuality. I have great respect for that unsung army of black men and women who trudged down back lanes and entered back doors, saying "Yes, sir" and "No, ma'am" in order to acquire a new roof for the schoolhouse, new books, a new chemistry lab, more

beds for the dormitories, more dormitories. They did not like
saying "Yes, sir" and "No, ma'am," but the country was in no
hurry to educate Negroes, these black men and women knew
that the job had to be done, and they put their pride in their
pockets in order to do it. It is very hard to believe that they
were in any way inferior to the white men and women who
opened those back doors. It is very hard to believe that those
men and women, raising their children, eating their greens,
crying their curses, weeping their tears, singing their songs,
making their love, as the sun rose, as the sun set, were in any
way inferior to the white men and women who crept over to
share these splendors after the sun went down. But we must
avoid the European error; we must not suppose that, because
the situation, the ways, the perceptions of black people so
radically differed from those of whites, they were racially
superior. I am proud of these people not because of their
color but because of their intelligence and their spiritual force
and their beauty. The country should be proud of them, too,
but, alas, not many people in this country even know of their
existence. And the reason for this ignorance is that a knowledge of the role these people played—and play—in American
life would reveal more about America to Americans than
Americans wish to know.

The American Negro has the great advantage of having
never believed that collection of myths to which white
Americans cling: that their ancestors were all freedom-loving
heroes, that they were born in the greatest country the world
has ever seen, or that Americans are invincible in battle and
wise in peace, that Americans have always dealt honorably
with Mexicans and Indians and all other neighbors or inferi-
ors, that American men are the world's most direct and virile,
that American women are pure. Negroes know far more
about white Americans than that; it can almost be said, in
fact, that they know about white Americans what parents—
or, anyway, mothers—know about their children, and that
they very often regard white Americans that way. And
perhaps this attitude, held in spite of what they know and
have endured, helps to explain why Negroes, on the whole,
and until lately, have allowed themselves to feel so little
hatred. The tendency has really been, insofar as this was
possible, to dismiss white people as the slightly mad victims of
their own brainwashing. One watched the lives they led. One
could not be fooled about that; one watched the things they

did and the excuses that they gave themselves, and if a white man was really in trouble, deep trouble, it was to the Negro's door that he came. And one felt that if one had had that white man's worldly advantages, one would never have become as bewildered and as joyless and as thoughtlessly cruel as he. The Negro came to the white man for a roof or for five dollars or for a letter to the judge; the white man came to the Negro for love. But he was not often able to give what he came seeking. The price was too high; he had too much to lose. And the Negro knew this, too. When one knows this about a man, it is impossible for one to hate him, but unless he becomes a man—becomes equal—it is also impossible for one to love him. Ultimately, one tends to avoid him, for the universal characteristic of children is to assume that they have a monopoly on trouble, and therefore a monopoly on *you*. (Ask any Negro what he knows about the white people with whom he works. And then ask the white people with whom he works what they know about *him*.)

How can the American Negro past be used? It is entirely possible that this dishonored past will rise up soon to smite all of us. There are some wars, for example (if anyone on the globe is still mad enough to go to war) that the American Negro will not support, however many of his people may be coerced—and there is a limit to the number of people any government can put in prison, and a rigid limit indeed to the practicality of such a course. A bill is coming in that I fear America is not prepared to pay. "The problem of the twentieth century," wrote W.E.B. Du Bois around sixty years ago, "is the problem of the color line." A fearful and delicate problem, which compromises, when it does not corrupt, all the American efforts to build a better world—here, there, or anywhere. It is for this reason that everything white Americans think they believe in must now be reexamined. What one would not like to see again is the consolidation of peoples on the basis of their color. But as long as we in the West place on color the value that we do, we make it impossible for the great unwashed to consolidate themselves according to any other principle. Color is not a human or a personal reality; it is a political reality. But this is a distinction so extremely hard to make that the West has not been able to make it yet. And at the center of this dreadful storm, this vast confusion, stand the black people of this nation, who must now share the fate of a nation that has never accepted them, to which they were brought in chains. Well, if this is so, one has no choice but to do all in one's power to change that fate, and at no matter what risk—eviction, imprisonment, torture, death. For the sake of one's children, in order to minimize the bill that *they* must pay, one must be careful not to take refuge in any delusion—and the value placed on the color of the skin is always and everywhere and forever a delusion. I know that what I am asking is impossible. But in our time, as in every time, the impossible is the least that one can demand—and one is, after all, emboldened by the spectacle of human history in general, and American Negro history in particular, for it testifies to nothing less than the perpetual achievement of the impossible.

When I was very young, and was dealing with my buddies in those wine- and urine-stained hallways, something in me wondered, *What will happen to all that beauty?* For black people, though I am aware that some of us, black and white, do not know it yet, are very beautiful. And when I sat at Elijah's table and watched the baby, the women, and the men, and we talked about God's—or Allah's—vengeance, I wondered, when that vengeance was achieved, *What will happen to all that beauty then?* I could also see that the intransigence and ignorance of the white world might make that vengeance inevitable—a vengeance that does not really depend on, and cannot really be executed by, any person or organization, and that cannot be prevented by any police force or army: historical vengeance, a cosmic vengeance, based on the law that we recognize when we say, "Whatever goes up must come down." And here we are, at the center of the arc, trapped in the gaudiest, most valuable, and most improbable water wheel the world has ever seen. Everything now, we must assume, is in our hands; we have no right to assume otherwise. If we—and now I mean the relatively conscious whites and the relatively conscious blacks, who must, like lovers, insist on, or create, the consciousness of the others—do not falter in our duty now, we may be able, handful that we are, to end the racial nightmare, and achieve our country, and change the history of the world. If we do not now dare everything, the fulfilment of that prophecy, re-created from the Bible in song by a slave, is upon us: *God gave Noah the rainbow sign, No more water, the fire next time!*

# Domestic Law
# and International Order

## Eldridge Cleaver

The police department and the armed forces are the two arms of the power structure, the muscles of control and enforcement. They have deadly weapons with which to inflict pain on the human body. They know how to bring about horrible deaths. They have clubs with which to beat the body and the head. They have bullets and guns with which to tear holes in the flesh, to smash bones, to disable and kill. They use force, to make you do what the deciders have decided you must do.

Every country on earth has these agencies of force. The people everywhere fear this terror and force. To them it is like a snarling wild beast which can put an end to one's dreams. They punish. They have cells and prisons to lock you up in. They pass out sentences. They won't let you go when you want to. You have to stay put until they give the word. If your mother is dying, you can't go to her bedside to say goodbye or to her graveside to see her lowered into the earth, to see her, for the last time, swallowed up by that black hole.

The techniques of the enforcers are many: firing squads, gas chambers, electric chairs, torture chambers, the garrote, the guillotine, the tightening rope around your throat. It has been found that the death penalty is necessary to back up the

From *Soul On Ice* (McGraw-Hill Book Company, 1968).

law, to make it easier to enforce, to deter transgressions against the penal code. That everybody doesn't believe in the same laws is beside the point.

Which laws get enforced depends on who is in power. If the capitalists are in power, they enforce laws designed to protect their system, their way of life. They have a particular abhorrence for crimes against property, but are prepared to be liberal and show a modicum of compassion for crimes against the person—unless, of course, an instance of the latter is combined with an instance of the former. In such cases, nothing can stop them from throwing the whole book at the offender. For instance, armed robbery with violence, to a capitalist, is the very epitome of evil. Ask any banker what he thinks of it.

If Communists are in power, they enforce laws designed to protect their system, their way of life. To them, the horror of horrors is the speculator, that man of magic who has mastered the art of getting something with nothing and who in America would be a member in good standing of his local Chamber of Commerce.

"The people," however, are nowhere consulted, although everywhere everything is done always in their name and ostensibly for their betterment, while their real-life problems go unsolved. "The people" are a rubber stamp for the crafty and sly. And no problem can be solved without taking the police department and the armed forces into account. Both kings and bookies understand this, as do first ladies and common prostitutes.

The police do on the domestic level what the armed forces do on the international level: protect the way of life of those in power. The police patrol the city, cordon off communities, blockade neighborhoods, invade homes, search for that which is hidden. The armed forces patrol the world, invade countries and continents, cordon off nations, blockade islands and whole peoples; they will also overrun villages, neighborhoods, enter homes, huts, caves, searching for that which is hidden. The policeman and the soldier will violate your person, smoke you out with various gases. Each will shoot you, beat your head and body with sticks and clubs, with rifle butts, run you through with bayonets, shoot holes in your flesh, kill you. They each have unlimited firepower. They will use all that is necessary to bring you to your knees. They won't take no for an answer. If you resist their sticks, they draw their guns. If you resist their guns, they call for reinforcements with bigger guns. Eventually they will come in tanks, in jets, in ships. They will not rest until you surrender or are killed. The policeman and the soldier will have the last word.

Both police and the armed forces follow orders. Orders. Orders flow from the top down. Up there, behind closed doors, in antechambers, in conference rooms, gavels bang on the tables, the tinkling of silver decanters can be heard as icewater is poured by well-fed, conservatively dressed men in hornrimmed glasses, fashionably dressed American widows with rejuvenated faces and tinted hair, the air permeated with the square humor of Bob Hope jokes. Here all the talking is done, all the thinking, all the deciding. Gray rabbits of men scurry forth from the conference room to spread the decisions throughout the city, as News. Carrying out orders is a job, a way of meeting the payments on the house, a way of providing for one's kiddies. In the armed forces it is also a duty, patriotism. Not to do so is treason.

Every city has its police department. No city would be complete without one. It would be sheer madness to try operating an American city without the heat, the fuzz, the man. Americans are too far gone, or else they haven't arrived yet; the center does not exist, only the extremes. Take away the cops and Americans would have a coast-to-coast free-for-all. There are, of course, a few citizens who carry their own private cops around with them, built into their souls. But there is robbery in the land, and larceny, murder, rape, burglary, theft, swindles, all brands of crime, profit, rent, interest—and these blasé descendants of Pilgrims are at each other's throats. To complicate matters, there are also rich people and poor people in America. There are Negroes and whites, Indians, Puerto Ricans, Mexicans, Jews, Chinese, Arabs, Japanese—all with equal rights but unequal possessions. Some are haves and some are have-nots. All have been taught to worship at the shrine of General Motors. The whites are on top in America and they want to stay there, up there. They are also on top in the world, on the international level, and they want to stay up there, too. Everywhere there are those who want to smash this precious toy clock of a system, they want ever so much to change it, to rearrange things, to pull the whites down off their high horse and make them equal. Everywhere the whites are fighting to prolong their status, to retard the erosion of their position. In America, when everything else fails, they call out the police. On the international level, when everything else fails, they call out the armed forces.

A strange thing happened in Watts, in 1965, August. The blacks, who in this land of private property have all private and no property, got excited into an uproar because they noticed a cop before he had a chance to wash the blood off his hands. Usually the police department can handle such flare-ups. But this time it was different. Things got out of hand. The blacks were running amok, burning, shooting, breaking. The police department was powerless to control them; the chief called for reinforcements. Out came the National Guard, that ambiguous hybrid from the twilight zone where the domestic army merges with the international; that hypocritical force poised within America and capable of action on either level, capable of backing up either the police or the armed forces. Unleashing their formidable firepower, they crushed the blacks. But things will never be the same again. Too many people saw that those who turned the other cheek in Watts got their whole head blown off. At the same time, heads were being blown off in Vietnam. America was embarrassed, not by the quality of her deeds but by the surplus of publicity focused upon her negative selling points, and a little frightened because of what all those dead bodies, on two fronts, implied. Those corpses spoke eloquently of potential allies and alliances. A community of interest began to emerge, dripping with blood, out of the ashes of Watts. The blacks in Watts and all over America could now see the Viet Cong's point: both were on the receiving end of what the armed forces were dishing out.

So now the blacks, stung by the new knowledge they have unearthed, cry out: *"POLICE BRUTALITY!"* From one end of the country to the other, the new war cry is raised. The youth, those nodes of compulsive energy who are all fuel and muscle, race their motors, itch to do something. The Uncle Toms, no longer willing to get down on their knees to lick boots, do so from a squatting position. The black bourgeoisie call for Citizens' Review Boards, to assert civilian control over the activity of the police. In back rooms, in dark stinking corners of the ghettos, self-conscious black men curse their own cowardice and stare at their rifles and pistols and shotguns laid out on tables before them, trembling as they wish for a manly impulse to course through their bodies and send them screaming mad into the streets shooting from the hip. Black women look at their men as if they are bugs, curious growths of flesh playing an inscrutable waiting game. Violence becomes a homing pigeon floating through the ghettos seeking a black brain in which to roost for a season.

In their rage against the police, against police brutality, the blacks lose sight of the fundamental reality: that the police are only an instrument for the implementation of the policies of those who make the decisions. Police brutality is only one facet of the crystal of terror and oppression. Behind police brutality there is social brutality, economic brutality, and political brutality. From the perspective of the ghetto, this is not easy to discern: the TV newscaster and the radio announcer and the editorialists of the newspapers are wizards of the smoke screen and the snow job.

What is true on the international level is true also at home: except that the ace up the sleeve is easier to detect in the international arena. Who would maintain that American soldiers are in Vietnam on their own motion? They were conscripted into the armed forces and taught the wisdom of obeying orders. They were sent to Vietnam by orders of the generals in the Pentagon, who receive them from the Secretary of Defense, who receives them from the President, who is shrouded in mystery. The soldier in the field in Vietnam, the man who lies in the grass and squeezes the trigger when a little half-starved, trembling Vietnamese peasant crosses his sights, is only following orders, carrying out a policy and a plan. He hardly knows what it is all about. They have him wired-up tight with the slogans of TV and the World Series. All he knows is that he has been assigned to carry out a certain ritual of duties. He is well trained and does the best he can. He does a good job. He may want to please those above him with the quality of his performance. He may want to make sergeant, or better. This man is from some hicky farm in Shit Creek, Georgia. He only knew whom to kill after passing through boot camp. He could just as well come out ready to kill Swedes. He will kill a Swede dead, if he is ordered to do so.

Same for the policeman in Watts. He is not there on his own. They have all been assigned. They have been told what to do and what not to do. They have also been told what they better not do. So when they continually do something, in every filthy ghetto in this shitty land, it means only that they are following orders.

It's no secret that in America the blacks are in total rebellion against the System. They want to get their nuts out of the sand. They don't like the way America is run, from top to bottom. In America, everything is owned. Everything is held as private property. Someone has a brand on everything. There is nothing left over. Until recently, the blacks themselves were counted as part of somebody's private property, along with the chickens and goats. The blacks have not forgotten this, principally because they are still treated as if they are part of someone's inventory of assets—or perhaps, in this day of rage against the costs of welfare, blacks are listed among the nation's liabilities. On any account, however, blacks are in no position to respect or help maintain the institution of private property. What they want is to figure out a way to get some of that property for themselves, to divert it to their own needs. This is what it is all about, and this is the real brutality involved. This is the source of all brutality.

The police are the armed guardians of the social order. The blacks are the chief domestic victims of the American social order. A conflict of interest exists, therefore, between the blacks and the police. It is not solely a matter of trigger-happy cops, of brutal cops who love to crack black heads. Mostly it's a job to them. It pays good. And there are numerous fringe benefits. The real problem is a trigger-happy social order.

The Utopians speak of a day when there will be no police. There will be nothing for them to do. Every man will do his duty, will respect the rights of his neighbor, will not disturb the peace. The needs of all will be taken care of. Everyone will have sympathy for his fellow man. There will be no such thing as crime. There will be, of course, no prisons. No electric chairs, no gas chambers. The hangman's rope will be the thing of the past. The entire earth will be a land of plenty. There will be no crimes against property, no speculation.

It is easy to see that we are not on the verge of entering Utopia: there are cops everywhere. North and South, the Negroes are the have-nots. They see property all around them, property that is owned by whites. In this regard, the black bourgeoisie has become nothing but a ridiculous nuisance. Having waged a battle for entrance into the American mainstream continually for fifty years, all of the black bourgeoisie's defenses are directed outward, against the whites.

They have no defenses against the blacks and no time to erect any. The black masses can handle them any time they choose, with one mighty blow. But the white bourgeoisie presents a bigger problem, those whites who own everything. With many shackled by unemployment, hatred in black hearts for this system of private property increases daily. The sanctity surrounding property is being called into question. The mystique of the deed of ownership is melting away. In other parts of the world, peasants rise up and expropriate the land from the former owners. Blacks in America see that the deed is not eternal, that it is not signed by God, and that new deeds, making blacks the owners, can be drawn up.

The Black Muslims raised the cry, *"WE MUST HAVE SOME LAND!" "SOME LAND OF OUR OWN OR ELSE!"* Blacks in America shrink from the colossus of General Motors. They can't see how to wade through that thicket of common stocks, preferred stocks, bonds and debentures. They only know that General Motors is huge, that it has billions of dollars under its control, that it owns land, that its subsidiaries are legion, that it is a repository of vast powers. The blacks want to crack the nut of General Motors. They are meditating on it. Meanwhile, they must learn that the police take orders from General Motors. And that the Bank of America has something to do with them even though they don't have a righteous penny in the bank. They have no bank accounts, only bills to pay. The only way they know of making withdrawals from the bank is at the point of a gun. The shiny fronts of skyscrapers intimidate them. They do not own them. They feel alienated from the very sidewalks on which they walk. This white man's country, this white man's world. Overflowing with men of color. An economy consecrated to the succor of the whites. Blacks are incidental. The war on poverty, that monstrous insult to the rippling muscles in a black man's arms, is an index of how men actually sit down and plot each other's deaths, actually sit down with slide rules and calculate how to hide bread from the hungry. And the black bourgeoisie greedily sopping up what crumbs are tossed into their dark corner.

There are 20,000,000 of these blacks in America, probably more. Today they repeat, in awe, this magic number to themselves: there are 20,000,000 of us! They shout this to each other in humiliated astonishment. No one need tell them that there is vast power latent in their mass. They know that

20,000,000 of anything is enough to get some recognition and consideration. They know also that they must harness their number and hone it into a sword with a sharp cutting edge. White General Motors also knows that the unity of these 20,000,000 ragamuffins will spell the death of the system of its being. At all costs, then, they will seek to keep these blacks from uniting, from becoming bold and revolutionary. These white property owners know that they must keep the blacks cowardly and intimidated. By a complex communications system of hints and signals, certain orders are given to the chief of police and the sheriff, who pass them on to their men, the footsoldiers in the trenches of the ghetto.

We experience this system of control as madness. So that Leonard Deadwyler, one of these 20,000,000 blacks, is rushing his pregnant wife to the hospital and is shot dead by a policeman. An accident. That the sun rises in the east and sets in the west is also an accident, by design. The blacks are up in arms. From one end of America to the other, blacks are outraged at this accident, this latest evidence of what an accident-prone people they are, of the cruelty and pain of their lives, these blacks at the mercy of trigger-happy Yankees and Rebs in coalition against their skin. They want the policeman's blood as a sign that the Viet Cong is not the only answer. A sign to save them from the deaths they must die, and inflict. The power structure, without so much as blinking an eye, wouldn't mind tossing Bova to the mob, to restore law and order, but it knows in the vaults of its strength that at all cost the blacks must be kept at bay, that it must uphold the police department, its Guardian. Nothing must be allowed to threaten the set-up. Justice is secondary. Security is the byword.

Meanwhile, blacks are looking on and asking tactical questions. They are asked to die for the System in Vietnam. In Watts they are killed by it. Now—*NOW!*—they are asking each other, in dead earnest: Why not die right here in Babylon fighting for a better life, like the Viet Cong? If those little cats can do it, what's wrong with big studs like us?

A mood sets in, spreads across America, across the face of Babylon, jells in black hearts everywhere.

# II

---

# Some New Sensibilities

They're busy spreading a rumor that I had a nervous break-down. It's not true. What I had was a nervous breakthrough.

—Ronald Sukenick, *Up*

The only performance that makes it, that really makes it, that makes it all the way, is the one that achieves madness.

—Mick Jagger as Turner in *Performance*

We're traveling fast
from a dream of the past
to a Brave New World.
Where nothing will last
that comes from the past,
it's a Brave New World.

—Steve Miller, "Brave New World"

"I don't know," I said. "I'd like to do something more religious. Explore America in the screaming night. You know. Yin and yang in Kansas. That scene."

—Don DeLillo, *Americana*

Of the many millions of words written about John Fitzgerald Kennedy and about the Kennedy phenomenon before and after his assassination, the ten thousand or so in Norman Mailer's 1960 *Esquire* piece that opens this section remain perhaps the most vivid, if not the most veracious. Any dispassionate account of Kennedy's performance as President —and there have been a good number of them as the grip of the Camelot mystique on our minds loosens—has to take into account his earlier mediocre record as a Senator from Massachusetts, his unquestioning acceptance of Cold War ideology, his shameful waffling on civil rights legislation, his taste for style, toughness and (a Kennedy administration cant word) pragmatism and his deference to military and intelligence "experts" that was to lead us into such debacles as the abortive Bay of Pigs operation and, ultimately, the Vietnam war.

But no major writer of our time has been less capable of dispassion than Normal Mailer. He was one of the first to perceive that it was JFK the authentic war hero, the wit, the handsome rake, the symbol of youth, vigor and adventure who would fire the imagination of an America flush with postwar prosperity and about to burst out spectacularly from the blandness, smugness and conformity of the Eisenhower years. So Mailer turned his rhetorical arts to the task of making up a hero for us, one who would deliver us from the totalitarian technocracy of his paranoid dreams and restore a sense of progress and risk to our national life.

It worked. The Kennedy that fascinated Mailer fascinated the country in the same way, appealing to an atavistic American need for a sense of forward movement on whatever frontiers were available, whether it was "conquering space," "bringing the twentieth century to the backward peoples of the world," or "meeting the worldwide challenge of communism." He was just the President the decade needed; he unlocked a huge reservoir of idealism and invention in the American spirit in much the way Mailer suggested he would. (Mailer was not alone in this somewhat metaphysical view of Kennedy. Eldridge Cleaver wrote, for instance, in *Soul on Ice* that "It could . . . be argued that the same collective urge that gave rise to the Twist swept Kennedy into office.")

He was most certainly the President Mailer needed, with his (Mailer's) outsized ambitions, his utter loathing for everything the Fifties represented, his need to measure himself as a writer against every challenge this amazing, appalling new America had to offer. After a decade in which his two novels, *Barbary Shore* and *The Deer Park*, were very badly received, a decade that he says almost killed him with its torpor and hypocrisy, Mailer had cleared his psychic decks in 1959 with *Advertisements for Myself*, an infuriating and fascinating compilation of articles, manifestoes (most notably that capsule bible of Hip, "The White Negro"), stories, marginalia and critical snubs of his contemporaries, all glued together with Tarzan yodels and breast thumpings of literary ambition. It opens, famously, "Like many another vain, empty, and bullying body of our time, I have been running for President these last ten years in the privacy of my mind. . . ." A couple of years later Mailer was to title the collection in which "Superman Comes to the Supermarket" appears *The Presidential Papers*, the conceit being that the book constituted a long and essential memorandum to Kennedy on the spiritual state of the nation.

After a performance like this there was no turning back, and, shifting his energies largely away from fiction, Mailer transformed himself into a protean compound of Ahab, Hemingway and Don Quixote, sometimes heroically, sometimes just plain fatuously in search of American Big Game. He made forays into filmmaking, playwriting, journalism, criticism, poetry, politics, boxing, bull fighting and, most especially, celebrity, imposing his vision of life as an existential struggle on whatever came within range. In the resulting books—the collections *The Presidential Papers* (1963), *Cannibals and Christians* (1966) and *Existential Errands* (1972); his accounts of the March on the Pentagon, *The Armies of the Night* (1968); the 1968 Republican and Democratic conventions, *Miami and the Siege of Chicago* (1968); the Apollo 11 moon landing, *Of a Fire on the Moon* (1971); and his crossing of swords with women's liberation, *The Prisoner of Sex* (1971)—Mailer emerges as the archetypal figure of the decade. His headlong, decade-long gamble that the radically subjective strategies of, in Richard Poirier's phrase, "the performing self" can yield new meaning and insight to history and an expanded sense of the possibilities of literature and identity paid off handsomely and excitingly.

Quite another region of selfhood and celebrityhood (though not unrelated) comes to spastic life in Tom Wolfe's "profile" of 1964's It Girl, Baby Jane Holzer, "The Girl of the Year." A sometime-model, sometime-actress, sometime-socialite, Jane Holzer was mostly, in Daniel Boorstin's well-known complaint, "famous for being famous." In his introduction to the book in which this piece appears, *The Kandy-Kolored Tangerine-Flake Streamline Baby* (1965), Wolfe dubbed the utterly artificial milieu in which such hothouse celebrities as Jane Holzer bloomed and as quickly faded "Pop Society." This new kind of social democracy was a promiscuous mingling of the erstwhile high society, the fashion world, the avant-garde and pop musicians in a scene in which girls could be "created" by photographers, "superstars" minted by fiat and "raw vital proles" like the Rolling Stones could call the stylistic shots. Notoriety and style, rather than money or social position, scored the status points, and this reflected the extraordinary openness and energy of an American society hungry for new sensations. (For a closer look at Tom Wolfe and the "New Journalism" of which "The Girl of the Year" is such a spiffy example, see Dwight Macdonald's piece, "Parajournalism: Tom Wolfe and His Magic Writing Machine" in the media section of this book.)

With the next four selections we begin to move deep into the sacerdotal precincts of the counterculture—that amorphous but undeniably amazing rebellion of youth that in the mid- to late Sixties turned the always tense gap between the generations into a battleground. Theodore Roszak, perhaps the most cogent and persuasive apologist for the counterculture, found in *The Making of a Counter Culture* the common thread that gave unity to this farrago of anarchic politics, visionary mysticism, communitarian social arrangements, Reichian psychology, Dadaesque entertainments, cosmic consciousness, rock music, pharmaceutical expertise and every other variety of esoterica to be its implacable opposition to technocracy and its scientific values. Against "the final consolidation of a technocratic totalitarianism in which we shall find ourselves ingeniously adapted to an existence wholly estranged from anything that has ever made the life of man an interesting adventure" (a possibility warned against by Mailer, Marcuse, Goodman, Mills and many others), the counterculture opposed sex and drugs and rock 'n' roll and magic and millenarianism and anything else it could find to get the Establishment's goat. It was surely one of the strangest, most unlikely revolutions in history, an outbreak in rationalized, prosperous, and powerful mid-twentieth century America of passions more associated with the rise of primitive Christianity in the Roman Empire or a medieval children's crusade. It gave adult America a terrible case of the willies.

Norman O. Brown's 1960 Phi Beta Kappa address, "Apocalypse: The Place of Mystery in the Life of the Mind," may be considered something of an opening salvo in the war, delivered, appropriately enough, to an assembly of scholarly technocrats at a university—Columbia—where some of the most heated action was later to occur. In the Fifties an obscure professor of classics at Wesleyan University, Brown had been catapulted to fame by his 1959 work *Life Against Death: The Psychoanalytic Meaning of History,* one of the most demanding and exciting works of scholarship ever written by an American. Along with Herbert Marcuse's *Eros and Civilization,* which is more overtly political in its approach, Brown had made bold and uncompromising use of the Freudian mechanisms of repression and sublimation as a tool to reveal the subtle and prevailing psychopathology of society and history. (The selection from Herbert Marcuse's *One-Dimensional Man* in the preceding section is in a related vein.) Both Brown and Marcuse preferred to ignore the pessimistic Freud of *Civilization and Its Discontents,* the Freud resigned to universal neurosis as the tribute the pleasure principle pays to the reality principle, to beckon instead toward a promised land of instinctual liberation and of "polymorphous perversity." Marcuse was the more superficially radical of the two thinkers, but Brown was more explosive; in his dogged insistence on the primacy of the body and on Freudian first principles he was able to show convincingly that the very categories of time and history so intrinsic to Western man spring from the inability, at the earliest and most deeply instinctual level, to face death. As an antidote to this "sickness that is man," the Apollonian sublimation of instinct in art, thought and life, Brown prescribes a Dionysiac excess in which individual identity dissolves, instinctual opposites reunite and an overtly Christian "resurrection of the body" occurs. Reversing Freud, Brown proclaims "Where ego is, there id shall be."

The address reprinted here, with its exhortation to "holy madness," had an electrifying effect on its audience of sober scholars comparable to that of the Phi Beta Kappa address by Ralph Waldo Emerson in 1837, "The American Scholar." It is an important midpoint in Brown's career between the still relatively linear *Life Against Death* and his incantory, aphoristic *Love's Body*, a book in form and prophetic spirit similar to Nietzsche's *Thus Spake Zarathustra*.

Many of the passages in the latter book, such as "The mad truth: the boundary between sanity and insanity is a false one. The proper outcome of psychoanalysis is the abolition of the boundary, the healing of the split, the integration of the human race. The proper posture is to listen and learn from lunatics as in former times . . ." could have been written by the British psychiatrist R. D. Laing, another prophet of the holy mystery of madness and the insanity of ordinary life. In his book *The Politics of Experience*, from which the selection "Transcendental Experience" is taken, Laing, drawing on Gregory Bateson's groundbreaking work on the "double binds" that can occur in family communication, analyzed schizophrenia as the only "sane" response to an insane environment, and proclaimed an almost terminal sense of cultural crisis: "The condition of alienation, of being asleep, of being unconscious, of being out of one's mind, is the condition of normal man." Echoing Marcuse, Laing meant literally "out of one's mind." He saw contemporary man as hopelessly estranged from his inner reality in the process of adjusting to alienating social reality. The function of a certain type of experience we call madness is to heal this radical split between inner and outer in our modern experience: "We respect the voyager, the explorer, the spaceman. It makes far more sense to me as a valid project—indeed as a desperately and urgently required project for our time—to explore the inner space and time of consciousness." This is the journey Laing believed the schizophrenic makes.

The fallout from the viewpoints of Brown and Laing is obvious throughout Sixties culture: in the Living Theatre's Dionysiac excesses, its recourse to the primitive mysteries of the theater, its use of the famous final words of *The Politics of Experience*, "If I could turn you on, if I could drive you out of your wretched mind, if I could tell you I would let you know" (see Leslie Epstein's piece on the Living Theatre in the arts section, "Walking Wounded, Living Dead"); in the widespread acceptance of Antonin Artaud's theories on the Theatre of Cruelty, and in such plays as Peter Weiss's *Marat/Sade*, an acting out by the inmates of an insane asylum in France, under the direction of the libertine Marquis de Sade, of scenes from the French Revolution; and in the immense success of Ken Kesey's pop-cult novel set in an Oregon insane asylum, *One Flew Over the Cuckoo's Nest*.

In the next piece, Warren Hinckle's funny "A Social History of the Hippies," we see Kesey in his later incarnation as master of the psychedelic revels and leader of the Merry Pranksters, in all a logical extension of his novelistic preoccupations. The discovery of the easily manufactured psychedelic drug LSD in the late Fifties dovetailed perfectly with a burgeoning segment of the culture eager for a skeleton key to the doors of perception and for some temporary schizophrenia. Kesey and the Pranksters set off in the mid-Sixties on an acid-fueled odyssey across America in a day-glo painted bus and publicized the faith in widely imitated freakouts called "Acid Tests" and "Trips Festivals." (For the full story, see Tom Wolfe's supremely entertaining *Electric Kool-Aid Acid Test*, whose veracity is attested to by Kesey himself.)

Kesey's scene was blessedly free of bullshit: Who needed overblown excuses to bend one's mind, indulge in sensory overloads, play mind games and psychedelic chicken with usually homocidal Hell's Angels? It was all good clean American fun, square in the Huck Finn/superhero tradition. The mystagogue and medicine man of acid culture was Timothy Leary, a defrocked Harvard psychologist who

pushed the drug energetically and irresponsibly as the panacea for the ills of Western man and cloaked his efforts in a
heavy fog of mystic mumbo-jumbo. ("We were part of an
ancient and honorable fellowship which had pursued this
journey since the dawn of recorded history. We began to read
the accounts of early trippers—Dante, Hesse, René Daumal,
Tolkien, Homer, Blake, George Fox, Swedenborg, Bosch—
and the explorers from the Orient—tantrics, Sufis, Bauls,
Gnostics, hermetics, Sivaites, sadhus." ("Turning On the
World," *Esquire,* July 1968.) Leary even founded his own
"church," the League for Spiritual Discovery.*

Kesey, Leary, and others called, and millions followed—to
San Francisco, Berkeley, Harvard Square, the East Village
and other outposts of the new culture. It's an index of how
seriously all this was taken that Hinckle's article, printed in
the March 1967 issue of *Ramparts,* occasioned a huge flap in
the hip Bay Area community; it seems Hinckle should have
kept his tongue farther from the vicinity of his cheek while
writing this still good-natured piece. All that free-floating
belief on the part of all those young people naturally searched
for its proper objects, and Leary, Kesey and various rock
stars were not alone in finding themselves the object of
adoring cults. Marco Vassi's hilarious account, excerpted
from one of the most sheerly enjoyable Sixties memoirs, *The
Stoned Apocalypse,* of how he became a holy man in the
space of a couple of weeks gives us an insider's look at the
creation of a Sixties archetype, the Jive Guru, and of the
forces that could get wildly out of the control of well-meaning
amateurs in the human-potential business. The workshop
Vassi set up and describes was typical of the kind of instant
spiritual transformation retailed by such spas for the psyche
as the Esalen Foundation in the Sixties, whose techniques

---

*No catalogue of Sixties mystagogues would be complete without mention of
Marshall McLuhan, the Delphic oracle of the age of electronics. A selection from
his incredibly influential work *Understanding Media* appears, naturally, in the
media section of this book. But much like Brown, McLuhan in the Sixties made
the transition from intellectual to teleological prophet, foretelling Western man's
redemption from "the typographical trance" of visual literacy by the electronic
media into a kind of global tribal awareness in which the barriers of individual
identity dissolve into mythical, corporate awareness: "In the electronic age we
wear all mankind as our skin." When McLuhan wrote that "Electric speed
creates centers everywhere. Margins cease to exist on the planet," the echoes of
Pascal's definition, "God is a sphere whose center is everywhere and whose
circumference is nowhere," were exactly intended.

were adopted in the Seventies by a host of sharks and psychological quick-buck artists.

The whole counterculture, in fact, got exploited and over-exposed to death in the late Sixties and early Seventies, which resulted in a slaughter of the innocents; whatever energies the counterculture may have generated are completely absorbed or dissipated by now. Roszak speaks of "a cynical smothering of dissent by saturation coverage," suggesting a kind of Marcusian mechanism of repression in the hyperfascination lavished by the media on the hippie phenomenon. There is also the irony that immense amounts of money were made, legally and illegally, on the mass-marketing of spinoffs from the supposedly cashless hippie society.

A more severe view of the matter can be found in Joan Didion's essay "Slouching Towards Bethlehem" (too long, unfortunately, to include in this book). While much of America was in the midst of being charmed by the exotic ways of the flower children, Didion had the Yeatsian perception to see that the disordered life of the vagabond teenagers in Haight-Ashbury was evidence that things were falling apart, the center was not holding, mere anarchy was being loosed throughout the entire fabric of American culture. The Armageddon of the counterculture, the Stones concert at the Altamont speedway, and the Tate-LaBianca murders by Charles Manson and his waifs gave frightening credibility to Didion's vision. (A somewhat less portentous type of disorder, though one no less destructive of cultural cohesion, is suggested by the texture of life described by Raymond Mungo in the selection from his book *Famous Long Ago* in the media section of this book.)

The final selection in this section, from George Dennison's beautiful and passionate account of the experience of teaching at the short-lived libertarian First Street School, *The Lives of Children,* may stand as an elegy for the entire range of plans and projects conceived in the Sixties to give a humane face to our institutions. A whole genre of books emerged in the Sixties from young teachers—Jonathan Kozol's *Death at an Early Age,* Herbert Kohl's *36 Children,* James Herndon's *Way It Spozed to Be* and *Survivor in Your Native Land,* John Holt's *How Children Fail* and *How Children Learn*—that described in poignant detail the human damage done to children, particularly Black children, by our senseless, thoughtless, racist, impersonal, regimented schools. These books struck a particular nerve in Americans, who historically have based a disproportionate amount of their faith in social progress and personal advancement on the efficacy of the schools; the news that the young children's lives were instead being blighted hit home with great force.

The First Street School, in contrast, was a shoestring operation at the other end of the spectrum from those institutions described above—a small, racially mixed school integrated firmly and intimately into its Lower East Side community and run completely along the noncoercive lines of A. S. Neill's famous Summerhill school in England. (Dennison, it should also be noted, was an associate and disciple of Paul Goodman.) For the impedimenta of lesson plans, curricula, schedules, homework, report cards and other crutches of bureaucratized education, the teachers at the First Street School substituted forbearance, trust, love, patience and a stubborn insistence that true learning only occurs when children experience education within the continuum of experience. The resulting progress, even with children who had experienced abject failure in the regular school system, was spectacular. After two years, however, the school was forced to close for lack of funds. Dennison's radiantly commonsensical account communicates especially how "arduous in the doing" the demanding set of educational practices taken from Neill, Dewey and Tolstoy that the school followed were, and how much was asked of the teachers. It suggests the uneasy thought that the larger "failures" of liberalism and other forms of social reform now widely advertised may have resulted less from faulty ideas and policies than from a lack of stamina and commitment.

# Superman Comes to the Supermarket

## Norman Mailer

**N**ot too much need be said for this piece; it is possible it can stand by itself. But perhaps its title should have been "Filling the Holes in No Man's Land."

American politics is rarely interesting for its men, its ideas, or the style of its movements. It is usually more fascinating in its gaps, its absences, its uninvaded territories. We have used up our frontier, but the psychological frontier talked about in this piece is still alive with untouched possibilities and dire unhappy all-but-lost opportunities. In European politics the spaces are filled—the average politician, like the average European, knows what is possible and what is impossible for him. Their politics is like close trench warfare. But in America, one knows such close combat only for the more banal political activities. The play of political ideas is flaccid here in America because opposing armies never meet. The Right, the Center, and what there is of the Left have set up encampments on separate hills, they face one another across valleys, they send out small patrols to their front and vast communiqués to their rear. No Man's Land predominates. It is a situation which calls for guerrilla raiders. Any army which would dare to enter the valley in force might not only determine a few new

From *Esquire*, November 1960. Reprinted in *The Presidential Papers* (G. P. Putnam's Sons, 1963); The italicized introduction is from this collection.

*political formations, but indeed could create more politics itself, even as the guerrilla raids of the Negro Left and Negro Right, the Freedom Riders and the Black Muslims, have discovered much of the secret nature of the American reality for us.*

*I wonder if I make myself clear. Conventional politics has had so little to do with the real subterranean life of America that none of us know much about the real—which is to say the potential—historic nature of America. That lies buried under apathy, platitudes, Rightist encomiums for the FBI, programmatic welfare from the liberal Center, and furious pips of protest from the Peace Movement's Left. The mass of Americans are not felt as a political reality. No one has any idea of how they would react to radically new sense. It is only when their heartland, their no man's land, their valley is invaded, that one discovers the reality. In Birmingham during the days of this writing, the jails are filled with Negro children, 2000 of them. The militancy of the Negroes in Birmingham is startling, so too is the stubbornness of the Southern white, so too and unbelievable is the procrastination of the Kennedy Administration. Three new realities have been discovered. The potential Left and potential Right of America are more vigorous than one would have expected and the Center is more irresolute. An existential political act, the drive by Southern Negroes, led by Martin Luther King, to end segregation in restaurants in Birmingham, an act which is existential precisely because its end is unknown, has succeeded en route in discovering more of the American reality to us.*

*If a public speaker in a small Midwestern town were to say, "J. Edgar Hoover has done more harm to the freedoms of America than Joseph Stalin," the act would be existential. Depending on the occasion and the town, he would be manhandled physically or secretly applauded. But he would create a new reality which would displace the old psychological reality that such a remark could not be made, even as for example the old Southern psychological reality that you couldn't get two Negroes to do anything together, let alone two thousand has now been destroyed by a new and more accurate psychological reality: you can get two thousand Negroes to work in cooperation. The new psychological realities are closer to history and so closer to sanity and they exist because, and only because, the event has taken place.*

*It was Kennedy's potentiality to excite such activity which interested me most; that he was young, that he was physically handsome, and that his wife was attractive were not trifling accidental details but, rather, new major political facts. I knew if he became President, it would be an existential event: he would touch depths in American life which were uncharted. Regardless of his politics, and even then one could expect his politics would be as conventional as his personality was unconventional, indeed one could expect his politics to be pushed toward conventionality precisely to counteract his essential unconventionality, one knew nonetheless that regardless of his overt politics, America's tortured psychotic search for security would finally be torn loose from the feverish ghosts of its old generals, its MacArthurs and Eisenhowers—ghosts which Nixon could cling to—and we as a nation would finally be loose again in the historic seas of a national psyche which was willy-nilly and at last, again, adventurous. And that, I thought, that was the hope for America. So I swallowed my doubts, my disquiets, and my certain distastes for Kennedy's dullness of mind and prefabricated politics, and did my best to write a piece which would help him to get elected.*

For once let us try to think about a political convention without losing ourselves in housing projects of fact and issue. Politics has its virtues, all too many of them—it would not rank with baseball as a topic of conversation if it did not satisfy a great many things—but one can suspect that its secret appeal is close to nicotine. Smoking cigarettes insulates one from one's life, one does not feel as much, often happily so, and politics quarantines one from history; most of the people who nourish themselves in the political life are in the game not to make history but to be diverted from the history which is being made.

If that Democratic Convention which has now receded behind the brow of the Summer of 1960 is only half-remembered in the excitements of moving toward the election, it may be exactly the time to consider it again, because the mountain of facts which concealed its features last July has been blown away in the winds of High Television, and the man-in-the-street (that peculiar political term which refers to the quixotic voter who will pull the lever for some reason so salient as: "I had a brown-nose lieutenant once with Nixon's looks," or "that Kennedy must have false teeth"), the not so easily estimated man-in-the-street has forgotten most of what happened and could no more tell you who Kennedy was fighting against than you or I could place a bet on who was leading the American League in batting during the month of June.

So to try to talk about what happened is easier now than in the days of the convention, one does not have to put everything in—an act of writing which calls for a bulldozer rather than a pen—one can try to make one's little point and dress it with a ribbon or two of metaphor. All to the good. Because mysteries are irritated by facts, and the 1960 Democratic Convention began as one mystery and ended as another.

Since mystery is an emotion which is repugnant to a political animal (why else lead a life of bad banquet dinners, cigar smoke, camp chairs, foul breath, and excruciatingly dull jargon if not to avoid the echoes of what is not known), the psychic separation between what was happening on the floor, in the caucus rooms, in the headquarters, and what was happening in parallel to the history of the nation was mystery enough to drown the proceedings in gloom. It was on the one hand a dull convention, one of the less interesting by general agreement, relieved by local bits of color, given two half hours of excitement by two demonstrations for Stevenson, buoyed up by the class of the Kennedy machine, turned by the surprise of Johnson's nomination as vice-president, but, all the same, dull, depressed in its overall tone, the big fiestas subdued, the gossip flat, no real air of excitement, just moments—or as they say in bullfighting—details. Yet it was also, one could argue—and one may argue this yet—it was also one of the most important conventions in America's history, it could prove conceivably to be the most important. The man it nominated was unlike any politician who had ever run for President in the history of the land, and if elected he would come to power in a year when America was in danger of drifting into a profound decline.

**A Descriptive of the Delegates: Sons and Daughters
of the Republic in a Legitimate Panic;
Small-time Practitioners of Small-town Political
Judo in the Big Town and the Big Time**

Depression obviously has its several roots: it is the doubtful
protection which comes from not recognizing failure, it is the
psychic burden of exhaustion, and it is also, and very often,
that discipline of the will or the ego which enables one to
continue working when one's unadmitted emotion is panic.
And panic it was I think which sat as the largest single
sentiment in the breast of the collective delegates as they
came to convene in Los Angeles. Delegates are not the
noblest sons and daughters of the Republic; a man of taste,
arrived from Mars, would take one look at a convention floor
and leave forever, convinced he had seen one of the drearier
squats of Hell. If one still smells the faint living echo of a
carnival wine, the pepper of a bullfight, the rag, drag, and
panoply of a jousting tourney, it is all swallowed and regurgi-
tated by the senses into the fouler cud of a death gas one must
rid oneself of—a cigar-smoking, stale-aired, slack-jawed,
butt-littered, foul, bleak, hard-working, bureaucratic death
gas of language and faces ("Yes, those *faces*," says the man
from Mars: lawyers, judges, ward heelers, *mafiosos*, Southern goons and grandees, grand old ladies, trade unionists and
finks), of pompous words and long pauses which lay like a
leaden pain over fever, the fever that one is in, over, or is it
that one is just behind history? A legitimate panic for a
delegate. America is a nation of experts without roots; we are
always creating tacticians who are blind to strategy and
strategists who cannot take a step, and when the culture has
finished its work the institutions handcuff the infirmity. A
delegate is a man who picks a candidate for the largest office
in the land, a President who must live with problems whose
borders are in ethics, metaphysics, and now ontology; the
delegate is prepared for this office of selection by emptying
wastebaskets, toting garbage and saying yes at the right time
for twenty years in the small political machine of some small
or large town; his reward, one of them anyway, is that he
arrives at an invitation to the convention. An expert on local
catch-as-catch-can, a small-time, often mediocre practitioner
of small-town political judo, he comes to the big city with

nine-tenths of his mind made up, he will follow the orders of the boss who brought him. Yet of course it is not altogether so mean as that: his opinion is listened to—the boss will consider what he has to say as one interesting factor among five hundred, and what is most important to the delegate, he has the illusion of partial freedom. He can, unless he is severely honest with himself—and if he is, why sweat out the low levels of a political machine?—he can have the illusion that he has helped to choose the candidate, he can even worry most sincerely about his choice, flirt with defection from the boss, work out his own small political gains by the road of loyalty or the way of hard bargain. But even if he is there for no more than the ride, his vote a certainty in the mind of the political boss, able to be thrown here or switched there as the boss decides, still in some peculiar sense he is reality to the boss, the delegate is the great American public, the bar he owns or the law practice, the piece of the union he represents, or the real-estate office, is a part of the political landscape which the boss uses as his own image of how the votes will go, and if the people will like the candidate. And if the boss is depressed by what he sees, if the candidate does not feel right to him, if he has a dull intimation that the candidate is not his sort (as, let us say, Harry Truman was his sort, or Symington might be his sort, or Lyndon Johnson), then vote for him the boss will if he must; he cannot be caught on the wrong side, but he does not feel the pleasure of a personal choice. Which is the center of the panic. Because if the boss is depressed, the delegate is doubly depressed, and the emotional fact is that Kennedy is not in focus, not in the old political focus, he is not comfortable; in fact it is a mystery to the boss how Kennedy got to where he is, not a mystery in its structures; Kennedy is rolling in money, Kennedy got the votes in primaries, and, most of all, Kennedy has a jewel of a political machine. It is as good as a crack Notre Dame team, all discipline and savvy and go-go-go, sound, drilled, never dull, quick as a knife, full of the salt of hipper-dipper, a beautiful machine; the boss could adore it if only a sensible candidate were driving it, a Truman, even a Stevenson, please God a Northern Lyndon Johnson, but it is run by a man who looks young enough to be coach of the Freshman team, and that is not comfortable at all. The boss knows political machines, he knows issues, farm parity, Forand health bill, Landrum-Griffin, but this is not all so adequate after all to revolutionaries in Cuba who look like beatniks, competitions in missiles, Negroes looting whites in the Congo, intricacies of nuclear fallout, and NAACP men one does well to call Sir. It is all out of hand, everything important is off the center, foreign affairs is now the lick of the heat, and senators are candidates instead of governors, a disaster to the old family style of political measure where a political boss knows his governor and knows who his governor knows. So the boss is depressed, profoundly depressed. He comes to this convention resigned to nominating a man he does not understand, or let us say that, so far as he understands the candidate who is to be nominated, he is not happy about the secrets of his appeal, not so far as he divines these secrets; they seem to have too little to do with politics and all too much to do with the private madnesses of the nation which had thousands—or was it hundreds of thousands—of people demonstrating in the long night before Chessman was killed, and a movie star, the greatest, Marlon the Brando out in the night with them. Yes, this candidate for all his record, his good, sound, conventional liberal record has a patina of that other life, the second American life, the long electric night with the fires of neon leading down the highway to the murmur of jazz.

### An Apparent Digression: A Vivid View of the "City of Lost Angels"; The Democrats Defined; A Pentagon of Traveling Salesmen; Some Pointed Portraits of the Politicians

"I was seeing Pershing Square, Los Angeles, now for the first time . . . the nervous fruithustlers darting in and out of the shadows, fugitives from Times Square, Market Street SF, the French Quarter—masculine hustlers looking for lonely fruits to score from, anything from the legendary $20 to a pad at night and breakfast in the morning and whatever you can clinch or clip; and the heat in their holy cop uniforms, holy because of the Almighty Stick and the Almightier Vagrancy Law; the scattered junkies, the small-time pushers, the queens, the sad panhandlers, the lonely, exiled nymphs haunting the entrance to the men's head, the fruits

with the hungry eyes and the jingling coins; the tough
teen-age chicks—'dittybops'—making it with the lost
hustlers . . . and amid the incongruous piped music and
the flowers—twin fountains gushing rainbow colored:
the world of Lonely America squeezed into Pershing
Square, of the Cities of Terrible Night, downtown now
trapped in the City of Lost Angels . . . and the trees
hang over it all like some type of apathetic fate."

—John Rechy, *Big Table 3*

Seeing Los Angeles after ten years away, one realizes all
over again that America is an unhappy contract between the
East (that Faustian thrust of a most determined human will
which reaches up and out above the eye into the skyscrapers
of New York) and those flat lands of compromise and
mediocre self-expression, those endless half-pretty repetitive
small towns of the Middle and the West, whose spirit is
forever horizontal and whose marrow comes to rendezvous in
the pastel monotonies of Los Angeles architecture.

So far as America has a history, one can see it in the severe
heights of New York City, in the glare from the Pittsburgh
mills, by the color in the brick of Louisburg Square, along the
knotted greedy façades of the small mansions on Chicago's
North Side, in Natchez' antebellum homes, the wrought-iron
balconies off Bourbon Street, a captain's house in Nantucket,
by the curve of Commercial Street in Provincetown. One can
make a list; it is probably finite. What culture we have made
and what history has collected to it can be found in those few
hard examples of an architecture which came to its artistic
term, was born, lived and so collected some history about it.
Not all the roots of American life are uprooted, but almost
all, and the spirit of the supermarket, that homogenous
extension of stainless surfaces and psychoanalyzed people,
packaged commodities and ranch homes, interchangeable,
geographically unrecognizable, that essence of the new postwar SuperAmerica is found nowhere so perfectly as in Los
Angeles' ubiquitous acres. One gets the impression that
people come to Los Angeles in order to divorce themselves
from the past, here to live or try to live in the rootless
pleasure world of an adult child. One knows that if the cities
of the world were destroyed by a new war, the architecture of
the rebuilding would create a landscape which looked, sub-

ject to specifications of climate, exactly and entirely like the
San Fernando Valley.

It is not that Los Angeles is altogether hideous, it is even by
degrees pleasant, but for an Easterner there is never any salt
in the wind; it is like Mexican cooking without chili, or
Chinese egg rolls missing their mustard; as one travels
through the endless repetitions of that city which is the capital
of suburbia with its milky pinks, its washed-out oranges, its
tainted lime-yellows of pastel on one pretty little architectural
monstrosity after another, the colors not intense enough, the
styles never pure, and never sufficiently impure to collide on
the eye, one conceives the people who live here—they have
come out to express themselves, Los Angeles is the home of
self-expression, but the artists are middle-class and middling-
minded; no passions will calcify here for years in the gloom to
be revealed a decade later as the tessellations of a hard and
fertile work, no, it is all open, promiscuous, borrowed, half
bought, a city without iron, eschewing wood, a kingdom of
stucco, the playground for mass men—one has the feeling it
was built by television sets giving orders to men. And in this
land of the pretty-pretty, the virility is in the barbarisms, the
vulgarities, it is in the huge billboards, the screamers of the
neon lighting, the shouting farm-utensil colors of the gas
stations and the monster drugstores, it is in the swing of the
sports cars, hot rods, convertibles, Los Angeles is a city to
drive in, the boulevards are wide, the traffic is nervous and
fast, the radio stations play bouncing, blooping, rippling
tunes, one digs the pop in a pop tune, no one of character
would make love by it but the sound is good for swinging a
car, electronic guitars and Hawaiian harps.

So this is the town the Democrats came to, and with their
unerring instinct (after being with them a week, one thinks of
this party as a crazy, half-rich family, loaded with poor
cousins, traveling always in caravans with Cadillacs and Okie
Fords, Lincolns and quarter-horse mules, putting up every
night in tents to hear the chamber quartet of Great Cousin
Eleanor invaded by the Texas-twanging steel-stringing geetar-
ists of Bubber Lyndon, carrying its own mean highschool
principal, Doc Symington, chided for its manners by good
Uncle Adlai, told the route of march by Navigator Jack, cut
off every six months from the rich will of Uncle Jim Farley,
never listening to the mechanic of the caravan, Bald Sam
Rayburn, who assures them they'll all break down unless

Cousin Bubber gets the concession on the garage; it's the Snopes family married to Henry James, with the labor unions thrown in like a Yankee dollar, and yet it's true, in tranquility one recollects them with affection, their instinct is good, crazy family good) and this instinct now led the caravan to pick the Biltmore Hotel in downtown Los Angeles for their family get-together and reunion.

The Biltmore is one of the ugliest hotels in the world. Patterned after the flat roofs of an Italian Renaissance palace, it is eighty-eight times as large, and one-millionth as valuable to the continuation of man, and it would be intolerable if it were not for the presence of Pershing Square, that square block of park with cactus and palm trees, the three-hundred-and-sixty-five-day-a-year convention of every junkie, pot-head, pusher, queen (but you have read that good writing already). For years Pershing Square has been one of the three or four places in America famous to homosexuals, famous not for its posh, the chic is round-heeled here, but because it is one of the avatars of the good old masturbatory sex, dirty with the crusted sugars of smut, dirty rooming houses around the corner where the score is made, dirty book and photograph stores down the street, old-fashioned out-of-the-Thirties burlesque houses, cruising bars, jukeboxes, movie houses; Pershing Square is the town plaza for all those lonely, respectable, small-town homosexuals who lead a family life, make children, and have the Philbrick psychology (How I Joined the Communist Party and Led Three Lives). Yes, it is the open-air convention hall for the small-town inverts who live like spies, and it sits in the center of Los Angeles, facing the Biltmore, that hotel which is a mausoleum, that Pentagon of traveling salesmen the Party chose to house the headquarters of the convention.

So here came that family, cursed before it began by the thundering absence of Great-Uncle Truman, the delegates dispersed over a run of thirty miles and twenty-seven hotels: the Olympian Motor Hotel, the Ambassador, the Beverly Wilshire, the Santa Ynez Inn (where rumor has it the delegates from Louisiana had some midnight swim), the Mayan, the Commodore, the Mayfair, the Sheraton-West, the Huntington-Sheraton, the Green, the Hayward, the Gates, the Figueroa, the Statler Hilton, the Hollywood Knickerbocker—does one have to be a collector to list such names?—beauties all, with that up-from-the-farm Los Angeles décor, plate-glass windows, patio and terrace, foam-rubber mattress, pastel paints, all of them pretty as an ad in full-page color, all but the Biltmore where everybody gathered every day—the newsmen, the TV, radio, magazine, and foreign newspapermen, the delegates, the politicos, the tourists, the campaign managers, the runners, the flunkies, the cousins and aunts, the wives, the grandfathers, the eight-year-old girls, and the twenty-eight-year-old girls in the Kennedy costumes, red and white and blue, the Symingteeners, the Johnson Ladies, the Stevenson Ladies, everybody—and for three days before the convention and four days into it, everybody collected at the Biltmore, in the lobby, in the grill, in the Biltmore Bowl, in the elevators, along the corridors, three hundred deep always outside the Kennedy suite, milling everywhere, every dark-carpeted grey-brown hall of the hotel, but it was in the Gallery of the Biltmore where one first felt the mood which pervaded all proceedings until the convention was almost over, that heavy, thick, witless depression which was to dominate every move as the delegates wandered and gawked and paraded and set for a spell, there in the Gallery of the Biltmore, that huge depressing alley with its inimitable hotel color, that faded depth of chiaroscuro which unhappily has no depth, that brown which is not a brown, that grey which has no pearl in it, that color which can be described only as hotel-color because the beiges, the tans, the walnuts, the mahoganies, the dull blood rugs, the moaning yellows, the sick greens, the greys and all those dumb browns merge into that lack of color which is an over-large hotel at convention time, with all the small-towners wearing their set, starched faces, that look they get at carnival, all fever and suspicion, and proud to be there, eddying slowly back and forth in that high block-long tunnel of a room with its arched ceiling and square recesses filling every rib of the arch with art work, escutcheons and blazons and other art, pictures I think, I cannot even remember, there was such a hill of cigar smoke the eye had to travel on its way to the ceiling, and at one end there was galvanized-pipe scaffolding and workmen repairing some part of the ceiling, one of them touching up one of the endless squares of painted plaster in the arch, and another worker, passing by, yelled up to the one who was working on the ceiling: "Hey, Michelangelo!"

Later, of course, it began to emerge and there were portraits one could keep, Symington, dogged at a press conference, declaring with no conviction that he knew he had a good chance to win, the disappointment eating at his good looks so that he came off hard-faced, mean, and yet slack—a desperate dullness came off the best of his intentions. There was Johnson who had compromised too many contradictions and now the contradictions were in his face: when he smiled the corners of his mouth squeezed gloom; when he was pious, his eyes twinkled irony; when he spoke in a righteous tone, he looked corrupt; when he jested, the ham in his jowls looked to quiver. He was not convincing. He was a Southern politician, a Texas Democrat, a liberal Eisenhower; he would do no harm, he would do no good, he would react to the machine, good fellow, nice friend—the Russians would understand him better than his own.

Stevenson had the patina. He came into the room and the room was different, not stronger perhaps (which is why ultimately he did not win), but warmer. One knew why some adored him; he did not look like other people, not with press lights on his flesh; he looked like a lover, the simple truth, he had the sweet happiness of an adolescent who has just been given his first major kiss. And so he glowed, and one was reminded of Chaplin, not because they were the least alike in features, but because Charlie Chaplin was luminous when one met him and Stevenson had something of that light.

There was Eleanor Roosevelt, fine, precise, hand-worked like ivory. Her voice was almost attractive as she explained in the firm, sad tones of the first lady in this small town why she could not admit Mr. Kennedy, who was no doubt a gentleman, into her political house. One had the impression of a lady who was finally becoming a woman, which is to say that she was just a little bitchy about it all; nice bitchy, charming, it had a touch of art to it, but it made one wonder if she were not now satisfying the last passion of them all, which was to become physically attractive, for she was better-looking than she had ever been as she spurned the possibilities of a young suitor.

Jim Farley. Huge. Cold as a bishop. The hell he would consign you to was cold as ice.

Bobby Kennedy, that archetype Bobby Kennedy, looked like a West Point cadet, or, better, one of those unreconstructed Irishmen from Kirkland House one always used to have to face in the line in Harvard house football games. "Hello," you would say to the ones who looked like him as you lined up for the scrimmage after the kickoff, and his type would nod and look away, one rock glint of recognition your due for living across the hall from one another all through Freshman year, and then bang, as the ball was passed back, you'd get a bony king-hell knee in the crotch. He was the kind of man never to put on the gloves with if you wanted to do some social boxing, because after two minutes it would be a war, and ego-bastards last long in a war.

Carmine DeSapio and Kenneth Galbraith on the same part of the convention floor. DeSapio is bigger than one expects, keen and florid, great big smoked glasses, a suntan like Man-tan—he is the kind of heavyweight Italian who could get by with a name like Romeo—and Galbraith is tall-tall, as actors say; six foot six it could be, terribly thin, enormously attentive, exquisitely polite, birdlike, he is sensitive to the stirring of reeds in a wind over the next hill. "Our grey eminence," whispered the intelligent observer next to me.

Bob Wagner, the mayor of New York, a little man, plump, groomed, blank. He had the blank, pomaded, slightly worried look of the first barber in a good barbershop, the kind who would go to the track on his day off and wear a green transparent stone in a gold ring.

And then there was Kennedy, the edge of the mystery. But a sketch will no longer suffice.

### Perspective from the Biltmore Balcony: The Colorful Arrival of the Hero with the Orange-brown Suntan and Amazingly White Teeth; Revelation of the Two Rivers Political Theory

". . . it can be said with a fair amount of certainty that the essence of his political attractiveness is his extraordinary political intelligence. He has a mind quite unlike that of any other Democrat of this century. It is not literary, metaphysical and moral, as Adlai Stevenson's is. Kennedy is articulate and often witty, but he does not seek verbal polish. No one can doubt the seriousness of his concern with the most serious political matters, but one feels that whereas Mr. Stevenson's political views derive from a view of life that holds politics to be a mere fraction of existence, Senator Kennedy's primary interest is in politics. The easy way in which he disposes of the question of Church and State—as if he felt that any reasonable man could quite easily resolve any possible conflict of loyalties—suggests that the organization of society is the one thing that really engages his interest."

—Richard Rovere, *The New Yorker,* July 23, 1960

The afternoon he arrived at the convention from the airport, there was of course a large crowd on the street outside the Biltmore, and the best way to get a view was to get up on an outdoor balcony of the Biltmore, two flights above the street, and look down on the event. One waited thirty minutes, and then a honking of horns as wild as the getaway after an Italian wedding sounded around the corner, and the Kennedy cortege came into sight, circled Pershing Square, the men in the open and leading convertibles sitting backwards to look at their leader, and finally came to a halt in a space cleared for them by the police in the crowd. The television cameras were out, and a Kennedy band was playing some circus music. One saw him immediately. He had the deep orange-brown suntan of a ski instructor, and when he smiled at the crowd his teeth were amazingly white and clearly visible at a distance of fifty yards. For one moment he saluted Pershing Square, and Pershing Square saluted him back, the prince and the beggars of glamor staring at one another across a city street, one of those very special moments in the underground history of the world, and then with a quick move he was out of the car and by choice headed into the crowd instead of the lane cleared for him into the hotel by the police, so that he made his way inside surrounded by a mob, and one expected at any moment to see him lifted to its shoulders like a matador being carried back to the city after a triumph in the plaza. All the while the band kept playing the campaign tunes, sashaying circus music, and one had a moment of clarity, intense as a *déjà vu,* for the scene which had taken place had been glimpsed before in a dozen musical comedies; it was the scene where the hero, the matinee idol, the movie star comes to the palace to claim the princess, or what is the same, and more to our soil, the football hero, the campus king, arrives at the dean's home surrounded by a court of open-singing students to plead with the dean for his daughter's kiss and permission to put on the big musical that night. And suddenly I saw the convention, it came into focus for me, and I understood the mood of depression which had lain over the convention, because finally it was simple: the Democrats were going to nominate a man who, no matter how serious his political dedication might be, was indisputably and willy-nilly going to be seen as a great box-office actor, and the consequences of that were staggering and not at all easy to calculate.

Since the First World War Americans have been leading a double life, and our history has moved on two rivers, one visible, the other underground; there has been the history of politics which is concrete, factual, practical and unbelievably dull if not for the consequences of the actions of some of these men; and there is a subterranean river of untapped, ferocious, lonely and romantic desires, that concentration of ecstasy and violence which is the dream life of the nation.

The twentieth century may yet be seen as that era when civilized man and underprivileged man were melted together into mass man, the iron and steel of the nineteenth century giving way to electronic circuits which communicated their messages into men, the unmistakable tendency of the new century seeming to be the creation of men as interchangeable as commodities, their extremes of personality singed out of existence by the psychic fields of force the communicators would impose. This loss of personality was a catastrophe to the future of the imagination, but billions of people might first benefit from it by having enough to eat—one did not know—and there remained citadels of resistance in Europe where the culture was deep and roots were visible in the architecture of the past.

Nowhere, as in America, however, was this fall from individual man to mass man felt so acutely, for America was at once the first and most prolific creator of mass communications, and the most rootless of countries, since almost no American could lay claim to the line of a family which had not once at least severed its roots by migrating here. But, if rootless, it was then the most vulnerable of countries to its own homogenization. Yet America was also the country in which the dynamic myth of the Renaissance—that every man was potentially extraordinary—knew its most passionate persistence. Simply, America was the land where people still believed in heroes: George Washington; Billy the Kid; Lincoln, Jefferson; Mark Twain, Jack London, Hemingway; Joe Louis, Dempsey, Gentleman Jim; America believed in athletes, rum-runners, aviators; even lovers, by the time Valentino died. It was a country which had grown by the leap of one hero past another—is there a county in all of our ground which does not have its legendary figure? And when the West was filled, the expansion turned inward, became part of an agitated, overexcited, superheated dream life. The film studios threw up their searchlights as the frontier was finally sealed, and the romantic possibilities of the old conquest of land turned into a vertical myth, trapped within the skull, of a new kind of heroic life, each choosing his own archetype of a neo-renaissance man, be it Barrymore, Cagney, Flynn, Bogart, Brando or Sinatra, but it was almost as if there were no peace unless one could fight well, kill well (if always with honor), love well and love many, be cool, be daring, be dashing, be wild, be wily, be resourceful, be a brave gun. And this myth, that each of us was born to be free, to wander, to have adventure and to grow on the waves of the violent, the perfumed, and the unexpected, had a force which could not be tamed no matter how the nation's regulators—politicians, medicos, policemen, professors, priests, rabbis, ministers, *idéologues*, psychoanalysts, builders, executives and endless communicators—would brick-in the modern life with hygiene upon sanity, and middle-brow homily over platitude; the myth would not die. Indeed a quarter of the nation's business must have depended upon its existence. But it stayed alive for more than that—it was as if the message in the labyrinth of the genes would insist that violence was locked with creativity, and adventure was the secret of love.

Once, in the Second World War and in the year or two which followed, the underground river returned to earth, and the life of the nation was intense, of the present, electric; as a lady said, "That was the time when we gave parties which changed people's lives." The Forties was a decade when the speed with which one's own events occurred seemed as rapid as the history of the battlefields, and for the mass of people in America a forced march into a new jungle of emotion was the result. The surprises, the failures, and the dangers of that life must have terrified some nerve of awareness in the power and the mass, for, as if stricken by the orgiastic vistas the myth had carried up from underground, the retreat to a more conservative existence was disorderly, the fear of communism

spread like an irrational hail of boils. To anyone who could
see, the excessive hysteria of the Red wave was no preparation to face an enemy, but rather a terror of the national self:
free-loving, lust-looting, atheistic, implacable—absurdity beyond absurdity to label communism so, for the moral products of Stalinism had been Victorian sex and a ponderous
machine of material theology.

Forced underground again, deep beneath all *Reader's
Digest* hospital dressings of Mental Health in Your Community, the myth continued to flow, fed by television and the
film. The fissure in the national psyche widened to the danger
point. The last large appearance of the myth was the vote
which tricked the polls and gave Harry Truman his victory in
'48. That was the last. Came the Korean War, the shadow of
the H-bomb, and we were ready for the General. Uncle
Harry gave way to Father, and security, regularity, order, and
the life of no imagination were the command of the day. If
one had any doubt of this, there was Joe McCarthy with his
built-in treason detector, furnished by God, and the damage
was done. In the totalitarian wind of those days, anyone who
worked in Government formed the habit of being not too
original. At the summit there was benevolence without
leadership, regularity without vision, security without safety,
rhetoric without life. The ship drifted on, that enormous
warship of the United States, led by a Secretary of State
whose cells were seceding to cancer, and as the world became
more fantastic—Africa burning itself upside down, while
some new kind of machine man was being made in China—
two events occurred which stunned the confidence of America into a new night: the Russians put up their Sputnik, and
Civil Rights—that reluctant gift to the American Negro,
granted for its effect on foreign affairs—spewed into real life
at Little Rock. The national Ego was in shock: the Russians
were now in some ways our technological superiors, and we
had an internal problem of subject populations equal conceivably in its difficulty to the Soviet and its satellites. The
fatherly calm of the General began to seem like the uxorious
mellifluences of the undertaker.

Underneath it all was a larger problem. The life of politics
and the life of myth had diverged too far, and the energies of
the people one knew everywhere had slowed down. Twenty
years ago a post-Depression generation had gone to war and
formed a lively, grousing, by times inefficient, carousing,

pleasure-seeking, not altogether inadequate army. It did part of what it was supposed to do, and many, out of combat, picked up a kind of private life on the fly, and had their good time despite the yaws of the military system. But today in America the generation which respected the code of the myth was Beat, a horde of half-begotten Christs with scraggly beards, heroes none, saints all, weak before the strong, empty conformisms of the authority. The sanction for finding one's growth was no longer one's flag, one's career, one's sex, one's adventure, not even one's booze. Among the best in this newest of the generations, the myth had found its voice in marijuana, and the joke of the underground was that when the Russians came over they could never dare to occupy us for long because America was too Hip. Gallows humor. The poorer truth might be that America was too Beat, the instinct of the nation so separated from its public mind that apathy, schizophrenia, and private beatitudes might be the pride of the welcoming committee any underground could offer.

Yes, the life of politics and the life of the myth had diverged too far. There was nothing to return them to one another, no common danger, no cause, no desire, and, most essentially, no hero. It was a hero America needed, a hero central to his time, a man whose personality might suggest contradictions and mysteries which could reach into the alienated circuits of the underground, because only a hero can capture the secret imagination of a people, and so be good for the vitality of his nation; a hero embodies the fantasy and so allows each private mind the liberty to consider its fantasy and find a way to grow. Each mind can become more conscious of its desire and waste less strength in hiding from itself. Roosevelt was such a hero, and Churchill, Lenin and De Gaulle; even Hitler, to take the most odious example of this thesis, was a hero, the hero-as-monster, embodying what had become the monstrous fantasy of a people, but the horror upon which the radical mind and liberal temperament foundered was that he gave outlet to the energies of the Germans and so presented the twentieth century with an index of how horrible had become the secret heart of its desire. Roosevelt is of course a happier example of the hero; from his paralytic leg to the royal elegance of his geniality he seemed to contain the country within himself; everyone from the meanest starving cripple to an ambitious young man could expand into the optimism of an improving future because the man offered an unspoken promise of a future which would be rich. The sexual and the sex-starved, the poor, the hard-working and the imaginative well-to-do could see themselves in the President, could believe him to be like themselves. So a large part of the country was able to discover its energies because not as much was wasted in feeling that the country was a poisonous nutrient which stifled the day.

Too simple? No doubt. One tried to construct a simple model. The thesis is after all not so mysterious; it would merely nudge the notion that a hero embodies his time and is not so very much better than his time, but he is larger than life and so is capable of giving direction to the time, able to encourage a nation to discover the deepest colors of its character. At bottom the concept of the hero is antagonistic to impersonal social progress, to the belief that social ills can be solved by social legislating, for it sees a country as all-but-trapped in its character until it has a hero who reveals the character of the country to itself. The implication is that without such a hero the nation turns sluggish. Truman for example was not such a hero, he was not sufficiently larger than life, he inspired familiarity without excitement, he was a character but his proportions came from soap opera: Uncle Harry, full of salty common-sense and small-minded certainty, a storekeeping uncle.

Whereas Eisenhower has been the anti-Hero, the regulator. Nations do not necessarily and inevitably seek for heroes. In periods of dull anxiety, one is more likely to look for security than a dramatic confrontation, and Eisenhower could stand as a hero only for that large number of Americans who were most proud of their lack of imagination. In American life, the unspoken war of the century has taken place between the city and the small town: the city which is dynamic, orgiastic, unsettling, explosive and accelerating to the psyche; the small town which is rooted, narrow, cautious and planted in the life-logic of the family. The need for the city is to accelerate growth; the pride of the small town is to retard it. But since America has been passing through a period of enormous expansion since the war, the double-four years of Dwight Eisenhower could not retard the expansion, it could only denude it of color, character, and the development of novelty. The small-town mind is rooted—it is rooted in the small town—and when it attempts to direct history the results are disastrously colorless because the instrument of world power which is used by the small-town mind is the committee. Committees do not create, they merely proliferate, and the incredible dullness wreaked upon the American landscape in Eisenhower's eight years has been the triumph of the corporation. A tasteless, sexless, odorless sanctity in architecture, manners, modes, styles has been the result. Eisenhower embodied half the needs of the nation, the needs of the timid, the petrified, the sanctimonious, and the sluggish. What was even worse, he did not divide the nation as a hero might (with a dramatic dialogue as the result); he merely excluded one part of the nation from the other. The result was an alienation of the best minds and bravest impulses from the faltering history which was made. America's need in those years was to take an existential turn, to walk into the nightmare, to face into that terrible logic of history which demanded that the country and its people must become more extraordinary and more adventurous, or else perish, since the only alternative was to offer a false security in the power and the panacea of organized religion, family, and the FBI, a totalitarianization of the psyche by the stultifying techniques of the mass media which would seep into everyone's most private associations and so leave the country powerless against the Russians even if the denouement were to take fifty years, for in a competition between totalitarianisms the first maxim of the prizefight manager would doubtless apply: "Hungry fighters win fights."

### The Hipster as Presidential Candidate: Thoughts on a Public Man's Eighteenth-Century Wife; Face-to-Face with the Hero; Significance of a Personal Note, or the Meaning of His Having Read an Author's Novel

Some part of these thoughts must have been in one's mind at the moment there was that first glimpse of Kennedy entering the Biltmore Hotel; and in the days which followed, the first mystery—the profound air of depression which hung over the convention—gave way to a second mystery which can be answered only by history. The depression of the delegates was understandable: no one had too much doubt that Kennedy would be nominated, but if elected he would be not only the youngest President ever to be chosen by voters, he would be the most conventionally attractive young man ever to sit in the White House, and his wife—some would claim it—might be the most beautiful first lady in our history. Of necessity the myth would emerge once more, because America's politics would now be also America's favorite movie, America's first soap opera, America's best-seller. One thinks of the talents of writers like Taylor Caldwell or Frank Yerby, or is it rather *The Fountainhead* which would contain such a fleshing of the romantic prescription? Or is it indeed one's own work which is called into question? "Well, there's your first hipster," says a writer one knows at the convention, "Sergius O'Shaugnessy born rich," and the temptation is to nod, for it could be true, a war hero, and the heroism is bona-fide, even exceptional, a man who has lived with death, who, crippled in the back, took on an operation which would kill him or restore him to power, who chose to marry a lady whose face might be too imaginative for the taste of a democracy which likes its first ladies to be executives of home-management, a man who courts political suicide by choosing to go all out for a nomination four, eight, or twelve years before his political elders think he is ready, a man who announces a week prior to the convention that the young are better fitted to direct history than the old. Yes, it captures the attention. This is no routine candidate calling every shot by safety's routine book ("Yes," Nixon said, naturally but terribly tired an hour after his nomination, the TV cameras and lights and microphones bringing out a sweat of fatigue on his face, the words coming very slowly from the tired brain, somber, modest, sober, slow, slow enough so that one could touch emphatically the cautions behind each word, "Yes, I want to say," said Nixon, "that whatever abilities I have, I got from my mother." A tired pause . . . dull moment of warning, ". . . and my father." The connection now made, the rest comes easy, ". . . and my school and my church." Such men are capable of anything.)

One had the opportunity to study Kennedy a bit in the days that followed. His style in the press conferences was interesting. Not terribly popular with the reporters (too much a contemporary, and yet too difficult to understand, he received nothing like the rounds of applause given to Eleanor Roosevelt, Stevenson, Humphrey, or even Johnson), he carried himself nonetheless with a cool grace which seemed indifferent to applause, his manner somehow similar to the poise of a fine boxer, quick with his hands, neat in his timing, and two feet away from his corner when the bell ended the round. There was a good lithe wit to his responses, a dry Harvard wit, a keen sense of proportion in disposing of difficult questions—invariably he gave enough of an answer to be formally satisfactory without ever opening himself to a new question which might go further than the first. Asked by a reporter, "Are you for Adlai as vice-president?" the grin came forth and the voice turned very dry, "No, I cannot say we have considered *Adlai* as a vice-president." Yet there was an elusive detachment to everything he did. One did not have the feeling of a man present in the room with all his weight and all his mind. Johnson gave you all of himself, he was a political animal, he breathed like an animal, sweated like one, you knew his mind was entirely absorbed with the compendium of political fact and maneuver; Kennedy seemed at times like a young professor whose manner was adequate for the classroom, but whose mind was off in some intricacy of the Ph.D. thesis he was writing. Perhaps one can give a sense of the discrepancy by saying that he was like an actor who had been cast as the candidate, a good actor, but not a great one—you were aware all the time that the role was one thing and the man another—they did not coincide, the actor seemed a touch too aloof (as, let us say, Gregory Peck is usually too aloof) to become the part. Yet one had little sense of whether to value this elusiveness, or to beware of it. One could be witnessing the fortitude of a superior sensitivity or the detachment of a man who was not quite real to himself. And his voice gave no clue. When Johnson spoke, one could separate what was fraudulent from what was felt, he would have been satisfying as an actor the way Broderick Crawford or Paul Douglas are satisfying; one saw into his emotions, or at least had the illusion that one did. Kennedy's voice, however, was only a fair voice, too reedy, near to strident, it had the metallic snap of a cricket in it somewhere, it was more impersonal than the man, and so became the least-impressive quality in a face, a body, a selection of language, and a style of movement which made up a better-than-decent presentation, better than one had expected.

With all of that, it would not do to pass over the quality in Kennedy which is most difficult to describe. And in fact some

touches should be added to this hint of a portrait, for later
(after the convention), one had a short session alone with
him, and the next day, another. As one had suspected in
advance the interviews were not altogether satisfactory, they
hardly could have been. A man running for President is
altogether different from a man elected President: the haz-
ards of the campaign make it impossible for a candidate to be
as interesting as he might like to be (assuming he has such a
desire). One kept advancing the argument that this campaign
would be a contest of personalities, and Kennedy kept
returning the discussion to politics. After a while one recognized this was an inevitable caution for him. So there would
be not too much point to reconstructing the dialogue since
Kennedy is hardly inarticulate about his political attitudes
and there will be a library vault of text devoted to it in the
newspapers. What struck me most about the interview was a
passing remark whose importance was invisible on the scale
of politics, but was altogether meaningful to my particular
competence. As we sat down for the first time, Kennedy
smiled nicely and said that he had read my books. One
muttered one's pleasure. "Yes," he said, "I've read . . ." and
then there was a short pause which did not last long enough to
be embarrassing in which it was yet obvious no title came
instantly to his mind, an omission one was not ready to mind
altogether since a man in such a position must be obligated to
carry a hundred thousand facts and names in his head, but the
hesitation lasted no longer than three seconds or four, and
then he said, "I've read *The Deer Park* and . . . the others,"
which startled me for it was the first time in a hundred similar
situations, talking to someone whose knowledge of my work
was casual, that the sentence did not come out, "I've read
*The Naked and the Dead* . . . and the others." If one is to
take the worst and assume that Kennedy was briefed for this
interview (which is most doubtful), it still speaks well for the
striking instincts of his advisers.

What was retained later is an impression of Kennedy's
manners which were excellent, even artful, better than the
formal good manners of Choate and Harvard, almost as if
what was creative in the man had been given to the manners.
In a room with one or two people, his voice improved,
became low-pitched, even pleasant—it seemed obvious that
in all these years he had never become a natural public
speaker and so his voice was constricted in public, the

symptom of all orators who are ambitious, throttled, and determined.

His personal quality had a subtle, not quite describable intensity, a suggestion of dry pent heat perhaps, his eyes large, the pupils grey, the whites prominent, almost shocking, his most forceful feature: he had the eyes of a mountaineer. His appearance changed with his mood, strikingly so, and this made him always more interesting than what he was saying. He would seem at one moment older than his age, forty-eight or fifty, a tall, slim, sunburned professor with a pleasant weathered face, not even particularly handsome; five minutes later, talking to a press conference on his lawn, three microphones before him, a television camera turning, his appearance would have gone through a metamorphosis, he would look again like a movie star, his coloring vivid, his manner rich, his gestures strong and quick, alive with that concentration of vitality a successful actor always seems to radiate. Kennedy had a dozen faces. Although they were not at all similar as people, the quality was reminiscent of someone like Brando whose expression rarely changes, but whose appearance seems to shift from one person into another as the minutes go by, and one bothers with this comparison because, like Brando, Kennedy's most characteristic quality is the remote and private air of a man who has traversed some lonely terrain of experience, of loss and gain, of nearness to death, which leaves him isolated from the mass of others.

The next day while they waited in vain for rescuers, the wrecked half of the boat turned over in the water and they saw that it would soon sink. The group decided to swim to a small island three miles away. There were other islands bigger and nearer, but the Navy officers knew that they were occupied by the Japanese. On one island, only one mile to the south, they could see a Japanese camp. McMahon, the engineer whose legs were disabled by burns, was unable to swim. Despite his own painfully crippled back, Kennedy swam the three miles with a breast stroke, towing behind him by a life-belt strap that he held between his teeth the helpless McMahon . . . it took Kennedy and the suffering engineer five hours to reach the island.

\* \* \*

The quotation is from a book which has for its dedicated unilateral title, *The Remarkable Kennedys,* but the prose is by one of the best of the war reporters, the former *Yank* editor, Joe McCarthy, and so presumably may be trusted in such details as this. Physical bravery does not of course guarantee a man's abilities in the White House—all too often men with physical courage are disappointing in their moral imagination —but the heroism here is remarkable for its tenacity. The above is merely one episode in a continuing saga which went on for five days in and out of the water, and left Kennedy at one point "miraculously saved from drowning (in a storm) by a group of Solomon Island natives who suddenly came up beside him in a large dugout canoe." Afterward, his back still injured (that precise back injury which was to put him on crutches eleven years later, and have him search for "spinal-fusion surgery" despite a warning that his chances of living through the operation were "extremely limited") afterward, he asked to go back on duty and became so bold in the attacks he made with his PT boat "that the crew didn't like to go out with him because he took so many chances."

It is the wisdom of a man who senses death within him and gambles that he can cure it by risking his life. It is the therapy of the instinct, and who is so wise as to call it irrational? Before he went into the Navy, Kennedy had been ailing. Washed out of Freshman year at Princeton by a prolonged trough of yellow jaundice, sick for a year at Harvard, weak already in the back from an injury at football, his trials suggest the self-hatred of a man whose resentment and ambition are too large for his body. Not everyone can discharge their furies on an analyst's couch, for some angers can be relaxed only by winning power, some rages are sufficiently monumental to demand that one try to become a hero or else fall back into that death which is already within the cells. But if one succeeds, the energy aroused can be exceptional. Talking to a man who had been with Kennedy in Hyannis Port the week before the convention, I heard that he was in a state of deep fatigue.

"Well, he didn't look tired at the convention," one commented.

"Oh, he had three days of rest. Three days of rest for him is like six months for us."

One thinks of that three-mile swim with the belt in his mouth and McMahon holding it behind him. There are pestilences which sit in the mouth and rot the teeth—in those five hours how much of the psyche must have been remade, for to give vent to the bite in one's jaws and yet use that rage to save a life: it is not so very many men who have the apocalyptic sense that heroism is the First Doctor.

If one had a profound criticism of Kennedy it was that his public mind was too conventional, but that seemed to matter less than the fact of such a man in office because the law of political life had become so dreary that only a conventional mind could win an election. Indeed there could be no politics which gave warmth to one's body until the country had recovered its imagination, its pioneer lust for the unexpected and incalculable. It was the changes that might come afterward on which one could put one's hope. With such a man in office the myth of the nation would again be engaged, and the fact that he was Catholic would shiver a first existential vibration of consciousness into the mind of the White Protestant. For the first time in our history, the Protestant would have the pain and creative luxury of feeling himself in some tiny degree part of a minority, and that was an experience which might be incommensurable in its value to the best of them.

### A Vignette of Adlai Stevenson; The Speeches: What Happened When the Teleprompter Jammed: How U.S. Senator Eugene McCarthy Played the Matador. An Observation on the Name Fitzgerald

As yet we have said hardly a word about Stevenson. And his actions must remain a puzzle unless one dares a speculation about his motive, or was it his need?

So far as the people at the convention had affection for anyone, it was Stevenson, so far as they were able to generate any spontaneous enthusiasm, their cheers were again for Stevenson. Yet it was obvious he never had much chance because so soon as a chance would present itself he seemed quick to dissipate the opportunity. The day before the nominations, he entered the Sports Arena to take his seat as a delegate—the demonstration was spontaneous, noisy and prolonged; it was quieted only by Governor Collins's invitation for Stevenson to speak to the delegates. In obedience perhaps to the scruple that a candidate must not appear before the convention until nominations are done, Stevenson said no more than: "I am grateful for this tumultuous and moving welcome. After getting in and out of the Biltmore Hotel and this hall, I have decided I know whom you are going to nominate. It will be the last survivor." This dry reminder of the ruthlessness of politics broke the roar of excitement for his presence. The applause as he left the platform was like the dying fall-and-moan of a baseball crowd when a home run curves foul. The next day, a New York columnist talking about it said bitterly, "If he'd only gone through the motions, if he had just said that now he wanted to run, that he would work hard, and he hoped the delegates would vote for him. Instead he made that lame joke." One wonders. It seems almost as if he did not wish to win unless victory came despite himself, and then was overwhelming. There are men who are not heroes because they are too good for their time, and it is natural that defeats leave them bitter, tired, and doubtful of their right to make new history. If Stevenson had campaigned for a year before the convention, it is possible that he could have stopped Kennedy. At the least, the convention would have been enormously more exciting, and the nominations might have gone through half-a-dozen ballots before a winner was hammered into shape. But then Stevenson might also have shortened his life. One had the impression of a tired man who (for a politician) was sickened unduly by compromise. A year of maneuvering, broken promises, and detestable partners might have gutted him for the election campaign. If elected, it might have ruined him as a President. There is the possibility that he sensed his situation exactly this way, and knew that if he were to run for President, win and make a good one, he would first have to be restored, as one can indeed be restored, by an exceptional demonstration of love—love, in this case, meaning that the Party had a profound desire to keep him as their leader. The emotional truth of a last-minute victory for Stevenson over the Kennedy machine might have given him new energy; it would certainly have given him new faith in a country and a party whose good motives he was possibly beginning to doubt. Perhaps the fault he saw with his candidacy was that he attracted only the nicest people to himself and there were not enough of them. (One of the private amusements of the convention was to divine some of the qualities of the candidates by the style of the young women who put on hats and clothing and politicked in the colors of one presidential gent or another. Of course, half of them must have been hired models, but someone did the hiring and so it was fair to look for a common denominator. The Johnson girls tended to be plump, pie-faced, dumb sexy Southern; the Symingteeners seemed a touch mulish, stubborn, good-looking pluggers; the Kennedy ladies were the handsomest; healthy, attractive, tough, a little spoiled—they looked like the kind of girls who had gotten all the dances in high school and/or worked for a year as an airline hostess before marrying well. But the Stevenson girls looked to be doing it for no money; they were good sorts, slightly horsy-faced, one had the impression they played field hockey in college.) It was indeed the pure, the saintly, the clean-living, the pacifistic, the vegetarian who seemed most for Stevenson, and the less humorous in the Kennedy camp were heard to remark bitterly that Stevenson had nothing going for him but a bunch of Goddamn Beatniks. This might even have had its sour truth. The demonstrations outside the Sports Arena for Stevenson seemed to have more than a fair proportion of tall, emaciated young men with thin, wry beards and three-string guitars accompanied (again in undue proportion) by a contingent of ascetic, face-washed young Beat ladies in sweaters and dungarees. Not to mention all the Holden Caulfields one could see from here to the horizon. But of course it is unfair to limit it so, for the Democratic gentry were also committed half en masse for Stevenson, as well as a considerable number of movie stars, Shelley Winters for one: after the convention she remarked sweetly, "Tell me something nice about Kennedy so I can get excited about him."

What was properly astonishing was the way this horde of political half-breeds and amateurs came within distance of turning the convention from its preconceived purpose, and managed at the least to bring the only hour of thoroughgoing excitement the convention could offer.

But then nominating day was the best day of the week and enough happened to suggest that a convention out of control would be a spectacle as extraordinary in the American scale of spectator values as a close seventh game in the World Series or a tied fourth quarter in a professional-football championship. A political convention is after all not a meeting of a corporation's board of directors; it is a fiesta, a carnival, a pig-rooting, horse-snorting, band-playing, voice-screaming medieval get-together of greed, practical lust, compromised idealism, career-advancement, meeting, feud, vendetta, conciliation, of rabble-rousers, fist fights (as it used to be), embraces, drunks (again as it used to be) and collective rivers of animal sweat. It is a reminder that no matter how the country might pretend it has grown up and become tidy in its manners, bodiless in its legislative language, hygienic in its separation of high politics from private life, that the roots still come grubby from the soil, and that politics in America is still different from politics anywhere else because the politics has arisen out of the immediate needs, ambitions, and cupidities of the people, that our politics still smell of the bedroom and the kitchen, rather than having descended to us from the chill punctilio of aristocratic negotiation.

So. The Sports Arena was new, too pretty of course, tasteless in its design—it was somehow pleasing that the acoustics were so bad for one did not wish the architects well; there had been so little imagination in their design, and this arena would have none of the harsh grandeur of Madison Square Garden when it was aged by spectators' phlegm and feet over the next twenty years. Still it had some atmosphere; seen from the streets, with the spectators moving to the ticket gates, the bands playing, the green hot-shot special editions of the Los Angeles newspapers being hawked by the newsboys, there was a touch of the air of promise that precedes a bullfight, not something so good as the approach to the Plaza Mexico, but good, let us say, like the entrance into El Toreo of Mexico City, another architectural monstrosity, also with seats painted, as I remember, in rose-pink, and dark, milky sky-blue.

Inside, it was also different this nominating day. On Monday and Tuesday the air had been desultory, no one listened to the speakers, and everybody milled from one easy chatting conversation to another—it had been like a tepid Kaffeeklatsch for fifteen thousand people. But today there was a whip of anticipation in the air, the seats on the floor were filled, the press section was working, and in the gallery people were sitting in the aisles.

Sam Rayburn had just finished nominating Johnson as one

came in, and the rebel yells went up, delegates started filing out of their seats and climbing over seats, and a pullulating dance of bodies and bands began to snake through the aisles, the posters jogging and whirling in time to the music. The dun color of the floor (faces, suits, seats and floor boards), so monotonous the first two days, now lit up with life as if an iridescent caterpillar had emerged from a fold of wet leaves. It was more vivid than one had expected, it was right, it felt finally like a convention, and from up close when you got down to the floor (where your presence was illegal and so consummated by sneaking in one time as demonstrators were going out, and again by slipping a five-dollar bill to a guard) the nearness to the demonstrators took on high color, that electric vividness one feels on the side lines of a football game when it is necessary to duck back as the ballcarrier goes by, his face tortured in the concentration of the moment, the thwomp of his tackle as acute as if one had been hit oneself.

That was the way the demonstrators looked on the floor. Nearly all had the rapt, private look of a passion or a tension which would finally be worked off by one's limbs, three hundred football players, everything from seedy delegates with jowl-sweating shivers to livid models, paid for their work that day, but stomping out their beat on the floor with the hypnotic adulatory grimaces of ladies who had lived for Lyndon these last ten years.

Then from the funereal rostrum, whose color was not so rich as mahogany nor so dead as a cigar, came the last of the requests for the delegates to take their seats. The seconding speeches began, one minute each; they ran for three and four, the minor-league speakers running on the longest as if the electric antenna of television was the lure of the Sirens, leading them out. Bored cheers applauded their concluding Götterdämmerungen and the nominations were open again. A favorite son, a modest demonstration, five seconding speeches, tedium.

Next was Kennedy's occasion. Governor Freeman of Minnesota made the speech. On the second or third sentence his television prompter jammed, an accident. Few could be aware of it at the moment; the speech seemed merely flat and surprisingly void of bravura. He was obviously no giant of extempore. Then the demonstration. Well-run, bigger than Johnson's, jazzier, the caliber of the costumes and decorations better chosen: the placards were broad enough, "Let's

Back Jack," the floats were garish, particularly a papier-mâché or plastic balloon of Kennedy's head, six feet in diameter, which had nonetheless the slightly shrunken, over-red, rubbery look of a toy for practical jokers in one of those sleazy off-Times Square magic-and-gimmick stores; the band was suitably corny; and yet one had the impression this demonstration had been designed by some hands-to-hip interior decorator who said, "Oh, joy, let's have fun, let's make this *true* beer hall."

Besides, the personnel had something of the Kennedy *élan*, those paper hats designed to look like straw boaters with Kennedy's face on the crown, and small photographs of him on the ribbon, those hats which had come to symbolize the crack speed of the Kennedy team, that Madison Avenue cachet which one finds in bars like P. J. Clarke's, the elegance always giving its subtle echo of the Twenties so that the raccoon coats seem more numerous than their real count, and the colored waistcoats are measured by the charm they would have drawn from Scott Fitzgerald's eye. But there, it occurred to one for the first time that Kennedy's middle name was just that, Fitzgerald, and the tone of his crack lieutenants, the unstated style, was true to Scott. The legend of Fitzgerald had an army at last, formed around the self-image in the mind of every superior Madison Avenue opportunist that he was hard, he was young, he was In, his conversation was lean as wit, and if the work was not always scrupulous, well the style could aspire. If there came a good day . . . he could meet the occasion.

The Kennedy snake dance ran its thirty lively minutes, cheered its seconding speeches, and sat back. They were so sure of winning, there had been so many victories before this one, and this one had been scouted and managed so well, that hysteria could hardly be the mood. Besides, everyone was waiting for the Stevenson barrage which should be at least diverting. But now came a long tedium. Favorite sons were nominated, fat mayors shook their hips, seconders told the word to constituents back in Ponderwaygot County, treacly demonstrations tried to hold the floor, and the afternoon went by; Symington's hour came and went, a good demonstration, good as Johnson's (for good cause—they had pooled their demonstrators). More favorite sons, Governor Docking of Kansas declared "a genius" by one of his lady speakers in a tense go-back-to-religion voice. The hours went by, two, three, four hours, it seemed forever before they would get to Stevenson. It was evening when Senator Eugene McCarthy of Minnesota got up to nominate him.

The gallery was ready, the floor was responsive, the demonstrators were milling like bulls in their pen waiting for the *toril* to fly open—it would have been hard not to wake the crowd up, not to make a good speech. McCarthy made a great one. Great it was by the measure of convention oratory, and he held the crowd like a matador, timing their *oles!*, building them up, easing them back, correcting any sag in attention, gathering their emotion, discharging it, creating new emotion on the wave of the last, driving his passes tighter and tighter as he readied for the kill. "Do not reject this man who made us all proud to be called Democrats, do not leave this prophet without honor in his own party." One had not heard a speech like this since 1948 when Vito Marcantonio's voice, his harsh, shrill, bitter, street urchin's voice screeched through the loud-speakers at Yankee Stadium and lashed seventy thousand people into an uproar.

"There was only one man who said let's talk sense to the American people," McCarthy went on, his muleta furled for the *naturales*. "There was only one man who said let's talk sense to the American people," he repeated. "He said the promise of America is the promise of greatness. This was his call to greatness. . . . Do not forget this man. . . . Ladies and Gentlemen, I present to you not the favorite son of one state, but the favorite son of the fifty states, the favorite son of every country he has visited, the favorite son of every country which has not seen him but is secretly thrilled by his name." Bedlam. The kill. "Ladies and Gentlemen, I present to you Adlai Stevenson of Illinois." Ears and tail. Hooves and bull. A roar went up like the roar one heard the day Bobby Thompson hit his home run at the Polo Grounds and the Giants won the pennant from the Dodgers in the third playoff game of the 1951 season. The demonstration cascaded onto the floor, the gallery came to its feet, the Sports Arena sounded like the inside of a marching drum. A tidal pulse of hysteria, exaltation, defiance, exhilaration, anger and roaring desire flooded over the floor. The cry which had gone up on McCarthy's last sentence had not paused for breath in five minutes, and troop after troop of demonstrators jammed the floor (the Stevenson people to be scolded the next day for having collected floor passes and sent them out to bring in new demonstrators) and still the sound mounted. One felt the convention coming apart. There was a Kennedy girl in the seat in front of me, the Kennedy hat on her head, a dimpled healthy brunette; she had sat silently through McCarthy's speech, but now, like a woman paying her respects to the power of natural thrust, she took off her hat and began to clap herself. I saw a writer I knew in the next aisle; he had spent a year studying the Kennedy machine in order to write a book on how a nomination is won. If Stevenson stampeded the convention, his work was lost. Like a reporter at a mine cave-in I inquired the present view of the widow. "Who can think," was the answer, half frantic, half elated, "just watch it, that's all." I found a cool one, a New York reporter, who smiled in rueful respect. "It's the biggest demonstration I've seen since Wendell Willkie's in 1940," he said, and added, "God, if Stevenson takes it, I can wire my wife and move the family on to Hawaii."

"I don't get it."

"Well, every story I wrote said it was locked up for Kennedy."

Still it went on, twenty minutes, thirty minutes, the chairman could hardly be heard, the demonstrators refused to leave. The lights were turned out, giving a sudden theatrical shift to the sense of a crowded church at midnight, and a new roar went up, louder, more passionate than anything heard before. It was the voice, it was the passion, if one insisted to call it that, of everything in America which was defeated, idealistic, innocent, alienated, outside and Beat, it was the potential voice of a new third of the nation whose psyche was ill from cultural malnutrition, it was powerful, it was extraordinary, it was larger than the decent, humorous, finicky, half-noble man who had called it forth, it was a cry from the Thirties when Time was simple, it was a resentment of the slick technique, the oiled gears, and the superior generals of Fitzgerald's Army; but it was also—and for this reason one could not admire it altogether, except with one's excitement—it was also the plea of the bewildered who hunger for simplicity again, it was the adolescent counterpart of the boss's depression before the unpredictable dynamic of Kennedy as President, it was the return to the sentimental dream of Roosevelt rather than the approaching nightmare of history's oncoming night, and it was inspired by a terror of the future as much as a revulsion of the present.

Fitz's Army held; after the demonstration was finally down, the convention languished for ninety minutes while Meyner and others were nominated, a fatal lapse of time because Stevenson had perhaps a chance to stop Kennedy if the voting had begun on the echo of the last cry for him, but in an hour and a half depression crept in again and emotions spent, the delegates who had wavered were rounded into line. When the vote was taken, Stevenson had made no gains. The brunette who had taken off her hat was wearing it again, and she clapped and squealed when Wyoming delivered the duke and Kennedy was in. The air was sheepish, like the mood of a suburban couple who forgive each other for cutting in and out of somebody else's automobile while the country club dance is on. Again, tonight, no miracle would occur. In the morning the papers would be moderate in their description of Stevenson's last charge.

# The Girl of the Year

## Tom Wolfe

Bangs manes bouffants beehives Beatle caps butter faces
brush-on lashes decal eyes puffy sweaters French thrust bras
flailing leather blue jeans stretch pants stretch jeans honey-
dew bottoms eclair shanks elf boots ballerinas Knight slippers, hundreds of them, these flaming little buds, bobbing
and screaming, rocketing around inside the Academy of
Music Theater underneath that vast old mouldering cherub
dome up there—aren't they super-marvelous!

"Aren't they super-marvelous!" says Baby Jane, and then:
"Hi, Isabel! Isabel! You want to sit backstage—with the
Stones!"

The show hasn't even started yet, the Rolling Stones aren't
even on the stage, the place is full of a great shabby
mouldering dimness, and these flaming little buds.

Girls are reeling this way and that way in the aisle and
through their huge black decal eyes, sagging with Tiger
Tongue Lick Me brush-on eyelashes and black appliqués,
sagging like display window Christmas trees, they keep staring at—her—Baby Jane—on the aisle. What the hell is this?
She is gorgeous in the most outrageous way. Her hair rises up
from her head in a huge hairy corona, a huge tan mane

From *The Kandy-Kolored Tangerine-Flake Streamline Baby* (Farrar, Straus &
Giroux, 1965).

around a narrow face and two eyes opened—swock!—like umbrellas, with all that hair flowing down over a coat made of . . . *zebra!* Those motherless stripes! Oh, damn! Here she is with her friends, looking like some kind of queen bee for all flaming little buds everywhere. She twists around to shout to one of her friends and that incredible mane swings around on her shoulders, over the zebra coat.

"Isabel!" says Baby Jane, "Isabel, hi! I just saw the Stones! They look super-divine!"

That girl on the aisle, Baby Jane, is a fabulous girl. She comprehends what the Rolling Stones *mean*. Any columnist in New York could tell them who she is . . . a celebrity of New York's new era of Wog Hip . . . Baby Jane Holzer. Jane Holzer in *Vogue*, Jane Holzer in *Life*, Jane Holzer in Andy Warhol's underground movies, Jane Holzer in the world of High Camp, Jane Holzer at the rock and roll, Jane Holzer is—well, how can one put it into words? Jane Holzer is This Year's Girl, at least, the New Celebrity, none of your old idea of sexpots, prima donnas, romantic tragediennes, she is the girl who knows . . . The Stones, East End vitality . . .

"Isabel!" says Jane Holzer in the small, high, excited voice of hers, her Baby Jane voice, "Hi, Isabel! Hi!"

Down the row, Isabel, Isabel Eberstadt, the beautiful socialite who is Ogden Nash's daughter, has just come in. She doesn't seem to hear Jane. But she is down the row a ways. Next to Jane is some fellow in a chocolate-colored Borsalino hat, and next there is Andy Warhol, the famous pop artist.

"Isabel!" says Jane.

"What?" says Isabel.

"Hi, Isabel!" says Jane.

"Hello, Jane," says Isabel.

"You want to go backstage?" says Jane, who has to speak across everybody.

"Backstage?" says Isabel.

"With the Stones!" says Jane. "I was backstage with the Stones. They look *divine!* You know what Mick said to me? He said, 'Koom on, love, give us a kiss!'"

But Isabel has turned away to say something to somebody.

"Isabel!" says Jane.

And all around, the little buds are batting around in the rococo gloom of the Academy of Music Theater, trying to crash into good seats or just sit in the aisle near the stage, shrieking. And in the rear the Voice of Fifteen-year-old

America cries out in a post-pubertal contralto apropos of nothing, into the mouldering void: "Yaaaagh! Yuh dirty fag!"

Well, so what; Jane laughs. Then she leans over and says to the fellow in the Borsalino hat:

"Wait'll you see the Stones! They're so sexy! They're pure sex. They're di*vine!* The Beatles, well, you know, Paul McCartney—*sweet* Paul McCartney. You know what I mean. He's such a *sweet person.* I mean, the Stones are *bitter—*" the words seem to spring from her lungs like some kind of wonderful lavender-yellow Charles Kingsley bubbles "—They're all from the working class, you know? the East End. Mick Jagger—well, it's all Mick. You know what they say about his lips? They say his lips are *diabolical.* That was in one of the magazines.

"When Mick comes into the Ad Lib in London—I mean, there's nothing like the Ad Lib in New York. You can go into the Ad Lib and everybody is there. They're all young, and they're taking over, it's like a whole revolution. I mean, it's *exciting,* they're all from the lower classes, East End-sort-of-thing. There's nobody exciting from the upper classes anymore, except for Nicole and Alec Londonderry, Alec is a British marquis, the Marquis of Londonderry, and, O.K., Nicole has to put in an appearance at this country fair or something, well, O.K., she does it, but that doesn't mean—you know what I mean? Alec is so—you should see the way he walks, I could just watch him walk—*Undoes-one-ship!* They're *young.* They're all young, it's a whole new thing. It's not the Beatles. Bailey says the Beatles are *passé,* because now everybody's mum pats the Beatles on the head. The Beatles are getting fat. The Beatles—well, John Lennon's still thin, but Paul McCartney is getting a big bottom. That's all right, but I don't particularly care for that. The Stones are thin. I mean, that's why they're beautiful, they're so thin. Mick Jagger—wait'll you see Mick."

Then the show begins. An electronic blast begins, electric guitars, electric bass, enormous speakers up there on a vast yellow-gray stage. Murray the K, the D. J. and M. C., O.K.?, comes out from the wings, doing a kind of twist soft shoe, wiggling around, a stocky chap, thirty-eight years old, wearing Italian pants and a Sun Valley snow lodge sweater and a Stingy Brim straw hat. Murray the K! Girls throw balls of paper at him, and as they arc onto the stage, the stage lights explode off them and they look like falling balls of flame.

And, finally, the Stones, now—how can one express it? the Stones come on stage—

"Oh, God, Andy, aren't they di*vine!*"

—and spread out over the stage, the five Rolling Stones from England, who are modeled after the Beatles, only more lower-class-deformed. One, Brian Jones, has an enormous blonde Beatle bouffant.

"Oh, Andy, look at Mick! Isn't he *beautiful!* Mick! Mick!"

In the center of the stage a short thin boy with a sweat shirt on, the neck of the sweat shirt almost falling over his shoulders, they are so narrow, all surmounted by this . . . enormous head . . . with the hair puffing down over the forehead and ears, this boy has exceptional lips. He has two peculiarly gross and extraordinary red lips. They hang off his face like giblets. Slowly his eyes pour over the flaming bud horde soft as Karo syrup and then close and then the lips start spreading into the most languid, most confidential, the wettest, most labial, most concupiscent grin imaginable. Nirvana! The buds start shrieking, pawing toward the stage.

The girls have Their Experience. They stand up on their seats. They begin to ululate, even between songs. The looks on their faces! Rapturous agony! There, right up there, under the sulphur lights, that is *them.* God, they're right there! Mick Jagger takes the microphone with his tabescent hands and puts his huge head against it, opens his giblet lips and begins to sing . . . with the voice of a bull Negro. Bo Diddley. You movung boo meb bee-uhtul, bah-bee, oh vona breemb you' honey snurks oh crim pulzy yo' min down, and, camping again, then turning toward the shrieking girls with his wet giblet lips dissolving . . .

And, occasionally, breaking through the ululation:

"Get off the stage, you finks!"

"Maybe we ought to scream," says Jane. Then she says to the fellow in the hat: "Tell me when it's five o'clock, will you, pussycat? I have to get dressed and go see Sam Spiegel." And then Baby Jane goes: "Eeeeeeeeeeeeeeeeeeeeeee

eeeeeeeeeeeeeeeeeeeyes!" says Diana Vreeland, the editor of *Vogue.* "Jane Holzer is the most contemporary girl I know."

Jane Holzer at the rock and roll—

Jane Holzer in the underground movies—in Andy's studio, Andy Warhol, the famous Pop artist, experiencing the rare world of Jonas and Adolph Mekas, truth and culture in a new holy medium, underground movie-making on the lower East Side. And Jane is wearing a Jax shirt, strung like a Christmas tree with Diamonds, and they are making *Dracula,* or *Thirteen Beautiful Women* or *Soap Opera* or *Kiss*—in which Jane's lips . . . but how can one describe an underground movie? It is . . . avant-garde. "Andy calls everything super," says Jane. "I'm a super star, he's a super director, we make super epics—and I mean, it's a completely new and natural way of acting. You can't imagine what really beautiful things can happen!"

Jane Holzer—with The New Artists, photographers like Jerry Schatzberg, David Bailey and Brian Duffy, and Nicky Haslam, the art director of *Show.* Bailey, Duffy and Haslam are English. Schatzberg says the photographers are the modern-day equivalents of the Impressionists in Paris around 1910, the men with a sense of New Art, the excitement of the salon, the excitement of the artistic style of life, while all the painters, the old artists, have moved uptown to West End Avenue and live in apartment buildings with Kwik-Fiks parquet floors and run around the corner to get a new cover for the ironing board before the stores close.

Jane in the world of High Camp—a world of thin young men in an environment, a decor, an atmosphere so—how can one say it?—so indefinably Yellow Book. Jane in the world of Teen Savage—Jane modeling here and there—wearing Jean Harlow dresses for *Life* and Italian fashions for *Vogue* and doing the most fabulous cover for Nicky at *Show,* David took the photograph, showing Jane barebacked wearing a little yacht cap and a pair of "World's Fair" sunglasses and holding an American flag in her teeth, so—so Beyond Pop Art, if you comprehend.

Jane Holzer at the LBJ Discotheque—where they were handing out aprons with a target design on them, and Jane Holzer put it on backward so that the target was behind and *then* did The Swim, a new dance.

Jane Holzer—well, there is no easy term available, Baby Jane has appeared constantly this year in just about every society and show business column in New York. The magazines have used her as a kind of combination of model, celebrity and socialite. And yet none of them have been able to do much more than, in effect, set down her name, Baby Jane Holzer, and surround it with a few asterisks and exploding stars, as if to say, well, here we have . . . What's Happening.

She is a socialite in the sense that she lives in a twelve-room apartment on Park Avenue with a wealthy husband, Leonard Holzer, heir to a real estate fortune, amid a lot of old Dutch and Flemish paintings, and she goes to a great many exciting parties. And yet she is not in Society the way the Good Book, the *Social Register,* thinks of Society, and the list of hostesses who have not thought of inviting Jane Holzer would be impressive. Furthermore, her stance is that she doesn't care, and she would rather be known as a friend of the Stones, anyway—and here she is at the April in Paris Ball, $150 per ticket, amid the heaving white and gold swag of the Astor Hotel ballroom, yelling to somebody: "If you aren't nice to me, I'll tell everybody you were here!"

Jane Holzer—the sum of it is glamor, of a sort very specific to New York. With her enormous corona of hair and her long straight nose, Jane Holzer can be quite beautiful, but she never comes on as A Beauty. "Some people look at my pictures and say I look very mature and sophisticated," Jane says. "Some people say I look like a child, you know, Baby Jane. And, I mean, I don't know what I look like, I guess it's just 1964 Jewish." She does not attempt to come on sexy. Her excitement is something else. It is almost pure excitement. It is the excitement of the New Style, the New Chic. The press watches Jane Holzer as if she were an exquisite piece of . . . radar. It is as if that entire ciliate corona of hers were spread out as an antenna for new waves of style. To the magazine editors, the newspaper columnists, the photographers and art directors, suddenly here is a single flamboyant girl who sums up everything new and chic in the way of fashion in the Girl of the Year.

How can one explain the Girl of the Year? The Girl of the Year is a symbolic figure the press has looked for annually in New York since World War I because of the breakdown of conventional High Society. The old establishment still holds forth, it still has its clubs, cotillions and coming-out balls, it is still basically Protestant and it still rules two enormously powerful areas of New York, finance and corporate law. But alongside it, all the while, there has existed a large and ever more dazzling society, Cafe Society it was called in the

twenties and thirties, made up of people whose status rests
not on property and ancestry but on various brilliant ephemera, show business, advertising, public relations, the arts,
journalism or simply new money of various sorts, people with
a great deal of ambition who have congregated in New York
to satisfy it and who look for styles to symbolize it.

The establishment's own styles—well, for one thing they
were too dull. And those understated clothes, dark woods,
high ceilings, silver-smithery, respectable nannies, and so
forth and so on. For centuries their kind of power created
styles—Palladian buildings, starched cravats—but with the
thickening democratic façade of American life, it has degen-
erated to various esoteric understatements, often cryptic—
Topsiders instead of tennis sneakers, calling cards with "Mr."
preceding the name, the right fork.

The magazines and newspapers began looking for heroines
to symbolize the Other Society, Cafe Society, or whatever it
should be called. At first, in the twenties, they chose the more
flamboyant debutantes, girls with social credentials who also
moved in Cafe Society. But the Other Society's styles began
to shift and change at a madder and madder rate, and the
Flaming Deb idea no longer worked. The last of the Flaming
Debs, the kind of Deb who made The Cover of *Life,* was
Brenda Frazier, and Brenda Frazierism went out with the
thirties. More recently the Girl of the Year has had to be
more and more exotic . . . and extraordinary. Christina Paolozzi! Her exploits! Christina Paolozzi threw a twenty-first
birthday party for herself at a Puerto Rican pachanga palace,
the Palladium, and after that the spinning got faster and faster
until with one last grand centripetal gesture she appeared in
the nude, face on, in *Harper's Bazaar.* Some became Girls of
the Year because their fame suddenly shed a light on their
style of life, and their style of life could be easily exhibited,
such as Jackie Kennedy and Barbra Streisand.

But Baby Jane Holzer is a purer manifestation. Her style of
life has created her fame—rock and roll, underground movies, decaying lofts, models, photographers, Living Pop Art,
the twist, the frug, the mashed potatoes, stretch pants,
pre-Raphaelite hair, Le Style Camp. All of it has a common
denominator. Once it was power that created high style. But
now high styles come from low places, from people who have
no power, who slink away from it, in fact, who are marginal,
who carve out worlds for themselves in the nether depths, in

tainted "undergrounds." The Rolling Stones, like rock and roll itself and the twist—they come out of the netherworld of modern teen-age life, out of what was for years the marginal outcast corner of the world of art, photography, populated by poor boys, pretenders. "Underground" movies—a mixture of camp and Artistic Alienation, with Jonas Mekas crying out like some foggy echo from Harold Stearn's last boat for Le Havre in 1921: "You filthy bourgeois pseudo-culturati! You say you love art—then why don't you give us money to buy the films to make our masterpieces and stop blubbering about the naked asses we show?—you mucky pseuds." Teen-agers, bohos, camp culturati, photographers—they have won by default, because, after all, they *do* create styles. And now the Other Society goes to them for styles, like the decadenti of another age going down to the wharves in Rio to find those raw-vital devils, damn their potent hides, those proles, doing the tango. Yes! Oh my God, those raw-vital proles!

The ice floe is breaking, and can't one see, as Jane Holzer sees, that all these people—well, they *feel,* they are alive, and what does it mean simply to be sitting up in her Park Avenue apartment in the room with the two Rubenses on the wall, worth half a million dollars, if they are firmly authenticated? It means almost nothing. One doesn't feel it.

Jane has on a "Poor" sweater, clinging to the ribs, a new fashion, with short sleeves. Her hair is up in rollers. She is wearing tight slacks. Her hips are very small. She has a boyish body. She has thin arms and long, long fingers. She sits twisted about on a couch, up in her apartment on Park Avenue, talking on the telephone.

"Oh, I know what you mean," she says, "but, I mean, couldn't you wait just two weeks? I'm expecting something to jell, it's a movie, and then you'd have a real story. You know what I mean? I mean you would have something to write about and not just Baby Jane sitting up in her Park Avenue apartment with her gotrocks. You know what I mean? . . . well, all right, but I think you'll have more of a story— . . . well, all right . . . bye, pussycat."

Then she hangs up and swings around and says, "That makes me mad. That was ———. He wants to do a story about me and do you know what he told me? 'We want to do a story about you,' he told me, 'because you're very big this year.' Do you know what that made me feel like? That made me feel like, All right, Baby Jane, we'll let you play this year, so get out there and dance, but next year, well, it's all over for you next year, Baby Jane, I mean, —! You know? I mean, I felt like telling him, 'Well, pussycat, you're the Editor of the Minute, and you know what? Your minute's up.'"

The thought leaves Jane looking excited but worried. Usually she looks excited about things but open, happy, her eyes wide open and taking it all in. Now she looks worried, as if the world could be such a simple and exhilarating place if there weren't so many old and arteriosclerotic people around to muck it up. There are two dogs on the floor at her feet, a toy poodle and a Yorkshire terrier, who rise up from time to time in some kind of secret needle-toothed fury, barking coloratura.

"Oh, ————," says Jane, and then, "You know, if you have anything at all, there are so many bitchy people just *waiting* to carve you up. I mean, I went to the opening of the Met and I wore a white mink coat, and do you know what a woman did? A woman called up a columnist and said, 'Ha, ha, Baby Jane rented that coat she went to the Met in. Baby Jane rents her clothes.' That's how bitchy they are. Well, that coat happens to be a coat my mother gave me two years ago when I was married. I mean, I don't care if somebody thinks I rent clothes. O.K. ————! Who cares?"

Inez, the maid, brings in lunch on a tray, one rare hamburger, one cheeseburger and a glass of tomato juice. Jane tastes the tomato juice.

"Oh, ————!" she says. "It's diet."

The Girl of the Year. It is as though nobody wants to give anyone credit for anything. They're only a *phenomenon*. Well, Jane Holzer did a great deal of modeling before she got married and still models, for that matter, and now some very wonderful things may be about to happen in the movies. Some of it, well, she cannot go into it exactly, because it is at that precarious stage—you know? But she has one of the best managers, a woman who manages the McGuire Sisters. And there has been talk about Baby Jane for *Who's Afraid of Virginia Woolf,* the movie, and *Candy*—

"Well, I haven't heard anything about it—but I'd *love* to play Candy."

And this afternoon, later on, she is going over to see Sam Spiegel, the producer.

"He's wonderful. He's, you know, sort of advising me on things at this point."

And somewhere out there in the apartment the dogs are loose in a midget coloratura rage amid patina-green walls and paintings by old Lowland masters. There is a great atmosphere in the apartment, an atmosphere of patina-green, faded plush and the ashy light of Park Avenue reflecting on the great black and umber slicks of the paintings. All that stretches on for twelve rooms. The apartment belongs to the Holzers, who have built a lot of New York's new apartment houses. Jane's husband, Leonard, is a slim, good-looking young man. He went to Princeton. He and Jane were married two years ago. Jane came from Florida, where her father, Carl Brookenfeld, also made a lot of money in real estate. But in a way they were from New York, too, because they were always coming to New York and her father had a place here. There was something so stimulating, so flamboyant, about New York, you know? Fine men with anointed blue jowls combed their hair straight back and had their shirts made at Sulka's or Nica-Rattner's, and their wives had copper-gold hair, real chignons and things, and heavy apricot voices that said the funniest things—"Honey, I've got news for you, you're crazy!"—things like that, and they went to El Morocco. Jane went to Cherry Lawn School in Darien, Connecticut. It was a progressive school.

And then she went to Finch Junior College:

"Oh, that was just ghastly. I wanted to flunk out and go to work. If you miss too many classes, they campus you, if you have a messy room, they campus you, they were always campusing me, and I always sneaked out. The last spring term I didn't spend one night there. I was supposed to be campused and I'd be out dancing at El Morocco. I didn't take my exams because I wanted to flunk out, but do you know what they did? They just said I was out, period. I didn't care about that, because I wanted to flunk out and go to work anyway— but the way they did it. I have a lot of good paintings to give away, and it's too bad, they're not getting any. They were not *educators*. They could have at least kept the door open. They could have said, 'You're not ready to be a serious student, but when you decide to settle down and be a serious student, the door will be open.' I mean, I had already paid for the whole term, they *had* the money. I always wanted to go there and tell them, well, ha ha, too bad, you're not getting any of the paintings. So henceforth, Princeton, which was super-marvelous, will get all the paintings."

Jane's spirits pick up over that. Princeton! Well, Jane left Finch and then she did quite a bit of modeling. Then she married Lennie, and she still did some modeling, but the real break—well, the whole *thing* started in summer in London, the summer of 1963.

"Bailey is fantastic," says Jane. "Bailey created four girls that summer. He created Jean Shrimpton, he created me, he created Angela Howard and Susan Murray. There's no photographer like that in America. Avedon hasn't done that for a girl, Penn hasn't, and Bailey created four girls in one summer. He did some pictures of me for the English *Vogue,* and that was all it took."

But how does one really explain about the Stones, about Bailey, Shrimp and Mick—well, it's not so much what they *do,* that's such an old idea, what people *do*—it's what they *are,* it's a revolution, and it's the kids from the East End, Cockneys, if you want, who are making it.

"I mean today Drexel Duke sits next to Weinstein, and why shouldn't he? They both made their money the same way, you know? The furniture king sits next to the catsup king, and why shouldn't he-sort-of-thing. I mean, that's the way it was at the opening of the Met. A friend of mine was going to write an article about it.

"I mean, we don't lie to ourselves. Our mothers taught us to be pure and you'll fall in love and get married and stay in love with one man all your life. O.K. But we know it doesn't happen that way and we don't lie to ourselves about it. Maybe you won't ever find anybody you love. Or maybe you find somebody you love four minutes, maybe ten minutes. But I mean, why lie to yourself? We know we're not going to love one man all our lives. Maybe it's the Bomb—we know it could all be over tomorrow, so why try to fool yourself today. Shrimp was talking about that last night. She's here now, she'll be at the party tonight—"

The two dogs, the toy poodle and the Yorkshire terrier, are yapping, in the patina-green. Inez is looking for something besides diet. The two Rubenses hang up on the walls. A couple of horns come up through the ashy light of Park Avenue. The high wind of East End London is in the air—whhhooooooooooo

ooooooooooooooosh! Baby Jane blows out all the candles. It is her twenty-fourth birthday. She and everybody, Shrimp,

Nicky, Jerry, everybody but Bailey, who is off in Egypt or something, they are all up in Jerry Schatzberg's . . . *pad* . . . his lavish apartment at 333 Park Avenue South, up above his studio. There is a skylight. The cook brings out the cake and Jane blows out the candles. Twenty-four! Jerry and Nicky are giving a huge party, a dance, in honor of the Stones, and already the people are coming into the studio downstairs. But it is also Jane's birthday. She is wearing a black velvet jump suit by Luis Estevez, the designer. It has huge bell-bottom pants. She puts her legs together . . . it looks like an evening dress. But she can also spread them apart, like so, and strike very Jane-like poses. This is like the Upper Room or something. Downstairs, they're all coming in for the party, all those people one sees at parties, everybody who goes to the parties in New York, but up here it is like a tableau, like a tableau of . . . Us. Shrimp is sitting there with her glorious pout and her textured white stockings, Barbara Steele, who was so terrific in *8½*, with thin black lips and wrought-iron eyelashes. Nicky Haslam is there with his Byron shirt on and his tiger skin vest and blue jeans and boots. Jerry is there with his hair flowing back in curls. Lennie, Jane's husband, is there in a British suit and a dark blue shirt he bought on 42nd Street for this party, because this is a party for the Rolling Stones. The Stones are not here yet, but here in the upper room are Goldie and the Gingerbreads, four girls in gold lamé tights who will play the rock and roll for the party. Nicky discovered them at the Wagon Wheel. Gold lamé, can you imagine? Goldie, the leader, is a young girl with a husky voice and nice kind of slightly thick—you know—glorious sort of *East End* features, only she is from New York—ah, the delicacy of minor grossness, unabashed. The Stones' music is playing over the hi-fi.

Finally the Stones come in, in blue jeans, sweat shirts, the usual, and people get up and Mick Jagger comes in with his mouth open and his eyes down, faintly weary with success, and everybody goes downstairs to the studio, where people are now piling in, hundreds of them. Goldie and the Gingerbreads are on a stand at one end of the studio, all electric, electric guitars, electric bass, drums, loudspeakers, and a couple of spotlights exploding off the gold lamé. *Baby baby baby where did our love go*. The music suddenly fills up the room like a giant egg slicer. Sally Kirkland, Jr., a young actress, is out on the studio floor in a leopard print dress with her vast mane flying, doing the frug with Jerry Schatzberg. And then the other Girl of the Year, Caterine Milinaire, is out there in a black dress, and then Baby Jane is out there with her incredible mane and her Luis Estevez jump suit, frugging, and then everybody is out there. Suddenly it is very odd. Suddenly everybody is out there in the gloaming, bobbing up and down with the music plugged into *Baby baby baby*. The whole floor of the studio begins to bounce up and down, like a trampoline, the whole floor, some people are afraid and edge off to the side, but most keep bobbing in the gloaming, and—pow!—glasses begin to hit the floor, but everyone keeps bouncing up and down, crushing the glass underfoot, while the brown whiskey slicks around. So many heads bobbing, so many bodies jiggling, so many giblets jiggling, so much anointed flesh shaking and jiggling this way and that, so many faces one wanted so desperately to see, and here they are, red the color of dried peppers in the gloaming, bouncing up and down with just a few fights, wrenching in the gloaming, until 5 A.M.—gleeeang—Goldie pulls all the electric cords out and the studio is suddenly just a dim ochre studio with broken glass all over the floor, crushed underfoot, and the sweet high smell of brown whiskey rising from the floor.

Monday's papers will record it as the Mods and Rockers Ball, as the Party of the Year, but that is Monday, a long way off. So they all decide they should go to the Brasserie. It is the only place in town where anybody would still be around. So they all get into cabs and go up to the Brasserie, up on 53rd Street between Park and Lexington. The Brasserie is the right place, all right. The Brasserie has a great entrance, elevated over the tables like a fashion show almost. There are, what?, 35 people in the Brasserie. They all look up, and as the first salmon light of dawn comes through the front window, here come . . . four teen-age girls in gold lamé tights, and a chap in a tiger skin vest and blue jeans and a gentleman in an English suit who seems to be wearing a 42nd Street hood shirt and a fellow in a sweater who has flowing curly hair . . . and then, a girl with an incredible mane, a vast tawny corona, wearing a black velvet jump suit. One never knows who is in the Brasserie at this hour—but are there any so dead in here that they do not get the point? Girl of the Year? Listen, they will *never* forget.

# Apocalypse
## The Place of Mystery in the Life of the Mind

### Norman O. Brown

I didn't know whether I should appear before you—there is a time to show and a time to hide; there is a time to speak, and also a time to be silent. What time is it? It is fifteen years since H. G. Wells said Mind was at the End of its Tether—with a frightful queerness come into life: there is no way out or around or through, he said; it is the end. It is because I think mind is at the end of its tether that I would be silent. It is because I think there is a way out—a way down and out—the title of Mr. John Senior's new book on the occult tradition in literature—that I will speak.

Mind at the end of its tether: I can guess what some of you are thinking—*his* mind is at the end of its tether—and this could be; it scares me but it deters me not. The alternative to mind is certainly madness. Our greatest blessings, says Socrates in the *Phaedrus*, come to us by way of madness—provided, he adds, that the madness comes from the god. Our real choice is between holy and unholy madness: open your eyes and look around you—madness is in the saddle anyhow. Freud is the measure of our unholy madness, as Nietzsche is the prophet of the holy madness, of Dionysus, the mad truth. Dionysus has returned to his native Thebes; mind—at the end

Reprinted from *Harper's Magazine*, May 1961.

of its tether—is another Pentheus, up a tree. Resisting madness can be the maddest way of being mad.

And there is a way out—the blessed madness of the maenad and the bacchant: "Blessed is he who has the good fortune to know the mysteries of the gods, who sanctifies his life and initiates his soul, a bacchant on the mountains, in holy purifications." It is possible to be mad and to be unblest; but it is not possible to get the blessing without the madness; it is not possible to get the illuminations without the derangement. Derangement is disorder: the Dionysian faith is that order as we have known it is crippling, and for cripples; that what is past is prologue; that we can throw away our crutches and discover the supernatural power of walking; that human history goes from man to superman.

No superman I; I come to you not as one who has supernatural powers, but as one who seeks for them, and who has some notions which way to go to find them.

Sometimes—most times—I think that the way down and out leads out of the university, out of the academy. But perhaps it is rather that we should recover the academy of earlier days—the Academy of Plato in Athens, the Academy of Ficino in Florence. Ficino who says, "The spirit of the god Dionysus was believed by the ancient theologians and Platonists to be the ecstasy and abandon of disencumbered minds, when partly by innate love, partly at the instigation of the god, they transgress the natural limits of intelligence and are miraculously transformed into the beloved god himself: where, inebriated by a certain new draft of nectar and by an immeasurable joy, they rage, as it were, in a bacchic frenzy. In the drunkenness of this Dionysian wine, our Dionysius (the Areopagite) expresses his exultation. He pours forth enigmas, he sings in dithyrambs. To penetrate the profundity of his meanings, to imitate his quasi-Orphic manner of speech, we too require the divine fury."

At any rate the point is first of all to find again the mysteries. By which I do not mean simply the sense of wonder—that sense of wonder which is indeed the source of all true philosophy—by mystery I mean secret and occult; therefore unpublishable; therefore outside the university as we know it; but not outside Plato's Academy, or Ficino's.

Why are mysteries unpublishable? First because they cannot be put into words, at least not the kind of words which earned you your Phi Beta Kappa keys. Mysteries display themselves in words only if they can remain concealed; this is poetry, isn't it? We must return to the old doctrine of the Platonists and Neo-Platonists, that poetry is veiled truth; as Dionysus is the god who is both manifest and hidden; and as John Donne declared, with the Pillar of Fire goes the Pillar of Cloud. This is also the new doctrine of Ezra Pound, who says: "Prose is not education but the outer courts of the same. Beyond its doors are the mysteries. Eleusis. Things not to be spoken of save in secret. The mysteries self-defended, the mysteries that cannot be revealed. Fools can only profane them. The dull can neither penetrate the secretum nor divulge it to others." The mystic academies, whether Plato's or Ficino's, knew the limitations of words and drove us on beyond them, to go over, to go under, to the learned ignorance, in which God is better honored and loved by silence than by words, and better seen by closing the eyes to images than by opening them.

And second, mysteries are unpublishable because only some can see them, not all. Mysteries are intrinsically esoteric, and as such an offense to democracy: is not publicity a democratic principle? Publication makes it republican—a thing of the people. The pristine academies were esoteric and aristocratic, self-consciously separate from the profane vulgar. Democratic resentment denies that there can be anything that can't be seen by everybody; in the democratic academy truth is subject to public verification; truth is what any fool can see. This is what is meant by the so-called scientific method: so-called science is the attempt to democratize knowledge—the attempt to substitute method for insight, mediocrity for genius, by getting a standard operating procedure. The great equalizers dispensed by the scientific method are the tools, those analytical tools. The miracle of genius is replaced by the standardized mechanism. But fools with tools are still fools, and don't let your Phi Beta Kappa key fool you. Tibetan prayer wheels are another way of arriving at the same result: the degeneration of mysticism into mechanism—so that any fool can do it. Perhaps the advantage is with Tibet; for there the mechanism is external while the mind is left vacant; and vacancy is not the worst condition of the mind. And the resultant prayers make no futile claim to originality or immortality; being nonexistent, they do not have to be catalogued or stored.

The sociologist Simmel sees showing and hiding, secrecy

and publicity, as two poles, like Yin and Yang, between which societies oscillate in their historical development. I sometimes think I see that civilizations originate in the disclosure of some mystery, some secret; and expand with the progressive publication of their secret; and end in exhaustion when there is no longer any secret, when the mystery has been divulged, that is to say profaned. The whole story is illustrated in the difference between ideogram and alphabet. The alphabet is indeed a democratic triumph; and the enigmatic ideogram, as Ezra Pound has taught us, is a piece of mystery, a piece of poetry, not yet profaned. And so there comes a time—I believe we are in such a time—when civilization has to be renewed by the discovery of new mysteries, by the undemocratic but sovereign power of the imagination, by the undemocratic power which makes poets the unacknowledged legislators of mankind, the power which makes all things new.

The power which makes all things new is magic. What our time needs is mystery: what our time needs is magic. Who would not say that only a miracle can save us? In Tibet the degree-granting institution is, or used to be, the College of Magic Ritual. It offers courses in such fields as clairvoyance and telepathy; also (attention physics majors) internal heat: internal heat is a yoga bestowing supernatural control over body temperature. Let me succumb for a moment to the fascination of the mysterious East and tell you of the examination procedure for the course in internal heat. Candidates assemble naked, in midwinter, at night, on a frozen Himalayan lake. Beside each one is placed a pile of wet frozen undershirts; the assignment is to wear, until they are dry, as many as possible of these undershirts before dawn. Where the power is real, the test is real, and the grading system dumfoundingly objective. I say no more. I say no more; Eastern Yoga does indeed demonstrate the existence of supernatural powers, but it does not have the particular power our Western society needs; or rather I think that each society has access only to its own proper powers; or rather each society will only get the kind of power it knows how to ask for.

The Western consciousness has always asked for freedom: the human mind was born free, or at any rate born to be free, but everywhere it is in chains; and now at the end of its tether. It will take a miracle to free the human mind: because the chains are magical in the first place. We are in bondage to authority outside ourselves: most obviously—here in a great university it must be said—in bondage to the authority of books. There is a Transcendentalist anticipation of what I want to say in Emerson's Phi Beta Kappa address on the American Scholar:

"The books of an older period will not fit this. Yet hence arises a grave mischief. The sacredness which attaches to the act of creation, the act of thought, is transferred to the record. Instantly the book becomes noxious: the guide is a tyrant. The sluggish and perverted mind of the multitude having once received this book, stands upon it, and makes an outcry if it is destroyed. Colleges are built on it. Meek young men grow up in libraries. Hence, instead of Man Thinking, we have the bookworm. I had better never see a book than to be warped by its attraction clean out of my own orbit, and made a satellite instead of a system. The one thing in the world, of value, is the active soul."

How far this university is from that ideal is the measure of the defeat of our American dream.

This bondage to books compels us not to see with our own eyes; compels us to see with the eyes of the dead, with dead eyes. Whitman, likewise in a Transcendentalist sermon, says, "You shall no longer take things at second or third hand, nor look through the eyes of the dead, nor feed on the specters in books." There is a hex on us, the specters in books, the authority of the past; and to exorcise these ghosts is the great work of magical self-liberation. Then the eyes of the spirit would become one with the eyes of the body, and god would be in us, not outside. God in us: *entheos:* enthusiasm; this is the essence of the holy madness. In the fire of the holy madness even books lose their gravity, and let themselves go up into the flame: "Properly," says Ezra Pound, "we should read for power. Man reading should be man intensely alive. The book should be a ball of light in one's hand."

I began with the name of Dionysus; let me be permitted to end with the name of Christ: for the power I seek is also Christian. Nietzsche indeed said the whole question was Dionysus versus Christ: but only the fool will take these as mutually exclusive opposites. There is a Dionysian Christianity, an apocalyptic Christianity, a Christianity of miracles and revelations. And there always have been some Christians for whom the age of miracle and revelation is not over: Christians who claim the spirit: enthusiasts. The power I look for is the power of enthusiasm; as condemned by John Locke; as possessed by George Fox, the Quaker; through whom the houses were shaken; who saw the channel of blood running down the streets of the city of Litchfield; to whom, as a matter of fact, was even given the magic internal heat—"The fire of the Lord was so in my feet, and all around me, that I did not matter to put on my shoes any more."

Read again the controversies of the seventeenth century and discover our choice: we are either in an age of miracles, says Hobbes, miracles which authenticate fresh revelations; or else we are in an age of reasoning from already received Scripture. Either miracle or Scripture. George Fox, who came up in spirit through the flaming sword into the paradise of God, so that all things were new, he being renewed to the state of Adam which he was in before he fell, sees that none can read Moses aright without Moses' spirit; none can read John's words aright, and with a true understanding of them, but in and with the same divine spirit by which John spake them, and by his burning shining light which is sent from God. Thus the authority of the past is swallowed up in new creation; the word is made flesh. We see with our own eyes and to see with our own eyes is second sight. To see with our own eyes is second sight.

> Twofold Always. May God us keep
> From single vision and Newton's sleep.

*Columbia University*
*May 31, 1960*

# Transcendental Experience

## R. D. Laing

We are living in an age in which the ground is shifting and the foundations are shaking. I cannot answer for other times and places. Perhaps it has always been so. We know it is true today.

In these circumstances, we have every reason to be insecure. When the ultimate basis of our world is in question, we run to different holes in the ground, we scurry into roles, statuses, identities, interpersonal relations. We attempt to live in castles that can only be in the air because there is no firm ground in the social cosmos on which to build. We are all witnesses to this state of affairs. Each sometimes sees the same fragment of the whole situation differently; often our concern is with different presentations of the original catastrophe.

In this chapter I wish to relate the transcendental experiences that *sometimes* break through in psychosis, to those experiences of the divine that are the living fount of all religion.

In the last chapter I outlined the way in which some psychiatrists are beginning to dissolve their clinical-medical categories of understanding madness. If we can begin to understand sanity and madness in existential social terms, we

From *The Politics of Experience* (Pantheon Books, 1967).

shall be more able to see clearly the extent to which we all
confront common problems and share common dilemmas.

Experience may be judged as invalidly mad or as validly
mystical. The distinction is not easy. In either case, from a
social point of view, such judgments characterize different
forms of behavior, regarded in our society as deviant. People
behave in such ways because their experience of themselves is
different. It is on the existential meaning of such unusual
experience that I wish to focus.

Psychotic experience goes beyond the horizons of our
common, that is, our communal, sense.

What regions of experience does this lead to? It entails a
loss of the usual foundations of the "sense" of the world that
we share with one another. Old purposes no longer seem
viable; old meanings are senseless; the distinctions between
imagination, dream, external perceptions often seem no
longer to apply in the old way. External events may seem
magically conjured up. Dreams may seem to be direct
communications from others; imagination may seem to be
objective reality.

But most radical of all, the very ontological foundations are
shaken. The being of phenomena shifts and the phenomenon
of being may no longer present itself to us as before. There
are no supports, nothing to cling to, except perhaps some
fragments from the wreck, a few memories, names, sounds,
one or two objects, that retain a link with a world long lost.
This void may not be empty. It may be peopled by visions and
voices, ghosts, strange shapes and apparitions. No one who
has not experienced how insubstantial the pageant of external
reality can be, how it may fade, can fully realize the sublime
and grotesque presences that can replace it, or that can exist
alongside it.

When a person goes mad, a profound transposition of his
place in relation to all domains of being occurs. His center of
experience moves from ego to self. Mundane time becomes
merely anecdotal, only the eternal matters. The madman is,
however, confused. He muddles ego with self, inner with
outer, natural and supernatural. Nevertheless, he can often
be to us, even through his profound wretchedness and
disintegration, the hierophant of the sacred. An exile from
the scene of being as we know it, he is an alien, a stranger
signaling to us from the void in which he is foundering, a void
which may be peopled by presences that we do not even

dream of. They used to be called demons and spirits, and they used to be known and named. He has lost his sense of self, his feelings, his place in the world as we know it. He tells us he is dead. But we are distracted from our cozy security by this mad ghost who haunts us with his visions and voices which seem so senseless and of which we feel impelled to rid him, cleanse him, cure him.

Madness need not be all breakdown. It may also be breakthrough. It is potentially liberation and renewal as well as enslavement and existential death.

There are now a growing number of accounts by people who have been through the experience of madness.*

The following is part of one of the earlier contemporary accounts, as recorded by Karl Jaspers in his *General Psychopathology*.†

I believe I caused the illness myself. In my attempt to penetrate the other world I met its natural guardians, the embodiment of my own weaknesses and faults. I first thought these demons were lowly inhabitants of the other world who could play me like a ball because I went into these regions unprepared and lost my way. Later I thought they were split-off parts of my own mind (passions) which existed near me in free space and thrived on my feelings. I believed everyone else had these too but did not perceive them, thanks to the protective successful deceit of the feeling of personal existence. I thought the latter was an artifact of memory, thought-complexes, etc., a doll that was nice enough to look at from outside but nothing real inside it.

In my case the personal self had grown porous because of my dimmed consciousness. Through it I wanted to bring myself closer to the higher sources of life. I should have prepared myself for this over a long period by invoking in me a higher, impersonal self, since "nectar" is not for mortal lips. It acted destructively on the animal-human self, split it up into its parts. These

---

*See, for example, the anthology *The Inner World of Mental Illness*, edited by Bert Kaplan (New York and London: Harper and Row, 1964), and *Beyond All Reason*, by Morag Coate (London: Constable and Co., 1964; Philadelphia: Lippincott, 1965).

†Manchester: Manchester University Press, 1962, pages 417-18.

gradually disintegrated, the doll was really broken and the body damaged. I had forced untimely access to the "source of life," the curse of the "gods" descended on me. I recognized too late that murky elements had taken a hand. I got to know them after they had already too much power. There was no way back. I now had the world of spirits I had wanted to see. The demons came up from the abyss, as guardian Cerberi, denying admission to the unauthorized. I decided to take up the life-and-death struggle. This meant for me in the end a decision to die, since I had to put aside everything that maintained the enemy, but this was also everything that maintained life. I wanted to enter death without going mad and stood before the Sphinx: either thou into the abyss or I!

Then came illumination. I fasted and so penetrated into the true nature of my seducers. They were pimps and deceivers of my dear personal self which seemed as much a thing of naught as they. A larger and more comprehensive self emerged and I could abandon the previous personality with its entire entourage. I saw this earlier personality could never enter transcendental realms. I felt as a result a terrible pain, like an annihilating blow, but I was rescued, the demons shriveled, vanished and perished. A new life began for me and from now on I felt different from other people. A self that consisted of conventional lies, shams, self-deceptions, memory images, a self just like that of other people, grew in me again but behind and above it stood a greater and more comprehensive self which impressed me with something of what is eternal, unchanging, immortal and inviolable and which ever since that time has been my protector and refuge. I believe it would be good for many if they were acquainted with such a higher self and that there are people who have attained this goal in fact by kinder means.

Jaspers comments:

Such self-interpretations are obviously made under the influence of delusion-like tendencies and deep psychic forces. They originate from profound experiences and the wealth of such schizophrenic experience calls on the observer as well as on the reflective patient not to take all this merely as a chaotic jumble of contents. Mind and spirit are present in the morbid psychic life as well as in the healthy. But interpretations of this sort must be divested of any casual importance. All they can do is to throw light on content and bring it into some sort of context.

This patient has described, with a lucidity I could not improve upon, a very ancient quest, with its pitfalls and dangers. Jaspers still speaks of this experience as morbid and tends to discount the patient's own construction. Yet both the experience and the construction may be valid in their own terms.

Certain *transcendental experiences* seem to me to be the original wellspring of all religions. Some psychotic people have transcendental experiences. Often (to the best of their recollection), they have never had such experiences before, and frequently they will never have them again. I am not saying, however, that psychotic experience necessarily contains this element more manifestly than sane experience.

We experience in different modes. We perceive external realities, we dream, imagine, have semiconscious reveries. Some people have visions, hallucinations, experience faces transfigured, see auras and so on. Most people most of the time experience themselves and others in one or another way that I shall call *egoic*. That is, centrally or peripherally, they experience the world and themselves in terms of a consistent identity, a me-here over against a you-there, within a framework of certain ground structures of space and time shared with other members of their society.

This identity-anchored, space-and-time-bound experience has been studied philosophically by Kant, and later by the phenomenologists, e.g. Husserl, Merleau-Ponty. Its historical and ontological relativity should be fully realized by any contemporary student of the human scene. Its cultural, socioeconomic relativity has become a commonplace among anthropologists and a platitude to the Marxists and neo-Marxists. And yet, with the consensual and interpersonal confirmation it offers, it gives us a sense of ontological security, whose validity we *experience* as self-validating, although metaphysically-historically-ontologically-socioeconomically-culturally we know its apparent absolute validity as an illusion.

In fact all religious and all existential philosophies have agreed that such *egoic experience* is a preliminary illusion, a veil, a film of *maya*—a dream to Heraclitus, and to Lao Tzu, the fundamental illusion of all Buddhism, a state of sleep, of death, of socially accepted madness, a womb state to which one has to die, from which one has to be born.

The person going through ego-loss or transcendental experiences may or may not become in different ways confused. Then he might legitimately be regarded as mad. But to be mad is not necessarily to be ill, notwithstanding that in our culture the two categories have become confused. It is assumed that if a person is mad (whatever that means) then *ipso facto* he is ill (whatever that means). The experience that a person may be absorbed in, while to others he appears simply ill-mad, may be for him veritable manna from heaven. The person's whole life may be changed, but it is difficult not to doubt the validity of such vision. Also, not everyone comes back to us again.

Are these experiences simply the effulgence of a pathological process or of a particular alienation? I do not think they are.

In certain cases, a man blind from birth may have an operation performed which gives him his sight. The result—frequently misery, confusion, disorientation. The light that illumines the madman is an unearthly light. It is not always a distorted refraction of his mundane life situation. He may be irradiated by light from other worlds. It may burn him out.

This "other" world is not essentially a battlefield wherein psychological forces, derived or diverted, displaced or sublimated from their original object-cathexes, are engaged in an illusionary fight—although such forces may obscure these realities, just as they may obscure so-called external realities. When Ivan in *The Brothers Karamazov* says, "If God does not exist, everything is permissible," he is *not* saying, "If my super-ego, in projected form, can be abolished, I can do anything with a good conscience." He *is* saying, "If there is *only* my conscience, then there is no ultimate validity for my will."

Among physicians and priests there should be some who are guides, who can educt the person from this world and induct him to the other. To guide him in it and to lead him back again.

One enters the other world by breaking a shell: or through a door: through a partition: the curtains part or rise: a veil is lifted. Seven veils: seven seals, seven heavens.

The "ego" is the instrument for living in *this* world. If the "ego" is broken up or destroyed (by the insurmountable contradictions of certain life situations, by toxins, chemical changes, etc.), then the person may be exposed to other worlds, "real" in different ways from the more familiar territory of dreams, imagination, perception or fantasy.

The world that one enters, one's capacity to experience it, seem to be partly conditional on the state of one's "ego."

Our time has been distinguished, more than by anything else, by a drive to control the external world, and by an almost total forgetfulness of the internal world. If one estimates human evolution from the point of view of knowledge of the external world, then we are in many respects progressing.

If our estimate is from the point of view of the internal world and of oneness of internal and external, then the judgment must be very different.

Phenomenologically the terms "internal" and "external" have little validity. But in this whole realm one is reduced to mere verbal expedients—words are simply the finger pointing at the moon. One of the difficulties of talking in the present day of these matters is that the very existence of inner realities is now called in question.

By "inner" I mean our way of seeing the external world and all those realities that have no "external," "objective" presence—imagination, dreams, fantasies, trances, the realities of contemplative and meditative states, realities of which modern man, for the most part, has not the slightest direct awareness.

For example, nowhere in the Bible is there any argument about the *existence* of gods, demons, angels. People did not first "believe in" God: they experienced His presence, as was true of other spiritual agencies. The question was not whether God existed, but whether this particular God was the greatest god of all, or the only God; and what was the relation of the various spiritual agencies to each other. Today, there is a public debate, not as to the trustworthiness of God, the particular place in the spiritual hierarchy of different spirits, etc., but whether God or such spirits *even exist* or ever have existed.

Sanity today appears to rest very largely on a capacity to adapt to the external world—the interpersonal world, and the realm of human collectivities.

As this external human world is almost completely and totally estranged from the inner, any personal direct awareness of the inner world already has grave risks.

But since society, without knowing it, is *starving* for the inner, the demands on people to evoke its presence in a "safe" way, in a way that need not be taken seriously, etc., is tremendous—while the ambivalence is equally intense. Small wonder that the list of artists, in say the last 150 years, who have become shipwrecked on these reefs is so long— Hölderlin, John Clare, Rimbaud, Van Gogh, Nietzsche, Antonin Artaud. . . .

Those who survived have had exceptional qualities—a capacity for secrecy, slyness, cunning—a thoroughly realistic appraisal of the risks they run, not only from the spiritual realms they frequent, but from the hatred of their fellows for anyone engaged in this pursuit.

Let us *cure* them. The poet who mistakes a real woman for his Muse and acts accordingly. . . . The young man who sets off in a yacht in search of God. . . .

The outer divorced from any illumination from the inner is in a state of darkness. We are in an age of darkness. The state of outer darkness is a state of sin—i.e., alienation or estrangement from the *inner light*.* Certain actions lead to greater estrangement; certain others help one not to be so far removed. The former used to be called sinful.

The ways of losing one's way are legion. Madness is certainly not the least unambiguous. The countermadness of Kraepelinian psychiatry is the exact counterpart of "official" psychosis. Literally, and absolutely seriously, it is *mad*, if by madness we mean any radical estrangement from the totality of what is the case. Remember Kierkegaard's objective madness.

As we experience the world, so we act. We conduct ourselves in the light of our view of what is the case and what is not the case. That is, each person is a more or less naïve

---

*M. Eliade, *The Two and the One* (London: Harvill Press, 1965), especially Chapter I.

ontologist. Each person has views of what is and what is not..

There is no doubt, it seems to me, that there have been profound changes in the experience of man in the last thousand years. In some ways this is more evident than changes in the patterns of his behavior. There is everything to suggest that man experienced God. Faith was never a matter of believing. He existed, but of trusting, in the presence that was experienced and known to exist as a self-validating datum. It seems likely that far more people in our time experience neither the presence of God, nor the presence of his absence, but the absence of his presence.

We require a history of phenomena, not simply more phenomena of history.

As it is, the secular psychotherapist is often in the role of the blind leading the half-blind.

The fountain has not played itself out, the frame still shines, the river still flows, the spring still bubbles forth, the light has not faded. But between *us* and It, there is a veil which is more like fifty feet of solid concrete. *Deus absconditus.* Or we have absconded.

Already everything in our time is directed to categorizing and segregating this reality from objective facts. This is precisely the concrete wall. Intellectually, emotionally, interpersonally, organizationally, intuitively, theoretically, we have to blast our way through the solid wall, even if at the risk of chaos, madness and death. For from *this* side of the wall, this is the risk. There are no assurances, no guarantees.

Many people are prepared to have faith in the sense of scientifically indefensible belief in an untested hypothesis. Few have trust enough to test it. Many people make-believe what they experience. Few are made to believe by their experience. Paul of Tarsus was picked up by the scruff of the neck, thrown to the ground and blinded for three days. This direct experience was self-validating.

We live in a secular world. To adapt to this world the child abdicates its ecstasy. *("L'enfant abdique son extase"*: Mallarmé.) Having lost our experience of the spirit, we are expected to have faith. But this faith comes to be a belief in a reality which is not evident. There is a prophecy in Amos that a time will come when there will be a famine in the land, "not a famine for bread, nor a thirst for water, but of *hearing* the words of the Lord." That time has now come to pass. It is the present age.

From the alienated starting point of our pseudo-sanity, everything is equivocal. Our sanity is not "true" sanity. Their madness is not "true" madness. The madness of our patients is an artifact of the destruction wreaked on them by us and by them on themselves. Let no one suppose that we meet "true" madness any more than that we are truly sane. The madness that we encounter in "patients" is a gross travesty, a mockery, a grotesque caricature of what the natural healing of that estranged integration we call sanity might be. True sanity entails in one way or another the dissolution of the normal ego, that false self competently adjusted to our alienated social reality; the emergence of the "inner" archetypal mediators of divine power, and through this death a rebirth, and the eventual reestablishment of a new kind of ego-functioning, the ego now being the servant of the divine, no longer its betrayer.

# A Social History of the Hippies

## Warren Hinckle

An elderly school bus, painted like a fluorescent Easter egg in orange, chartreuse, cerise, white, green, blue, and, yes, black, was parked outside the solitary mountain cabin, which made it an easy guess that Ken Kesey, the novelist turned psychedelic Hotspur, was inside. So, of course, was Neal Cassady, the Tristram Shandy of the Beat Generation, proto-type hero of Jack Kerouac's *On the Road*, who had sworn off allegiance to Kerouac when the beat scene became meno-pausal and signed up as the driver of Kesey's fun and games bus, which is rumored to run on LSD. Except for these notorious luminaries, the Summit Meeting of the leaders of the new hippie subculture, convened in the lowlands of California's High Sierras during an early spring weekend last month, seemed a little like an Appalachian Mafia gathering without Joe Bananas.

Where was Allen Ginsberg, father goddam to two genera-tions of the underground? In New York, reading his poetry to freshmen. And where was Timothy Leary, self-styled guru to tens or is it hundreds of thousands of turned-on people? Off to some nowhere place like Stockton, to preach the gospel of Lysergic Acid Diethylamide to nice ladies in drip-dry dresses.

Reprinted from *Ramparts*, March 1967.

The absence of the elder statesmen of America's synthetic gypsy movement meant something. It meant that the leaders of the booming psychedelic bohemia in the seminal city of San Francisco were their own men—and strangely serious men, indeed, for hippies. Ginsberg and Leary may be Pied Pipers, but they are largely playing old tunes. The young men who make the new scene accept Ginsberg as a revered observer from the elder generation; Leary they abide as an Elmer Gantry on their side, to be used for proselytizing squares, only.

The mountain symposium had been called for the extraordinary purpose of discussing the political future of the hippies. Hippies are many things, but most prominently the bearded and beaded inhabitants of the Haight–Ashbury, a little psychedelic city-state edging Golden Gate Park. There, in a daily street-fair atmosphere, upwards of fifteen thousand unbonded girls and boys interact in a tribal, love-free, free-swinging, acid-based type of society where, if you are a hippie and you have a dime, you can put it in a parking meter and lie down in the street for an hour's suntan (thirty minutes for a nickel) and most drivers will be careful not to run you over.

Speaking, sometimes all at once, inside the Sierra cabin were many voices of conscience and vision of the Haight–Ashbury—belonging to men who, except for their Raggedy Andy hair, paisley shirts, and pre-mod western Levi jackets, sounded for all the world like Young Republicans.

They talked about reducing governmental controls, the sanctity of the individual, the need for equality among men. They talked, very seriously, about the kind of society they wanted to live in, and the fact that if they wanted an ideal world they would have to go out and make it for themselves, because nobody, least of all the government, was going to do it for them.

The utopian sentiments of these hippies were not to be put down lightly. Hippies have a clear vision of the ideal community—a psychedelic community, to be sure—where everyone is turned on and beautiful and loving and happy and floating free. But it is a vision that, despite the Alice in Wonderland phraseology hippies usually breathlessly employ to describe it, necessarily embodies a radical political philosophy: communal life, drastic restriction of private property, rejection of violence, creativity before consumption, freedom before authority, de-emphasis of government and traditional forms of leadership.

Despite a disturbing tendency to quietism, all hippies *ipso facto* have a political posture—one of unremitting opposition to the Establishment which insists on branding them criminals because they take LSD and marijuana, and hating them, anyway, because they enjoy sleeping nine in a room and three to a bed, seem to have free sex and guiltless minds, and can raise healthy children in dirty clothes.

The hippie choice of weapons is to love the Establishment to death rather than protest it or blow it up (hippies possess a confounding disconcern about traditional political methods or issues). But they are decidedly and forever outside the Consensus on which this society places such a premium, and since the hippie scene is so much the scene of those people under twenty-five that *Time* magazine warns will soon constitute half our population, this is a significant political fact.

This is all very solemn talk about people who like to skip rope and wear bright colors, but after spending some time with these fun and fey individuals you realize that, in a very unexpected way, they are as serious about what they're doing as the John Birch Society or the Junior League. It is not improbable, after a few more mountain seminars by those purposeful young men wearing beads, that the Haight–Ashbury may spawn the first utopian collectivist community since Brook Farm.

That this society finds it so difficult to take such rascally looking types seriously is no doubt the indication of a deep-rooted hang-up. But to comprehend the psychosis of America in the computer age, you have to know what's with the hippies.

[KEN KESEY—I]

## Games people play, Merry Prankster Division

Let us go, then, on a trip.

You can't miss the Tripmaster: the thick-necked lad in the blue and white striped pants with the red belt and the golden

eagle buckle, a watershed of wasted promise in his pale blue
eyes, one front tooth capped in patriotic red, white and blue,
his hair downy, flaxen, straddling the incredibly wide divide
of his high forehead like two small toupees pasted on
sideways. Ken Kesey, Heir Apparent Number One to the
grand American tradition of blowing one's artistic talent to
do some other thing, was sitting in a surprisingly comfortable
chair inside the bus with the psychedelic crust, puffing
absentmindedly on a harmonica.

The bus itself was ambulatory at about fifty miles an
hour jogging along a back road in sylvan Marin County,
four loudspeakers turned all the way up, broadcasting
both inside and outside Carl Orff's *Carmina Burana,* and
filled with two dozen people simultaneously smoking marijuana and looking for an open ice cream store. It was the
Thursday night before the Summit Meeting weekend and
Kesey, along with some fifteen members of the turned-
on yes men and women who call him "Chief" and whom
he calls the "Merry Pranksters" in return, was demonstrating a "game" to a delegation of visiting hippie fire-
men.

Crossing north over the Golden Gate Bridge from San
Francisco to Marin County to pay Kesey a state visit were
seven members of The Diggers, a radical organization even
by Haight–Ashbury standards, which exists to give things
away, free. The Diggers started out giving out free food,
free clothes, free lodging, and free legal advice, and hope
eventually to create a totally free cooperative community.
They had come to ask Kesey to get serious and attend
the weekend meeting on the state of the nation of the hippies.

The dialogue had hardly begun, however, before Kesey
loaded all comers into the bus and pushed off into the dark
to search for a nocturnal ice cream store. The bus, which
may be the closest modern man has yet come to aping
the self-sufficiency of Captain Nemo's submarine, has
its own power supply and is equipped with instruments for
a full rock band, microphones, loudspeakers, spotlights,
and comfortable seats all around. The Pranksters are presently installing microphones every three feet on the bus
walls so everybody can broadcast to everybody else all at
once.

At the helm was the Intrepid Traveler, Ken Babbs, who is auxiliary chief of the Merry Pranksters when Kesey is out of town or incommunicado or in jail, all three of which he has recently been. Babbs, who is said to be the model for the heroes of both Kesey novels, *One Flew Over the Cuckoo's Nest* and *Sometimes A Great Notion,* picked up a microphone to address the guests in the rear of the bus, like the driver of a Grayline tour: "We are being followed by a police car. Will someone watch and tell me when he turns on his red light."

The law was not unexpected, of course, because any cop who sees Kesey's bus just about *has* to follow it, would probably end up with some form of professional D.T.'s if he didn't. It is part of the game: the cop was now playing on their terms, and Kesey and his Pranksters were delighted. In fact, a discernible wave of disappointment swept across the bus when the cop finally gave up chasing this particular U.F.O. and turned onto another road.

The games he plays are very important to Kesey. In many ways his intellectual rebellion has come full circle; he has long ago rejected the structured nature of society—the foolscap rings of success, conformity, and acceptance "normal" people must regularly jump through. To the liberated intellect, no doubt, these requirements constitute the most sordid type of game. But, once rejecting all the norms of society, the artist is free to create his own structures—and along with any new set of rules however personal, there is necessarily, the shell to the tortoise, a new set of games. In Kesey's case, at least, the games are usually fun. Running around the outside of an insane society, the healthiest thing you can do is laugh.

It helps to look at this sort of complicated if not confused intellectual proposition in bas relief, as if you were looking at the simple pictures on Wedgwood china. Stand Successful Author Ken Kesey off against, say, Successful Author Truman Capote. Capote, as long as his game is accepted by the system, is free to be as mad as he can. So he tosses the biggest, most vulgar ball in a long history of vulgar balls, and achieves the perfect idiot synthesis of the upper middle and lower royal classes. Kesey, who cares as much about the system as he does about the Eddie Cantor Memorial Forest, invents his own game. He purchases a pre-'40s International

Harvester school bus, paints it psychedelic, fills it with undistinguished though lovable individuals in varying stages of eccentricity, and drives brazenly down the nation's highways, high on LSD, watching and waiting for the cops to blow their minds.

At the least, Kesey's posture has the advantage of being intellectually consistent with the point of view of his novels. In *One Flew Over the Cuckoo's Nest,* he uses the setting of an insane asylum as a metaphor for what he considers to be the basic insanity, or at least the fundamentally bizarre illogic, of American society. Since the world forces you into a game that is both mad and unfair, you are better off inventing your own game. Then, at least, you have a chance of winning. At least that's what Kesey thinks.

## [KEN KESEY—II]

### The Curry Is Very Hot;
### Merry Pranksters Are Having Pot

There wasn't much doing on late afternoon television, and the Merry Pranksters were a little restless. A few were turning on; one Prankster amused himself squirting his friends with a yellow plastic watergun; another staggered into the living room, exhausted from peddling a bicycle in everdiminishing circles in the middle of the street. They were all waiting, quite patiently, for dinner, which the Chief was whipping up himself. It was a curry, the recipe of no doubt cabalistic origin. Kesey evidently took his cooking seriously, because he stood guard by the pot for an hour and a half, stirring, concentrating on the little clock on the stove that didn't work.

There you have a slice of domestic life, February, 1967, from the swish Marin County home of Attorney Brian Rohan. As might be surmised, Rohan is Kesey's attorney, and the novelist and his *aides de camp* had parked their bus outside for the duration. The duration might last a long time, because Kesey has dropped out of the hippie scene. Some might say that he was pushed, because he fell, very hard, from favor among the hippies last year when he announced that he, Kesey, personally, was going to help reform the psychedelic scene. This sudden social conscience may have had something to do with beating a jail sentence on a compounded marijuana charge, but when Kesey obtained his freedom with instructions from the judge "to preach an anti-LSD warning to teenagers" it was a little too much for the Haight–Ashbury set. Kesey, after all, was the man who had turned on the Hell's Angels.

That was when the novelist was living in La Honda, a small community in the Skyline mountain range overgrown with trees and, after Kesey invited the Hell's Angels to several house parties, overgrown with sheriff's deputies. It was in this Sherwood Forest setting, after he had finished his second novel with LSD as his co-pilot, that Kesey inaugurated his band of Merry Pranksters (they have an official seal from the State of California incorporating them as "Intrepid Trips, Inc."), painted the school bus in glow sock colors, announced he would write no more ("Rather than write, I will ride buses, study the insides of jails, and see what goes on"), and set up funtime housekeeping on a full-time basis with the Pranksters, his wife and their three small children (one confounding thing about Kesey is the amorphous quality of the personal relationships in his entourage—the several attractive women don't seem, from the outside, to belong to any particular man; children are loved enough, but seem to be held in common).

When the Hell's Angels rumbled by, Kesey welcomed them with LSD. "We're in the same business. You break people's bones, I break people's heads," he told them. The Angels seem to like the whole acid thing, because today they are a fairly constant act in the Haight–Ashbury show, while Kesey has abdicated his role as Scoutmaster to fledgling acid heads and exiled himself across the Bay. This self-imposed Elba came about when Kesey sensed that the hippie community had soured on him. He had committed the one mortal sin in the hippie ethic: *telling* people what to do. "Get into a responsibility bag," he urged some four hundred friends attending a private Halloween party. Kesey hasn't been seen much in the Haight–Ashbury since that night, and though the Diggers did succeed in getting him to attend the weekend discussion, it is doubtful they will succeed in getting the

novelist involved in any serious effort to shape the Haight–
Ashbury future. At thirty-one, Ken Kesey is a hippie has-
been.

[KEN KESEY—III]

## The Acid Tests—From Unitarians to Watts

Kesey is now a self-sufficient but lonely figure—if you can be
lonely with dozens of Merry Pranksters running around your
house all day. If he ever gets maudlin, which is doubtful, he
can look back fondly on his hippie memories, which are
definitely in the wow! category, because Ken Kesey did for
acid roughly what Johnny Appleseed did for trees, and
probably more.

He did it through a unique and short-lived American
institution called the Acid Test. A lot of things happened at
an Acid Test, but the main thing was that, in the Haight–
Ashbury vernacular, everyone in the audience got zonked out
of their minds on LSD. LSD in Pepsi. LSD in coffee. LSD in
cake. LSD in the community punch. Most people were
generally surprised, because they didn't know they were
getting any LSD until it was too late. Later, when word got
around that this sort of mad thing was happening at Acid
Tests, Kesey sometimes didn't give out LSD on purpose, just
so people wouldn't know whether they did or did not have
LSD. Another game.

The Acid Tests began calmly enough. In the early versions
Kesey merely gave a heart-to-heart psychedelic talk and
handed LSD around like the Eucharist, which first happened
at a Unitarian conference in Big Sur in August of 1965. He
repeated this ritual several times, at private gatherings in his
home in La Honda, on college campuses, and once at a
Vietnam Day Committee rally at Berkeley. Then Kesey
added the Grateful Dead, a pioneer San Francisco rock
group, to his Acid Tests and, the cherry on the matzos, the
light show atmospheric technique of projecting slides and
wild colors on the walls during rock dances. This combination
he called "trips." Trip is the word for an LSD experience, but
in Kesey's lexicon it also meant kicks, which were achieved by
rapidly changing the audience's sensory environment what

seemed like approximately ten million times during an evening by manipulating bright colored lights, tape recorders, slide projectors, weird sound machines, and whatever else may be found in the electronic sink, while the participants danced under stroboscopic lights to a wild rock band or just played around on the floor.

It was a fulgurous, electronically orgiastic thing (the most advanced Tests had closed circuit television sets on the dance floor so you could see what you were doing), which made psychedelics very "fun" indeed, and the hippies came in droves. Almost every hippie in the Bay Area went to at least one Acid Test, and it is not exceeding the bounds of reasonable speculation to say that Kesey may have turned on at least ten thousand people to LSD during the twenty-four presentations of the Acid Test. (During these Tests the Merry Pranksters painted everything including themselves in fluorescent tones, and bright colors became the permanent in-thing in psychedelic dress.)

Turning so many unsuspecting people on to LSD at once could be dangerous, as the Pranksters discovered on a 1965 psychedelic road show when they staged the ill-fated Watts Acid Test. Many of the leading citizens of Watts came to the show, which was all very fine except that whoever put the LSD in the free punch that was passed around put in too much by a factor of about four. This served to make for a very wild Acid Test, and one or two participants "freaked out" and had a very hard time of it for the next few days.

After the California legislature played Prohibition and outlawed LSD on October 6, 1966, Kesey wound up the Acid Test syndrome with what was billed as a huge "Trips Festival" in San Francisco. People who regularly turn on say the Trips Festival was a bore: it embodied all the Acid Test elements except acid and, happily for the coffers of Intrepid Trips, Inc., attracted a huge crowd of newspapermen, narcotics agents and other squares, but very few hippies. The Merry Pranksters slyly passed out plain sugar cubes for the benefit of the undercover agents.

Suddenly, San Francisco, which for a grown-up city gets excited very easily, was talking about almost nothing but "trips" and LSD. Hippies, like overnight, had become fashionable.

If you are inclined to give thanks for this sort of thing, they go to the bad boy wonder of Psychedelphia, disappearing there over the horizon in his wayward bus.

[HISTORIAN CHESTER ANDERSON—I]

## The Ghosts of Scenes Past, or How We Got Here from There

Like Frederick J. Turner and Arnold Toynbee, Chester Anderson has a theory of history. His theory is psychedelic, but that is perfectly natural since he is a veteran acid head. Anderson, a thirty-five-year-old professional bohemian who looks forty-five, considers himself the unofficial historian of the psychedelic movement and has amassed enough footnotes to argue somewhat convincingly that the past fifteen years of social change in the United States—all the underground movements, and a significant part of the cultural changes—have been intimately connected with drugs.

If he is going to press his argument all the way, he may have to punch it out with Marshall McLuhan, who no doubt would assert that such phenomena as hippie colonies are nothing but a return to "tribal" culture, an inevitable reaction to our electronic age. And any social historian worth his salt will put it that every society has found some way to allow the sons and daughters of its middle class to drop out and cut up (most hippies by the way, are from middle-class stock, so what's the difference from, say, the Teddy Boys?) Maybe lots, maybe none. But there is no disputing the cultural and artistic flip-flops this country has gone through in the last decade. The jazz musicians' vogue meant something. So did the Beat Generation. So, we suppose, did Pop Art, and Rock and Roll, and so, of course, the hippies. If, in briefly tracing the derivation of the hippies from their seminal reasons in the intellectual uneasiness of the early 1950s, we chance to favor the testimony of Chester Anderson, it is only because he was there.

That was some bad year, 1953. There was a war on in Korea, a confusing, undefined war, the first big American war that wasn't the one to end all wars, because the aftermath of World War II had blown that phobia. And now the Bomb was with us, and with it the staccato series of disturbing headline events that stood for the Cold War; college was the only escape from the draft, but eggheads were becoming unpopular; Stevenson had lost the election and the Rosenbergs had been executed. It was all gloom, gloom, and dullsville, and if you were young and intellectual you were hard-pressed to find a hero or even a beautiful person. The only really alive, free thing, it seemed, was jazz—and the arrival of the long playing record had sparked a jazz renaissance, and with it the first drug heroes: most kids sympathized with Gene Krupa's marijuana busts, the agony of Lady Day's junk hang-up was universal, and Charlie Parker had his own drugstore.

Lady Day's way wasn't the way of the new generation, Chester Anderson will be quick to tell you, because she was on "body" drugs. Whatever else body drugs—heroin, opium, barbiturates, alcohol, tranquilizers—may do, they eventually turn you off, and contemporary heads like to be turned on—i.e., senses intensified, stimulated rather than depressed. "Head" drugs, which do the latter, are both cheaper and easier to get than body drugs, and come in approximately eighteen varieties in three different classifications—natural drugs like marijuana, hashish, peyote, morning glory seeds, Hawaiian wood rose seeds, and certain types of Mexican mushrooms; artificial psychedelics like mescaline, LSD, psilocybin and psilocin, and whatever the ingredient is that makes Romilar cough syrup so popular with young heads; and synthetic stimulants which, used in large doses by heads, are known as "speed"—dexedrine, benzedrine, and methedrine.

But in the early 1950s there wasn't such a complete psychedelic medicine shelf to choose from, and the culturally disenchanted pioneers who began to settle new colonies in New York's Village and San Francisco's North Beach had to make do with pot. In a climate dominated by Dwight Eisenhower in the newspapers and Ed Sullivan on television, they also began to turn on to the pacifist, humanist philosophies of Asia—particularly Buddhism, most especially Zen—while Christianity as a workable concept became more meaningless, despite the exemplary efforts of such men as Brother

Antoninus and Thomas Merton. American churchmen seemed to have neither the patience nor the fortitude to deal with people who were, well *unsettled*. Folk music, which had been slowly dying, perked up a little, and there was a new interest in fresh, tuned-in poetry. As the '50s approached middle age and McCarthy went on the rampage, the few signs of life in a stagnant society centered around the disoriented peace movement, the fledgling civil rights movement, the young political Left, jazz and folk music, poetry, and Zen. Most of these followers were, of course, taking pot, while the rest of the country remained on booze and sleeping pills.

(If, in memory of the 85th anniversary of Anthony Trollope's death, we may be permitted an aside to the reader, it would be to say that one of the things that is considered original, but is in fact not, about the hippies is the concept of "dropping out" of society. Without adopting the histtronics of Hogarth crusading against the masses drinking gin, it is true that alcohol is an opiate which serves to help tens of millions of busy businessmen and lethargic housewives to "drop out" of any essential involvement in life and remain political and artistic boors. But alcohol is legal so nobody cares. If pot and LSD were ever legalized, it would be a mortal blow to this bohemia. Hippies have a political posture essentially because of the enforced criminality of their daily dose, and if taking LSD meant no more in society than the commuter slugging down his seventh martini, the conspiratorial magic would go out of the movement.)

Meanwhile, in San Francisco, Allen Ginsberg remembers an evening in 1955 which could stand as well as any for the starting point of what was to become the most thorough repudiation of America's middlebrow culture since the expatriates walked out on the country in the 1930s. The vanguard of what was to be the Beat Generation had gathered at the 6 Gallery on Fillmore Street for a poetry reading moderated by Kenneth Rexroth, a respectable leftish intellectual who was later to become the Public Defender of the beats. Lawrence Ferlinghetti was in the audience, and so were Kerouac and his then sidekick, Neal Cassady, listening to Michael McClure, Phil Lamantia, Gary Snyder, and Philip Whalen read their poetry. Ginsberg was there too, and delighted everyone with a section of the still unfinished "Howl," better known to beats as the Declaration of Independence.

Two distinct strains in the underground movement of the '50s were represented at this salient gathering. One was a distinctly fascist trend, embodied in Kerouac, which can be recognized by a totalitarian insistence on action and nihilism, and usually accompanied by a Superman concept. This strain runs, deeper and less silent, through the hippie scene today. It is into this fascist bag that you can put Kesey and his friends, the Hell's Angels, and, in a more subtle way, Dr. Timothy Leary.

The other, majority, side of the beats was a cultural reaction to the existential brinkmanship forced on them by the Cold War, and a lively attack on the concurrent rhetoric of complacency and self-satisfaction that pervaded the literary establishment all the way from the *Atlantic Monthly* to Lionel Trilling. Led by men like Ginsberg and Ferlinghetti, the early beats weighed America by its words and deeds, and found it pennyweight. They took upon themselves the role of conscience for the machine. They rejected all values and when, in attempting to carve a new creative force, they told America to "go fuck itself," America reacted, predictably, with an obscenity trial.

The early distant warnings of the drug-based culture that would dominate the Haight–Ashbury a decade later were there in the early days of North Beach. Marijuana was as popular as Coke at a Baptist wedding, and the available hallucinogens—peyote and mescaline—were part of the beat rebellion. Gary Snyder, poet, mountain climber, formal Yamabushi Buddhist, and a highly respected leader of the hippie scene today, first experimented with peyote while living with the Indian tribe of the same name in 1948; Ginsberg first took it in New York in 1951; Lamantia, Kerouac and Cassady were turned on by beat impresario Hymie D'Angolo at his Big Sur retreat in 1952. And beat parties, whether they served peyote, marijuana or near beer, were rituals, community sacraments, setting the format for contemporary hippie rituals.

But the psychedelic community didn't really begin

to flourish until late 1957 and 1958 in New York, and for that story we take you to Chester Anderson in the Village.

### [HISTORIAN CHESTER ANDERSON—II]

## Was the Kingston Trio Really Red Guards?

On Thanksgiving Day, 1957, Chester Anderson was turned on to grass by a bongo-playing superhippie who went by the code name of Mr. Sulks. Grass, if you don't know and don't have an underground glossary handy, is translated marijuana, and from that day forward, Anderson, who once studied music at the University of Miami so he could write string quartets like Brahms, became a professional Turn-On and migrated with bohemia, east to west to east to west, from the Village to North Beach back to the Village to the Haight-Ashbury, where he can be found today—a prototype of the older psychedelic type who mixes with the drifting, turning-on kids to form the central nervous system of any body of hippies.

The first psychedelic drug to reach the Village in any quantity was peyote, an obscure hallucinatory cactus bud used by Indians in religious ceremonies. Peyote was cheap and plentiful (it can still be ordered by mail from Laredo at $10 for 100 "buttons") and became highly touted—Havelock Ellis and Aldous Huxley recommended it. The only problem with peyote was that it tasted absolutely terrible, and, as peyote cults sprang up, peyote cookbooks came out with recipes for preparing the awful stuff in ways that would kill the taste. "Man," Chester recalls a head telling him at the time, "if I thought it'd get me high, I'd eat shit." As with most new head drugs, the taking of peyote was treated as a quasi-religious event. The first time Chester took it, he did so with great ritual before a statue of the Buddha.

Peyote was the thing in late 1957, and by the summer of 1958 mescaline, the first synthetic psychedelic, was widely distributed. The heads reacted like unwed mothers being handed birth control pills—they were no longer dependent on nature. Turn-ons could be *manufactured!*

According to Chester's files, LSD didn't arrive in any large, consumer-intended supply in the Village until the winter of

1961-62, and not in the Bay Area until the summer of 1964, but by that time something unusual had happened to America's psychedelic gypsies: they had become formal enemies of the State. Massive harassment by the cops in San Francisco, by the coffeehouse license inspectors in New York, had led the heads and the young middle-class types who came in caravan proportions, to test the no-more-teachers, no-more-books way of bohemian life, to view the Establishment as the bad guy who would crush their individuality and spirituality in any way he could. This is the derivation of whatever political posture the hippies have today. It will be significant, of course, only if the Haight–Ashbury scene doesn't go the way of the Beat Generation—assimilated by a kick-hungry society. For the serious, literary beats, it was all over but the shouting when the Co-existence Bagel Shop became a stop on sightseeing tours.

In 1962, the Village was pulsating with psychedelic evangelism. LSD was so cheap and so plentiful that it became a big thing among heads to turn on new people as fast as they could give LSD away.

Pot, also, was being used more widely than ever by middle-class adults, and spread from the urban bohemias to the hinterlands by small folk music circles that were to be found everywhere from Jacksonville, Florida, to Wausau, Wisconsin. At the same time, almost the entire Village was treating LSD like it was a selection on a free lunch counter, and a scruffy folknik called Bobby Dylan was beginning to play charitable guest sets in the Washington Square coffeehouses. "Things," Chester said, "were happening more rapidly than we knew."

What was happening, Mr. Jones, was that folk music, under the influence of early acid culture, was giving way to rock and roll. Rock spread the hippie way of life like a psychedelic plague, and it metamorphosed in such rapid fashion from the popularity of folk music, that a very suspicious person might ask if seemingly safe groups like the Kingston Trio were not, in fact, the Red Guards of the hippie cultural revolution.

There was a rock and roll before, of course, but it was all bad seed. The likes of Frankie Avalon, Fabian, and Elvis Presley sent good rock and roll musicians running to folk music. Then absolutely the world's greatest musical blitz fell and the Beatles landed, everywhere, all at once. The impact of their popular music was analogous to the Industrial Revolution on the nineteenth century. They brought music out of the juke box and into the street. The Beatles' ecstatic, alive, electric sound had a total sensory impact, and was inescapably participational. It was "psychedelic music." "The Beatles are a trip," Chester said. Whether the Beatles or Dylan or the Rolling Stones actually came to their style through psychedelic involvement (Kenneth Tynan says a recent Beatles song "Tomorrow Never Knows" is "the best musical evocation of LSD I've ever heard") is not as important as the fact that their songs reflect LSD values—love, life, getting along with other people, and that this type of involving, turn-on music galvanized the entire hippie underground into overt, brassy existence—particularly in San Francisco.

Drug song lyrics may, in fact, be the entire literary output of the hippie generation. The hippies' general disregard for anything as static as a book is a fact over which Chester Anderson and Marshall McLuhan can shake hands. For acid heads are, in McLuhan's phrase, "post-literate." Hippies do not share our written, linear society—they like textures better than surfaces, prefer the electronic to the mechanical, like group, tribal activities. Theirs is an ecstatic, do-it-now culture, and rock and roll is their art form.

[THE MERCHANT PRINCES—I]

## Dr. Leary—Pretender to the Hippie Throne

The suit was Brooks Brothers '59, and the paisley tie J. Press contemporary, but the bone-carved Egyptian mandala hanging around his neck, unless it was made in occupied Japan, had to be at least two thousand years old. Dr. Timothy Leary, B.A. University of Alabama, Ph.D. University of California, LSD Cuernavaca, and 86'd Harvard College, was dressed up for a night on the town, but as his devotees say of this tireless proselytizer of the psychedelic cause, it was work, work, work. Tonight Leary was scouting somebody else's act, a Swami's at that, who was turning on the hippies at the Avalon Ballroom by leading them in an hour-long Hindu chant without stopping much for breath. The Avalon is one of the two great, drafty ballrooms where San Francisco hippies, hippie-hangers-on, and young hippies-to-be congregate each weekend to participate in the psychedelic rock and light shows that are now as much a part of San Francisco as cable cars and a lot noisier.

This dance was a benefit for the new Swami, recently installed in a Haight–Ashbury storefront, with a fair passage sign from Allen Ginsberg whom he had bumped into in India. The hippies were turning out to see just what the Swami's *schtick* was, but Dr. Leary had a different purpose. He has a vested, professional interest in turning people on, and here was this Swami, trying to do it with just a chant, like it was natural childbirth or something.

The word professional is not used lightly. There is a large group of professionals making it by servicing and stimulating the hippie world—in the spirit of the Haight–Ashbury we should refer to these men as merchant princes—and Timothy Leary is the pretender to the throne.

Dr. Leary claims to have launched the first indigenous religion in America. That may very well be, though as a religious leader he is Aimee Semple McPherson in drag. Dr. Leary, who identifies himself as a "prophet," recently played the Bay Area in his LSD road show, where he sold $4 seats to lots of squares but few hippies (Dr. Leary's pitch is to the straight world), showed a technicolor movie billed as simulating an LSD experience (it was big on close-ups of enlarged blood vessels), burned incense, dressed like a holy man in white cotton pajamas, and told everybody to "turn on, tune in, and drop out."

In case you are inclined to make light of this philosophic advice you should not laugh out loud. Because Dr. Leary is serious about his work, he can not be dismissed as a cross between a white Father Divine and Nietzsche, no matter how tempting the analogy. He has made a substantial historical contribution to the psychedelic scene, although his arrest records may figure more prominently than his philosophy in future hippie histories.

Since, something like Eve, he first bit into the sacred psychedelic mushroom while lounging beside a swimming pool in Cuernavaca, he has been hounded by the consequences of his act. Since Dr. Leary discovered LSD, he has been booted out of Harvard for experimenting a little too widely with it among the undergraduate population, asked to leave several foreign countries for roughly the same reasons, and is now comfortably if temporarily ensconced in a turned-on billionaire friend's estate near Poughkeepsie, New York, while awaiting judicial determination of a thirty-year prison sentence for transporting a half-ounce of marijuana across the Rio Grande without paying the Texas marijuana tax, which has not been enforced since the time of the Lone Ranger.

If he were asked to contribute to the "L" volume of the World Book Encyclopedia, Dr. Leary would no doubt sum up his work as "having turned on American culture," though his actual accomplishments are somewhat more prosaic. Together with Richard Alpert, who was to Dr. Leary what Bill Moyers was to President Johnson, Leary wrote an article in May, 1962, in, surprise, *The Bulletin of the Atomic Scientists*. The article warned that in event of war, the Russians were likely to douse all our reservoirs with LSD in order to make people so complacent that they wouldn't particularly care about being invaded, and as a civil defense precaution we ought to do it ourselves first—you know, douse our own reservoirs—so that when the reds got *their* chance the country would know just what was coming off. It was back to the old drawing board after that article, but Alpert and Dr. Leary made their main contribution to the incredibly swift spread of LSD through the nation in 1964 by the simple act of publishing a formula for LSD, all that was needed by any enterprising housewife with a B-plus in high school chemistry and an inclination for black market activity. Dr. Leary's religious crusade has been a bust, convert-wise, and not so salutary financially, either, so he announced recently that he was dropping out himself, to contemplate his navel under the influence. It would be easier to take Dr. Leary seriously if he could overcome his penchant for treating LSD as a patent snake-bite medicine.

An enlightening example of this panacea philosophy is found back among the truss ads in the September, 1966, issue of *Playboy*. In the midst of a lengthy interview when, as happens in *Playboy*, the subject got around to sex, Dr. Leary was all answers. "An LSD session that does not involve an ultimate merging with a person of the opposite sex isn't really complete," he said, a facet of the drug he neglected to mention to the Methodist ladies he was attempting to turn on in Stockton, California. But this time, Dr. Leary was out to turn on the *Playboy* audience.

The following selection from the interview is reprinted in its entirety. Italics are *Playboy*'s.

PLAYBOY: We've heard that some women who ordinarily have difficulty achieving orgasm find themselves capable of multiple orgasms under LSD. Is that true?

LEARY: In a carefully prepared, loving LSD session, a woman will inevitably have several hundred orgasms.

PLAYBOY: Several *hundred*?

LEARY: Yes. Several hundred.

After recovering from that intelligence, the *Playboy* interviewer, phrasing the question as diplomatically as possible, asked Dr. Leary if he got much, being such a handsome LSD turn-on figure. Dr. Leary allowed that women are always falling over him, but responded with the decorum of Pope Paul being translated from the Latin: "Any charismatic person who is conscious of his own mythic potency awakens this basic hunger in women and pays reverence to it at the level that is harmonious and appropriate at the time."

Dr. Leary also said that LSD is a "specific *cure* for homosexuality."

The final measurement of the tilt of Dr. Leary's windmill, his no doubt earnest claim to be the prophet of this generation, must be made by weighing such recorded conversations against his frequent and urgent pleas to young people to "drop out of politics, protest, petitions and pickets" and join his "new religion" where, as he said recently:

"You have to be out of your mind to pray."

Perhaps, and quite probably so.

[THE MERCHANT PRINCES—II]

## Where Dun & Bradstreet Fears to Tread

Allen Ginsberg asked ten thousand people to turn towards the sea and chant with him. They all did just that, and then picked up the papers and miscellaneous droppings on the turf of Golden Gate Park's Polo Field and went contentedly home. This was the end of the first Human Be-In, a gargantuan hippy happening held only for the joy of it in mid-

January. The hippie tribes gathered under clear skies with rock bands, incense, chimes, flutes, feathers, candles, banners, and drums. Even the Hell's Angels were on their good behavior—announcing that they would guard the sound truck against unspecified evil forces. It was all so successful that the organizers are talking about another be-in this summer to be held at the bottom of the Grand Canyon with maybe two hundred thousand hippies being-in.

The local papers didn't quite know how to treat this one, except for the San Francisco *Chronicle's* ace society editor Frances Moffat, who ran through the crowd picking out local socialites and taking notes on the fashions.

Mrs. Moffat's intense interest reflects the very in, very marketable character of San Francisco Hippiedom. Relatively high-priced mod clothing and trinket stores are as common in the Haight–Ashbury as *pissoirs* used to be in Paris. They are run by hippie merchants mostly for square customers, but that doesn't mean that the hippies themselves aren't brand name conscious. Professing a distaste for competitive society, hippies are, contradictorily, frantic consumers. Unlike the beats, they do not disdain money. Indeed, when they have it, which with many is often, they use it to buy something pretty or pleasureful. You will find only the best hi-fi sets in hippie flats.

In this commercial sense, the hippies have not only accepted assimilation (the beats fought it, and lost), they have swallowed it whole. The hippie culture is in many ways a prototype of the most ephemeral aspects of the larger American society; if the people looking in from the suburbs want change, clothes, fun, and some lightheadedness from the new gypsies, the hippies are delivering—and some of them are becoming rich hippies because of it.

The biggest Robber Baron is dance promoter Bill Graham, a Jewish boy from New York who made it big in San Francisco by cornering the hippie bread and circuses concession. His weekend combination rock and roll dances and light shows at the cavernous, creaky old Fillmore Auditorium on the main street of San Francisco's Negro ghetto are jammed every night. Even Andy Warhol played the Fillmore. Although Graham is happy providing these weekend spiritual experiences, he's not trying to be a leader. "I don't want to make cadres, just money," he said. Graham's cross-town competitor is Chet Helms, a rimless-glasses variety hippie from Texas who has turned the pioneer, non-profit San Francisco rock group called The Family Dog, into a very profit-making enterprise at the Avalon Ballroom.

A side-product of the light show dances, and probably the only other permanent manifestation of hippie culture to date, is the revival in a gangbusters way of Art Nouveau poster art. Wes Wilson, who letters his posters in 18, 24 and 36 point Illegible, originated the basic style in posters for the Fillmore dances. Graham found he could make as much money selling posters as dance tickets, so he is now in the poster business, too.

The posters, at $1 apiece, as common as window shades in the Haight–Ashbury, demand total involvement from the reader, and are thus considered psychedelic manifestations of the existential, nonverbal character of hippie culture.

Haight Street, the Fifth Avenue of Hippiedom, is geographically parallel to Golden Gate Park but several blocks uphill, where rows of half vacant store fronts once indicated the gradual decline of a middle-class neighborhood. But all that changed, dramatically, during the past eighteen months. Haight Street now looks like the Metropolitan Opera Company backstage on the opening night of *Aida*. The stores are all occupied, but with mercantile ventures that might give Dun & Bradstreet cause to wonder. Threaded among the older meat markets, discount furniture stores, laundromats, and proletarian bars are a variety of leather goods shops, art galleries, mod clothing stores, and boutiques specializing in psychedelic paraphernalia like beads, prisms, and marijuana pipes, and of course there is the Psychedelic Shop itself.

The Psychedelic Shop is treated as a hippie landmark of sorts, but the Haight–Ashbury scene was percolating long before the Thelin brothers, Ron and Jay, stuffed a disconcertingly modern glass and steel store front full of amulets, psychedelic books, a large stock of the underground press, and some effete gadgetry for acid heads. The hippie phenomena began to metamorphose from a personal to a social happening around the fall of 1965 after the kids at Berkeley turned on to LSD, Ken Kesey started holding Acid Tests, and The Family Dog staged its first dance.

Instrumental in spreading the word was the *Chronicle*'s highly regarded jazz critic, Ralph J. Gleason. Gleason is read religiously by hippies. Besides explaining to his square readers what is happening, he is also the unofficial arbitrator of good taste in the Haight–Ashbury community. Gleason was quick to tell Ken Kesey, in print, when he was out of line, and did the same for Dr. Leary. Gleason's writings tuned in other members of the *Chronicle* staff, and the extensive, often headline publicity the newspaper gave to the hippie scene (Kesey's return from a self-imposed Mexican exile was treated with the seriousness of a reasonably large earthquake) helped escalate the Haight–Ashbury population explosion.

So there is plenty of business for the hippie merchants, but some of them, like the Thelin brothers, are beginning to wonder where it will all lead. At the prodding of The Diggers, the Thelins are considering making the store a nonprofit cooperative that will help "the kids get high and stay high" at low cost. They may also take the same steps with *The Oracle*, the Haight–Ashbury monthly tabloid. The majority of the hip merchants, however, are very comfortable with the ascending publicity and sales, and have as little vision of what they are helping create as did Alexander Bell when he spilled acid on himself.

[EMMETT GROGAN—I]

## Will the Real Frodo Baggins Please Stand Up?

Except for the obvious fact that he wasn't covered with fur, you would have said to yourself that for sure there was old Frodo Baggins, crossing Haight Street. Frodo Baggins is the hero of the English antiquarian J. R. R. Tolkien's classic trilogy, *Lord of the Rings*, absolutely the favorite book of every hippie, about a race of little people called Hobbits who live somewhere in prehistory in a place called Middle Earth. Hobbits are hedonistic, happy little fellows who love beauty and pretty colors. Hobbits have their own scene and resent intrusion, pass the time eating three or four meals a day and smoke burning leaves of herb in pipes of clay. You can see why hippies would like Hobbits.

The hustling, heroic-looking fellow with the mistaken identity was Emmett Grogan, kingpin of The Diggers and the closest thing the hippies in the Haight–Ashbury have to a real live hero. Grogan, twenty-three, with blond, unruly hair, and a fair, freckled Irish face, has the aquiline nose of a leader, but he would prefer to say that he "just presents alternatives." He is in and out of jail seventeen times a week, sometimes busted for smashing a cop in the nose (Grogan has a very intolerant attitude toward policemen), sometimes bailing out a friend, and sometimes, like Monopoly, just visiting. The alternatives he presents are rather disturbing to the hippie bourgeoisie, since he thinks they have no business charging hippies money for their daily needs and should have the decency to give things away free, like The Diggers do, or at least charge the squares and help out the hippies.

Grogan has a very clear view of what freedom means in society ("Why can't I stand on the corner and wait for nobody? Why can't everyone?") and an even clearer view of the social position of the hippie merchants ("They just want to expand their sales, they don't care what happens to people here; they're nothing but goddamn shopkeepers with beards").

Everyone is a little afraid of Grogan in the Haight–Ashbury, including the cops. A one-man crusade for purity of purpose, he is the conscience of the hippie community. He is also a bit of a daredevil and a madman, and could easily pass for McMurphy, the roguish hero in Kesey's novel set in an insane asylum. There is a bit of J. P. Donleavy's *Ginger Man* in him, too.

A few weeks ago, out collecting supplies for The Diggers' daily free feed, Grogan went into a San Francisco wholesale butcher and asked for soup bones and meat scraps. "No free food here, we work for what we eat," said the head butcher, a tattooed Bulgar named Louie, who was in the icebox flanked by his seven assistant butchers. "You're a fascist pig and a coward," replied Grogan, whom Louie immediately smashed in the skull with the blunt side of a carving knife. That turned out to be a mistake, because the seven assistant butchers didn't like Louie much, and all jumped him. While all those white coats were grunting and rolling in the sawdust, a bleeding Grogan crawled out with four cardboard boxes full of meat.

This was a typical day in Dogpatch for Grogan, who has had his share of knocks. A Brooklyn boy, he ran away from home at fifteen and spent the next six years in Europe, working as a busboy in the Alps, and, later, studying film making in Italy under Antonioni. Grogan had naturally forgotten to register for the draft, so when he returned to the United States he was in the Army four days later. That didn't last long, however, because the first thing Grogan had to do was clean the barracks. His idea of cleaning barracks was to throw all the guns out the window, plus a few of the rusty beds, and artistically displeasing footlockers. Then he began painting the remaining bed frames yellow. "I threw out everything that was not esthetically pleasing," he told the sergeant.

Two days later Grogan was in the psychiatric ward of Letterman Hospital in San Francisco where he stayed for six months before the authorities decided they couldn't quite afford to keep him. That was shortly after an Army doctor, learning of his film training, ordered Grogan to the photo lab for "work therapy." It was a "beautiful, tremendously equipped lab," Grogan recalls, and since it wasn't used very much, he took a picture of his own big blond face and proceeded to make 5000 prints. When the doctors caught up with him, he had some 4700 nine by twelve glossies of Emmett Grogan neatly stacked on the floor, and all lab machines: driers, enlargers, developers were going like mad, and the water was running over on the floor. "What did you do *that* for?" a doctor screamed.

Grogan shrugged. "I'm crazy," he said.

He was released a little later, and acted for a while with the San Francisco Mime Troupe, the city's original and brilliant radical theater ensemble. Then last fall, when the Negro riots broke out in San Francisco and the National Guard put a curfew on the Haight–Ashbury, The Diggers happened. "Everybody was trying to figure how to react to the curfew. The SDS came down and said ignore it, go to jail. The merchants put up chicken posters saying 'for your own safety, get off the street.' Somehow, none of those ideas seemed right. If you had something to do on the streets, you should do it and tell the cops to go screw off. If you didn't, you might as well be inside."

Something to do, to Grogan, was to eat if you were hungry, so at 8 P.M., at the curfew witching hour, he and an actor friend named Billy Landau set up a delicious free dinner in the park, right under the cops' noses, and the hippies came and ate and have been chowing down, free, every night since. The Haight–Ashbury has never been quite the same.

[EMMETT GROGAN—II]

## A Psychedelic Grapes of Wrath

Every Bohemian community has its inevitable coterie of visionaries who claim to know what it is all about. But The Diggers are, somehow, different. They are bent on creating a wholly cooperative subculture and, so far, they are not just hallucinating, they are doing it.

Free clothes (used) are there for whomever wants them. Free meals are served every day. Next, Grogan plans to open a smart mod clothing store on Haight Street and give the clothes away free, too (the hippie merchants accused him of "trying to undercut our prices"). He wants to start Digger farms where participants will raise their own produce. He wants to give away free acid, to eliminate junky stuff and end profiteering. He wants cooperative living to forestall inevitable rent exploitation when the Haight–Ashbury becomes chic.

Not since Brook Farm, not since the Catholic Workers, has any group in this dreadfully co-optive, consumer society been so serious about a utopian community.

If Grogan succeeds or fails in the Haight–Ashbury it will not be as important as the fact that he has tried. For he is, at least, providing the real possibility of what he calls "alternatives" in the down-the-rabbit-hole-culture of the hippies.

Grogan is very hung up on freedom. "Do your thing, what you are, and nothing will ever bother you," he says. His heroes are the Mad Bomber of New York who blissfully blew up all kinds of things around Manhattan over thirty years because he just liked to blow things up, and poet Gary Snyder, whom he considers the "most important person in the Haight–Ashbury" because instead of sitting around sniffing incense and talking about it, he went off to Japan and became a Zen master. "He did it, man."

This is an interesting activist ethic, but it remains doubtful just what the hippies will do. Not that many, certainly, will join Grogan's utopia, because utopias, after all, have a size limit.

The New Left has been flirting with the hippies lately, even to the extent of singing "The Yellow Submarine" at a Berkeley protest rally, but it looks from here like a largely unrequited love.

The hip merchants will, of course, go on making money.

And the youngsters will continue to come to the Haight–Ashbury and do—what?

That was the question put to the hippie leaders at their Summit Meeting. They resolved their goals, but not the means, and the loud noise you heard from outside was probably Emmett Grogan pounding the table with his shoe.

The crisis of the happy hippie ethic is precisely this: it is all right to turn on, but it is not enough to drop out. Grogan sees the issue in the gap "between the radical political philosophy of Jerry Rubin and Mario Savio and psychedelic love philosophy." He, himself, is not interested in the war in Vietnam, but on the other hand he does not want to spend his days like Ferdinand sniffing pretty flowers.

This is why he is so furious at the hip merchants. "They created the myth of this utopia; now they aren't going to do anything about it." Grogan takes the evils of society very personally, and he gets very angry, almost physically sick, when a pregnant fifteen-year-old hippie's baby starves in her stomach, a disaster which is not untypical in the Haight–Ashbury, and which Grogan sees being repeated ten-fold this summer when upwards of two hundred thousand migrant teen-agers and college kids come, as a psychedelic *Grapes of Wrath*, to utopia in search of the heralded turn-on.

The danger in the hippie movement is more than over-crowded streets and possible hunger riots this summer. If more and more youngsters begin to share the hippie political posture of unrelenting quietism, the future of activist, serious politics is bound to be affected. The hippies have shown that it can be pleasant to drop out of the arduous task of attempting to steer a difficult, unrewarding society. But when that is done, you leave the driving to the Hell's Angels.

# Relaxation, Awareness, and Breathing

## Marco Vassi

I found a place in San Francisco's Bernal Heights, a hippie hobbitland at the end of the Mission District. It was an old Italian neighborhood where goats had once grazed on the hill which now served as the base for a giant Army radar screen. It was now peopled by a goodly number of *heads* who had much of the gentle anonymity of the early Haight love children. Aster and I came to an abrupt parting of the ways since the excitement of travel had somewhat supplanted the intensity of our sexual trip, and we were left with only the hate portion of the relationship. She split for a farm in Oregon and within a few weeks I found myself the sole inhabitant of a damp apartment that overlooked a dead-end street in the front, and opened on to a garden in the back.

Next door were Fred and Melissa who had been living together for two years, erupting every two months in another "final" separation which lasted for a week or so. Pat lived upstairs, a wise old/young lady of twenty-six years who read Doris Lessing and listened to Satie as she smoked each day away in vaguely pointed yearnings. Later, for a while, Leah was to be with me, my bisexual sister of a hundred encounters, with abyss-suggesting brown Taurus eyes and entrancingly small breasts. Across the way were Harry and Mary, a

From *The Stoned Apocalypse* (Trident Press, 1972).

psychedelic version of the nice American couple. He played guitar and fixed motorcycles, while she tried to keep the house together and make babies. Above them were Paul and Cheryl who were later to become Christians.

Although I had about two thousand dollars and a car, easily enough to live on for six months on the Coast, I still had my New York habits, and was soon busy looking for something to "do." My best gig was, ironically enough, teaching classes in relaxation, which involved getting people just to lie down and breathe, until they entered a state of light hypnotism, at which time I would take them on mind trips. I had learned the gimmick some years earlier while working with a fearless and feckless therapist who kept rediscovering the psychological wheel. Every month she would come roaring in with a new theory, only to have it pointed out to her that Freud or Aristotle or Buddha or somebody had written it all down years before. I was her patient for a year, her partner for six months, and her therapist for six months after that. It was a strange relationship, but one which taught me more than a little about how simple it is to mold people in any direction whatsoever. During that time we stumbled onto Reichian breathing, thought transfer, body language, and the whole panoply of jargonized insights which has since made Esalen such a pile of loot.

I now began tracking down encounter group leaders through the *Barb,* and finally found myself at San Francisco State College, where the Experimental College on campus was in the midst of transforming the structure of education.

My introduction to the scene was through Loren Jones. Loren is a rare combination of scholar and revolutionary. He had been initiated by one of the secret esoteric orders, and could make a candle flame do tricks at ten paces. He was short, due to a spine defect which kept him in continual pain, and wore a noble beard. In all, a kind of hippie Toulouse-Lautrec.

The Experimental College was one of a group of student organizations, along with the Black Student Union and the Third World Liberation Front, which was in the process of radicalizing the almost thirty thousand students on campus. In addition, there were the usual splinter groups of political crazies, SDS, PL, and ad hoc freak brigades who wanted everything from instant assassination of Reagan to an end of Western civilization.

The EC was, unquestionably, the most successful and least overtly threatening of all the groups. It was looked upon benignly by the administration because its courses consisted largely of things like astrology, dance, poetry, and the other unmartial arts. When I arrived in September, they were about to hold an open registration, to run for an entire day. The approach was simplicity itself. Anyone who wanted to teach wrote up his course description in a catalogue. On registration day, each would-be teacher would stand under a sign listing his course, and students would have a chance to dig on the person teaching as well as the formal catalogue blurb. The class size was limited by the appeal of the teacher. The college allowed no credits for any courses taken at the EC, but this didn't stop students from signing up for as many as six courses, while letting their official schoolwork drop.

The reason was clear. Most of the people at the EC were young, or knew what the young mind is about. The course descriptions covered a general area, but almost every course at the EC had a single subject matter: life. How to live well, fully. The aridity of the academic curriculum stood out in sharp contrast to the joyously pragmatic attitude of the counter-college. And the beauty of the entire scene was that the administration was so busy looking in the closets of the overtly political organizations that they missed the fact that the real revolution was taking place in that hotbed of freaks in the gaudily painted barracks at the center of campus. Because the EC was allowing the students to dance and laugh and exult, to let their minds roam freely, to take pride in their sex and demand honor in their relations with their fellow men. And this is what the right- and left-wing fascists cannot stand: the sheer exuberance of living. It is not a political question; it is a question of being.

That year, the registration was to take in over three thousand students, and this was only in its second year of functioning. Registration day was like a flea market of the mind, with every frustrated teacher, homegrown guru, and visionary in the Bay Area hawking his psychic wares to the young people coming through. It was held in the Gallery Lounge, a great flat building which someone had the sense to leave completely empty. Of course, everyone was stoned, on grass, on good vibrations, and the wild music of the young Hassidim from the House of Love and Prayer. It was a day of Renaissance, a birthday party for the new culture.

The EC itself was autocratically run, by the EC "staff." At their head was Evan Standard, a twenty-six-year-old leonine and pockmarked saint. He was gaunt, with teeth missing, and a shock of hair and beard that totally covered his face and shoulders. As with most of the heavies there, he was thoroughly well-read in all matters of the metaphysical and occult, mostly through an Oriental bias. His major mode of expression was the guffaw.

Loren Jones was his right-hand man. During meetings Evan would sit, his six-inch aura dominating the room, with Loren next to him, cooling off the vibes. The rest of the staff were second-stringers, good people but not in the same class as the boss. Later, when I had precipitated a crisis by attempting to force my admission to the staff, Evan blocked my entry and disillusioned the others, who were under the impression that the staff was a democratic group. At the meeting, Loren announced to the group, "Evan *is* the EC. And I am here to protect him. That's the way it is, and nobody here have any notions to the contrary." I had succeeded in blowing the lid off the scene, and for my pains suffered ostracism from the overlord and his underlings.

It is odd that the single most radical force on the campus should have been run dictatorially, and that period of my life once and for all dispelled the idea in my mind that there is something inherently better about democracy as a social form. I suspect that the health of a state depends on the quality of the people, and it doesn't matter what particular form they choose to express their sanity or their madness.

By registration day, I had written up a blurb for a workshop in "Relaxation, Awareness, and Breathing." At the time, I was floating in a more or less continual euphoria. The sheer joy of San Francisco, the golden rich September days, the freedom from all the habits of my New York life, came together to keep me permanently high. The campus was such a continual feast day that soon I had shed all the gray eastern film, and had begun going barefoot, wearing a leopard-skin cloak, carrying a wooden staff, and playing a harmonica instead of talking. It was a perfect time. I could do nothing wrong. If I danced in the street, I would have an appreciative audience. If I wanted a particular girl, I had only to smile at her.

I was getting very deeply into the power of dance and mime, learning that in any given communication, if one responds to breathing patterns, muscle tensions, and eye contact, and if one is sensitive to the nonverbal vibrations in any given group, then one is like the man with one eye in the land of the blind. I found that charisma was nothing more than letting this multileveled awareness, and its concomitant energy, glow. In short, I was becoming a strangely influential force, and the fear of the EC rulers had a basis in fact.

All around the Gallery Lounge we stood and sat. All the current legends were there, and as the morning progressed, and the crowds grew, and music swelled, and the grass circulated, the entire place began to lift off the ground. The vibes were so high that just to walk through the door was like smoking a joint of good-grade dope.

Michael Parker had the booth next to mine, and just to be in Michael's presence is the equivalent of a lick of acid, so by mid-afternoon I was infatuated with enlightenment. The energy poured out of me like sweat. When I went to the john, my eyes in the mirror were like strobe kaleidoscopes. The Spirit was in me, and the people saw. I started dancing, and soon, scores of students were flocking to the booth, wanting to sign up, not even knowing what it was I was teaching, not caring. It was the classic guru scene; one judged the master not by what he says, but by the force of life which flows through him.

By day's end, I had over two hundred people sign up for a workshop which was designed for no more than twelve. The other high tally was for Michael's Monday Night Class, and he drew almost three hundred. Michael continued his class even after the EC closed down, and eventually went on to become perhaps the foremost American-born spiritual teacher, with over fifteen hundred people coming every Monday night to hear his rap, and share in the circle of beauty and truth he and his family have created.

My first class was for a Wednesday night, and all that week, I prepared. I drew up a list of graduated exercises, beginning with deep physical relaxation, and going into mutual support workouts, and ending with group movement and chanting. The point was to get everyone into the same psychic space by relaxing the normal tensions of uptight daily life. There was a danger of creating a cheap instant-intimacy, such as the kind that Esalen thrives on, but I was guarding against that. It was possible to keep critical intelligence even in the midst of the most turgid touchie-feelies.

That Wednesday I held silence until evening, eating lightly, spending a good deal of time sitting quietly. I hitched to the campus, finding that a freer way of travel than driving, and loosened up with a light rap with the cats who were driving. On campus, I went to the Lounge, and spent an hour moving chairs and picking trash up off the floor. This was the necessary self-humbling that the religious cookbooks recommended for any holy venture.

I went out onto the grounds and sat under a tree, smoking three joints, and watching the evening star emerge from the growing dusk. I made peace with the universe, switched my consciousness onto No-Mind, and prepared to begin an adventure the parameters of which were totally unknown to me. At least, consciously. As always, the twin threads of sexuality and mysticism wove their fantastic pattern through all my actions, but the final result of that mix wasn't to be seen until four weeks later.

A hundred and ten people showed up. All young, all beautiful, all stoned. When the class began, I sat crosslegged on the floor, and watched all those eyes looking at me, waiting, expecting. All of my preparation steadied me, and I gazed slowly over the crowd which I had to transform into a single organism before three hours. Countless thoughts tumbled through my mind, so quickly and profusely that I couldn't even check them as they passed. I merely watched and let them register.

"What do they want?" I wondered. "Here are a bunch of kids who are healthy, pretty, and living in the most beautiful city of the richest nation on earth. They have access to some of the earth's most wondrous offerings. Their government is becoming militarily fascistic and their heads are being wooed by psychedelics. Their parents and teachers are wooden automatons for the most part. Why aren't they somewhere else, fucking or turning on or blowing up banks? What do they hope to get here, in this public place, from this stranger from New York?"

I checked my catalogue of basics: food, shelter, clothing, recognition, meditation, orgasms, truth, and love. The first three were out of my domain. So I went to the other five. Each of these people was starved for recognition; not the surface hello we give to one another. But every one of them wanted that deep inner part, that part that is most central, to be seen and known as valuable and beautiful. As far as meditation, it was clear that not a one of them had any notion what that meant. Those who were even at all familiar with the word had probably been introduced through one of the Maharishi-type charlatans who infest the nation with their lotus poses and self-induced visions. Orgasm was always a problem; men could ejaculate and women could clitorally twitch, but few could sail into that totally convulsive realm of pure vegetative release. Truth, of course, being practically nonexistent among the human race, was to be another necessary element, but the transmission of truth can never be articulated in any symbology whatsoever. And as for love, I put that on the shelf of hopefulness. The best thing to do was prime the subconscious with an awareness of the elements and then not consider them again.

The workshop was successful but unspectacular. I ran through several of the standard routines, including facial relaxation and eye contact, mutual massage and suggestion of imagery. That night I ended with an exercise I had originated, called "the Puppet." After having everyone go into very deep physical relaxation lying in the corpse pose, I had them imagine a guillotine above them, with the blade dropping down at intervals to chop off, one by one, each of the limbs and head. The sense of imagining one's body being cut to pieces allows a muscular relaxation not otherwise attained. At least, in most cases. Several of the people that night, when I said, "Now let the blade drop down and slice off your head," sat bolt upright, blinking in sheer terror. But, to paraphrase Lenin, "You can't make a revolution without blowing a few minds."

Afterward, I put on a recording of Ravi Shankar's, and led the group in a period of spontaneous movement, telling them to imagine that they were puppets, and that each of their severed parts was attached by strings to the fingers of a great puppet master. Using this artifice allowed them to let their bodies move without the usual tension clichés, and the total effect of over a hundred people moving easily and sensually was glorious. We ended by chanting Om, and when the class was over, the strangers had shared a moment of pleasant ease. I left very quickly, before anyone could talk to me; the night had exhausted me and I just needed to crash. What I didn't know was that my honest performance and sudden departure planted the seeds of a myth. The people began to whisper that a true holy man had come among them.

Meanwhile, the guru was having his problems. I had just begun a ménage with Rita and Leah. It was a blind attempt at union which swung between ecstasy and despair, during the course of which I learned how two women can make love, and have since been forever humbled in my own sexuality. We were swept up in the beauty of what happens when three people can, even for a brief time, become one organism on at least two levels of consciousness. But we also suffered the pain and paranoia which follows the tearing of the fabric, when all the delicacy of give-to-get builds higher and finer until the slim foundation of time-shared can't sustain the great elaborations of the erotic superstructure. We were at a point where I was finding out the difference between male chauvinism and manhood, and the women were struggling between the desire for wider communion and the biological instinct of possessiveness of the mate.

That week, my preparation for the class navigated the tricky rhythms of our troika. By the time Wednesday came, my subconscious was totally enmeshed in questions of human sexual relationship. I arrived only two hours early this time, cleaned up the Lounge in a hurry, and on my way back from smoking a joint sent up a prayer to Venus, which had just begun to glow. It was getting darker earlier as the year dipped toward winter.

Once again I put the crew through their paces. This time there were almost a hundred and fifty of them. When I started my opening rap, I found myself talking about sensuality. I spun an elaborate schema of the way in which sexuality tends to burn out the more delicate needs of touch and glance and breath, and ended by noting that many people wind up fucking someone just because they need to be held. The admiration from the psychically pubescent women in the class was palpable.

But I was feeling expansive and depleted from my efforts of the week. It suddenly came upon me that tonight I should teach the men how to make love to the women, how to be gentle and responsive. So, after the softening-up relaxation period, I broke the class down into groups of four, and led them into a mutual feeling session, in which three people massage the fourth, until all have been both active and passive. I took great pains to outline what to look for, what kinaesthetic clues lurked inside the body, and what could be learned from observing another's breathing and skin tone and subtle motions. Halfway through the exercise, the air started getting steamy. Everywhere I looked half-erect cocks bulged through jeans, female crotches yawned over the entire floor, and succulent buttocks contracted and expanded as unimaginable eddies of exquisite sensation ran through dozens of nearly virginal thighs.

By the end of that round, I was slightly out of control. I took an unexpected turn, and had them all lie down again, and once again took them on an inner voyage, feeling their bodies with their bodies, or letting the bodies be aware of themselves. But this time I lingered over the genitals, spinning out fantasies about what the inside of a cunt feels like, of what happens inside a penis when it expands. Aroused, half-hypnotized, willing, they let themselves be swayed, and soon sighs of rapture and moans of pleasure began to erupt. They were beginning to let it all hang out.

The music I used that night was from the Stones, which perfectly took the amorphous sexual flow and coagulated it into a driving hard rhythm. At the end of the first side of the album, everyone had blood in their eyes. I took the vibes down again, and ended with a large circle, with everyone's arms around everyone else's shoulders. Of course, with all that kundalini running free, the circle became electric, and soon, eyes closed, they were swaying in the single most beautiful jellyfish I had ever seen. I asked them to let sounds out, and within a minute the room was filled with all those different voices, each in a different pitch, with the whole blending into a giant sound of praise. My eyes began tearing, and I couldn't absorb any more, so before they finished, I quietly left.

I learned later that they stayed for a half hour after the class, not wanting to leave one another's physical presence, and talking about the mysterious man who comes to perform miracles and then leaves before anyone can speak to him.

During the next week, the thing with Leah and Rita fell totally apart. We reached the point where we were criticizing one another's method of washing dishes. The viciousness was barely ameliorated by its pettiness. We were all heartbroken, because we all loved the hurting moments when we sat at the kitchen table, holding hands before dinner, listening to the silence of the house. But the scene was beyond our ability to manage, and we knew it, and now had to do the deadly business of getting to hate one another before we could garner the energy to split.

I took refuge, as I often did in those days, in *The Tibetan Book of the Great Liberation.* Between the heavy blows dealt my mind by that book and the emotional upheaval I was experiencing, and the growing unreality of my scene at the college, I freaked. It suddenly occurred to me that I was gathering hubris at a rapid rate. The underbelly of megalomania showed its greenish light, and all of a sudden I saw myself as a charlatan, a breaker of hearts, and agreed with Evan that I was a black magician.

My mind turned around. I remembered that I had forgotten God, and had fallen into the modern heresy of thinking that man was the supreme entity in the universe, that I had forgotten my own limitations. I decided that I was leading the people astray, and during the next class, would call for a spiritual regeneration. That this fell in with the image they were forming of me as a spiritual leader was the type of coincidence that would have delighted Jung.

I got to the campus very early the next morning. To my surprise, strangers kept approaching me, asking me if they might join the class. One girl came up to me, and after some preliminary small talk, suddenly grabbed my hand and said urgently, "I can't come. Please help me. I know you can." I gave her my phone number and told her to call me in a few days. The scene was too much out of Feiffer to be erotic. Members of my class, as they recognized me sitting on the grass, would come up and sit silently in front of me for long periods of time and then, reverentially, get up and leave without saying a word. Without doing a single thing but following the inner logic of my madness to its most baroque extension, I was becoming a guru to an entire generation.

The third week's class was a masterpiece of metatheater. I *very* humbly cleaned up the Lounge this time, picking up every cigarette butt by hand. I found that four or five women were helping me, and I realized that my first group of inner disciples was forming. Then I sat on a piano bench in full lotus, and waited for the throngs to arrive. They came slowly and made a giant crowd at my feet. One thin blond girl came up and laid a bouquet of flowers before me. Here and there, joss sticks were lit.

And, in a phosphorescent flash before my third eye, the solution hit. To blend the erotic and the godly, the path was through Tantra.

My talk that night was all about that superhedonistic yoga of quintessential fucking, that marvelous ritual whereby color and scent and fabric and food and long, careful preparation go into making that consummate human action. I spoke of the way in which the male sits rigid and knowing, moving the kundalini up from the base of his spine to the thousand-petaled lotus above his head, while the female works in the ecstatic movements of Sirasvati until, at one grand moment, the male explodes in cosmic consciousness and full physical orgasm, and the female rides the tumultuous waves of universal orgasm, that of the Great Mother giving birth to existence itself.

Everyone got stoned on the image.

The class that night was all breathing, very slow movement, and exercises in penetrating perception. I did a very long facial relaxation, and then had everyone let themselves be seen in their full inner nakedness, while they gazed on all the others in that state. At the very end, I allowed the gentlest of touching to take place. It all went so beautifully that I forgot to check my meters, to see what kinds and levels of energy were building beneath the surface of appearances.

I asked them all to form a large circle, and begin closing in on the center, my idea being to bring together on the physical plane the communion that was taking place spiritually. But no sooner did that troupe of bodies pass a certain critical mass than the tension snapped, and in a flash the Gallery Lounge was a pile of writhing, meshing, groping bodies. I was horrified, much as the old Tibetan monk leading a group of novices in Tantric practices, and leaving the room for a minute to come back to find his charges fucking merrily on the floor.

It grew orgiastic. Hands grabbed cunts, mouths went to nipples, asses flashed and rolled. I stepped to the edge. "Stop," I cried. "Stop." As an answer, three pairs of arms reached up and grabbed me, and before I could react, I was pulled into the sea of flesh.

It was a most peculiar experience, for on the one hand I was sinking under the sheer sensuality of the scene, and at the same time I was trying to maintain my spiritual stance. It took me minutes to crawl out, and I fled from the scene, shaken. They went on like that for almost an hour and many of them went off by twos and threes and fours to the beach and various apartments.

During the following week, I struggled for the proper way to continue the class, but during that time, I was converted to Christianity. . . .

# The Whole Child:
# Summerhill and
# the First Street School

## George Dennison

In our own time, the most important example of freedom in education has been A. S. Neill's Summerhill school in England. It is a residence school—a community, really—and its laws and customs are worked out by all participants. In spite of the great popularity of Neill's book, *Summerhill: A Radical Approach to Child-Rearing*, the school itself still has an undeserved reputation for anarchy. Its actual distinctiveness lies not in the absence of regulations but in the kinds of regulations it makes use of, and in its manner of arriving at them. There is a General School Meeting every Saturday night. All questions pertaining to the life of the community are discussed here and are settled by vote. Where certain kinds of rules (e.g., bedtime regulations for the young) tend to survive in one basic form, others are changed frequently or refined. Penalties are extremely specific. One lonely boy, for example, was cured of stealing when his fellows voted to give him money for each offense.

But there is no need to describe Summerhill here. Most interested persons will have read the book by now, which in its paperback edition was a long-term best-seller in this country. Instead, I would like to quote from John Holt's

From *The Lives of Children: The Story of the First Street School* (Random House, 1969).

observation of the school, as it appeared in the *Bulletin of the Summerhill Society, USA,* in 1965:

> It was the young children, six, seven, and eight, who made the strongest impression on me. The older children, though free, seemed not to have had their freedom long enough to be able to relax with it and take it for granted. The little ones were quite different. Occasionally, very rarely, in a particularly happy family, I have seen little children who have seemed wholly secure, at ease, natural, and happy. But never before this meeting had I seen so many of them in one place, least of all in a school. They were joyous, spontaneous, unaffected. I wondered why this should be, and at the party I thought I saw why. More times than I could count, I would see a little child come up to a big one, and with a word, or a gesture, or a clutch of the hand, claim his attention. I never saw one rebuffed, or treated anything but lovingly. The big kids were always picking them up, hugging them, swinging them around, dancing with them, carrying them on their shoulders. For the little children, Summerhill was a world full of big people, all of whom could be enjoyed, trusted, and counted on. It was like living in an enormous family, but without the rivalries and jealousies that too often plague our too small and too possessive families. . . .
>
> One of the rules is that bedtime in the cottage, where the little kids live, is at 8:30. Further down the page I read another rule, obviously passed under pressure of necessity: "All kissing goodnight involving cottagers must be over by 8:30."

The two issues most frequently discussed by those who are interested in Summerhill—either for or against—are its sexual mores and the children's freedom to stay away from classes.

In sexual matters, Neill's point of view is a simple one: the evils of repression can be avoided. We are not *sexual* beings, but human beings. Sexuality cannot be excluded from our lives; neither will it dominate our lives under conditions of freedom. Neill detests pornography, prurience, and priggishness. To be anti-sex is to be anti-life.

In short, sex is not treated as an evil at Summerhill. In

fact—so I infer from Neill's pages, and so I gather from talks with Summerhill alumni—it is not much "treated" at all. The boys and girls are let alone. One might say that nature takes its course—but the fact is that nature always takes its course. I doubt if there is any more sex at Summerhill than at American high schools, but certainly the air is cleaner than ours, the lives of the students freer of cant and hypocrisy and lame-duck psychology.

Neill speaks often of the "free child," and in many respects his book is intended as a manual of child-rearing. The idea of "sexual freedom," however, is not a Neillian idea. We hear it rather from his critics and from some few enthusiasts, whom Neill on several occasions has taken pains to correct. One of Neill's great virtues is that he keeps his eyes on persons. We tend to do the opposite here in America, and lose ourselves among issues. The distinction is crucial in practice, and is worth going into in some detail.

The phrase "sexual freedom," like almost every phrase involving the word *freedom,* is a polemical abstraction. Its background is a long series of heated arguments. When we turn from these arguments to the phenomena of lives, we see immediately that what we call *freedom* is not ours to give, and what we call *sexuality* cannot be defined by kissing, caressing, and making love. I have listened to arguments about sexual freedom at conferences sponsored by the Summerhill Society in New York. They were often touching, almost always excited and urgent. Adults cannot speak of this issue except in tones of longing, regret, resentment, anxiety, bitterness. One finds housewives in the audience who seem to be speaking of their children, but whose tones and facial expressions are saying, "I am yearning for love! Absolve me of my sexual guilt!"; and others who, in effect, cry bitterly, "I was denied it, and by God I won't grant it to anyone else!" Some speak with sadness and regret, and soon find themselves reassuring the anxious ones. Both band together and attack the authoritarians in their midst. I have observed all this when adolescent students were also present. One had only to look at their faces to understand the truth: they preferred the dignity of being let alone, but come what may, they would certainly fuck. Nor were they interested in "sexual freedom" but in Jane and Leroy, Harriet and Dick. Love, after all, is love. It may tolerate poets, but *spokesmen* are anathema, whether they're for or against.

Yet these young persons were extremely interested in the arguments. There was something they shared immediately with the adults.

Aside from regret for the past, and the anxious fear of regret itself, the adults were not speaking (either pro or con) of the actual behavior of particular young persons. They were speaking of their own willingness to sanction sexuality, or their desire to confine it. Nor were the young who were present worried very much that their own pleasures would be denied them. They would outwit the adults, as always. They would tell lies, etc. Yet they were extremely interested, and their interest, like that of the adults, lay in the question of sanction.

Sanction is not a matter of *what happens,* but of methods of control and ideals of life: what sort of world must we build? The young understand this question with great immediacy. And they want a great deal more than "sexual freedom." They want *wholeness.* They do not want to lie and evade and suffer guilt, but to affirm themselves in the largest possible harmony of self and society, passion and intellect, duty and pleasure. They want the esteem of their elders, and they cannot help but want the excitement that rises so imperiously in their own experience. They know very well, too, that where sanction is involved, the attitudes of a few teachers are mere grains on a sandy shore. The problem begins in infancy and runs through the whole of society. Slogans and attitudes are of little value, and there is a terrible, naïve *hubris* in the behavior of a teacher who believes that he can sanction sexuality by conferring freedom. He can no more sanction it than sanction the law of gravity. All he can do is cease to attempt to control the young. Beyond this he can ally himself with the student's quest for wholeness. Here the teacher's own quest for wholeness is extremely valuable. Life being what it is, there is no man who can stand before the young and acclaim himself an exemplar of liberated energies. The "do as I do" cannot be put in this form, for if he boasts of sexual freedom, the young will wonder about the propaganda: why does he boast? Why is so much energy being devoted to polemics? A good example of this attitude can be found in the writings of Henry Miller, which carry a heavy theme of self- and sexual liberation. One observes, however, that the liberated self constructs a peculiar and hermetic environment, one of proselytizing: endless rhapsodies on liberation, preaching freedom in order to retain the illusion of it. The loss is obvious: it is the world. Euphoria, in this context, might be defined as anxiety masquerading as pride.

In life, as in art, the healing truth is the whole truth. The libertarian teacher cannot give freedom. He can only cease to control. He cannot sanction sexuality. He can only seek to allay guilt. He cannot eradicate sexual embarrassment either in himself or in his students by an act of will, but he *can* identify embarrassment as a problem, just as he can hold forth a human ideal in which hatred of the body, distrust of emotion, and repugnance toward sex will find no part. At best, the libertarian can demonstrate reason, faith, generosity, and hope struggling against the damages he himself has already sustained and which he hopes to mitigate in the lives of his students. This attitude is a far cry from the banner-waving of *sexual freedom*.

Let me give an example to make this more plain. I visited a school ostensibly modeled on Summerhill, but in fact (so I believe) not much like it. I noticed two teen-agers who were pathologically depressed. I learned that they were suffering severe conflicts with their parents. I was informed, too, that their parents were small-minded, narrow, repressive, status-seeking *petit bourgeois*—which is to say that the suffering of the two students had been invested with a programmatic radical meaning: their detestation of their parents appeared as a form of loyalty to the school. The two students, in short, were in a hopeless quandary, being tugged in opposite directions by self-interested adults. To make matters worse, the tugging at school was largely *sub rosa*, implicit rather than overt, and the foreground was filled by "freedom," that is by lack of contact, lack of guidance, lack of structure, lack of everything that young people experiencing such disorders absolutely require. Let me hasten to say that such lacks as these cannot be filled by rules and regulations. They must be filled by persons—and not just any persons, but persons capable of true encounter and properly motivated for work with the young. The problem at this school was that the director himself regarded staff and students less as people than as events in his own protracted crusade against middle-class America. The faculty, too, consisted of True Believers—and I had never before seen such a listless, resentful bunch, or heard the words "creativity" and "spontaneity" bandied about quite so often.

When the young are experiencing conflicts within themselves, it is disastrous for the teacher to "take sides"—and no vice is more prevalent among teachers than taking sides against the parents. What the student needs is not an ally in one quarter of his own psychic economy—which tends to perpetuate his conflict precisely as conflict—but an ally in the world. This is what I mean by supporting his quest for wholeness. It is the difference between saying, "You are right to detest your parents," and "You are obviously suffering because you detest your parents." It is the difference between saying, "Transcend your sexual guilt! Be free!" and saying, "Let us take your guilt seriously. How do you experience it?" I am not suggesting that every teacher be a psychotherapist. I am insisting that every teacher put himself in relation with the person before him, and not with one portion of that person's conflicts. Just to the extent that a teacher will do this, he will recognize, too, that sexuality permeates everything and it cannot be set aside and given special treatment. When, in the classroom, the child is allowed to speak freely and experience the creative unity of feelings, hunches, thoughts, humor, etc., we are in fact supporting a positive sexuality. When we create conditions that do away with shame and self-contempt, we are supporting a positive sexuality. And so on.

The notion of "sexual freedom," in short, is another of the many symptoms of the massive sickness of our world. It is not an idea we can use, but an idea that needs to be dissolved until its atoms come to rest again in the phenomena of life. It would be helpful, too, to recognize that sexuality is a world phenomenon, not merely an individual one. There is an ecology of the emotions. No better example can be found than that of the hippies of New York's East Village. They are remarkably good-looking and sweet-natured young people. They believe earnestly in sexual freedom and the beauty of the human body. And they act upon their beliefs. But alas! alas! the erotic élan of youth simply isn't there. And all their modest or desperate bravery, and their earnest believing, cannot put it there. The conditions of their lives are decisive. Their lot is anxious, insecure, badly nourished, cut off from the future, alienated from the past, anonymous in the present. They are haunted by the bomb and deadened by crises of identity. Where will the joy of life come from?

Another example, showing again the meager effect of ideology and opinion where such broad, primitive phenomena as sexuality are involved: I attended a showing at an avant-garde film house, and after the main course a little divertissement was thrown on the screen for laughs, one of those all-girl-orchestra "shorts" of the early 1930s, two dozen marimba players in low-cut gowns and long-enduring smiles. Members of the audience (not all, for I think some must have felt as I did) laughed complacently at their provincial style and the bouncy banality of their music. None of that meant much to me. I was absolutely astonished by the sensual appearance of those girls. Their smiles were in fact naïve smiles of pleasure, their eyes were bright, their faces vivacious, their arms and shoulders softly rounded and relaxed, and there was something melting and fluid in the way their torsos rode upon their hips. Would any one of them have come out for "sexual freedom"? One might well suppose that they had few attitudes at all, and if asked would simply affirm for the moment the most conventional—and by our standards, retrograde—morality. But that was pre-war America, not yet so hugely organized, still rich in space and time, its future undarkened by the bomb and the present by unending war, hot and cold. I need not list the other differences. Flesh and psyche were simply better off, and they certainly looked it. The lights went on and the girls in the audience stood up, adjusting their plastic coats and mini-skirts. Some were still smiling. All, most likely, were digesting the Pill they had taken that morning. And how put-upon they looked! I do not mean that they were spiritless. Not at all. There was something strong in them, something admirable. But the verve and color was all in their clothes. Their eyes were lightless or fixed, their faces drawn tight by lines of strain. Tension showed in their throats and the unyielding motions of their gaits. Some, no doubt, had a style in bed, as they had a style in clothes and a style in cars. They would quite routinely speak in affirmation of sex—and confess to the psychotherapist that the issue was not sex but meaning, joy, life, passion, love, and describe a nightmare of growing cold, not unrelated to the style of being "cool." As for the therapist, he will have heard the identical story, in essence, a thousand times. These tales are not produced by family strife alone, or by America destroying itself in isolation. They are the landscape of the modern world.

If we want to release and sustain and civilize, in the true sense, the sexuality of the young, we can begin by putting "sexuality" back into the person. It is the whole child we are interested in. We can increase his security, treat him with justice and consideration, respect his pride of life, value the independence of his spirit, be his ally in a world that needs to be changed. We can do nothing more directly than this about his sexuality.

The practice at Summerhill is a case in point. The security of the individual, his constructive role in the community, the absence of punishment and coercion, the student's responsible awareness of other lives—these things taken all together promote a healthy, positive sexuality for the same reason that they promote unusual courtesy (many visitors have remarked on this) and vigorous self-reliance: the whole person is encouraged to flourish. If many problems still remain, it is not surprising, since Summerhill is a small part of a large and troubled world.

Nor is it odd that some few of Neill's disciples should have distorted his meaning. This happens inevitably to every innovator—another way of saying this is that Neill is not a Summerhillian, no more than Freud was a Freudian, or Reich a Reichian. Pioneers of this kind emerge into history in severe conflict with the value systems of their youth. In their own persons they represent profound resolutions of conflicting experience. Their conflicts, however, tend to become background. I mean that their chief appearance in the writing is a stylistic one. Freud, for example, was adopted as the patron saint of the French Surrealists, but after an interview with their leader, Breton, he refused to take seriously their use of his insights. They had not understood him. For one thing they had paid no attention to the meaning of his style—his reverence for reason, and for ordinary virtue—but had seized upon the revelation of the unconscious as if it were the key to the whole of life. Reich, similarly, believed in the self-regulation of the organism. But by *regulation* he meant its harmony in a world which included rationality and duty. Just so, the character of Neill was not formed in a Summerhillian universe, but in a difficult world containing both traditional and revolutionary values. This world is present at Summerhill in the person of Neill, which is to say that many of its values are present by active demonstration, though they may not be much spoken of: values of rectitude, courage, patience, duty, pragmatic common sense. These are much in evidence, too, in Neill's writing—which helps to account, I think, for its popularity in this country, surfeited as we are with the voiceless "objectivity" of our hordes of experts. If some few of Neill's disciples have minimized these things, it is because they have seized impatiently upon certain insights, namely those which justify their own anger at a world that has injured them.

Summerhill is our chief point of reference, too, for the question of compulsory attendance. This is an issue much discussed by libertarian teachers, and is one that will become important on a larger scale if the present liberalizing tendency in education should ever really alter our public schools. Should we compel attendance or not? Neill tells us that at Summerhill the children are in no way pressured into attending classes. Unfortunately, he does not tell us enough about what happens in the meantime. Some few purists that I have observed have bent over backwards on this issue, creating a kind of vacuum between themselves and their students in order to give the students' volition enough room to mature. This, it seems to me, is an error. It arises, in good part, from posing the problem in terms of attendance and compulsion.

But the whole issue, as we know it in this country, testifies to a really peculiar anxiety and lack of faith on the part of adults. Would children really abandon school if they were no longer compelled to attend? Or, more properly, would the acquisition of skills and knowledge, and the participation in large-scale social life with their peers suddenly lose all attractiveness? The idea of school—though not in its present bureaucratized form—is one of the most powerful social inventions that we possess. It rests squarely on the deepest of necessities and draws on motives we could not disavow even if we wished to. Teaching is one of the few natural functions of adults. Vis à vis the young, we simply cannot escape it. Further, our legitimate demand of the young—that in one style or another they be worthy inheritors of our world—is deeply respected by the young themselves. They form their notions of selfhood, individual pride, citizenship, etc., in precisely the terms that we put forward, converting our demands into goals and even into ideas of glory. I cannot believe that all this is so feeble that we need to rest the function of education upon acts of compulsion, with all the damage that this entails.

If compulsion is damaging and unwise, its antithesis—a vacuum of free choice—is unreal. And in fact, we cannot deal with the problem in these terms, for the real question is not, "What shall we do about classes?" but, "What shall we do about our relationships with the young? How shall we deepen them, enliven them, make them freer, more amiable, and at the same time more serious? How shall we broaden the area of mutual experience?" If these things can be done, the question of school attendance, or classroom attendance, will take a simpler and more logical form, will lie closer to the fact that classroom instruction is after all a *method* (one among many) and deserves to be criticized in terms of its efficiency. It is not the be-all and end-all of a child's existence.

Let me put this in terms of our experience at the First Street School. We were located in Manhattan's East Village, where we rented classrooms in the old Emanu-El Midtown Y. Our twenty-three children were black, white, and Puerto Rican in about equal proportions. Most were poor. Many were on welfare. There were three full-time teachers and one part-time, an obviously luxurious teacher/pupil ratio, but a realistic one considering that about half of our children were "problem cases." As at Summerhill, the children were free to refuse instruction. But what does this mean in practice? Where does the refusal begin? And the teacher's insistence? Is the teacher sitting in the classroom, and the child simply refuses to go in? I have spoken earlier in these pages of thirteen-year-old José, and of how he could read Spanish at the age of seven when he first arrived from Puerto Rico, and of how, after six years in the public schools of New York he could read neither English nor Spanish. Let me refer to him again in order to make clear that *lessons* and *refusals* are small events occurring within a large and relatively powerful context. If we want to know their meaning, we must find out what their context is. For José, the context was something like this:

1. He was thirteen, and was disadvantaged even among his peers because he could not read. He did his best to hide his mortification, but his suffering was obvious, especially in his endless bluffing, which at times veered dangerously into a world of dreams. He was convinced that he was stupid, and he was afraid to expose himself once again to failure—yet he wanted desperately to learn.

2. We established a relationship. This was not difficult, for I liked him, though liking him would not have been essential. We spent several weeks getting to know each other, roughly three hours a day of conversations, games in the gym,

outings, etc. We lived in the same neighborhood and saw each other on the streets. He knew me as George, not as "Teacher."

3. He understood immediately that our school was different, that the teachers were present for reasons of their own and that the kind of concern they evinced was unusual, for there were no progress reports, or teacher ratings, or supervisors. Yet this concern, which appeared so unusual in a school setting, was identical with the everyday concern of his relatives and grown-up neighbors, who often asked him about his schoolwork and were obviously serious when they expressed their hopes for his future.

4. He understood that I had interests of my own, a life of my own that could not be defined by the word *teacher*. And he knew that he, though not a large part of my life, was nevertheless a part of it.

Now given this background, what must José have thought about my wanting to teach him to read? For I did want to, and I made no bones about it. He saw that I considered it far more important than many of the fleeting feelings he expressed or exhibited.

The fact is, he took it for granted. It was the right and proper relationship, not of teacher and student, but of adult and child—for his relatives wanted him to read, and so did his neighbors, and if it were not for the dreadful pressures of life in the slums, among which are the public institutions and the general hatred thereof, many of them could have taught him. But the idea occurred to no one, least of all José.

And so I did not wait for José to decide for himself. When I thought that the time was ripe, I insisted that we begin our lessons. My insistence carried a great deal of weight with him, since for reasons of his own he respected me. Too, his volition, in any event, could arise only from a background in which I myself already figured, with my own interests and my own manifestation of an adult concern he was accustomed to everywhere but in school. He did *not* feel that his own motives were no concern of mine. No child feels this. This belongs to the hang-ups of adolescence and the neuroses of the hippies. To a child, the motives of adults belong quite simply to the environment. They are like icebergs or attractive islands: one navigates between, or heads straight for them. The child's own motives, similarly, are projected outward; they become occasions for dissimulation or closer

contact. It is because of this that both affection and straight-
out conflict come so easily. They come inevitably, and they
belong, both together, to the teaching/learning experience.

My own demands, then, were an important part of José's
experience. They were not simply the demands of a teacher
nor, either, of an adult, but belonged to my own way of caring
about José. And he sensed this. There was something he
prized in the fact that I made demands on him. This became
all the more evident once he realized that I wasn't simply
processing him, that is, grading, measuring, etc. And when he
learned that he *could* refuse—could refuse altogether, could
terminate the lesson, could change its direction, could insist
on something else—our mutual interest in his development
was taken quite for granted. We became collaborators in the
business of life.

Obviously, if I had tried to compel him, none of this would
have been possible. And if I had made no demand—had
simply waited for him to come to class—I would in some
sense have been false to my own motives, my own engagement in the life of the school and the community. In his eyes I
would have lost immediacy, would have lost reality, as it
were, for I would have seemed, more and more, like *just* "a
teacher." What he prized, after all, was this: that an adult,
with a life of his own, was willing to teach him.

How odd it is to have to say this! What a vast perversion of
the natural relations of children and adults has been worked
by our bureaucratized system of public education! It was
important to José that I was not just a teacher, but was a
writer as well, that I was interested in painting and had
friends who were artists, that I took part in civil rights
demonstrations. To the extent that he sensed my life stretch-
ing out beyond him into (for him) the unknown, my meaning
as an adult was enhanced, and the things I already knew and
might teach him gained the luster they really possess in life.
This is true for every teacher, every student. No teacher is
just a teacher, no student just a student. The life-meaning
which joins them is the *sine qua non* for the process of
education, yet precisely this is destroyed in the public schools
because everything is standardized and the persons are made
to vanish into their roles. This is exactly Sartre's definition of
*inauthenticity*. I am reminded here, too, of how often John
Dewey, and in our own time Paul Goodman and Elliot
Shapiro, have urged the direct use of the community. The

world *as it exists* is what the young are hungry for—and we give them road maps, mere diagrams of the world-at-a-distance.

What I have just described of my relations with José might also be said of the other teachers and their pupils. Some were perhaps more demanding than I; nevertheless, all of the children could refuse. They needed a good reason, and they had to stand up to the adults. But they discovered that good reasons were respected. Boredom, for instance, is a good reason. The beautiful days of spring are good reasons. An ardent desire for something else is a good reason. Anxiety is a good reason. So is a headache or a toothache. And there are many things which if they arise during the course of a lesson deserve and must be given full precedence, such things as considerations of justice, self-respect, friendship. We and the children, in short, were in an ongoing experience of attraction and repulsion, of cooperation and conflict. Out of this flexible and many-faceted encounter, the actual structure of our time together evolved. The essential thing was the absence of compulsion. For every child there was always *a way out* and *a way in,* and—most important—a Bill of Personal Rights equal to that of the teachers. The children *could* win—not by availing themselves of an empty foreground of "freedom," but by encountering the adults head-on. It was a noisy school, as should be, though often, as should be, an electrically quiet one.

It is so easy to underestimate the importance of conflict that I would like to stress that it is both inevitable and desirable—I mean desirable in a developmental sense, for it certainly hurts a teacher's ears and frays his nerves. I am referring, of course, to the noisy conflicts, the kinds that *do* arise, and that only rarely have a parliamentary outcome. It boils down to this: that two strong motives exist side by side and are, innately, not antagonistic but incongruous. The one is that we adults are entitled to demand much of our children, and in fact lose immediacy as persons when we cease to do so. The other is that the children are entitled to demand that they be treated as individuals, since that is what they are. The rub is this: that we press our demands, inevitably, in a far more generalized way than is quite fitting for any particular child. And there is nothing in this process that is self-correcting. We must rely upon the children to correct us. They'll do it in their own interests, however, not in ours. In fact, they'll throw us off, perhaps with much yelling and jumping, like a man in a pair of shoes that pinch his feet. Let any teacher think back over the course of a month and ask himself how often this has occurred—and ask himself, too, if he would knowingly eliminate it, however much he might like to in the interests of his nerves. These mutual adjustments occur steadily in a broad, broad stream, and we notice everything about them—their noise, duration, obduracy, etc.—everything but the fact that their additive shape is beautifully rational and exceeds anything we might invent by the exercise of our wits.

I must admit that I have mentioned conflict just here because I have always been annoyed by the way some Summerhillians speak of love, of "giving love," or "creating an atmosphere of love." I have noticed, not infrequently, that the "love" of such enthusiasts is actually inhibited aggression. But this is by the way. The point itself, however, is worth making: we cannot "give love" to children. If we do feel love, it will be for some particular child, or some few, and we will not give *it* but give ourselves, because we are much more in the love than it is in us. What we *can* give to all children is attention, forbearance, patience, care, and, above all, justice. This last is certainly a form of love: it is—precisely—love in a form that *can* be given, given without distinction to all, since just this is the anatomy of justice; it is the self-conscious, thoroughly generalized human love of humankind. This can be seen negatively in the fact that while a child (past infancy) can survive, grow, and—if not flourish—do well enough in an environment that is largely without love, his development in an environment that is largely without justice will be profoundly disturbed. The absence of justice demands a generalized suspicion of others and alters the sense of reality down to its very roots. The environments I have just referred to are not hypothetical, but institutional. The former is an orphanage I had a chance to observe; the latter is Youth House, a New York detention home.

I have said nothing of the times when the children don't want to go to class. What happens then? But there are no such times, any more than there are times when we adults cross the street because we don't want to stay on the same side, or go to a ball game because we don't want to stay in the house. Often, at First Street, the children knew fairly well what they wanted to do instead of sit in class: a trip, a picnic, a project of some sort. But usually they did not know *quite* what they wanted, though a lesson was clearly not it. Some dim figure of what they wanted—perhaps of what they needed—was present in their minds and they could not quite see it or name it. And isn't it traditionally the role of adults to help them discover what will truly engage them? It is part of a teacher's job, then, to help his students find out what to do instead of sitting in class. Here is an example. The five older boys had passed through a period of strife (largely racial) and had suddenly become united, almost as a gang. The warm weather had arrived. They were restless, hated the idea of lessons, ran out of the school, ran back, milled around in the hall, went out again and sat on the front steps, moping ferociously. They didn't know what to do. We suggested that they go out on bikes. That wasn't quite right. And they didn't want dodge-ball or games in the park. They didn't want a supervised trip, either. It became apparent that something real was lurking in their minds, something they vaguely agreed upon or vaguely sensed was important. What was it? One of the other teachers intuited what it was: they wanted to do something *together,* some shared and purposeful activity that would confirm their new relationships. She suggested that they make a pool table—and that was it! They trooped off to the lumberyard and bought a big piece of plywood, and strips for the sides, and some foam rubber, and green felt, and glue, and a coping saw to make the holes, and a file to smooth them. They worked at their table almost a week and it came out surprisingly well, and they used it when it was finished. And it was evident all along that this table was an embryonic clubhouse—exactly what they needed.

In sum, we cannot, as teachers, define our relations with children in terms of lessons, or even school. School itself is merely one feature of the ongoing relationship of children and adults. Or rather, it should be. Our society as it is is dreadfully closed to children, dreadfully compartmentalized. And between home and school there is no provision at present but the truant officer.

In comparison with residence schools in the country, we were fortunate in having the city all around us. I am not thinking so much of the activities that were available as of the fact that in our relationships with the students we were not so unremittingly confined to our roles as teachers, as if to say that classes and lessons were all that we shared with them. We shared the world with them, and this brought lessons, and school itself, into a much healthier and more realistic perspective. We tried to understand our school in the larger setting of the children's lives. Their sexual interest in each other—which was largely horseplay—never appeared to us as infractions of rules, but as the inevitable and necessary energy of a growth that would continue, with or without us. So too, the refusal of a lesson meant something real, and one searched for its meaning not in the routines of the school, but in the life of the child. Family and neighborhood events, our chance encounters with the children in the street, and their frequent visits to our homes, the growing friendships between parents and teachers and among parents themselves—one would say that all this was the true context of the school, but in fact these things and our school were all of a piece. I have mentioned the wholeness that is desired instinctively by the young. The most accurate way to describe it would be in evolutionary terms: life perpetuates itself in whole forms. Our psychological and physical *ideal types,* the perfect specimens of our botanic plates—these are not ideals at all, but represent quite accurately the inevitable tendencies of growth. We need do nothing to *create* wholeness. Wholeness is a natural norm. The necessary thing is not to destroy it.

# The Exploding Arts

We like books that have a lot of *dreck* in them, matter which presents itself as not wholly relevant (or indeed, at all relevant) but which, carefully attended to, can supply a kind of "sense" of what is going on. This "sense" is not to be obtained by reading between the lines (for there is nothing there, in those white spaces) but by reading the lines themselves—looking at them and so arriving at a feeling not of satisfaction exactly, that is too much to expect, but of having read them, of having "completed" them.

—Donald Barthelme, *Snow White*

I am for the art of underwear and the art of taxicabs. I am for the art of ice cream cones dropped on concrete. I am for the blinking art, lighting up the night. I am for falling, splashing, wiggling, jumping, going on and off. I am for the art of fat truck-tires and black eyes. I am for Kool Art, 7-up Art, Pepsi Art, Sunkist Art, Dro-bomp Art, Vam Art, Pamryl Art, San-O-Med Art, 39 cents Art and 9.99 Art.

—Claes Oldenburg, *Environments Situations Spaces*

One fine morning she turned on that
  New York station.
She couldn't believe what she heard at all.
She started dancin' to that fine fine music.
Her life was saved by rock and roll.

—Lou Reed, "Rock and Roll"

The editor and critic Theodore Solotaroff tells a funny/sad story on himself in the course of his essay about Wanting to Be a Writer in the Fifties, "Silence, Exile, and Cunning" (*New American Review* No.8, January 1970). University educated in an irredeemably serious era, Solotaroff was in thrall to the prevailing mystiques about literature: the Stephen Dedalus archetype of the writer as heroic isolate, the later models of radical alienation and renunciation provided by Beckett and Genêt, the cult of the masterpiece fostered by the High Moderns, the Flaubertian insistence on an impossibly high standard of craft and the prevailing air of religiosity lent to the whole enterprise by T.S. Eliot. As a result, he spent most of the Fifties laboring in understandable artistic constipation trying to achieve a handful of stories that would have the requisite gem-like perfection of surface and the resonant depths. The irony, one you don't have to have gone to graduate school to appreciate, was that none of the rich life he managed to live as a young husband, professional waiter, psychiatric attendant, office temporary, gardener and gambler got anywhere near his fiction. It didn't seem to him to be the stuff you could make Art from.

The Fifties weren't any easier for painters. The scholarly theorist of the Abstract Expressionists, Robert Motherwell,

had asserted that every painting was a response to the entire
history of art that had gone before it, and had written as well
that "it is the artists who guard the spiritual in the modern
world." Barnett Newman, Clyfford Still, Mark Rothko,
David Smith and other Abstract Expressionists were vocal in
their declarations of the heroic dimensions of their struggle to
create a great indigenous American art, and of the tragic
content of their outsized abstractions.

It is against this background of an almost impossible
burden of seriousness that we can best appreciate the liberating quality of the style and sensibility of the characteristic art
of the Sixties. In literature fresh winds of vulgarity, playfulness, experimentation and a new kind of comic hysteria made
writing possible again, if still problematic. In the visual arts
irony, formalism, impersonality and the determination to
explore, in Robert Rauschenberg's much-quoted formula,
the gap between art and life, demolished the notion of art as a
secular cathedral and gave it a new accessibility. Above all, in
both realms there was an eagerness to exploit the unself-
conscious energies of popular culture artifacts too declassé to
notice or utilize in the Fifties: comic books, advertising and
especially film and popular music. In a word, Pop.

A good place to begin to examine the complexities of this
shift is Philip Roth's influential essay "Writing American
Fiction." Roth, not incidentally a friend of Solotaroff's,
emerged from a similar literary background and felt the
similar pull of high seriousness. In that essay he discussed the
difficulties of the conventional literary sensibility (circa 1960)
in connecting with the stupefying quality of postwar American life, delivering one of the most influential statements on
the writer's situation in the postwar years. Roth acutely
diagnosed the directions and strategies the fiction writer is
likely to adopt when realism, imaginatively speaking, seems
beside the point.

Roth's own work provides an excellent case in point. His
*Letting Go* (1962) and *When She Was Good* (1967) were
respectably conventional novels. But in 1969 his *Portnoy's
Complaint,* a hilarious comic exercise in the return of the
repressed—Alexander Portnoy's life as a guilt-ridden Jewish
son, as told to his analyst—made Roth the most notorious
writer in America. The novel, narrated at a manic pitch and
hysterically frank about loathsome male adolescent practices,
re-created the Oedipal complex as a situation comedy and

was strongly reminiscent of another renegade Jewish monologist, Lenny Bruce.

The catch-all term for this kind of calculated incorrigibility was "black humor," a literary vogue of the Sixties in which *Portnoy's Complaint* was a late, but completely successful, entry. Morris Dickstein, in an illuminating discussion of black humor in his book *The Gates of Eden,* assigns Roth to the category of "verbal" black humorists, a school that also includes Stanley Elkin (*Boswell, A Bad Man, Criers and Kibitzers, Kibitzers and Criers, The Dick Gibson Show*), Bruce Jay Friedman (*The Dick, Stern,* and also as editor of the anthology *Black Humor*), Terry Southern (*Candy, Red-Dirt Marijuana* and *The Magic Christian,* for my money one of the few books that can literally injure you with laughter) and even Saul Bellow in his more frantic moments, such as *Herzog.* Black humor trafficked in the strategies of aggression, outrage and perversity, and may be seen as a response to the situation Roth described in "Writing American Fiction": If you can't bring yourself to do justice to the sickening American scene, then do it the most outlandish injustice. Naturally, however, the ante of outrage was upped with each book, and the weak suit of the verbal black humorists was precisely the need to top themselves and each other, book after book.

But Dickstein also isolates a darker, more durable strain of black humor, one he calls the structural. His discussion, excerpted here, of some of the best novels in this genre—Joseph Heller's *Catch-22,* Kurt Vonnegut's *Mother Night* and Thomas Pynchon's *V* and *The Crying of Lot 49*—shows how eerily accurate these works of deadly comedy were in mirroring our collective paranoia. Their ostensible milieu may have been World War II or Nazi Germany, or Fifties New York, but the real subject of these books was the secret history of our time. Alfred Kazin, in his masterful study of postwar American fiction, *The Bright Book of Life,* maintains that these novelists were in fact writing about the apocalyptic "Next War"—"a war which will be without limits and without meaning, a war that will end when no one is alive to fight it."

This selection barely scratches the surface of the fascinating variety of riches in the American fiction of the 1960s. Any decade in which such writers (in addition to those mentioned above) as Robert Coover, John Updike, E. L. Doctorow, Joan Didion, Ken Kesey, Leonard Michaels, Ronald Sukenick,

Harry Matthews, Thomas Berger, Ishmael Reed, William Burroughs, Joseph McElroy, Grace Paley, Don DeLillo, Walker Percy and Donald Barthelme emerged, and in which such writers of older vintage as John Barth, John Cheever, Flannery O'Connor, Bernard Malamud, James Baldwin, William Styron, Vladimir Nabokov and John Hawkes did notable work as well has to be reckoned as some kind of golden period. A selected bibliography of Sixties fiction appears at the end of this book.

Susan Sontag also wrote two characteristically "difficult" and European-feeling novels in the Sixties, *The Benefactor* (1963) and *Death Kit* (1967). But it was as an essayist and polemicist of rigor, vision and forbidding range and erudition that she made her strongest impact. Her 1966 collection *Against Interpretation* is without question the most influential statement of the new aesthetic thinking necessary to appreciate the bewildering changes that were well under way in the arts by that time. Her favorite targets of attack were the literary intellectuals who held sway in Anglo-American circles. She castigated them repeatedly for their tendencies to discuss the form and content of works of art as separable qualities and to interpret them unto death—psychoanalytically, textually, politically, anthropologically. As she wrote in the title essay, "Today is . . . a time when the project of interpretation is largely reactionary, stifling. Like the fumes of the automobile and of heavy industry which befoul the urban atmosphere, the effusions of interpretations of art poison our sensibilities." This essay ends with the clarion call, "In place of a hermeneutics we need an erotics of art."

Just how this "erotics" of art might work receives its clearest formulation in the essay reprinted here, "One Culture and the New Sensibility." In contrast to C.P. Snow's declaration of two mutually exclusive cultures in the modern world, the literary/humanistic and the scientific, Sontag notes that science and the arts alike are progressing in tandem, and that the aim of art is no longer the stimulation of (wonderful phrase!) "the Matthew Arnold apparatus" of moral sentiment, but the modification of sensation and consciousness. This open-ended new sensibility could receive with equal delight and aesthetic intelligence Pop art, camp artifacts, Godard films, Rauschenberg combine paintings, literary pornography, science fiction movies, *Marat/Sade,* underground film epics and Motown.

Sontag's calls for a species of intellectual hedonism were understandably regarded by many established critics as so many hand grenades lobbed in their direction. But she remains the most instructive writer we have on the anti-romantic aesthetics of the Sixties and the ways the revolutionary explosions in the arts paralleled and fed upon the radical politics. In fairness, it should be noted that Sontag has retreated considerably today from these combative critical positions. She is now inclined to attack Leni Riefenstahl's *Triumph of the Will,* for instance, for its propagandistic content, and in a recent interview in *The New York Times,* (November 11, 1980) stated that "A decade long residence in the '60s, with its inexorable conversion of moral and political radicalisms into 'style' has convinced me of the perils of overgeneralizing the aesthetic view of the world."

Two outstanding avatars of the New Sensibility were the species of free-form, Dadaist painters' theater known as Happenings, and the coolest, emptiest, most famous Pop artist of all, Andy Warhol. Calvin Tomkins titled his recent (1980) history of the American art world of the Sixties *Off the Wall,* meaning it as an exact description of where the art object actually went. But Happenings were "off the wall" in both senses of that phrase, in where they literally happened and in their somewhat lunatic quality. Despite the screwy goings-on, however, Happenings were informed by an impressive battery of ideas, many borrowed from Marcel Duchamp and composer John Cage. Many of the artists who fall under the rubric of Pop—Rauschenberg, Claes Oldenburg, Jim Dines, Red Grooms and Warhol—perpetrated Happenings, which, in their improvisatory, participatory, transitory nature, were Pop in spirit.

At bottom Happenings were attempts by painters to escape the burdens of the self and self-expression, the cult of success, the mythology of artistic progress, the overweaning solicitude of the newly with-it art audience and a lot of other constricting notions by jumping into the ambiguous, contingent, aleatory territory between art and life. Despite the fact that Happenings were often elaborate put-ons or near-physical assaults on the audience, they were quite the rage in the early Sixties with the well-heeled art crowd, a development that Tom Wolfe and Thorstein Veblen together could nicely explain.

With Warhol we face a phenomenon that achieves perfect

opacity through perfect transparency. In his profile Tomkins is correct in calling Warhol one of *the* representative figures of his time—he's the newest New Sensibility we possess. His art, financial considerations aside, seems perfectly beside the point to his persona. Blank-visaged, he silk-screened images of soup cans, flowers, Jackie Kennedys and Liz Taylors on an assembly-line basis. His films—twelve hours' worth of the Empire State Building in *Empire; My Hustler,* the story of butch, blond Paul America and the many men who want to meet him; the horny Western epic *Lonesome Cowboys; Chelsea Girls,* the Canterbury Tales of the Chelsea Hotel; enough footage of the legendary socialite "superstar" Edie Sedgewick to mount a retrospective; and much more—were studies in the limits of voyeurism. With Warhol we get as far from the Fifties and from commonly accepted notions about humanity as possible—which makes him an archetypal figure of the Sixties.

Warhol's *real* art was publicity and the put-on, though. He was famous the way Muhammad Ali, Norman Mailer, Marilyn Monroe were famous—megafamous. Here is Warhol in his memoir, *POPism:* "A week or so after Philadelphia I got a real lesson in show business and Pop style. Just when you think you're getting famous, somebody comes along and makes you look like a warm-up act for amateur night. Pope Paul VI. Talk about advance PR—I mean, for centuries! Definitely the most Pop appearance of the Sixties was the visit of the Pope to New York City." The envy here is one of the few real emotions in the book. Tomkins' profile of Warhol should be read along with Tom Wolfe's profile of the Warhol "superstar" Baby Jane Holzer in the preceding section for the full effect. I recommend Warhol's *POPism* as an entertaining, strangely evocative memoir, an East coast version of the story Tom Wolfe tells in *The Electric Kool-Aid Acid Test.*

Because film communicates so directly and so sensuously with its audience (*vide* Jean-Luc Godard's definition of cinema: "Truth at twenty-four frames a second"), and had not, at least at that time, been befouled by overinterpretation, Sontag had declared that "Cinema is the most alive, the most exciting, the most important of the art forms right now." The young in particular eagerly assented to this, so much so that Stanley Kauffmann dubbed them "The Film Generation." In the Sixties film took on a special mystique for intellectuals as well that it had never had before. European directors who were making film do new tricks such as Godard, Antonioni, Truffaut and Bergman became true culture heroes, as did, in part from their dedicated sponsorship by these same Europeans, the older generation of commercial American directors: Howard Hawks, Raoul Walsh, George Cukor, John Ford, John Huston, and Preston Sturges among them. This rediscovery and reappreciation of the American film heritage was in large part made possible by the New Sensibility, which cherished surfaces, artifice, accessibility.

These two streams of film sensibility—European self-consciousness and American bang-bang action orientation—finally merged in this country with explosive force in 1967 with *Bonnie and Clyde* (screenplay by Robert Benton and David Newman, directed by Arthur Penn). Up to that point the New Sensibility in the contemporary American commercial film had been confined for the most part to the absolute lack of sincerity and seriousness of the James Bond spy thrillers and the *Mad Magazine*-style black humor of Stanley Kubrick and Terry Southern's apocalyptic comedy, *Dr. Strangelove*. (There was plenty of New Sensibility to be found in the underground film scene, however, a unique Sixties invention that, much like the counterculture, got co-opted or overexposed to death.) But *Bonnie and Clyde,* a slapstick comedy with real bullets in it that shifted tones from lyrical to comic to brutal with no warning, caught many people badly off guard. Pauline Kael's superb review captures exactly what the ensuing flap was all about and offers, as her best work always does, a precise reading of the cultural temper of the times. The film was immensely influential in a number of ways; to this day one can still see car commercials scored for hyperactive banjos, for instance.

Hollywood was subsequently to discover Youth with a vengeance in the late Sixties and early Seventies, when such films as Mike Nichols' *The Graduate* (1967) and Dennis Hopper's *Easy Rider* (1970), with their themes of youthful rebellion and alienation, became unexpectedly huge successes. But absolutely the greatest thing about being young in the Sixties was not movies, but rock 'n' roll. Everybody knew that the most important people in the world were not the movie stars or athletes or politicians, but rock stars. John Lennon was not far from the mark when he said that the Beatles were more popular than Jesus Christ, and save for

John Kennedy's assassination, the most widely shared and remembered moment in time from the Sixties is their 1964 American television debut on the Ed Sullivan Show.* To be young was very heaven indeed, especially with a new Stones album and the door to your room closed, or a ticket to see the Dead, Cream, Sly, Janis, the Doors, the Airplane, Traffic, Jimi or a dozen other groups or performers at the Fillmore. Rock was a secret language shared by umpteen million teenagers. The Beatles, Dylan, the Stones and others spoke to them with the authority of electronic oracles.

Albert Goldman was a Columbia professor, not a teenager, in the Sixties, but nevertheless his piece beautifully captures the ambience of the Sixties rock scene and the fact that some of the music turned into an art that managed to be both completely fresh and highly sophisticated. This intersection of pop and art occurred with complete ease in the case of rock, making it a central paradigm for the creative sensibility of the Sixties. Goldman also gives us a salutary reminder of the unpayable debt white rock owes to black musical forms, and of the sheer genius of such black performers as James Brown, Aretha Franklin, Ray Charles, and the Motown stable of artists. As happened with the best of the Hollywood movies, the renaissance in popular music gave us a native American art of the utmost vitality (even if much of this art came back by way of England).

The final piece in this section, Leslie Epstein's searching, ambivalent response to the fall 1968 American tour of David Beck and Judith Malina's Living Theater, conveys better than any other piece in this book, I think, the politically super-heated, *Walpurgisnacht* atmosphere of the late Sixties. The year or so before Barbara Garson's *MacBird!*, a play notable not for its dramatic art but for its scurrilous, if scarcely serious imputation that Lyndon Johnson (MacBird) had murdered John Kennedy (John Ken O'Dunc) and hired Earl Warren (The Earl of Warren) to cover up the deed, was widely applauded for its courage by many members of the intellectual community. By this time the put-ons had a murderous

---

*It is very much to the point to note here that the senseless shooting of John Lennon in December 1980 unleashed a flood of emotions strongly reminiscent of the reactions to the assassinations of John and Robert Kennedy and Martin Luther King, Jr., in the Sixties. The Beatles and these three men held extraordinary sway over people's inner lives in ways that have not been equaled by public figures since.

edge to them; driven beyond reason by the continuing escalation of the Vietnam war, intellectuals were after LBJ's scalp. On another front a whole new theater of aggression had developed, based on the proposition that that theater audience was composed of an emotionally blocked bourgeoisie who required shock therapy: a hefty dose of shouted insults concerning their political opinions, racial prejudices and impoverished sex lives, followed by an invitation to doff their clothes for a liberating group grope up on the stage.

The Living Theater, a communal group that had been in exile in Europe through the mid-Sixties, represented the culmination and apotheosis of these trends. They returned to the United States just at the cultural flashpoint, and like a lightning rod they attracted—and also sought—every kind of roiling passion and controversy. Nobody could agree whether the Living Theater was re-creating the primitive Dionysiac mysteries of the theater or acting out a new kind of nude therapy or stylizing an antiwar rally or practicing emotional assault and battery. What is clear is that in Epstein's troubling piece we see a frightening reflection of a culture coming apart at the seams.

# Black Humor and History

## Morris Dickstein

In the pages that follow I'd like to look more closely at three representative black humor novels of the early sixties, *Mother Night*, *Catch-22*, and *The Crying of Lot 49*. These books are neither antiquarian nor excessively literary; in a complex way they develop a striking and unusual sense of history that in the end tells us less about history than about the cultural tone of the period when they were written. Vonnegut and Heller return to World War II not for purposes of historical recreation, not simply because it was their own great formative experience, and certainly not to provide the vicarious thrills of the conventional war novel. Rather, it's because the unsolved moral enigma of that period and that experience most closely expresses the conundrum of contemporary life fifteen years later. Earlier writers had been able to approach World War II with a certain moral simplicity; here after all was a "just war" if there ever was one. But after fifteen more years of continuous cold war and the shadow of thermonuclear war, all war seemed morally ambiguous if not outright insane; in the prolonged state of siege the whole culture seemed edged with insanity. With that special prescience that

From Chapter 6, "Black Humor and History: The Early Sixties" in *Gates of Eden: American Culture in the Sixties* (Basic Books, 1977).

novelists sometimes have, *Catch-22*, though published in 1961, anticipates the moral nausea of the Vietnam war, even famously anticipates the flight of deserters to neutral Sweden. Similarly Vonnegut in *Mother Night* chooses a morally ambiguous double agent as his "hero," just as he writes about the problematic Allied bombing of Dresden rather than a Nazi atrocity in *Slaughterhouse-Five*.

Like Pynchon, but in a different way, both Vonnegut and Heller are interested in international intrigue; they marvel at the zany and unpredictable personal element at work or play within the lumbering forces of history. Heller's Milo Minderbinder is a satire not simply on the American capitalist entrepreneur but also on the international wheeler-dealer, whose amoral machinations, so hilarious at first, become increasingly somber, ugly, and deadly—like so much else in the book—so that we readers become implicated in our own earlier laughter. Yet Milo is particularly close to the book's hero, Yossarian: the two understand each other. They share an ethic of self-interest that in Yossarian comes close to providing the book's moral: as in Céline, it's all a crock, look out for Number One. In the figure of Milo the book and its protagonist confront their seamy underside, a hideous caricature of their own values.

This doubling effect is typical of works of structural black humor. In the historical plot of [Pynchon's] *V.* the central character is called Stencil, and one key structural element is the pairing of fathers and sons—Hugh Godolphin and Evan Godolphin, Sidney Stencil and Herbert Stencil. The younger Stencil's quest for V., which is also a search for parents and identity, is an attempt to decipher a history whose meaning is encoded in the fragmentary remains of previous histories and earlier generations. On this point there's a striking resemblance between *V.* and the Oedipal detective novels that Ross Macdonald has been writing since *The Galton Case* in 1959. In Macdonald the mysteries of the present are always solved by decoding the past; there's an abundance of missing parents, traumatized children, and buried corpses that have been moldering for a generation, waiting for their secrets to be unearthed. In late novels like *The Underground Man* and *Sleeping Beauty* these Oedipal tangles are doubled and redoubled into a plot of appalling complexity, even repetitiveness, so that individual identity pales—it becomes hard to keep track of the characters or to separate them, and the solution comes to interest the author far less than the obsessive mesh of parallel relationships. In *V.* the detective, Herbert Stencil, is himself a cipher (as his name implies) who merely organizes an immense range of partial perspectives into one large diagram, a pattern of possible coherence and meaning. But where detective novels really do deliver a final secret that solves and abolishes all puzzles—Edmund Wilson objected that "this secret is nothing at all" after the big buildup—Pynchon is a modernist who leaves open the possibility that this final solution may be a mirage . . . a mirage or a shocking confirmation of a plot-ridden and mysteriously overorganized world. The mystery writer creates the pattern, but the modernist makes it more truly resonant, mysterious, and contingent.

The doubling and proliferation in the plot of these novels—which approaches a point of surfeit, even nausea, in the dense, choked pages of *Gravity's Rainbow*—always points to an ambiguity of identity, to mysterious correspondences behind the plenitude of the world's surfaces. In Pynchon the ambiguity is historical, ontological: who am I, where do I come from, who's pulling my strings, how can I wrench some meaning from my hieroglyphic surroundings? In Vonnegut the ambiguity is moral: what's the relation within Howard W. Campbell, Jr., the double agent who is the protagonist in *Mother Night* (1961), between the writer, the lover, the Nazi propagandist, and the American spy? Vonnegut himself tells us that the moral of the story ("the only story of mine whose moral I know") is that "we are what we pretend to be, so we must be careful what we pretend to be." In fact the book seems more of a fictional anticipation of Hannah Arendt's thesis that Eichmann represented "the banality of evil." Campbell does indeed encounter a very banal Eichmann while both are awaiting trial as Nazi criminals in an Israeli jail. Campbell's own specific gravity is not banal but mediocre. He's a mediocre but utterly facile and amoral man with a horrible talent for survival.

If Vonnegut's fascination with the bombing of Dresden suggests a degree of survivor-guilt—he lived while 135,000 others died—*Mother Night* is a positive brief against survival and adaptability in a murderous age. "If I'd been born in Germany, I suppose I would have *been* a Nazi, bopping Jews and gypsies and Poles around," says Vonnegut. He feels no superiority to the passive, pliable Everyman. His naive persona, which many critics have reviled as false simplicity, seems to me utterly true to his view of the world. What makes Vonnegut appeal so much to adolescents is probably a certain adolescent pessimism and moral absolutism, a modern Welt-schmerz, which often threatens to reduce complex human problems to simple dichotomies, easy formulas. This is especially true when he speaks in his own person, in essays, prefaces, and interviews, where the mask of the wise simpleton quickly becomes cloying.

But in the novels something else happens. Simplicity of statement begins to have a quite different function. The manner becomes flat and factual, the chapters very brief, like the précis of an action rather than a full-scale novelization. Descriptive and psychological texture are reduced to mere notation, the action to pure plot, and the plot proliferates to a high degree of complexity, taking amazing twists and turns that double back on one another. Like most writers attracted to science fiction, Vonnegut has a precise, logical turn of mind; he loves to scatter the action in twenty separate strands, some of them quite fantastic, only to loop them all neatly together at the end. In this, like Pynchon in *V.*, he resembles the genre-writer or the old-fashioned crafter of well-made plots more than the modernist addicted to problematic and open-ended forms. But Vonnegut crowds the three-decker story into a book the length of a novella so that the emphasis on plot and incident, on Aristotelian changes of fortune, becomes overwhelming, becomes in fact the meaning, not simply a device. (This is especially true of *Mother Night* and *Cat's Cradle*, his strongest books, which both belong to the early sixties.)

The result is a subtle alteration of our sense of reality, at least as we read the book. Despite the promiscuous mixture of fact and fantasy, Vonnegut's flat, declarative manner and the simple-man persona give his narrators a sort of man-to-man reliability in the mind of the reader. They put everything in the story on the same plane: the most bizarre events seem more matter-of-fact, while flat-out realities take on the glow of lunacy they would naturally have if we weren't so inured to them. Vonnegut is attracted to such subjects as the Nazis or the Minutemen not so much because of his German descent

or his own participation in World War II, but because, like
other garish and spectacular subjects that appeal to him, they
accord better with his sense of reality. Unlike the personal
novelist of the fifties, who stakes his claim on the ground of
immediate experience, who desires above all to be credible,
Vonnegut finds life truer in its more extreme, more lunatic
manifestations. Such a sense of the modern world could be
fatal to a novelist; it could make him the ringmaster of a freak
show, or a trivial, harmless fantasist, as it does some of the
verbal black humorists. (Alfred Kazin complains, with some
justice, of their "typed extremism" and of "the passion for
collecting all possible accidents, oddities, lunacies and giving
them an enormous presence in one's own mind.") But the
mentality of Vonnegut, Heller, and Pynchon is not the
collector's mentality but a more truly novelistic one, seizing
on a genuine subject, a piece of world, and finding the
imaginative means for making it a separate world, a convincing, coherent artifice.

The Jewish novelists of the fifties were drawn to extreme
emotional states; they saw life's problems and glories in the
involutions of the self. A writer like Vonnegut is drawn to
extreme conditions of reality, conditions which have addled
our minds or dulled our capacity for *any* emotional response.
Perhaps under the influence of the death camps or the Bomb,
but responding as well to the general tenor of modern life,
Vonnegut and Heller are drawn to situations in which the
arbitrary, the terrible, and the irrational have been *routi-
nized*. They find it maniacally comic that men should learn to
adjust to insane conditions, cultivate their private lives, go
about their business. Howard Campbell is both an American
spy and a Nazi propagandist, a game he plays so well that he
frequently overdoes it; if not more Catholic than the Pope
he's surely more Nazi than the Führer. "How else could I
have survived?" he asks his American superior. "That was
your problem," he's told. "Very few men could have solved it
as thoroughly as you did." (This combination of virtuosity
and amorality intrigues Vonnegut; Campbell turns pliability
and time-serving into a fine art.) His father-in-law Werner
Noth, the police chief of Berlin, is a different sort of
time-server. Though hanged summarily from an apple tree as
a Nazi, it turns out that "terror and torture were the
provinces of other branches of the German police," that

Noth's province was to keep up ordinary law and order and keep the traffic moving. "Noth's principal offense," we are told, "was that he introduced persons suspected of misdemeanors and crimes into a system of courts and penal institutions that was insane. Noth did his best to distinguish between the guilty and the innocent, using the most modern police methods; but those to whom he handed over his prisoners found the distinction of no importance. Merely to be in custody, with or without trial, was a crime."

Much of the comedy of *Catch-22* comes from the same effort to maintain business as usual under "insane" conditions. The painstaking records the Nazis kept were perhaps rooted in a similar impulse. Werner Noth is a great admirer of his son-in-law's propaganda broadcasts and, though a Nazi, is unconcerned that Campbell may also have been an American spy, "because," as he tells him, "you could never have served the enemy as well as you served us. . . . Almost all the ideas that I hold now, that make me unashamed of anything I may have felt or done as a Nazi, came not from Hitler, not from Goebbels, not from Himmler—but from you. . . . You alone kept me from concluding that Germany had gone insane." Out of pure play-acting, unhampered by any real disorderly commitment, Campbell has amusingly (!) become the Ur-Nazi, whose work still turns up twenty years later as the staple of right-wing lunatic fringe groups. You are what you do, you become what you seem to be. No wonder Vonnegut and Heller became classics of the anti-Vietnam generation, curious comic bibles of protest, so different from the protest literature of the thirties, while writers like Malamud, who took the fifties posture of stoicism and endurance, or else Jamesian renunciation, gradually lost favor.* Vonnegut's zany, cartoon-like plot, his distaste for violence and heroic posturing, and his affinity for a few simple human verities help make his work the moral equivalent of the New Politics of the early sixties, which substituted communitarian good

---

*This is not to say that established writers were unaffected by the new cultural mood; Mailer and Roth, for example, changed styles completely, as did numbers of poets. Saul Bellow was galvanized into oppositional fury by his total loathing of the new culture and all its works. But some fifties writers lost energy and force even when they lamely adopted a more militant message their imagination couldn't fully sustain—notably Baldwin after *The Fire Next Time* and Malamud in *The Fixer* and *The Tenants*.

will, anarchic individualism, and ethical fervor for the old
staples of ideology. Thus Vonnegut, in a key passage of
*Mother Night,* likens the totalitarian mind to "a system of
gears whose teeth have been filed off at random. . . . The
missing teeth, of course, are simple, obvious truths, truths
available and comprehensible even to ten-year-olds, in most
cases. . . . This is the closest I can come to explaining the
legions, the nations of lunatics I've seen in my time." Like the
New Left, however, Vonnegut is more impressive as happening than as explanation: the "at random" seems particularly
inadequate. But the ingenious reversals of Vonnegut's plots
go well beyond the simple verities of his own moralizing, and
provide as full a helping of moral ambiguity as any modernist
could want.

The final twist of Vonnegut's book is Howard Campbell's
last-minute exoneration by the system of "justice," which he
refutes by committing suicide. After all, unlike Eichmann, he
had surrendered to the Israelis precisely to counteract his
miserable gift for survival; now he takes more definitive
action. By writing this book and then taking his life he
becomes his own prosecutor, judge, and executioner.
Vonnegut is sure that there are no heroes, that he himself
might have gone along with the Nazis had he lived in
Germany, and therefore that no one has the right to stand in
judgment of another. By executing judgment on himself
Campbell cuts through the fog of moral ambiguity and
becomes the book's true protagonist and center of value.

I said earlier that characters in black humor novels tend to
be cartoon-like and two-dimensional, without the capacity to
grow or change. To this we must add the qualification that the
protagonist is usually different: he doesn't completely belong
to this mode of reality or system of representation. As
Richard Poirier has suggested apropos of Pynchon, the
central character of these novels often moves on a different
plane: he shows at least the capacity to become a fuller, more
sentient human being, a character in a realistic novel. In the
first part of the book the "hero" is typically enmeshed in a
system of comic repetition: tics of speech and behavior,
entanglements of plot, all the "routines" of verbal black
humor, life imitating vaudeville. Heller, for example, like
Dickens, knows how to make his own comic technique
approximate poignant human realities. And as the comedy in
*Catch-22* darkens, the system of dehumanization becomes

clearer, and the central character becomes increasingly isolated in his impulse to challenge and step outside it.

In Yossarian Heller introduces a new figure into postwar American fiction, descended from the schlemiel of the Jewish novel but finally an inversion of that passive and unhappy figure. Heller tells us he's an Assyrian, but only because (as he said to an interviewer) "I wanted to get an extinct culture. . . . [M]y purpose in doing so was to get an outsider, a man who was intrinsically an outsider." The typical schlemiel is certainly no hero, but like Yossarian has a real instinct for survival. In earlier days Yossarian had really tried to bomb the targets, as he was supposed to do. Now his only goal is to avoid flak, to keep alive. "Yossarian was the best man in the group at evasive action." This Yossarian is concerned only with saving his skin, obsessed by the things that threaten his life. "There were too many dangers for Yossarian to keep track of." And Heller gives us a wonderful catalogue of them, from Hitler, Mussolini, and Tojo ("they all wanted him dead") to all the insane and fanatical people in his own army ("they wanted to kill him, too") to all the organs of his body, with their arsenal of fatal diseases:

There were diseases of the skin, diseases of the bone, diseases of the lung, diseases of the stomach, diseases of the heart, blood and arteries. There were diseases of the head, diseases of the neck, diseases of the chest, diseases of the intestines, diseases of the crotch. There were even diseases of the feet. There were billions of conscientious body cells oxidating away day and night like dumb animals at their complicated job of keeping him alive and healthy, and every one was a potential traitor and foe. There were so many diseases that it took a truly diseased mind to even think about them as often as he and Hungry Joe did.

Yossarian seems perilously close to the Sterling Hayden character in *Dr. Strangelove,* the general who fears that women are sapping his vital bodily fluids. The insanity of the system, in this case the army, breeds a defensive counterinsanity, a mentality of organized survival that mirrors the whole system of rationalized human waste and devaluation. The self itself becomes an army, a totalitarian body politic, demanding total vigilance against the threat of betrayal and insurrection. Each individual organ, each cell, becomes an object of paranoid anxiety. I remember as a child being afraid I might forget to breathe, holding my breath as long as I could, to be reassured it would still happen without me. Yossarian too has the "childish" wish to assert the sort of outside control that he himself feels gripped by.

The pattern of *Catch-22* is similar to that of *Mother Night:* a world gone mad, a protagonist caught up in the madness, who eventually steps outside it in a slightly mad way. The Sweden to which Yossarian flees at the end of the book is something of a pipe dream, a pure elsewhere. Yossarian's friend Orr has made it there (from the Mediterranean in a rowboat!), but Orr is Yossarian's opposite, utterly at home in the world, as idiotically free of anxiety as Yossarian is dominated by it. Orr is the unkillable imp, the irrepressible innocent, a "likable dwarf with a smutty mind and a thousand valuable skills that would keep him in a low income group all his life." Orr is the gentile Crusoe to Yossarian's Jewish neurotic; along with the diabolical Milo they form a spectrum of the possibilities of survival in extreme situations, which include not only wartime but just about all of modern life, indeed the whole human condition, for which the war is ultimately a metaphor.

But Yossarian goes through a second change before the book ends: he becomes a troublemaker and, worse still, the unwilling keeper of the book's conscience, just as Nately's whore becomes the figure of Nemesis, the haunting, surreal spirit of female revenge for the callous inhumanity of a man-made world. The earlier Yossarian saw through the no-win bind of Catch-22 and set out monomaniacally to survive. But as each of the others goes separately, uncomplainingly, to his predictable fate, Yossarian becomes more and more the somber registrar of their deaths and exits:

> Nately's whore was on his mind, as were Kraft and Orr and Nately and Dunbar, and Kid Sampson and McWatt, and all the poor and stupid and diseased people he had seen in Italy, Egypt and North Africa and knew about in other areas of the world, and Snowden and Nately's whore's kid sister were on his conscience, too.

Yossarian has come willy-nilly to brood about more than his own inner organs. Other people have become a desperate reality to him, and with it has come a sense of their common fate, their mutual essence. The secret of Snowden, who spills his guts in the tail of a plane, is revealed to Yossarian alone:

> His teeth were chattering in horror. He forced himself to look again. Here was God's plenty, all right, he thought bitterly as he stared—liver, lungs, kidneys, ribs, stomach and bits of the stewed tomatoes Snowden had eaten that day for lunch. Yossarian hated stewed tomatoes. . . . He wondered how in the world to begin to save him.
>
> "I'm cold," Snowden whispered. "I'm cold."
>
> "There, there," Yossarian mumbled in a voice too low to be heard. "There, there."
>
> Yossarian was cold, too, and shivering uncontrollably. . . . It was easy to read the message in his entrails. Man was matter, that was Snowden's secret. Drop him out a window and he'll fall. Set fire to him and he'll burn. Bury him and he'll rot, like other kinds of garbage. The spirit gone, man is garbage. That was Snowden's secret. Ripeness was all.

Impelled perhaps by the unconscious Jewish identification, Heller paraphrases the famous "humanizing" speech of Shylock ("If you prick us, do we not bleed? if you tickle us, do we not laugh? if you poison us, do we not die?"). But the final allusion to *Lear* is breathtaking: an impertinence to do it, the height of *chutzpah* to bring it off. The scene must be read as a whole to see how well it works—it's the penultimate moment of the book—but even the delicate texture of these pages of prose would be nothing had not the "secret" of Snowden been such an important leitmotif throughout the book. (Snowden's death had taken place before the book opened, but it's fully remembered and decoded as he lies on an operating table in the next-to-last chapter, as if its meaning, which underlies the whole book, had taken that long to be reduced to its terrifying simplicity and finality.) The somber tone of this passage—despite the necessary farcical touch of Yossarian's dislike of stewed tomatoes—is something that's not available to verbal black humor, which aims for wild incongruities at every turn, which is more at home with disgust and humiliation and absurdity than with the simple terror of the world as it is; such a poignant effect requires a more fully human respondent, which Yossarian has by now become. Heller's "structural" use of the secret of Snowden

makes it a time bomb of ineluctable tragic fact ticking away
beneath the book's surface of farce and rollicking insanity;
except that the secret unfolds its revelations gradually, alongside the story, until it finally *becomes* the story.*

When I first read *Catch-22* I felt strongly that except for the
Snowden chapter the book's final shift in tone in the last
seventy-five pages didn't work, that after doing an amazing
*comic* adaptation of Kafka and Dostoevsky most of the way,
Heller unaccountably switched to imitating them directly in
the finale, a contest he couldn't win. Rereading the book I
can see why I felt that way—we miss the sheer gratuitous
pleasure of the comedy—but I also see how much the somber
and even ugly side was present from the beginning and how
gradually the book modulates into it: for such laughter we
have the devil to pay. The *Mr. Roberts* element won't carry us
all the way through. I'm now sure the last section works and
makes the whole book work; up against a wall, I'd have to call
*Catch-22* the best novel of the sixties.

But what can we learn about the sixties from *Catch-22?* I
think the popular success of the book can be attributed to the
widespread spiritual revulsion in the sixties against many of
our most sacrosanct institutions, including the army; to which
our leaders replied by heightening just those things that had
caused the disgust in the first place, especially the quality of
fraud, illusion, and manipulation in our public life. Just as the
response to war-protest was escalation and the solution to the
failures of the bombing was more bombing, so the push for
more honesty in public debate was met by more public
relations and bigger lies. The Johnson Administration's unshakable insistence that black was white, that escalation was
really the search for peace, and that the war was being won
was a perfect realization of the structure of unreality and
insanity that runs as a theme through both *Mother Night* and

---

*I wonder if Heller was aware of Wordsworth's use of Snowdon, the Welsh
mountain, as the penultimate scene of revelation before the conclusion of *The
Prelude;* if so he inverts Wordsworth's brooding "recognitions of transcendent
power" into his own more nihilistic *Lear*-like epiphany. He does refer to Villon's
rueful "snows of yesteryear"—"Où sont les Neigedens d'antan?"—but not to
Wordsworth. The name itself may mean "snowed-in," for the scene in the plane,
with Snowden whimpering and Yossarian "shivering uncontrollably," is infused
with the terror of frozen entrapment, life ebbing away in preternatural cold.
Kazin aptly calls this the "primal scene" of the novel. It's surely the book's
primal experience and the master-image of Yossarian's anxieties.

*Catch-22.* "We're all in this business of illusion together," says Doc Daneeka, who himself later suffers from the general illusion that he is dead (which, morally speaking, he is). Daneeka's merely physical presence proves powerless to contradict his "official" demise, and he is destroyed as much by his own insane survival ethic as by the structure of unreality that is the army. When he asks Yossarian to substitute for a dead soldier whose parents are coming to see him die, he says: "As far as we're concerned, one dying boy is just as good as any other, or just as bad. . . . All you've got to do is lie there a few minutes and die a little." Surprisingly, when Yossarian does it, the parents go along:

> "Giuseppe."
> "It's not Giuseppe, Ma. It's Yossarian."
> "What difference does it make?" the mother answered in the same mourning tone, without looking up. "He's dying."

When the whole family starts crying, Yossarian cries too. It's not a show anymore. Somehow they're right, Daneeka's right, they *are* all dying; in some sense it *doesn't* matter. A piece of ghoulish humor has turned into something exceptionally moving. The same point is made with the Soldier in White, a mummy in bandages whose only sign of life is an interchange of fluids. What *is* a man, anyway, when things have come to this extremity? The ground is being readied for revealing Snowden's secret. The *Lear* theme is at the heart of the book, no mere device for concluding it.

Unlike the realistic novelists of the fifties, the black humorists suggest that besides our personal dilemmas, which often loom so large in our imagination, we all share features of a common fate, enforced by society and the general human condition. Though the quest for identity must inevitably be personal, in some sense we *are* interchangeable. Furthermore, the quest will surely be thwarted if society becomes a vast structure of illusion and duplicity, and hence treats us as even more interchangeable and manipulable than we necessarily are. One effect of Vietnam and Watergate was that the official organs of our society lost much of the respect and credence they had commanded. Even middle Americans began to live with less of a mystified and paternalistic sense of Authority. The disillusionment and ruthless skepticism—

really, spoiled idealism—of *Catch-22*, outlived the sixties to become a pervasive national mood. With Célinean cynics and paranoids installed in the White House, people at large became that much more cynical and paranoid themselves. And the paranoia had some basis in fact, for in a highly polarized society, where the self-imposed limitations of tradition and civility have been cast away, it's likely that somebody really is out to get you, by any means fair or foul. During the Johnson and Nixon Administrations we learned that even in this country Authority's talent for abusing power is greater, or at least more nimble, than society's ability to check the abuse. The Watergate revelations showed how close we came to an internal *coup d' état*, perhaps on the Indian model, if not to the paranoid nightmare of manipulation and control foreshadowed by the black humor novel.

During the Eisenhower Administration American power, though it had not withdrawn from its new world role, was quietly exercised in what seemed like a paternal and benign way. When Kennedy challenged the phlegmatic and restrained tendencies that underlay the saber-rattling of a Dulles, he called attention to American power and position in a new way. Kennedy demanded a more flexible military posture, the ability to fight two and a half wars simultaneously (a typical maniac vision), and hence the tactical power to combat so-called wars of national liberation, one of which was already in progress in Indochina. Kennedy's liberalism, like the whole liberal tradition since 1945, was internationalist, while Eisenhower and the conservatives still labored under a faint shadow of isolationism, the precedent of the period after World War I, when America had pulled back from its international "responsibilities." Hence Vietnam was in large measure the liberals' war, not only because many liberals were crucial in prosecuting and defending it but because its rationale emerged directly from the cold war liberalism of the forties and fifties, which accepted the worldwide mission of "containing" the Communists wherever they might appear, in whatever national form. By attacking the old general for a nonexistent "missile gap" and for overall military weakness, Kennedy seized the initiative of anti Communism for the Democratic Party, less than a decade after McCarthy had snatched it away from Truman and Acheson. And predictably, the first two years of the Kennedy Administration—from the Bay of Pigs, to the summit meeting with Khrushchev in Vienna, to the Berlin crisis of the summer of 1961, to the Cuban missile crisis of 1962—were a period of substantial intensification of the cold war, while our defense establishment was being vastly expanded and retooled for hot wars. The more soft-centered liberals like Stevenson, Bowles, Galbraith, and Schlesinger, who might have opposed this tendency, all were confined to window-dressing positions that were more or less marginal to the making of policy.

While few of these things "caused" any writers to write their books, I think this climate helps explain why black humor began its great efflorescence during the Kennedy years, in apparent contradiction to the idealism, optimism, and high style that we still like to attribute to that period. Mailer's *An American Dream* can be read as a testament about the Kennedy years, ultimately shrewder than all the tendentious memoirs and eulogies that were published after the assassination. When I first came upon the references to Kennedy in the opening pages I thought them meretricious: one more piece of megalomania for Mailer to associate his all-too-Mailerian hero with the dashing, fallen president. But Mailer's identification with Kennedy had come much earlier and ran much deeper. His first major piece of journalism was about Kennedy's nomination. A would-be courtier and counselor, he'd addressed a whole book of essays to Kennedy as president. Sexually rivalrous, he'd written an open letter to Jackie, half-scolding her but implicitly trying to woo her away. Like others Mailer saw Kennedy as some kind of union of style and power—both Irish and Harvard, moneyed and *macho*—whose classy imperial court had a use for the arts. But in the novel his hero, Rojack, complains that

The real difference between the President and myself may be that I ended with too large an appreciation of the moon, for I looked down the abyss on the first night I killed: four men, four very separate Germans, dead under a full moon—whereas Jack, for all I know, never saw the abyss.

Recall the premise that Kennedy and Rojack are alter egos, both war heroes, both elected to Congress in the same year. (Even his name may be an amalgam of Robert and Jack.) But Mailer's Rojack has explored the nether side of violence and power, explores it again in the course of the book, coming out only "something like sane again" in the last line. The book's plot can be seen as an enactment of his fantasies, his irrationalities, his madness. Dangling over the balcony of a skyscraper to probe his courage and manhood, he hears voices that tell him he can fly. The whole book is steeped in magic and dread, the dark underside of a too-purely Apollonian Kennedy vision of power without price or penalty. Rojack is not Mailer but Mailer's ambiguous self-portrait as an archetype of the age. Only the best writers have the gift of using the accidents of their own experience, the stuff of their fantasy life, in that significant way, and we can hardly blame the book's first readers, myself included, who were still under the sway of Camelot's idealized Apollonian self-image, for seeing bad taste and confessional self-aggrandizement in its allusions to both Kennedy and the author's own recent bad-boy history.

Today time allows us quite another perspective on that period and its literature. From *Catch-22*, *Mother Night*, and *V.* to *Cat's Cradle*, *Little Big Man*, and *An American Dream*, the black humor novels of the first half of the sixties, even when conceived earlier, are like a secret history of the Kennedy years, when the terrifying specter of thermonuclear war flared garishly one last time before beginning to dim, when fond hopes for building a better society were repeatedly mocked by our inability to deal with the society we have, when a President's civilized, cosmopolitan vision helped conceal the expansion of our imperial role. Pynchon and Heller, like Mailer and Berger, are the first novelists of a new imperial America, even when they write about World War II, that just war, or about German Southwest Africa, or about the Fashoda crisis of the 1880s (which neatly foreshadows the Suez crisis of the 1950s), or about the political machinations of Argentine exiles in Florence in 1902. *V.* especially is a novel whose wide-ranging imagination, strongly influenced by European novelists of imperialism like Conrad and Graham Greene, peculiarly parallels America's new world role. Just as *An American Dream* is ambivalent toward power—sexual power, political power, American power—*V.* is ambivalent toward history, seeing in it an exhilarating if frighteningly comprehensive shape and design, but seeing it also as perhaps a fraud, an illusion, the ultimate unreality compared to the individual's humblest private need. The early sixties was itself an ambiguous period, for like these novels it did really have an exuberant and expansive side that was not mere Camelot rhetoric.

Let me stress again the positive side of that cultural moment before descending once more into the maelstrom of its hidden history. The early sixties really were a hopeful period, a dizzying time when things everywhere seemed to be opening up after the stagnation of the Eisenhower years. There were many portents of change in society. The decisions of the Supreme Court in cases of civil rights, civil liberties, reapportionment, and the separation of church and state seemed to foreshadow significant change in areas where the two other branches of government had proved cowardly, helpless, or paralyzed. A nascent civil rights movement, then still in its hand-in-hand, "We Shall Overcome" mood, was translating the stirrings of the Court into direct action. A nascent New Left, humanistic in its values, spontaneous and American in its methods, but potentially radical in its goals, seemed determined to avoid the ideological rigidity and conspiratorial mentality of the Old. In Beat poetry and the new vogue of folk music these social movements found their artistic accompaniment, as poets and folksingers reached past the academic insularity and pop commercialism of the fifties toward the positive cultural side of the left-wing heritage of the thirties, the populism of the Popular Front. When a very young Bob Dylan made his pilgrimage from Hibbing, Minnesota, to the bedside of a dying Woody Guthrie, the spirit of two epochs was symbolically joined. Songs of protest and solidarity helped create a tenuous tissue of brotherhood at every civil rights event, just as poets would later lend their bardic daimon to the antiwar movement.

But the opening up of the novel was a deeper, more ambiguous development, and I think it revealed more about the changing sensibility of the early sixties. Grandiose and experimental in form, these books partook of the imperial buoyancy of the Kennedy years. But their vision sometimes had a bleak, dead-end character that belied any official optimism. *Catch-22* had a plastic creative freedom and energy hardly present in the novels of the fifties, but it imagines a world wholly unredeemed by rational purpose or humanistic uplift. A similar ambiguity attaches to the theme of paranoia and the vision of history in Pynchon's novels. His form and language, his historical range and complexity of plot, match Heller in creative exuberance, and many in his endless cast of cartoonish characters are pure products of the comic or satiric spirit. Even his paranoid theme has its exhilarating side: it enables him to make astonishing connections and fantasize breathtaking possibilities, to subvert and intimidate our pedestrian sense of reality and causation, "to bring the estate into pulsing stelliferous Meaning" (as Oedipa Maas muses). *"Shall I project a world?"* Oedipa asks herself in *The Crying of Lot 49,* situating herself neatly somewhere between the novelist and the psychotic. She is neither, but the elaborate plot that her sleuthing gradually intuits makes for a novel that's both impressively somber in tone and yet amazingly conditional and tentative in substance. For those who entirely associate black humor with apocalyptic farce and a tone of raucous extremity, *The Crying of Lot 49* should come as a revelation. *V.* embodies more of the positive side of the paranoid vision, with its immense assortment of characters, plots, historical periods, and narrative modes, all spun together into a dazzling web of possible meanings—which still don't measure up to the pleasure of the telling, the joy of imaginative construction, where the paranoid and the novelist *do* come together. But in the spare, perfectly controlled novella that Pynchon wrote next, Oedipa, the heroine, imagines a vast plot that the author mostly doesn't care to enact. *Lot 49* is *about* plotting, and Oedipa is less the projector than the object, the possible victim. Herbert Stencil, the sleuth of *V.,* is an eccentric bird in search of his own identity, who in the process happens to construct an immense historical mosaic. Himself nothing, Stencil could only become; but since the cartoon of history is enough for him, he probably won't. But Oedipa Maas, despite her piquant Pynchonesque name, has the pulse of a full-blooded woman. The California cartoon world that surrounds her can't possibly satisfy her, but the richer baroque underworld she glimpses won't necessarily do so either. It might be a way out, but not to anything better. The ambiguity of history in *V.*—does it have no meaning or too much meaning? is it a chaos of random hints or a tightly organized totalitarian web?—becomes the more direct subject of *The Crying of Lot 49*. In trying to sort out the estate of the late Pierce Inverarity, Oedipa gets in a classic double bind, which eventually comes to represent reality itself, particularly the American reality. Either Oedipa has stumbled onto an immense plot—or into an immense hoax—that has the "secret richness and concealed density of dream" but also a dream-like pointlessness and ineffectuality, or else there is nothing, no "real alternative to the exit-lessness, to the absence of surprise to life, that harrows the head of everybody American you know," nothing but the official surfaces of life, the "lies, recitations of routine, arid betrayals of spiritual poverty." Oedipa hopes none of these things is true. "She didn't like any of them, but hoped she was mentally ill; that that's all it was." Either no exit, or an exit into rich but unhinging, even appalling realities, or perhaps an exit into madness, clinical paranoia, inner space.

It's astonishing how well the book locates itself on this narrow shelf of ambiguity, this edge of contingency, beauti-fully epitomized in a small moment when Oedipa comes upon what looks like an ordinary trash can, hand-painted with the initials W.A.S.T.E. "She had to look closely to see the periods between the letters." It's a witty touch, for those tiny periods flickering near the vanishing-point could mean noth-ing at all, but might also make all the difference between a simple trash can and a system of secret communication going back centuries; she may have stumbled into the dense under-brush of a hidden reality, something she might have uncov-ered "anywhere in her Republic, through any of a hundred lightly concealed entranceways, a hundred alienations, if only she'd looked." "Behind the hieroglyphic streets there would either be a transcendent meaning, or only the earth."

It should be clear why Pynchon's paranoid myth makes some claim on us, without demanding that we be paranoid ourselves or give any credence to the reality of V. or the Tristero System. Pynchon's paranoia is neither a clinical paranoia nor a literal paranoid view of history but instead a metaphor for something the novelist shares with the mystic, the drug-taker, the philosopher, and the scientist: a desperate appetite for meaning, a sense at once joyful and threatening that things are not what they seem, that reality is mysteriously over-organized and can be decoded if only we attend to the hundred innocent hints and byways that beckon to us, that life is tasteless and insipid without this hidden order of meaning but perhaps appalling *with* it.

Without farce or violence, Pynchon's paranoia reveals an alienation from American life greater than that of Heller or any other comic-apocalyptic writer. Society commands no loyalty in *Lot 49,* though the freaked-out scene of California n the sixties evokes an anthropological fascination; the rest is a tissue of falsehood and spiritual deadness. The drifter ambiance of *V.*, which Pynchon himself has evidently continued to live out, has ripened in good sixties fashion into a complete rejection of official cant and the square world. Pynchon's sensibility, like that of some of the earlier Beat figures (whom he resembles in many ways, not including his highly structured style of writing and his aversion to personal publicity), strikingly foreshadowed the mood of young people in the late sixties. For them paranoia, like radicalism, drug-taking, and communal life, was both a rejection of the official culture and a form of group solidarity, promising a more fully authentic life-possibility.

For Pynchon the paranoid imagination is a special way of rebelling or dropping out, but it's also more than that. He compares it to a hallucinogenic drug. For him it rends the veil of life's banal and numbing surfaces, putting him in touch with something more deep and rich, which may also unfortunately be quite unreal. Above all it makes him feel more fully alive, with a more intense and absolute self than the official rational culture dares allow. It's "a delirium tremens, a trembling unfurrowing of the mind's plowshare." It's also analogous to the powerful sentiment of being that marks certain religious experiences: "the saint whose water can light lamps, the clairvoyant whose lapse in recall is the breath of God, the true paranoid for whom all is organized in spheres joyful or threatening about the central pulse of himself. . . ." It's important that Oedipa herself does not really have such an experience, only a glimmering and conditional intimation of it. Her mind trembles and is unfurrowed, but down to the end she passively receives these intimations and continues to weigh and judge them, caught in her double bind:

> Another mode of meaning behind the obvious, or none. Either Oedipa in the orbiting ecstasy of a true paranoia, or a real Tristero. For there either was some Tristero beyond the appearance of the legacy America, or there was just America and if there was just America then it seemed the only way she could continue, and manage to be at all relevant to it, was as an alien, unfurrowed, assumed full circle into some paranoia.

Evidently Pynchon is tempted to romanticize Oedipa into a figure or rebellion, just as he briefly inflates Pierce Inverarity's "legacy" into an allegory of America; but this is not where the book is really impressive. In the final scene Oedipa, "with the courage you find you have when there is nothing more to lose," prepares to make a final gesture to expose the Tristero secret. But she's far from a heroic figure, only—like Yossarian, like most of Vonnegut's heroes—a modest center of value in a world where human values have been misplaced or forgotten; she's caught between two worlds, the conventional and the paranoid, that each have gone amok in their own way. Oedipa is not simply the drifter and the bumbling amateur sleuth on loan from *V*. She grows more real and human as the book proceeds, trying to make connections but more impressive in her quiet despair and sexual *dis*connection, a mood that heightens gradually into a sense of apocalyptic foreboding. What really moves us in *Lot 49* is not the paranoid myth itself—we care almost as little about the Tristero System as about the impossibly elaborate plot of the Jacobean play Pynchon parodies—but rather the state of mind, the rhythm of perception it makes possible. The big novels of the early sixties really do belong to the expansive, world-projecting mood of that period. *The Crying of Lot 49,* published in 1966, already anticipates the more somber expectations of the late sixties, when paranoia gradually ceased to be an ecstatic enlargement of the possibilities of meaning and being, a positive subversion of ordinary reality, and instead darkened into an apocalyptic and pervasive anxiety. The paranoid became the victim of the plot or the helpless onlooker waiting to be engulfed, not the imaginative projector. If *Catch-22* foreshadows the soul-destroying madness of the Vietnam war, *The Crying of Lot 49* foreshadows the darkening green of the end of the sixties, when a government of lawless desperadoes and a half-crazed remnant of young radicals would pair off in an unequal contest of mutual paranoia, helping to destroy each other and confirming also Delmore Schwartz's much-quoted adage that "even paranoids have enemies."

The black humor novels of the sixties are not only deeply interested in history but create amazing parallels to the history of their own times, less in their actual subjects than in their whole mode of imagination. The sense of incongruity and absurdity, the mixture of farce, violence, and hysteria, that we find in these books we can also find in the wars, riots, movements, assassinations, conspiracies, as well as in much subtler and less spectacular manifestations of the spirit of the sixties. The black humor novel of the sixties, like the radicalism of the sixties, indeed like the American government and the architects of social policy in the sixties, began with elaborate efforts to assimilate history, to comprehend and shape it along the lines of private mythology, public planning, the enlightened will. By the end of the sixties—in both fiction and reality—this confidence was displaced by a sense that history was out of control, or that the Others had their hands on the wheel and were preparing to do us in completely. By the end of the sixties paranoia was the last fuel for direct action, the last gasp of a coherent world-view, which soon itself collapsed into fragments. "Fragments are the only forms I trust," wrote Donald Barthelme, as the influence of more titanic modernists like Joyce gave way to such inspired miniaturists as Kafka and Borges, negative visionaries whose work undercut all mythic inclusiveness. In late-sixties writers like Barthelme or Wurlitzer the sense of disconnection is complete, as it is in the Weatherman phase of sixties radicalism, where futility and frustration spawn random violence. Barthelme and Wurlitzer write as if they were surrounded by the curious artifacts of an extinct culture, which they plunder like collectors, or stroll past vacantly like sleepwalkers.

# One Culture and the New Sensibility

## Susan Sontag

In the last few years there has been a good deal of discussion of a purported chasm which opened up some two centuries ago, with the advent of the Industrial Revolution, between "two cultures," the literary-artistic and the scientific. According to this diagnosis, any intelligent and articulate modern person is likely to inhabit one culture to the exclusion of the other. He will be concerned with different documents, different techniques, different problems; he will speak a different language. Most important, the type of effort required for the mastery of these two cultures will differ vastly. For the literary-artistic culture is understood as a general culture. It is addressed to man insofar as he is man; it is culture or, rather, it promotes culture, in the sense of culture defined by Ortega y Gasset: that which a man has in his possession when he has forgotten everything that he has read. The scientific culture, in contrast, is a culture for specialists; it is founded on remembering and is set down in ways that require complete dedication of the effort to comprehend. While the literary-artistic culture aims at internalization, ingestion—in other words, cultivation—the scientific culture aims at accumulation and externalization in complex instruments for problem-solving and specific techniques for mastery.

from *Against Interpretaion* (Farrar, Straus & Giroux, 1966).

Though T. S. Eliot derived the chasm between the two cultures from a period more remote in modern history, speaking in a famous essay of a "dissociation of sensibility" which opened up in the 17th century, the connection of the problem with the Industrial Revolution seems well taken. There is a historic antipathy on the part of many literary intellectuals and artists to those changes which characterize modern society—above all, industrialization and those of its effects which everyone has experienced, such as the proliferation of huge impersonal cities and the predominance of the anonymous style of urban life. It has mattered little whether industrialization, the creature of modern "science," is seen on the 19th and early 20th century model, as noisy smoky artificial processes which defile nature and standardize culture, or on the newer model, the clean automated technology that is coming into being in the second half of the 20th century. The judgment has been mostly the same. Literary men, feeling that the status of humanity itself was being challenged by the new science and the new technology, abhorred and deplored the change. But the literary men, whether one thinks of Emerson and Thoreau and Ruskin in the 19th century, or of 20th century intellectuals who talk of modern society as being in some new way incomprehensible, "alienated," are inevitably on the defensive. They know that the scientific culture, the coming of the machine, cannot be stopped.

The standard response to the problem of "the two cultures"—and the issue long antedates by many decades the crude and philistine statement of the problem by C. P. Snow in a famous lecture some years ago—has been a facile defense of the function of the arts (in terms of an ever vaguer ideology of "humanism") or a premature surrender of the function of the arts to science. By the second response, I am not referring to the philistinism of scientists (and those of their party among artists and philosophers) who dismiss the arts as imprecise, untrue, at best mere toys. I am speaking of serious doubts which have arisen among those who are passionately engaged in the arts. The role of the individual artist, in the business of making unique objects for the purpose of giving pleasure and educating conscience and sensibility, has repeatedly been called into question. Some literary intellectuals and artists have gone so far as to prophesy the ultimate demise of the art-making activity of man. Art, in an automated scientific society, would be unfunctional, useless.

But this conclusion, I should argue, is plainly unwarranted. Indeed, the whole issue seems to me crudely put. For the question of "the two cultures" assumes that science and technology are changing, in motion, while the arts are static, fulfilling some perennial generic human function (consolation? edification? diversion?). Only on the basis of this false assumption would anyone reason that the arts might be in danger of becoming obsolete.

Art does not progress, in the sense that science and technology do. But the arts do develop and change. For instance, in our own time, art is becoming increasingly the terrain of specialists. The most interesting and creative art of our time is *not* open to the generally educated; it demands special effort; it speaks a specialized language. The music of Milton Babbitt and Morton Feldman, the painting of Mark Rothko and Frank Stella, the dance of Merce Cunningham and James Waring demand an education of sensibility whose difficulties and length of apprenticeship are at least comparable to the difficulties of mastering physics or engineering. (Only the novel, among the arts, at least in America, fails to provide similar examples.) The parallel between the abstruseness of contemporary art and that of modern science is too obvious to be missed. Another likeness to the scientific culture is the history-mindedness of contemporary art. The most interesting works of contemporary art are full of references to the history of the medium; so far as they comment on past art, they demand a knowledge of at least the recent past. As Harold Rosenberg has pointed out, contemporary paintings are themselves acts of criticism as much as of creation. The point could be made as well of much recent work in the films, music, the dance, poetry, and (in Europe) literature. Again, a similarity with the style of science—this time, with the accumulative aspect of science—can be discerned.

The conflict between "the two cultures" is in fact an illusion, a temporary phenomenon born of a period of profound and bewildering historical change. What we are witnessing is not so much a conflict of cultures as the creation of a new (potentially unitary) kind of sensibility. This new sensibility is rooted, as it must be, in *our* experience, experi-

ences which are new in the history of humanity—in extreme
social and physical mobility; in the crowdedness of the human
scene (both people and material commodities multiplying at a
dizzying rate); in the availability of new sensations such as
speed (physical speed, as in airplane travel; speed of images,
as in the cinema); and in the pan-cultural perspective on the
arts that is possible through the mass reproduction of art
objects.

What we are getting is not the demise of art, but a
transformation of the function of art. Art, which arose in
human society as a magical-religious operation, and passed
over into a technique for depicting and commenting on
secular reality, has in our own time arrogated to itself a new
function—neither religious, nor serving a secularized religious function, nor merely secular or profane (a notion which
breaks down when its opposite, the "religious" or "sacred,"
becomes obsolescent). Art today is a new kind of instrument,
an instrument for modifying consciousness and organizing
new modes of sensibility. And the means for practicing art
have been radically extended. Indeed, in response to this new
function (more felt than clearly articulated), artists have had
to become self-conscious aestheticians: continually challeng-
ing their means, their materials and methods. Often, the
conquest and exploitation of new materials and methods
drawn from the world of "non-art"—for example, from
industrial technology, from commercial processes and imagery, from purely private and subjective fantasies and dreams—
seems to be the principal effort of many artists. Painters no
longer feel themselves confined to canvas and paint, but
employ hair, photographs, wax, sand, bicycle tires, their own
toothbrushes and socks. Musicians have reached beyond the
sounds of the traditional instruments to use tampered instruments and (usually on tape) synthetic sounds and industrial
noises.

All kinds of conventionally accepted boundaries have
thereby been challenged: not just the one between the
"scientific" and the "literary-artistic" cultures, or the one
between "art" and "non-art"; but also many established
distinctions within the world of culture itself—that between
form and content, the frivolous and the serious, and (a
favorite of literary intellectuals) "high" and "low" culture.

The distinction between "high" and "low" (or "mass" or
"popular") culture is based partly on an evaluation of the

difference between unique and mass-produced objects. In an era of mass technological reproduction, the work of the serious artist had a special value simply because it was unique, because it bore his personal, individual signature. The works of popular culture (and even films were for a long time included in this category) were seen as having little value because they were manufactured objects, bearing no individual stamp—group concoctions made for an undifferentiated audience. But in the light of contemporary practice in the arts, this distinction appears extremely shallow. Many of the serious works of art of recent decades have a decidedly impersonal character. The work of art is reasserting its existence as "object" (even as manufactured or mass-produced object, drawing on the popular arts) rather than as "individual personal expression."

The exploration of the impersonal (and trans-personal) in contemporary art is the new classicism; at least, a reaction against what is understood as the romantic spirit dominates most of the interesting art of today. Today's art, with its insistence on coolness, its refusal of what it considers to be sentimentality, its spirit of exactness, its sense of "research" and "problems," is closer to the spirit of science than of art in the old-fashioned sense. Often, the artist's work is only his idea, his concept. This is a familiar practice in architecture, of course. And one remembers that painters in the Renaissance often left parts of their canvases to be worked out by students, and that in the flourishing period of the concerto the cadenza at the end of the first movement was left to the inventiveness and discretion of the performing soloist. But similar practices have a different, more polemical meaning today, in the present post-romantic era of the arts. When painters such as Joseph Albers, Ellsworth Kelly, and Andy Warhol assign portions of the work, say, the painting in of the colors themselves, to a friend or the local gardener; when musicians such as Stockhausen, John Cage, and Luigi Nono invite collaboration from performers by leaving opportunities for random effects, switching around the order of the score, and improvisations—they are changing the ground rules which most of us employ to recognize a work of art. They are saying what art need not be. At least, not necessarily.

The primary feature of the new sensibility is that its model product is not the literary work, above all, the novel. A new non-literary culture exists today, of whose very existence, not to mention significance, most literary intellectuals are entirely unaware. This new establishment includes certain painters, sculptors, architects, social planners, film-makers, TV technicians, neurologists, musicians, electronics engineers, dancers, philosophers, and sociologists. (A few poets and prose writers can be included.) Some of the basic texts for this new cultural alignment are to be found in the writings of Nietzsche, Wittgenstein, Antonin Artaud, C. S. Sherrington, Buckminster Fuller, Marshall McLuhan, John Cage, André Breton, Roland Barthes, Claude Lévi-Strauss, Siegfried Gideion, Norman O. Brown, and Gyorgy Kepes.

Those who worry about the gap between "the two cultures," and this means virtually all literary intellectuals in England and America, take for granted a notion of culture which decidedly needs reexamining. It is the notion perhaps best expressed by Matthew Arnold (in which the central cultural act is the making of literature, which is itself understood as the criticism of culture). Simply ignorant of the vital and enthralling (so called "avant-garde") developments in the other arts, and blinded by their personal investment in the perpetuation of the older notion of culture, they continue to cling to literature as the model for creative statement.

What gives literature its preeminence is its heavy burden of "content," both reportage and moral judgment. (This makes it possible for most English and American literary critics to use literary works mainly as texts, or even pretexts, for social and cultural diagnosis—rather than concentrating on the properties of, say, a given novel or a play, as an art work.) But the model arts of our time are actually those with much less content, and a much cooler mode of moral judgment—like music, films, dance, architecture, painting, sculpture. The practice of these arts—all of which draw profusely, naturally, and without embarrassment, upon science and technology—are the locus of the new sensibility.

The problem of "the two cultures," in short, rests upon an uneducated, uncontemporary grasp of our present cultural situation. It arises from the ignorance of literary intellectuals (and of scientists with a shallow knowledge of the arts, like the scientist-novelist C. P. Snow himself) of a new culture, and its emerging sensibility. In fact, there can be no divorce between science and technology, on the one hand, and art, on the other, any more than there can be a divorce between art and the forms of social life. Works of art, psychological forms, and social forms all reflect each other, and change with each other. But, of course, most people are slow to come to terms with such changes—especially today, when the changes are occurring with an unprecedented rapidity. Marshall McLuhan has described human history as a succession of acts of technological extension of human capacity, each of which works a radical change upon our environment and our ways of thinking, feeling, and valuing. The tendency, he remarks, is to upgrade the old environment into art form (thus Nature became a vessel of aesthetic and spiritual values in the new industrial environment) "while the new conditions are regarded as corrupt and degrading." Typically, it is only certain artists in any given era who "have the resources and temerity to live in immediate contact with the environment of their age . . . That is why they may seem to be 'ahead of their time' . . . More timid people prefer to accept the . . . previous environment's values as the continuing reality of their time. Our natural bias is to accept the new gimmick (automation, say) as a thing that can be accommodated in the old ethical order." Only in the terms of what McLuhan calls the old ethical order does the problem of "the two cultures" appear to be a genuine problem. It is not a problem for most of the creative artists of our time (among whom one could include very few novelists) because most of these artists have broken, whether they know it or not, with the Matthew Arnold notion of culture, finding it historically and humanly obsolescent.

The Matthew Arnold notion of culture defines art as the criticism of life—this being understood as the propounding of moral, social, and political ideas. The new sensibility understands art as the extension of life—this being understood as the representation of (new) modes of vivacity. There is no necessary denial of the role of moral evaluation here. Only the scale has changed; it has become less gross, and what it sacrifices in discursive explicitness it gains in accuracy and subliminal power. For we are what we are able to see (hear, taste, smell, feel) even more powerfully and profoundly than we are what furniture of ideas we have stocked in our heads. Of course, the proponents of "the two cultures" crisis continue to observe a desperate contrast between unintelligible, morally neutral science and technology, on the one hand, and morally committed, human-scale art on the other. But matters are not that simple, and never were. A great work of art is never simply (or even mainly) a vehicle of ideas or of moral sentiments. It is, first of all, an object modifying our consciousness and sensibility, changing the composition, however slightly, of the humus that nourishes all specific ideas and sentiments. Outraged humanists, please note. There is no need for alarm. A work of art does not cease being a moment in the conscience of mankind, when moral conscience is understood as only one of the functions of consciousness.

Sensations, feelings, the abstract forms and styles of sensibility count. It is to these that contemporary art addresses itself. The basic unit for contemporary art is not the idea, but the analysis of and extension of sensations. (Or if it is an "idea," it is about the form of sensibility.) Rilke described the artist as someone who works "toward an extension of the regions of the individual senses"; McLuhan calls artists "experts in sensory awareness." And the most interesting works of contemporary art (one can begin at least as far back as French symbolist poetry) are adventures in sensation, new "sensory mixes." Such art is, in principle, experimental—not out of an elitist disdain for what is accessible to the majority, but precisely in the sense that science is experimental. Such an art is also notably apolitical and undidactic, or rather, infradidactic.

When Ortega y Gasset wrote his famous essay *The Dehumanization of Art* in the early 1920s, he ascribed the qualities of modern art (such as impersonality, the ban on pathos, hostility to the past, playfulness, willful stylization, absence of ethical and political commitment) to the spirit of youth which he thought dominated our age.[*] In retrospect, it seems this "dehumanization" did not signify the recovery of childlike innocence, but was rather a very adult, knowing response. What other response than anguish, followed by anesthesia and then by wit and the elevating of intelligence over sentiment, is possible as a response to the social disorder and mass atrocities of our time, and—equally important for our sensibilities, but less often remarked on—to the unprecedented change in what rules our environment from the intelligible and visible to that which is only with difficulty intelligible and is invisible? Art, which I have characterized as an instrument

---

[*]Ortega remarks, in this essay: "Were art to redeem man, it could do so only by saving him from the seriousness of life and restoring him to an unexpected boyishness."

for modifying and educating sensibility and consciousness, now operates in an environment which cannot be grasped by the senses.

Buckminister Fuller has written:

> In World War I industry suddenly went from the visible to the invisible base, from the track to the trackless, from the wire to the wireless, from visible structuring to invisible structuring in alloys. The big thing about World War I is that man went off the sensorial spectrum forever *as the prime criterion of accrediting innovations* . . . All major advances since World War I have been in the infra and the ultrasensorial frequencies of the electromagnetic spectrum. All the important technical affairs of men today are invisible . . . The old masters, who were sensorialists, have unleased a Pandora's box of non-sensorially controllable phenomena, which they had avoided accrediting up to that time . . . Suddenly they lost their true mastery, because from then on they didn't personally understand what was going on. If you don't understand you cannot master . . . Since World War I, the old masters have been extinct . . .

But, of course, art remains permanently tied to the senses. Just as one cannot float colors in space (a painter needs some sort of surface, like a canvas, however neutral and textureless), one cannot have a work of art that does not impinge upon the human sensorium. But it is important to realize that human sensory awareness has not merely a biology but a specific history, each culture placing a premium on certain senses and inhibiting others. (The same is true for the range of primary human emotions.) Here is where art (among other things) enters, and why the interesting art of our time has such a feeling of anguish and crisis about it, however playful and abstract and ostensibly neutral morally it may appear. Western man may be said to have been undergoing a massive sensory anesthesia (a concomitant of the process that Max Weber calls "bureaucratic rationalization") at least since the Industrial Revolution, with modern art functioning as a kind of shock therapy for both confounding and unclosing our senses.

One important consequence of the new sensibility (with its abandonment of the Matthew Arnold idea of culture) has already been alluded to—namely, that the distinction between "high" and "low" culture seems less and less meaningful. For such a distinction—inseparable from the Matthew Arnold apparatus—simply does not make sense for a creative community of artists and scientists engaged in programming sensations, uninterested in art as a species of moral journalism. Art has always been more than that, anyway.

Another way of characterizing the present cultural situation, in its most creative aspects, would be to speak of a new attitude toward pleasure. In one sense, the new art and the new sensibility take a rather dim view of pleasure. (The great contemporary French composer, Pierre Boulez, entitled an important essay of his twelve years ago, "Against Hedonism in Music.") The seriousness of modern art precludes pleasure in the familiar sense—the pleasure of a melody that one can hum after leaving the concert hall, of characters in a novel or play whom one can recognize, identify with, and dissect in terms of realistic psychological motives, of a beautiful landscape or a dramatic moment represented on a canvas. If hedonism means sustaining the old ways in which we have found pleasure in art (the old sensory and psychic modalities), then the new art is anti-hedonistic. Having one's sensorium challenged or stretched hurts. The new serious music hurts one's ears, the new painting does not graciously reward one's sight, the new films and the few interesting new prose works do not go down easily. The commonest complaint about the films of Antonioni or the narratives of Beckett or Burroughs is that they are hard to look at or to read, that they are "boring." But the charge of boredom is really hypocritical. There is, in a sense, no such thing as boredom. Boredom is only another name for a certain species of frustration. And the new languages which the interesting art of our time speaks are frustrating to the sensibilities of most educated people.

But the purpose of art is always, ultimately, to give pleasure—though our sensibilities may take time to catch up with the forms of pleasure that art in a given time may offer. And, one can also say that, balancing the ostensible anti-hedonism of serious contemporary art, the modern sensibility is more involved with pleasure in the familiar sense than ever. Because the new sensibility demands less "content" in art, and is more open to the pleasures of "form" and style, it is also less snobbish, less moralistic—in that it does not demand that pleasure in art necessarily be associated with edification. If art is understood as a form of discipline of the feelings and a programming of sensations, then the feeling (or sensation) given off by a Rauschenberg painting might be like that of a song by the Supremes. The brio and elegance of Budd Boetticher's *The Rise and Fall of Legs Diamond* or the singing style of Dionne Warwick can be appreciated as a complex and pleasurable event. They are experienced without condescension.

This last point seems to me worth underscoring. For it is important to understand that the affection which many younger artists and intellectuals feel for the popular arts is not a new philistinism (as has so often been charged) or a species of anti-intellectualism or some kind of abdication from culture. The fact that many of the most serious American painters, for example, are also fans of "the new sound" in popular music is *not* the result of the search for mere diversion or relaxation; it is not, say, like Schoenberg also playing tennis. It reflects a new, more open way of looking at the world and at things in the world, our world. It does not mean the renunciation of all standards: there is plenty of stupid popular music, as well as inferior and pretentious "avant-garde" paintings, films, and music. The point is that there *are* new standards, new standards of beauty and style and taste. The new sensibility is defiantly pluralistic; it is dedicated both to an excruciating seriousness and to fun and wit and nostalgia. It is also extremely history-conscious; and the voracity of its enthusiasms (and of the supercession of these enthusiasms) is very high-speed and hectic. From the vantage point of this new sensibility, the beauty of a machine or of the solution to a mathematical problem, of a painting by Jasper Johns, of a film by Jean-Luc Godard, and of the Beatles is equally accessible.

# Raggedy Andy

## Calvin Tomkins

> I'd prefer to remain a mystery.
> I never give my background,
> and anyway, I make it all up
> different every time I'm asked.

There is a snapshot of Andy Warhol at the age of fourteen, taken in one of those do-it-yourself booths in a bus station. The features are delicate and well formed, the expression trusting, angelic. Time treated him unfairly. His face grew coarse, Slavic, with a fleshy nose and narrow eyes weak as a mole's. And of course the famous pallor—an almost total absence of pigmentation, the result of a childhood disease that may have been rheumatic fever, although his mother's reference to "nervous fits" suggests other causes. In spite of time's jokes, however, the face of that beautiful fourteen-year-old is instantly recognizable.

The first year Andy came to New York he lived with a whole group of boys and girls in a basement apartment at 103rd Street and Manhattan Avenue. This was in 1949. Everybody did something interesting or planned to—study dance, paint, write, make jewelry. Andy was very much the baby of the family. Although he may or may not have been

From *The Scene: Reports on Post-Modern Art* (Viking, 1976).

nineteen at the time (his birth date varies each time he is asked), he seemed even younger. And so shy—he rarely spoke at all. One of the girls in the apartment remembers getting so mad at Andy for not talking to her that she threw an egg and hit him on the head with it. They all had a lot of fun, sharing food, money, and clothes and being such good friends—there was no sex involved. They went to the movies a lot, and had a communal crush on Judy Garland. When one of her films played the neighborhood Loews they all saw it six times.

Andy had no money at all then. Lila Davies, who went through art school at Carnegie Tech with him and who brought him into the Manhattan Avenue kibbutz, knew that he came from very poor people. Andy's father, a coal miner and part-time construction worker, had come over from Czechoslovakia in 1912 to make his fortune, but fortunes were elusive even in America and it had been nine years before he was able to send back for his wife. Andy and his two older brothers grew up in McKeesport, Pennsylvania. Their name was Warhola—Andy shortened it when he came to New York. Not even Lila knew where the money had come from to send Andy through Carnegie Tech. The father had died in 1941, and for a while after that Andy had worked part time in the Five and Ten and had sold vegetables from a truck. He occasionally mentioned his mother and his two brothers, but never his father.

To the others in the apartment Andy seemed unbelievably naïve—so innocent that you felt the need to protect him. He spent a lot of his time in the apartment, drawing. Andy had worked out an unusual technique. He would sketch with a pencil until he got what he wanted, then copy the sketch very rapidly in ink on tissue and press the tissue down on watercolor paper before the ink dried. The result was a blotted, broken line that looked spontaneous and fluid and, oddly enough, highly sophisticated. Periodically, Andy would take his drawings around to magazines and advertising agencies. He couldn't afford a portfolio, so he took them around in a brown paper bag from the A & P.

One day he took his paper bag into the office of Tina Fredericks, who at that time was art director of *Glamour* magazine. She was intrigued both by the drawings and by Andy, pale and shy and a little forlorn in his old chino pants and dirty sneakers. She told him the drawings were good, but that what *Glamour* really needed at the moment were drawings of shoes. Andy came back the next day with fifty shoe drawings in the brown paper bag. *Glamour* eventually used several of them, and this led to his first commission from I. Miller. For the next few years I. Miller was Andy's meal ticket. Nobody had ever drawn shoes the way Andy did. He somehow gave each shoe a temperament of its own, a sort of sly, Toulouse-Lautrec kind of sophistication, but the shape and the style came through accurately and the buckle was always in the right place. The kids in the apartment noticed that the vamps on Andy's shoe drawings kept getting longer and longer, but I. Miller didn't mind. I. Miller loved them.

Andy never seemed to be working terribly hard. When his eyes began bothering him, though, Lila made him go to an oculist who told him he had "lazy eyes" and prescribed rather grotesque glasses to strengthen the muscles—the lenses were opaque, with a tiny pinhole to see through. To everyone's surprise, Andy wore them dutifully when he was working and a lot of the time when he was not. It began to occur to the others that Andy worked pretty hard. Still, he wasn't what you'd call ambitious, although he did have this thing about famous people. He was always writing to movie stars to get their autographs. He once wrote a letter to Truman Capote, to ask if he could illustrate *Other Voices, Other Rooms* (Capote did not answer), and then he had some wild idea about movie stars' underwear, that you could go into business selling underwear that had been worn by the stars; it would cost $5 washed and $50 unwashed. But all that was just fun and games, and nobody took it seriously when Andy said that he was going to be famous himself. Andy was so naïve, so fragile. The kids in the apartment would have done anything to shield him from the hard, aggressive, urban rat race.

* * *

> Money doesn't worry me, either,
> though I sometimes wonder where
> is it? Somebody's got it all!

Fritzie Miller felt that her husband, a commercial artist, was not getting the attention he deserved from his agent, so she said, "Why don't you let me take your stuff around?" and he said, "All right, why don't you?" Her husband and a couple of friends were her first clients. One day in the 1950s, soon after she started out as an agent, she went to see an art director named Will Burton. In Burton's office when she arrived was a slender boy in paint-splattered clothes, holding a hand-painted Easter egg. The egg was a present for Burton. "Andy, meet Fritzie," Burton said. "You need her."

They never signed a formal contract. In fact, a month or so after this first meeting, Andy called up Fritzie in great agitation and said that a friend of his, who had taken his stuff around to the agencies in the past, had just returned from Europe and was angry with Andy for getting an agent. Andy, who was subject to a lot of anxieties at this time, worried that his friend might be going to beat him up. (The group in the Manhattan Avenue apartment had broken up by this time because the building was being torn down, and Andy had moved into a cold-water flat in the East Seventies with his mother, who had come to New York to visit him one day and just stayed on.) "Listen, Andy, forget it," Fritzie told him. "You don't owe me anything." But a month later Andy called up again and said he wanted Fritzie to represent him, and that's what happened.

Andy was still doing shoes for I. Miller, and quite a few other things as well. He designed stationery for Bergdorf-Goodman, Christmas cards for Tiffany's and for the Tiber Press, and record jackets for Columbia Records. For a brief period he drew the little suns and clouds in the weather chart on an early-morning television program—only his hand was visible on screen, but he had to get up at 5 a.m. and go to the studio to have his hand made up because otherwise it looked too white. He took any job he was offered, and everything he did was done professionally and stylishly, and on time.

Fritzie got him into the big women's magazines, first *McCalls* and *The Ladies' Home Journal,* and later *Vogue* and *Harper's Bazaar.* A lot of people in the industry began to notice Andy's magazine work. Whatever he illustrated— shampoo or bras or jewelry or lipstick or perfume—there was a decorative originality about his work that made it eye-catching. It was amazing, Fritzie thought, how someone with Andy's background could hit the right note so unerringly. The childish hearts and flowers and the androgynous pink cherubs that he used were not quite what they seemed to be; there was a slight suggestiveness about them that people in the business recognized and approved. He could kid the product so subtly that he made the client feel witty.

Andy never wore anything but old clothes. He would show up at *Vogue* or *Bazaar* looking like some street urchin in his torn chinos and dirty sneakers—Raggedy Andy—and the editors and art directors found this irresistible. Imagine coming in here looking like that! Actually he was starting to make quite a lot of money—enough, at any rate, to rent two nonconsecutive floors in an apartment building on East Seventy-fourth Street, over a bar called Shirley's Pin-Up. Andy and Mrs. Warhola had their living quarters on the lower floor. Andy bought some furniture and other objects from Serendipity, but the place never really got to look furnished because Andy was always too busy. He was out all day and half the night, taking art directors to lunch at expensive restaurants, keeping appointments, going to parties. Andy went to all kinds of parties, even the ones given by somebody's secretary, because you could never be sure whom you'd meet or what it might lead to. Shy, inarticulate Andy, using his shyness and inarticulateness to superb effect, made a lot of contacts that way; most people found him charming and oddly fascinating. He hardly ever got home until past midnight, and then he would spend the next three or four hours working. Luckily he had a quick technique and could sketch a whole layout in a couple of hours. He worked on the top floor of the building, in a large, incredibly littered room. Magazines and newspapers and clothes and half-full coffee containers and swatches of this and that and discarded drawings and unanswered mail piled up in drifts on the floor, providing sport and concealment for Andy's cats. There were eight cats, all named Sam. Nathan Gluck, a designer who came in part time to help with layouts, occasionally tried to clean the place up a little, but it was hopeless. The cats lived there. The smell was something.

Through Emile de Antonio, a dropout college English teacher who knew everybody and made a sort of living in those days by putting artists and other talents in touch with people who could help them (he is now a film-maker), Andy went to see Eugene Moore at Bonwit Teller. Gene Moore, one of New York's little-known geniuses, was then in charge of window display at Bonwit's and also at Tiffany's, and he made a point of using serious young artists to do window decoration—Robert Rauschenberg and Jasper Johns supported themselves in this way for several years in the 1950s. According to Moore, Andy was unfailingly cooperative. "He worked hard and made it seem easy." Moore remembers. "On the surface he always seemed so nice and uncompli-cated. He had a sweet, fey, little-boy quality, which he used, but it was pleasant even so—and that was the quality of his work, too. It was light, it had great charm, yet there was always a real beauty of line and composition. There was nobody else around then who worked quite that way."

Dan Arje, who took over the display department at Bonwit's when Moore went to Tiffany's full time, was equally enthusiastic about Andy. Andy was a real pro. He under-stood deadlines, and where other artists might freeze up under the pressure of having to do a window in two or three evening hours Andy would just come in and go right to work, painting freehand on the inside of the glass his witty and whimsical images—cherubs, pincushions, ice-cream fanta-sies. Once he built a wood fence out of scrap lumber and decorated it with graffiti and flowers and suns and the kind of stick people that kids draw. The mannequins looked fabulous against it.

Andy never stopped pushing. Every week or so, the art directors and fashion editors and display people would get some little reminder—a wash drawing of butterflies in candy-mint colors, for example, or a fanciful shoe on gold paper, just in case they forgot that Andy was around. He was furious when other illustrators started to imitate his blotted line and his cherubs. Gene Moore and others explained to him that he had to expect this, anybody with talent was bound to have imitators, but Andy didn't like it a bit. He seemed to want all the accounts, all the windows, all the business. Was it the memory of his grim childhood that drove him? "He does love money," Fritzie Miller conceded. "Not for himself, though—for what he can do with it."

But what was he doing with it?

* * *

I delight in the world.
I get great joy out of it,
but I'm not sensuous.

Could that be Andy? In chinos and sneakers, a handkerchief knotted at the four corners on his head to ward off the sun, stepping gingerly around the ruins of Angkor Wat? Accompa-nied by Floyd Davis, the well-known *Saturday Evening Post*

illustrator, and Gladys Rockmore Davis, the well-known
Floyd's even better-known wife?

Andy and his friend Charles Lisanby were on a trip around
the world. Lisanby, who designs sets for television and is an
inveterate traveler, happened to mention that he was thinking
of such a trip, and Andy, who had never been anywhere
except Pittsburgh and New York and McKeesport, said,
"Gee, can I come?" Lisanby was delighted. He and Andy had
met at a party the year before, and they had taken an
immediate liking to one another. As is the case with so many
New Yorkers who came from somewhere else, Lisanby, who
was born on a farm in Kentucky, had the easy assurance and
polish that Andy so much admired; Lisanby was fascinated by
Andy's oddness, by the contrast between his naïveté and the
extraordinary sophistication of his work. They left in June
1956, flying first to San Francisco and then out to Japan.

Lisanby planned the trip. From Japan they went to Hong
Kong, Formosa, Djakarta, and Bali, and then to Cambodia,
where they met the Davises. Andy did a lot of sketching. He
seemed interested most of the time, although not what you'd
call thrilled about anything; he particularly liked the gold-
and-black-lacquer work they saw in Bangkok. After Angkor
Wat they went on to India. Lisanby wanted to go up to Nepal,
which had recently been opened to tourists, but just before
they were to go there he came down with a fever. An Indian
doctor pumped him full of antibiotics, but the fever hung on
and so instead of going to Nepal they booked tickets on a
plane to Rome.

It was August by this time. As their plane came down for a
landing at Cairo airport, they looked out the window and saw
a great many tanks, soldiers, and machine guns ringing the
perimeter; no one was permitted to disembark. Both Andy
and Lisanby were quite surprised to learn, later, that there
had been some sort of international crisis over Suez and that
they had landed right in the middle of it.

In Rome they stayed at the Grand Hotel until Lisanby had
fully recovered. Lisanby kept urging Andy to go out and see
the sights, but Andy didn't feel like going out alone; he
seemed quite content to stay in the hotel. When they got to
Florence, however, Lisanby, who had been there several
times, insisted on Andy's going into every church and museum, and Andy seemed to enjoy that. Andy's reactions to
art were never very verbal. Faced with a Titian or a Botticelli,

he might produce a mild "Wow!" or "Great!" but that would be the end of it. Lisanby once asked him what he really wanted out of life, and Andy replied, rather memorably, "I want to be Matisse." Lisanby interpreted this to mean that he wanted to be as famous as Matisse, so that anything he did would instantly become marvelous. Fame was certainly very much on his mind.

From Florence they went to Amsterdam for a week and from there they flew directly home, stopping in neither Paris nor London.

• • •

The artificial fascinates me,
the bright and shiny.

The boys at Serendipity helped Andy decorate the apartment over Shirley's Pin-Up. Serendipity, which was partly a restaurant and partly a shop, catered to the kind of taste that had not yet been identified as camp. It had Tiffany glass before people were buying Tiffany glass. Andy bought a Tiffany lamp and some bentwood chairs, a long, soft couch, and a lot of white-painted wicker furniture, and from other shops on Third Avenue he picked up some American antiques. He had also started to buy pictures—a Magritte, some Miró lithographs, things like that. One of his friends from this period described the apartment's style as "Victorian Surrealist."

Serendipity also carried Andy's work. The original drawings for his I. Miller shoe ads were for sale there, and so were the drawings of imaginary footgear that he had taken to designing, fantastically ornate boots and slippers "dedicated" to famous personalities such as Truman Capote, Julie Andrews, Zsa Zsa Gabor, and James Dean. Serendipity carried Andy's books as well. The first of these was called *25 Cats Named Sam and One Blue Pussy.* Andy did the drawings, had them printed and bound, then got his friends to come in and help hand-color them. After the cat book came *The Gold Book,* a collection of Andy's blotted line drawings of friends, flowers, shoes, and other images on gold paper (the idea came from the gold lacquer work he had seen in Bangkok). Then there was *In the Bottom of My Garden* (slightly suspect cherubs), and *Wild Raspberries,* a joke cookbook with Suzie Frankfurt's recipes for dishes like "Salade de Alf Landon" and "Seared Roebuck." The recipes in the cookbook were

written out in longhand by Andy's mother, Mrs. Warhola,
who could barely speak English, could not write it at all, but
Andy liked her handwriting and so he would give her the text
and have her copy it letter for letter, laboriously, missing or
transposing a letter here and there, which always delighted
Andy enormously. Serendipity also had a book called *Holy
Cats* that really was by Andy's mother—she did the drawings
herself, as well as the captions, the rather risqué innuendoes
of which she probably did not understand.

Andy's friends all thought Mrs. Warhola was fabulous.
Although her English never improved very much, she was
cheerful and sweet, and she liked all of Andy's friends. Some
of his friends thought it a shame that Andy didn't let his
mother come to the parties that Serendipity gave whenever
one of his books appeared. Even when he had a show of his
gold-shoe drawings in 1959 at the Bodley Gallery, a few doors
down from Serendipity's new store, on Sixtieth Street,
Andy's mother didn't come to the opening. But Mrs. Warhola
never seemed to mind. She was happy taking care of Andy,
and seeing to it that he went to mass every Sunday. Once,
when Andy talked about going somewhere in an airplane,
Mrs. Warhola got very upset. "Too many big shot die in the
air," she said. Mrs. Warhola knew Andy was a big shot.

• • •

I never wanted to be a painter.
I wanted to be a tap dancer.

In the late 1950s, the fashion crowd started to take an active
interest in the New York art scene. This was not without
precedent, but it was a change from the recent past. Throughout the heroic period of American art in the 1940s and early
1950s, the era that saw New York painting achieve international fame and influence, the artists had kept pretty much to
themselves, fighting private battles and forging private myths.
*Vogue* and *Harper's Bazaar* had duly noted the emergence of
the New York School, had posed their mannequins against
Abstract Expressionist, dripped-paint backdrops and informed their readers that "people are talking about" Jackson
Pollock and Willem de Kooning, but there had been no real
interaction between the worlds of art and fashion. Now,
however, a new spirit was coming into vanguard art. Robert
Rauschenberg and Jasper Johns had broken out of the

Abstract Expressionist nest. Rauschenberg's paintings, which incorporated everyday images from the urban environment and actual everyday objects such as Coke bottles and street signs, had opened the way for a whole generation of artists who tended to look out at the world, rather than in upon their own reactions to it. Magazines such as *Life* and *Newsweek*, discovering that art was news, had begun to devote considerable coverage to the New York art scene, and in doing so had helped to swell the public that was already flocking in ever-increasing numbers to galleries and museums. Art was *in*. The fashion crowd, which knew Rauschenberg and Johns as display artists, realized with a slight start that people really *were* talking about Rauschenberg and Johns.

No one realized it more keenly than Andy. "Jasper is such a star," Andy would say, wistfully, to Emile de Antonio. It bothered Andy that Rauschenberg and Johns, who were also friends of de Antonio's, seemed to have no interest in becoming friends of his. Andy often asked very naïve questions, and he couldn't resist asking de Antonio ("Dee") why Bob and Jap didn't like him. Dee said that, among other things, they found Andy too frigging commercial. Bob and Jap took only enough window-display jobs to pay the rent on their studios. They clearly did not consider the drawings that Andy showed at the Bodley and at Serendipity essentially different from his commercial work, for which he made close to $50,000 a year.

De Antonio's wife could not imagine what her husband saw in Andy. To her Andy was just a silly little boy. But behind the innocence and the naïveté, de Antonio thought he could discern an iron streak. "Andy was blindingly ambitious," he said. "I was sure he was going to make it, although not necessarily in art—he could have made it in just about anything he tried."

● ● ●

Q.  Do you think Pop Art is—?
A.  No.
Q.  What?
A.  No.
Q.  Do you think Pop Art is—?
A.  No. No, I don't.

Andy called up Charles Lisanby one day in 1962. "Listen," he said, "there's something new we're starting. It's called Pop Art, and you better get in on it because you can do it, too." Lisanby thought Andy was putting him on. Oddly enough, the whole thing happened so fast that Andy himself almost didn't get in on it.

For two years Andy had been more and more intrigued by the art scene. He went around to the galleries with his friend Ted Carey, and occasionally they bought things—paintings by Robert Goodnough and Larry Rivers, a Jasper Johns drawing of a light bulb, a double portrait of themselves by Fairfield Porter. Andy wouldn't buy anything if he thought it was too expensive—in fact, if you ask him today what impressed him about the Johns drawing he will say it was the price: "I couldn't understand how he could get five hundred dollars for a drawing. Even Picasso didn't get that much, did he?" Andy decided against a small Rauschenberg collage that Carey wanted to buy because it cost $250. "I could do that myself," Andy said.

"Well," said Carey, "why don't you?"

Andy lost the I. Miller account around this time. A new art director had come in and decided to change the I. Miller image: since Andy was totally responsible for the image, that meant no more Andy. His income dropped off as a result, although he was still making more than almost any other illustrator in the business. Andy had started to make some friends in the art world, and he saw fewer of his friends in the commercial field. At some point in 1960 he did a series of paintings that had no apparent relation either to his commercial work or to the drawings for his books. The new pictures were based on comic strips—Popeye, Superman, The Little King, Dick Tracy. They were painted in the broad, crude style of the originals, from which he would select some detail and present it on a greatly enlarged scale. He also did two large paintings of Coca-Cola bottles. One of them showed a pure, literal, unadorned Coke bottle, greatly enlarged, while the other had a lot of Abstract Expressionist hashmarks— dripped paint and agitated brushwork—at the bottom. Andy asked de Antonio which of the Coke bottle paintings he liked best, and Dee said the unadorned one, absolutely.

Some of Andy's friends from the commercial field didn't like the new paintings at all. They couldn't understand why he had chosen those images, and they said there was nothing of Andy in them. What bothered Andy more than his friends' opinions was that he could not get a gallery to show the pictures. For a while he toyed with the idea of renting the Bodley again, but renting was so expensive and anyway it no longer seemed like the thing to do. By this time Andy was feeling pretty depressed.

Several factors had contributed to his depression. From Ivan Karp, the associate director of the Castelli Gallery, he had learned about Roy Lichtenstein's comic-strip paintings. Lichtenstein had done some paintings based on *Nancy and Sluggo* and *Mickey Mouse*, among others, and Ivan and Leo Castelli and Andy himself agreed that Lichtenstein's were much more authoritative than Andy's. Soon after this, Andy also learned for the first time about James Rosenquist, whose pictures were made up of greatly enlarged details of common objects—one of them featured a Seven-Up bottle.

Pop Art, in fact, was just about to burst upon the scene. Claes Oldenburg's plaster replicas of food and merchandise were shown at his "Store" on East Second Street during the winter of 1961-62. Jim Dine's necktie paintings, George Segal's plaster casts, Lichtenstein's comic strips had been discovered by the newsmagazines, and the artists involved, who in most cases had not previously known one another or been aware of each other's work, found themselves the leaders of the most swiftly recognized and efficiently promoted art movement in history. Almost before the older generation of artists and critics could get around to registering their disapproval, Pop had established an impregnable beachhead and set about colonizing the natives. But where was Andy? Leo Castelli liked his work, but Castelli had already taken Lichtenstein into the gallery and he was reluctant to take on another artist who seemed at the moment so similar. Richard Bellamy, the other leading promotor of Pop, had taken Oldenburg, Rosenquist and Tom Wesselmann into the Green Gallery; he, too, balked at Warhol. Andy's paintings were all over town—Castelli, Bellamy, and Allan Stone all had a few in the back room—and in the summer of 1962 Andy's comic strip pictures were even seen briefly in the window of Bonwit's annex on Fifty-seventh Street. But nobody was buying them.

Andy was desperate for ideas. "What'll I do next?" he kept asking his new art-world friends. Ivan Karp and Henry Geldzahler had urged Andy to develop images that were not being used by anyone else, but he couldn't think of any. One evening in early 1962, in the apartment over Shirley's Pin-Up, Muriel Latow told Andy she had an idea but it would cost him money to hear it. Muriel ran an art gallery that was going broke. "How much?" Andy asked her. Muriel said, "Fifty dollars." Andy went straight to the desk and wrote out a check.

"All right," Muriel said. "Now, tell me, Andy, what do you love more than anything else?"

"I don't know," Andy said. "What?"

"Money," Muriel said. "Why don't you paint money?"

Andy thought that was a terrific idea. Later on that evening Muriel also suggested (gratis, this time) that he paint something that was so familiar that nobody even noticed it any more, "something like a can of Campbell's soup."

The next day Andy went out and bought a whole lot of canvas and painted the money pictures and the first of the Campbell's soup pictures. This was before he had discovered the silk-screen process, so everything was painted by hand; when he learned about silk-screening it went much faster. The soup-can paintings were exhibited that summer, but not in New York. Irving Blum, who owned the Ferus Gallery in Los Angeles, saw them and offered to show them there, which he did in July. The show came in for a lot of heavy ridicule. A gallery next door to the Ferus piled up Campbell's soup cans in its window and advertised "the real thing" for twenty-nine cents a can. Irving Blum sold six of the thirty-two soup-can paintings for $100 apiece, but later he bought them back from the customers so that he could have the complete set himself.

In addition to soup cans and dollar bills Andy began doing silk-screen portraits of Marilyn Monroe and other stars. (Andy and his friends thought Marilyn was just great, even better than Judy Garland.) Eleanor Ward, who ran the Stable Gallery in New York, had come to the apartment that spring of 1962 to see Andy's work, and although she had liked it she could not offer him a show because she had just given the only free spot on her next season's exhibition calendar to Robert Indiana. During the summer, however, one of her older artists left the gallery, and so she called Andy from her summer place in Connecticut and said he could have a show at the Stable in November. Andy was just ecstatic, she remembers. "I'll never forget the sight of him coming into the gallery that September, in his dirty, filthy clothes and hi worn-out sneakers with the laces untied, and a big bunch of canvases rolled up under his arm. 'Look what the cat dragged in,' he said. Oh, he was so *happy* to have a gallery!"

Examples of nearly all the paintings that Andy had been doing since 1960 were in the Stable show, with the exception of the comic-strip paintings. The show caused a huge sensation. It was widely reported in the press, and it virtually sold out. That same month, November 1962, Sidney Janis put on his two-gallery show of Pop Art, and in December the Museum of Modern Art sponsored a symposium devoted to the new movement. Andy had got in just under the wire.

•  •  •

> I feel I'm very much a part of
> my times, of my culture,
> as much a part of it as
> rockets and television.

In the group of artists who gained prominence through the triumph of Pop, not one knows fame on the level that Andy does. As Alan Solomon once remarked, Andy is the first real art celebrity since Picasso and Dali. Housewives in Keokuk who may never have heard of Lichtenstein, or even of Rauschenberg and Johns, are aware of Andy Warhol. His dream has come true.

It all happened so fast, this stardom. After the first Stable show Andy went into mass production. He had taken a studio on East Forty-seventh Street—"The Factory," he called it—and with the help of his new friend Gerard Malanga he turned out hundreds of pictures during the next few months: multiple-image silk-screen portraits of Troy Donahue, Roger Maris, Liz Taylor, Ethel Scull; Campbell's soup cans by the hundred on single canvases; the new "death" series (suggested originally by Geldzahler) of grisly automobile wrecks, a suicide in mid-air, the electric chair at Sing-Sing. Every week he would show up at the Stable with another roll of canvases under his arm for the gallery assistants to stretch and mount, and everything he did was immediately bought. *Almost* everything, that is—the auto wrecks proved too tough for most buyers, although for some reason the electric chairs were hugely popular. For his next show, Andy filled the Stable with boxes—wooden boxes made to his order and silk-screened on all sides to look exactly like the cartons of

Brillo pads and Mott's Apple Juice and Heinz Tomato
Ketchup that you saw in the supermarkets. Visitors threaded
their way through narrow aisles between the piled-up boxes.
So many people came to the opening that there was a long
line on the street outside waiting to get in. After that Andy
moved to the Leo Castelli Gallery, where he had two shows.
The first, in 1964, was all flowers, silk-screened from a photo
in a photography magazine; the second, in 1966, consisted of
Andy's cow portrait repeated over and over on wallpaper,
together with silver, helium-filled pillows that floated. Production at the Factory continued at full blast. Then, with
awesome timing, Andy declared Pop Art dead and moved on
to the next phase.

The Factory, by now a famous Pop artifact lined from floor
to ceiling with silver foil, was converted from silk screens to
movies. The flickering strobe light of Andy's energy illuminated a series of his girls-and-boys-of-the-year: Baby Jane
Holzer, Gerard Malanga, Edie Sedgwick, Henry Geldzahler.
Andy's early films celebrating the splendors of total boredom
won the Independent Film Award—the highest accolade of
the underground cinema. Andy's Exploding Plastic Inevitable
group act plugged into the rock-music scene at the Electric
Circus, and boomed the fad for multimedia light shows of all
kinds. The fashion crowd went gaga with admiration; artists
were now dictating the new clothing styles and everyone wore
a costume. Andy, whose soiled chinos and sneakers had been
superseded by a black leather jacket and silver-sprayed hair,
seemed to be everywhere at once. For two years he was out
every night. Passive, pale as death, wearing his strange
melancholia like a second skin, he was supremely visible. At
the opening of Andy's 1965 show at the Institute of Contemporary Art in Philadelphia, the huge crowd went berserk at
their first sight of Andy and Edie Sedgwick on a balcony; they
had to be smuggled out a side door to escape being crushed.
Andy-Matisse.

But why? Surely those monotonously repetitive flowers and
cows, those gaudy portraits, and those torpid films were not
all that compelling. Not more so, at any rate, than Lichtenstein's drowning heroines or Oldenburg's giant hamburgers.
True, Andy went further than the other Pop artists. The
death series, the endless repetitions, the mass-production
methods carried certain ideas implicit in Pop to an extreme
point, but a point not unknown to earlier and more radical

artists than Andy. After all, Duchamp removed the artist's
hand from art in 1913, when he began signing "readymade"
objects. It has been said that Andy's real art is publicity, but
even this is debatable. Although Andy knows more or less
precisely what he is doing at all times, and continues to
capitalize brilliantly on his own drawbacks, he does not really
manipulate events. Andy remains essentially a voyeur, letting
things take their course and looking on with cool detachment,
interested but uninvolved. Then how do we explain the fact of
his celebrity?

The word, I think, is resonance. From time to time an
individual appears—not necessarily an artist—who seems to
be in phase with certain signals not yet receivable by standard
equipment. The clairvoyance with which Andy touched the
nerve of fashion and commercial art, the energy emanating
from God knows where, the inarticulateness and naïveté, the
very mystery and emptiness of his persona—all suggest the
presence of an uncanny intuition. Always somewhat unearthly, Warhol became in the 1960s a speechless and rather
terrifying oracle. He made visible something that was happening beneath the surface of American life.

• • •

I've always had this philosophy
of: it doesn't really matter.

A great deal of what took place in America during the 1960s
decade is missing, of course, from Warhol's house of mirrors.
He has had nothing whatsoever to say to the young militants,
the activists on either side of our contemporary conflicts.
Participation, confrontation, and martyrdom do not interest
him; if Andy contributes a painting to a liberal benefit it is
only because a refusal would be awkward and uncool. And no
one in the history of cool has ever been cooler than Andy.

One feels that Lichtenstein got to his Pop image intellectually, by logical steps, while Andy just *was* there by instinct.
Take the soup can, for example. Although the idea may have
come from Muriel Latow, it was Andy who sensed its
absolute rightness and saw just how to present it. Banal,
stupid, loaded with sentimental associations as it was, Andy
painted his soup can with icy precision and utter objectivity.
No interpretation, no reaction, no judgment, no emotion, no
comment—and not an echo of his former I. Miller insouci-

ance. The same is true of his other paintings (a possible exception being the Jackie Kennedy series, where some emotion seems evident on the part of the artist), and it is equally true of the films. Every Warhol image comes across frontally nude, without a shred of feeling attached. Andy's camera lens is the ultimate voyeur, but his films, for all their funny-sad sex scenes and their preoccupation with drugs and transvestism and pubic hair, are antierotic and utterly, numbingly cool.

The cool style requires a mastery of the put-on, of course, and in this area Andy knows no peer. Asked by a reporter why he painted the soup cans, Andy replies that for twenty years he has eaten soup for lunch. To an interviewer he gives deadpan nonanswers and asks at the end, "Have I lied enough?" Alan Midgette, the actor hired to impersonate Andy on a lecture tour, lectures at a dozen or more colleges before the hoax is discovered, whereupon Andy explains that Midgette is "more like what people expect than I could ever be." The put-on, another talisman of the 1960s, has been raised by Andy to the status of a minor art. It is also, let us note, a perfectly valid means of anesthesizing despair, without resort to hypocrisy. The absurd public world and the even more absurd private world are both treated as an in-joke, and sanity is preserved a little longer.

Over it all, however, lies the shadow. Vietnam, racism, urban blight, the poisoning of the environment, the alienation of the young, the murder of those few leaders who showed any real stomach for attacking the problems, and the sickening hypocrisy of our elected officials have drained us of hope. Even Andy has been ripped from grace, shot twice in the stomach by a woman who mistook him for a god ("He had too much control over my life," she told the police), his life nearly extinguished and still not wholly restored to him (one of the wounds would not heal for months). By a truly supernatural irony he was denied even the fruits of publicity that were due him; forty-eight hours after he was shot another assassin killed Robert Kennedy in Los Angeles. Afterward, he would say that his own life had come to seem like a dream, that he could not be sure whether he was alive or dead. Nor can we.

Andy kept his cool, but things are not the same. At the new Factory, down on Union Square (Andy moved out of the old one after a man walked in off the street and started to play

Russian roulette with a loaded gun—another irony), Andy's friend and business manager Paul Morrissey has more or less taken over the Warhol films operation. Andy comes in for an hour or so each afternoon but his heart is not in it. Brigid Polk, who has been around since the early 1960s and is one of Andy's established confidantes, thinks he may get out of films. "Andy buried painting," Brigid says, "and he may just bury movies, too." Andy is said to be interested in videotape. He wants his own television show, where people come on and talk and do whatever they like, while Andy watches.

Will his face inhabit the future as it has the past? Ivan Karp suggests that Andy's reputation may rest as much on his face as on anything else—the pale cast of those Slavic features, sensitive/ugly, angelic/satanic, not-quite-of-this-world. "One of the things he would have liked most," says another friend, "was to have been beautiful." Perhaps he is. At the moment, though, what we seem to see reflected in that strange face is a sickness for which there may be no cure. This is the new shudder brought by Warhol's art. Andy, in what one fervently hopes is just another put-on, begins to look more and more like the angel of death.

---

*Note:* Since this was written in 1970, Warhol has shown new signs of life: a series of surprisingly painterly portraits, some on commission (Philip Johnson, Leo Castelli), others on intuition (Chairman Mao); *Andy Warhol's Interview Magazine,* which charts the folk wisdom of various stars and superstars; a book, *The Philosophy of Andy Warhol (From A to B & Back Again).* He goes out more, is seen at parties and theaters wearing a Brooks Brothers suit and a rep tie. Andy endures.

# Bonnie and Clyde

## Pauline Kael

How do you make a good movie in this country without
being jumped on? *Bonnie and Clyde* is the most excitingly
American American movie since *The Manchurian Candidate*.
The audience is alive to it. Our experience as we watch it has
some connection with the way we reacted to movies in
childhood: with how we came to love them and to feel they
were ours—not an art that we learned over the years to
appreciate but simply and immediately ours. When an American movie is contemporary in feeling, like this one, it makes a
different kind of contact with an American audience from the
kind that is made by European films, however contemporary.
Yet any movie that is contemporary in feeling is likely to go
further than other movies—go too far for some tastes—and
*Bonnie and Clyde* divides audiences, as *The Manchurian
Candidate* did, and it is being jumped on almost as hard.
Though we may dismiss the attacks with "What good movie
doesn't give some offense?," the fact that it is generally *only*
good movies that provoke attacks by many people suggests
that the innocuousness of most of our movies is accepted with
such complacence that when an American movie reaches
people, when it makes them react, some of them think there

From *Kiss Kiss Bang Bang* (Little Brown and Co./ Atlantic Monthly Press, 1968).
First published in *The New Yorker*, October 1967.

must be something the matter with it—perhaps a law should be passed against it. *Bonnie and Clyde* brings into the almost frighteningly public world of movies things that people have been feeling and saying and writing about. And once something is said or done on the screens of the world, once it has entered mass art, it can never again belong to a minority, never again be the private possession of an educated, or "knowing," group. But even for that group there is an excitement in hearing its own private thoughts expressed out loud and in seeing something of its own sensibility become part of our common culture.

Our best movies have always made entertainment out of the anti-heroism of American life; they bring to the surface what, in its newest forms and fashions, is always just below the surface. The romanticism in American movies lies in the cynical tough guy's independence, the sentimentality lies, traditionally, in the falsified finish when the anti-hero turns hero. In 1967, this kind of sentimentality wouldn't work with the audience, and *Bonnie and Clyde* substitutes sexual fulfillment for a change of heart. (This doesn't quite work, either; audiences sophisticated enough to enjoy a movie like this one are too sophisticated for the dramatic uplift of the triumph over impotence.)

Structurally, *Bonnie and Clyde* is a story of love on the run, like the old Clark Gable–Claudette Colbert *It Happened One Night* but turned inside out; the walls of Jericho are psychological this time, but they fall anyway. If the story of Bonnie Parker and Clyde Barrow seemed almost from the start, and even to them while they were living it, to be the material of legend, it's because robbers who are loyal to each other—like the James brothers—are a grade up from garden-variety robbers, and if they're male and female partners in crime and young and attractive they're a rare breed. The Barrow gang had both family loyalty and sex appeal working for their legend. David Newman and Robert Benton, who wrote the script for *Bonnie and Clyde,* were able to use the knowledge that, like many of our other famous outlaws and gangsters, the real Bonnie and Clyde seemed to others to be acting out forbidden roles and to relish their roles. In contrast with secret criminals—the furtive embezzlers and other crooks who lead seemingly honest lives—the known outlaws capture the public imagination, because they take chances, and because, often, they enjoy dramatizing their lives. They know

that newspaper readers want all the details they can get about
the criminals who do the terrible things they themselves don't
dare to do, and also want the satisfaction of reading about the
punishment after feasting on the crimes. Outlaws play to this
public; they show off their big guns and fancy clothes and
their defiance of the law. Bonnie and Clyde established the
images for their own legend in the photographs they posed
for: the gunman and the gun moll. The naïve, touching
doggerel ballad that Bonnie Parker wrote and had published
in newspapers is about the roles they play for other people
contrasted with the coming end for them. It concludes:

> Someday they'll go down together;
> They'll bury them side by side;
> To few it'll be grief—
> To the law a relief—
> But it's death for Bonnie and Clyde.

That they did capture the public imagination is evidenced
by the many movies based on their lives. In the late forties,
there were *They Live by Night,* with Farley Granger and
Cathy O'Donnell, and *Gun Crazy,* with John Dall and Peggy
Cummins. (Alfred Hitchcock, in the same period, cast these
two Clyde Barrows, Dall and Granger, as Loeb and Leopold,
in *Rope.*) And there was a cheap—in every sense—1958
exploitation film, *The Bonnie Parker Story,* starring Dorothy
Provine. But the most important earlier version was Fritz
Lang's *You Only Live Once,* starring Sylvia Sidney as "Joan"
and Henry Fonda as "Eddie," which was made in 1937; this
version, which was one of the best American films of the
thirties, as *Bonnie and Clyde* is of the sixties, expressed
certain feelings of its time, as this film expresses certain
feelings of ours. (*They Live by Night,* produced by John
Houseman under the aegis of Dore Schary, and directed by
Nicholas Ray, was a very serious and socially significant tragic
melodrama, but its attitudes were already dated thirties
attitudes: the lovers were very young and pure and frightened
and underprivileged; the hardened criminals were sordid; the
settings were committedly grim. It made no impact on the
postwar audience, though it was a great success in England,
where our moldy socially significant movies could pass for
courageous.)

Just how contemporary in feeling *Bonnie and Clyde* is may

be indicated by contrasting it with *You Only Live Once,* which, though almost totally false to the historical facts, was *told* straight. It is a peculiarity of our times—perhaps it's one of the few specifically modern characteristics—that we don't take our stories straight any more. This isn't necessarily bad. *Bonnie and Clyde* is the first film demonstration that the put-on can be used for the purposes of art. *The Manchurian Candidate* almost succeeded in that, but what was implicitly wild and far-out in the material was nevertheless presented on screen as a straight thriller. *Bonnie and Clyde* keeps the audience in a kind of eager, nervous imbalance—holds our attention by throwing our disbelief back in our faces. To be put on is to be put on the spot, put on the stage, made the stooge in a comedy act. People in the audience at *Bonnie and Clyde* are laughing, demonstrating that they're not stooges—that they appreciate the joke—when they catch the first bullet right in the face. The movie keeps them off balance to the end. During the first part of the picture, a woman in my row was gleefully assuring her companions, "It's a comedy. It's a comedy." After a while, she didn't say anything. Instead of the movie spoof, which tells the audience that it doesn't need to feel or care, that it's all just in fun, that "we were only kidding," *Bonnie and Clyde* disrupts us with "And you thought we were only kidding."

This is the way the story was told in 1937. Eddie (Clyde) is a three-time loser who wants to work for a living, but nobody will give him a chance. Once you get on the wrong side of the law, "they" won't let you get back. Eddie knows it's hopeless —once a loser, always a loser. But his girl, Joan (Bonnie)— the only person who believes in him—thinks that an innocent man has nothing to fear. She marries him, and learns better. Arrested again and sentenced to death for a crime he didn't commit, Eddie asks her to smuggle a gun to him in prison, and she protests, "If I get you a gun, you'll kill somebody." He stares at her sullenly and asks, "What do you think they're going to do to me?" He becomes a murderer while escaping from prison; "society" has made him what it thought he was all along. *You Only Live Once* was an indictment of "society," of the forces of order that will not give Eddie the outcast a chance. "We have a right to live," Joan says as they set out across the country. During the time they are on the run, they become notorious outlaws; they are blamed for a series of crimes they didn't commit. (They do commit holdups, but only to get gas or groceries or medicine.) While the press pictures them as desperadoes robbing and killing and living high on the proceeds of crime, she is having a baby in a shack in a hobo jungle, and Eddie brings her a bouquet of wild flowers. Caught in a police trap, they die in each other's arms; they have been denied the right to live.

Because *You Only Live Once* was so well done, and because the audience in the thirties shared this view of the indifference and cruelty of "society," there were no protests against the sympathetic way the outlaws were pictured—and, indeed, there was no reason for any. In 1958, in *I Want to Live!* (a very popular, though not very good, movie), Barbara Graham, a drug-addict prostitute who had been executed for her share in the bludgeoning to death of an elderly woman, was presented as gallant, wronged, morally superior to everybody else in the movie, in order to strengthen the argument against capital punishment, and the director, Robert Wise, and his associates weren't accused of glorifying criminals, because the "criminals," as in *You Only Live Once,* weren't criminals but innocent victims. Why the protests, why are so many people upset (and not just the people who enjoy indignation), about *Bonnie and Clyde,* in which the criminals *are* criminals—Clyde an ignorant, sly near psychopath who thinks his crimes are accomplishments, and Bonnie a bored, restless waitress-slut who robs for excitement? And why so many accusations of historical inaccuracy, particularly against a work that is far more accurate historically than most and in which historical accuracy hardly matters anyway? There is always an issue of historical accuracy involved in any dramatic or literary work set in the past; indeed, it's fun to read about Richard III vs. Shakespeare's Richard III. The issue is always with us, and will always be with us as long as artists find stimulus in historical figures and want to present their versions of them. But why didn't movie critics attack, for example, *A Man for All Seasons*—which involves material of much more historical importance—for being historically inaccurate? Why attack *Bonnie and Clyde* more than the other movies based on the same pair, or more than the movie treatments of Jesse James or Billy the Kid or Dillinger or Capone or any of our other fictionalized outlaws? I would suggest that when a movie so clearly conceived as a new version of a legend is attacked as historically inaccurate, it's because it shakes people a little. I know this is based on some pretty sneaky psychological suppositions, but I don't see how else to account for the use only against a *good* movie of arguments that could be used against almost all movies. When I asked a nineteen-year-old boy who was raging against the movie as "a cliché-ridden fraud" if he got so worked up about other movies, he informed me that that was an argument *ad hominem*. And it is indeed. To ask why people react so angrily to the best movies and have so little negative reaction to poor ones is to imply that they are so unused to the experience of art in movies that they fight it.

Audiences at *Bonnie and Clyde* are not given a simple, secure basis for identification; they are made to feel but are not told *how* to feel. *Bonnie and Clyde* is not a serious melodrama involving us in the plight of the innocent but a movie that assumes—as William Wellman did in 1931 when he made *The Public Enemy*, with James Cagney as a smart, cocky, mean little crook—that we don't need to pretend we're interested only in the falsely accused, as if real criminals had no connection with us. There wouldn't be the popular excitement there is about outlaws if we didn't all suspect that—in some cases, at least—gangsters must take pleasure in the profits and glory of a life of crime. Outlaws wouldn't become legendary figures if we didn't suspect that there's more to crime than the social workers' case studies may show. And though what we've always been told will happen to them—that they'll come to a bad end—does seem to happen, some part of us wants to believe in the tiny possibility that they can get away with it. Is that really so terrible? Yet when it comes to movies people get nervous about acknowledging that there must be some fun in crime (though the gleam in Cagney's eye told its own story). *Bonnie and Clyde* shows the fun but uses it, too, making comedy out of the banality and conventionality of that fun. What looks ludicrous in this movie isn't *merely* ludicrous, and after we have laughed at ignorance and helplessness and emptiness and stupidity and idiotic deviltry, the laughs keep sticking in our throats, because what's funny isn't only funny.

In 1937, the movie-makers knew that the audience wanted to believe in the innocence of Joan and Eddie, because these two were lovers, and innocent lovers hunted down like animals made a tragic love story. In 1967, the movie-makers know that the audience wants to believe—maybe even prefers to believe—that Bonnie and Clyde were guilty of crimes, all right, but that they were innocent in general; that is naïve and ignorant *compared with us*. The distancing of the sixties version shows the gangsters in an already legendary period, and part of what makes a legend for Americans is viewing anything that happened in the past as much simpler than what we are involved in now. We tend to find the past funny and the recent past campy-funny. The getaway cars of the early thirties are made to seem hilarious. (Imagine anyone getting away from a bank holdup in a tin lizzie like that!) In *You Only Live Once*, the outlaws existed in the same present as the audience, and there was (and still is, I'm sure) nothing funny about them; in *Bonnie and Clyde* that audience is in the movie, transformed into the poor people, the Depression people, of legend—with faces and poses out of Dorothea Lange and Walker Evans and *Let Us Now Praise Famous Men*. In 1937, the audience felt sympathy for the fugitives because they weren't allowed to lead normal lives; in 1967, the "normality" of the Barrow gang and their individual aspirations toward respectability are the craziest things about them—not just because they're killers but because thirties "normality" is in itself funny to us. The writers and the director of *Bonnie and Clyde* play upon our attitudes toward the American past by making the hats and guns and holdups look as dated as two-reel comedy; emphasizing the absurdity with banjo music, they make the period seem even farther away than it is. The Depression reminiscences are not used for purposes of social consciousness; hard times are not the reason for the Barrows' crimes, just the excuse. "We" didn't make Clyde a killer; the movie deliberately avoids easy sympathy by picking up Clyde when he is already a cheap crook. But Clyde is not the urban sharpster of *The Public Enemy;* he is the hick as bank robber—a countrified gangster, a hillbilly killer who doesn't mean any harm. People so simple that they are alienated from the results of their actions—like the primitives who don't connect babies with copulation— provide a kind of archetypal comedy for us. It may seem like a minor point that Bonnie and Clyde are presented as not mean and sadistic, as having killed only when cornered; but in terms of legend, and particularly movie legend, it's a major one. The "classic" gangster films showed gang members betraying each other and viciously murdering the renegade who left to join another gang; the gang-leader hero no sooner got to the top than he was betrayed by someone he had trusted or someone he had double-crossed. In contrast, the Barrow gang represent family-style crime. And Newman and Benton have been acute in emphasizing this—not making them victims of society (they are never that, despite Penn's cloudy efforts along these lines) but making them absurdly "just-folks" ordinary. When Bonnie tells Clyde to pull off the road—"I want to talk to you"—they are in a getaway car, leaving the scene of a robbery, with the police right behind them, but they are absorbed in family bickering: the traditional all-American use of the family automobile. In a sense, it is the absence of sadism—it is the violence without sadism —that throws the audience off balance at *Bonnie and Clyde*. The brutality that comes out of this innocence is far more shocking than the calculated brutalities of mean killers.

Playfully posing with their guns, the real Bonnie and Clyde mocked the "Bloody Barrows" of the Hearst press. One photograph shows slim, pretty Bonnie, smiling and impeccably dressed, pointing a huge gun at Clyde's chest as he, a dimpled dude with a cigar, smiles back. The famous picture of Bonnie in the same clothes but looking ugly squinting into the sun, with a foot on the car, a gun on her hip, and a cigar in her mouth, is obviously a joke—her caricature of herself as a gun moll. Probably, since they never meant to kill, they thought the "Bloody Barrows," were a joke—a creation of the lying newspapers.

There's something new working for the Bonnie-and-Clyde legend now: our nostalgia for the thirties—the unpredictable, contrary affection of the prosperous for poverty, or at least for the artifacts, the tokens, of poverty, for Pop culture seen in the dreariest rural settings, where it truly seems to belong. Did people in the cities listen to the Eddie Cantor show? No doubt they did, but the sound of his voice, like the sound of Ed Sullivan now, evokes a primordial, pre-urban existence— the childhood of the race. Our comic-melancholic affection for thirties Pop has become sixties Pop, and those who made *Bonnie and Clyde* are smart enough to use it that way. Being knowing is not an artist's highest gift, but it can make a hell of a lot of difference in a movie. In the American experience, the miseries of the Depression are funny in the way that the Army is funny to draftees—a shared catastrophe, a leveling, forming part of our common background. Those too young to

remember the Depression have heard about it from their
parents. (When I was at college, we used to top each other's
stories about how our families had survived: the fathers who
had committed suicide so that their wives and children could
live off the insurance; the mothers trying to make a game out
of the meals of potatoes cooked on an open fire.) Though the
American derision of the past has many offensive aspects, it
has some good ones, too, because it's a way of making fun not
only of our forebears but of ourselves and our pretensions.
The toughness about what we've come out of and what we've
been through—the honesty to see ourselves as the Yahoo
children of yokels—is a good part of American popular art.
There is a kind of American poetry in a stickup gang seen
chasing across the bedraggled backdrop of the Depression (as
true in its way as Nabokov's vision of Humbert Humbert and
Lolita in the cross-country world of motels)—as if crime were
the only activity in a country stupefied by poverty. But
Arthur Penn doesn't quite have the toughness of mind to
know it; it's not what he means by poetry. His squatters'-
jungle scene is too "eloquent," like a poster making an
appeal, and the Parker-family-reunion sequence is poetic in
the gauzy mode. He makes the sequence a fancy lyric
interlude, like a number in a musical (*Funny Face*, to be
exact); it's too "imaginative"—a literal dust bowl, as thoroughly becalmed as Sleeping Beauty's garden. The movie
becomes dreamy-soft where it should be hard (and hard-
edged).

If there is such a thing as an American tragedy, it must be
funny. O'Neill undoubtedly felt this when he had James
Tyrone get up to turn off the lights in *Long Day's Journey Into
Night*. We are bumpkins, haunted by the bottle of ketchup on
the dining table at San Simeon. We garble our foreign words
and phrases and hope that at least we've used them right. Our
heroes pick up the wrong fork, and the basic figure of fun in
the American theatre and American movies is the man who
puts on airs. Children of peddlers and hod carriers don't feel
at home in tragedy; we are used to failure. But, because of
the quality of American life at the present time, perhaps there
can be no real comedy—nothing more than stupidity and
"spoof"—without true horror in it. Bonnie and Clyde and
their partners in crime are comically bad bank robbers,
and the backdrop of poverty makes their holdups seem
pathetically tacky, yet they rob banks and kill people; Clyde

and his good-natured brother are so shallow they never think much about anything, yet they suffer and die.

If this way of holding more than one attitude toward life is already familiar to us—if we recognize the make-believe robbers whose toy guns produce real blood, and the Keystone cops who shoot them dead, from Truffaut's *Shoot the Piano Player* and Godard's gangster pictures, *Breathless* and *Band of Outsiders*—it's because the young French directors discovered the poetry of crime in American life (from our movies) and showed the Americans how to put it on the screen in a new, "existential" way. Melodramas and gangster movies and comedies were always more our speed than "prestigious," "distinguished" pictures; the French directors who grew up on American pictures found poetry in our fast action, laconic speech, plain gestures. And because they understood that you don't express your love of life by denying the comedy or the horror of it, they brought out the poetry in our tawdry subjects. Now Arthur Penn, working with a script heavily influenced—one might almost say inspired—by Truffaut's *Shoot the Piano Player,* unfortunately imitates Truffaut's artistry instead of going back to its tough American sources. The French may tenderize their American material, but we shouldn't. That turns into another way of making "prestigious," "distinguished" pictures.

Probably part of the discomfort that people feel about *Bonnie and Clyde* grows out of its compromises and its failures. I wish the script hadn't provided the upbeat of the hero's sexual success as a kind of sop to the audience. I think what makes us not believe in it is that it isn't consistent with the intelligence of the rest of the writing—that it isn't on the same level, because it's too manipulatively clever, too much of a gimmick. (The scene that shows the gnomish gang member called C.W. sleeping in the same room with Bonnie and Clyde suggests other possibilities, perhaps discarded, as does C.W.'s reference to Bonnie's liking his tattoo.) Compromises are not new to the Bonnie-and-Clyde story; *You Only Live Once* had a tacked-on coda featuring a Heavenly choir and William Gargan as a dead priest, patronizing Eddie even in the afterlife, welcoming him to Heaven with "You're free, Eddie!" The kind of people who make a movie like *You Only Live Once* are not the kind who write endings like that, and, by the same sort of internal evidence, I'd guess that Newman and Benton, whose Bonnie seems to owe so much to Catherine in *Jules and Jim,* had more interesting ideas originally about Bonnie's and Clyde's (and maybe C.W.'s) sex lives.

But people also feel uncomfortable about the violence, and here I think they're wrong. That is to say, they *should* feel uncomfortable, but this isn't an argument *against* the movie. Only a few years ago, a good director would have suggested the violence obliquely, with reaction shots (like the famous one in *The Golden Coach,* when we see a whole bullfight reflected in Anna Magnani's face), and death might have been symbolized by a light going out, or stylized, with blood and wounds kept to a minimum. In many ways, this method is more effective; we feel the violence more because so much is left to our imaginations. But the whole point of *Bonnie and Clyde* is to rub our noses in it, to make us pay our dues for laughing. The dirty reality of death—not suggestions but blood and holes—is necessary. Though I generally respect a director's skill and intelligence in inverse ratio to the violence he shows on the screen, and though I questioned even the Annie Sullivan–Helen Keller fight scenes in Arthur Penn's *The Miracle Worker,* I think that this time Penn is right. (I think he was also right when he showed violence in his first film, *The Left Handed Gun,* in 1958.) Suddenly, in the last few years, our view of the world has gone beyond "good taste." Tasteful suggestions of violence would at this point be a more grotesque form of comedy than *Bonnie and Clyde* attempts. *Bonnie and Clyde* needs violence; violence is its meaning. When, during a comically botched-up getaway, a man is shot in the face, the image is obviously based on one of the most famous sequences in Eisenstein's *Potemkin,* and the startled face is used the same way it was in *Potemkin*—to convey in an instant how someone who just happens to be in the wrong place at the wrong time, the irrelevant "innocent" bystander, can get it full in the face. And at that instant the meaning of Clyde Barrow's character changes; he's still a clown, but *we've* become the butt of the joke.

It is a kind of violence that says something to us; it is something that movies must be free to use. And it is just because artists must be free to use violence—a legal right that is beginning to come under attack—that we must also defend the legal rights of those film-makers who use violence to sell tickets, for it is not the province of the law to decide that one man is an artist and another man a no-talent. The no-talen has as much right to produce works as the artist has, and not only because he has a surprising way of shifting from one category to the other but also because men have an inalienable right to be untalented, and the law should not discriminate against lousy "artists." I am not saying that the violence in *Bonnie and Clyde* is legally acceptable because the film is a work of art; I think that *Bonnie and Clyde,* though flawed, is a work of art, but I think that the violence in *The Dirty Dozen,* which isn't a work of art, and whose violence offends me *personally,* should also be legally defensible, however morally questionable. Too many people—including some movie reviewers—want the law to take over the job of movie criticism; perhaps what they really want is for their own criticisms to have the force of law. Such people see *Bonnie and Clyde* as a danger to public morality; they think an audience goes to a play or a movie and takes the actions in it as examples for imitation. They look at the world and blame the movies. But if women who are angry with their husbands take it out on the kids, I don't think we can blame *Medea* for it; if, as has been said, we are a nation of mother-lovers, I don't think we can place the blame on *Oedipus Rex.* Part of the power of art lies in showing us what we are *not* capable of. We see that killers are not a different breed but are *us* without the insight or understanding or self-control that works of art strengthen. The tragedy of *Macbeth* is in the fall from nobility to horror; the comic tragedy of *Bonnie and Clyde* is that although you can't fall from the bottom you can reach the same horror. The movies may set styles in dress- or love-making, they may advertise cars or beverages, but art is not examples for imitation—that is not what a work of art does for us—though that is what guardians of morality *think* art is and what they want it to be and why they think a good movie is one that sets "healthy," "cheerful" examples of behavior, like a giant all-purpose commercial for the American way of life. But people don't "buy" what they see in a movie quite so simply; Louis B. Mayer did not turn us into a nation of Andy Hardys, and if, in a film, we see a frightened man wantonly take the life of another, it does not encourage us to do the same, any more than seeing an ivory hunter shoot an elephant makes us want to shoot one. It may, on the contrary, so sensitize us that we get a pang in the gut if we accidentally step on a moth.

Will we, as some people have suggested, be lured into

imitating the violent crimes of Clyde and Bonnie because Warren Beatty and Faye Dunaway are "glamorous"? Do they, as some people have charged, confer glamour on violence? It's difficult to see how, since the characters they play are horrified by it and ultimately destroyed by it. Nobody in the movie gets pleasure from violence. Is the charge based on the notion that simply by their presence in the movie Warren Beatty and Faye Dunaway make crime attractive? If movie stars can't play criminals without our all wanting to be criminals, then maybe the only safe roles for them to play are movie stars—which, in this assumption, everybody wants to be anyway. After all, if they played factory workers, the economy might be dislocated by everybody's trying to become a factory worker. (Would having criminals played by dwarfs or fatties discourage crime? It seems rather doubtful.) The accusation that the beauty of movie stars makes the anti-social acts of their characters dangerously attractive is the kind of contrived argument we get from people who are bothered by something and are clutching at straws. Actors and actresses are *usually* more beautiful than ordinary people. And why not? Garbo's beauty notwithstanding, her Anna Christie did not turn us into whores, her Mata Hari did not turn us into spies, her Anna Karenina did not make us suicides. We did not want her to be ordinary looking. Why should we be deprived of the pleasure of beauty? Garbo could be all women in love because, being more beautiful than life, she could more beautifully express emotions. It is a supreme asset for actors and actresses to be beautiful; it gives them greater range and greater possibilities for expressiveness. The handsomer they are, the more roles they can play; Olivier can be anything, but who would want to see Ralph Richardson, great as he is, play Antony? Actors and actresses who are beautiful start with an enormous advantage, because we love to look at them. The joke in the glamour charge is that Faye Dunaway has the magazine-illustration look of countless uninterestingly pretty girls, and Warren Beatty has the kind of high-school good looks that are generally lost fast. It's the roles that make *them* seem glamorous. Good roles do that for actors.

There is a story told against Beatty in a recent *Esquire*—how during the shooting of *Lilith* he "delayed a scene for three days demanding the line 'I've read *Crime and Punishment* and *The Brothers Karamazov*' be changed to 'I've read

*Crime and Punishment* and *half* of *The Brothers Karamazov.*'" Considerations of professional conduct aside, what is odd is why his adversaries waited three days to give in, because, of course, he was right. That's what the character he played *should* say; the other way, the line has no point at all. But this kind of intuition isn't enough to make an actor, and in a number of roles Beatty, probably because he doesn't have the technique to make the most of his lines in the least possible time, has depended too much on intuitive non-acting —holding the screen far too long as he acted out self-preoccupied characters in a lifelike, boringly self-conscious way. He has a gift for slyness, though, as he showed in *The Roman Spring of Mrs. Stone,* and in most of his films he could hold the screen—maybe because there seemed to be something going on in his mind, some kind of calculation. There was something smart about him—something shrewdly private in those squeezed-up little non-actor's eyes—that didn't fit the clean-cut juvenile roles. Beatty was the producer of *Bonnie and Clyde,* responsible for keeping the company on schedule, and he has been quoted as saying, "There's not a scene that we have done that we couldn't do better by taking another day." This is the hell of the expensive way of making movies, but it probably helps to explain why Beatty is more intense than he has been before and why he has picked up his pace. His business sense may have improved his timing. The role of Clyde Barrow seems to have released something in him. As Clyde, Beatty is good with his eyes and mouth and his hat, but his body is still inexpressive; he doesn't have a trained actor's use of his body, and, watching him move, one is never for a minute convinced he's impotent. It is, however, a tribute to his performance that one singles this failure out. His slow timing works perfectly in the sequence in which he offers the dispossessed farmer his gun; there may not be another actor who would have dared to prolong the scene that way, and the prolongation until the final "We rob banks" gives the sequence its comic force. I have suggested elsewhere that one of the reasons that rules are impossible in the arts is that in movies (and in the other arts, too) the new "genius"—the genuine as well as the fraudulent or the dubious—is often the man who has enough audacity, or is simpleminded enough, to do what others had the good taste not to do. Actors before Brando did not mumble and scratch and show their sweat; dramatists before Tennessee Williams did not make explicit a particular substratum of American erotic fantasy; movie directors before Orson Welles did not dramatize the techniques of film-making; directors before Richard Lester did not lay out the whole movie as cleverly as the opening credits; actresses before Marilyn Monroe did not make an asset of their ineptitude by turning faltering misreadings into an appealing style. Each, in a large way, did something that people had always enjoyed and were often embarrassed or ashamed about enjoying. Their "bad taste" shaped a new accepted taste. Beatty's non-actor's "bad" timing may be this kind of "genius"; we seem to be watching him *think out* his next move.

It's difficult to know how Bonnie should have been played, because the character isn't worked out. Here the script seems weak. She is made too warmly sympathetic—and sympathetic in a style that antedates the style of the movie. Being frustrated and moody, she's not funny enough—neither ordinary, which, in the circumstances, would be comic, nor perverse, which might be rather funny, too. Her attitude toward her mother is too loving. There could be something funny about her wanting to run home to her mama, but, as it has been done, her heading home, running off through the fields, is unconvincing—incompletely motivated. And because the element of the ridiculous that makes the others so individual has been left out of her character she doesn't seem to belong to the period as the others do. Faye Dunaway has a sixties look anyway—not just because her eyes are made up in a sixties way and her hair is wrong but because her personal style and her acting are sixties. (This may help to make her popular; she can seem prettier to those who don't recognize prettiness except in the latest styles.) Furthermore, in some difficult-to-define way, Faye Dunaway as Bonnie doesn't keep her distance—that is to say, an *actor's* distance—either from the role or from the audience. She doesn't hold a characterization; she's in and out of emotions all the time, and though she often hits effective ones, the emotions seem *hers*, not the character's. She has some talent, but she comes on too strong; she makes one conscious that she's a willing worker, but she doesn't seem to know what she's doing—rather like Bonnie in her attempts to overcome Clyde's sexual difficulties.

Although many daily movie reviewers judge a movie in isolation, as if the people who made it had no previous history, more serious critics now commonly attempt to judge a movie as an expressive vehicle of the director, and a working out of his personal themes. Auden has written, "Our judgment of an established author is never simply an aesthetic judgment. In addition to any literary merit it may have, a new book by him has a historic interest for us as the act of a person in whom we have long been interested. He is not only a poet . . . he is also a character in our biography." For a while, people went to the newest Bergman and the newest Fellini that way; these movies were greeted like the latest novels of a favorite author. But Arthur Penn is not a writer-director like Bergman or Fellini, both of whom began as writers, and who (even though Fellini employs several collaborators) compose their spiritual autobiographies step by step on film. Penn is far more dependent on the talents of others, and his primary material—what he starts with—does not come out of his own experience. If the popular audience is generally uninterested in the director (unless he is heavily publicized, like DeMille or Hitchcock), the audience that is interested in the art of movies has begun, with many of the critics, to think of movies as a directors' medium to the point where they tend to ignore the contribution of the writers— and the directors may be almost obscenely content to omit mention of the writers. The history of the movies is being rewritten to disregard facts in favor of celebrating the director as the sole "creative" force. One can read Josef von Sternberg's autobiography and the text of the latest books on his movies without ever finding the name of Jules Furthman, the writer who worked on nine of his most famous movies (including *Morocco* and *Shanghai Express*). Yet the appearance of Furthman's name in the credits of such Howard Hawks films as *Only Angels Have Wings, To Have and Have Not, The Big Sleep,* and *Rio Bravo* suggests the reason for the similar qualities of good-bad-girl glamour in the roles played by Dietrich and Bacall and in other von Sternberg and Hawks heroines, and also in the Jean Harlow and Constance Bennett roles in the movies he wrote for *them*. Furthman, who has written about half of the most entertaining movies to come out of Hollywood (Ben Hecht wrote most of the other half), isn't even listed in new encyclopedias of the film. David Newman and Robert Benton may be good enough to join this category of unmentionable men who do what the directors are glorified for. The Hollywood writer is becoming a ghostwriter. The writers who succeed in the struggle to protect their identity and their material by becoming writer-directors or writer-producers soon become too rich and powerful to bother doing their own writing. And they rarely have the visual sense or the training to make good movie directors.

Anyone who goes to big American movies like *Grand Prix* and *The Sand Pebbles* recognizes that movies with scripts like those don't have a chance to be anything more than exercises in technology, and that this is what is meant by the decadence of American movies. In the past, directors used to say that they were no better than their material. (Sometimes they said it when they weren't even up to their material.) A good director can attempt to camouflage poor writing with craftsmanship and style, but ultimately no amount of director's skill can conceal a writer's failure; a poor script, even well directed, results in a stupid movie—as, unfortunately, does a good script poorly directed. Despite the new notion that the direction is everything, Penn can't redeem bad material, nor, as one may surmise from his *Mickey One,* does he necessarily know when it's bad. It is not fair to judge Penn by a film like *The Chase,* because he evidently did not have artistic control over the production, but what happens when he does have control and is working with a poor, pretentious mess of a script is painfully apparent in *Mickey One*—an art film in the worst sense of that term. Though one cannot say of *Bonnie and Clyde* to what degree it shows the work of Newman and Benton and to what degree they merely enabled Penn to "express himself," there are ways of making guesses. As we hear the lines, we can detect the intentions even when the intentions are not quite carried out. Penn is a little clumsy and rather too fancy; he's too much interested in being cinematically creative and artistic to know when to trust the script. *Bonnie and Clyde* could be better if it were simpler. Nevertheless, Penn is a remarkable director when he has something to work with. His most interesting previous work was in his first film, *The Left Handed Gun* (and a few bits of *The Miracle Worker,* a good movie version of the William Gibson play, which he had also directed on the stage and on television). *The Left Handed Gun,* with Paul Newman as an ignorant Billy the Kid in the sex-starved, male-dominated Old West, has the same kind of violent, legendary, nostalgic material as *Bonnie and Clyde;* its script, a rather startling one, was adapted by Leslie Stevens from a Gore Vidal television play.

In interviews, Penn makes high, dull sounds—more like a politician than a movie director. But he has a gift for violence, and, despite all the violence in movies, a gift for it is rare. (Eisenstein had it, and Dovzhenko, and Buñuel, but not many others.) There are few memorable violent moments in American movies, but there is one in Penn's first film: Billy's shotgun blasts a man right out of one of his boots; the man falls in the street, but his boot remains upright; a little girl's giggle at the boot is interrupted by her mother's slapping her. The mother's slap—the seal of the awareness of horror—says that even children must learn that some things that look funny are not only funny. That slap, saying that only idiots would laugh at pain and death, that a child must develop sensibility, is the same slap that *Bonnie and Clyde* delivers to the woman saying "It's a comedy." In *The Left Handed Gun*, the slap is itself funny, and yet we suck in our breath; we do not dare to laugh.

Some of the best American movies show the seams of cuts and the confusions of compromises and still hold together, because there is enough energy and spirit to carry the audience over each of the weak episodes to the next good one. The solid intelligence of the writing and Penn's aura of sensitivity help *Bonnie and Clyde* triumph over many poorly directed scenes: Bonnie posing for the photograph with the Texas Ranger, or—the worst sequence—the Ranger getting information out of Blanche Barrow in the hospital. The attempt to make the Texas Ranger an old-time villain doesn't work. He's in the tradition of the mustachioed heavy who foreclosed mortgages and pursued heroines in turn-of-the-century plays, and this one-dimensional villainy belongs, glaringly, to spoof. In some cases, I think, the writing and the conception of the scenes are better (potentially, that is) than the way the scenes have been directed and acted. If Gene Hackman's Buck Barrow is a beautifully controlled performance, the best in the film, several of the other players—though they are very good—needed a tighter rein. They act too much. But it is in other ways that Penn's limitations show—in his excessive reliance on meaning-laden closeups, for one. And it's no wonder he wasn't able to bring out the character of Bonnie in scenes like the one showing her appreciation of the fingernails on the figurine, for in other scenes his own sense of beauty appears to be only a few rungs farther up that same cultural ladder.

The showpiece sequence, Bonnie's visit to her mother (which is a bit reminiscent of Humphrey Bogart's confrontation with his mother, Marjorie Main, in the movie version of *Dead End*), aims for an effect of alienation, but that effect is confused by all the other things attempted in the sequence: the poetic echoes of childhood (which also echo the child sliding down the hill in *Jules and Jim*) and a general attempt to create a frieze from our national past—a poetry of poverty. Penn isn't quite up to it, though he is at least good enough to communicate what he is trying to do, and it is an attempt that one can respect. In 1939, John Ford attempted a similar poetic evocation of the legendary American past in *Young Mr. Lincoln;* this kind of evocation, by getting at how we *feel* about the past, moves us far more than attempts at historical re-creation. When Ford's Western evocations fail, they become languorous; when they succeed, they are the West of our dreams, and his Lincoln, the man so humane and so smart that he can outwit the unjust and save the innocent, is the Lincoln of our dreams, as the Depression of *Bonnie and Clyde* is the Depression of our dreams—the nation in a kind of trance, as in a dim memory. In this sense, the effect of blur is justified, is "right." Our memories *have* become hazy; this is what the Depression has faded into. But we are too conscious of the technical means used to achieve this blur, of the *attempt* at poetry. We are aware that the filtered effects already include our responses, and it's too easy; the lines are good enough so that the stylization wouldn't have been necessary if the scene had been played right. A simple frozen frame might have been more appropriate.

The editing of this movie is, however, the best editing in an American movie in a long time, and one may assume that Penn deserves credit for it along with the editor, Dede Allen. It's particularly inventive in the robberies and in the comedy sequence of Blanche running through the police barricades with her kitchen spatula in her hand. (There is, however, one bad bit of editing: the end of the hospital scene, when Blanche's voice makes an emotional shift without a corresponding change in her facial position.) The quick panic of Bonnie and Clyde looking at each other's face for the last time is a stunning example of the art of editing.

The end of the picture, the rag-doll dance of death as the gun blasts keep the bodies of Bonnie and Clyde in motion, is brilliant. It is a horror that seems to go on for eternity, and yet it doesn't last a second beyond what it should. The audience leaving the theatre is the quietest audience imaginable.

Still, that woman near me was saying "It's a comedy" for a little too long, and although this could have been, and probably was, a demonstration of plain old-fashioned insensitivity, it suggests that those who have attuned themselves to the "total" comedy of the last few years may not know when to stop laughing. Movie audiences have been getting a steady diet of "black" comedy since 1964 and *Dr. Strangelove, Or: How I Learned to Stop Worrying and Love the Bomb.* Spoof and satire have been entertaining audiences since the two-reelers; because it is so easy to do on film things that are difficult or impossible in nature, movies are ideally suited to exaggerations of heroic prowess and to the kind of light-hearted nonsense we used to get when even the newsreels couldn't resist the kidding finish of the speeded-up athletic competition or the diver flying up from the water. The targets have usually been social and political fads and abuses, together with the heroes and the clichés of the just preceding period of film-making. *Dr. Strangelove* opened a new movie era. It ridiculed *everything* and *everybody* it showed, but concealed its own liberal pieties, thus protecting itself from ridicule. A professor who had told me that *The Manchurian Candidate* was "irresponsible," adding, "I didn't like it—I can suspend disbelief only so far," was overwhelmed by *Dr. Strangelove:* "I've never been so involved. I had to keep reminding myself it was only a movie." *Dr. Strangelove* was clearly intended as a cautionary movie; it meant to jolt us awake to the dangers of the bomb by showing us the insanity of the course we were pursuing. But artists' warnings about war and the dangers of total annihilation never tell us how we are supposed to regain control, and *Dr. Strangelove,* chortling over madness, did not indicate any possibilities for sanity. It was experienced not as satire but as a confirmation of fears. Total laughter carried the day. A new generation enjoyed seeing the world as insane; they *literally* learned to stop worrying and love the bomb. Conceptually, we had already been living with the bomb; now the mass audience of the movies—which is the youth of America—grasped the idea that the threat of extinction can be used to devaluate everything, to turn it all into a joke. And the members of this

audience do love the bomb; they love feeling that the worst
has happened and the irrational are the sane, because there is
the bomb as the proof that the rational are insane. They love
the bomb because it intensifies their feelings of hopelessness
and powerlessness and innocence. It's only three years since
Lewis Mumford was widely acclaimed for saying about *Dr.
Strangelove* that "unless the spectator was purged by laughter
he would be paralyzed by the unendurable anxiety this policy,
once it were honestly appraised, would produce." Far from
being purged, the spectators are paralyzed, but they're still
laughing. And how odd it is now to read, *"Dr. Strangelove*
would be a silly, ineffective picture if its purpose were to
ridicule the characters of our military and political leaders by
showing them as clownish monsters—stupid, psychotic, obsessed." From *Dr. Strangelove* it's a quick leap to *MacBird*
and to a belief in exactly what it was said we weren't meant to
find in *Dr. Strangelove*. It is not war that has been laughed to
scorn but the possibility of sane action.

Once something enters mass culture, it travels fast. In the
spoofs of the last few years, everything is gross, ridiculous,
insane; to make sense would be to risk being square. A brutal
new melodrama is called *Point Blank* and it is. So are most of
the new movies. This is the context in which *Bonnie and
Clyde,* an entertaining movie that has some feeling in it,
upsets people—people who didn't get upset even by *Mondo
Cane.* Maybe it's because *Bonnie and Clyde,* by making us
care about the robber lovers, has put the sting back into
death.

# The Emergence of Rock

## Albert Goldman

To experience the Age of Rock full-blast and to begin to grasp its weird complexities, one can't do much better than spend a Saturday night at The Electric Circus, the most elaborate discothèque in New York. Located on St. Marks Place, the main nexus of East Village otherness, The Electric Circus is up a flight of stairs from The DOM (one of the early landmarks of the rock scene which has since evolved into a "soul" club). One makes his way through a gaggle of very young hippies sprawled on the porch steps, and enters a long, narrow alcove where the faithful, the tourists, and those somewhere in between wait in line for admission in a mood of quiet expectancy, like people waiting to get into one of the more exciting exhibits at the World's Fair. Once inside, the spectator moves along a corridor bathed in ultraviolet light in which every speck of white takes on a lurid glow, climbs a steep staircase, and passes through a dark antechamber. Here the young sit packed together on benches and, already initiated into the mysteries beyond, stare back at the newcomer with glazed, indifferent expressions as though they had been sitting there for days. Then, suddenly, there is a cleft in the wall, and the spectator follows the crowd pressing through

Reprinted from *New American Review* No. 3, April 1968.

it into a gigantic hall that suggests a huge bleached skull. Its dark hollows are pierced by beams of colored light that stain the walls with slowly pulsing patterns and pictures: glowing amoeba shapes, strips of home movies, and giant mandalas filled with fluid colors. The scream of a rock singer comes at one, the beat amplified to a deafening blast of sound. Housed within this electronic cave are hundreds of dancers, a number of them in exotic, flowing garments, their faces marked with phosphorescent insignia, hands clutching sticks of incense. Some of the dancers are gyrating frantically, as if trying to screw themselves down through the floor; others hold up their fists, ducking and bobbing like sparring partners; while others wrench their heads and thrust out their hands as if to ward off evil spirits. For all of its futuristic magic, the dance hall brings to mind those great painted caves such as Altamira in Spain where prehistoric man practiced his religious rites by dancing before the glowing images of his animal gods.

Magnetized by the crowd, impelled by the relentless pounding beat of the music, one is then drawn out on the floor. Here there is a feeling of total immersion: one is inside the mob, inside the skull, inside the music, which comes from all sides, buffeting the dancers like a powerful surf. Strangest of all, in the midst of this frantic activity, one soon feels supremely alone; and this aloneness produces a giddy sense of freedom, even of exultation. At last one is free to move and act and mime the secret motions of his mind. Everywhere about him are people focused deep within themselves, working to bring to the surfaces of their bodies their deep-seated erotic fantasies. Their faces are drugged, their heads thrown back, their limbs extended, their bodies dissolving into the arcs of the dance. The erotic intensity becomes so great that one wonders what sustains the frail partition of reserve that prevents the final spilling of this endlessly incited energy.

If one withdraws from the crowd and climbs to the gallery overlooking the dance floor, he soon succumbs to the other spell cast by this cave of dreams. Falling into a passive trance, his perceptions heightened perhaps by exhaustion or drugs (no liquor is served here), the spectator can enjoy simultaneously the pleasures of the theater, the movies, and the sidewalk cafe. At The Electric Circus the spectacle of the

dancers alternates with the surrealistic acts of professional
performers. An immaculate chef on stilts will stride to the
center of the floor, where he looms high above the dancers.
They gather around him like children, while he entertains
them by juggling three apples. Then, taking out a knife, he
slices the fruit and feeds it to his flock. High on a circular
platform, a performer dressed to look like a little girl in her
nightie struggles ineffectually with a Yo-Yo. A blinding white
strobe light flashes across her body, chopping her absurd
actions into the frames of an ancient flickering movie. Another girl comes sliding down a rope; someone dressed as a
gorilla seizes her and carries her off with a lurching gait.
Sitting in the dark gallery, one watches the crepitating
spectacle below; the thumping music now sinks slowly
through his mind like a narcotic; eventually he closes his
eyes and surrenders to a longing for silence, darkness, and
rest.

## II

Like those fabled cities whose walls rose to the sounds
of music, The Electric Circus and other such dance halls
have been drawn into being and charged with their electric atmosphere by the magical power of the beat.
The total-environment discothèque is principally an attempt to capture and concentrate, as in a giant orgone
box, the multiple energies of rock which have evolved
during the past decade into a veritable witches' brew—
part aphrodisiac, part narcotic, and part hallucinogen.
There is no simple way of comprehending the extra-
ordinarily rapid and complex development of the rock
sound and culture. But perhaps the clearest way is to begin at the beginning and try to follow the principal trends
of the music, along with their respective cultural ambi-
ences and meanings, both in the Negro and in the white
world.

Rock was born in a flashback, a celluloid loop doubled
back inside a time machine. The date was 1954; the place was
Cleveland, Ohio; the occasion, the first broadcast of Negro
race records to an audience of white teen-agers. Alan Freed,
a local disk jockey, made the experiment. Almost immediately, it became apparent that he had struck a nerve that

was ready to vibrate. The records he played were known in the trade as "rhythm and blues." Ground out by tiny Negro record companies in the South, they were aimed at the black ghettos of the North. What they contained was a particularly potent strain of the same urban blues that had swept over the country in the late thirties during the vogue of the big bands. Indeed, if one can imagine an old Kansas City blues band crushed like a tin can so that nothing remains of it but top, bottom, and lots of rusty ragged edges, he will have a fair idea of how the early r&b combos sounded. Concentrating on essentials, these groups used a disproportionate number of instruments (electric rhythm and bass guitars, plus piano and drums) to hammer out the beat, while the solo performers, vocal or instrumental, worked way out in front, using a primitive style compounded of honks and cries and words bawled out like curses.

It was, therefore, an old and radically racial sound that Freed offered to his listeners in the Midwest, and later in New York: a sound that told of dirt and fear and pain and lust. But the white kids loved it; and soon, as if to signify that the music had been adopted by a new public, Freed changed its name to "rock 'n' roll," though even this new name came from an old blues, "My baby rocks me with a steady roll." The success of rock attracted white performers: the first r&b song recorded by a white singer was "Rock Around the Clock" by Bill Haley and the Comets. Haley initiated that process of white assimilation of Negro style that for many years has been a basic feature of the movement; but the tendency of early rock was to pull away from the heavy racial sound in favor of the lighter, swifter beat of hillbilly music, which was to be one of rock's more durable elements, and a subject matter (cars, Cokes, and heartaches) more suitable to white teenagers. On this new wave of country blues, Chuck Berry and then Elvis Presley rode to fame. When Presley entered the army at the end of the decade, one expected the fad to recede and vanish. But the culture remained firmly rockbound.

While rock was enjoying this first surge of popularity, Negro music was undergoing a series of changes among the most profound in its history. The music of the ghetto was being revived and recharged by powerful new performers bent on outdoing their white imitators, while its basic genres

—blues and gospel—were coalescing to produce a new style of enormous strength and popularity.

The greatest of these singers—indeed, the greatest of all the basic rock performers—was Little Richard. Richard's records all sounded as if they were made in the Saturday night uproar of a turpentine logging camp. His raw strident voice was torn from his throat in a bawling, shouting torrent that battered and scattered the words until they sounded like raving. Behind this desperately naked voice worked a boogie-woogie rhythm section tightened to viselike rigidity. The furious energy of the singing caught in the iron cage of the rhythm produced an almost unbearable tension. Instead of illustrating the words, which often spoke of pleasure ("I'm gonna ball tonight!"), the music conveyed the agonizing effort to break through to joy. (Or just to break through: Richard usually ended his chorus with the bloodcurdling scream of a man hurling himself over a precipice.) What Little Richard was saying musically—and the Negro ghetto with him —was not that he was having a good time, but that he had the right to one and would "cut" anyone who got in his way. His note was erotic defiance. As such, Little Richard represented a new type of Negro youth. Reckless and rebellious, he gave us the first taste of the voice that was later to holler, "Burn, baby, burn!"

Oddly enough, the other great performer who emerged in this period expressed a character of precisely the opposite sort. Ray Charles was the eternal Negro, a poor blind man crying out of his darkness, singing to assuage his pain. Yet as a musician he was far from being a traditionalist; in fact, in undertaking to mix gospel and blues he violated one of the strictest taboos of Negro music. Throughout modern times, gospel and blues had always been rigidly segregated expressions of the sacred and the profane. Blues worked cathartically, urging that everything painful be confronted, named, lamented, and exorcised in a lonely, impersonal, almost aloof style. Gospel had functioned in a completely opposite manner, one that overwhelmed unhappiness by a swelling evocation of the joys of life beyond the present world. Just as the blues was traditionally depressed, understated, ironic, and resigned, gospel was typically ebullient, extravagant, even at times orgiastic in its affirmation. The Negro community had preserved the solace of each of these traditions by maintaining a total separation between them. The singing of blues in church was forbidden, while the blues singer steadfastly confronted his troubles without ever looking heavenward.

That is, until Ray Charles and his followers stepped boldly over the boundary and ended the prohibition. One of the first effects of this revolution was an inversion of traditional modes. Not only did these singers perform minor blues in the style of plaintive dirges, such as one might hear in church; they also added blues lyrics to the hand-clapping, footstamping, tambourine-banging gospel shouts. On stage they adopted many of the mannerisms, practices, and rituals of the storefront Negro church. They testified, danced ecstatically, called for witnesses, appeared to be led from above, tore off their clothes, and fell and rose again like men in the grip of a religious revelation.

Charles's own manner was often that of the preacher: the voice deliberately crude, cracked, thickened with Southern Negro pronunciations; the style figured with cantorial embellishments. The effect was that of a man seized by emotion, spilling out his feelings with absolute candor. Typical of the original gospel-blues mix was "Yes, Indeed," one of Charles's most successful early numbers. The piece opens with soft church chords played on a harmonium; next, Charles gives out the text in his deep deacon's voice, a word or two—then the gospel beat, heavy and lurching, comes crashing in with a chorus of "Amen girls" hypnotically chanting after every phrase, "Yaas, indeed!" As the piece stomps through its traditional 16-bar course, the confidently rising intervals generate an aura of optimism that reaches its climax in a moment of pure "salvation." The horns riff joyously, the chord changes signal that we are coming home, and the lead voice sings: "Well, I know when it gets ya, you get a feelin' deep down in your soul, every time you hear that good old rock 'n' roll. Yaas, indeed." The lyrics tumble here to a dreadful anticlimax, just at the point where the music becomes most transcendent, for what would have been in the original a religious affirmation has been rubbed out and a pop music cliché scribbled in its place.

Once the barrier was down between gospel and blues, the distinctions between other Negro musical traditions also began to disappear. Singers, composers, instrumentalists, and arrangers began to take what they wanted from a racial ragbag of Delta blues, hillbilly strumming, gutbucket jazz, boogie-woogie piano, pop lyricism, and storefront shouting. The result—less a new genre than a mélange of musical materials—was called "soul."

When one thinks of soul today, the image that presents itself is of a monotonously revolving kaleidoscope loaded with dozens of factory-stamped, smoky-colored bits of gospel, rock, blues, jazz, pop, folk, rock, blues, and so on in endlessly shifting combinations of this week's, last month's, tomorrow's "sound." The agency most responsible for this commercialization of Negro music is Motown, the General Motors of rock. Its founder, owner, and manager is Berry Gordy, Jr., a one-time assembly-line worker, who since the early sixties has been turning out hit tunes produced by teams of composers, arrangers, and performers, all working closely to the specifications of the Motown formula.

The basic ingredient of the formula is the beat. Pushing beyond the traditional "and *two* and *four*" style of drumming, Berry's arrangers trained the drums to bark on every beat. Then they strengthened and enlarged the new beat by over-amplification and by doubling it with tambourine, tom-tom, cymbals, bass, and, eventually, anything that would bounce. Today, Motown rocks with a driving, slogging rhythm that rumbles up through the floor of a discothèque like an earthquake.

The other active ingredient of the formula is the "shout," a short, arresting phrase that flashes the song's message. This is underscored and embellished with every resource provided by Negro tradition and the Hollywood sound stage. The most primitive types of plantation music—the sounds of Jew's harps, tambourines, pipes, and quills—have been unearthed to fill the formula's demand for a "funky" core. Around this core have been wrapped some fairly complicated arrangements, entailing the integration of strings, symphonic percussion sections, choirs, and soloists.

Motown's effort to concentrate all the sounds of Negro tradition into a super-soul has often produced the opposite of the intended effect—a typically commercial dilution of the Negro essence. But sometimes Detroit's stylists, especially the gifted team of Eddie and Bryant Holland and Lamont Dozier, have updated tradition so skillfully that they succeed in adding a genuinely contemporary voice to Negro music. Not content to paste pop lyrics over old church tunes, this team has approached gospel in a sophisticated spirit, seeking to exploit its ritual of salvation without sacrificing the love story indispensable to the pop ballad. In their best work they can telescope into three relentless minutes the events of a whole evening in a storefront church without dislodging the conventional facade of the ballad.

"I'll Be There," the most admired song of Motown's The Four Tops, opens on a characteristically exotic note: pipes and slap bass evoking a movie image of Genghis Khan and his men trotting across the steppes of Central Asia. Then this mirage is suddenly blown away and we are down to the bedrock of soul: the drums pounding, the tambourines jingling, and the anguished voice of Levi Stubbs exhorting his sweetheart in the manner of an evangelist preacher:

> If you feel that you can't go on,
> Because all of your hope is gone,
> And your life is filled with much confusion,
> Until happiness is just an illusion:

"Reach out!" cry the wraithlike voices that have been trailing and echoing Stubbs. "Reach out for *me!*" he adds, distending the word with a flourish of emotion. Then for one suspenseful moment, all the voices cease, and we gaze into a void in which there is nothing but the nakedly writhing beat. Suddenly the emptiness is filled with the solemn sound of the "shout," "I'll be there," sung in unison by leader and chorus and accompanied by the exotic pipes of the introduction, which now assume their proper place as a kind of stained-glass window behind the singers. The final touch of religious excitement was added during the recording session: when the break in the melody opened for the last time, Levi shouted to the girl, "Look over your shoulder!" For a Negro audience this phrase summons up one of the most intense moments at a gospel service: the sight of some believer pointing wildly toward a corner of the church where he has caught a glimpse of the Holy Spirit.

Motown does a dizzying business with its exploitation of classic Negro styles, and most of this business is done in the Negro ghettos (where nobody pays any attention to The Beatles). Generally, the success of the style is attributed to Negro pride, to the joy with which Negroes respond to the basic expressions of their culture. But the regressive, almost caricatured Negritude of soul, and even more importantly, the desperately naked avowal of suffering made in the more seriously expressive songs, suggest that this music celebrates blackness less for its beauty than for its strength as a revived resource against the white terror.

Soul's revival of gospel music has been accompanied by a return to archaic patterns of body movement which combine gestures of incantation and exorcism. In the currently popular boogaloo, for example, there is a complete pantomime of terror. The dancer's neck is twisted spasmodically as if by a lynch rope, his eyes roll up into his head, his hands shoot out past his face as if to avert a blow, and his whole body tips as though he were about to collapse. The imagery of anxiety in such a performance accords perfectly with the character of the words and music which excite it, and all three qualify drastically the notion that rock is simply the revelry of orgy.

### III

Not the least reason for the exaggeration of Negritude in soul music has been the emergence in recent years of rock groups composed of pale English boys. What The Beatles represented in their early unregenerate years was a Liverpudlian impression of Little Richard, Chuck Berry, and Bo Diddley, precisely the roughest, raunchiest Negro rhythm and blues men accessible through American records. When their manager, Brian Epstein, styled the boys' hair and dressed them in chic suits, he didn't comb any of the fuzz out of their sound. The result was that English dandyism was wedded to Negro eroticism, and every teeny-bopper in the Western world began to dream of possessing a mod moppet with soul. Other

English groups have since become so adept at mimicking Negroes that the listener (white or black) can only identify the singer's race by the record liner. In fact, one may even prefer Stevie Winwood or Spencer Davis to the ordinary Detroit sound just because the English product seems more authentic, less bedecked with the gaudy trappings of Motown. This authenticity is, of course, only skin-deep; it is a mask that the singer sustains only because his narrow expressive gambit does not oblige him to flex his features with a full range of expression. For three minutes, the length of a "45" side, he can hold this pose; but it is just as unnatural for him as the spraddling stance is for the model who is out to make a "smashing" appearance in *Queen* or *Vogue*. It takes only one record like Aretha Franklin's recent virtuoso treatment of "I Can't Get No Satisfaction," written by Mick Jagger of The Rolling Stones, to remind us of the great gap that exists between those who have soul and those who merely pay it the compliment of imitation.

Once Negritude had been synthesized so that it could be manufactured anywhere in the world, rock began to cast about for fresh game. But this was less a matter of the normal development of popular music than of the cultural disorientation of the rock generation. On the face of it, there was no reason why the music that developed from white imitations of Negro styles should not have continued to evolve along the same path that swing had followed in the forties. Starting with a basic style derived largely from Negro sources, the swing bands added more and more non-Negro elements until they had created a new pop sound. At that time, as today, there had been a dialogue between black and white, with plenty of give and take. Miles Davis, for example, borrowed the arranger of the most refined white band (Gil Evans of the Claude Thornhill band) to act as midwife at the birth of the cool. But rock was not destined to play with counters that were only white and black.

The youth of the swing era thought they knew who they were; today's youth has no such illusion. But lacking any clear-cut sense of identity has only made them more keenly aware of everyone else's. Rock is, in one sense, a direct

direct reflection of their hunger for the essence of every people or period that displays a striking or exotic style. The Rock Age has assimilated everything in sight, commencing with the whole of American music: urban and country blues, gospel, hillbilly, Western, "good-time" (the ricky-tick of the twenties), and Tin Pan Alley. It has reached across the oceans for the sounds and rhythms of Africa, the Middle East, and India. It has reached back in time for the baroque trumpet, the madrigal, and the Gregorian chant; and forward into the future for electronic music and the noise collages of *musique concrète*.

By virtue of its cultural alliances, the Beat has also become the pulse of pop culture. The creators of the new milieu vie with one another in proclaiming rock the inspirational force of the day. A discothèque like The Electric Circus is a votive temple to the electronic muse, crammed with offerings from all her devotees. The patterns on the walls derive from Pop and Op art; the circus acts are Dada and Camp; the costumes of the dancers are mod and hippie; the technology is the most successful realization to date of the ideal of "art and engineering"; the milieu as a whole is psychedelic, and the discothèque is itself a prime example of mixed-media or total-environment art. The only elements of rock culture that are not conspicuous there are the literary ones: the underground newspapers that report the news and gossip of this world; the put-on critiques of the New Journalism; and the social and political rhetoric of the folk-rock singers, the finger-pointers, like Bob Dylan, Janis Ian, and Joan Baez.

As for the audience for rock, they are apt to manifest the same eager feeling for cultural essences that is revealed by the musicians. They like to fashion modish simulacra of cherished periods like the twenties, thirties, or the Edwardian Age; they are strong on certain ethnic types, like the American Indian and the Slavic peasant; their holdings in the East are large and constantly increasing—and they all can do a pretty good take-off on W. C. Fields. They like to dress up in cast-off clothes purchased in thrift shops or old theatrical costume warehouses; on Saturday afternoons they make King's Road in Chelsea the scene of one of the most extraordinary pageants ever seen on the streets of a European city. To describe their dress as "masquerade" is not quite accurate because, like all true decadents, they prefer to the pure forms those piquant mixtures of unrelated things that show wit and fancy as opposed to mere mimicry. Yet their ideal costume is not obviously hybrid. It aims to achieve the integrity of familiar things. The first glance at it elicits the sense of *déjà vu;* the second, a frown of perplexity. "What country do you come from?" is a query often directed at The Beatles costume designers, a Dutch group known as The Apple, as they walk about London in their enchanting peasant drag.

As this mode of dressing makes clear, the time has now passed when it was enough to seize a single style and make it one's own—as Bob Dylan first transformed himself into an Okie or Monti Rock III into a Harlem Negro. Today, the grand cultural ideal is encapsulated in the tiny word "mix." The goal is to blend various exotic essences into mysterious alchemical compounds.

Take for example The Beatles' "Strawberry Fields Forever," with its mixture of hippie argot, classic myth, and baroque music. Grave Elysian flutes lead the way as the singers chant, "Let me take you *down,";* then, swooning on the wave of an Hawaiian guitar, the voices drift into their subterranean lotus land. Gradually, the atmosphere grows heavy and murky; the tone of the singers is stoned; their speech is muddled and ambiguous ("No one, I think, is in my tree; I mean, it must be high or low; that is, you can't, you know, tune in, but it's all right; that is, I think it's not too bad"). As the music advances in trance-like time, the baroque bass line presses relentlessly downward, the drums beat a tattoo, and trumpets sound like autos jamming. The song swells into a massive affirmation of meaninglessness— a junkie anthem. After a final crescendo, the end is signaled by the conventional fade-out; but this is swiftly countermanded by an unexpected fade-in which brings delicate Indian sounds bubbling to the surface of the heavily doctored soundtrack. The effect is magical—The Beatles sink into the ground in London and pop to the surface again at Bombay.

The more farfetched and unlikely the ingredients, the better for the mix; and likewise, the more arts and media laid under contribution, the greater the impact. The ideal is strongly reminiscent of surrealism, of Max Ernst's formula of "the fortuitous meeting of distant realities." It would be a mistake, however, to attribute any direct influence to such doctrines, no matter how prophetic they have proved to be. Life, not theory, and, more particularly, the electronic maelstrom that has shaped the sensibility of our youth best explain the syncretism of the present moment. Our youth are accustomed to being bombarded from every side by sounds and images that have been torn loose, distorted, and scrambled in a thousand ways. Nothing more is needed to suggest the frantic mix than the everyday act of twirling a radio or TV dial. It is not surprising that the archetypal image of so much Pop art is the fun house. Distorting mirrors, grotesque images, spooky vistas, traps, tricks, and shocks to every sense constitute in their aggregate a very brilliant metaphor for the contemporary experience. And, as if this were not enough, the youth have given their bizarre world one last crazy spin by turning on with anything they can get into their mouths or veins—narcotics, stimulants, hypnotics, hallucinogens.

Every contemporary medium has evolved some version of the mix, whether it be called collage, montage, assemblage, or *musique concrète*. The form most often associated with rock is the light show. Two seasons ago, Bob Goldstein installed his "Lightworks" in a roadhouse called L'Oursin at Southampton, Long Island. To date the finest multimedia discothèque, Goldstein's club revealed a great deal about the potentialities of the mix. It was designed, like a giant Scopitone jukebox, to light up with a complete picture show every time a new record dropped on the turntable. The images that flashed upon its three towering screens (which were played contrapuntally, one against the other) were drawn from every source dear to the Pop sensibility. There were glass slides of New York's turn-of-the-century *haute monde,* film clips from Hollywood musicals of the thirties, twist films, old newsreels, poster patterns, and light paintings. The effect of this streaming phantasmagoria, which shuttled the spectator's mind back and forth along invisible tracks of association —from past to present, comic to sentimental, nostalgic to erotic—was that of a fantastic variety show, a Psychedelic Follies.

In such discothèques as L'Oursin, rock became a medium for producing a range of new sensations. Associating rock with images induces that sense of poring scrutiny, of lens-in-eye obsession, that is one of the most distinctive modes of contemporary sensibility. (Consider the excitement it generates in the central episode of *Blow-Up*.) Like the effect of LSD, that of rocking things is to spotlight them in a field of high concentration and merge them with the spectator in a union that is almost mystical. Few discothèque designers, to be sure, have Goldstein's taste and theatrical flair; most are content to break off bits and pieces of cultural imagery and embed them in the beat to produce a haphazard rock terrazzo. But the beguiling and tranquilizing effect of spending an evening in the contemplation of "Lightworks" assures us—far more than all the current theorizing—that the ideal of the synesthetic art work is perfectly valid and closer to realization today than at any time since its first statement in the writings of Wagner and Baudelaire.

## IV

The concept of a psychedelic variety show is strikingly akin to the form evolved by The Beatles in the last two years. Young men of imagination who have grown up in the cultural greenhouse of show business, The Beatles have developed their own exotic blooms of parody and hallucination. Like all the members of their generation, but to a far greater degree than most, they have fashioned themselves out of borrowed materials. Year after year they have added other idioms to their vocabulary, and now speak a language that is as rich as any in the history of the popular arts. The terms of their recent work are sophistication and ambiguity. But looking back over their history, one finds a logical progression toward these higher qualities, for the art of which The Beatles are masters has always had a complex and somewhat factitious character.

The story of The Beatles is pop culture's redaction of the myth of innocence and experience. When the famous four set out on their careers, they knew nothing of art or life. At home only in the rough-and-tumble world of the

Liverpool cellar club or the Hamburg *Lokal,* they were a shaggy and ignorant crew. They could not read music, they could barely play their instruments, and their idea of a joke was to come out on the bandstand wearing toilet seats around their necks. Since then their careers and lives have mounted upward and outward in dizzying gyres that have swept them around the whole world of twentieth-century life and culture and set them on terms of respect and familiarity with some of the most sophisticated minds in the contemporary arts. In the course of their jet-age development, they have already been twice transformed bodily and spiritually; now they stand poised on the verge of yet another metamorphosis as the result of their studies with Maharishi Mahesh Yogi, the apostle of transcendental meditation.

It was their manager Brian Epstein who transformed these coarse rockers into the adorable Eton boys known to fame, a change of costume that proved to be the shrewdest packaging job in the history of popular music. It would be a mistake, however, to claim, as LeRoi Jones has done, that The Beatles owe their early success entirely to the Epstein formula; for paradoxically, just as their imitations of Negro rock began to achieve universal popularity, the boys began to modify their sound in obedience to the promptings of their own souls. What emerged was a sort of ancestral reverberation, echoes of ancient English music reaching back to a time before the New World had been settled. In his recent book *Caliban Reborn,* Wilfred Mellers, the distinguished British musicologist, provides an interesting analysis of the traditional English elements in The Beatles' music, identifying bits and pieces that once belonged to the musical vocabulary of Giles Farnaby and of Orlando Gibbons, the master of the sixteenth-century madrigalists. From this analysis, it would appear that The Beatles stand in somewhat the same relation to their culture as do the Negroes and hillbillies to ours: they, too, play by ear, and what they hear is still attuned partially to a kind of scale and tonality that has long since been forgotten by literate musicians. If Mellers is right, the tension between the "illiterate" and "literate" elements in the work of these quasi-folk artists may be what accounts for their unique effect, the resonance in their simple songs of something deep and agelessly innocent. One might add that The

Beatles' feeling for baroque music is characteristically British: it is Handel that sounds the affirmative note in "Strawberry Fields Forever," as it is the Purcell of the trumpet voluntaries that wells up with such purity in "Penny Lane."

The appearance in 1966 of their album *Revolver* signaled an important transformation of The Beatles. First, the album soured the milky innocence of "I Want to Hold Your Hand" and "Michelle" with the sardonic tone of the city citizen, personified in the acrid sounds and sarcastic lyrics of "Taxman." The sound change was formal: instead of singing in their one basic style, The Beatles became virtuosos and produced a pastiche of modes.

"Eleanor Rigby," one of the two most impressive songs, is couched in a nineteenth-century string idiom, suggestive alternately of a country fiddle and a Beethoven string quartet. Its old-fashioned style, urgent, chopping rhythm, and lovely plangent melody provide a setting rich in sentiment for the series of genre pictures sketched in the verses. There is Eleanor Rigby, a solitary spinster picking up the rice after a wedding; and Father McKenzie darning a sock in his room late at night. They are the lonely people who live outside the modern world. The very thought of their existence wrings from The Beatles a cry of bewildered innocence: "All the lonely people! Where *do* they all come from? Where *do* they all belong?"

"Tomorrow Never Knows" is composed in an antithetical mode and provides this generation's answer to the poignant sense of human futility expressed in "Eleanor Rigby." A futuristic chant intoned by a robot voice over a hubbub of jungle noises, squiggling strings, and sore boil guitar riffs—all this underscored by the pounding of a primitive drum—the song mechanically announces its message like an electronic oracle. The message is that of the hippies:

> Turn off your mind,
> Relax and float downstream;
> It is not dying.

*Revolver* also contains a number of other "answers": a pioneer effort to assimilate the sound of the Indian raga

("Love You To"); a street chanty, widely interpreted as a
comical drug song ("Yellow Submarine"); "For No One,"
which evokes the Edwardian parlor musicale, with Auntie
Ellen strumming the cottage piano and Uncle Wembley
winding the French horn; "Good Day Sunshine," a perky
tune sweetly reminiscent of straw-hat vaudeville; and
"Here, There and Everywhere," an exquisite ballad. Altogether this album offers a remarkable range of material,
comprising the nostalgic, the futuristic, the hortatory,
the contemplative, the Oriental, and the American. It
also demonstrates a great expansion of The Beatles' resources of instrumentation and recording technique. For
the first time, one really feels the presence of George
Martin, the so-called "Fifth Beatle," a record producer
and academy-trained musician of considerable sophistication who has supervised all The Beatles' record-
ings.

*Revolver* points the way to the variety mix, but it furnishes
no general context for its excellent songs, and hence they gain
nothing from being on one record. *Sgt. Pepper* remedies
this deficiency by assembling its tunes inside the framework
of an old-time band concert. Offering itself as a record of
such an occasion, it harmonizes the stylistic eclecticism of
its contents by presenting each song as an individual vaudeville turn. At the same time the opportunity is created to
step beyond the artificial glare of the footlights and deliver
with chilling effect the final revelation of "A Day in the
Life."

The effect of this last song is like that of awakening from
turbulent but colorful dreams to stare at the patch of gray that
signals dawn in the city. What we awake to in the song is the
modern oscillation between anomie and anxiety punctuated
periodically by the sound of a dynamo that has just been
switched on. This sound is itself the ultimate symbol of The
Beatles' world. It represents the state of being turned on, of
getting high and escaping from our deadened selves; but at
the same time, its alarming crescendo of speed and power
suggests an acceleration to the point of explosion (an implication underscored by the Beethoven-like chords of a symphony
orchestra, portending doom). The end of the song is a single tonic chord struck on the piano and then allowed to
float away for half a minute, like a slowly dissolving puff of
smoke.

"A Day in the Life" is a skillfully contrived microcosm of the contemporary world. Called by one critic "the Beatles' *Waste Land*," and by another "a little Antonioni movie," its brilliance lies in the exquisite adjustment of its tone, calibrated finely between apathy and terror. Reflecting meaning from every facet, the song not only evokes the chug chug of a mechanistic society and the numbed sensibilites of its anonymous inhabitants, but also sounds with conviction the note of apocalypse.

## V

That a song of such intellectual sophistication and artistic resourcefulness should arise out of the same tradition that only a dozen years ago was spawning ditties like "Rock Around the Clock" seems almost unbelievable. But the very swiftness of the development indicates its real nature. Unlike other popular arts, rock has not been forced to spin its substance out of itself. Instead, it has acted like a magnet, drawing into its field a host of heterogeneous materials that has fallen quickly into patterns. No other cultural force in modern times has possessed its power of synthesis. Indeed, one of the common complaints of cultural critics has been that there were no coherent movements to animate and order the vast piles of cultural detritus under which we seemed destined to smother. Evidently, the only impulse at all equal to the task has been the primitive power of the beat.

Having assumed a role of cultural authority, rock has not, as was feared, dragged us down into the mire of cultural regression. The Spenglerian anxieties have proven once again to be unfounded. Rather than either lowering or elevating us, rock has served to equalize cultural pressures and forces. It has cleared a channel from the lowest and most archaic to the highest and most recent, and through that conduit is now flowing a revitalizing current of energy and of ideas. The result has been the elevation of rock to the summit of popular culture and the accelerating expansion of its interests and resources.

Thus The Beatles have already journeyed so far from their starting point in American rock 'n' roll that their relation to the tradition has become problematic, perhaps irrelevant. In their steady drift toward the international avant-garde, however, The Beatles, and the other English groups like The Procol Harum that have followed in their wake, represent only one end of the lengthening rock spectrum. At the other end, stand the new musicians who have developed the sensuousness and violence of the original beat. Outstanding among these are the acid-rock groups of San Francisco and Los Angeles: groups with exotic names like The Grateful Dead, The Moby Grape, The Jefferson Airplane, Big Brother and the Holding Company, or Country Joe and the Fish. The California sound has sublimated the basic essence of rock and mixed it with the idiom of the hippies, the motorcycle gangs, and the surfers in a cultural fusion that is reminiscent of soul. Indeed, acid-rock is the closest approximation yet to an authentic white soul.

The finest of these West Coast groups is The Doors, four young Californians whose prior experience included college, jazz, and film-making school. The Doors think of themselves —as their name signifies—as the means or channel through which their audiences pass from ignorance to knowledge, from ordinary consciousness to ecstasy, from control and inhibition to revolt and freedom. They think of themselves as "erotic politicians" and as pioneers in a libidinal wilderness: "The world we suggest should be of a new wild West," proclaims Jim Morrison, the group's writer and singer. "A sensuous evil world, strange and haunting, the path of the sun. . . . We're all centered around the end of the zodiac, the Pacific."

Constrained in recording studios and falsified in their stage and TV appearances, The Doors need to be heard in their own milieu. They really do belong to the misty littoral of Southern California, facing the setting sun and leading a hippie tribe in their shamanistic rites. One can see Jim Morrison in the center of the circle, immense electric totems behind him, as he stands limply, his snaky body encased in black vinyl, his finely chiseled features framed in flowing Dionysian hair, his hands clutching, his mouth almost devouring the mike, as he chants with closed eyes the hallucinatory verses of "The End."

"The End" commences by evoking with solemn drones and

shimmering metal the shadowy, consecrated atmosphere that surrounds the performance of an Indian temple dancer. But instead of sacred pantomime, we hear a voice—husky, pale, and weary—intoning words of farewell. Like all of The Doors' music, the theme hovers abstractly between sex, drugs, and death. What is ending: a love affair, an acid trip, the world? We cannot tell but it hardly matters. The emotion is produced by the ritual. First, the shaman or soul voyager launches himself with the aid of drugs and music into the spirit world; then he travels among its terrors, calling out his adventures to the awestruck tribe. Sometimes his language is fragmentary and symbolic: he sings of an ancient snake, a gold mine, the summer rain. Sometimes the words are literal and dramatic, as in the climactic episode. "The killer awakes before dawn. He puts his boots on. He took a face from the ancient gallery. And he walks on down the hall. . . . And he came to a door and he looked inside." The Oedipal theme emerges with the cool violence of a Capote novel, "' Father?' 'Yes, son?' 'I want to kill you. Mother? I want to—.'" The words explode into an incredible scream; the drums thunder and crash. But this is not the end. The tumult subsides, and the shaman croons like a seductive snake: "Come on baby, take a chance with us, and meet me at the back of the blue bus. Tonight, tomorrow night, blue bus, tonight, come on, yeah!" As he repeats the phrase with mounting urgency and indistinctness, the music—which has been coiling as if to strike—slips into a rocking raga and then races upward to an enormous crescendo. At the peak of the excitement, a sinister whine is heard (like The Beatles' dynamo) and then the sound erupts in crashing waves. Behind the uproar Morrison can be heard chanting hoarsely: "Kill! Kill! Kill! Fuck! Fuck! Fuck!" Then comes the end, not violently or cruelly but with a gradual subsidence into the dark and mysterious sounds of the beginning.

The mood of The Doors is revolutionary in that it represents a deliberate break with the mentality of the hippies— and for that matter, with that of the whole rock generation. Instead of "flower power" and "love, love, love," The Doors project real and undisguised anger. The seriousness of their anger varies from the Lear-like rage of "The End" to the deadpan mockery of "She's a Twentieth Century Fox," one of many songs that score off the modern woman. But the important point about this anger is its calculated violation of a taboo. For in the overthrow of so many old prohibitions, there has grown up a new structure of forbidden things and denied emotions—and the first of these is anger. By venting their rage in the ceremony of the tribe, The Doors both express their own freedom and achieve their purpose as gurus, which is to confront their audience with the most basic unbearable truths. At the same time they achieve artistic effects that are finer than the adolescent moralism of Janis Ian or the monotonous, unmusical irony of Bob Dylan. They produce a purifying catharsis that leaves their audiences shaken but surer in themselves.

The Doors are no less revolutionary as musicians. Faced with the rigidifying conventions of hard rock, they have opened the door of free improvisation. The great moments at their recent concerts have been the extended treatments of tunes that were originally the constrictively patterned products of the rock formulary. By recovering the valuable skills that were lost to popular music through the abandonment of jazz, The Doors have begun to reestablish jazz on a rock foundation. But their development is completely independent of traditional jazz. The finest performing musicians on the scene today, their instrumental language owes more to Bach than bop and more than either to B movies. When The Doors jam, the effect is that of a mad organist tracing his fugue across an electric keyboard while beside him hovers a crazy chemist concocting psychedelics out of the sonorities of a steel guitar. Obviously, the boys have done a lot of their tripping in the vicinity of Hollywood.

Ultimately, what is most impressive about The Doors is the completeness of their commitment. Whether it be acid, sex, ritual, or rock, they are further into it than any other group. Perhaps this explains the air of dignity that accompanies all their actions. No matter how wild or strange this group behaves, one feels they are in the American grain—indigenous artists like Walt Whitman or Charlie Parker.

## VI

By pushing toward higher levels of imaginative excellence, rock has begun to realize one of the most cherished dreams of mass culture: to cultivate from the vigorous but crude growth of the popular arts a new serious art that would combine the strength of native roots with the beauty flowering from the highest art. In America this hope had been baffled time and time again by the failure of any of our popular arts (with minor exceptions) to achieve, after generations of development, the stature implicit in their beginnings. Like thundering geysers from underground, the geniuses of jazz, for example, have hurled themselves at their lofty goals only to fall back, spent by their unaided efforts. And this hope would have remained futile had it not been for the simultaneous emergence of two necessary conditions: first, the widespread assimilation through the mass media of the themes and technical resources of the fine arts; second, the tendency of serious artists today to exploit the myths and devices of the popular culture.

The difficulty of such a convergence of high and low modern art is well attested by recent history. On two memorable occasions in recent decades, a self-taught genius of popular music has sought unsuccessfully to study with a contemporary master. In the twenties George Gershwin approached Maurice Ravel in Paris, only to be told that there was no way he could improve what he was already doing so perfectly. Again in the forties, in New York, Charlie Parker implored Edgar Varèse to take him on in any capacity (even as a cook) in exchange for lessons in composition. But again the artist demurred—not because he lacked appreciation of Parker's gifts but simply because he could not imagine what two such sundered arts might have to contribute to each other. Today the situation is radically different—so much so that if John Lennon were to sit down with John Cage to discuss music, one wonders who would come away the wiser.

# Walking Wounded,
# Living Dead

## Leslie Epstein

The ride to the Living Theater—hurtling under a river, pressed among swaying, hostile blacks, sparks flying from Hephaestus' anvil, the ominous clank of chains—was one that any Greek would recognize as a journey to the Underworld, or, perhaps, as the hallucinations and thunderings which accompany the Eleusinian mysteries, though in fact I was only going to Brooklyn on the IRT. *Kogx! Ompax!* The performance was scheduled for eight-thirty and I arrived at the Academy about forty-five minutes early. Even at that hour patrons swarmed through the lobby and out onto the steps leading to Lafayette Street; they were dressed much as the Eleusinian initiates have been described, wearing garlands, crowned with myrtle, and wearing sandals ("having under their feet the skin of a victim offered to [the] god," J. Lemprière, *A Classical Dictionary*, 1951). There was about them, and their intense conversation, that same sense of excitement which, somewhat more feebly, had breached the faculty dining hall at Queens College: colleagues growing red in the face, trading insults, throwing down a

Reprinted from *New American Review* No. 6, April 1969.

gauntlet of napkins, letting their meat loaf grow cold. And all this over the theater! I retreated to the Bickford's in the Long Island Rail Road station, bought a paper, and ordered English muffins. JACKIE TO MARRY ONASSIS, the headline ran, in what was to be a final salute to Aristotle. The woman who brought my order stood to the side in the classic waitress's contraposto: head to the left, the back of one foot against a wall, one hand on her skewered hip, the other, in violation of everything her posture testified to, lightly, gracefully, touching her hair.

"What's going on here tonight?" she asked.

"The Living Theater," I replied. "Have you seen it yet?"

"Seen it? They're weirdos! In and out of here all day long, with the beards and the beads and the whole production! You can't show me anything. I've been all over the world a couple of times, you know it, and before the war I lived on the West Bank of Paris. The whole time I was there I never knew an ugly person. It wasn't like this, a filthy generation."

"Why not go back?" I asked, thinking, *the heckling's started already.* "Why stay on here?"

"I'm fifty-four, what more can I see? All I'm doing is making up time for Social Security. Believe me," she said, making a vague gesture around the room, empty now save for the two of us and an elderly gentleman decomposing in whiskers and steam from his tea, "it's a living death."

*Mysteries and Smaller Pieces* (the Eleusinian rites were also divided into Greater and Lesser Mysteries) began with a young man, black beard, black pigtail, Indian-looking despite his round glasses and thermal undershirt, standing breathless at the front of the stage. His arms were turned biceps forward and slightly bent, as were his legs, as if he were bearing and transmitting a burden, the middle carving of a totem pole, altogether oblivious of the members of the tribe filing in beneath him. The difficulty was that, except for an almost imperceptible fluttering of the diaphragm, he remained that way long after the last spectator had found his seat and come, after some reflection, to the conclusion that this was mystery number one. A good twenty minutes passed. The man behind me, a middle-aged critic, finished off a chapter in a handsome new copy of *Man's Fate* and began a mean conversation with a colleague about a third critic who a few nights earlier had taken off his clothes ("he's loathsome enough with them on") and danced in these aisles. Still the Kwakiutl stood, like an illustration for an absent lecturer, unmoving, unblinking, *This, gentlemen, is an atavism,* until, some time close to nine o'clock, a voice cried out from the depths of the orchestra, "*Nu?*" and the catcalls began: "I thought this was the *Living* Theater!" "Draw, pardner!" "Author! Author!" When I saw *Dionysus 69* (a work which also seeks to revive Greek rituals of communion), a Maenad approached a dapper spectator and clutched him with her bloodstained hand. "Do you not admire our trophy of the chase?" she asked, indicating the corpse of Pentheus, slain for asserting the order of his mind and kingdom against the arrows of instinct. "Trophy of the chaste?" cried the spectator as he pinched his date's neat bottom, "You have the wrong trophy, my dear!" The play, already moribund, never recovered. But as the heckling continued in the Brooklyn Academy, it became increasingly clear that, far from being susceptible to wisecracks, the Living Theater needed them, used them—just as it needed and used the responses of the audience in everything it did—as demonstrations of faith. In this instance, it did not take long for their point to emerge. The catatonic savage—mute, unbending, with hardly a breath of life—was in fact so much *less* rigid than the audience confronting him. He stood peacefully while they could not sit still in their seats; and the longer he remained there, the softer, more passive, more thoughtful he became, while the audience, which at first had been driven to creative, or at any rate witty, participation, became increasingly impatient, antagonistic, vulgar. The wooden Indian was a shaman, sucking away at, testing, drawing our defenses—the hierophant of Eleusis, revealing how far, in the course of the evening, we had to go.

The *Smaller Pieces*—the marching of *The Brig* turned into a dance, Yoga exercises, improvisations, a raga, living snapshots—stood to the *Mysteries* as the Lesser Eleusinian rites did to the Greater: that is, they were preparatory, meant to bring the uninitiated to a deeper awareness of the sacred in order that they might confront the ultimate mystery. Hence, each Piece was an attempt to ritualize essentially profane objects, acts, relationships, as when white, clean, important-looking toilet paper was solemnly unrolled and the cast hawked and blew into it with such terrific energy and serious-ness that, surely, they were clearing their souls. It is for this reason—the irrelevance of ritual time to theatrical "timing"—that everything the Living Theater does takes so long. I once saw a film of a medicine man—a bisexual Tiresias, the skin of his breasts drawn and pinched into waggling dugs, long hair mud-matted becomingly—cutting the nails of his client and burying them, with appropriate incantations, in the ground. It made Antonioni look like Mack Sennett. There were ten separate funeral ceremonies (one for each toe), ten little mounds of earth, ten individual charms, ten identical tears running down the painted cheek. A manicure for a centipede! But anything less, a single intermission, a corner cut ("And so forth," as my grandfather used to say before the hard-boiled eggs at Passover), might liven the proceedings but ruin the magic. The Living Theater, while never so boring as the witch doctor, practices the same medicine and shares the same logic. Instead of the theater, the imitation of an action—they perform the act itself; instead of the representa-tion of an idea, of art—they think primitive thoughts, enact primitive science, which is designed not to interpret but to manipulate the world, to produce immediately, magically, *presto!* what the Living Theater calls "the Permanent Revo-lution," though Pentheus knew it as the religion of Diony-sus.

That religion, contrary to what we are taught in the drama schools, had nothing to do with tragedy, or indeed with any art that seeks through words, images, ideas, emotions—that is, through imagined instead of actual processes, through psychology—to interpose itself between desire and fulfill-ment. Antonin Artaud has declared, "Psychology, which works relentlessly to reduce the unknown to the known, to the quotidian and the ordinary, is the cause of the theater's abasement and its fearful loss of energy." A tragedian or a psychologist would say "elevate" instead of "reduce" "the unknown to the known," for both systems are based upon a necessary distinction between conscious and unconscious, reality and illusion, intellect and instinct, and both are committed to extending the domain of the former over the latter through a policy of territorial expansion called catharsis. Dionysus, however, tosses his curls, waves his wand, and all the boundaries vanish. There is no audience at his ritual, only participants, no isolated Corybant, only the single congregation. Here there is no distinction between the known and the unknown for the very concept of distinctions, along with consciousness itself, is lost in the ecstasy of the dance, the forgetfulness of wine, the intoxication of laurel leaves, the passion of orgasm, and above all the exultation of the slaughter of the goat-god and the feast. In tragedy, as in all rituals of catharsis, the goat who bears our fantasies and sins is led away into the wilderness. In the religion of Dionysus he is torn apart and eaten, so that all things—the god and his worshipers, sacred and profane, mind and body, self and other, wish and the joy of the wish coming true—are one. It is precisely this unity and this energy, which the drama has sought to dissipate, that the Living Theater seeks to revive in the communal mystery.

There were, I think, two Greater Mysteries that evening. The first sequence began with moving lights on the darkened stage, pinpricks, clustered in groups of five or six, fading like so many constellations when the house lights went on, leaving the glowing sticks of incense clutched in twenty pairs of hands. The cast descended to the aisles; the sticks, reed-thin, trembling, scattering ash, smoke, smell about us, candlesticks for heroines, spikes in a palm. (The fifth day of the Eleusinian rites "was called *The Torch Day,* because on the following night the people ran about with torches in their hands," Lemprière.) On-stage Julian Beck—bald pate, long locks on the fringe, a Chinese monkey—sits cross-legged and chants, first, lines from a poem, "End the wars, End the wars, End the wars," then, whatever we shout at him: "Free the schools!" someone yells; "Free the schools . . ." Beck intones; "Free the schools . . ." many reply. *"Sieg Heil!"* A nondescript man objects to the liturgy. I jump from my seat, cross the aisle, ask why he should want to say such a thing. "What do you think is going on?" he asks. "That's what this is all about, this chanting and shouting in unison. You ought to know your history."

"But listen to *what* they're saying," I respond. "And what about the *spirit* behind the words. Don't you hear that?"

"Sure I do. When people follow a leader they always end up saying *Sieg Heil. SIEG HEIL!*"

"There *is* no leader!" I exclaim, at the same time managing to register the man's fixed smile and how the knuckles of his hand gripping a book had gone white.

"Yeah, well, just listen to them; in a minute they'll be following *me! SIEG HEIL! Sieg Heil!*" But no one does. The song ends; the cast pinches out the incense and gathers on the stage, where they throw the burnt sticks into the center of the circle they have somehow formed. Hands on each other's shoulders, facing inwards, once again the Living Theater has turned its back to us—we are ignored. But there is less rigidity on both sides now. After a time the circle begins to sway, hardly visibly, back and forth, and from it, or from over it, a low humming sound begins, at once angelic and like the sound of bombers, so that the group onstage seems simultaneously full of grace and surrounded by doom. Then, at first singly or in pairs, then in groups, then, seemingly, all at once, the audience begins to scale the stage, those above reaching down to those below, as if it were a barricade and they realize they are storming what had always stood between them and their deepest instincts. So the circle swelled, exfoliated, became a concentric series, swaying, humming still, as massive as Stonehenge, and light, quick, mobile, shifting as Stonehenge too, when the sun triggers its rocks and turns them about in their own shadows. Watching this, I glimpsed the man, now silent, across from me. He hadn't been wrong. Mass movements *do* end in *Sieg Heil.* There is no morality apart from the individual. Yet this Mystery was in the process of accomplishing the extinction not only of leaders and led, actors and audiences, but of the separate man as well; and with his dissolution there was no sense of nihilism, only, surprisingly, the feeling of shared goodness, the conviction, always revolutionary, always discredited, yet here once again affirmed and—moment by moment, as the auditorium emptied and the stage filled —*verified*, that man is more perfect in concert than he is alone.

The humming sound was tremendous and still ambiguous, a portent of a blessing or imminent destruction. I thought suddenly of the scene in *Man's Fate* in which the revolutionaries are waiting to be thrown into the boiler of a locomotive and of how each merry blast of the glutted whistle draws them closer together until the leader, Katov, hands one of his two companions a capsule of poison, and, wounded, he drops it to the pitch-black floor. All three begin a desperate search for the cyanide and the communion it offers:

> He was looking too, trying to control his nervousness, to place his hand flat, at regular intervals, wherever he could reach. Their hands brushed his. And suddenly one of them took his, pressed it, held it.
>
> "Even if we don't find it—" said one of the voices. Katov also pressed his hand, on the verge of tears, held by that pitiful fraternity, without a face, almost without a real voice (all whispers resemble one another), which was being offered him in this darkness. . . .

I turned to the critic behind me. "It's the same as *Man's Fate*," I cried. "Where they're looking for the capsule and clasp hands. Isn't it just the same!" Icy smile, supercilious nod, another man with a book. Papyrus not priapus! But I was a third, scribbling these thoughts in my spiral notebook, fast to my seat, while all around me stragglers rushed forward to touch their comrades in the dark.

The second Mystery began when the cast started to cough and gasp and clutch at their throats. The lights dimmed and a yellow haze trickled about the staggering, tottering, collapsing forms. My fingers pushed involuntarily between my shirt collar and my neck, for, as any resident of the city knows, a plague is raging, and its appropriate symptom is not, as was the case in Thebes, sterility, but asphyxiation. One after the other the cast fell to their knees, to their bellies and backs, writhing, squirming, turning, at last, arms and legs up to the thickened air. Once again the sheer duration of their agony was, by the usual standards, undramatic; yet—perhaps because the symptoms were not pathological but, a cough, a wheeze, legs giving way on the street, common reactions to an atmosphere—the effect was of speed, not slowness, as if a time-lapse film were reeling off the perishing of us all, the nighttime death I often experience, particularly in winter, when every furnace burns number-six oil and nimbostratus clouds hang layer on layer, an iron lid upon the city, trapping sulfur and smoke, which then trundled downward to where I lie on my bed, a little Jew in a gigantic oven.

"*Sieg Heil!*" It is the same man across the aisle, now standing in his seat, craning to catch my eye, pointing to the figures expiring before us. "What did I tell you? Wasn't I right to shout *Sieg Heil?*"

"No! No!" I cry. "They're not killing us, they're telling us we're dying." But he doesn't hear, doesn't see, only taps his skull knowingly with his index finger, and all at once I realize that this Mystery does not mean to evoke the asphyxiation that descends upon us from without, but to exorcise that inner suffocation, that necessary repression, which life in any city demands. Raskolnikov, for example, strides about the dusty, stinking streets of St. Petersburg, stepping over and around the drunken men who lie in his path, strangling himself: ". . . he might even more truly be said to have fallen into a kind of coma, and he went on his way without even giving them a thought." Still alive, a few members of the cast manage to crawl up the aisle to die at our feet. Plague-stricken, comatose, we watch: a hand stretches out, a body shudders, a mouth opens, closes, a rattle, a sigh, silence. Around me now people fall from their seats, kneel by the dying, embrace them. A few rows back a girl is weeping hysterically over the body that stiffens in her arms. My heart clatters but I do not move. Too late. From somewhere a last, defiant wisecrack—"I told you we shouldn't eat in Brooklyn!"—and immediately, in magical response, the aisles are filled with corpses; yet once again, though the bodies are picked up by the surviving cast as if they were planks, and though they are stacked, too, like wood, head to toe to toe to head, in a ziggurat at the center of the stage, they remain so much less rigid than we.

For one thing, they are surrounded by tender gestures: their shoes are removed and placed, saints' relics, along the apron; a girl's hair is moved from the face of the person lying two layers beneath her; a blouse is folded over an exposed breast; a lost ribbon is picked up and placed across the owner's shoe. They are cared for. Moreover, like Oedipus at *his* burial ("I pray that you and this your land and all your people may be blessed"), they retain, even enhance, their magic and their influence with the gods after death. A number of times during the *Smaller Pieces* a little girl of perhaps four, obviously the child of one of the cast, had wandered onto the stage to see what was happening and even take part, usually by tugging the beard of one of the cast. Now she appeared again in the dim light, a mound of corpses behind her and another graveyard yawning before, holding, as proof against each, a balloon tucked under her arm. She walked among the dead shoes, picking them up, looking at them, setting them down. Then she turned, laughed, and, as if she had seen the bodies for the first time, walked curiously and calmly to them. With a flat palm, at the end of a straight, awkward arm, she slid her hand over the faces heaped in the pyramid. I have since talked to a number of people who have seen different performances of *Mysteries and Smaller Pieces*. The child was not there. She belonged to us, in fact she was each one of us, whoever, earlier, had not the courage to join the circle of rocks, whoever, later, had not the compassion to comfort the dying, whoever had remained so stone-hearted, or of such little faith, as to shout or mock. The power that the ritual had generated is brought in this final Mystery to such a pitch that reality gives. These dead may work miracles, may call up a perfect image of grace to play upon their faces and, with a laugh, set these other dead free.

I rode the subway home amazed. That I should rediscover the theater—and myself—in this way was astonishing, for when it comes to drama (and other things) I am Pentheus' man, willing to lock Dionysus in jail, and all for boundaries, particularly the one that distinguishes the illusion onstage from the reality I must bear with me. Nothing in the avant-garde theater—least of all the threat in *Dionysus 69* to cut me up and eat me—has led me to think I am wrong. No, there is one exception. Not long before attending *Mysteries* I had seen *The Concept*, in which a number of young addicts go through the sort of therapeutic encounters that take place (or used to) in their home, Daytop Village. At the end of the evening the cast, having touched one another, reach for the audience. They leave the stage and ask whatever spectator they happen to stand before, "Will you love me?" My reaction was to huddle in my seat, making myself as small as possible—like a student dematerializing before his teacher— and, as the soft questions and soft embraces went on around me, to think, making magic, *notmenotmenotme*. Eric Bentley has used this moment in *The Concept* to attack the Living Theater and participatory drama in general. *Will you love me? Of course not*, he replies, *I hardly know you*. Bentley's failure here—one that is crucial, given the task of the contemporary critic—is that he has been insensitive to the distinction between realism as a technique and reality as an experience, an imitation of an action and the act itself. These are addicts, not actors; the tears, the trembling, the tongue-tied evasions are not part of what a group therapy session is *like*, but of a genuine encounter. What friends have we— friends whom we profess to love and whom we casually and constantly embrace—who dare to reveal themselves so deeply before us? What friends have we whom we know so well? By living, instead of providing an impression of life, the people of *The Concept*, no less than those of *Mysteries*, refuse to enact the audience's fantasies or atone for its sins; instead, the burden of action, and of decision, is shifted from actor to spectator, who may shrink in his seat, praying *not me!*, or step boldly into the circle of waiting arms.

Alas, my amazement, and that world of possibilities, disintegrated one night later. Bickford's was my Delphi, its oracle a woman who sat at a table near the window, out of her mind. She would have been attractive in a thin-faced, ravaged, tubercular way, had it not been for her mouth, which was snaggle-toothed and leering, and which twisted downward—as if she were crying—whenever she laughed. Her dress was hiked up her crossed legs, and she sat in such a way that the dark, flat-nosed, white-eyed faces pressed to the window glass could see, without straining the length of her thigh. Each time one of these spectators gave up, turned away, floated back into the avenue lights, she laughed and pivoted the heel of her grounded foot beneath the table. It was a prophetic performance—for the evening that followed, with all its pleasures, belonged to the mad.

*Paradise Now* has a script, or at any rate a chart, a ladder, whose rungs are arranged to take us from the sort of hostility displayed by the audience at *Mysteries* to a condition of "Permanent Revolution" in which all differences will be reconciled. In other words, the motto printed at the bottom of the chart, "The essential trip is the voyage from the many to the one," is precisely that carved on the tablets of the Dionysian religion. The voyagers sat crowded on the stage, ready to embark, instantly recognizable to one another as either the most serene or the most hysterical citizens of New York. It would be a fair test, I thought, if these people could be brought to communion.

For the next five hours the Living Theater tried, doggedly moving from rung to rung, prayer to prayer, ritual to ritual, burning money, baring bodies, flying through the air; but the magic was not working, the congregation cracked into a perceptible chaos of the disinterested and the deranged. Arguments broke out all over the Brooklyn Academy. A plump Passionaria spat into the face of one of the cast, and then, changing roles, pulled up her sweater, mad madonna, and began to suckle her infant child. Youth Against War and Fascism screamed slogans and started pushing people around. An old man stood on his seat and read a political statement. Coins, heavy, dangerous, flew back and forth between the auditorium and the stage, and eyes began to fill with the points of paper gliders raining down from the sky. "Do what you want! Free Theater! Do what you want!" shouted Julian Beck, a kindly, punch-drunk Cadmus, first henchman of the horned god. A few seats from me a man reached beneath the brassiere of the loveliest girl in the cast, who was standing in the aisle, and began kneading her breasts from behind. On stage, another man, fully clothed, pulled a participant from the Rite of Universal Intercourse and dragged her on her bare back to the wings, where he knelt between her legs. If he took her, no jury could convict him of rape. We had all been solicited.

Someone—a young Sinatra, curly black hair, protruding ears, and liquid eyes—bent his knees, threw out his arms, and began to croon, "O moon over Manhattan . . ." Three black cats in bright green pants and alligator shoes jumped up on the apron; for a moment one could see their faces grinning beneath square Lenin caps—the same ubiquitous faces that seem to peek over shoulders into the camera at any civic disaster—before they were swallowed up by the crowd in a flash of iridescent vines. In all the confusion the cast succeeded in maneuvering to the front of the stage, where, linking together, contorting their bodies, they coalesced into the word ANARCHY. In an instant the woman with the baby had thrown herself on her back at the lip of the stage and was holding her red squalling infant over her head in the palm of her hand: "THIS IS ANARCHY MOTHA-FUCKERS!" It was a blood-curdling scream, but its impact came not so much from the intensity of the demon-woman who had uttered it as from the fact that it was true. The premise, the possibility tendered us the evening before—the revolutionary assertion of the innate goodness of man—had just been revoked by the face of the revolution itself. What was heartbreaking about the spectacle was its ordinariness, its familiarity, its profaneness. Mysteries, its shining vision, was submerged by movies and their hackneyed version of the Reign of Terror, full of cackling hags and banging in the gutter and lunatics running about breaking beautiful things. I sat there, a counterrevolutionary, an aristocrat, male Antoinette, thinking, most horribly, Jackie, marry him quick.

Yet there was something sacred in the catastrophe of Paradise Now, and that was the reassertion of the spirit of Dionysus in the life of the theater. The woman who had been, in turn, Passionaria, Madonna, and Statue of Anarchy, was also possessed by the spirit of the god. "Why don't you put real bullets in your guns?" she screamed at one of the cast, and blew smoke in his face like so much steam from the oracle's thighs. She was right again. Violence was at least as pervasive that night as sexuality. The logic of the ritual—do what you want, free theater, do what you want—leads inescapably to making murder sacrifice, just as it had transformed rape into an act of consent. At still another point in the spectacle, this same woman—she was no plant, for by then I recognized her as a marcher in various peace parades, a taut banner fluttering near her head—turned to those of us attending her argument and cried, "Look at them! They're masturbating under their programs! You're not a theater, you're a wet dream!" What is this but a call for a theater that will go beyond the drama—traditional, illusory, frustrating —performed on either side of the cafeteria window glass? One can hear in that cry, as one can see only too well in the course of *Paradise Now*, the theater of the future, participatory, ritualistic, though hardly based on comforting the fallen or responding to an appeal for love. Instead, there will be ravishment at random, or, more likely, a member of the audience will be haphazardly shot, picked by lot and sacrificed, one at each performance, Bacchus' favorite, with golden curls. Perhaps that is the theater of the present as well. It is difficult to interpret otherwise a nation's willingness to tolerate a distant war whose day-in and day-out dramatization involves the killing of some young man, vaguely familiar, a neighbor's son, and his subsequent flight to Hades slung from a whirlybird.

It was raining the next day, and in Bickford's the madwoman sat, her hair wet, her legs in a lull, calmly eating a bacon and lettuce and tomato sandwich. A man with impressive leonine hair and beard, whom I recognized as a spectator at *Mysteries* and *Paradise Now,* came into the cafeteria section, balancing a tray. Victim of the age-old association of wisdom and facial hair (from which the cleverest and glandularly most advanced of my students benefit), I asked him what he thought of the Living Theater and was shocked by the banality of his reply—"How can they charge money, if we put on the show?"—and the high-pitched silly voice with which he uttered it. C-minus and a sigh.

I do not mean to strain the powers of English muffins, but there is a sense in which this contradiction between form and content was mirrored in the production of the Sophocles/ Brecht *Antigone* I saw that afternoon. What, after all, did the Living Theater have to do with Bert Brecht, that disciplinarian, who sought communion only from the Party with a thousand eyes? Indeed, what had it to do with Sophocles, himself, or his *Antigone?* Of course I remembered Haemon's famous speech about flexibility ("Have you not seen the trees beside the torrent, the ones that bend them saving every leaf, while the resistant perish root and branch?") and saw its relevance to the quotation from Beck reprinted in each of the Brooklyn Academy programs: "If we can reduce the amount of aggression in one person, or change one person from being more rigid to less rigid, then the effort is worth while." But the Living Theater was not in the business of delivering messages, any more than it was interested in making itself felt through images. It was not propaganda, but it was not art either, and the spirit of tragedy, dedicated to desacralizing the individual, dividing him from his fellow man and his own wounded soul, is clearly inimicable to the communal impulse and magical practice that linked this company to that which danced for Dionysus.

This confusion in purpose and spirit—which is surely related to the contradiction in effect between *Mysteries and Smaller Pieces* and *Paradise Now*—permeated the *Antigone.* Undeniably, there were moments which did tend to catch the audience up in a ritual action larger than the play itself: the opening with its lowing sirens and sense of alarm; the closing, in which the entire cast retreats to the rear wall of the stage, horrified by what they see staring at them from the audience's eyes; the way in which Creon strips the black shirt from the back of his dying son and holds it in front of his face, erasing himself; the series of symbolic dismemberings and emasculations that decimate the cast, the executions (a hand reaches up, shhhhhhhhhhhhhhhk, my throat is slit) that riddle the spectators—each of these moments helps to create an experience which, in savagery and passion, is very close to what the Greeks must have seen, far closer, in fact, than those refined "classical" productions of Euripides at the Circle in the Square, in which white handkerchiefs are summoned to our eyes. The trouble is that these images are vitiated by being everywhere subject to relentless interpretation. The war with the Argives becomes ours with the Vietnamese; the leader of the Thebans is the President; his willful daughter, our own dissent. On the face of it—the Greeks certainly used the myths to examine their own society—there is nothing wrong with this method. Nor are the conclusions it suggests invalid or its parallels uninteresting. Beck's Creon, in particular, made a marvelous LBJ, full of sanctimoniousness and a fierce yearning for love, threatening and bullying, wheeling and dealing, yet competent, a good father, and with a certain measure of courage in the face of adversity that lifts the characterization (as it has the President) from clinging vulgarity. There is a poster by Bernard Aptekar which quotes Catullus in order to capture one of the most disquieting and elusive of Johnson's traits, his indisguisable glee in the midst of catastrophe, the relish of disaster, bliss at suffering: "Whatever's the deal he smiles and smiles; it's a disease he's got." The idiot grin of the Bacchus mask, into which Beck twists his face, was that disease in its advanced stage, each muscle paralyzed, everything gone numb save for the Dionysian capacity to find in destruction quantities of sheer fun.

Why, then, should this technique, intrinsic to many Greek tragedies, produce here comedy on the order of a postgraduate *MacBird!*? The answer is that it is precisely because it *is* a technique, because the company is acting, interpreting, satirizing, commenting, holding us apart from them with the stiff arm of a point of view. Heretofore, it was the intensity of their belief, their personal grace, which transformed us; in *Antigone* it is the conception and not their conviction of which we become aware, and we are forced to judge it by a quality of execution rather than a degree of faith. The results are not happy. When the Living Theater speaks or sings through any other mouths than their own, when they seek, in short, to impersonate anything other than what they have learned of themselves, it is like spying, beneath the star-chased robes, the sorcerer's store-bought shoes. And Judith Malina, who possesses perhaps the greatest theatrical imagination in the world today, has no stage presence whatsoever. And she plays Antigone. *O hirsute paradox!*

We are returned to the realm of what Artaud would call art; a theater of cruelty is replaced by one of language, illusion, and above all psychology—one in which we are more comfortable, surely, but in which the Living Theater is so misplaced we laugh more from embarrassment than relief. It is a tribute to what *Mysteries* had worked in me, and what *Paradise Now* failed to destroy, that in this familiar territory I

felt a sense of displacement, I think it was because I somehow
had realized that the best and worst of the Living Theater was
the best and worst the world could do; and I had returned
that third day ready to risk the conflict, to respond, to decide, to act. Or not to. Instead I got a peep show. The
one lesson I had learned was that, given Punch and Judy,
we become rag dolls. And so I sat, sawdust spilling from
the gash in my throat, collapsing into my native daze,
biting the thumbs of irresolution down to their bloodless
quick.

Two weeks later I drove to Cambridge to see *Frankenstein*.
Cars were backed up on either side of Bridgeport, first for a
crazy man—yet another!—who danced around his disabled
Chevrolet, waggling his head at a clutch of dumbfounded
cops, then for a jackknifed truck, leaking something brown. I
rolled up the window and—the Raskolnikov effect—stepped
on it. At M.I.T. the Permanent Revolution was on. A soldier
had gone AWOL and taken refuge in the Union, where
hundreds of students had gathered to prevent his arrest. The
influence of the Becks, who were setting up their scenery
in the Kresge Auditorium nearby, had penetrated this refuge; for here indeed was a ritual communion—great red
cans of S.S. Pierce Chow Mein, and on the side, crispy
noodles; ecstasy—Friday night Jews *davening* in the corner and praying through the nose; and the Dionysian
principle of all-inclusiveness—"Friendly Fuzz Welcome"
on a hand-lettered sign. Hearts blossomed on a poster for
*Tufts SDS*, a heterotopy matched by the pillows flourishing everywhere on cold cement and the merry smiles on
double-breasted Communists. Signs warned, *no guns, no
billy clubs, no acid, no grass*, and indeed these communi-
cants possessed nothing to protect either the lost soldier
from the authorities in pursuit or themselves from the ob-
stinate armies of reality, save for the moral power of their
cause, the strength of their commitment, and the magic of
their example, in whose contagiousness lay their only sanctuary.

Meanwhile, across the courtyard, the other Living Theater
had begun a similar rite. Most of the cast were on stage,
working their minds in whatever way necessary to levitate a
young girl seated in their midst. Every now and then a voice

would announce on a loudspeaker how much time was left before she would start to ascend. Quite a lot of time, it turned out, and while it passed I noticed the woman from *Paradise Now* and her sleeping baby. *If we can reduce the amount of aggression in one person . . .* The sanctity of the Living Theater, if not its success, may be measured by the fact that from the calamity of that earlier evening, through their patience and gentleness, they had made this single convert, this one follower. Whether owing to the effects of her redemption, or to this soothing audience of square-jawed engineers in pink eyeglass frames—*by golly we're going to lick pollution!*—she remained calm and in her seat until the final exit. Back onstage the countdown had begun. Brows knit, eyes rolled, the full force of the Living Theater's collective personality shot outward in waves of energy and enveloped the squatting figure, who shuddered visibly but did not rise. The ritual had failed; yet only because it miscarried, because of the hidden imperfection of spirit, the worm in the rose, could *Frankenstein* continue. In this way the opening meditation acted as a preface not only to our own lives—that sense of vision blurred, pleasure denied, Eden forbidden, from which disconnectedness, our only sin, derives—but to the life of the Living Theater as well. If *Mysteries* had succeeded more completely than it had, if *Paradise Now* had been less a ruin, the Permanent Revolution would cease. The hidden doctrine of *Frankenstein* is that of the Fortunate Fall, for as a doctor needs disease and an artist ugliness, the Living Theater requires failure in order to survive.

The remainder of the play is in a sense the view from the high Hill, "This top of Speculation," the panorama of life after the Fall which the Angel Michael depicts for bedazzled Adam, and then says:

This having learnt, thou has attain'd the sum
Of wisdom; hope no higher, though all the Stars
Thou knew'st by name, and all the ethereal Powers . . .
                     only add
Deeds to thy knowledge answerable, add Faith,
Add Virtue, Patience, Temperance, add Love,
By name to come call'd Charity, the soul
Of all the rest: then wilt thou not be loath

To leave this Paradise, but shalt possess
A paradise within thee, happier far.

In the Becks' version, the expulsion from Eden, alienation,
is brought on by the failure of the specific ritual of communion we had witnessed at the start of the play. Because, before time, in a prelude to the action, men were
unable to love each other, their history is the story of how
they chose to execute each other: "They are hunted, they
are electrocuted, they are gassed, they are guillotined, they
are racked, they are hanged, they are garrotted, they are
beheaded, they are crucified, they are shot" (the entire
program gloss is studiedly Miltonian). But the lesson Adam
learned was at one and the same time of suffering and
redemption, history and history's end ("Eternity, whose end
no eye can reach"). In the play, the symbol of that
curse and blessing is Doctor Frankenstein's monster. The
ritual, once so pure, has become black magic; the evolution of science is, from what we see here, the painting
of a circle on the victim's stomach to what we read in the
newspapers, the naming of the stars and the circling of the
moon.

In theatrical terms, the sum of Adam's wisdom is the need
for tragedy, that is, for a redeemer, a scapegoat to act out his
fantasies and atone for his sins. The Doctor's monster is that
hero, and his creation and manipulation is a study of the role
of drama in the life of man. The entire middle part of the play
consists of the education of the newborn monster, a form of
socialization in which dozens of theatrical forms (the program
notes list a few, "children's Greek-myth theater, shadow-
play, Buddha legends, Grand-Guignol, circus, magic-show,
mime, collage, silence, climactic speech, the chase") are
staged in the platform of his sleeping mind. The content of
these many dramas is made up of the collective dreams of the
race, from the Flight of Icarus and the Rape of Europa to,
once again, the weirdly appropriate headlines from that day's
newspaper: SCORPION FOUND ON BOTTOM OF SEA; ISRAELIS
PENETRATE TO BANKS OF NILE. Thus the hero assimilates to
himself the mythological and actual life of mankind, just as he
incorporates into his mind the dozens of men who portray
his shifting, various thoughts. What this section suggests is
that, for all the experimentation, we, and the monster who

is to save us, are being subjected to the effects of traditional drama: art as a dream, an illusion, a flicker in slumber—from which we wake not to refreshment, our souls buoyant and delighted, but to discover ourselves brainwashed.

That is why, when the monster escapes into the wilderness there is no freedom, no sanctuary; instead, "the authorities take over," and we are back where we began. Rituals of catharsis do not work either. In the last act, history resumes. The world is a jailhouse, tier on tier of identical cells, into which the population is pushed, endlessly, until the place is full. Art's cry has always been that it can set men free ("Stone walls do not a prison make/Nor iron bars a cage") but it is a cry directed to "minds innocent and quiet." This prison is an asylum. We are back in New York, in the tenements of the mad, and the only means of escape is rebellion, the only remaining ceremony a trial by fire. At the end of the play the prisoners collect their strength and, like Dionysus in Pentheus' jail, burst the walls of their cells. They join in a new communion, a common body, a single creature, not a monster this time, no one else's image, merely man, arms outstretched, knees slightly bent, bringer of his own salvation. Artaud speaks of "a fabricated Being, made of wood and cloth, entirely invented, corresponding to nothing, yet disquieting by nature, capable of reintroducing on the stage a little breath of . . . metaphysical fear." Most who see this production feel this fear. I did not. It was true that *Frankenstein* (rather, the whole experience of the Living Theater) would make it difficult to attend the Broadway theater again, but it did not make it impossible to go on living. I had made the mistake, perhaps, of seeing how Paradise was to be regained before I had seen how it had been lost, for on balance, and uneasily, it seemed less difficult to exist in the abattoir of history than join the asylum (in both senses) of eternity.

Before going to bed I stopped off at my motel's nightclub, the Cockatoo Lounge. A trio was going through the last set. The smoke and laughter and lowered lights reminded me less of *Mysteries* than of fraternity initiations. A singer jumped up on the stage and announced a Lebanese melody: "S-a-a-a-a-lami, oh! oh! S-a-a-a-a-lami, oh! oh! oh!" A waitress bent across a nearby table, joking with the patrons, and her skirt rose to the hem of her panties. My wish to put my hand on her forbidden, perfect rump was stronger, a thousand times so, than anything I had felt when invited to work my will upon the naked cast. The singer introduced his partner, a comic. He was fifty-five or sixty and his tuxedo pants ended far above his split and ancient patent leather shoes. He did a little dance. The waitress turned to take my order. Sweat shone between her hanging breasts, reflecting the ecstatic candle writhing on my tabletop. The comic had put a mop on his head and was doing an imitation of Tiny Tim. The singer played the straight man for gags about queers. The piano player leaned into his mike and said the show was over. The room started to empty to a series of trills. A group of men who had failed to pick up any girls stood for a moment in the center of the room, laughing, joking, fondling each other, pinching, as consolation, their own behinds. The lights came up and decorations left over from Halloween loomed from the walls, orange pumpkins and black cats and a skeleton jiggling on a string. Boo! Boo! Boo! I lingered at the doorway, looking back: *"then wilt thou not be loath to leave this Paradise, but shalt possess a Paradise within thee, happier far."*

Driving back to the city the next night I hit a patch of fog on the Massachusetts Turnpike. I plowed forward cockily, whistling to the faded radio, when ahead, too close to stop, I saw a car turned perpendicular to the highway, all lights off, blocking two lanes of road. I managed to swerve around him and pull off to the right. As I sat in my car, I heard a screech of brakes and the terrific impact of a second car hitting the first broadside. I jumped out onto the road. There was complete silence and the fog had grown too thick to see a thing. I started to walk toward the accident. Out of nowhere there was an identical screech of brakes and an identical collision, and then, before I could react, there was a third crash. It was a nightmare. Once again I was torn by a decision. I did not want to face multiple collisions, to pull dead people from flaming cars, to risk my life. I wanted to get in my own car, drive off, hunch over the wheel, *Not me! Not me!* Through a rent in the fog I saw the tangle of cars on the highway. I ran across the road to the median divider and worked my way back to where a few figures were staggering about on the strip of grass. A police car pulled up from the opposite direction and I took an armload of magnesium flares and ran up the road to warn approaching traffic. I stood there for an hour, my torch sputtering like the monster's red eye, the Angel's flaming sword, while cars slowed and swerved and their drivers rolled down their windows to gaze at the walking wounded in the land of the living dead.

# IV

# Messages from the Media

We read napalm and imagine napalm.
Since we cannot imagine napalm
we read about napalm until
by napalm we can imagine more.
Now we protest against napalm.

—Günter Grass, "Powerless, with a Guitar"

Within two hours I was on the steps of San Francisco City Hall in front of four television cameras, five photographers, four newspaper reporters, and seven radio stations, denouncing HUAC as a "witch hunter" . . . I raved, "The government is trying to stifle antiwar dissent." The press hung on every word. I was playing Angry Radical, but inside I was laughing, standing on my hands and turning somersaults. HUAC was not stifling dissent, but stimulating it—to greater and greater heights.

—Jerry Rubin in *Do It!* on being subpoenaed by HUAC

mcluhan etc:

so what does all this mean in practical political terms? for one thing we're talking at the same time to two quite differently conditioned generations: the visual, linear older generation, and the aural, tactile, suffusing younger generation.

the bobby phenomenon: his screaming appeal to the tv generation. this certainly has nothing to do with logical persuasion; it's a total *experience*, a tactile sense—thousands of little girls who want him to be president so they can have him on the tv screen and run their fingers through the image of his hair.

Memo by William Gavin of Richard Nixon's 1968 reelection staff, quoted in *The Selling of the President 1968* by Joe McGinniss

Although he lived until late 1980, the last years of Marshall McLuhan's life amounted to a sad falling-off from the glory days of the Sixties. Just before he died the University of Toronto dismantled his Center for Culture and Technology and, worse yet, forced the retirement of the 68-year-old McLuhan himself. While he died somewhat in the position of a millennial prophet who had predicted the precise date of the apocalypse, only to have that date pass, in the Sixties McLuhan did bestride the media like a colossus. His books— *The Gutenberg Galaxy* (1962), *Understanding Media* (1964), *The Medium Is the Massage* (1967), *Counterblast* (1969) and others—sold hundreds of thousands of copies. Newsmagazines did cover stories on McLuhan and his work, and enough other articles were written to eventually make up *two* paperback readers, *McLuhan Hot and Cold* and *McLuhan Pro and Con*. He produced his own distinctly nonlinear television specials, and broadcasting and advertising groups around the country listened eagerly to his gnomic lectures on the explosive implications of their business. His message of an effortless cultural transformation mediated by the ubiquitous television set was warmly assented to by the "aural, tactile, suffusing younger generation." He was the first pop philosopher, and he got more people upset and/or excited than any other intellectual figure of the decade.

What was McLuhan saying? In its stripped-down form, the basic argument underlying his most influential book, *Understanding Media*, was this: The invention of movable type in the fifteenth century and the subsequent spread of literacy throughout Western culture was a fall from grace, from an oral, tribal, "sacred" culture to an atomized, specialized, visual and linear one. The habit of reading type shuts man within the illusion of a fixed point of view and a three-dimensional perspective. From this form of hypervisual consciousness comes the individualization, specialization, centralization and fragmentation of work characteristic of Western culture in the past few centuries. These ways of apprehending and remaking the world have made our spectacular progress possible, but at the cost of a drastic narrowing in our range of experience.

But with the rise of the electronic media—the telegraph, telephone, radio, phonograph and, ultimately, television—a new psychic and social implosion is taking place, a worldwide retribalization through a kind of electronic central nervous system, whose "current transformation of our entire lives into the spiritual form of information seems to make of the entire globe, and of the human family, a single consciousness"—the famous global village. According to McLuhan this implosion is taking place not because of, but *in spite of*, the "content" of these media, "for the 'content' of the medium is like the juicy piece of meat carried by the burglar to distract the watchdog of the mind." Note the affinity here with Susan Sontag's aesthetic preference for effectively "contentless," but consciousness-altering art in "One Culture and the New Sensibility." In other places, where he describes the forthcoming electronic state of grace, McLuhan echoes Norman O. Brown's *Love's Body:* "Electricity points the way to an extension of the process of consciousness itself, on a world scale, and without any verbalization whatsoever. Such a state of collective awareness may have been the preverbal condition of man."

All of this and much more was put across in *Understanding Media* in a vague and oracular prose style—startling asides delivered *ex cathedra*, with synaptic rather than logical jumps of exposition. And even more than Sontag or Brown, McLuhan infuriated literary intellectuals with his blithe assertions that the print medium had had it. Nowhere did McLuhan make more enemies and converts than in his thoughts on television, a medium he defined as "cool"—that is, of low definition, thereby requiring the "depth involvement" of the viewer to "fill in" the image. Thus, according to McLuhan, the generation raised on television participates "mythically" in events, and aspires to "wholeness, empathy, and depth of awareness." Presumably this explained the appearance of hippies, and many other things as well. McLuhan's analysis, reprinted here, of the reasons for John Kennedy's stunning defeat (in media terms) of Richard Nixon in the first televised presidential debate in 1960, and of the kind of cool, low-key personal image that comes across best on television, was one of the hardest-read passages of the decade.

One needn't subscribe to McLuhan's metaphysics, however, to appreciate just how skillfully and effortlessly John Kennedy used television as a presidential tool. In the process he revolutionized our politics. The Kennedy style was born for the television screen, and politicians quickly awoke to the power of the television image to mold the thoughts and perceptions of the electorate. They handed crucial parts of their campaigns over to the men whose arts had previously been employed to sell soap, cigarettes, cars and deodorants, and the way politicians and their messages were presented took on a new sheen.

George Lois, the maverick advertising genius, describes in *George, Be Careful* shooting miles of videotape during Robert Kennedy's 1964 New York senatorial campaign of the candidate answering unrehearsed questions around the state. Then "it was edited down to TV spots that showed the real RFK, who could field the tough ones—even when the answers came out with pain. We were showing the real man." Everyone "remembers," though not that many have actually seen, the famous Lyndon Johnson television commercial in 1964 of a young girl picking daisies in a field while a voice-over counts down to a nuclear explosion—an unsubtle allusion to Republican Barry Goldwater's supposedly itchy trigger finger. The spot was shown once on network television before heated protests made the Democrats take it off the air.

The process of this manipulation of reality and images for political ends was hilariously, devastatingly laid bare in Joe McGinniss' bestselling *The Selling of the President 1968,* an *in camera* exposé of the Madison Avenue techniques used to package the "New Nixon." The 1968 Republican Convention had been precisely orchestrated to play television's tune, and

Nixon's corps of media pros made sure that not only was a repeat of the 1960 debacle avoided, but that every element of the Nixon campaign presentation was calibrated to produce a desired effect. Panels of "real" people were screened with exquisite care to question Nixon on television (though once a Jewish psychiatrist got through the net, occasioning a blow-up by campaign manager Len Garment—Nixon could not abide a psychiatrist, especially a Jewish one, in the same room). With cynical skill filmmakers crafted swift, suggestive montages of race riots, demonstrations, and battle scenes that implied everything and said nothing. ("The public sits home and watches *Gunsmoke* and when they're fed pap about Nixon, they think they're getting something worthwhile."— this from someone who *edited* that pap!) Meanwhile a campaign aide and later speechwriter William Gavin typed out stream-of-consciousness strategy memos that reduced McLuhan, none too clear to begin with, to laughable gibberish—a good index of how poorly he could be understood. McGinniss' book, as the excerpt that follows demonstrates, was one of the funniest and scariest of the decade, and we are still living with its implications.

Questions of reality and illusion and fairness and accuracy arose most explosively in the case of the press and television coverage of the Vietnam war. In the introduction to his book *Living Room War,* from which "Television and the Press in Vietnam" is taken, Michael Arlen wrote that in the mid- to late Sixties "the war seemed to be the central fact in American life, seemed to be there, whether one talked about it or not at first, whether one claimed to be bored by it or not, later offended, later outraged, later bored. It was a changing shape beneath everything else in American life in that period, in a way that no other war we'd experienced had been, and most of us knew about it from television." As the Günter Grass quotation that opens this section is meant to suggest, for all the moral passion that many Americans poured into trying to grasp the reality of the war and to bring it to a halt, it eluded our grasp. We were in the position of voyeurs, watching and reading about our government's devastation of another country in the name of abstractions crazily inappropriate to the facts. And nothing anybody did seemed to make the "enemy" go away or the war stop coming over our television sets. In the place of results the entire country was left with a dangerous sense of frustration and impotence, a situation that resulted in the worst national political divisions since the Civil War.

As the Arlen piece demonstrates, the print and television media's immense technical and logistic efforts in covering the war in many ways only exacerbated Americans' sense of the war's irreality. The images and information communicated were constant and impressive, but with rare exceptions the reporting did not or could not penetrate much past the government's version of events. In this piece, and also in Michael Herr's superb *Dispatches* (published in 1977, although chapters began appearing in *Esquire* and *New American Review* in the late Sixties), one reads of military press briefings that seem straight out of *Catch-22*. But quite beyond the numerical absurdities put forth by the government as to body counts, hamlets secured and hills taken, Vietnam as a suffering country, the war as a wrenching, confused struggle, and the real politics underlying the whole conflict rarely came across. It is a journalistic truism that in war truth is the first casualty. But in the case of the Vietnam war the disjuncture between what we were told and shown and what we sensed and learned for ourselves was so great that the ultimate casualty was this country's cohesion and sense of self-respect.

Another phenomenon of the Sixties that eluded—this time deliberately—understanding was the put-on. Along with, and related in spirit to, black humor (see Terry Southern's *The Magic Christian*), the put-on was one of the characteristic forms of comedy in the Sixties—although the laughter it evoked was meant to be either knowing or uneasy. The whole notion of the put-on, an aggressive, subversive form of humor which never quite paid off in a punchline or an identifiable point of view, may have originated in the art world. Marcel Duchamp had made a career out of putting on the very idea of art, painting mustaches on reproductions of the Mona Lisa and solemnly presenting a urinal or a bicycle wheel mounted on a bench as "ready-made" works of art. In addition, a new art crowd, unsure of its taste to begin with and uneasily aware of the many sainted avant-gardists who had first been greeted by derisive howls of "fake" and "phony," almost begged to have their aesthetic deficiencies mercilessly kidded.

But this attitude soon spread throughout every form of cultural expression. Jerry Rubin in *Do It!* recalls Allen Ginsberg's thoughts on how to get Bob Dylan to attend a peace march: "Dylan might come if the march says nothing about the war. Like if everyone carries a placard with a picture of a different kind of fruit." Richard Rovere, the respected political columnist, wrote a mock-scholarly article spoofing the notion of an all-powerful, cabalistic "American Establishment." (One footnote cites "Masters' first-rate monograph, *Establishment Watering Holes,* Shekomeko Press, 1957.") Most people took the piece straight. Jacob Brackman perpetrated a vintage put-on in the form of a "review" of a nonexistent self-published book on the Kennedy assassination, *Time of the Assassins* by one Ulov G. K. LeBoeuf, which supposedly tied in the killing with the deaths of Marilyn Monroe, Aldous Huxley and Adlai Stevenson, and with George Hamilton's draft evasion. Meant to spoof the baroque paranoia of assassination buffs, the put-on only proved it the more: some 300 people sent in $24 checks for the four-volume set to *Ramparts,* and booksellers across the country were frantic when they could not place calls to LeBoeuf in Levittown, N.Y., where the review had placed him.

Why was the put-on so popular? A McLuhanesque explanation might say that the abandonment of the fixed point of view by the perpetrators and the penalizing of it in the victims paralleled the larger cultural transformation taking place, making it the perfect form of humor for the aural, tactile, suffusing younger generation. Brackman suggests in his *New Yorker* article on the phenomenon (June 24, 1967) that one can square the taste for put-ons with the quest for sincerity and authenticity by seeing it as a form of aggression born out of deep hurt and disappointment—a knowing con aimed against an outside world full of nothing but cons. Whatever the root causes, the put-on was the perfect way to guarantee that one's cool was maintained, a matter of great importance in the Sixties.

A perfect example of how the ethos of the put-on infiltrated commercial as well as artistic culture can be found in George Lois's brash account of his creation of a decade's worth of electrifying *Esquire* covers. Artists may be the antennae of the race, but art directors are crucial relay stations in transmitting the signals to the rest of us. Along with every other area of our cultural life, Madison Avenue experienced a refreshing renaissance in the Sixties, and Lois's memoir, *Be Careful, George,* from which this selection is excerpted, may be read as a latter-day *Autobiography of Benvenuto Cellini—*

the artist doing continually brilliant work amid a welter of
scrapes and blow-ups with his accounts/patrons. Among his
most memorable achievements were his work on the fondly
remembered Volkswagen campaign; the previously mentioned adaptation of *cinéma vérité* techniques to the exigen-
cies of political advertising; and such indelible *Esquire* covers
as Sonny Liston in a Santa Claus suit, Muhammad Ali posed
as the St. Sebastian of the fight game, and Lieutenant Calley
surrounded by a clutch of cute Asian kids. In his piece Lois
seems convinced that these covers made hard-hitting statements on America's burning issues. They hit hard, all right,
but where and what they were hitting—what he or *Esquire*
meant precisely by these covers—nobody quite knew. Asking
branded you as uptight. Whatever was meant, the covers sold
magazines, and worked perfectly as the outward and visible
sign of *Esquire*'s beautifully achieved Sixties irreverence.

An inward and readable sign of that irreverence was the
birth and flowering within its pages of the much-vaunted new
journalism. Tom Wolfe, one of whose signature pieces, "The
Girl of the Year," appears in the section "Some New
Sensibilities," described the Damascus of the new journalism
as the breakthrough he experienced in the midst of clutching
on a piece for *Esquire* on the West Coast custom-car scene;
that piece was eventually to become the title article of his first
collection, *The Kandy-Kolored Tangerine-Flake Streamline
Baby.* Two other pieces from that book, "The Last American
Hero Is Junior Johnson. Yes!" and "Las Vegas (What?) Las
Vegas (Can't Hear You! Too Noisy) *Las Vegas!!!*" also
appeared in *Esquire,* creating a stir with their celebrations of
the disorienting qualities of contemporary life. If any writer
has known how to turn the imitative fallacy to good use, it is
Wolfe. Dwight Macdonald's review of Wolfe's first collection
pinpointed the factual and artistic shortcomings of Wolfe's
journalistic method and capsulized (very early on in the
game, it should be noted) the issues raised by this ostensibly
"new" journalism. The footnotes that Macdonald added to
his review when it was reprinted some years later in his
collection *Discriminations* provide a useful running commentary on the progress of this debate.

What was new about the new journalism was the way that
the distance between the ostensible journalistic subject and
the writer/observer disappeared, with the point of view often
being located *within* the subject. But the traffic sometimes

went in the other direction: instead of effacing himself, the writer would often unabashedly thrust himself forward, using his subjectivity as a literary probe. In the Sixties, then, journalism often seemed to be aspiring to the condition of fiction. Finally, in the introduction to his 1972 anthology *The New Journalism,* Wolfe was to claim with stunning philistinism that the new journalism, with its careful, sometimes obsessive attention to status detail and its fidelity to "real" life as it is lived today had entirely superseded contemporary novelists, supposedly all in thrall to the poetics of alienation.

Without for a second assenting to this view, it does bear emphasizing that journalists and novelists-turned-journalists brought important innovations of craft and modifications of sensibility to bear in the Sixties on the spectacle of American life. In the process they often created something no more classifiable than "nonfiction," but no less deserving of the appellations "literature" or "history." To cite the most successful examples of the genre: Truman Capote's exhaustively researched "nonfiction novel" about the murder of the Clutter family in Kansas by two drifters, *In Cold Blood;* Joan Didion's astringent, eerily composed reports on the varieties of California experience, *Slouching Towards Bethlehem;* Marshall Frady's lush and vivid dispatches from a South in the throes of the racial passage and its delayed entrance into the mid-twentieth century, and his astonishing 1968 biography, *Wallace;* Tom Wolfe's extraordinary account of the cultural odyssey of Key Kesey and the Merry Prankster's, *The Electric Kool-Aid Acid Test,* and his murderously on-target ribbing of the Leonard Bernsteins for their high-society benefit for the Black Panthers, "Radical Chic"; and especially Norman Mailer's epic report on the 1967 antiwar March on the Pentagon, *The Armies of the Night,* arguably the greatest book of the decade.

The final selection in this section highlights a somewhat ephemeral, but in its time vital media development: the birth of the underground or alternative press. Such papers as the *Berkeley Barb,* the *East Village Other, The Avatar,* the *San Francisco Oracle* and the *Los Angeles Free Press* blossomed with the birth of the counterculture and became its tribal organs. Editorial content ran heavily toward the cultural revolution, drugs, rock music, radical politics and occultism; ditto for advertising, with graphics and layout running to a distinctly McLuhanesque nonlinearity. In many ways these new alternative papers were, like the counterculture that they served, the victims of their own successes. As the mass marketing of hip began in earnest in the Summer of Love, 1967, these papers' advertising revenues and circulations grew until the charm and authenticity of their underground anarchism bloated beyond recovery. At a particular point— right about the weekend of the Woodstock Festival, say—so many people considered themselves members of the cultural underground that the term lost whatever meaning it once had.

While never really an underground magazine, the case of *Ramparts* is instructive. As he tells the story in his memoir *If You Have a Lemon, Make Lemonade*, Warren Hinckle, its renegade Jesuit-educated editor, was determined to rescue this tiny "radical" Catholic magazine from "the shadow circulation caves and butcher paper ghettoes" of the old-time leftist press. To this end he embarked on a program of "radical slick" financed largely by fast talk and boldfaced lies to well-heeled philanthropists: highly professional layouts, coated paper, four-color graphics, and scrupulously re-searched and edited muckraking articles on various and sundry governmental indiscretions. With nerve, talent, and incessant promotion of their frequent scoops of the establish-ment press, Hinckle & Co. largely succeeded: *Ramparts* reached a circulation high of 250,000 in the late Sixties and spawned a rebirth of the great American tradition of adver-sary journalism.

Hinckle calls his *Ramparts* approach "Kamikaze journal-ism." But the office style there was probably positively IBM compared to the countercultural catch-as-catch-can approach of the Liberation News Service described in the Raymond Mungo selection that ends this section. From their revolution-ary warren at Three Thomas Circle Northwest in Washing-ton, D.C., the LNS staff fed college and underground papers across the country with articles ranging from left-wing report-age to handy recipes for psilocybin. With the large exception of the drug abuse, the hang-loose, make-do approach of LNS was in fact square in the classic revolutionary tradition. Here, for instance, is Ross Terrill's description of the young Mao Tse-tung's life in Peking:

Mao rented part of the old and crumbling Fuxu lamasery on North Avenue by the moat of the Imperial Palace. He slept in

the main hall of the unheated temple, under the eyes of gilded
Tibetan gods. His desk for the night reading and writing was an
incense table made eerie by the glow of an oil lamp. A
mimeograph machine—chalice of the new era of political
organization—stood by the incense table. It formed the plant for
what the young provincial politician grandly called Common
People's News Agency. . . . *(Mao,* p. 47)

Mao had somewhat more luck and staying power in his
revolutionary task, of course. LNS was eventually to founder
on the schism between the original cadre of free spirits and
the more militantly political and ideological faction that later
took power. Mungo and his associates, who took the existential radicalism of the early New Left to its logical conclusion,
complain bitterly throughout *Famous Long Ago* of the ideological lockstep imposed by this later LNS generation. Yet
Mungo, Jerry Rubin and others, heads full of acid, turned a
Eugene McCarthy press conference with college newspaper
editors into a shambles in the summer of 1968, more or less as
a goof. This incident crystallizes the confusion between
blitzing one's brain and smashing the state that reigned
throughout the counterculture. Mungo and others of the
founding generation of LNS were eventually to flee Babylon
for the New Age in Vermont, leaving the LNS name to the
remaining hard-core militants.

# Television: The Timid Giant

## Marshall McLuhan

The power of the TV mosaic to transform American innocence into depth sophistication, independently of "content,"
is not mysterious if looked at directly. This mosaic TV image
had already been adumbrated in the popular press that grew
up with the telegraph. The commercial use of the telegraph
began in 1844 in America, and earlier in England. The
electric principle and its implications received much attention
in Shelley's poetry. Artistic rule-of-thumb usually anticipates
the science and technology in these matters by a full generation or more. The meaning of the telegraph mosaic in its
*journalistic* manifestations was not lost to the mind of Edgar
Allan Poe. He used it to establish two startlingly new
inventions, the symbolist poem and the detective story. Both
of these forms require do-it-yourself participation on the part
of the reader. By offering an incomplete image or process,
Poe *involved* his readers in the creative process in a way that
Baudelaire, Valéry, T. S. Eliot, and many others have
admired and followed. Poe had grasped at once the electric
dynamic as one of public participation in creativity. Nevertheless, even today the homogenized consumer complains
when asked to participate in creating or completing an

From *Understanding Media: The Extensions of Man* (McGraw Hill Book
Company, 1964).

abstract poem or painting or structure of any kind. Yet Poe knew even then that participation in depth followed at once from the telegraph mosaic. The more lineal and literal-minded of the literary brahmins "just couldn't see it." They still can't see it. They prefer not to participate in the creative process. They have accommodated themselves to the tactile and nonpictorial modes of symbolist and mythic structures, thanks to the TV image.

*Life* magazine for August 10, 1962, had a feature on how "Too Many Subteens Grow Up Too Soon and Too Fast." There was no observation of the fact that similar speed of growth and precociousness have always been the normal in tribal cultures and in nonliterate societies. England and America fostered the institution of prolonged adolescence by the negation of the tactile participation that is sex. In this, there was no conscious strategy, but rather a general accept-ance of the consequences of prime stress on the printed word and visual values as a means of organizing personal and social life. This stress led to triumphs of industrial production and political conformity that were their own sufficient warrant.

Respectability, or the ability to sustain visual inspection of one's life, became dominant. No European country allowed print such precedence. Visually, Europe has always been shoddy in American eyes. American women, on the other hand, who have never been equaled in any culture for visual turnout, have always seemed abstract, mechanical dolls to Europeans. Tactility is a supreme value in European life. For that reason, on the Continent there is no adolescence, but only the leap from childhood to adult ways. Such is now the American state since TV, and this state of evasion of adoles-cence will continue. The introspective life of long, long thoughts and distant goals, to be pursued in lines of Siberian railroad kind, cannot coexist with the mosaic form of the TV image that commands immediate participation in *depth* and admits of no delays. The mandates of that image are so various yet so consistent that even to mention them is to describe the revolution of the past decade.

The phenomenon of the paperback, the book in "cool" version can head this list of TV mandates, because the TV transformation of book culture into something else is mani-fested at that point. Europeans have had paperbacks from the first. From the beginnings of the automobile they have preferred the wraparound space of the small car. The pictorial value of "enclosed space" for book, car, or house has never appealed to them. The paperback, especially in its highbrow form, was tried in America in the 1920s and thirties and forties. It was not, however, until 1953 that it suddenly became acceptable. No publisher really knows why. Not only is the paperback a tactile, rather than a visual, package; it can be as readily concerned with profound matters as with froth. The American since TV has lost his inhibitions and his innocence about depth culture. The paperback reader has discovered that he can enjoy Aristotle or Confucius by simply slowing down. The old literate habit of racing ahead on uniform lines of print yielded suddenly to depth reading. Reading in depth is, of course, not proper to the printed word as such. Depth probing of words and language is a normal feature of oral and manuscript cultures, rather than of print. Europeans have always felt that the English and Americans lacked depth in their culture. Since radio, and especially since TV, English and American literary critics have exceeded the performance of any European in depth and subtlety. The beatnik reaching out for Zen is only carrying the mandate of the TV mosaic out into the world of words and perception. The paperback itself has become a vast mosaic world in depth, expressive of the changed sense-life of Americans, for whom depth experience in words, as in physics, has become entirely acceptable, and even sought after.

Just where to begin to examine the transformation of American attitudes since TV is a most arbitrary affair, as can be seen in a change so great as the abrupt decline of baseball. The removal of the Brooklyn Dodgers to Los Angeles was a portent in itself. Baseball moved West in an attempt to retain an audience after TV struck. The characteristic mode of the baseball game is that it features one-thing-at-a-time. It is a lineal, expansive game which, like golf, is perfectly adapted to the outlook of an individualist and inner-directed society. Timing and waiting are of the essence, with the entire field in suspense waiting upon the performance of a single player. By contrast, football, basketball, and ice hockey are games in which many events occur simultaneously, with the entire team involved at the same time. With the advent of TV, such isolation of the individual performance as occurs in baseball became unacceptable. Interest in baseball declined, and its stars, quite as much as movie stars, found that fame had some very cramping dimensions. Baseball had been, like the movies, a hot medium featuring individual virtuosity and stellar performers. The real ball fan is a store of statistical information about previous explosions of batters and pitchers in numerous games. Nothing could indicate more clearly the peculiar satisfaction provided by a game that belonged to the industrial metropolis of ceaselessly exploding populations, stocks and bonds, and production and sales records. Baseball belonged to the age of the first onset of the hot press and the movie medium. It will always remain a symbol of the era of the hot mommas, jazz babies, of sheiks and shebas, of vamps and gold-diggers and the fast buck. Baseball, in a word, is a hot game that got cooled off in the new TV climate, as did most of the hot politicians and hot issues of the earlier decade.

There is no cooler medium or hotter issue at present than the small car. It is like a badly wired woofer in a hi-fi circuit that produces a tremendous flutter in the bottom. The small European car, like the European paperback and the European belle, for that matter, was no visual package job. Visually, the entire batch of European cars are so poor an affair that it is obvious their makers never thought of them as something to look at. They are something to put on, like pants or a pullover. Theirs is the kind of space sought by the skin-diver, the water-skier, and the dinghy sailor. In an immediate tactile sense, this new space is akin to that to which the picture-window fad had catered. In terms of "view," the picture window never made any sense. In terms of an attempt to discover a new dimension in the out-of-doors by pretending to be a goldfish, the picture window does make sense. So do the frantic efforts to roughen up the indoor walls and textures as if they were the outside of the house. Exactly the same impulse sends the indoor spaces and furniture out into the patios in an attempt to experience the outside as inside. The TV viewer is in just that role at all times. He is submarine. He is bombarded by atoms that reveal the outside as inside in an endless adventure amidst blurred images and mysterious contours.

However, the American car has been fashioned in accordance with the *visual* mandates of the typographic and the movie images. The American car was an enclosed space, not a tactile space. And an enclosed space, as was shown in the chapter on Print, is one in which all spatial qualities have been reduced to visual terms. So in the American car, as the French observed decades ago, "one is not on the road, one is in the car." By contrast, the European car aims to drag you along the road and to provide a great deal of vibration from the bottom. Brigitte Bardot got into the news when it was discovered that she liked to drive barefoot in order to get the maximal vibration. Even English cars, weak on visual appearance as they are, have been guilty of advertising that "at sixty miles an hour all you can hear is the ticking of the clock." That would be a very poor ad, indeed, for a TV generation that has to be *with* everything and has to *dig* things in order to get at them. So avid is the TV viewer for rich tactile effects that he could be counted on to revert to skis. The wheel, so far as he is concerned, lacks the requisite abrasiveness.

Clothes in this first TV decade repeat the same story as vehicles. The revolution was heralded by bobby-soxers who dumped the whole cargo of visual effects for a set of tactile ones so extreme as to create a dead level of flat-footed deadpanism. Part of the cool dimension of TV is the cool, deadpan mug that came in with the teenager. Adolescence, in the age of hot media, of radio and movie, and of the ancient book, had been a time of fresh, eager, and expressive countenances. No elder statesman or senior executive of the 1940s would have ventured to wear so dead and sculptural a pan as the child of the TV age. The dances that came in with TV were to match—all the way to the Twist, which is merely a form of very unanimated dialogue, the gestures and grimaces of which indicate involvement in depth, but "nothing to say."

Clothing and styling in the past decade have gone so tactile and sculptural that they present a sort of exaggerated evidence of the new qualities of the TV mosaic. The TV extension of our nerves in hirsute pattern possesses the power to evoke a flood of related imagery in clothing, hairdo, walk, and gesture.

All this adds up to the compressional implosion—the return to nonspecialized forms of clothes and spaces, the seeking of multi-uses for rooms and things and objects, in a single word—the iconic. In music and poetry and painting, the tactile implosion means the insistence on qualities that are close to casual speech. Thus Schönberg and Stravinsky and

Carl Orff and Bartok, far from being advanced seekers of
esoteric effects, seem now to have brought music very close to
the condition of ordinary human speech. It is this colloquial
rhythm that once seemed so unmelodious about their work.
Anyone who listens to the medieval works of Perotinus or
Dufay will find them very close to Stravinsky and Bartok. The
great explosion of the Renaissance that split musical instruments off from song and speech and gave them specialist
functions is now being played backward in our age of
electronic implosion.

One of the most vivid examples of the tactile quality of the
TV image occurs in medical experience. In closed-circuit
instruction in surgery, medical students from the first reported a strange effect—that they seemed not to be watching
an operation, but performing it. They felt that they were
holding the scalpel. Thus the TV image, in fostering a passion
for depth involvement in every aspect of experience, creates
an obsession with bodily welfare. The sudden emergence of
the TV medico and the hospital ward as a program to rival the
western is perfectly natural. It would be possible to list a
dozen untried kinds of programs that would prove immediately popular for the same reasons. Tom Dooley and his epic
of Medicare for the backward society was a natural outgrowth
of the first TV decade.

Now that we have considered the sublimed force of the TV
image in a redundant scattering of samples, the question
would seem to arise: "What possible *immunity* can there be
from the subliminal operation of a new medium like television?" People have long supposed that bulldog opacity,
backed by firm disapproval, is adequate enough protection
against any new experience. It is the theme of this book that
not even the most lucid understanding of the peculiar force of
a medium can head off the ordinary "closure" of the senses
that causes us to conform to the pattern of experience
presented. The utmost purity of mind is no defense against
bacteria, though the confreres of Louis Pasteur tossed him
out of the medical profession for his base allegations about
the invisible operation of bacteria. To resist TV, therefore,
one must acquire the antidote of related media like print.

It is an especially touchy area that presents itself with the
question: "What has been the effect of TV on our political
life?" Here, at least, great traditions of critical awareness and

vigilance testify to the safeguards we have posted against the dastardly uses of power.

When Theodore White's *The Making of the President: 1960* is opened at the section on "The Television Debates," the TV student will experience dismay. White offers statistics on the number of sets in American homes and the number of hours of daily use of these sets, but not one clue as to the nature of the TV image or its effects on candidates or viewers. White considers the "content" of the debates and the deportment of the debaters, but it never occurs to him to ask why TV would inevitably be a disaster for a sharp intense image like Nixon's, and a boon for the blurry, shaggy texture of Kennedy.

At the end of the debates, Philip Deane of the London *Observer* explained my idea of the coming TV impact on the election to the *Toronto Globe and Mail* under the headline of "The Sheriff and the Lawyer," October 15, 1960. It was that TV would prove so entirely in Kennedy's favor that he would win the election. Without TV, Nixon had it made. Deane, toward the end of his article, wrote:

> Now the press has tended to say that Mr. Nixon has been gaining in the last two debates and that he was bad in the first. Professor McLuhan thinks that Mr. Nixon has been sounding progressively more definite; regardless of the value of the Vice-President's views and principles, he has been defending them with too much flourish for the TV medium. Mr. Kennedy's rather sharp responses have been a mistake, but he still presents an image closer to the TV hero, Professor McLuhan says— something like the shy young Sheriff—while Mr. Nixon with his very dark eyes that tend to stare, with his slicker circumlocution, has resembled more the railway lawyer who signs leases that are not in the interests of the folks in the little town.
>
> In fact, by counterattacking and by claiming for himself, as he does in the TV debates, the same goals as the Democrats have, Mr. Nixon may be helping his opponent by blurring the Kennedy image, by confusing what exactly it is that Mr. Kennedy wants to change.
>
> Mr. Kennedy is thus not handicapped by clear-cut issues; he is visually a less well-defined image, and appears more nonchalant. He seems less anxious to sell

himself than does Mr. Nixon. So far, then, Professor
McLuhan gives Mr. Kennedy the lead without underesti-
mating Mr. Nixon's formidable appeal to the vast conservative forces of the United States.

Another way of explaining the acceptable, as opposed to
the unacceptable, TV personality is to say that anybody
whose *appearance* strongly declares his role and status in life
is wrong for TV. Anybody who looks as if he might be a
teacher, a doctor, a businessman, or any of a dozen other
things all at the same time is right for TV. When the person
presented *looks* classifiable, as Nixon did, the TV viewer has
nothing to fill in. He feels uncomfortable with his TV image.
He says uneasily, "There's something about the guy that isn't
right." The viewer feels exactly the same about an exceed-
ingly pretty girl on TV, or about any of the intense "high
definition" images and messages from the sponsors. It is not
accidental that advertising has become a vast new source of
comic effects since the advent of TV. Mr. Khrushchev is a
very filled-in or completed image that appears on TV as a
comic cartoon. In wirephoto and on TV, Mr. Khrushchev is a
jovial comic, an entirely disarming presence. Likewise, precisely the formula that recommends anybody for a movie role
disqualifies the same person for TV acceptance. For the hot
movie medium needs people who look very definitely a *type*
of some kind. The cool TV medium cannot abide the typical
because it leaves the viewer frustrated of his job of "closure"
or completion of image. President Kennedy did not look like
a rich man or like a politician. He could have been anything
from a grocer or a professor to a football coach. He was not
too precise or too ready of speech in such a way as to spoil his
pleasantly tweedy blur of countenance and outline. He went
from palace to log cabin, from wealth to the White House, in
a pattern of TV reversal and upset.

The same components will be found in any popular TV
figure. Ed Sullivan, "the great stone face," as he was known
from the first, has the much needed harshness of texture and
general sculptural quality demanded for serious regard on
TV. Jack Paar is quite otherwise—neither shaggy nor sculptural. But on the other hand, his presence is entirely acceptable on TV because of his utterly cool and casual verbal agility.
The Jack Paar show revealed the inherent need of TV for

spontaneous chat and dialogue. Jack discovered how to extend the TV mosaic image into the entire format of his show, seemingly snaffling up just anybody from anywhere at the drop of a hat. In fact, however, he understood very well how to create a mosaic from other media, from the world of journalism and politics, books, Broadway, and the arts in general, until he became a formidable rival to the press mosaic itself. As Amos and Andy had lowered church attendance on Sunday evenings in the old days of radio, so Jack Paar certainly cut night-club patronage with his late show.

How about Educational Television? When the three-year-old sits watching the President's press conference with Dad and Grandad, that illustrates the serious educational role of TV. If we ask what is the relation of TV to the learning process, the answer is surely that the TV image, by its stress on participation, dialogue, and depth, has brought to America new demand for crash-programming in education. Whether there ever will be TV in every classroom is a small matter. The revolution has already taken place at home. TV has changed our sense-lives and our mental processes. It has created a taste for all experience *in depth* that affects language teaching as much as car styles. Since TV, nobody is happy with a mere book knowledge of French or English poetry. The unanimous cry now is, "Let's *talk* French," and "Let the bard be *heard*." And oddly enough, with the demand for depth, goes the demand for crash-programming. Not only deeper, but further, into all knowledge has become the normal popular demand since TV. Perhaps enough has been said about the nature of the TV image to explain why this should be. How could it possibly pervade our lives any more than it does? Mere classroom use could not extend its influence. Of course, in the classroom its role compels a reshuffling of subjects, and approaches to subjects. Merely to put the present classroom on TV would be like putting movies on TV. The result would be a hybrid that is neither. The right approach is to ask, "What can TV do that the classroom cannot do for French, or for physics?" The answer is: "TV can illustrate the interplay of process and the growth of forms of all kinds as nothing else can."

The other side of the story concerns the fact that, in the visually organized educational and social world, the TV child is an underprivileged cripple. An oblique indication of this startling reversal has been given by William Golding's *Lord of the Flies*. On the one hand, it is very flattering for hordes of docile children to be told that, once out of the sight of their governesses, the seething savage passions within them would boil over and sweep away pram and playpen, alike. On the other hand, Mr. Golding's little pastoral parable does have some meaning in terms of the psychic changes in the TV child. This matter is so important for any future strategy of culture or politics that it demands a headline prominence, and capsulated summary:

## Why the TV Child Cannot See Ahead

The plunge into depth experience via the TV image can only be explained in terms of the differences between visual and mosaic space. Ability to discriminate between these radically different forms is quite rare in our Western world. It has been pointed out that, in the country of the blind, the one-eyed man is not king. He is taken to be an hallucinated lunatic. In a highly visual culture, it is as difficult to communicate the nonvisual properties of spatial forms as to explain visuality to the blind. In *The ABC of Relativity* Bertrand Russell began by explaining that there is nothing difficult about Einstein's ideas, but that they do call for total reorganization of our imaginative lives. It is precisely this imaginative reorganization that has occurred via the TV image.

The ordinary inability to discriminate between the photographic and the TV image is not merely a crippling factor in the learning process today; it is symptomatic of an age-old failure in Western culture. The literate man, accustomed to an environment in which the visual sense is extended everywhere as a principle of organization, sometimes supposes that the mosaic world of primitive art, or even the world of Byzantine art, represents a mere difference in degree, a sort of failure to bring their visual portrayals up to the level of full visual effectiveness. Nothing could be further from the truth. This, in fact, is a misconception that has impaired understanding between East and West for many centuries. Today it impairs relations between colored and white societies.

Most technology produces an amplification that is quite explicit in its separation of the senses. Radio is an extension of the aural, high-fidelity photography of the visual. But TV is, above all, an extension of the sense of touch, which involves maximal interplay of all the senses. For Western man, however, the all-embracing extension had occurred by means of phonetic writing, which is a technology for extending the sense of sight. All non-phonetic forms of writing are, by contrast, artistic modes that retain much variety of sensuous orchestration. Phonetic writing, alone, has the power of separating and fragmenting the senses and of sloughing off the semantic complexities. The TV image reverses this literate process of analytic fragmentation of sensory life.

The visual stress on continuity, uniformity, and connectedness, as it derives from literacy, confronts us with the great technological means of implementing continuity and lineality by fragmented repetition. The ancient world found this means in the brick, whether for wall or road. The repetitive, uniform brick, indispensable agent of road and wall, of cities and empires, is an extension, via letters, of the visual sense. *The brick wall is not a mosaic form,* and neither is the mosaic form a visual structure. The mosaic can be *seen* as dancing can, but is not *structured* visually; nor is it an extension of the visual power. For the mosaic is not uniform, continuous, or repetitive. It is discontinuous, skew, and nonlineal, like the tactual TV image. To the sense of touch, all things are sudden, counter, original, spare, strange. The "Pied Beauty" of G. M. Hopkins is a catalogue of the notes of the sense of touch. The poem is a manifesto of the nonvisual, and like Cézanne or Seurat, or Rouault it provides an indispensable approach to understanding TV. The nonvisual mosaic structures of modern art, like those of modern physics and electric-information patterns, permit little detachment. The mosaic form of the TV image demands participation and involvement in depth of the whole being, as does the sense of touch. Literacy, in contrast, had, by extending the visual power to the uniform organization of time and space, psychically and socially, conferred the power of detachment and noninvolvement.

The visual sense when extended by phonetic literacy fosters the analytic habit of perceiving the single facet in the life of forms. The visual power enables us to isolate the single incident in time and space, as in representational art. In visual representation of a person or an object, a single phase or moment or aspect is separated from the multitude of known and felt phases, moments and aspects of the person or object. By contrast, iconographic art uses the eye as we use our hand in seeking to create an inclusive image, made up of many moments, phases, and aspects of the person or thing. Thus the iconic mode is not visual representation, nor the single position. The tactual mode of perceiving is sudden but not specialist. It is total, synesthetic, involving all the senses. Pervaded by the mosaic TV image, the TV child encounters the world in a spirit antithetic to literacy.

The TV image, that is to say, even more than the icon, is an extension of the sense of touch. Where it encounters a literate culture, it necessarily thickens the sense-mix, transforming fragmented and specialist extensions into a seamless web of experience. Such transformation is, of course, a "disaster" for a literate, specialist culture. It blurs many cherished attitudes and procedures. It dims the efficacy of the basic pedagogic techniques, and the relevance of the curriculum. If for no other reason, it would be well to understand the dynamic life of these forms as they intrude upon us and upon one another. TV makes for myopia.

The young people who have experienced a decade of TV have naturally imbibed an urge toward involvement in depth that makes all the remote visualized goals of usual culture seem not only unreal but irrelevant, and not only irrelevant but anemic. It is the total involvement in all-inclusive *nowness* that occurs in young lives via TV's mosaic image. This change of attitude has nothing to do with the programming in any way, and would be the same if the programs consisted entirely of the highest cultural content. The change in attitude by means of relating themselves to the mosaic TV image would occur in any event. It is, of course, our job not only to understand this change but to exploit it for its pedagogical richness. The TV child expects involvement and doesn't want a specialist *job* in the future. He does want a *role* and a deep commitment to his society. Unbridled and misunderstood, this richly human need can manifest itself in the distorted forms portrayed in *West Side Story*.

The TV child cannot see ahead because he wants involvement, and he cannot accept a fragmentary and merely visualized goal or destiny in learning or in life.

## Murder by Television

Jack Ruby shot Lee Oswald while tightly surrounded by guards who were paralyzed by television cameras. The fascinating and involving power of television scarcely needed this additional proof of its peculiar operation upon human perceptions. The Kennedy assassination gave people an immediate sense of the television power to create depth involvement, on the one hand, and a numbing effect as deep as grief itself, on the other hand. Most people were amazed at the depth of meaning which the event communicated to them. Many more were surprised by the coolness and calm of the mass reaction. The same event, handled by press or radio (in the absence of television), would have provided a totally different experience. The national "lid" would have "blown off." Excitement would have been enormously greater and depth participation in a common awareness very much less.

As explained earlier, Kennedy was an excellent TV image. He had used the medium with the same effectiveness that Roosevelt had learned to achieve by radio. With TV, Kennedy found it natural to involve the nation in the office of the Presidency, both as an operation and as an image. TV reaches out for the corporate attributes of office. Potentially, it can transform the Presidency into a monarchic dynasty. A merely elective Presidency scarcely affords the depth of dedication and commitment demanded by the TV form. Even teachers on TV seem to be endowed by the student audiences with a charismatic or mystic character that much exceeds the feelings developed in the classroom or lecture hall. In the course of many studies of audience reactions to TV teaching, there recurs this puzzling fact. The viewers feel that the teacher has a dimension almost of sacredness. This feeling does not have its basis in concepts or ideas, but seems to creep in uninvited and unexplained. It baffles both the students and the analysts of their reactions. Surely, there could be no more telling touch to tip us off to the character of TV. This is not so much a visual as a tactual-auditory medium that involves all of our senses in depth interplay. For people long accustomed to the merely visual experience of the typographic and photographic varieties, it would seem to be the *synesthesia,* or tactual depth of TV experience, that dislocates them from their usual attitudes of passivity and detachment.

The banal and ritual remark of the conventionally literate, that TV presents an experience for passive viewers, is wide of the mark. TV is above all a medium that demands a creatively participant response. The guards who failed to protect Lee Oswald were not passive. They were so involved by the mere sight of the TV cameras that they lost their sense of their merely practical and specialist task.

Perhaps it was the Kennedy funeral that most strongly impressed the audience with the power of TV to invest an occasion with the character of corporate participation. No national event except in sports has ever had such coverage or such an audience. It revealed the unrivaled power of TV to achieve the involvement of the audience in a complex *process.* The funeral as a corporate process caused even the image of sport to pale and dwindle into puny proportions. The Kennedy funeral, in short, manifested the power of TV to involve an entire population in a ritual process. By comparison, press, movie, and even radio are mere packaging devices for consumers.

Most of all, the Kennedy event provides an opportunity for noting a paradoxical feature of the "cool" TV medium. It involves us in moving depth, but it does not excite, agitate or arouse. Presumably, this is a feature of all depth experience.

# Vietnam. Look at America.
# Black Capitalism

## Joe McGinniss

One day Harry Treleaven came into his office with two reels of movie film under his arm.

"Come on," he said. "I think you'd like to see this." We went into the big meeting room and he gave the film to a man in the projection booth.

The film was in black and white. There was a title: *A Face of War*. It had been made in Vietnam. It was the story of three months of fighting done by a single infantry platoon. There was no music or narration. Just the faces and sounds of jungle war.

Halfway through the first reel, Len Garment and Frank Shakespeare came in. They were there for a one o'clock meeting. They took seats and began to watch the film. Neither spoke. They watched the men crawling single file through the jungle, heard the sound the leaves made as they brushed the faces of the men and heard the sound of rain and bullets and mortar shells in the night. The reel ended. The meeting was due to begin. Harry Treleaven turned to the projection booth. "Play the second reel," he said. Ruth Jones came in for the meeting and watched the film for three minutes and left. "I can't sit through that," she said.

From *The Selling of the President 1968* (Trident Press, 1969).

No one else spoke. There were only the men trying to kill and trying to avoid being killed in the jungle.

Twenty minutes later, with the film still running, Art Duram said, "Don't you think we'd better start?" No one moved or gave any sign of having heard.

"It's half past one already."

Harry Treleaven sat up in his chair and looked at his watch. "All right, that's enough," he said to the man in the projection booth.

The lights came on in the room. No one spoke for a moment. Each man was still staring at where the film had been.

"That's the most powerful thing I've ever seen," Len Garment said.

"What is it?" Frank Shakespeare said.

Harry Treleaven stood and stepped toward the projection booth. "It's called *A Face of War*," he said, "and it was made by the man I want to hire to do our spot commercials."

Originally, Treleaven had wanted David Douglas Duncan, the photographer, to make commercials. Duncan was a friend of Richard Nixon's but when Treleaven took him out to lunch he said no, he would be too busy. Then Duncan mentioned Eugene Jones.

Treleaven had wanted Duncan because he had decided to make still photography the basis of Richard Nixon's sixty-second television commercial campaign. He had learned a little about stills at J. Walter Thompson when he used them for some Pan American spots. Now he thought they were the perfect thing for Nixon because Nixon himself would not have to appear.

Treleaven could use Nixon's voice to accompany the stills but his face would not be on the screen. Instead there would be pictures, and hopefully, the pictures would prevent people from paying too much attention to the words.

The words would be the same ones Nixon always used—the words of the acceptance speech. But they would all seem fresh and lively because a series of still pictures would flash on the screen while Nixon spoke. If it were done right, it would permit Treleaven to create a Nixon image that was entirely independent of the words. Nixon would say his same old tiresome things but no one would have to listen. The words would become Muzak. Something pleasant and lulling in the background. The flashing pictures would be carefully selected to create the impression that somehow Nixon represented competence, respect for tradition, serenity, faith that the American people were better than people anywhere else, and that all these problems others shouted about meant nothing in a land blessed with the tallest buildings, strongest armies, biggest factories, cutest children, and rosiest sunsets in the world. Even better: through association with the pictures, Richard Nixon could *become* these very things.

Obviously, some technical skill would be required. David Douglas Duncan said Gene Jones was the man.

Treleaven met Jones and was impressed. "He's low-key," Treleaven said, "He doesn't come at you as a know-it-all."

Gene Jones, also in his middle forties, had been taking movies of wars half his life. He did it perhaps as well as any man ever has. Besides that, he had produced the Today show on NBC for eight years and had done a documentary series on famous people called *The World of* . . . Billy Graham, Sophia Loren, anyone who had been famous and was willing to be surrounded by Jones's cameras for a month.

Jones understood perfectly what Treleaven was after. A technique through which Richard Nixon would seem to be contemporary, imaginative, involved—without having to say anything of substance. Jones had never done commercial work before but for $110,000 from which he would pay salaries to a nine-man staff, he said he would do it for Nixon.

"A hundred and ten thousand dollars," Frank Shakespeare said after seeing *A Face of War*. "That's pretty steep."

"I wouldn't know," Treleaven said. "I have nothing to compare it to."

"It's pretty steep."

"He's pretty good."

"Yes, he is."

"What do you think?"

"Oh, I have no objection. That just hit me as a very high price."

"I'd like approval to pay it right now. I want to hire him immediately."

"Fine," Frank Shakespeare said. "You've got it."

A day or two later Jones came down to Treleaven's office to discuss details such as where he should set up a studio and what areas the first set of spots should cover.

"This will not be a commercial sell," Jones said. "It will not have the feel of something a—pardon the expression—an agency would turn out. I see it as sort of a miniature *Project 20*. And I can't see anyone turning it off a television set, quite frankly."

That same day Jones rented two floors of the building at 303 East Fifty-third Street, one flight up from a nightclub called Chuck's Composite. Within three days, he had his staff at work. Buying pictures, taking pictures, taking motion pictures of still pictures that Jones himself had cropped and arranged in a sequence.

"I'm pretty excited about this," Jones said. "I think we can give it an artistic dimension."

Harry Treleaven did not get excited about anything but he was at least intrigued by this. "It will be interesting to see how he translates his approach into political usefulness," Treleaven said.

"Yes," Frank Shakespeare said, "if he can."

Gene Jones would start work at five o'clock in the morning. Laying coffee and doughnuts on his desk, he would spread a hundred or so pictures on the floor, taken from boxes into which his staff already had filed them. The boxes had labels like VIETNAM . . . DEMOCRATIC CONVENTION . . . POVERTY: HARLEM, CITY SLUMS, GHETTOS . . . FACES; HAPPY AMERICAN PEOPLE AT WORK AND LEISURE . . .

He would select a category to fit the first line of whatever script he happened to be working with that day. The script would contain the words of Richard Nixon. Often they would be exactly the words he had used in the acceptance speech, but re-recorded in a hotel room somewhere so the tone would be better suited to commercial use.

Jones would select the most appropriate of the pictures and then arrange and rearrange, as in a game of solitaire. When he had the effect he thought he wanted he would work with a stopwatch and red pencil, marking each picture on the back to indicate what sort of angle and distance the movie camera should shoot from and how long it should linger on each still.

"The secret is in juxtaposition," Jones said. "The relationships, the arrangement. After twenty-five years, the other things—the framing and the panning, are easy."

Everyone was excited about the technique and the way it could be used to make people feel that Richard Nixon belonged in the White House. The only person who was not impressed was Nixon. He was in a hotel room in San Francisco one day, recording the words for one of the early commercials. The machine was turned on before Nixon realized it and the end of his conversation was picked up.

"I'm not sure I like this kind of a . . . of a format, incidentally," Nixon said. "Ah . . . I've seen these kinds of things and I don't think they're very . . . very effective . . ."

Still, Nixon read the words he had been told to read:

"In recent years crime in this country has grown nine times as fast as the population. At the current rate, the crimes of violence in America will double by nineteen seventy-two. We cannot accept that kind of future. We owe it to the decent and law-abiding citizens of America to take the offensive against the criminal forces that threaten their peace and security and to rebuild respect for law across this country. I pledge to you that the wave of crime is not going to be the wave of the future in America."

There was nothing new in these words. Harry Treleaven had simply paraphrased and condensed the standard law and order message Nixon had been preaching since New Hampshire. But when the words were coupled with quickly flashing colored pictures of criminals, of policemen patrolling deserted streets, of bars on storefront windows, of disorder on a college campus, of peace demonstrators being led bleeding into a police van, then the words became something more than what they actually were. It was the whole being greater than the sum of its parts.

In the afternoons, Treleaven, Garment and Shakespeare would go to Gene Jones' studio to look at the films on a little machine called a movieola. If they were approved, Jones would take them to a sound studio down the street to blend in music, but they never were approved right away. There was not one film that Garment or Shakespeare did not order changed for a "political" reason. Anything that might offend Strom Thurmond, that might annoy the Wallace voter whom Nixon was trying so hard for; any ethnic nuance that Jones, in his preoccupation with artistic viewpoint, might have missed: these came out.

"Gene is good," Treleaven explained, "but he needs a lot of political guidance. He doesn't always seem to be aware of the point we're trying to make."

Jones didn't like the changes. "I'm not an apprentice," he said. "I'm an experienced pro and never before in my career have I had anyone stand over my shoulder telling me to change this and change that. It might sound like bullshit, but when you pull out a shot or two it destroys the dynamism, the whole flow."

The first spot was called simply *Vietnam*. Gene Jones had been there for ninety days, under fire, watching men kill and die, and he had been wounded in the neck himself. Out of the experience had come *A Face of War*. And out of it now came E.S.J. [for Eugene S. Jones] #1, designed to help Richard Nixon become President. Created for no other purpose.

| VIDEO | AUDIO |
|---|---|
| 1. OPENING NETWORK DISCLAIMER: "A POLITICAL ANNOUNCEMENT." | |
| 2. FADEUP ON FAST PACED SCENES OF HELO ASSAULT IN VIETNAM. | SFX AND UNDER |
| 3. WOUNDED AMERICANS AND VIETNAMESE. | R.N. |
| | Never has so much military, economic, and diplomatic power been used as ineffectively as in Vietnam. |
| 4. MONTAGE OF FACIAL CU'S OF AMERICAN SERVICEMEN AND VIETNAMESE NATIVES WITH QUESTIONING, ANXIOUS, PERPLEXED ATTITUDE. | And if after all of this time and all of this sacrifice and all of this support there is still no end in sight, then I say the |

| VIDEO | AUDIO |
|-------|-------|
| 5. PROUD FACES OF VIETNAM-ESE PEASANTS ENDING IN CU OF THE WORD "LOVE" SCRAWLED ON THE HELMET OF AMERICAN G.I. AND PULL BACK TO REVEAL HIS FACE. | time has come for the American people to turn to new leadership—not tied to the policies and mistakes of the past.<br><br>I pledge to you: we will have an honorable end to the war in Vietnam.<br><br>MUSIC UP AND OUT. |

Harry Treleaven and Len Garment and Frank Shakespeare thought this commercial was splendid.

"Wow, that's powerful," Treleaven said.

Dead soldiers and empty words. The war was not bad because of insane suffering and death. The war was bad because it was *ineffective.*

So Richard Nixon, in his commercial, talked about new leadership for the war. New leadership like Ellsworth Bunker and Henry Cabot Lodge and U. Alexis Johnson.

*Vietnam* was shown across the country for the first time on September 18. Jack Gould did not like this one any more than he had liked Connie Francis.

"The advertising agency working in behalf of Richard Nixon unveiled another unattractive campaign spot announcement," he wrote. "Scenes of wounded GIs were the visual complement for Mr. Nixon's view that he is better equipped to handle the agony of the Vietnamese war. Rudimentary good taste in politics apparently is automatically ruled out when Madison Avenue gets into the act."

The fallen soldiers bothered other people in other ways. There was on the Nixon staff an "ethnic specialist" named Kevin Phillips, whose job it was to determine what specific appeals would work with specific nationalities and in specific parts of the country. He watched *Vietnam* and sent a quick and alarmed memo to Len Garment: "This has a decidedly dovish impact as a result of the visual content and it does not seem suitable for use in the South and Southwest."

His reasoning was quite simple. A picture of a wounded soldier was a reminder that the people who fight wars get hurt. This, he felt, might cause resentment among those Americans who got such a big kick out of cheering for wars from their Legion halls and barrooms half a world away. So bury the dead in silence, Kevin Phillips said, before you blow North Carolina.

Another problem arose in the Midwest: annoyance over the word "Love" written on the soldier's helmet.

"It reminds them of hippies," Harry Treleaven said. "We've gotten several calls already from congressmen complaining. They don't think it's the sort of thing soldiers should be writing on their helmets."

Len Garment ordered the picture taken out of the commercial. Gene Jones inserted another at the end; this time a soldier whose helmet was plain.

This was the first big case of "political" guidance, and for a full week the more sensitive members of the Gene Jones staff mourned the loss of their picture.

"It was such a beautiful touch," one of them said. "And we thought, what an interesting young man it must be who would write 'Love' on his helmet even as he went into combat."

Then E.S.J. Productions received a letter from the mother of the soldier. She told what a thrill it had been to see her son's picture in one of Mr. Nixon's commercials, and she asked if there were some way that she might obtain a copy of the photograph.

The letter was signed: Mrs. William Love.

Almost all the commercials ran sixty seconds. But Jones did one, called E.S.J. #3: *Look at America,* that went more than four minutes.

| VIDEO | AUDIO |
|---|---|
| 2. FADEUP ON FAST, DRAMATIC RIOT IN CITY, FLAMING BUILDINGS. | ELECTRONIC MUSIC UP FULL. |
| 3. VIETNAM COMBAT. | ELECTRONIC MUSIC CONTINUES AND UNDER. |
| 4. G.I. IN VIETNAM SLUMPS DEJECTEDLY. | R.N. America is in trouble today not because her people have failed, but because her leaders have failed. |

| VIDEO | AUDIO |
|---|---|
| | Let us look at America. Let us listen to America. |
| | We see Americans dying on distant battlefields abroad. |
| 5. RIOT & FIRES.   • | We see Americans hating each other; fighting each other; killing each other at home. |
| | We see cities enveloped in smoke and flame. |
| 6. FIRE ENGINES. | We hear sirens in the night. |
| 7. PERPLEXED FACES OF AMERICANS. | As we see and hear these things millions of Americans cry out in anguish. |
| | Did we come all the way for this? |
| 8. MONTAGE URBAN & RURAL DECAY—(hungry in Appalachia—poor in ghetto —ill-clothed on Indian reservations. Unemployment in cities and welfare in small towns). | MUSIC UP AND UNDER. |
| 9. MONTAGE OF AMERICANS "CREATING AND CONTRIBUTING" MOTIVATES INTO CU'S OF FACES. | R.N. Let us listen now to another voice. It is the voice of the great majority of Americans —the nonshouters; the nondemonstrators. |
| | They are not racists or sick; they are not guilty of the crime that plagues the land. • |

AUDIO

They are black and they are white—native born and foreign born—young and old.

They work in America's factories.

They run American business.

They serve in government.

They provide most of the soldiers who died to keep us free.

CONTINUING MONTAGE OF "CREATIVE & CONTRIBUTING FACES."

They give drive to the spirit of America.

They give lift to the American Dream.

They give steel to the backbone of America.

They are good people, decent people; they work, they save, they pay their taxes, they care. Like Theodore Roosevelt, they know that this country will not be a good place for any of us to live in unless it is a good place for all of us to live in.

This, I say, is the real voice of America. And in this year 1968, this is the message it will broadcast to America and to the world.

| VIDEO | AUDIO |
|---|---|
| 10. STRENGTH AND CHAR-ACTER OF AMERICANS—BUSY FACTORIES, FARMS, CROWDS & TRAFFIC, ETC. | Let's never forget that despite her faults, America is a great nation. |
| 11. INTO MONTAGE OF SCENIC VALUES OF AMERICA FROM THE PACIFIC OCEAN TO DESERTS, TO SNOW-COVERED MOUNTAIN. BESIDE A STILL POND A MAN WAITS. | R.N.<br>America is great because her people are great.<br><br>With Winston Churchill, we say: "We have not journeyed all this way across the centuries, across the oceans, across the mountains, across the prairies, because we are made of sugar candy." |
| 12. DOLLY TOWARD SUNRISE. HOLD. FADEOUT. | America is in trouble today not because her people have failed, but because her leaders have failed.<br><br>What America needs are leaders to match the greatness of her people.<br><br>MUSIC UP AND OUT. |

"Run it through again, would you please, Gene?" Len Garment said. "There's something there that bothers me."

The film was rewound and played again.

"There, that's it," Garment said. "Yeah, that will have to be changed."

"What will have to be changed?" Jones said.

The film had been stopped just as Richard Nixon, reciting his litany to the "forgotten Americans," had said, "They provide most of the soldiers who died to keep us free." The picture that went with those words was a close-up of a young American soldier in Vietnam. A young Negro soldier.

Len Garment was shaking his head.

"We can't show a Negro just as RN's saying 'most of the

soldiers who died to keep us free,'" he said. "That's been one of their big claims all along—that the draft is unfair to them—and this could be interpreted in a way that would make us appear to be taking their side."

"Hey, yes, good point, Len," Frank Shakespeare said. "That's a very good point."

Harry Treleaven was nodding.

Gene Jones said okay, he would put a white soldier there instead.

A couple of weeks later, when Treleaven told Gene Jones to shoot a commercial called *Black Capitalism*, he was surprised to hear the Negroes in Harlem were reluctant to pose for the pictures.

Jones had not been able to find any pictures that showed Negroes gainfully employed, so he decided to take his own. He hired his own photographer, a white man, and sent him to Harlem with instructions to take pictures of good Negroes, Negroes who worked and smiled and acted the way white folks thought they ought to. And to take these pictures in front of Negro-owned stores and factories to make the point that this is what honest labor can do for a race.

An hour after he started work, the photographer called Gene Jones and said when he started lining Negroes up on the street to pose he had been asked by a few young men what he was doing. When he told them he was taking pictures for a Richard Nixon commercial, it was suggested to him that he remove himself and his camera from the vicinity. Fast.

Gene Jones explained to Harry Treleaven.

"Gee, isn't that strange," Treleaven said. "I can't understand an attitude like that."

# Television and the Press in Vietnam; or, Yes, I Can Hear You Very Well—Just What Was It You Were Saying?

## Michael Arlen

There's still rubber, of course—the rubber that finds its way from the large French plantations in the south and in the Central Highlands into Michelin and other Free World tires— but, aside from that, probably the largest and most valued single export item from South Vietnam these days is American journalism. The stuff pours out of Saigon each day in a torrent of television film, still photographs, and words—the film and the photographs heading east toward relay stations in Tokyo or San Francisco on the now daily jet flights out of Tan Son Nhut Airport, and the words rushing along the new cable that links Saigon, Guam, Honolulu, and the West Coast and that makes a phone conversation between Saigon and Chicago infinitely clearer than anything that can usually be managed between one Saigon hotel room and another. General William Westmoreland has a telephone in his quarters that enables him to speak instantly with the Commander-in-Chief in Washington. Simmons Fentress, of *Time-Life,* has a telephone that enables *him* to communicate instantly with the *Time-Life* news bureau in Rockefeller Center. Most bureaus are not quite that up-to-the-minute; in fact, many bureaus, the *Times* among them, borrow the Reuters lease line, the *Times* men trudging up to their small office on Tu-Do

From *Living Room War* (Viking Press, 1969).

Street after dinner in order to file their three or four daily stories by one or two in the morning, which is one or two in the afternoon (the previous afternoon) in New York, and thus get them there in time for the next morning's edition. All the same, there is a staggering amount of communication going on in Vietnam: the military, with all its field radios and private telephones and teletype machines, communicating within the military; the embassy and the CIA and USAID and so forth communicating within "the mission"; all of them communicating, when they choose to, with the journalists; the journalists communicating with their editors, and the editors with the public—hundreds of teletypes and Telexes clackety-clacking away all over the bloody country, roughly five-hundred working journalists (and working pretty hard for the most part, too), and where it all ends up, where it all ends up is Fred leans forward in his chair at eleven-thirty in the evening, stares briefly and intensely at the floor, sticks his chin out a bit, adopts a thoughtful look, and, speaking somewhere in the direction of his left shoe, declares, "Well, it's certainly, um, you have to say, ah . . . a very . . . *complex* situation."

After even a little time in Vietnam, a couple of things seem fairly clear. One is that although in a certain sense one can hardly avoid calling the situation in Vietnam "complex" (for that matter, the cell structure of the Arizona tree frog is complex), on a number of possibly more useful levels (for instance, the level of operable communication, of what can be sent out and what can be received) it isn't so complex after all. (The word "complex" tends to be one of our contemporary talismans; whatever you touch with it becomes somehow embalmed and unreachable, and the "complexity" itself is likely to become more interesting or important than the subject it is supposed to enfold.) The situation in Vietnam is obviously composed of many different parts—parts involving such seemingly disparate elements as power politics, South Vietnamese peasant life, the United States Congress, military firepower and tactics, local politics, and corruption—but the parts themselves are relatively simple, or, at any rate, relatively comprehensible. One will never know everything there is to know about politics in the United States. One will never know everything there is to know about politics in Vietnam.

Still, if one had the time, or took the trouble, to get in touch with a certain number of reliable Vietnamese political authorities and ask them what was actually happening as a result of such-and-such a power alignment, or what might happen if such-and-such a Cabinet change was effected, they could probably tell one enough so that one could put together a fairly concrete, useful analysis of the subject, so that, for example, in the aftermath of the recent Vietnamese elections, with the Buddhists marching and the students getting beaten up and the Assembly threatening to throw out the vote, one wouldn't get stuck, as most of the American television stations and newspapers got stuck, with trying hastily to explain to the public at the end of September what it was that had been going on for more than a month and had been pointing in the direction of such an outburst (and for the most part not even trying to explain, just giving the bare facts or running around trying to illustrate them), and with the public, responding to yet another overquick, undercooked explanation, once again nodding its head and muttering, "I told you so. Another mixed-up South American republic."

Vietnam may be the Number 1 story, but journalists don't have that smooth a time covering it. Virtually none of them speaks Vietnamese. Most newspapermen and TV men are here nowadays on only six-month tours of duty, which is hardly enough time to find out the name of the province chief in Binh Dinh, let alone ask him how the corruption situation is coming along—and, in any case, most of the six months is usually spent in chasing Vietnamese fire engines for the New York desk. When somebody gets on a story, as CBS did with Con Thien early in September, then everyone goes chasing after it—wire services, newspapers, rival networks—the Saigon bureau chiefs receiving "rockets" from New York to get competitive (not really much different from the way the papers and TV cover a fast-breaking news event back home). The trouble is, Vietnam isn't a fast-breaking news event most of the time. The papers back home have their headlines; the TV stations have their scheduled news broadcasts. The journalists here try to feed the stuff back—there's usually some kind of stuff to feed back, some of it technically useful, and now and then it's good (R. W. Apple had a fine long piece in the *Times* this August on the "stalemate" in the war);

sometimes it's ridiculous (as are the solemn transmissions of enemy casualty figures that are often obtained by a pilot looking down from a spotter plane a couple of thousand feet in the air)—and a lot of chatter comes out of the newspapers and picture tubes, but sometimes nothing really happens. Or, when it does happen, it happens in a time and space that often isn't very meaningfully evoked in terms of standard hard-news copy. People have this feeling that they're not getting the "true picture" of Vietnam from daily journalism. (Just about the first thing anyone asks a returning visitor from Vietnam is "What's *really* going on there?") People are, on the whole, right, and what makes the failure of the press to communicate the reality of the Vietnam war something well worth looking into is that the Vietnam war isn't such an isolated phenomenon as many people seem to think it is. "Not like the Second World War," people say. Indeed it isn't: no formal front lines, no supportive religious illusions about a Holy War, no happy embrace of propaganda ("We're all in this together, Fred. Hang the Kaiser. Down with Tojo. Here's a toast to Winnie, Uncle Joe, and Madame Chiang"). A different world now, a different war. The Detroit riots of 1967 are qualitatively, not just chronologically, different from the Detroit riots of 1943. The waves of energy emanating from the hippies in California are qualitatively different from those that emanated from the Lindy Hoppers that short while ago. It isn't, perhaps, that the world is deeper in chaos than it used to be, but that the element of chaos which has always been there in life, which really *is* life (after all, there were minority groups and emerging nations in the eleventh century too), is now coming more and more out from under wraps: Father has left the house, and the children have some new toys and are threatening to knock the house to pieces, and that would be all right, it would be manageable, if we could somehow get inside the house and really find out what was going on, could sit down and try to understand the children, listen to them, at any rate if we could confront what it was that they were doing (let alone thinking about), but, as things are, we make this big thing about how we know everything that's going on— *nothing* escapes us, because we too have new toys, which tell us things—but what really happens is that we sit outside the house and every now and then a maid comes out onto the porch and stamps one foot lightly for attention and then reads us a brief announcement, and we sit there looking thoughtful or impatient and listening to the sounds of breaking furniture from somewhere on the second story. We have this great arrogance about communications. We've given up much of our capacity for first-hand experience—certainly for first-hand sensory experience—cheerfully sitting at home shrouded in plastic, film, magnetic tape, peering out at the world through lenses, electronic tubes, photographs, lines of type. And we've also, at a time when the ability of a people to order and enhance its existence depends increasingly on its ability to know what is really going on (no more just getting the word from Father or the King; no more milling around in front of Whitehall to find out what really gives with Kitchener in the Sudan)—we've also given up the ideal of knowing first hand about ourselves and the world in favor of receiving sometimes arbitrary and often nearly stenographic reports through a machine system we call "communications," which for the most part neither recognizes the element of chaos in the world for what it is nor is able to make contact with it except on a single narrow-beam wavelength.

It's ironic, maybe, that among the methods men have devised for usefully reflecting the world back to themselves, only those methods that the population at large doesn't really take very seriously—one thinks especially of the novel and the film—have made any significant attempt to cope with the evolving human experience. Not so long ago, in the nineteenth century, when the world was held in place by nuts and bolts, when the doors to all the upstairs rooms were locked up tight, when Father was home and brooked no nonsense—in those days, because it seemed relevant and interesting to find out about the things in people's lives, what work they did, what trolley car they took from where to where, and whom they married, novelists wrote book after book after book that covered these things in an orderly way, and that often appeared to describe the universe largely in terms of stationary articles of furniture. Nowadays it seems more relevant to write about the inside of people's heads (or at least the writers' heads) and about how they really live—about how life doesn't always go in a straight line from here to there but moves forward, backward, upside down, inside the head, and outside. The nervier writers—the Mailers, the Pynchons, the

Updikes—go reaching out and grabbing at how things seem
to be right now. A book by Mailer, or a film by Antonioni,
may not define the world, and you may not like it, but, taken
all in all, the novels and films being turned out today seem to
attempt to reflect more of the shifting dynamism of present-
day life than does even the best of daily journalism (both
press and television), which we take *very* seriously and defer
to for most of our public and private impressions of the world
and, one imagines, of ourselves. Daily journalism, in fact,
seems to have changed very little over the last few decades—
as if nobody quite knew what to do with it (except for adding
more white space, syndicating Clayton Fritchey, and "liven-
ing up" the women's page), as if its conventions were
somehow eternal. The *Times*, which has editors and reporters
with sufficient imagination and sense of history to recognize
that there is more to be reflected upon in our evolving
experience in Vietnam than the daily bombing reports,
continues for the most part to treat the war as an accounting
exercise—and "treat" is right, for the hurly-burly of the world
emerges in the pages of the *Times* somehow ordered and
dignified, a bit the way a man's ridiculous life emerges as so
splendidly established (all those "estate"'s and "issue"'s and so
forth) when he listens to the lawyer read him out his will.
Television, with all its technical resources, with all the
possibilities of film and film-editing for revealing fluid motion,
continues for the most part to report the war as a long, long
narrative broken into two-minute, three-minute, or four-
minute stretches of visual incident. Now, it's obvious that
there are plenty of events in the war, or anywhere, that ought
to be treated in an accountant's manner, and also that there
are plenty of incidents that are inherently visual and can most
accurately be revealed on film. If there's an important battle,
it ought to be put down, covered—just that. The thing is,
though, that it doesn't take one very long in Vietnam to
realize—perhaps "feel" would be closer than "realize"—that
there is a crucial difference between what seems to be *here*
and what is reflected of it back home on television and in
newspapers. It isn't so much a matter of the press distorting
the picture (one of the favorite themes of our embassy in
Saigon), because, although there's a certain amount of
that—a certain amount of deferring to official pronouncements that one knows are biased, a certain amount of

translating battles in which we lost a cruel number of men into gallant actions that were "gallant" because we took so many losses—somehow the concept of press distortion implies a demonology that for the most part just doesn't exist. What really seems to be standing in the way of an accurate reflection of Vietnam right now isn't that the press is "lying" or not telling all it knows. It's partly that much of the press, especially the wire services and television, just doesn't have either the time or the inclination to investigate the various parts of the Vietnam picture—what's the true military situation, what's being done with new technology, what can't be done, how solid is the government's hold on the villages, how solid is the government, how good or bad is the ARVN, and so on. And, more important, when they do get hold of one of these parts, neither most of the newspapers nor most of television seems to be able to do anything more with it than to treat it as an isolated piece of detail—maybe an important piece of detail, maybe unimportant, but isolated in any case, cut off by the rigors and conventions of journalism from the events and forces that brought it into being, cut off, too, from the events and forces that it will in turn animate. The other week, as a small example, a crew from ABC flew in here to do an interview with Ambassador Ellsworth Bunker. The ambassador sat behind his desk and, in response to questions gently shoved at him by ABC's John Scali, discoursed at length on such matters as the "new stability" that would, he said, result from the Thieu-Ky election, and on the fine prospects for Thieu and Ky to work well together in the new government ("They have worked together very well in the last two years"). The program was presented a few days later in the United States—presented, naturally, at face value. At the end of the next week, Buddhists were marching in the streets here, students were getting clubbed by the police, reporters and TV crews (including ABC's) were tearing around Saigon trying to cover a situation that was, after all, a fairly predictable result of the unpopularity of the recent elections, of the fact that the "new stability" we are so hopefully committed to in many instances seems to depend largely on the ability of General Loan to hold down the lid on the kettle, even on the fact that Thieu and Ky have trouble staying in the same room with each other, let alone in the same government. The point isn't that Mr. Bunker shouldn't have said what he said, or that journalists shouldn't have been chasing after riot coverage, but that in life, after all, events don't sit stiffly, separately upon a page, don't take place in terms of three-minute narrative slices of film; they push and jostle and flow and mix against one another, and the process of this mixing is often a more important and revelatory part of what is really going on (this continuing reality that we so proudly call history when it has gone past us) than the isolated announcements that we usually have to make do with. It's obviously not fair—or, at any rate, not realistic—to expect a consistent resourcefulness in writing, political analysis, and so forth from a profession (journalism) that has traditionally been longer on energy than on anything else. But it seems true to say that most journalists here convey a more firmly realized picture of Vietnam in a couple of hours of conversation in the evening (with all those elisions made, the separate parts connected) than they've achieved sometimes (in complicity with their editors and their public) in six months of filing detached, hard-news reports. And it seems even truer to say that one of the notable results of all this has been the almost tangible inability of people back home to pay any very rigorous attention to Vietnam. It obsesses people, certainly, but more as a neurosis (which it's become, it often seems, largely as a result of this inability to confront it) than as a very real, evolving attempt of a large, important nation to relate outward to a large, important sector of the world, which, whether one finds the attempt good or bad, moral or immoral, useful or useless, is what it's all about.

People often refer to television's coverage of Vietnam as "television's war" (as one could probably describe television's coverage of civil rights as "television's civil war"), and although it seems fair to say that in general television has done very well strictly in terms of what it has set out to report about Vietnam—in terms of those usually combat-oriented film clips that appear on the morning and evening news programs—it also seems fair to say that for the most part television in Vietnam has operated on a level not much more perceptive than that of a sort of illustrated wire service, with the television crews racketing around the countryside seeking to illustrate the various stories that are chalked on the assignment boards in Saigon ("4th Div. Opn.," "Chopper story," "Hobo Woods Opn.," "Buddhist march"), constantly under pressure to feed the New York news programs new stories (ideally, combat stories), moving in here, moving out, moving in there the next day. Recently, the major effort of the military war has been taking place up north in the I Corps area, and, as a result, many of the television and newspaper correspondents are now working out of the Danang press center. Ordinarily, though, much of the work is done almost in bankerish fashion from Saigon, and one says "bankerish" not to disparage the factor of risk-taking in their covering of various operations (a factor that ranges from slight to very considerable), but as an indication of how difficult it is to get close to a strange war in an unfamiliar country by a process that more often than not consists in your having breakfast at the Hotel Caravelle at seven-thirty, driving out to a helicopter base, going by chopper to where some military operation is occurring (say, a search of an area where a Vietcong ammunition dump supposedly exists, the possible picture value being in the blowing up of the ammo dump), wandering around in the woods taking pictures until three-thirty, maybe getting shot at a bit and maybe not, then taking the chopper back, doing all your paperwork and film-shipment arrangements, and meeting friends in the Continental bar at seven o'clock. The correspondents tend to have mixed feelings about all this themselves. Many of them, to be sure, are older men with families and are not crazy about spending more time than necessary out in the field, and, doubtless like journalists everywhere, they complain of not having enough time to cover the "right stories," and of the pressure from New York to provide combat coverage. Of the newspapermen and magazine correspondents, in fact, except for a couple of people like Peter Arnett and Henri Huet of the AP, and David Greenway of *Time*, and Dana Stone of UPI, virtually none are doing the combat work that television is now doing almost on a routine basis (a seemingly routine basis, anyway). And although it's true that the Vietnam story is more than the story of men shooting at one another (the television people themselves refer to it as "bang-bang" coverage, and have a healthy respect for what goes into the getting of it), it's also true that American men (and Vietnamese men) are indeed getting shot and killed, and are shooting and killing others, and one would have to be a pretty self-indulgent pacifist to say that it wasn't somebody's job to record and witness something of that. The trouble is that television doesn't do much more than that. It doesn't try. There are the highly structured news programs, with correspondents from around the world coming on for a few minutes at a time. And then, as a way of circumventing this limitation, there are the "news specials," which up to now have generally been done with the same hasty, unfeeling, technically skillful professionalism that (more justifiably) characterizes the shorter film clips. For the most part, "television's war" is a prisoner of its own structure, a prisoner of such facts as that although television is the chief source of news and information for the majority of the people, the News & Information act is still just another aspect of the world's greatest continuous floating variety show; that the scope and cost of television news require an immense weight of administrative managing from above; that for TV the newsworthiness of daily events is still so restrictively determined by visual criteria. For example, people watching an evening news show about an ammo dump being blown up in the Hobo Woods might reasonably conclude, on a day, say, when a nationwide strike was averted in San Diego, when a rebel army was captured in Nigeria, when the Pope fell sick, and when Indonesia broke relations with Red China, that there was some special significance to the blowing up of this particular ammo dump, or not even anything special about it, just some significance—that its presentation on the screen in front of one said something useful about the war. In all too many cases, though, what the blowing up of the ammo dump says is that when you blow up an ammo dump it goes boom-boom-boom and there is a lot of smoke, and that is about it. Daily journalism in general seems to be virtually rooted in its traditional single-minded way of presenting the actuality of daily life, as if some invisible sacred bond existed between the conventional structures of daily journalism and the conventional attitudes of so many of the people whom daily journalism serves. This has been increasingly noticeable in journalism's severely conventional covering of most of the major matters of our time—covering civil rights, for instance, with its technically proficient battle-action accounts of rioting, and its distracted, uncomprehending, essentially uninterested sliding over of the dark silences that fill the empty spaces in between the riots. It is now especially evident, and damaging, in Vietnam, where, for the most part, American journalism has practically surrendered itself to a consecutive, activist, piecemeal, the-next-day-the-First-Army-forged-onward-to-ward-Aachen approach to a war that even the journalists covering it know to be non-consecutive, non-activist, a war of silences, strange motions, where a bang on the table gets you nothing and an inadvertent blink causes things to happen in rooms you haven't even looked into yet, where there is no Aachen, and "onward" is a word that doesn't seem to translate very well into the local language. The journalists reorder the actuality of Vietnam into these isolated hard-news incidents for the benefit of their editors. The editors say that that's what the public wants, and, to a great extent, the editors are right about that. The public does indeed want and need hard news, something concrete amid the chaos, something you can reach out to over the morning coffee and almost touch—a hill number, for example. Hill 63. Hill 881. It's a truism, especially among wire-service reporters in Vietnam, that if you can somehow get a hill number attached to a military operation (most operations start at one latitude-longitude point and move to another), regardless of the number of casualties, regardless, especially, of the relevance of this operation to the rest of the war, the story will run on for days, particularly in the pages of the small-to-medium-circulation newspapers that buy most of the wire-service copy. The public also presumably wants and needs a sense of progress, and since this is a public that tends to measure progress numerically—so many yards gained rushing, so many villages pacified, earnings per share up, body counts down, carloadings steady—there is a tendency on the part of the dispensers of information, the military and the government, to scour Vietnam for positive statistics and dole them out to newsmen, who are always under pressure to supply copy, and who know that there is nearly always a market back home for these firm-sounding stories that seem to be about numbers, which in turn seem to mean something, but in fact are often just about the numbers. One of the better *Catch-22* effects over here is to pick up the daily *Stars & Stripes* and read the wire-service lead, datelined Saigon—"Hurtling out of an overcast sky, warplanes of the United States Seventh

Fleet delivered another massive air strike against the port city of Haiphong," and so on—and try to recall the atmosphere and the phrasing when the source information was delivered in the course of the daily briefing, the famous "five-o' clock follies" held each day at the Mission Press Center. A couple of dozen correspondents are slouched in chairs in the briefing room, a bored Air Force major is reading aloud in a flat, uninflected voice the summary of the various air strikes conducted that morning and earlier that afternoon: "Airplanes of the United States Seventh Fleet flew 267 missions against targets in the south. . . . Airplanes of the 12th Tactical Fighter Wing flew 245 missions and 62 sorties against selected targets, including the warehouse system outside Hanoi and bridges in the Loc Binh area. . . ." Everybody has been dozing along, except that now someone asks, "Say, Major, isn't that Loc Binh just five miles from the Chinese border?" The major will acknowledge that it is. "Say, Major, isn't that the closest we've yet come to the Chinese border?" The major will acknowledge that it is. "Major," another voice will ask, "wouldn't you say that was a 'first'—I mean in proximity terms?" The major looks thoughtful for a moment. "In proximity terms," he will reply, "I would say 'affirmative.'"

Television correspondents try to get around the limitations, not of their medium but of what they are structurally required to cover (at least, the more political and thoughtful among them do), by inserting some sort of verbal point of view in the taped narrative they send off with their brief film reports, as though to say, Okay, fellows, here's your bang-bang footage, but if I put a little edge in my voice maybe it will come out a bit closer to the way things were. Morley Safer used to do this with a vengeance on CBS, and CBS's David Schoumacher and NBC's Dean Brelis do it to a certain degree now, and in some ways it's effective—it sharpens a point of view, if there should be one to begin with, and it allows for a slight intrusion of irony into a war that most news organizations are attempting to report without irony. (Trying to report a war without irony is a bit like trying to keep sex out of a discussion of the relations between men and women.) The fact is, though, that if you show some film of, say, half a dozen helicopters whirring in onto the ground, our men rushing out with rifles at the ready amid sounds of gunfire here and there, a platoon commander on the radio, men running by with stretchers amid more gunfire, what you are really doing is adding another centimeter or millimeter to what is often no more than an illusion of American military progress (our boys rushing forward, those roaring helicopters, the authoritative voice of the captain). And to stand up there afterward, microphone in hand, and say, with all the edge in your voice you can muster, as Safer used to do, "Another typical engagement in Vietnam. . . . A couple of battalions of the Army went into these woods looking for the enemy. The enemy was gone. There was a little sniper fire at one moment; three of our men were hit, but not seriously. It was pretty much the way it usually goes," doesn't pull the picture back quite straight—or perhaps, to be a bit more accurate, it focuses one's eyes on a picture that may not really have any useful connection with the situation it claims to be communicating about. Communications. One is so terribly serious about some things. One has a direct circuit installed between Rockefeller Center and the Hotel Caravelle. One can whoosh eight cans of 16-millimeter film two-thirds of the way around the world in less than twenty hours. For around seventy-five hundred bucks, one can buy thirty minutes' worth of satellite time and relay the film in from Tokyo. The television people work like hell in Vietnam—Saturdays, Sundays, all the time, really. Many of the journalists there work like hell—able men, responsible men, pasting detail upon detail into some sort of continuing scrapbook of stories about bombing raids, and pacification programs, and bombing raids, and about the Buddhist march, and the new infrared searchlight, and bombing raids, and about the fact that forty thousand Vietcong defected in the last six months. And the detail accretes, day in, day out; paragraphs clatter out over the cable, film by the bagload heads home for processing, detail, detail, detail, and people back home, who have been fed more words and pictures on Vietnam than on any other event in the last twenty years, have the vague, unhappy feeling that they still haven't been told it straight. And, of course, it's true. When President Johnson stands behind the podium in the East Room, looks into the cameras, and declares that he has "read all the reports" and that the reports tell him "progress is being made," it isn't that he's lying. He doesn't need to lie for the situation to be potentially disastrous; all he needs to do is defer to the authority of a reportorial system (one is thinking especially of the government's) that, in terms of the sensitivities, the writing skill, and the general bias of the reporters, is unlikely to be automatically accurate, or anywhere near it. Patriotism doesn't have much to do with it, any more than inaccuracy or distortion has much to do with whatever it is that gives old Fred—after three years in which he has read 725,000 words about Vietnam—the feeling that he couldn't write three intelligible sentences about the subject on a postcard to his mother.

There are a couple of things one could probably do to improve the situation. In television, the most likely would be to loosen up and expand the evening news programs so that the correspondents could handle larger themes, and then be less restrictively visual about the assignments. (The networks might also get some correspondents whose interest in daily events wasn't entirely confined to hustling 450 feet of film into a can.) In newspapers (the best of which are far less limited, obviously, than television), one might conceivably do the same sort of thing—loosen the paper up, get some new writers, encourage them to at least allow themselves the possibility of breaking through the barriers of the orthodox good-newspaper-writing declarative sentence ("McCormick Place, the huge exposition center that draws more than a million visitors a year to Chicago, was ravaged by fire today. Damage was estimated at $100 million" is the way *The New York Times* sings it). In television, again—although this, admittedly, isn't very likely, at least in this Golden Age—it might even happen that a network official would someday have the nerve and imagination to call on a few of the really inventive movie-makers, like Godard, Antonioni, and Richardson, or, since they might be a bit hard to get, on some of the young inventive movie-makers like Stan Vanderbeek, Shirley Clarke, Donn Pennebaker, and say, "How about you and you and you going in there for a while, to Vietnam, Harlem, Texas, and bringing home some film of what you think is going on?" After all, there *are* these really inventive movie-makers, and one of the reasons they're in movies, and not TV, is that TV tends to remain so consistently nerveless and conventional in its use of film. And both the papers and TV could stand being a great deal more investigative, because if the emperor doesn't have any clothes on you're surely not doing the empire much of a favor by saying he does. Right now, for example, there's a big public-relations push going on among the military and the embassy people here to get across the idea that the ARVN is a fine, competent, reliable modern army, which it certainly isn't—partly because we spent three years (between 1959 and 1961) training it to be an old-fashioned army, and partly for reasons having to do with corruption and such matters. With the exception of Peter Arnett of the AP, and Merton Perry of *Newsweek,* and a very few others, however, nobody has really gone into the ARVN story, which isn't to say that everyone has been praising the ARVN; even *Time* qualifies its statements about it to the extent of acknowledging that the ARVN hasn't yet fully "found itself." Still, it's an important story to do (many of the things you find out about the ARVN are inextricably connected with the rest of Vietnamese life), and it's here, it's here all the time (maybe a bit the way Negro slums are there all the time back home), and nobody really looks into it until something happens—a victory, a defeat, a campaign. Or, when somebody does, he does it in the way ABC looked into the ARVN the other day, which was to run a three-minute film clip on one of its few decent battalions receiving a Presidential citation from General Westmoreland, concluding with a few well-chosen words from the general on the great improvement he had lately detected in the South Vietnamese Army—all presented absolutely straight. The thing is, one takes note of these various deficiencies, inabilities, disinclinations; one dutifully nudges forward one's little "constructive suggestions"—but they're no more than that. We're all prisoners of the same landscape, and it hardly seems realistic to expect that we'll ever derive a truly intelligent, accurate, sensitive reflection of actuality from a free-market communications system that is manned and operated by people like us, and that will, inevitably, tell us for the most part what we want to know. In Vietnam recently the war has shifted—superficially, maybe, but shifted anyway—up into the I Corps area, where, just below the DMZ, we have some batteries of Marine artillery, which were placed there last February in an aggressive move to fire upon the enemy infiltration routes, and which have now become exposed, potentially isolated, and subjected to extremely heavy shelling from the enemy's guns, these being in the main well camouflaged, dug in behind the hills within the DMZ, and hard to hit. The other day, after a month-long period in which Con Thien in particular had taken as many as a thousand rounds of artillery fire in a single day, the military headquarters in Saigon (four hundred miles to the south) suddenly announced that the enemy had pulled back from his positions, that we had in fact won at Con Thien, had punished him too severely with our artillery and bombers, and instantly there was a great outpouring of cables and messages back home. U.S. GUNS BATTER REDS AT CON THIEN, headlined the *New York Post*. REDS FLEE GUN POSTS; CON THIEN SIEGE ENDS, said the *Denver Post*. The AP put a big story on the wire which began, "Massive American firepower has broken the back of the Communists' month-long artillery siege of Con Thien," and went on to quote General West-moreland as having said, "We made it a Dien Bien Phu in reverse." One of the few exceptions was Charles Mohr of the *Times*, who had recently been up there and who filed a long piece to his paper two days later to the effect that Con Thien was still extremely exposed, that "aerial photos confirmed a limited withdrawal but did not necessarily prove that the bulk of the gun pits—most of which have never been located— were hit by B-52 bombing raids and United States artillery," and that "few sources believe that more than a respite has been gained." There is disagreement among journalists here as to the real likelihood of our suffering a military defeat in I Corps, at a place say, such as Con Thien. There are those who point out that two weeks ago eighteen inches of rain fell on Con Thien in two days, that air strikes could not get in, that trucks could not supply the base with ammunition, or even with water, that it is not totally implausible, considering the fact that the enemy has superior forces in the area, for a combination of circumstances to occur in which the enemy might indeed overrun Con Thien, destroy the guns, raise hell, get out—and then you really would have a sort of mini-Dien Bien Phu disaster. There are also those—the majority—who regard a successful enemy attack on Con Thien as very unlikely, who think that Con Thien could never get that exposed, and who cite as evidence the fact that the enemy is as impeded by monsoon weather as we are. The majority view is probably right. ("The United States Command disclosed today that about 4000 men of the First Air Cavalry Division had been moved north to within 20 miles of Danang," the AP filed a few days later, forgetting perhaps to disclose that Danang is the central staging area for I Corps and the outposts near the DMZ, or that the reinforcement of the Marine Corps by the Army is not yet an everyday occurrence in Vietnam or anywhere else.) But, in either case, most journalists who have been up north (some of the same men, indeed, who seem to have so blithely passed along those "Victory at Con Thien" announcements) recognize that the shifting situation in I Corps, and notably around Con Thien (where for the first time Vietnam has turned into a conventional war; in fact, not just a conventional war—a small-scale replica of the First World War), not only says a great deal about the military possibilities in Vietnam right now but, even more important, raises a good many questions about the limits of technology as a cure-all in every modern military situation, about the hazards of trying to fight what appears increasingly to be a ground war with insufficient troops, about the possibilities of negotiating a peace settlement with an enemy who seems to be able to effectively increase his infantry capabilities more than we can. ("Long-range Communist artillery and Red mortars opened up again yesterday and today on U.S. Marine positions south of the Demilitarized Zone," the AP dispatch began on October 11, as if the previous ones had never existed.) Con Thien—lately, anyway—raises these sorts of questions, but, with few exceptions, such as Mohr, and Lee Lescaze of the *Washington Post*, nobody seems to even hear the questions, let alone try to pass them on. (Television, it should be pointed out, first broke the Con Thien story, first took note of the fact that the situation had shifted from an aggressive gun emplacement last February to a defensive battery holding on for dear life in the fall, but, in terms of the three-minute film clips on the evening news, it hasn't done much beyond showing what the place is like—no mean trick itself.) Back home now, one gathers, the tide of impatience and unhappiness with the war keeps growing. Governor Reagan, one reads, advises that we should use the "full technological resources of the United States" to win the war. An eminent Midwestern senator visiting Saigon the other day slammed his thick hand upon the

table and declared in anguish and frustration (the special
anguish and frustration of eminent people) that he could see
"no alternative remaining" except that we "step up the
bombing" or "pack up and leave." A journalist was talking
here recently, a young man who works for television and who
has been up to Con Thien. "The real hazard about Con
Thien," he was saying, "is that we'll get so frustrated trying to
win a ground war without enough troops that we'll indeed
step up the technology, whatever that means. I hate to think
what that means." There are so many real and possible
tragedies connected with Vietnam—the tragedies of men and
women dead, of men and women dying, of nations dying.
(Perhaps there's no worse tragedy than people dying.) But
sometimes, listening to the note of anger and impatience that
arises above the towns and cities in our country, that hovers
over daily life, feeling the growing swell of semi-automatic
hawkishness and doveishness that pushes so many people
nowadays, and seems to say less for what they rigorously,
intelligently believe is right than for the inability of many
persons to stand in uncertainty much longer when there are
firm choices to be seen on either side, sometimes one has the
sense that maybe as great a tragedy as any other will be that
we will indeed *do* something shortly (this nation of men and
women that always has to be doing something to keep sane),
distracted, numbed, isolated by detail that seemed to have
been information but was only detail, isolated by a journalism
that too often told us only what we thought we wanted to
hear, isolated, in fact, by communications—expressing pieties, firmness, regrets, what you will, citizens patting each
other on the back ("We did the right thing, Fred"); and not
know what we did. Or why. And, once again, will have
learned nothing.

# Too Bad Lieutenant Calley Killed Aunt Jemima

## George Lois with Bill Pitts

Take my word for it, Harold, even though there ain't a bookmaker in Las Vegas who gives a million-to-one odds, his chances of keeping the title are one in a million because when those sledgehammer hands connect, he'll land flat on his ass. So what we oughtta show is a black guy in the champ's trunks lying cold-cocked on the canvas, but in an *empty* arena. It may *look* as though we're calling the fight, and even if that's the intention, which it ain't, everyone knows how it'll end. But when you show a black heavyweight left for *dead*, you get a mood on the cover that makes people stop at every newsstand in America and say, 'What the fuck goes on? Is that Patterson? Is *Esquire* saying that Liston's gonna knock him out? But how come the whole goddam place is empty? There's something going on here that I don't understand, so I'll buy the magazine and find out.' A cover, in other words, has to be ballsy, but not completely literal— you gotta raise a big question after you get attention. The fight's on September 25 and you'll hit the stands a week before, so you can be sure that some people are gonna bitch because they'll say you're calling the fight, which ain't very cricket for a national magazine. But if you want

From *Be Careful, George* (Saturday Review Press, 1972).

to grab people's interest you have to go for the guts, and when they holler you just say, 'Listen, if you don't like what's on my cover you can always buy *Vogue*, sweetheart.'"

In 1962 *Esquire* asked my advice on their covers—they knew something was needed to juice up the magazine's face, something powerful to jack up newsstand sales. After expressing myself on the special relationship between covers and contents, I was asked to do their October cover. Harold T. P. Hayes, one of *Esquire*'s editors, sent me all the articles slated for that issue and gave me carte blanche. He had no idea what I might come up with. When I saw a short piece on the upcoming Patterson-Liston fight I told Hayes I wanted to show a flattened black fighter in an empty arena. "Can you find out the color of Patterson's trunks?" I asked him. Harold Hayes was a midtown Mark Twain from North Carolina, stylishly decked out in a white suit when the weather was warm, and usually waggling a handsome stogie, not the Little Caesar gorillas that Baum chomped, but slender beauties in keeping with his white getup and poker-player eyes. He fingered his stogie and told me to do the cover. But he couldn't find out the color of Patterson's trunks because that was traditionally the champ's option; if his manager leaked it before a fight that might put a whammy on the champ.

So I took a black model built like Floyd Patterson to empty St. Nicholas Arena with *two* pairs of Everlasts and we shot him on the canvas twice—in black trunks with white stripes and vice versa. St. Nick's was set to be razed a few weeks after our shot. The empty joint was like a vast funeral parlor, especially with our model lying there like a corpse, the last stiff to hit the canvas in that historic arena—and with its smallest gate: one photographer and a Greek art director.

"Run the shot with the black trunks," I told Hayes when the photos were done. *"Surreal,"* said Harold, looking at the tiny figure of the flattened black man surrounded by tiers of empty seats. We went with the black trunks. A few days after that issue came out, Liston put away Patterson in the first round to become the new champ. But calling Patterson's trunks on a million covers of *Esquire* was tougher than calling the fight. He wore the black Everlasts, which convinced lots of people that we *were* predicting the outcome. Some insiders may have felt that we even put the whammy on Patterson, but I was really showing how fast the world runs from losers. The reams of bullshit about heavyweight bouts don't matter for a minute because performance is the only word that counts and no amount of talk can hide the fact that someone landed on the canvas and suddenly he's dead meat.

*Esquire*'s publisher saw it as a prediction. "Sly editorializing," said Arnold Gingrich, but with a wry smile to his words because newsstand sales went up as his magazine became an eyestopper. With that first cover I began a decade of visual editorials for *Esquire*.

A year later Liston, the ex-con ghetto *nigger,* was still king of the ring, with a media-made image as the meanest man in the world. For the 1963 Christmas cover I told Hayes that Sonny Liston would make a fine Santa. Harold was a southerner and many advertisers don't like to buy ad pages from niggerlovers. That may have stacked the odds against doing Santa Liston, but *Esquire*'s editor saw its jolting symbolism at a time when America was being rocked by the black revolution. Hayes leaned across our table at the Four Seasons, where we often discussed each month's cover, lined up his fine Carolinian nose against my crooked schnozz and said he would put his Dixie neck on the chopping block if I could pull Liston away from the crap tables in Las Vegas long enough to pose as Santa without winging his thirteen-inch fist at an artist prick who was fool enough to interrupt his favorite fun. I told Harold if I couldn't get Liston to pose I knew someone who could.

Sonny Liston was living in Las Vegas, where he loved to gamble, and while the "mean man" image was mostly hoked up, he was one of the roughest mothers who ever wore the heavyweight crown. Liston's arrival in the national limelight by decking the *Negro* Floyd Patterson, a devout Catholic who was hated by many *blacks* for being an Uncle Tom, belted America like a rabbit punch. There were freedom rides then and Martin Luther King was making black waves in the big white sea. Liston had served time for armed robbery and was hardly a white man's black man. But he idolized one of the finest human beings of the century. "Name your intermediary," said Hayes. I rubbed my gorgeous nose and said, "Joe Louis." Hayes leaned away, dragged on his stogie and said, "This meal's on me."

When I called Joe Louis in Las Vegas to tell him I wanted to shoot a black Santa Claus, he said, "That'll be the day." But he promised to help and I headed west with Carl Fischer, the photographer who has worked with me on most of my *Esquire* covers. Joe Louis was Sonny's idol, advisor and big brother. In our Las Vegas hotel room Carl set up his equipment and Joe Louis brought in the biggest, blackest, meanest-looking sonofabitch I ever saw. And Sonny Liston was plenty pissed-off as he plopped into a camp chair under Carl's lights. I placed a Santa cap over his enormous head, dipping the white fleece over his black forehead while Joe Louis sized up his boy and told Liston that if he didn't go through with the shooting he would get his ass kicked. Then Joe left us to our work as Carl clicked out Polaroid test shots.

"Sensational," I whispered to Carl, "but move fast—he's getting ready to bust heads." Carl quickly switched cameras while I adjusted the fleece and whispered to Liston, "Great shot, Champ, we'll be done in five minutes." He was turning beautifully fierce. *"Now!"* I shouted to Carl, but as he was focusing, Sonny bolted from his chair and flung off Santa's cap. "Had me enough of this motherfuckin crap," he muttered, lumbering back to the crap tables. Instead of blocking the door, Fischer ran to the lounge, where he spotted Joe Louis and told him what happened. As Liston blew on the dice for a new roll, Joe grabbed his collar, twirled him around and pointed him toward the elevator. "Git," he whispered in Sonny's ear, "git, *git!*" We returned to the room and Fischer clicked the meanest, blackest Santa of them all.

Liston, I later found out, was the twenty-fourth of twenty-five children. He described his mother as "helpless" and his father "didn't care about any of us." I found that out in 1971 in his obituary, after he was found dead in Las Vegas, with narcotics in his room. "A nice thoughtful man," was the way his wife described him. She always called him "Charles." Five years after I shot Charles Sonny Liston as Santa Claus in Las Vegas he did a great TV commercial for me with Andy

Warhol, one of the best pieces of advertising I ever did (which also helped me lose the biggest account of my career), but there was something awesome in watching this black, brooding mountain of a man under the white fleece. I was looking into the eyes of a changing America, and I was showing what was coming *before* it became the most agonizing change in our history since Lincoln freed Sonny's ancestors.

After that issue went on sale a Hunter College professor of art history described Santa Liston in a letter to *Esquire* as "one of the greatest social statements of the plastic arts since Picasso's *Guernica*." But a few advertisers said shove it and yanked their ads out of *Esquire*. "Rude raspberry," was Hayes' buzzword for Santa Liston. Six months later Arnold Gingrich wrote in his monthly column, ". . . you'd never believe the number of hours we devoted to long and earnest exchanges of correspondence with people who kept asking why we ran that particular cover." John Kennedy was killed a few days before that issue was released. When black Santa showed his face I wasn't sorry about the coincidence.

The big reason *Esquire*'s covers succeeded when they did was Mark Twain Hayes' hands-off attitude toward my work. Two months before each issue he told me all he knew of its contents, and I called my own shots. The Liston cover was inspired by a minor item on his terrible ferocity in *Esquire*'s fattest edition ever, their thirtieth anniversary issue, with articles by the top literary bananas of the era. I went for Santa Claus because I was free to come up with the rudest of raspberries. But a beautiful lemon was bound to hit the newsstands on other occasions when I thought I was thinking big.

A few months later a story was due on the American Indian, reason enough to tell Harold Hayes the time was ripe for a gem of Americana. I suggested a photo-portrait of the same redman who posed for the Indian-head nickel. But first I called the Washington bureau in charge of Indian Affairs to find out who the Indian was—and if he were still alive. I was astonished to hear the Washington official stammer on the phone after he had dug into his records, "Chief Johnny Big Tree . . . think he's still alive . . . the Onondaga Reservattion . . . outside of Syracuse."

He had posed for the nickel in the early 1900s when he was in his thirties. I called my Syracuse father-in-law, Joe Lewandowski, and asked him to drive out to the reservation to find out if the chief was indeed still alive—and if so, to see if he was willing and able to pose, because he would have to be about ninety. Carl and I would then go to the reservation for the shot.

Joe Lewandowski drove out to the reservation, where he located a ramshackle cabin without electricity. A few minutes later Chief Johnny Big Tree walked in, toting a bundle of twigs. He was eighty-seven years old and stood six feet two. I had given my father-in-law detailed instructions to work out the most convenient arrangements for a sitting at the reservation because if the chief was sick or senile I wanted him to be treated like a piece of fragile ancient pottery. If this relic of America's bloody past was indeed alive, I was sure he shouldn't come to Manhattan Island even if it cost *Esquire* more than $24.

My kid Harry, who was five by then, answered the phone that evening while watching a TV western. "It's Grandpa," he shouted to me. "Haralampos or Lewandowski?" I asked him. "Grandpa Joe," he said. "He says the redskins are coming." I grabbed the phone from Harry. "Get a room at the Beekman," said Joe, "and meet him at LaGuardia because he likes to fly and he wants to come to New York. The Beekman is his favorite hotel. He's in great shape, but there's something about the old guy that's not all there." I was so thrilled to hear the original nickel-Indian was on his way that I shouted at my father-in-law, "Joe, for God's sake, if he's senile or absent-minded and needs help, get somebody to fly down with him and we'll pick up the tab."

"George, George, calm down. All he needs is a new set of teeth. And listen—you know the Indian on the Pontiac? That's him too. Terrific old man. His father's name was Twenty Canoes. You'll love him."

In 1912 the sculptor James Earl Fraser spotted Chief John Big Tree in a Wild West show on Coney Island and asked him to pose for the Indian-head nickel. The chief was a Seneca, a descendant of the Iroquois Confederacy, dating back to the 1500s. When he arrived at Carl Fischer's studio he wore a business suit and a butch haircut. Makeup man

Eddie Senz dressed him in a black wig and built up his toothless mouth with cotton wads. We were about to start clicking when the chief yanked out the cotton and waved his hand. "Nickel is only me to the bottom of my nose. I pose for forehead and nose. Other chiefs, a Sioux and a Cheyenne, they pose for chin and hair." But Chief John with a cotton mouthful looked fine and we shot his historic profile. Then he flew back to Syracuse on Mohawk Airlines.

When the majestic face of Chief Johnny Big Tree hit the newsstands a half century after he posed for the Indian nickel I was more proud of that cover than any I had ever done for *Esquire*. It was pure Americana. But I found out that Indians don't sell magazines. "Not a rude raspberry this time," said Harold Hayes when he saw the newsstand sales of that issue. "A red lemon," I had to admit. "This meal's on you, Lois. Any pemmican on the menu?" asked Hayes, lighting a stogie.

Four years later, when I did a cover on the martyrdom of Muhammad Ali, I found out what was missing from the portrait of Chief John. Ali was out on bail at the time, waiting for his draft evasion appeal to reach the Supreme Court. Meanwhile he was getting the shaft while hanging in limbo. *Esquire* was planning an article on the agony of his exile from the ring. I decided to show Ali as St. Sebastian, the Roman soldier who survived execution by arrows for converting to Christianity, and was then clubbed to death.

I got a postcard miniature of Castagno's painting at the Metropolitan Museum and described the pose to Ali on the phone—a full photo of his body in a Crucifixion agony, pierced by arrows. He ran off at the mouth whenever I said *martyr,* but he seemed to understand what I had in mind, and agreed to pose. We went ahead and made arrows in pads of plastic blood, suspended by wires, to be glued against Ali's body, exactly like Castagno's Sebastian, a distinctly Christlike pose. When he arrived at Carl's studio I asked him again, "Muhammad, you're sure you know what we're trying to say with this cover?" Black Prince Ali was a complex kid, and while I was sure he knew what a martyr was, I was afraid he might have misunderstood the pose that I described in words. He hauled off again with a ten-minute spiel on how and where he was screwed, naming every place and date of his martyrdom. When I showed him the Castagno miniature he studied it closely and pointed out a serious contradiction: the painting was very *Christian*.

Sebastian looked like a suffering Christ, and Ali reminded me that he refused to be drafted because of his religious beliefs as a Muslim minister. He phoned his manager, Herbert Muhammad, in Chicago. After a long explanation of Castagno's painting by this semi-literate kid who played the fool to build his gates, Ali told us it was okay to pose. He changed into his Everlasts, we fixed the arrows to his body and he struck the stance of St. Sebastian better than a professional model.

After defeating Liston in 1964, the champion who was then known as Cassius Marcellus Clay announced to the world that he had become a Muslim and changed his name. "I don't have to be what you want me to be," said the new champ who now called himself Ali. "I'm free to be who I want." As I watched him pose, quiet and relaxed in the martyr's stance, I saw a completely free man.

Carl Fischer fell in love with that photo, framed a color blowup and hung it in the entrance to his studio. He wanted to come out with poster blowups, but no publisher would touch it. Carl printed it privately and ended up with a large inventory of unsold posters. Even in ghetto stores it fizzled. The photo showed Ali's suffering as an authentic black martyr too clearly. It was also chancy as a magazine cover, yet *Esquire* took the risk. And in arousing concern about the abuse of a black man who said screw you Charlie, I'll be black *my* way, "The Martyrdom of Muhammad Ali" drew attention to a terrible wrong that was righted in 1971 by the Supreme Court. But his four martyred years won't be brought back. All he has is a picture of those years.

After the Black Muslim Muhammad Ali, formerly a Baptist, posed as a martyr after the white Christian St. Sebastian, formerly a pagan, based on the painting by the Italian Catholic Castagno, directed by Greek Orthodox Lois, photographed by Carl Fischer, Jewish, the issue appeared on the newsstands by Syracuse and my Polish father-in-law called me. "If Chief Johnny were still alive," he said, "I could have brought you some great arrows."

At the Four Seasons with Harold Hayes I leaned across the table while he lit his pencil stogie to beat him to the buzzword. *"Ecumenical,"* I said. "What's that?" he asked, scanning the poster-size menu. "The Ali cover," I said. He exhaled a billow of fine smoke, shaking his head. "Wrong," said Harold T. P. Hayes. "Pictorial Zola. I'll start with the consommé."

"The consommé's lousy tonight, Harold."

"How do you know? You haven't tasted it."

"Mr. Hayes," I said, clearing the smoke, "we artists are clairvoyant." Across the room a guy came in who looked like Edward G. Robinson imitating Little Caesar, chewing on a bigger stogie than Harold T. P. Hayes', flicking ashes on the carpet. His face was meant for an *Esquire* cover.

I began to count the months of my life by these covers. Each one became a labor of love. I was paid $600 a month, and donated the money to a fund for Greek orphans. When the Colonels took over I stopped the donations. But as the turbulent decade raced on, I was given greater latitude than I ever thought possible from a mass periodical. In many ways it was more exciting than creating advertising. My cover messages were uncensored commentaries on serious issues in my own style. I was doing my hawk-nosed Columbus and Mussolini-the-fatman on one of the biggest blackboards of America. They outraged the mighty, they angered advertisers and they irritated readers—but they visualized America's changes and needled our hypocrisies. And nobody ever diddled with my work. The ruder the raspberry, the happier was Hayes.

In the late sixties we hit the torrid issues of race, war and politics. We blasted the silly hangups of pop culture and deflated the synthetic images of celebrities. I showed Andy Warhol drowning in a giant can of Campbell's tomato soup for an issue headlined "The final decline and total collapse of the American avant-garde." I created a notorious cover with poolside shots of a man who looked like Howard Hughes and a dame just like his wife, Jean Peters. The Hughes cover deceived a lot of people, but it was a tongue-in-cheek hoax. I showed four deliberately out-of-focus snapshots of an actor in a bathrobe playing Hughes. He spots a photographer hiding in the bushes and orders a bodyguard to get rid of him. Then the model who plays Hughes' wife pops out of the pool looking startled. Above the snapshots, all very authentic-looking, we said, "Howard Hughes: We see you! We see you!"

When that cover came out everyone thought it was the real thing. The issue sold like hotcakes because the "invisible" Hughes was finally "discovered," but *Time* magazine found out it was an elaborate put-on. When the press swarmed over Harold Hayes, he summed up the silly hoohah over the mystery celebrity: "What we're doing is an attempt to satirize the whole obsession with Mr. Hughes' anonymity—his idea that people are constantly pursuing him when they're not trying to pursue him." That was fully three years before the Clifford Irving affair.

A cover that never ran on black militancy would have been the rudest raspberry of them all. Brace yourself: I took the lovable Aunt Jemima trademark and superimposed a photo of her black hand, wielding a meat cleaver. When Hayes saw the layout he thought I was working a pun. *"Eldridge,"* he said. I hadn't thought of that, and it certainly fit, but the cover was replaced at the last minute by a bigger subject that came up suddenly. In almost a decade that was the only cover killed by Harold after I shot it. A great line to go with the symbol would have been "Aunt Jemima . . . what took you so long?"

During the Svetlana Stalin binge, *Esquire* ran a story on her weird hangups with assorted religions. It analyzed how she was taken in hand by the smart boys in publishing and international relations when she came to the United States with her hot manuscript about Life with Father Josef. By then all the women's magazines had gone ape with cover pictures of Stalin's little girl. "Ya father's mustache," I muttered as the *Esquire* deadline was drawing close; with all those pictures of Svetlana stuck on my wall, I couldn't see how one more cover would possibly stand out. Then it hit me: I grabbed a grease pencil and drew a graffiti mustache on Svetlana's face.

It was incredible—she looked just like her old man; she was completely transformed into Joe Stalin with long hair.

But like Chief Johnny Big Tree, it was one of my best covers and one of *Esquire*'s worst sellers. I think the world had had its full serving of St. Svetlana by then. But what probably hurt newsstand sales most was the realistic grease-pencil mustache against the photo of Svetlana. It was pure graffiti, as though some kid went by the newsstand and drew a mustache on each cover. People don't like to shell out a buck for a marked-up magazine. Edmund Wilson complained that it was disgraceful, so Harold Hayes got a photo of Wilson, put a mustache on him, and ran it as a one-page feature within the magazine. He looked okay with a mustache, but Svetlana looked more like the real Joe.

In early 1968, before Nixon was nominated, when he was thought of as a loser, I did a composite shot of our next President being made up before a TV appearance. In the wire service archives I found a good profile photo of Nixon snoozing. Then I had a separate photo taken by Carl Fischer of four hands working on the profile: one with an aerosol spray can to set his hair, a second with a makeup brush to paint out lines under his eyes, a third with a powder puff to dull the light bounce off his nose—while a fourth hand moved in with a tube of lipstick to give his mouth definition. The four hands were lighted with surgical care to match the perspective and lighting on the Nixon profile photo. It showed a routine makeup job prior to a TV appearance. But I got a call from some guy on his staff, bitching about that cover; he said it was an attack on Nixon's masculinity. I explained that it was a satirical comment on the 1960 TV debates when his man lost to JFK by a shadow because he looked like hell in front of the cameras. In fact, the cover's title was "Nixon's last chance. This time he'd better look right!"

I was amazed at the gripe. I've been working with makeup people ever since I've been in advertising. If I could use lipstick on Joe Louis, Joe Namath, Mickey Mantle and Johnny Unitas before a TV shoot, you can be sure it's not regarded as fag stuff. "That wasn't intended at all," I said. "I was simply carrying an idea to its very edge.

If you're put out because Mr. Nixon might appear vain, that's a justifiable knock and I accept that, but the *masculinity* stuff—you must be kidding." Well, these birds in Nixon's corner don't laugh too easily. He called me a sonofabitch and hung up. But Richard Nixon sure looked better on TV in 1968 than in 1960. I wonder if he used lipstick.

The fact is, I was much, much rougher on the man Nixon ran against. In 1966 I had a ventriloquist's dummy constructed to look like Hubert Humphrey. The cover showed him sitting on someone's knee. The HHH-dummy said, "I have known for sixteen years his courage, his wisdom, his tact, his persuasion, his judgment, and his leadership." Pretty rough on the Vice President, no? But the cover didn't end there. It continued as a foldout, springing Lyndon Johnson as the ventriloquist holding Hubert on his knee. *"You tell 'em, Hubert,"* said Lyndon the ventriloquist. There's a case where I carried an idea to the very edge of a President's knee at the expense of the Vice President. But nobody called me to chew me out. And two years later when I was in the Vice President's office for a meeting on political advertising, there it was, hanging on the wall of an anteroom. I told the Vice President that I was the wiseass who did it. "You no good sonofabitch," he told me straight out. He looked very miffed, but professional politicians like to collect stuff about themselves, the good and the bad; it wouldn't have been in his office if he felt it went *too* far. "Well then why do you have it hanging there?" I asked the Vice President. "Because," he said, "it's a wonderful cover."

The rude raspberries played no favorites. After Chappaquiddick I showed Teddy Kennedy in a Santa cap for an article on the "Re-shaping of Teddy's Image." When Roy Cohn told his side of the Army-McCarthy hearings in *Esquire* I propped a gold halo behind his head and showed him like the angel that he claimed to be. I showed Aristotle Onassis, the man who had everything, with the one thing he lacked— youth; I superimposed his head against a muscleman body. I later superimposed a movie marquee featuring *Easy Rider* against St. Patrick's Cathedral for an article on the impact of our new youth culture. But among the rude raspberries we planted a sweet grape—a cover that knocked nobody. It led to an unusual gathering one afternoon in Carl Fischer's studio.

In the front of the group sat Norman Thomas, by then a very old man with a painful spinal paralysis that had spread across his shoulders and up through his neck. Joe Louis stood directly behind Norman Thomas. Marianne Moore was at his right, a link between the two great fighters. She clasped one hand of Joe Louis and one hand of Norman Thomas—who needed all the support he could get. In a grouping around them were Helen Hayes, Jimmy Durante, Kate Smith, Eddie Bracken and John Cameron Swayze. They were, "The Unknockables," eight Americans for a 1966 cover. The headline explained why these eight men and women were looking up at the camera: "In a time when everybody hates somebody, nobody hates The Unknockables."

Carl Fischer was on a balcony above, asking them to look up at his camera. But Norman Thomas was having an agonizing time trying to look up because of his paralysis. Carl leaned over the balcony and asked him very softly, "Mr. Thomas, could you just lift your head up a *little* more?" The old Socialist strained from the guts just to look up at Carl. Without moving his head more than an inch, he said, "I . . . don't think . . . I can."

Joe Louis, who was standing behind the frail Thomas, leaned over very gently and said, "Oh, Mr. Thomas, *you* never had trouble sticking your neck out before." Tears welled up in Norman Thomas's eyes. He looked up and we shot the cover.

Vietnam, the biggest issue of the 1960s, became an obsessional subject with me from the war's earliest days. By the summer of 1963 we had lost a total of eighty-one Americans since its official start in December 1961—small stuff, just about the number of deaths in one bad plane crash. In the fall of 1963 I suggested to Harold Hayes that we run a full-face photo on the cover, life-size, of our hundredth casualty, with the simple epitaph: "The 100th American killed in Vietnam." The cover never ran because in those days it was a small war. There was talk of a truce each Christmas that might end the shooting. The hundredth GI was never shown and I did a more conventional cover for the holiday season: our first black Santa Claus.

Three years later 350,000 Americans were in Vietnam and six thousand GI's had died there. *Esquire* assigned the writer John Sack to report on the fate of an infantry company, from training in Fort Dix through its combat cycle in Vietnam. Sack's first article came out in October 1966. In his account of a search-and-destroy mission, he reported a GI's reaction when he found the body of a dead Vietnamese child. I put the GI's words on the cover of that issue, with no illustration and no visual—just the stark white words on a solid black page: "*Oh my God—we hit a little girl!*" Even the masthead was muted to give each word the power of a thousand pictures.

That was years before we became concerned about the civilian population of Vietnam. The world later heard about Mylai, and a lieutenant named Calley became the focal point for America's feelings about the war, pro and con. John Sack was writing Calley's story as a book. Harold Hayes ran a pre-publication excerpt from the book while Calley was awaiting trial. The lead article in *Esquire*'s November 1970 issue was the excerpt from Sack's book, "The Confessions of Lieutenant Calley."

"Tough subject for a cover," said Hayes at the Seasons. "He's innocent until the army decides. Think about it." I didn't think it was that difficult. "Can you get Calley to Carl's place for a sitting?" I asked Harold. "Sack probably can," he said, "but it depends on what you have in mind." I explained the shot: "We'll show him with a bunch of oriental kids. No guns or anything that suggests killing. Just Calley and the kids—happy, smiling, oriental kids. Those who think he's innocent will say *that* proves it. Those who think he's guilty will say that *proves* it." After Hayes got off the floor he went to call John Sack.

Sack came to Carl's place with the lieutenant. Calley came in civvies and changed into his uniform at the studio. He was edgy, almost suspicious; but the presence of this young nobody who suddenly caught the attention of the world and put a magnifying glass on the war gave the place an eerie feeling. It was like being on the inside of something terrible and momentous.

I took him aside before the shooting to calm him down. He had that shifty look as though he expected to get a royal screwing by the big media. Meanwhile four oriental kids were horsing around in the studio—two little girls nicely dressed in checkered dresses, a cute little boy in a white shirt, and a baby in a jumper. Carl had lined them up through a casting agency. Their mothers were with them, cooing over how the kids looked. The women were terribly excited about having their kids on a magazine cover.

I told Calley that I had seen action in Korea, and that I knew what it meant to protect men in combat. Then I explained the shooting: "Lieutenant, this picture will show that you're not afraid as far as your guilt is concerned. People can read that into the picture if they want to, or they'll refuse to see it there if they don't see you as guilty. The picture will say, 'Here I am with these children you're accusing me of killing. Whether you believe I'm guilty or innocent, at least read about my background and motivations.'"

The kids were fine at the shooting. The baby sat on Calley's knee while two kids leaned on his shoulder. The fourth kid leaned against the lieutenant's right arm. There were no props; not even the chair was seen. Only Calley's combat infantryman's badge was visible. The kids looked just a trifle tired, but Calley snapped out of his edgy mood long enough to grin from ear to ear. And we completed the shooting. The mothers were gaga about their kids appearing on the cover of a national magazine. They knew who Calley was, but they seemed to be unconcerned about the famous event for which the lieutenant was standing trial.

When I sent the finished shot to Harold Hayes he called to let me know that the office was plenty shook up. "Some detest it and some love it," he said.

"You going to chicken out?"

"Nope. It's your most outrageous work since Santa Claus."

The cover ran. Those who thought Calley was innocent said *that* proves it, and those who thought he was guilty said that *proves* it. But many who thought he was guilty detested it with a vengeance, although on one of Harold's campus lectures he asked for reactions to the Calley cover, and one student called it the statement of the century. Just one.

It was just a simple portrait of a young American lieutenant
from Miami with four Asian children, and the shooting went
off without a hitch, except for the mothers, who yakked a
little.

This was the cover that replaced Aunt Jemima with her
cleaver.

(Too bad Lieutenant Calley killed Aunt Jemima.)

# Parajournalism, or Tom Wolfe and His Magic Writing Machine

## Dwight Macdonald

A new kind of journalism is being born, or spawned. It might be called "parajournalism," from the Greek *para*, "beside" or "against": something similar in form but different in function. As is parody, from the *parodia*, or counter-ode, the satyr play of Athenian drama that was performed after the tragedy by the same actors in grotesque costumes. Or paranoia ("against-beside thought") in which rational forms are used to express delusions. Parajournalism seems to be journalism—"the collection and dissemination of current news"—but the appearance is deceptive. It is a bastard form, having it both ways, exploiting the factual authority of journalism and the atmospheric license of fiction. Entertainment rather than information is the aim of its producers, and the hope of its consumers.*

---

*(1973) This paragraph much too dismissive. True about Tom Wolfe *e tutti quanti*, but in more talented hands, parajournalism is a legitimate art form. How could I have forgotten James Agee's *Let Us Now Praise Famous Men* (1942)? And Norman Mailer's early essays in the genre—his fact-fiction reportage on the 1960 Democratic and the 1964 Republican convention—which later culminated in *The Armies of the Night*?

From *New York Review of Books*, August 26, 1965. Reprinted with footnotes in *Discriminations: Essays and Afterthoughts, 1938-1974* (Viking Grossman, 1974).

Parajournalism has an ancestry, from Daniel Defoe, whose *Journal of the Plague Year* was a hoax so convincingly circumstantial that it was long taken for a historical record, to the gossip columnists, sob sisters, fashion writers, and Hollywood reporters of this century. What is new is the pretension of our current parajournalists to be writing not hoaxes or publicity chitchat but the real thing; and the willingness of the public to accept this pretense. We convert everything into entertainment: *The New Yorker* recently quoted from a toy catalogue:

WATER PISTOL & "BLEEDING" TARGETS! Bang! Bang! I got 'cha! Now the kids can know for sure who's [sic] turn it is to play "dead"! New self-adhesive "stick-on" water wounds TURN RED WHEN WATER HITS THEM! Don't worry, Mom! Won't stain clothing! "Automatic" pistol is a copy of a famous gun. SHOOTS 30 FT. Water Pistol & Wounds . . . 59c. 40 Extra Wounds . . . 29c.

And there was the ninety-minute TV, pop-music, and dance spectacular put on at Sargent Shriver's official request, by a disc jockey who calls himself Murray the K, in the hope of "getting through" to high school dropouts about what Mr. Shriver's Office of Economic Opportunity could do for them. Some Republican senators objected on grounds of taste and dignity—the message was delivered by Murray the K jigging up and down in a funny hat as the big beat frugged on—but the program did stimulate a great many teen-age inquiries. It "worked" in the same sense that parajournalism does.

The genre originated in *Esquire* but it now appears most flamboyantly in the New York *Herald Tribune*, which used to be a staidly respectable newspaper but has been driven by chronic deficits—and by a competitive squeeze between the respectable, and profitable, *Times*, and the less substantial but also profitable *News*—into some very unstaid antics. Dick Schaap is one of the *Trib*'s parajournalists. "David Dubinsky began yelling, which means he was happy," he begins an account of a recent political meeting. Another is Jimmy Breslin, the tough-guy-with-heart-of-schmalz bard of the little man and the big celeb:

> Richard Burton, who had just driven in from Quogue . . . went straight for the ice-cubes when he came into his sixth-floor suite at the Regency Hotel. "Oh, I'd love a drink," he said. "Vodka." . . . "Humphrey Bogart," he laughed. "Bogey . . ." Burton has his tie pulled down and his eyes flashed as he told the stories. He tells a story maybe better than anybody I've ever heard. The stories are usually about somebody else. The big ones seem to have very little trouble thinking about something other than themselves. His wife kept hopping up and down getting drinks for everybody. She has long hair and striking eyes.

Right out of Fitzgerald, except he would have made a better job of describing Mr. Burton's wife.

But the king of the cats is, of course, Tom Wolfe, an *Esquire* alumnus who writes mostly for the *Trib*'s Sunday magazine, *New York,* which is edited by a former *Esquire* editor, Clay Felker, with whom his writer-editor relationship is practically symbiotic. Wolfe is thirty-four, has a Ph.D. from Yale in "American Studies," was a reporter first on the Springfield *Republican,* then on the *Washington Post,* and, after several years of writing tepid, old-fashioned para-journalism for *Esquire,* raised, or lowered, the genre to a new level. This happened when, after covering a Hot Rod and Custom Car show at the New York Coliseum and writing a conventional, poking-mild-fun article about it (what he calls a "totem story"), he got *Esquire* to send him out to California where the Brancusis of hot-rod custom, or kustom, car design are concentrated. He returned full of inchoate excitements that he found himself unable to express freely in the usual condescending "totem" story because he was inhibited by "the big amoeba god of Anglo-European sophistication that gets you in the East." At the ultra-last deadline, Byron Dobell, Felker's successor at *Esquire,* asked him just to type out his notes and send them over for somebody else to write up. What happened was a stylistic breakthrough: "I just started recording it all [at 8:00 P.M.] and inside of a couple of hours, typing along like a madman, I could tell that something was beginning to happen." By 6:15 next morning he had a forty-nine-page memo, typed straight along no revisions at five pages an hour, which he delivered to Dobell, who struck out the initial "Dear Byron" and ran it as was. A historic breakthrough.

The *Kandy-Kolored Tangerine-Flake Streamline Baby* is a collection of twenty-four articles written by Wolfe in the fifteen months after his stylistic retooling. It is amusing if one reads it the way it was written, hastily and loosely, skipping paragraphs, or pages, when the jazzed-up style and the mock-sociological pronouncements become oppressive. Since elaboration rather than development is Wolfe's forte, anything you miss will be repeated later, with bells on. He writes about topics like Las Vegas, Cassius Clay, Baby Jane Holzer, demolition car derbies, a pop-record entrepeneur named Phil Spector, and a stock-car racing driver named Junior Johnson. A good read, as the English say. The fifth and last section, "Love and Hate, New York Style," is more than that. He is a good observer, with an eye for the city's style, and he would do very well as a writer of light pieces for, say, *The New Yorker*. "Putting Daddy On" and "The Woman Who Has Everything" are parajournalism at its best, making no pretense at factuality but sketching with humor and poignancy urban dilemmas one recognizes as real. "The Voices of Village Square" and "The Big League Complex" are shrewd and funny social comments—not the bogus-inflated kind he makes in his more ambitious pieces. Even better was "Therapy and Corned Beef While You Wait," which was in the advance galleys but doesn't appear in the book. Doubtless for space reasons, but why is it always the best parts they can't find room for?

A nice little book, one might say, might go to five thousand with luck. One would be wrong. The *Kandy-Kolored* (etc.) is in its fourth printing, a month after publication, has sold over ten thousand and is still going strong. The reviews helped. Except for Wallace Markfield in the *Tribune*'s Sunday *Book Week*, and Conrad Knickerbocker's penetrating analysis in *Life*, they have been "selling" reviews. That Terry Southern should find it "a groove and a gas" and Seymour Krim "super-contemporary" is expectable, but less so other reactions: ". . . might well be required reading in courses like American studies" (*Time*); "He knows all the stuff that

Arthur Schlesinger, Jr., knows, keeps picking up brand-new, ultra-contemporary stuff that nobody else knows, and arrives at zonky conclusions couched in scholarly terms. . . . Verdict: excellent book by a genius who will do anything to attract attention." (Kurt Vonnegut, Jr., *New York Times Book Review.*) *Newsweek* summed it up: "This is a book that will be a sharp pleasure to reread years from now when it will bring back, like a falcon in the sky of memory, a whole world that is currently jetting and jazzing its way somewhere or other." I don't think Wolfe will be read with pleasure, or at all, years from now, for the same reasons the reviewers, and the reading public, are so taken with his book: because he has treated novel subjects—fairly novel, others have discovered our teen-age culture, including myself, seven years ago, in a *New Yorker* series—in a novel style. But I predict the subjects will prove of ephemeral interest and that the style will not wear well because its eccentricities, while novel, are monotonous; those italics, dots, exclamation points, odd words like "infarcted" and expressions like *Santa Barranza!* already look a little tired in his recent *Trib* pieces. As Mr. Knickerbocker writes, "There is no one as dead as last year's mannerist."*

The distinctive qualities of parajournalism appear in the lead to "The Nanny Mafia":

All right, Charlotte, you gorgeous White Anglo-Saxon Protestant socialite, all you are doing is giving a birthday party for your little boy. . . . So why are you sitting

---

*(1973) Eight years later, I think my prediction was accurate. Perhaps because his style has become boring to himself, Mr. Wolfe has written, or at least published, less and less of late years. He did edit a big anthology of what he calls "the new journalism" recently, with a nervous assertive preface staking out big claims to ultramodernity, but this I take to be whistling in the dark. Those who can, write; those who can't, anthologize. . . . I must admit, however, that a few years ago he did produce one indubitable parajournalistic triumph: *Radical Chic and Mau-Mauing the Flak Catchers*, a long report on the famous "cause party" Leonard Bernstein gave for the Black Panthers. It was as nasty, ungenerous, unfair, slanted, reactionary, racist, facist—take your pick—in viewpoint as it was successful aesthetically and polemically. I mean that his observation was acute, his style under perfect control, and his low-comedy kidding very funny in that exaggerated/grotesque style we all admire when Dickens uses it on the Veneerings or Mr. Pecksniff. Also that he had, I'm afraid, a real, solid sociocultural point, for once: there was in fact a vast amount of bad faith, hypocrisy, and role-playing on both sides; a false position all around; and Wolfe wolfed it up to the last bleeding morsel.

there by the telephone and your old malachite-top coffee-table gnashing on one thumbnail? Why are you staring out the Thermo-Plate glass toward the other towers on East 72nd Street with such vacant torture in your eyes?

"Damn it, I knew I'd forget something," says Charlotte. "I forgot the champagne."

The "knowing" details—Charlotte's malachite coffee table and her Thermo-Plate windows (and, later, her "Leslie II Prince Valiant coiffure") are fictional devices that remind me of similar touches in the young Kipling's Plain Tales from the Hills. But Wolfe, who has publicly promised to write eight novels by 1968* and the sooner he gets at it and gives up journalism the better, is no Kipling but a mere reporter who is, ostensibly, giving us information—in this case that there is a mafia of superior, British-born nurses who tyrannize over socially insecure Park Avenue employers like Charlotte to such an extent that they don't dare give a children's party without providing champagne for the nurses. This may or may not be true—he rarely gives data that can be checked up on—but if it isn't, I don't think we would be quite as interested. Unlike Kipling's tales, it doesn't stand up as fiction. Marianne Moore defines poetry as putting real toads into imaginary gardens. Wolfe has reversed the process: his decor is real but his toads are synthetic. Junior Johnson and Murray the K and Phil Spector and the kustom-kar designers are real persons—or so I assume—but somehow in his treatment come to seem as freely invented as Charlotte.

Stylistically, the above passage has the essential quality of kitsch, or a pseudocultural product manufactured for the market: the built-in reaction. The hastiest, most obtuse reader is left in no doubt as to how he is supposed to react to Charlotte with her malachite table and—later—"her alabaster legs and lamb-chop shanks . . . in hard, slippery, glistening skins of nylon and silk." As T. W. Adorno has noted of popular songs: "The composition hears for the listener." The specific kitsch device here is intimacy. Intimacy with the subject not in the old-fashioned sense of research, but an

---

*(1973) Five years after the deadline Wolfe's Three-Year Plan is 100 percent unfulfilled.

intimacy of style: the parajournalist cozies up, merges into the subject so completely that the viewpoint is wholly from the inside, like family gossip. "All right, Charlotte, you . . ." There is no space between writer and topic, no "distancing" to allow the most rudimentary objective judgment. Inside and outside are one. It might be called topological journalism after those experiments with folding and cutting a piece of paper until it has only one side. There is also an intimacy with the reader, who is grabbed by the lapels—the buttonhole school of writing. I've never met Jimmy Breslin but he often addressed me as "you"—in print.

It is hard to say just what Wolfe thinks of Charlotte, or of the real people he writes about. He melts into them so topologically that he seems to be celebrating them, and yet there is a peculiar and rather unpleasant ambivalence, as in his piece on Mrs. Leonard ("Baby Jane") Holzer, a rich young matron with lots of blond hair whom he says he made "The Girl of the Year" (that is, last year; there's another one now). I'm willing to grant this claim, but his piece seems to alternate between building up Baby Jane and tearing her down, damning with loud praise, assenting with not-so-civil leer. As for his readers, flattered though they may be to be taken so intimately into his confidence, made free of the creative kitchen so to speak, they are in the same ambiguous position. "Bangs manes bouffants bee-hives Beatle caps butter faces brush-on lashes decal eyes puffy sweaters French thrust bras" one article begins, continuing for six more unpunctuated lines of similar arcana and if you don't dig them you're dead, baby.

But there is one value Tom Wolfe asserts clearly, constantly, obsessively: old he bad, new he good. Although he is pushing thirty-five, or perhaps because of it, he carries the American teen-ager's contempt for adults to burlesque extremes. His forty-seven-page ode to Junior Johnson, "The Last American Hero," ends: "up with the automobile into their America, and the hell with the arteriosclerotic old boys trying to hold onto the whole pot with their arms of cotton seersucker. Junior!" He contrasts his teen-age tycoon, Phil Spector, with "the arteriosclerotic, larded adults, infarcted vultures . . . one meets in the music business." Even Baby Jane—Baby! Junior!—loses her cool when she thinks of all those . . . adults: "Now she looks worried, as if the world could be such a simple and exhilarating place if there weren't so many old and arteriosclerotic people around to muck it up."

Those ten-thousand-plus purchasers of Wolfe's book are probably almost all adults, arteriosclerotic or not, since there are so many of them still around mucking it up and also in a financial position to lay $5.50 on the line. So it's not a literal business of age—Junior and Baby Jane aren't exactly teen-agers. Maybe more like how you *feel* sort of—"in" (new) or "out" (old)? I think the vogue of Tom Wolfe may be explained by two *kultur-neuroses* common among adult, educated Americans today: a masochistic deference to the Young, who are also, by definition, new and so in; and a guilt feeling about class—maybe they don't deserve their status, maybe they aren't so cultivated—that makes them feel inse- cure when an articulate young—well, youngish—type like Wolfe assures them the "proles," the *young* proles that is, have created a cultural style which they either had been uncultivated enough to think vulgar or, worse, hadn't even noticed. Especially when his spiel is on the highest level —Wolfe is no Cholly Knickerbocker, he's even more impres- sive than Vance Packard—full of hard words like "ischium" and "panopticon" and heady concepts like "charisma" ("the [automobile] manufacturers may well be on their way to routinizing the charisma, as Max Weber used to say") and offhand references to "high-status sports cars of the Apollo- nian sort" as against, you understand, "the Dionysian custom kind." Or: "The people who end up in Hollywood are mostly Dionysian sorts and they feel alien and resentful when they are confronted with the Anglo-European ethos. They're a little slow to note the differences between topside and sneakers, but they appreciate Cuban sunglasses." A passage like that can shake the confidence of the most arrogant Ivy League WASP. Or this:

> The educated classes in this country [Wolfe writes in his Introduction] the people who grow up to control visual and printed communication media are all plugged into what is, when one gets down to it, an ancient, aristo- cratic aesthetic. Stock car racing, custom cars—and for that matter the jerk, the monkey, rock music—still seem

beneath serious consideration, still the preserve of ratty people with ratty hair and dermatitis and corroded thoracic boxes and so forth. Yet all these rancid people [one assumes "ratty," "rancid," etc., are rhetorical irony but one can't be sure; with Wolfe for the defense you don't need a D.A.] are creating new styles all the time and changing the whole life of the country in ways nobody even seems to record, much less analyze.

The publisher's handout puts it more frankly: "Tom Wolfe describes his beat as 'the status life of our time.' As he sees it, U.S. taste is being shaped by what were once its subcultures, largely teenage. . . . He zeroes in on the new, exotic forms of status-seeking of a young, dynamic social class, 'vulgar' and 'common' to the Establishment, that has emerged since the war and that expresses the ordinary American's sense of form and beauty." No wonder the book is selling. In addition to appealing to our adult masochisms, it also promises a new sociology of taste. The postwar "culture boom" has greatly increased the number of Americans who are educated, in the formal sense they have gone through college, without increasing proportionately the number who know or care much about culture. There is, therefore, a large and growing public that feels it really should Take An Interest and is looking for guidance as to what is, currently, The Real Thing. The old *kitsch* was directed to the masses but the reader of Edna Ferber or even Will Durant would be put off, if only by its title, by *The Kandy-Kolored Tangerine-Flake Streamline Baby*, which is *kitsch* addressed to what might be called a class-mass audience, smaller and, educationally, on a higher level but otherwise not so different from the old one.

I don't think they will get their money's worth, for their *arbiter elegantiarum* is as uncertain as they are, his only firm value being old-bad, new-good. Not enough. It forces him to abstract "style" so aseptically from all other contexts that it becomes ambiguous even as a guide to taste. Writing of those kandy-kolored automotive aberrations, he drops names desperately—Miró, Picasso, Cellini, and the Easter Island statues, "If Brancusi is any good, then this thing belongs on a pedestal"—but his actual description of them and of their

creators runs the other way. "Jane Holzer—and the Baby
Jane syndrome—there's nothing freakish about it," he protests. "Baby Jane is the hyper-version of a whole new style of
life in America. I think she is a very profound symbol. But
hers is not the super-hyper-version. The super-hyper-version
is Las Vegas." Rodomontade, whistling in the dark. He
doesn't explain why Baby Jane is not freakish or why she is a
profound symbol of the new American style or why Las Vegas
is a super-hyper-profounder one, and his articles on her, and
on Las Vegas ("the Versailles of America") lead me to
opposite conclusions, which he often seems to share as a
reporter if not as an ideologue. His most extreme effort is his
praise of Bernarr Macfadden's New York *Daily Graphic:*
"Everybody was outraged and called it 'gutter journalism'
and 'The Daily Pornographic.' But by god the whole thing
had style. . . . Even in the realm of the bogus, the *Graphic*
went after bogosity with a kind of Left Bank sense of
rebellious discovery. Those cosmographs, boy! Those confes-
sion yarns!" But the "cosmographs" were merely faked
news photos, the confessions dreary fabrications, and that
dear old *Graphic* in fact *was* gutter journalism in which
no kind of rebellion, Left or Right Bank, was involved.
Wolfe's term for its subtle quality is "the *aesthetique
du schlock*"—*schlock* being Yiddish for *ersatz* or phony—
and it applies to his other discoveries in "the new American style." Oh, we're tenting tonight on the old camping
ground!

There are two kinds of appropriate subjects for parajournalism. The kind Tom Wolfe exploits in the present book
is the world of the "celebs": prizefighters, gamblers, movie
and stage "personalities," racing drivers, pop singers and
their disc jockeys like Murray the K ("The Fifth Beatle"),
impresarios like Phil Spector ("The First Tycoon of Teen"),
entrepeneurs like Robert Harrison (whose *Confidential* magazine, the classic *old* one [1952–1958] you understand, Wolfe
salutes as "the most scandalous scandal magazine in the
history of the world," adding: *"Confidential* was beautiful.
This may be a hard idea to put across . . . but the fact is the
man is an aesthete, the original *aesthete du schlock,"* who as a
teen-age employee of the *Graphic* received the stigmata
direct from Bernarr Macfadden) and pop-art-*cum*-society
figures like Andy Warhol, Huntington Hartford (an antipop

popper), and Mrs. Leonard Holzer.* The other kind of suitable game for the parajournalist—though not Tom Wolfe's pigeon—is the Little Man (or Woman) who gets into trouble with the law; or who is interestingly poor or old or ill or, best, all three; or who has some other Little problem like delinquent children or a close relative who has been murdered for which they can count on Jimmy Breslin's heavy-breathing sympathy and prose.

Both celebs and uncelebs offer the same advantage: inaccuracy will have no serious consequences. The little people are unknown to the reader and, if they think they have been misrepresented, are in no position to do anything about it, nor, even if such a daring idea occurred to them, to object to the invasion of their privacy. The celebs are eager to have their privacy invaded, welcoming the attentions of the press for reasons of profession or of vanity. While the reader knows a great deal, too much, about them, this is not real knowledge because they are, in their public aspect, not real. They are not persons but *personae* ("artificial characters in a play or novel"—or in parajournalistic reportage) which have been manufactured for public consumption—with their enthusiastic cooperation. Notions of truth or accuracy are irrelevant in such a context of collusive fabrication on both sides; all that matters to anybody—subject, writer, reader—is that it be a good story. To complain of Wolfe's Pindaric ode to Junior Johnson that his hero couldn't be all that heroic is like objecting to Tarzan as unbelievable.

But of late Tom Wolfe has attempted more solid, resistant subjects. As his colleague, Mr. Breslin, might put it, he's been fighting above his weight. There was that front-page review of Norman Mailer's *An American Dream* in the Sunday Tribune's *Book Week* (which Richard Kluger edits in a more substantial and, to me, interesting way than Clay Felker's set-'em-up-in-the-other-alley technique with *New York*). As the French say, the most beautiful parajournalist

---

*Wolfe unaccountably missed Christina Paolozzi, a young Italian noblewoman who achieved celebdom by no more complicated strategy than stripping to the waist and allowing *Harper's Bazaar* to photograph her, from the front. But Gay Talese, an *Esquire* alumnus who now parajournalizes mostly in the *Times*—in a more dignified way, of course—includes her in his recent collection, *The Overreachers*, along with Joshua Logan, Floyd Patterson, Peter O'Toole, Frank Costello, and such.

cannot give any more than he has, and the only way Wolfe could explicate his low estimation of the novel was to jeer at the author's private life and personality—or rather his *persona*, this being the aspect of people Wolfe is at home with—followed by some satirical excursions on tangential matters like the ludicrous discrepancy between Mailer and Dostoevsky and the even more laughable crepancy between Mailer and James M. Cain. *C'est amusant mais ce n'est pas la critique*. Not that I disagree with his low estimate of *An American Dream*. Mr. Kluger asked me to review it and I declined for lack of time. If I had accepted, I should also have slated it but I don't think I would have thought of going into Mailer's personality and private life if only because there is so much in the printed text to criticize. But Tom Wolfe doesn't seem to be much of a reader.

A week or two later, he took on a subject of much greater mass and resistance: *The New Yorker,* with which he grappled in the April 11 and 18, 1965, issues of Felker's *New York.* The perfect target for two young(ish) men on the make with a new magazine competing for the same kind of readers and advertisers. Part One was headed "Tiny Mummies! The True Story of The Ruler of 43rd Street's Land of the Walking Dead!" It sketched in bold strokes, letting the facts fall where they may, an action painting of a bureaucratic, arteriosclerotic, infarcted organism that was dead but didn't know enough to lie down and of William Shawn, its editor, "the museum curator, the mummifier, the preserver-in-amber, the smiling embalmer" who took over after Harold Ross died in 1952.* The second part debunks the magazine itself: "For forty years it has maintained a strikingly low level of literary achievement"—compared, that is, to *Esquire* and the *Saturday Evening Post.* There is no space here to consider the truth of these propositions or the methods by which Wolfe attempts to demonstrate them beyond noting that, as a staff writer with an office at *The New Yorker* for the last thirteen years, I find his facts to be often not such, especially when some atmospheric touch depends on them; his snide caricature of Shawn to be a *persona* (convenient for his purpose) rather than the

---

*"Infarcted" sums up Wolfe's stance: *"Pathol.* a circumscribed portion of tissue which has been suddenly deprived of its blood supply by embolism or thrombosis and which, as a result, is undergoing death (necrosis), to be replaced by scar tissue." Necrosis! Scar tissue! Santa Barranza! Eeeeeeeeeee!

real person I know; and his evaluation of the magazine to be hung on a statistical gimmick it would be courteous to call flimsy. His "research" wouldn't get by the editor of a high school yearbook; and his ignorance of *The New Yorker's* present and past—he thinks Ross was trying to imitate *Punch*—is remarkable even for a Doctor of American Studies.

Somehow Tom Wolfe has managed to miss a target broad enough to have profited by sensible criticism. He has also revealed the ugly side of parajournalism when it tries to be serious. What with his own reading block and Shawn's refusal to be interviewed—his privilege, I should think, perhaps and in fact constitutional right, cf. Justice Brandeis on "the right to privacy"—Wolfe was reduced to speculations on the nature of the magazine and its editor. These are sometimes plausible, sometimes not, but they always fit into a pattern that has been determined in advance of the evidence, like Victorian melodrama or the political tracts we used to get from Germany and Russia in the thirties.* It is not surprising that Wolfe got away with it, making an instant reputation as a rebel and bad man which didn't do any harm to his book later. The first resource of a parajournalist is that his audience knows even less than he does—and it was a bold, slashing attack on a sacred cow, an Institution, the Establishment. That fellow Wolfe, he really gave it to *The New Yorker!* David and Goliath. It's hard for the class-mass audience to see that, today, Goliath is sometimes the good guy. He's so much less entertaining than David.

---

*These are generalizations and parajournalism, which thrives on generalization, cannot be understood unless it is examined in specific detail. For such an examination of Tom Wolfe's *New Yorker* Caper see my analysis of his technique, from boldly asserted unfacts to rhetorically insinuated untruths, in a forthcoming issue of this paper.

(1973) See the February 3, 1966, issue of *New York Review of Books* for perhaps the most complete, certainly the most detailed debunking job I've ever done. Even my case-hardened spirit began to falter (but managed to stagger on) as I discovered the extent of Wolfe's imposture. Practically every inference was either ingenuous or disingenuous, and almost the only actual fact was the magazine's address. "Tom Wolfe doesn't tell lies," I concluded, because "he seems to be honestly unaware of the distinction between fact and fabrication."

# Three Thomas Circle Northwest

## Raymond Mungo

"I wasn't talking about knowledge . . . I was talking about the mental life," laughed Dukes. "Real knowledge comes out of the whole corpus of the consciousness; out of your belly and your penis as much as out of your brain and mind. The mind can only analyse and rationalize. Set the mind and the reason to cock it over the rest, and all they can do is criticize, and make a deadness. I say *all* they can do. It is vastly important. My God the world needs criticizing today . . . criticizing to death. Therefore let's live the mental life, and glory in our spite and strip the rotten old show. But mind you, it's like this: while you *live* your life, you are in some way an organic whole with all life. But once you start the mental life you pluck the apple. You've severed the connexion between the apple and the tree: the organic connexion. And if you've got nothing in your life *but* the mental life, then you yourself are a plucked apple."

—D. H. Lawerence, *Lady Chatterley's Lover*, 1928

The Pentagon has been elevated, it seems, and everybody went home. Except for our group of new media freaks. We

From *Famous Long Ago: My Life and Hard Times with Liberation News Service* (Beacon Press, 1970).

suddenly realize that we *were* home, an island of living guerrilla energy amid the enemy's home camp. It was all so like Saigon, we fantasized, and our job, apart from "revolutionizing the national media," was then to build a Liberated Zone within Washington, a clump of Free Land from which the next, the *real*, Pentagon seizure could be directed. The months ahead were to fill out the metaphor elegantly—I lived to see machine-gun nests set up on the Capitol steps— but we had no way of knowing that the march on the Pentagon was to be the last massive group action for years to come. It was late 1967; Lyndon Johnson was President and would, we presumed, run again; and our movement was one of peace, sanity, and full enjoyment of the senses —we were in pursuit of happiness, LBJ in dictation of misery.

It is impossible for me to describe our "ideology," for we simply didn't have one; we never subscribed to a code of conduct or a clearly conceptualized Ideal Society and the people we chose to live with were not gathered together on the basis of any intellectual commitment to socialism, pacifism, anarchism, or the like. They were people who were homeless, could survive on perhaps five dollars a week in spending money, and could tolerate the others in the house. I guess we all agreed on some basic issues—the war is wrong, the draft is an abomination and a slavery, abortions are sometimes necessary and should be legal, universities are an impossible bore, LSD is Good and Good For You, etc., etc.—and I realize that marijuana, that precious weed, was our universal common denominator. And it was the introduction of formal ideology into the group which eventually destroyed it, or more properly split it into bitterly warring camps—but more on that story later. One reason why legislators could safely ignore irate anti-war letters from their constituents, I am sure, is that the lawmakers themselves, and the enormous majority of ordinary people, can find time to concern themselves only with that which directly affects their personal comforts and securities. Ideology, or the power of ideas, is a feeble power indeed in my country. Thus it is not surprising that the young, who have everything to lose (e.g., their lives) and nothing to gain from the war, not to mention the job-family-corporation cycle and the university's regimen, have carried on the principal burden of the fight.

In short, I am not about to recount the ideas which LNS published or describe the contents of your average underground newspaper—you know all that stuff anyway. It is important for you to understand *the way we lived:* because perhaps in retelling it I too will understand it better ("by-and-by"), for to paraphrase Dylan Thomas, I'm still living it and know it horribly well—and yet much remains to unseal the blind tombs of my mind.

*     *     *

On December 1, 1967, the Liberated Zone moved its physical reality from our sagging Church Street brownstone to a decrepit three-story office building at Number Three Thomas Circle Northwest, which boasted *two* underground levels. The building was an offshoot of Washington's curious urban development, in which shiny towers and purplish monuments rise alongside structures unfit for human habitation. The Liberated Zone shared Thomas Circle with Lyndon Johnson's own church, the National City Christian, which resembles a Greek temple with its phony acanthus and sleek marble columns; the Hotel Americana, a semicircular mold of glass and steel graced by a heated, domed swimming pool where a poor hip could, with luck, cop a free swim by *seeming* to be *with* some young hotel guest; the all-night People's Drug Store, which locks all but two of its doors at sundown to halt the flow of free merchandise out its portals, and sells plastic hamburgers wrapped in cellophane which you heat up yourself in a special two-minute X-ray machine; a variety of cheap rooming houses; an old red-brick Baptist church, where one may get free food during periods of civil insurrection; a tawdry grocery store where every known Girlie and Boyo magazine is sold; and a colorful assortment of pimps, hustlers, prostitutes, petty thieves, and alcoholics. The State Department and *Washington Post* are around the corner, the White House is six blocks away, the local police precinct nine blocks, and the heart of the Northwest ghetto—SNCC and SCLC country, 14th and U—ten blocks.

By the time we moved there the house on Church Street had become quite full and was no longer sufferable as an office as well—eight phones, each with five blinking buttons, assured irregular and difficult sleeping hours in all the bedrooms; and the bedrooms, as you shall see, were quite noisy enough as it was. Posters lined the walls in indiscriminate ideological conflict—the Beatles alongside Ché Guevara, and Mao Tse-tung with a disrespectful pink bubble pasted on his nose. Stereos copped from middle-class relatives, or purchased (as in my case) during the days when we held straight jobs, rang out with Bob Dylan, Phil Ochs, Ravi Shankar, Monteverdi, Bach, the Rolling Stones, Jimi Hendrix, and Walt Disney's Greatest Hits ("When you wish upon a starrr/Makes no difference who you arrrre"). And these were the people who lived in the rooms and ran the news service and Liberated the Zone:

First there was Marshall Irving Bloom, son of Denver's finest furniture dealer, past editor of the *Amherst Student* at Amherst College in western Massachusetts and founder of the Lecture Series there, and the face that launched the first genuine student uprising in Britain in centuries—London School of Economics, 1966. The issue in London was the appointment of Walter Adams, a white Briton given to strengthening the Empire's firm control over black natives of Rhodesia, as head of LSE. The student protest closed down LSE and killed an elderly porter, who suffered a heart attack at the sight of thousands of students marching on the catheral. Marshall took upon himself some responsibility for the entirely unforeseeable death of the old man, and today must be hard pressed to discuss the London affair at all—although the Sunday *New York Times* and various British journals occasionally resurrect the incident, usually when a new LSE protest erupts. The *London American*, published for and by U.S. citizens living in or visiting England, published a lead editorial entitled "Bloom, Go Home," and so he did; and at that a full year before Bobbie Dylan's famous advice (in "John Wesley Harding"): "One should never *be* where one does not belong."

Marshall was once described by Steve Lerner in the *Village Voice* as "a gaunt young man of insufferable allergies." That he continues to associate with Steve is testament to his boundless respect for the *truth*. He has what seems to some people a nervous and high-strung way of carrying himself, forever fleeing to some other engagement or taking notes or dreaming up apocalyptic schemes or speaking at a pace too rapid to imitate. To some his remarkable performance-in-life seems domineering, unstable, and disconcerting while to those, like me, who love him it is simply his way—unstable no more than any sensitive person would be unstable in our age, and never intimidating. Although Marshall would heatedly and sincerely deny it, everybody else involved would agree that the fortunes of Liberation New Service rose and fell on his shoulders alone; and to his enemies this was anathema while to us his friends it was a natural part of our lives, unobjectionable as the sun and stars and a fact we could understand was appropriate and necessary under the circumstances. His enemies insisted a "radical" news service must be managed by socialists who lived communally and conducted their endeavors as a group, a democratic Team. His friends liked what he did, knew it was good, and encouraged him to do more of it, knowing that *nobody else* could. And this extended argument over Marshall and how we felt about him at last came to be classified, by some, as a difference between "socialists" and "anarchists." An "ideological split" is born. It shall never be said that Marshall left anyone indifferent or unmoved.

He ped-xed all day and hallucinated all night: making the right phone calls, getting bills paid, finding someone to loan a mimeo machine, warding off the collection agencies as a ped-xer (*to ped-x: to manage, work out, solve unpleasant or tiresome duties, such as raising money to live or walking to the store while stoned; cf. San Francisco street-crossing signs, imbedded in the gravel: PED-XING);* and bringing home candy, playing Moroccan music, taking you for a ride in his ridiculous tiny car, understanding your hangups and cheering you up as a hallucinator (*to hallucinate: to have fun, feel free, be easy, be in tune with life, enjoy and understand; opposite of PED-X*). In short he is one of a small group of people alive in the world who can make something out of nothing, nurse an enterprise into a functioning if erratic organization, widely influential if fabulously in debt. Experience has taught me that such rare men often lose control over what they have created from a vacuum. If these were the days of Andrew Carnegie and youth aspired to industrial empire building, Marshall would be very rich—perhaps a furniture tycoon in Denver. As it is, he is quite poverty-stricken, but aren't we all? And he is too kindly and intelligent to be also worldly. In fact, very few of the people in this story are Of This World.

Marshall lived in the big room at the top of the staircase, a good lookout onto the troubled street below; he kept his room scattered with papers and journals atop a colorful Moroccan rug, on which he worked. He was then and is now too hyperthyroid to sit at a desk—and so Letters to the Editor of the *Post*, manifestos for the New Left, and everything else got written on the floor. He sometimes shared the room with Bala-Bala, whose "real" name is forever committed to silence since she is now in hiding from the forces of law, order, and orthodoxy in my country.

Bala-Bala was a secretary, a working girl, when she joined up with Bloom and me in Minneapolis. She lived in a clean, but barely furnished apartment, the address of which she kept secret from her employers and everyone else save Marshall and me. She'd been the kept woman at various times of the son of a former President of the United States, and had roomed with a black lady who later married one of America's most public black militants; she'd been a cocktail waitress, student, and inmate of a "mental hospital"; she'd lived in the mountains with Mexicans and in the cities with rankled business executives; lived high and low, but always *lived*, the apple and the tree all together. She was twenty-two. She lived with us for some months in Washington and later in San Francisco. She is one of the realest, truest persons I have ever fallen in love with. She is tall and blond and incognito, and she might be the ordinary girl sitting next to you on the drugstore lunch-counter stool. If so, if you see her, ask her if she remembers me at all, will you? And tell her, for me, that there is a great peace which lies beyond the war.

Bala-Bala's measure of greatness was that, like Marshall, she was an accomplished ped-xer with sense enough to hallucinate. Although she was decidedly a child of LSD (but aren't we all?), she can get confirmed reservations for The New Media Project on United's flight 308 to Chicago quicker than the Pentagon; and while your average acid-eating freak will be getting arrested for attempting to sit in the park under General Thomas' horse in Thomas Circle (for it is illegal to visit that park, which is picturesquely set in the middle of traffic without crosswalks), Bala-Bala will be tripping off into the night stars, having casually bounced a check off United's friendly hostess.

Next came Little Stevie Wonder, who was sixteen years old and prematurely experienced in the wonderful world of dope, women, and the underground press. He met Harvey Wasserman, a jolly two-hundred-pound Woodrow Wilson fellow (history) at the University of Chicago and former editor of the *Michigan Daily*, on the steps of the Pentagon—and Harvey, who bears uncanny resemblance to Sluggo in the "Nancy" cartoons, gave him a piece of carpet to sleep on in our house. By the time everyone had been bailed out of jail, Stevie had produced a series of magic photographs of the Pentagon event, one of which became a cover for the *San Francisco Oracle* and another an example of "antiwar activity" in the *Atlantic*, and he petitioned us to become LNS photographer in residence. He was gangly and tall and had a crop of curly black hair, not yet long, owing to high-school regulations. He was tired of suburban New Jersey, his parents, his school, and his childhood, and he presented himself to us as a peer while reserving himself the privilege of halcyon indifference to the needs of the news service since he was, after all, "only a growing boy." I was so old-age as to insist on a letter of consent from his father, and astonished when it arrived promptly in the mail; for we'd housed runaways before and always lived to regret it ("You seem like a nice, educated boy," I recall one harried mother saying as she yanked her daughter from our living room. "Why are you destroying your life like this?").

Stevie was living proof, in our own home, that in our early twenties we were already over the hill. He didn't know about Hesse, Keats, Kerouac, Marcuse, Norman O. Brown, Marx, Leary, or Alan Watts as we did but he lived a bit of all of them. Being two years too young for the draft, he had decided not to bother to register. Being too young to drink, he smoked pot, dropped acid, and at last sniffed heroin (but that's another story); and being too minor to sign contracts, he never worried about the rent, time payments on the press, or the nasty booger from Pitney-Bowes Inc. who periodically called to repossess the postage meter. He hadn't read Zinn,

Lacouture, Fall, Robert Scheer, Tom Hayden, or Staughton Lynd but he decided that the war in Vietnam was "bullshit" and he would have no part of it. He characterized Lyndon Johnson not as a war criminal, liar, thief, or any such common terms, but as "an asshole." He had dozens of Little friends around and there are thousands of kids like Stevie all over the United States. He learned faster than we could teach and soon outdistanced us in the lengths to which he would go to express his revolt against the system. He was wide-eyed and bewildered much of the time, picked up and repeated our political views when the occasion seemed to warrant it, and went fishing in Maryland when he was most needed to grind out photographs for the press run. He had an enormous army-surplus overcoat in the immense pockets of which he would shoplift dinner at the local chain grocery when the larder was absolutely bare.

Stevie lived in the basement on a concrete floor covered with mattresses and bamboo curtains rescued from the dump, with an eighty-pound, twenty-two-year-old speed-freak named Robin, who was sharp and tough and could, though white, make her own way in the jungle backstreets of Northwest, and a heroin addict, black, named Romeo, who slept most of the time. He was the classic No-good Boyo of Thomas's *Under Milkwood* and he taught us that an hour could be forever.

Too, there was Lisbeth Aschenbrenner Meisner—Mrs., not Miss. Liz was perhaps twenty-five, a friend of Marshall's at LSE, and just back from a year in the Soviet Union on a Fulbright scholarship. She had married Mr. Meisner in Poland, and until he arrived in the States via Montreal, she lived in the basement room adjoining Stevie's, and played Bach to his Beatles. She worked as a research assistant to I. F. Stone, who sometimes lunched with us on Wednesdays after dropping off the *Weekly* at the printer's, and who told us to make the news service "independent" of SDS and everybody else if we didn't want to end up the mouthpiece of an established political group. Liz had the credentials, degrees, experience, charm, and beauty to be something better than a secretary and mother to a mangy group of seekers, it seemed to me, but then what were the alternatives? The *Washington Post* pays much better than Izzy Stone (and, at that, LNS usurped much of her salary), but the mere presence of the *Post* on our doorstep was trying enough, and Lisbeth, who took seriously all the acts which America performs abroad in *her name*, could never see herself on the Russian Desk at the *Post* or "at State," for you must understand that those two desks are organically connected. She was physically in love with good food, fine wines, her old man in Poland, but even more fiercely partisan to the *idea* we were entertaining: a news agency to the dispossessed! A spokesman for the new culture! She had long brown hair, was strong and almost overwhelmingly well read and bright, and would lecture me on the importance of keeping the *idea* alive when it seemed most difficult, and being *kind* to myself and the others. If I, at twenty-one, could be Stevie's doddering prudent uncle, Liz, at twenty-five, could be my auntie in this microcosmic New Age family. The only known photograph of Lisbeth has her brandishing a strip of Franklin D. Roosevelt stamps (postage had gone to six cents, to our enormous chagrin since we spent more on stamps than on spaghetti) across her chest, with a wide grin. "Good old" Liz knew where the stamps were kept as well as how Lenin organized the masses.

About Elliot Blinder I could only say that he was free—and freedom cannot be adequately described; it must be experienced. Whereas we could be angry with Stevie for going fishing when all of the anti-war movement *needed* his photos, it was impossible to ever *expect* tireless devotion and slavish duty from Elliot's serene composure, although much of himself was freely given. He'd been editor of his high-school newspaper in Syosset, New York, and had worked with me as layout editor of the *Boston University News*—a good man on graphics, as they say in the trade. He was an inveterate head, forever floating through life, far more a hallucinator than a ped-xer, a serious disciple of Leary, Alpert, Watts, et al., and member of the Neo-American Church, whose sacraments are peyote and LSD. He managed, nonetheless, to successfully struggle for hours with the various duplicating machines at the Institute for Policy Studies, where we printed the first twenty-five or so issues of the news service under the somewhat reluctant aegis of the IPS staff of academic lefties; but he finally left Washington in reaction to the fact that LNS was "too political" and D.C.

too basically inferior to Boston as a home base for tripping and rapping. Elliot was soft-spoken, twenty, and very hairy, and lived in the tiny upstairs room-with-a-porch which overlooked the alley between Church and Q—the room which was later to become Miss Verandah Porche's worldwide headquarters of the Bay State Poets for Peace.

I found the words to describe Elliot, though they are not my own. They were written by William Gass, a philosopher and member of That *New York Review* Crowd, with whom I shared visions of Armageddon one dull morning at Purdue University. From his novel, *Omensetter's Luck:*

"The way you walked through town . . . carrying your back as easy and as careless as you would a towel, newly come from swimming always, barely dry you always seemed, you were a sign. Remember the first evening when you came? You were a stranger, bare to heaven really, and your soul dwelled in your tongue when you spoke to me, as if I were a friend and not a stranger, as if I were an ear of your own. You had mud beneath your arms, mud sliding down the sides of your boots, thick stormy hair, dirty nails, a button missing. The clouds were glowing, a rich warm rose, and I watched them sail 'til dark when I came home. It seemed to me that you were like those clouds, so natural and beautiful. You knew the secret: how to be."

Also there was Max Smith, who called himself just Smith, and his lover Abigail, a seer and card reader late of Berkeley, and they lived all over the house until Max's aunt died and left him enough of an inheritance to take a room elsewhere and write short stories for the hell of it. Smith was a Missouri hillbilly, thirty years old, who met Marshall at the New Politics Convention in Chicago in September, 1967, and came along for the ride; and who, though he wrote news stories very poorly, always leaving out the source of his information or the number arrested, played a heavy guitar and cheerfully cleaned up our generally filthy home and office. He spoke with his hands, seldom offered any opinion or advice, and nodded omnisciently to express approval. There is one known photo of him as well, holding a wet mop and grinning easily under his moustache.

And finally there was me. I lived in the big room next to Marshall's which looked out onto the everlasting alley and slept with a variety of friends on a big red double mattress on the floor. All I can say for myself is that I tried my best to keep the cockroaches from completely overtaking the house, but ultimately lost the battle. There have been cockroaches everywhere I have lived, from early childhood, except for the little Vermont mountain farm which I now inhabit (which has skunks, porcupines, and deer instead). I am thus relieved to learn at last that it was not me alone which brought the roaches, but something about class; and as I now live in the woods, in a frigid climate, the roaches will never come for it's Too Far to Walk, even considering the goodies I leave around.

\* \* \*

The sudden acquisition of an office building in a "respectable" (read "white") part of town raised the new problem of collaboration, since LNS alone could neither meet the monthly rent (three hundred dollars) nor fill all of the floors with people and equipment. Our people have been briefly introduced to you, although hosts of others were also involved and some of them will enter the picture a little later; our equipment consisted of one 1932 IBM electric typewriter ("The Crapola") purchased for eighty dollars from Sam the junkman up on 18th Street. Since nobody got a "salary," master's degree or not, our only expenses were for postage, paper, and telephones, which together quickly ran to two thousand dollars a month almost from the outset. Needless to say, we stole where we could, calling it "liberation of urgently-needed matériel," and we left many bills unpaid. All of our "news," which cut an astonishingly wide swath across the colleges, anti-war groups, government committees, sundry riots, GI bases, and many foreign countries, came by mail or phone at first—we knew reliable if slightly freaked-out people all over the U.S., and met more every day. Our friends told their friends, and before long we were getting signed, unsolicited articles from as far afield as Peking and as nearby as Baltimore. But the new building called for some serious furniture

—groups of like-minded people to rent the empty office space, and some superduper twentieth-century communications equipment. Or so it seemed to us in those giddy hours when we smoked dope in the long, empty corridors.

We had the idea then that it would be exciting and impressive for all the anti-war and hip groups in Washington to share one downtown center. I gather in retrospect that this notion was inspired in part by New York's 5 Beekman Street (now, after twenty years, moved to 339 Lafayette Street), where the War Resisters League provides quarters for a half-dozen related activities. The difference in our case was that LNS did not propose to coordinate or otherwise exercise judgment on the groups in the building, which were to be independent partners in a cooperative venture. It had also not occurred to us, although it well might have, that such centralization of "our people" was bound to make us an easy target for the police, the Congress, even the American Nazis over in Arlington. And we remained to learn that it is difficult to remain "independent" of aggressive young Trotskyites when you share a bathroom with them. The same danger which lay dormant beneath the concept of the news service, the impossibility of reconciling all the ferociously partisan outfits which claim a role in one movement, plagued the establishment of our Liberated Zone.

It seemed we had two alternatives: we could give over two floors to the National Welfare Rights Organization, an interracial lobbying group for welfare recipients, whose staff members were mostly in their thirties and clean-cropped; or we could split the floors into offices for the *Washington Free Press*, the local SDS chapter, the Washington Area Resistance (there was so little of this that Marshall and I once turned in our outdated draft classification notices with them in order to raise their public numbers to four), Washington Area Mobilization to End the War (mostly graying Jewish mamas and papas), Insurgent Graphics and Printing (the name was changed, as the mood turned, to *Yippie* Graphics and Printing), *Gordon Free News* (a junior high school underground monthly), Dick Gregory for President Campaign Headquarters, and, later, the Young Socialist Alliance (of the Trotsky persuasion).

We chose the latter course for we wanted to give all those fledgling groups a home and the young men of Welfare Rights wore *ties.* How shocking it is, a year or two later, to discover that welfare is suddenly *the issue,* and the young men with the ties are arousing people to a passion over their *own* rights which they could never reach over anything as distant and abstract as "socialism" or even "the war."

And so the freaks came, came from all the neighboring blocks and cities three thousand miles away, and the police and the press right on their heels. Posters of Malcolm X and Ho-Ho-Ho-Chi-Minh flyers flapped in the breeze in plain view of Lyndon Johnson's own Sunday refuge. The dirty windows of the old building were thrown open with a lusty yank. The old wooden signs identifying this as the home of Soul Records, Inc., were unscrewed and psychedelic name-plates nailed on the door with all the passion of Martin Luther. "Basement: Insurgent Graphics." "DEMO Thursday! Be there!" "Better Living Through Chemistry." Every one's unused back issues, mimeo equipment, battered suitcases, began to pile up in the halls until passage became wide enough for only one thin person at a time. (No problem there, there were no fatties in our midst.) Last week's half-eaten Eddie Leonard's Shop tuna sandwiches sent out a powerful beam to the neighborhood rats, who lost no time muscling in. Gary Rader, a handsome blond Green Beret who burned his draft card in uniform, was commissioned to carry black wooden desks up the dark stairwells on his back. A healthy army of beaded, painted stoop-sitters took up sitting on the stoop, while Stevie (always most resourceful in such matters) discovered that the roof could be as sunny and airy as Laguna, and group siestas at noon became the rage up there. The plumbing groaned, coughed, and went into a reluctant renaissance. I discovered the miracle of water-based paint. A local construction site was raided by night and enough sawhorses and planks stolen to make desks. Green filing cabinets with ten-degree tilts to starboard sat mutely on the sidewalk, waiting to go into creaking service, while curious pedestrians walked around them. A lad whose voice had not yet cracked, but who claimed to be sixteen, was living in the second-floor closet; Marshall give him five dollars to invest in *Free Presses* for street sale, but he spent it on grass. A man from the telephone company arrived—did we want to be listed in the Yellow Pages under "News Service—Radical" for as little as five dollars a month? We didn't. Just to make everything official, we startled the local bank teller with a new checking account, "The Liberated Zone." Four different people could sign it.

Deliveries began to be made. First five hundred, then a thousand pieces of mail a day in three separate bundles. A thousand pounds of blinding magenta paper from that nice Mrs. Shapiro at the paper warehouse, whose son had been drafted to Vietnam. Telegram for "Motha": COME HOME ALL IS FORGIVEN DAD. "I'm sposda deliver this collator to the Liberated Noose, this the place?" My FBI agent, Philip Mostrom, took up a stool at People's: "Just coffee." The precinct paddy wagon parked outside—just in case. Nonetheless the pungent odor of marryjuwanna floated out every open window, proof positive that even the clearest risk of arrest will never stop every mother's son from smoking the stuff that lifts him above the horrors and emptiness of American streets. Ugly. Ugly. Ugly. Got to make a Liberated Zone out of your mind and *in* your mind in order to escape the creeping meatball! That lovely joint stands between you and the White House. The Congressional Record was delivered:

AMERICONG OPEN HEADQUARTERS IN NATION'S CAPITAL

*"In the House:* Mr. YOUNG, Missouri: Ladies and Gentlemen, now the American Cong have blatantly announced revolutionary headquarters right here in our nation's capital! . . . Mr. and Mrs. America, how long will we allow this to go on?"

We immediately ordered two thousand orange-on-black lapel buttons: I AM THE AMERICONG. They too were delivered. The lights burned all night.

Down in the subbasement was Thomas Loves You (when directly addressed, "Thomas Loves *Me*"), the energetic fourteen-year-old commander of the *Gordon Free News,* who played hooky from junior high in order to study rare Semitic scrolls at the Smithsonian. His office was cold and dark at all times and very wet in the spring, so planks were found to make a bouncy floor and a cat was hired to chase the rats, and shit in the corners, giving the *Gordon Free News* the appearance and odor of a very far underground sheet. Just above Thomas, in the basement, was his mentor Dick Ochs, thirty, and his anti-war machine (Insurgent Graphics), which sported a live daffodil in its water trough and feebly printed posters and leaflets for the community; and Stevie's darkroom which, although it *was* dark, never acquired enough real equipment to be of much use. On some occasions, our photos were printed with *Washington Post* facilities since we had secret sympathizers riddled throughout that journalistic hippo. (In fact, although LNS used a considerable amount of talent and machinery from the *Post*, I am pleased to say we *never lost a man* to it. We were never even solicited.) The rest of the basement was given over to used collators and presses which never performed *properly*, bought and charged by LNS shortly after we occupied the building.

The first floor was the home of the *Free Press*, a bi-weekly specializing in lurid colors, wretched typography, and anguished struggle with the politics of communal living. Since the *Free Press* never had an "editor" or "business manager," it was presumed that the "entire staff" made all the decisions. But the newspaper gave the impression that nobody made any decisions. Meetings of the "entire staff" were periodically called (it was always difficult to determine exactly who could vote and who could not since tripping adolescents arrived yesterday would announce themselves members of the "entire staff" and nobody was authorized to deny it) and at times lasted as long as ten or twelve shouting hours. Ideological splits developed and people I had just become accustomed to seeing around the *Free Press* office were hitchhiking back to Texas. The paper was sold on the streets for twenty-cents-the-copy by whoever was poor enough to do it, and had a following among government employees as well as Georgetown freaks (a PR man for the Office of Economic Opportunity told me that "all the boys at OEO," not to mention at Peace Corps, bought and read the *Free Press* and liked to know "what you kids are thinking"). I am sure an occasional copy ended up in the White House. And I'm embarrassed in retrospect that the chief voice of the anti-war movement in the District of Columbia clouded its message with so much of what Lenny Bruce would call "ordinary tits-and-ass," as distinguished from *intelligent* tits-and-ass (like Paul Krassner's *Realist*). The leading lights of the *Free Press* ranged the full spectrum from Mike Grossman, a pudgy curlyheaded junior Norman Mailer always into fistfights (and who once broke the finger of Roly Koefud, editor of Boston's *Le Chronic*, in some fraternal argument or other) to Art Grosman (no relation) who was as gentle and fluid as Connie's Mellors in *Lady Chatterley's Lover*. Too, there were ex-professional men like Bill Blum, formerly with the State Department, and Allen Young, formerly with the *Post* and the *Christian Science Monitor*. Allen also worked with LNS and now heads the New York City office "opposite Grant's Tomb." Many of the *Free Press* folk lived in a haunted house at 12th and N Sts, a cavernous and utterly unfurnished affair where the vibes were nearly as chaotic as in the office.

The second floor housed Mobilization, known for its excellent electric typewriters, the Young Socialist Alliance, known for its evangelicism, Dick Gregory headquarters, known for its splendid namesake, SDS, and The Resistance— the latter two eventually merging to share the thirty-dollar monthly rent. Resisters kept a commune way out near Columbia Road, and SDS, on Corcoran Street. And the physical presence of SDS raised a new problem of collaboration.

In New Left circles at the time, Students for a Democratic Society was indisputably the largest and most influential organization; it has never been, as J. Edgar Hoover would have you believe, an organized cadre preparing to bring down the republic with howitzers and Molotov cocktails. Indeed, when the republic falls, it will be a case of self-destruction, I am convinced (for what civilized society *deliberately* poisons its air and water, makes fresh food illegal, gears for nuclear holocaust?). But it was impossible to get around SDS as something of a common denominator for young insurgents, and for LNS to criticize SDS, which it did, was exactly parallel to the *Post* criticizing Lyndon Johnson, which it didn't—at least not substantially. The White House, it is often whispered, will cease granting "favors" (such as scraps of information!) to correspondents of newspapers which publish a "negative" view of its affairs; just so would SDS cease to be quite "fraternal" with a radical news service which did not adhere to its line. At the very moment while the SDS national office in Chicago was condemning the Youth International Party's (YIPPIE) plans to piss on the Democratic Party convention, LNS was the chief agent publicizing YIPPIE in the subterranean prints. And the names of Bloom, Mungo, Blinder, et al. appeared alongside Jerry Rubin's on the YIP manifesto now held by Mayor Daley to be proof of, among other things, a sinister conspiracy to assassinate himself! The semiofficial view of SDS was that no national radical news agency could *survive* unless organically linked with a national radical Political Party—i.e., SDS. Carl Davidson wrote it up in *New Left Notes*, stating that SDS needed a better "propaganda machinery" and coyly suggesting that LNS should properly be It. For a few weeks I tried to convince myself that I was being *politically immature* to recoil at the word "propaganda," but I couldn't help myself. (Bourgeois hangup?) LNS rejected the proposed affiliation with Students for a Democratic Society.

Unfortunately, the official policemen of American mores, men like Hoover, Daley, and now Nixon, refuse to draw the fine distinctions between different kinds of dissident citizens which I am here laboring. Daley appears on my TV screen to say it is a conspiracy among three men—"Rubin, Hayden, and Dellinger, Rubin, Hayden, and Dellinger"—which led the assault on his fair burg. Rubin is a brilliant anarchist, Hayden a conscientious socialist, and Dellinger an uncompromising pacifist, but these labels conveniently fit into a single nefarious category in Richard Daley's crippled vision. Thus are we cast afloat in a dangerous sea, together in spite of ourselves yet forever separate by passionate will.

\* \* \*

Meanwhile up on the third floor, where LNS lived, everything was happening too fast. It soon took us all day just to open the mail and answer the phones, which were everywhere, it seemed. All attempts to divide and categorize the work—Stevie must answer mail requests for Howard Zinn's article "Dow Shalt Not Kill" (we sold twenty thousand), Liz must screen the phone calls and get rid of bill collectors, Allen Young must drive his Volkswagen to the post office— failed miserably in the rush of work undone. Everybody was trying to keep up with insurrection in colleges, ghettos, and hip communities all at the same time. "Max, have you called Orangeburg, South Carolina, yet?" Cleveland? St. Louis? Norman, Oklahoma? Everybody wondered aloud whether any checks had come in the day's mail (subscribers were advised to pay fifteen dollars monthly for the service, although many couldn't afford to and paid less or nothing)— and could we thus go to the movies tonight? The number of underground newspapers went from fifty to a hundred to three hundred in a matter of a few months, and as 1968 came upon us, there were suddenly *straight* newspapers too, dailies in Pennsylvania and Iowa and California, who wanted to print our copy, dying to know where it was *at*. The mass media— UPI, the *New York Times*, CBS News—decided that we were a reliable source of information about the movement, and we had to dance around their questions. Meanwhile, mailings of LNS were getting fat and frequent—three times a week.

We looked for help wherever we could find it. One apparent break came in December when SNCC founded an Aframerican News Service in Atlanta to specialize in news of black power. We instantly effected an exchange relationship with them, grateful for some hard stuff written by blacks, who were in those days justifiably suspect of the white left and its neuroses. ANS began to crowd out LNS in ghetto newspapers like Cleveland's *Plain Truth* and Albany's *Liberator,* but we were delighted. And, toward the end of December, came the remarkable Telex, easily the most sophisticated device ever put into the hands of movement freaks.

Telex is a trade name of the Western Union Company for a private teletype system used by many fat-cat corporations and the United States Senate and relatively bugproof. A half-dozen machines had been introduced in college newspaper offices while we were with the U.S. Student Press Association, and others were envisioned for Boston, New York, San Francisco, and Chicago. All but the latter came true. Best of all, anybody anywhere could cable news to us—collect, of course—by going to any Western Union office and producing our code number. The Telex news was instantaneous, cheaper than telephones, and already typed with carbons. And just at the moment when the infernal clatter was getting tiresome, we hit upon international Telex (this system is owned by the International Telephone and Telegraph Company, which does not charge a monthly rental fee, so that even the most insolvent enterprise can have one and pay only for time used). And that led to Harry Pincus and Danny Schechter, our friends in London, establishing a European News Service from their ramshackle house on Roslyn Hill and translating LNS into foreign languages at their office in Oxford.

A few days before the Lunar New Year, Howard Zinn and Dan Berrigan, professor and priest, had gone to Hanoi to supervise the release of three American pilots. The Telex rang loudly but I ignored it for a while, for unlike the phones, it did not require immediate tending. I returned to find a solidarity message from the Vietnam Peace Committee, doubtless written by some of the Vietnamese I'd met in Bratislava, and this from Zinn and Berrigan:

RELEASE OF THREE AIRMEN IMMINENT. NORTH VIETNAMESE OUTRAGED AT CONTINUING BOMBARDMENT BUT RETAIN COMPASSION FOR AIRMEN WHO ARE TRAPPED BY WASHINGTON DECISIONS. HOPE RELEASED AIRMEN NEVER AGAIN BOMB YET AWARE POSSIBILITY THREE RELEASED PILOTS RETURN TO BOMB VIETNAM. WE ARE MOVED BY NORTH VIETNAMESE STATEMENT "EVEN IF THIS HAPPENS WE RETAIN FAITH IN ULTIMATE DECENCY OF AMERICAN PEOPLE."

* * *

Window Poem at Thomas Circle

Green with age
and frozen in the saddle,
hat in hand,
with a humble nod
for a hundred-gun salute
(long silent)

sits the model major general George
while a pigeon nestles on his head.
She lifts her leg to lay an egg.

There is little to praise here,
Mother of Cities,
the Washington's Needle,
the Santa Maria,
the Presidential Christian Bank and Tomb;
SPQR on police cars,
Gestapo everywhere—with dogs;
there is little to praise.

And if we cannot praise you
we must bury you,
and while we bury you
how shall we sing?
If we do not smite you,
Gorgon of Cities,
your blood-feathered eagles
will carry us off
to make glue and soap
in our sleep.

I am a gentlewoman,
not given to murder, martyrdom,
or apocalyptic dreams.
Yet in well-lit rooms at midday
the images ooze like auto fumes
as they circle the green
where General Thomas,
greathearted mountie,
watches the traffic,
awaiting the moment to strike.

—Verandah Porche

\* \* \*

Marshall Bloom is now the chief Boo-Hoo of the Neo-American Church in western Massachusetts, where he resides at the LNS Farm in Montague and prepares for the birth of *The Journal of the New Age;* Bala-Bala is in hiding halfway to the Orient; Lisbeth Aschenbrenner Meisner is in Berkeley, doing whatever it is people do in that otherworldly town;

Elliot Blinder broadcasts acid rock on an FM radio station in Boston; Max Smith was last seen heading for the Ozarks; and I am winter-bound in Vermont and, of course, writing this story.

And Little Stevie Wonder died of fast cars and exotic pills, mixed, on a New Hampshire quarry road. "He went straight," Marshall said, "while the road turned." No-good Boyo is on the ultimate trip.

# V

---

## Coda

# Faust in the '60s

## Marshall Berman

We have followed Faust out from under the crushing gabled roofs of a traditional and feudal society, up the steep and jagged slopes of modernization, toward the great and beautiful vistas opened up by a new industrial world. Wherever Faust has found himself—alone in his study, in bed with Gretchen, at work contending with fretful elements and men—he has found himself driven by a relentless and overpowering will to change. This drive has led him into his three metamorphoses, as dreamer, lover, organizer—but also, sooner or later, it has led him through and out of and beyond them. Faust's restless urge to move and change and grow has filled his life with romance and resonance, and has turned him into a radically new, distinctively modern kind of hero: The Developer. But this Faustian drive for development is a deeply ambiguous and dangerous passion—not only heroic, but demonic—and its creativity is bound to be destructive, and tragic, in the end.

If we look back now on recent American life, and ask where in our exploding culture and society Faust would feel at home, it should be clear to us that the answer is—*everywhere*. Faust would have no trouble recognizing millions of Ameri-

From "Sympathy for the Devil: Faust, the '60s and the Tragedy of Development," in *American Review No. 19*, January 1974 (Bantam).

cans who, through all the storms of the '60s, steadfastly refused to recognize each other. He who has passed through so many different styles of life would understand how a radical conflict of styles can mask a deeper unity of drives and needs. He would see at once how our official culture and our radical "counter-culture" are animated by the same insatiable lust for development, the same heroic will and energy and largeness of vision and courage to move, the same reckless insensitivity to the lives and needs of the people in the way. The unity of Faust's life should help us grasp the underlying unit of our own collective life. His story should help us see how our own economic developers and our psychedelic visionaries and our revolutionary activists—Bernard Cornfeld and Eldridge Cleaver, Robert Moses and Norman Mailer, Tim Leary and Bob McNamara, Clark Kerr and Mark Rudd, Walt Whitman Rostow and Jerry Rubin, Janis Joplin and Lyndon Johnson—are all caught up and whirled in the same maelstrom, all actors and victims in the American tragedy of growth.

The cultural and political explosions of the '60s will make more sense to us if we remember that they came at the crest of an economic boom, the climax of a generation of spectacular growth. Since the start of World War II, American productive and financial power, technological capacity and creativity, political control and cultural influence, had been expanding at a fantastic rate. The dynamism and energy of our economy seemed boundless. Mutual funds and conglomeration were driving the market to dizzying heights. Enormous freeways were shooting out in every direction, whole new industries and teeming population centers were springing out of the ground. In settled areas, high-rise office and commercial and luxury housing and entertainment complexes were sprouting up in every empty lot—and even in lots that had been full, obliterating everything transmitted to us from the past. In this period, the figure of the developer came into his own. Sometimes he sprang from private industry, sometimes from government bureaucracy, usually he had links with both. Nothing was sacred to him. Armed with zoning variances, with eminent domain—and, as a last resort, with the police, the national guard, the marines—he sought the power to tear down and build up anything, anywhere, in the city, in the country, in the world. In a time when everything seemed, effortlessly, endlessly, to get bigger and bigger (though not necessarily better), and everybody seemed to get richer and richer (though not necessarily happier), the developer was the man of the hour. He thought and acted and spoke for a society that was buoyant, exhilarated, full of an easy confidence in its drives and its innate momentum.

In this climate, America was ready for a "cultural revolution." As the '60s began, Americans were growing steadily more permissive and expressive in their sexual and emotional lives, more open and experimental in their responses to literature and art, more playful and extravagant in the styles and manners with which they lived their everyday lives. And through it all, the market kept on going up, the economy grew and grew. This economic fact generated a decisive change in millions of people's sensibilities. For all of us had been brought up to believe that we (and everyone else) had to repress ourselves, grit our teeth and hold back our feelings and desires if we wanted to survive. But now, as the decade developed, and we began, tentatively at first, to let it all hang out, and act it all out and bring long-suppressed feelings into the open, and free our bodies and expand and implode our minds, we found—for a time at least—that our new self-expression, far from threatening our survival, was bringing us new sources of life and energy, and helping us cope, not only more happily, but even more effectively, than we ever had before.

No wonder, then, that we embraced the ebullient vision of the developers as our own. We enforced our own variety of zoning variance—this was the real meaning of so many of the sit-ins and teach-ins and love-ins and weird disruptions and outrages of the decade—with boundless confidence that everyone would adapt and everything would be fine, finer than ever, very soon. This expansive faith was especially striking in the knowledge and education and culture industries—industries that were uniquely spectacular in their growth. It is appropriate that LSD was first used and celebrated not in shadowy bohemian enclaves but at Harvard and at the UCLA Medical Center of TV serial fame. When Leary and Alpert were eventually forced to leave Harvard, many of their disciples hung on through the mid '60s, and proselytized for acid with the motto, "Better Living Through Chemistry." I remember asking one of them if this wasn't in fact the slogan of one of America's most sinister pharmaceutical combines. "Sure," he said, smiling, "but for our drug it's really true."

He went on to assure me that there were no bad trips on LSD, only slanderous stories spread by "them." That was the way people talked in the '60s. So many new sources of life and liberty and happiness, and so few dues to pay!

But even in our most euphoric moments we knew there were still some dues to pay. We knew that, for the time being at least, all existing institutions were controlled by "them." We knew, as we came out into the world in the late '60s, that many of us were going to have to pay for our personal growth and our cultural liberation—more for these than for our radical politics—with our jobs. But losing jobs did not seem so bad. We believed our parents' generation had been too hung up on jobs, and on the respectability and security that jobs could confer. We did not worry so much about a job, for we were sure there would always be other jobs, around the corner or across the country. New schools and colleges and institutes, and free schools and alternate universities and centers for social change, were being created ex nihilo every day. Or else, if we got tired of academic life, there were whole new industries opening up, from computers to rock to dope. Or else, if that didn't work out, we could always drop out, and drift around, and pick up odd jobs, and live on food stamps, and steal—ripping off the system, it was called, an act that was not only useful but righteous. It was easy, in those boom years, to live off the fat of the land. This made it easier to experiment, to take risks for the sake of our self-development, for we were secure in the knowledge that it was not only possible, but adventurous and exciting, to move on. Thus the growth and dynamism of the American economy provided for us—for an expanding and energetic new middle class—the same sort of support that Mephisto's money and mobility provide for Faust.

It was only natural that the Civil Rights Movement and the New Left, as they came to life early in the '60s, should share the joy in motion and momentum that animated American society as a whole in those days of fervid development. It was natural, too, though full of sad irony, that as the decade went on, and a new radical movement crystallized, its style turned out to be a mirror image of the style of those hotshot stock market operators and real estate developers whom we most despised. Our radical campaigns shared the contours of the "shooters," the hot new issues that were flooding the market late in the '60s—and that, ironically, turned out to be far more subversive to Wall Street than we were: short-term, high-risk, extravagantly speculative, full of flash and energy, but often built on the flimsiest of foundations, capable of sudden marvelous surges, but just as capable of catastrophic overnight collapse. Our movement thrived on extreme situations—gross and enormous spectacles, dramatic confrontations, "action" on the grandest and most desperate scale. When an extreme situation did not seem to exist, we tried to create one—to force the issue, to bring the moment to its crisis—because this was the only wavelength on which we felt at home. For the most part, of course, we did not need to create crises and catastrophes—the government did it very well. Our movement grew—along with the pressure under which we had to move. We loved the pressure and urgency, for we were caught up in the magic of our momentum, and didn't worry much about the steering, let alone the brakes. When we confronted the demons at the Pentagon, we rejoiced innocently in the spectacular growth of the radical counter-culture that was gathered together that day. How sweet it felt, as we converged on them, to shout the words of The Doors' latest apocalyptic song: "We want the world, and we want it—NOW!" We didn't realize then how close in spirit we were to the genial megalomaniac in the White House, who would have understood our words perfectly if he had heard them, who wanted the world even more than we did, and who was bombing it—for the sake of its future development, of course—even as we marched and sang. I am not trying to discredit the New Left when I argue that our style was a mirror of theirs; in the context of the '60s, this was the only style there was. As Marx said, the bourgeoisie creates a whole world—even its opponents—in its image.

There are many more ironies here. We must face the fact that, for all our Faustian desire to overreach, we didn't actually reach very far. We fantasized endlessly about drastic and horrific action, expended spirit psyching ourselves up for cataclysmic violence; but very few of us were actually willing to do it, and very little was done. When the radical violence of the '60s is compared with earlier troubled times—the 1890s, say, or the 1930s—it looks almost embarrassingly puny. For all the murderous rage of their language and imagery and gestures, the vast majority of '60s radicals showed by their behavior that they didn't want to hurt people, not even the people they hated. This is why the fate of the Weathermen was so traumatic: by going all the way in reality on a trip that many radicals had taken in fantasy, they showed us that this was not after all the way we wanted to go. We were capable of sympathy for the devil, but not of intimacy, let alone identity, with demonic ways and means. Any viable post-'60s radicalism is going to have to accept that fact and build on the self-awareness it brings.

Another irony is that, while we were talking about violence and violation, the official representatives of "straight" society were actually doing it. Under Lyndon Johnson, this was obvious: he was our Captain Ahab, and he was going to get that whale, if he had to drag us all down with him in the attempt. (Why did he quit? Might he have recognized that, if he stayed in power, he might indeed drag the whole world down with him? To quit, then, meant to pull back from an abyss he yearned for—Johnson's one indisputably heroic act.) Under Nixon, it was more masked—till the Watergate story tore the mask cleanly off—and more sinister. Even as he and his friends were shaking their heads over our violent language, condemning permissiveness and loose morality, celebrating law and order and the virtues of civilized restraint, they were killing and horribly maiming millions of people abroad, and systematically violating the rights of millions more—of all of us—at home. The continuing Watergate/ Ellsberg/ITT/Berrigan/Camden/Gainesville stories, among others, suggest that the radicals of the '60s, for all their riotous rhetoric, tended to behave with a touching propriety and probity—while the official guardians of law and order were in fact capable of anything. If we are looking for genuine diabolism, rampant nihilism, we should forget about characters in weird clothes who sing songs such as "Sympathy for the Devil"—people like that are bound to be dilettantes, amateurs at best. We should focus instead on the sober organization men in crew cuts and business suits—Mephisto appears as one of these men in the last act of *Faust*—doing their jobs in a calm and orderly way. This perspective may strip the powers of darkness of their romantic dash, but it will give us a clearer vision of their real power and dread.

As Johnson's administration went on, and the war escalated, and our lives grew bitterer, and people began to turn against the President ("Turn On Johnson," a nicely ambigu-

ous button worn at the Pentagon) as a personification of all
that was wrong with our country, it was his Faustian spirit that
they often blamed: the largeness of his presence, his enormous aims, his sense of a righteous mission, his obsessive will
to change the world. If we could only slow ourselves down,
reduce our energy level, stagnate a little—if we could learn to
benignly neglect the world—we would do ourselves and
everyone else a great deal less harm. When Nixon came in,
many people who detested him nevertheless sighed with
relief. There was a certain feeling that we had wrought so
much destruction, so much evil, by force of our great dreams
of our noblest virtues. After all this, a man who was utterly
devoid of these virtues could help us come down. We could
forestall Faustian tragedy if we forswore Faustian heroism.
Now, after five years of Nixonian ferocity and malevolence in
the service of nothing—of an abyss of cynicism, an ultimate
nothingness—we are rediscovering the banality of evil. In the
gray '70s, the devil is very much with us, even though Faust is
not.

Even those of us who most loved the '60s, as I did, were
relieved to feel them come to an end. But the tragedy had
different endings for different actors. Faust's tragedy is the
tragedy of a mature man, a man who has lived and grown
both intellectually and emotionally, who has developed survival skills and perspective on life, before he ventures into the
world. Those of us whose identities had already jelled and
crystallized in the '50s could take special delight in the '60s:
we could let ourselves go, knowing they would come back.
Our maturity made us always a bit ironic, reserved even in
our most luminous moments; but those reserves were what
kept us together when the bubble burst. When, after all our
hopes and struggles, the system didn't change much after
all—and in some ways even got worse, a repressive administration and an economic slump coming down on us at
once—we were sad, but didn't take it all that personally. We
could head for our local forests and caverns and mountain-
tops, as Faust does—studies or libraries or local coffeehouses
and bars will do just as well—and consolidate our personal
growth, and savor all the '60s had done for us. Gretchen's
tragedy, on the other hand, is the tragedy of youth, a youth
whose soul is more beautiful than Faust's, but whose self is far
less free. Like so many of the kids who lit up in the '60s, she

goes all the way, holds back nothing of herself, but consequently has nothing to fall back on when the catastrophe comes: she takes it all too personally, and her personality falls apart. She feels abandoned, not only by a society that hates her, but by the man who loves her—as, not so long ago, many of the kids we loved, or said we loved, felt abandoned by us. We really did love them, as Faust really loves Gretchen; but we did find ourselves getting bored after a while with the narrowness of their pure intensity; we longed for something more complex. And so, we Faustians went our separate ways, sad and tired, but opened and enlarged and deepened and developed by the storms we had passed through. And many, too many, of the kids, like Gretchen, hardly grown, fell apart or died alone.

No doubt I am being melodramatic here: after all, even though many did disintegrate and die, most of us, in fact, survived. Still, so many who survived the '60s brought another typical form of tragedy on themselves, the tragedy of the survivor, who cripples himself in body and soul rather than face again the terrors of being fully alive. Our campuses and mountain trails and highways are full of languid kids whose deepest ambition seems to be to retire at 25. (And some have actually made it: Woodstock and Marin County, for instance, are full of "retired" dope dealers, grazing in the sun, senior citizens at 30.) Bookstore shelves marked "Growth" or "Self-Realization" or "Getting Yourself Together" feature T-Groups or Tantric Yoga, Shamanism or Sensual Massage—everything but the Faustian project of growing and developing oneself through action in the world. The great thing now, it seems, is to be "mellow"—which means, as you know if you have ever sat through a few minutes of this mellowness, to be empty. The '60s brought these kids up so high, so fast; now, in the '70s, they want only to go down slow.

What hurts me even more is that my own generation of intellectuals, artists, teachers, ex-activists, seem only too glad to let them—even to help them go. This is especially sad because one of my generation's authentic political achievements was its insistence, in the midst of feverish expansion and construction, that man was not made for economic growth, economic growth was made for man. One of the crucial points of our many struggles over student power, neighborhood and community control, workers' self-management, was that the bureaucratic drive for unlimited development—whether capitalist or statist—had no right to ride roughshod over the needs and the lives of the people in the way. Even in our fight against the Indochina war, traditional opposition to imperialism was intertwined with a revulsion at the way the imperatives of America's development had ravaged and shattered traditional societies and given them nothing in return. Economic growth can be justified only where it contributes to human growth—the growth not of hypothetical human beings at some future date, but of the actual people who are here right now. This idea is part of the lasting legacy of the New Left. Alas, even as more and more Americans were learning to appreciate our vision and make it their own—see the Department of Labor's *Work in America* report—many old New Leftists were losing hold on the vision that they had been the first to see. Their sensitivity to the human costs of development desensitized them to its real human gains. Instead of grasping the process of modernization as a tragedy, they came to see it as a melodrama—all bad. Traumatized by the tragedy of their own development, they came to hate all their radical energy and creativity and overflowing of life. When their mocking inner voices, like the Goethean Earth Spirit, called out to them, "Where are you, Faust, whose voice rang out to me,/Who forced himself on me so urgently?" they pulled the covers over their heads and dreamed of forests and caverns of primal listlessness.

I don't mean to deny the terrible force of all the pain we saw and felt—and sometimes caused. But I do want to suggest that tragedies of development form the deepest core of modern experience: they are not ours alone. It is crucial for us to come to terms with the demonic potentialities of human growth, both individual and social, psychosexual and economic. But although we have to learn to accept responsibility, it is pointless to paralyze ourselves with cynicism or mutilate ourselves with blame. Indeed, if we repress our Faustian vision and energy and will, and recoil from action—as plenty of us have learned to do surprisingly fast and well—even then we will be to blame. We will be guilty of perpetuating the only alternative to the tragedy of development: the tragedy of *under*development—a story that most of our parents, and those who grew old in the silent night of the '50s, and the 40 million Americans still stuck beneath the poverty line, and millions more in the undeveloped Third World, know all too well.

It used to be said, back in the '60s, that we should throw out the tragic sense of life, because it made life seem too complex and thus enervated our will to change the world. On the contrary, I think, it is only in the context of militant activism and attempts to change the world that tragedy has any meaning at all. Max Weber, one of the great Faustian heros of modern times, spoke of this in his luminous essay, "Politics as a Vocation." Writing at a moment of revolutionary activity and exhilaration, Weber said that it required no special virtue to be active at a time like the present; the real test would come in the future, when the forces of reaction triumphed again—as they soon did, both in his Germany (though he did not live to see it) and in our America. Weber anticipated a time of torpor and dejection very like our '70s, and spoke to it in advance. He restated the discovery that Faust makes at the beginning of his tragedy, that "the world is governed by demons." In our modern, post-Christian world, personal devils have been rendered obsolete, and thrown out of work, by enormous impersonal organizations, what Weber called "human machines." Anyone who persists in the belief "that good can follow only from good, and evil only from evil"—who believes, in other words, that he can live in this world and still keep his innocence intact—"is a political infant." Human life is darkly ambiguous at its core. Nevertheless, everyone—not only everyone who wants to follow politics as a vocation, but "everyone who is not spiritually dead"—is "responsible for what may become of himself under the impact of these paradoxes." The requirements for being political are the requirements for being a *Mensch*, "a genuine man," a full human being. Who was he calling? "Only he," says Weber's last line, "who in the face of all this can say, 'In spite of all!' . . ." This is what tragic heroism, and authentic radicalism, and sympathy for the devil, are all about.

# Chronology

*January 2* John Fitzgerald Kennedy, Senator from Massachusetts, announces candidacy for presidency.

*February 1* Negro students begin spontaneous demonstrations and "sitdowns" in protest of segregation policies of Woolworth and Kress stores in Greensboro, N.C. Movement subsequently spreads to cities throughout South.

*March 25* U.S. Circuit Court of Appeals in New York rules that unexpurgated version of D. H. Lawrence's *Lady's Chatterley's Lover* is not obscene.

*April 5* JFK defeats Hubert Humphrey in Wisconsin primary.

*May 1* American U–2 high-altitude reconnaissance plane shot down over central Russia. The pilot, Lieutenant Francis Gary Powers, is captured. East–West Summit Conference subsequently collapses at May 16th opening session.

*May 6* President Eisenhower signs Civil Rights Act of 1960 into law.

*May 9* Federal Drug Administration approves first birth-control pill, Enovid, as safe for use.

*July 13* JFK nominated for president on first ballot by Democratic National Convention in Los Angeles; Lyndon Baines Johnson nominated for vice-president.

*July 27* Vice-President Richard Nixon nominated for president by Republican National Convention in Chicago on first ballot; Henry Cabot Lodge, chief United Nations delegate, nominated for vice-president.

*September 26* First televised presidential campaign debate between Kennedy and Nixon.

*October 12* Soviet Premier Khrushchev pounds shoe on table at UN 25th-anniversary session.

*November 8* Kennedy–Johnson ticket edges out Nixon–Lodge in squeaker.


## 1961

*January 3* U.S. breaks off diplomatic relations with Cuba.

*January 20* JFK inaugurated president.

*February 7* Jean-Luc Godard's *Breathless* released in U.S.

*March 1* JFK issues executive order creating the Peace Corps.

*March 21* U.S. sends military aid and advisers to Laos.

*April 12* Soviet cosmonaut Yuri Gagarin becomes first man to orbit earth.

*April 15–20* Air strikes at Bay of Pigs by CIA-trained Cuban-refugee pilots begin, followed by abortive invasion by Cuban exiles.

*May 4* Freedom Riders leave Washington by bus to test desegregation in southern cities.

*May 5* Alan Shepard rides Mercury capsule in suborbital flight to become the first American in space.

*June 3* JFK and Khrushchev meet at summit conference in Vienna.

*July 2* Ernest Hemingway commits suicide.

*August 13* East Germany closes Berlin border and begins to build wall.

*September 1* Soviet Union begins nuclear testing in atmosphere after three-year moratorium.

*October 1* Roger Maris hits 61st home run.

*October 10* Joseph Heller's *Catch–22* published.

*December* Pop artist Claes Oldenburg opens his "Store" on N.Y.C.'s Lower East Side, filled with plastic and papier maché reproductions of food and clothing.

*December 11* JFK sends first 400 American combat troops to South Vietnam.


## 1962

*February 1* Ken Kesey's *One Flew Over the Cuckoo's Nest* published.

*February 20* John Glenn becomes first American to orbit the earth.

*April 25* U.S. resumes atmospheric nuclear testing.

*June 11–15* Students for a Democratic Society (SDS) hold first national convention in Port Huron, Michigan.

*July 10* Telstar satellite broadcasts first live intercontinental television transmission.

*September 25* Sonny Liston KO's Floyd Patterson in first round to win heavyweight boxing title.

*September 30* James Meredith attempts to enroll at Old Miss; JFK forced to send U.S. marshals, then troops.

*October 22–November 2* Soviet missiles discovered in Cuba; JFK orders blockade until missiles are finally removed. Khrushchev agrees, ending crisis.

*November* Andy Warhol holds first major show of paintings at Stable Gallery in N.Y.C.

*November 17* James Baldwin's "Letter From a Region in My Mind" (later titled in book form *The Fire Next Time*) published in *The New Yorker*.

*December 31* 11,000 U.S. military personnel and technicians now aiding Sout,CVietnam.

# 1963

*February 19* Betty Friedan's *The Feminine Mystique* published.

*March 1* Major civil rights voter-registration drive begins in Mississippi.

*April 2* Martin Luther King, Jr., leads campaign against segregation in Birmingham, Alabama; Sheriff Bull Connor sets police dogs on demonstrators.

*June 11* Buddhist monk immolates himself in South Vietnam to protest religious persecution.

*June 12* Civil rights worker Medgar Evers murdered in Mississippi.

*August 5* Nuclear test ban treaty signed by U.S., USSR, and Great Britain.

*August 28* Martin Luther King, Jr., delivers "I have a dream" speech at conclusion of the March on Washington.

*September 7* Four black girls die in church bombing in Birmingham, Alabama.

*November 3* Ngo Dinh Diem, President of South Vietnam, and brother murdered in coup.

*November 22* John Fitzgerald Kennedy murdered in Dallas, Texas; Lyndon Baines Johnson assumes office.

*November 24* Lee Harvey Oswald murdered by Jack Ruby.

## 1964

*January 8* LBJ declares "unconditional war on poverty in America" in his State of the Union address.

*January 29* Stanley Kubrick and Terry Southern's *Dr. Strangelove* released.

*February 9* Beatles make U.S. television debut on the Ed Sullivan show; "I Want to Hold Your Hand" is number one song.

*February 25* Cassius Clay/Muhammad Ali defeats Sonny Liston for heavyweight crown; announces Muslim faith the next day.

*July 2* LBJ signs Civil Rights Act of 1964 into law.

*July 15* Barry Goldwater nominated as Republican candidate for president.

*August 4* Bodies of civil rights workers Schwerner, Goodman, and Chaney discovered in Philadelphia, Mississippi, after 44 days missing.

*August 10* Gulf of Tonkin Resolution passed in Congress; in Senate only Wayne Morse and Ernest Gruening vote no.

*August 20* LBJ signs Economic Opportunity Act calling for "maximum feasible participation of poor" into law.

*September–December* Berkeley Free Speech Movement erupts, led by Mario Savio, with sit-ins and calls for campus strike; ends December 3rd with 796 arrests.

*September 24* Warren Commission Report released, calling Kennedy assassination work of lone gunman.

*October 14* Martin Luther King, Jr., receives Nobel Peace Prize in Stockholm.

*November 3* Lyndon Baines Johnson elected president in landslide.

## 1965

*February 7* LBJ orders bombing raids on North Vietnam to begin.

*February 21* Malcolm X assassinated in the Audubon Ballroom in Harlem, New York.

*March 21* Civil rights march from Selma to Montgomery, Alabama takes place under National Guard protection.

*March 25* Civil rights marcher Viola Liuzzo murdered in Lownde County, Ala.

*April 28* 22,000 American troops sent to Dominican Republic to ai military junta.

*June 19* Nguyen Kao Ky appointed South Vietnamese premier.

*July 10* Rolling Stones' "Satisfaction" reaches number one.

*July 24* Bob Dylan "goes electric" with rock band at Newport Folk Festival.

*July 30* LBJ signs Medicare bill into law.

*August 5* Marilyn Monroe commits suicide.

*August 10–13* Black riots erupt in Watts ghetto in Los Angeles.

*November 8 Autobiography of Malcolm X* published.

*November 27* Ken Kesey and the Merry Pranksters hold first "acid test" open to the public.

*December 24* Christmas halt of bombing of North Vietnam.

## 1966

*January 21–22* San Francisco Trips Festival—first hippie conclave.

*January 21* U.S. resumes air raids over North Vietnam as peace effort fails.

*February 14* Truman Capote's *In Cold Blood* becomes best seller.

*April 8 Time* asks on cover, "Is God Dead?"

*June 6* James Meredith is wounded by sniper on march near Hernando, Mississippi.

Truman Capote holds famous "Black and White Ball"—widely regarded as most glittering bash of decade.

*June 13* Supreme Court rules in Miranda case that criminal suspects must be informed of their rights upon arrest.

*June 29* U.S. bombing raids now start on Hanoi and Haiphong.

*July* Negro riots in Chicago, Brooklyn, and Cleveland.

*August 3* Lenny Bruce dies of heroin overdose in N.Y.C.

*August 5* John Lennon states, with some justification, that Beatles are now more popular than Jesus Christ.

*September Chelsea Girls* by Andy Warhol opens at 41st Street Theatre—first "commercial" run of an underground film.

*October 15* U.S. troops in Vietnam now number 320,000—more than their South Vietnamese allies.

*December 15* Walt Disney dies.

## 1967

*January 14* San Francisco Human Be-In.

*February 22* Broadway premiere of Barbara Garson's *MacBird!*

*April 15* 100,000 attend antiwar demonstration in New York.

*April 28* Muhammad Ali stripped of his heavyweight crown for draft resistance.

*June–August* Summer of Love.

*June 16–18* Monterey Pop Festival.

*July* Negro riots in Detroit and Newark leave 69 dead.

*July 1 Sergeant Pepper's Lonely Hearts Club Band* heads album charts.

*July 17* John Coltrane dies of liver ailment.

*August 13 Bonnie and Clyde*, directed by Arthur Penn and starring Warren Beatty and Faye Dunaway, released.

*September 7* 464,000 American troops now in Vietnam; 13,000 Americans have died in war.

*October 21–22* The March on the Pentagon.

*November 9 Rolling Stone* publishes first issue.

*December 3* First successful heart transplant performed by Dr. Christian Barnard in Cape Town, South Africa.

*December 21 The Graduate*, directed by Mike Nichols, starring Dustin Hoffman, and with sound track by Simon & Garfunkel, released.

# 1968

*January 30* Viet Cong's Tet Offensive stuns American military leadership.

*February 8* Eldridge Cleaver's *Soul on Ice* published.

*March 1* Publication of the Kerner Commission Report on Civil Disorders—"Our nation is moving toward two societies—one white, one black—separate and unequal."

*March 13* Eugene McCarthy comes in second in New Hampshire presidential primary.

*March 31* LBJ announces that he will not seek re-election in wake of strong challenge in Democratic primaries from antiwar candidate Eugene McCarthy.

*April 4* Martin Luther King, Jr., shot dead in Memphis; violence erupts across country.

*April 23–30* Columbia University student strike and takeover of buildings.

*April 29 Hair!* premieres on Broadway.

*May 6* Norman Mailer's *Armies of the Night* published.

*June 4* Andy Warhol shot by crazed feminist Valerie Solanas in his studio, The Factory.

*June 6* Robert F. Kennedy assassinated in Los Angeles at victory party to celebrate his winning California primary.

*June 23* Vietnam becomes longest war in nation's history.

*August 1* Richard Nixon and Spiro Agnew nominated as Republican presidential ticket in Miami.

*August 25–28* Democratic National Convention in Chicago nominates Hubert Humphrey and Edmund Muskie amid demonstrations, civil disorders, and police brutality.

*November 5* Richard Nixon elected president in much closer election than expected.

*December 28* Both Beatles' *White Album* and Rolling Stones' *Beggars Banquet* on charts.

## 1969

*January 1* U.S. troop strength in Vietnam reaches peak of 542,000.

*March 10* James Earl Ray pleads guilty to the murder of Martin Luther King, Jr.

*March 21* Philip Roth's *Portnoy's Complaint* heads fiction bestseller list; Kurt Vonnegut's *Slaughterhouse-Five* published.

*April 19* Black students exit from occupied student union building at Cornell University carrying guns.

*April 21* Jack Kerouac dies of abdominal hemorrhaging at mother's home in St. Petersburg, Fla., while watching "The Galloping Gourmet."

*May 15* Squatters forcibly evicted by police from "People's Park" in Berkeley.

*July 3* Brian Jones of the Rolling Stones drowns in his swimming pool in England.

*July 8* President Nixon announces first troop withdrawals from Vietnam.

*July 20* Neil Armstrong and Buzz Aldrin become first human beings to walk on surface of the moon.

*July 14* *Easy Rider,* starring Dennis Hopper, Peter Fonda, and Jack Nicholson, premieres.

*August 9* Tate–LaBianca murders in Los Angeles committed by Charles Manson and gang.

*August 15–17* Woodstock Music and Art Festival in White Lake, New York, takes place.

*September 24* Chicago 8 conspiracy trial—defendants include Bobby Seale, Jerry Rubin, and Abbie Hoffman—begins under Judge Julius Hoffman in Chicago.

*October 8–11* Four violent "Days of Rage" by Weathermen, a splinter faction of SDS, take place in Chicago.

*October 15* Vietnam Moratorium Day.

*October 18* Opening party for Henry Geldzahler's "New York Painting and Sculpture: 1940–1970" show at Metropolitan Museum of Art.

*October 19* Spiro Agnew characterizes Vietnam Moratorium Day committee as "an effete corps of impudent snobs."

*November 12* Lieutenant William Calley charged with the multiple murders of civilians at Song My, South Vietnam.

*December 1* First draft lottery of decade held.

*December 6* Gun-wielding black man stabbed to death by Hell's Angels at huge Rolling Stones concert at Altamont Speedway at end their 1969 U.S. tour.

## 1970

*February 18* Jury acquits seven of Chicago 8 of conspiracy charges, but convicts five of individual acts of incitement to riot.

*February 26* Bank of America branch burned down by students in Santa Barbara, California.

*March 6* Greenwich Village townhouse demolished by explosion of Weatherman bomb factory.

*March 18* Prince Norodom Sianhouk of Cambodia overthrown in bloodless coup.

*May 1* President Nixon announces "incursion" of American combat troops into Cambodia.

*May 4* Four student demonstrators killed, nine wounded by National Guard gunfire at Kent State.

*May 9* 100,000 protest Cambodian invasion in Washington.

*May 15* Two black students killed, nine wounded by police gunfire at Jackson (Miss.) State College.

*June 29* U.S. ground troops complete withdrawal from Cambodia.

*August 7* Judge Harold Haley and three kidnappers killed in escape attempt by black militants from San Rafael, California, courthouse; warrant later issued for Angela Davis' arrest.

*September 7* U.S. troop strength in Vietnam falls below 400,000 for first time since January, 1967.

*September 18* Jimi Hendrix dies of drug overdose in London.

*September 26* President's Commission on Campus Unrest calls gap between youth culture and established society threat to American stability.

*October 4* Janis Joplin dies of drug overdose in Hollywood.

*December 18* Supreme Court rules that 18-year-olds can vote in federal elections.

## 1971

*March 8* Joe Frazier beats Muhammad Ali in 15-round decision at Madison Square Garden.

*March 29* Lieutenant Calley found guilty in court martial of the murder of at least 20 Vietnamese civilians.

*April 24* Several hundred Vietnam veterans throw away medals in Washington; 250,000 marchers protest continuation of war.

*May 5* Mass arrests of Mayday demonstrators reach 12,000 in three days.

*June 13* New York Times begins publication of classified "Pentagon Papers" history of U.S. involvement in South Vietnam.

*July 3* Jim Morrison, poet, lead singer of the Doors, and "erotic politician" dies of heart failure in Paris.

*August 15* President Nixon orders 90-day wage and price freeze.

## 1972

*January 25* President Nixon unveils previously secret eight-point plan for peace in South Vietnam calling for cease fire, return of POWs, and six-month pull-out of U.S. forces.

*February 21* President Nixon arrives in Peking to begin week-long visit to Communist China.

*March 22* Senate approves Equal Rights Amendment, sending it to the states for ratification.

*April 5* "Harrisburg 7" acquitted of conspiring to kidnap Henry Kissinger.

*May 5* U.S. mines Haiphong harbor.

*May 15* George Wallace shot and wounded while campaigning at rally for Maryland presidential primary.

*June 4* Angela Davis acquitted by all-white jury of murder, kidnap, and criminal conspiracy.

*June 17* Break-in at Democratic National Headquarters at the Watergate complex.

*July 12* George McGovern nominated as Democratic candidate for president; selects Senator Thomas Eagleton of Missouri as running mate, who later removes himself from race when news of previous hospitalization for nervous breakdowns emerge.

*October 26* Henry Kissinger announces that "peace is at hand."

*November 7* Richard Nixon is re-elected President in landslide victory, carrying 49 states.

*December 15–30* U.S. resumes "Christmas" bombing of North Vietnam as Paris peace talks break down.

## 1973

*January 27* Formal peace agreement signed in Paris ending Vietnam hostilities.

*February 7* U.S. Senate establishes select committee to investigate Watergate affair.

*March 29* Last U.S. combat troops withdraw from Vietnam, and last U.S. prisoners of war released.

# Bibliography

I have made a particular attempt in this bibliography to list current paperback editions of works, as these are the editions most likely to be available both to the general reader and for study. Where there are two publisher's listings for a title, the second listing is for the last paperback edition of the work to be listed in *Books in Print*. Unfortunately, a good many of the works listed here are no longer in print in either hard- or softcover; hence some of these listings are offered to show where the trail ends.

In the section on Sixties fiction—which selection of works is of necessity highly subjective—I have taken the liberty of including several works that either predate or antedate the Sixties but that seem to me either to have found their proper audience and greatest influence in that decade or to represent the final flowering (or decay) of trends in the fiction of the Sixties. Only one foreign writer, Jorge Luis Borges, is included, and he because the publication of his two collections of stories in the early Sixties had such a profound influence on the direction American fiction writing was to take.

A final note: Anyone in search of the sensibility of the Sixties at its most articulate, or interested in tracing its survival and metamorphosis into the Seventies, should be sure to look at the superb paperback literary magazine *New American Review* (later titled simply *American Review*). Edited by Theodore Solotaroff with laudable and

intelligent openmindedness, NAR was preeminently a *writer's* magazine; it opened its pages to fiction, poetry, criticism and political and
cultural commentary by many of the American writers likely to be
remembered as the most talented and attuned of our time, and they
responded in many cases with their best work. The fact that for most
of its eleven years NAR took the form of a widely distributed
mass-market paperback says something important about the nature
and scope of literacy in the Sixties as well. There is little point in a
formal bibliographic listing of issues, since only certain university
libraries and used bookstores are likely to harbor copies; finding
*NARs* requires scrounging and luck. For the record, though, *New
American Review*, Nos. 1–10, were published in mass-market format
by New American Library from 1967 to 1970; Nos. 11–15 were
published in trade-paperback format by Simon & Schuster/ Touchstone from 1971 to 1972; and in its final incarnation, Nos. 16–26 were
published once again in mass-market format by Bantam, under the
revised title *American Review*, from 1973 until its demise in 1978
from financial woes.

## General

Renata Adler, *Toward a Radical Middle: Fourteen Pieces of
    Reporting and Criticism* (Random House, 1969; Vin-
    tage, 1970)
Jane Alpert, *Growing Up Underground* (Morrow, 1981)
Morris Dickstein, *Gates of Eden: American Culture in the
    Sixties* (Basic Books, 1977; paperback, 1978)
Harold Hayes, editor, *Smiling Through the Apocalypse:
    Esquire's History of the Sixties* (McCall Publishing, 1970;
    Delta, 1971)
Abbie Hoffman, *Revolution for the Hell of It* (Dial, 1968;
    Pocket, 1970)
    *Steal This Book* (Grove, 1971)
    *Soon to Be a Major Motion Picture* (Putnam's, 1980,
    hardcover and paperback)
Lynda Rosen Obst, editor; Robert Kingsbury, designer, *The
    Sixties* (Random House/Rolling Stone Press, 1977)
Jerry Rubin, *Do It! Scenarios of the Revolution* (Simon &
    Schuster, 1969; Ballantine, 1970)
Nora Sayre, *Sixties Going on Seventies* (Arbor House, 1973)
Gore Vidal, *Homage to Daniel Shays: Collected Essays,
    1952–1972* (Random House, 1972; Vintage, 1973)
Rex Weiner and Deanne Stillman, *Woodstock Census: The*

*Nationwide Survey of the Sixties Generation* (Viking, 1979; Fawcett, 1980)

**History and Politics**

James Baldwin, *Nobody Knows My Name* (Dial, 1961; Dell, 1970)
  *The Fire Next Time* (Dial, 1963; Dell, 1970)
Daniel Bell, *The End of Ideology: On the Exhaustion of Political Ideas in the Fifties*, revised edition (The Free Press, 1962)
Chester Bowles, *Promises to Keep: My Years in Public Life* (Harper and Row, 1971)
Eldridge Cleaver, *Soul on Ice* (McGraw Hill/Ramparts, 1968; Delta, 1970)
  *Eldridge Cleaver: Post-Prison Writings and Speeches*, Robert Scheer, editor (Random House/Ramparts, 1969)
*Columbia Spectator* staff, *Up Against the Ivy Wall* (Atheneum, 1969)
Joe Esterhazas and Michael D. Roberts, *Thirteen Seconds: Confrontation at Kent State* (Dodd, Mead, 1970)
Frantz Fanon, *Wretched of the Earth* (Grove Press, 1965; paperback, 1968)
  *Black Skin, White Masks* (Grove Press, 1967; paperback, 1970)
Frances FitzGerald, *Fire in the Lake: The Vietnamese and the Americans in Vietnam* (Random House, 1972; Vintage, 1973)
Marshall Frady, *Wallace*, revised edition (Meridian, 1976)
  *Southerners: A Journalist's Odyssey* (New American Library, 1980)
Betty Friedan, *The Feminine Mystique* (Norton, 1963; Dell, 1977)
Paul Goodman, *Growing Up Absurd* (Random House, 1960; Vintage, 1962)
  *Utopian Essays and Practical Proposals* (Random House, 1962; Vintage, 1963)
  *Compulsory Mis-Education* (Random House, 1964; Vintage, 1965)
  *People or Personnel* (Random House, 1965; Vintage, 1966)
  *New Reformation: Notes of a Neolithic Conservative* (Random House, 1970; Vintage, 1971)

  *Drawing the Line: The Political Essays of Paul Goodman,* Taylor Stoehr, editor (Free Life, 1977; Dutton, 1979)

David Halberstam, *The Making of a Quagmire* (Random House, 1965)
  *The Best and the Brightest* (Random House, 1972; Fawcett, 1973)

Michael Harrington, *The Other America: Poverty in the United States* (Macmillan, 1962, revised, 1970; Penguin, 1971)
  *Toward a Democratic Left* (Macmillan, 1968; Penguin, 1969)

James Herndon, *Way It Spozed to Be* (Simon & Schuster, 1968; Touchstone, 1977)
  *Survivor in Your Native Land* (Simon & Schuster, 1971; Touchstone, 1977)

Godfrey Hodgson, *America in Our Time: From WWII to Nixon—What Happened and Why* (Doubleday, 1976; Vintage, 1978)

John Holt, *How Children Fail* (Pitman, 1964; Dell, 1970)
  *How Children Learn* (Pitman, 1967; Dell, 1970)

Irving Howe, *Steady Work: Essays in the Politics of Democratic Radicalism* (Harcourt, Brace and World, 1966)

George Jackson, *Soledad Brothers* (Bantam, 1970)

Doris Kearns, *Lyndon Johnson and the American Dream* (Harper and Row, 1976; Signet, 1977)

John F. Kennedy, *The Strategy of Peace* (Harper and Row, 1960)
  *Inaugural Address* (Acropolis, 1965)

Robert F. Kennedy, *Thirteen Days: A Memoir of the Cuban Missile Crisis* (Norton, 1969; paper, 1971)
  *To Seek a Newer World* (Doubleday, 1969)

Kerner Commission, *Report of the National Advisory Commission on Civil Disorders* (Dutton, hardcover; Bantam, paperback, 1968)

Martin Luther King, Jr., *Why We Can't Wait* (Harper and Row, 1963; Mentor, 1964)
  *Where Do We Go from Here: Chaos or Community* (Harper and Row, 1967; Beacon Press, 1968)

Jonathan Kozol, *Death at an Early Age* (Houghton Mifflin, 1967; Bantam, 1968)

James Simon Kunen, *The Strawberry Statement: Notes of a*

*College Revolutionary* (Random House, 1969; Avon, 1970)

Louis Lomax, *The Negro Revolt* (Harper and Row, 1962; Mentor, 1963)

Alasadair MacIntyre, *Herbert Marcuse* (Viking, 1970)

Norman Mailer, *The Armies of the Night* (New American Library, 1968; Signet, 1970)

*Miami and the Siege of Chicago* (Signet, 1968)

Malcolm X, *The Autobiography of Malcolm X* (Grove Press, 1965; Ballantine, 1977)

*Malcolm X Speaks* (Path Press, 1976; Grove Press, 1978)

William Manchester, *Death of a President* (Harper and Row, 1967; Penguin, 1977)

Herbert Marcuse, *Eros and Civilization* (Beacon Press, 1955; paperback, 1974)

*One-Dimensional Man* (Beacon Press, 1964; paperback, 1966)

*A Critique of Pure Tolerance*, with Robert Paul Wolf and Barrington Moore, Jr. (Beacon Press, 1965)

*An Essay on Liberation* (Beacon Press, 1969)

Kate Millett, *Sexual Politics* (Doubleday, 1970; Avon, 1971)

C. Wright Mills, *White Collar* (Oxford University Press, 1951; paperback, 1956)

*The Power Elite* (Oxford University Press, 1956; paperback, 1959)

*The Causes of World War Three* (Oxford University Press, 1958)

*Listen, Yankee: The Revolution in Cuba* (Oxford University Press, 1960)

*Sociological Imagination* (Oxford University Press, 1959; paperback, 1967)

*Power, Politics and People: The Collected Essays of C. Wright Mills*, Irving Louis Horowitz, editor (Oxford University Press, 1963; paperback, 1967)

Charles Morris, *The Cost of Good Intentions: New York City and the Liberal Experiment* (Norton, 1980; McGraw Hill, 1981)

Carl Oglesby, editor, *The New Left Reader* (Grove Press, 1969)

Norman Podhoretz, *Doings and Undoings* (Farrar, Straus and Giroux, 1964)

*Making It* (Random House, 1968)

*Breaking Ranks: A Political Memoir* (Harper and Row, 1979; paperback, 1980)

Howell Raines, *My Soul Is Rested: Movement Days in the Deep South Remembered* (Putnam's, 1977; Bantam, 1978)

Kirkpatrick Sale, *SDS* (Random House, 1973; Vintage, 1974)

Arthur Schlesinger, Jr., *A Thousand Days* (Houghton Mifflin, 1965; Fawcett, 1977)
   *Violence: America in the Sixties* (Signet Broadside, 1968)
   *Robert F. Kennedy and His Times* (Houghton Mifflin, 1978; Ballantine, 1979)

Sargent Shriver, *Point of the Lance* (Harper and Row, 1965)

Charles Silberman, *Crisis in Black and White* (Random House and Vintage, 1964)
   *Crisis in the Classroom: The Remaking of American Education* (Random House, 1970; Vintage, 1971)

Theodore Sorenson, *Kennedy* (Harper and Row, 1965)

I. F. Stone, *Polemics and Prophecies 1967–1970* (Random House, 1971; Vintage, 1972)
   *I. F. Stone Weekly Reader*, Neil Middleton, editor (Vintage, 1974)

Milton Viorst, *Fire in the Streets* (Simon & Schuster, 1980; Touchstone, 1981)

Gary Wills, *Nixon Agonistes: The Crisis of the Self-Made Man* (Houghton Mifflin, 1970; Mentor, 1971, revised edition, 1979)

Harris Wofford, *Of Kennedys and Kings: Making Sense of the Sixties* (Farrar, Straus and Giroux, 1980)

Theodore H. White, *The Making of the President 1960* (Atheneum, 1961; Mentor, 1967)
   *The Making of the President 1964* (Atheneum, 1965; Mentor, 1966)
   *The Making of the President 1968* (Atheneum, 1969; Pocket, 1970)

Tom Wolfe, *Radical Chic and Mau-mauing the Flak Catchers* (Farrar, Straus and Giroux, 1970; Bantam, 1971)

**New Sensibilities**

Gene Anthony, *The Summer of Love* (Celestial Arts, 1980)

Norman O. Brown, *Life Against Death: The Psychoanalytic*

*Meaning of History* (Wesleyan University Press, 1959; Vintage, 1960)

*Love's Body* (Random House, 1966; Vintage, 1968)

*Closing Time* (Random House, 1973; Vintage, 1974)

George Dennison, *The Lives of Children* (Random House, 1969; Vintage, 1970)

Joan Didion, *Slouching Towards Bethlehem* (Farrar, Straus and Giroux, 1968; Washington Square Press, 1980)

*The White Album* (Simon & Schuster, 1979; Pocket, 1980)

Nora Ephron, *Wallflower at the Orgy* (Viking, 1971; Bantam, 1980)

Allen Ginsberg, *Howl* (City Lights, 1956)

*Kaddish and Other Poems 1958–1960* (City Lights, 1961)

*Planet News 1961–1967* (City Lights, 1968)

Emmett Grogan, *Ringolevio: A Life Played for Keeps* (Little, Brown, 1972; Avon, 1973)

Dennis Hale and Jonathan Eisen, editors, *The California Dream* (Macmillan, 1968; paperback, 1969)

Jane Kramer, *Allen Ginsberg in America* (Random House, 1969; Vintage, 1970)

R. D. Laing, *The Divided Self* (Penguin, 1965)

*The Politics of Experience* (Pantheon, 1967; Penguin, 1979)

Anthony Lukas, *Don't Shoot—We Are Your Children* (Random House, 1971; Delta, 1973)

Norman Mailer, *Advertisements for Myself* (Putnam's, 1959; Berkley, 1963)

*Presidential Papers* (Putnam's, 1963; Berkley, 1964)

*Cannibals and Christians* (Dial, 1966; Pinnacle, 1981)

*Existential Errands* (Little, Brown, 1971; Signet, 1973)

*Of a Fire on the Moon* (Little, Brown and Signet, 1971)

Charles Reich, *The Greening of America* (Random House, 1970; Bantam, 1971)

Paul Robinson, *The Freudian Left* (Harper and Row, 1969)

Theodore Roszak, *The Making of a CounterCulture* (Anchor, 1969; also in paperback)

*Where the Wasteland Ends: Politics and Transcendence in Post-Industrial Society* (Anchor, 1973; also in paperback)

Hunter Thompson, *Hell's Angels* (Random House, 1966; Ballantine, 1967)

*Fear and Loathing in Las Vegas* (Random House, 1972; Popular Library, 1973)

Marco Vassi, *The Stoned Apocalypse* (Trident Press, 1972)

Tom Wolfe, *The Kandy-Kolored Tangerine-Flake Streamline Baby* (Farrar, Straus and Giroux, 1965; also in Noonday paperback)
*The Electric Kool-Aid Acid Test* (Farrar, Straus and Giroux, 1968; Bantam, 1969)
*The Pump House Gang* (Farrar, Straus and Giroux, 1968; Bantam, 1969)

## Literary Criticism

Leslie Fiedler, *Love and Death in the American Novel* (Stein and Day, 1960, revised edition, 1967; paperback, 1975)
*Waiting for the End* (Stein and Day, 1964; paperback, 1969)
*Return of the Vanishing American* (Stein and Day, 1969; paperback, 1970).
*Cross the Border—Close the Gap* (Stein and Day, 1969; paperback, 1970)

William Gass, *Fiction and the Figures of Life* (Knopf, 1971; Godine, 1978)

Richard Gilman, *The Confusion of Realms* (Random House, 1969)
*Common and Uncommon Masks: Writings on the Theatre 1960–1970* (Random House, 1971; Vintage, 1972)

Irving Howe, *The Decline of the New* (Harcourt Brace Jovanovich, 1970)
*The Critical Point* (Horizon Press, 1973; Delta, 1975)

Alfred Kazin, *Bright Book of Life* (Little, Brown, 1973; Delta, 1974)

Marcus Klein, *The American Novel Since World War II* (Fawcett, 1969)

Jerome Klinkowitz and John Somer, editors, *The Vonnegut Statement* (Delta, 1973)

Richard Kostelanetz, *On Contemporary Literature* (Avon, 1968)

Frank McConnell, *Four Postwar American Novelists: Bellow, Mailer, Barth, and Pynchon* (University of Chicago Press, 1978; paperback, 1979)

Richard Poirier, *The Performing Self* (Oxford University Press, 1971; also in paperback)
   *Norman Mailer* (Viking, 1972)
Philip Roth, *Reading Myself and Others* (Farrar, Straus and Giroux, 1975; also in paperback)
Wilfrid Sheed, *The Morning After: Selected Essays and Reviews* (Farrar, Straus and Giroux, 1971)
Theodore Solotaroff, *The Red Hot Vacuum and Other Pieces on the Writing of the Sixties* (Atheneum, 1970; Godine, 1979)
Susan Sontag, *Against Interpretation* (Farrar, Straus and Giroux, 1966; Delta, 1978)
   *Styles of Radical Will* (Farrar, Straus and Giroux, 1969; Delta, 1978)
Tony Tanner, *City of Words: American Fiction 1950–1970* (Harper and Row, 1971)
Diana Trilling, *We Must March, My Darlings* (Harcourt Brace Jovanovich, 1977)


**Fiction**

James Baldwin, *Another Country* (Dial, 1962; Dell, 1963)
   *Go Tell It on the Mountain* (Dial, 1963; Dell, 1970)
   *Tell Me How Long the Train's Been Gone* (Dial, 1968; Dell, 1969)
John Barth, *The Sot-Weed Factor* (Doubleday, 1960; Bantam, 1969)
   *Giles Goat-Boy* (Doubleday, 1966; Fawcett, 1967)
   *Lost in the Funhouse* (Doubleday, 1969; Bantam, 1970)
Donald Barthelme, *Come Back, Dr. Caligari* (Little, Brown Atlantic Monthly Press, 1964; paperback, 1971)
   *Snow White* (Atheneum, 1967; also in paperback)
   *Unspeakable Practices, Unnatural Acts* (Farrar, Straus and Giroux, 1968; Pocket, 1976)
   *City Life* (Farrar, Straus and Giroux, 1970; Pocket, 1976)
Joe David Bellamy, *Superfiction, or the American Story Transformed* (Vintage, 1975)
Saul Bellow, *Henderson the Rain King* (Viking, 1959; Penguin, Avon, 1976)
   *Herzog* (Viking, 1964; Penguin, 1972; Avon, 1976)
   *Mosby's Memoirs and Other Stories* (Viking, 1968; Penguin, 1977)
   *Mr. Sammler's Planet* (Viking, 1969; Penguin, 1977)

Thomas Berger, *Crazy in Berlin* (Scribner's, 1958; Ballantine, 1978)

> *Reinehart in Love* (Scribner's, 1962; Ballantine, 1978)
> *Little Big Man* (Dial, 1964; Fawcett, 1978)
> *Vital Parts* (R. W. Baron, 1969; Ballantine, 1978)

Jorge Luis Borges, *Ficciones* (Grove Press, 1962)

> *Labyrinths* (New Directions, 1962)

Richard Brautigan, *A Confederate General from Big Sur* (Grove Press, 1964; Dell, 1979)

> *Trout Fishing in America* (Four Seasons Foundation, 1967; Dell, 1969)

William Burroughs, *Naked Lunch* (Grove Press, 1962)

> *The Nova Express* (Grove Press, 1964)
> *The Soft Machine* (Grove Press, 1966)
> *The Ticket That Exploded* (Grove Press, 1967)

John Cheever, *Some People, Places, and Things That Will Not Appear in My Next Novel* (Harper and Row, 1961)

> *The Brigadier and the Golf Widow* (Harper and Row, 1964)
> *The Wapshot Scandal* (Harper and Row, 1964; paperback, 1973)
> *Bullet Park* (Knopf, 1969; Bantam, 1970)

Robert Coover, *The Origin of the Brunists* (Putnam's, 1966; Bantam, 1979)

> *The Universal Baseball Association, Inc., J. Henry Waugh, Prop.* (Random House, 1968; Plume, 1971)
> *Pricksongs and Descants* (Dutton, 1969; Plume, 1970)

Joan Didion, *Run River* (Obolensky, 1963; Pocket, 1980)

> *Play It as It Lays* (Farrar, Straus and Giroux, 1970; Pocket, 1980)

E. L. Doctorow, *Welcome to Hard Times* (Simon & Schuster, 1960; Bantam, 1976)

> *The Book of Daniel* (Random House, 1971; Bantam, 1979)

Stanley Elkin, *Boswell* (Random House, 1964; Warner, 1980)

> *Criers and Kibitzers, Kibitzers and Criers* (Random House, 1965; Plume, 1973)
> *A Bad Man* (Random House, 1967; Warner, 1980)
> *The Dick Gibson Show* (Random House, 1970; Warner, 1980)

Richard Fariña, *Been Down So Long It Looks Like Up to Me* (Random House, 1966; Dell, 1971)

William Gaddis, *The Recognitions* (Harcourt Brace and World, 1955; Avon, 1975)

William Gass, *Omensetter's Luck* (World, 1966; Meridian, 1969)
*In the Heart of the Heart of the Country* (Harper and Row, 1968; Pocket, 1977)
*Willie Master's Lonesome Wife* (Northwestern University Press, 1968)

John Hawkes, *The Lime Twig* (New Directions, 1960)
*Second Skin* (New Directions, 1964)

Joseph Heller, *Catch-22* (Simon & Schuster, 1961; Dell, 1970)

Ken Kesey, *One Flew Over the Cuckoo's Nest* (Viking, 1962; Signet, 1963; Penguin, 1977)
*Sometimes a Great Notion* (Viking, 1964; Bantam, 1965; Penguin, 1977)

Norman Mailer, *An American Dream* (Dial, 1964; Dell, 1966)
*Why Are We in Vietnam?* (Putnam's, 1967; Berkley, 1977)

Bernard Malamud, *A New Life* (Farrar, Straus and Giroux, 1961; Avon, 1980)
*The Fixer* (Farrar, Straus and Giroux, 1966; Pocket, 1975)
*Pictures of Fidelman* (Farrar, Straus and Giroux, 1968; Pocket, 1975)

Harry Matthews, *The Conversions* (Doubleday, 1962)
*Tlooth* (Doubleday, 1966)
*The Sinking of the Odradek Stadium and Other Novels* (includes *The Conversions* and *Tlooth*) (Harper and Row, 1975, hardcover and paperback)

Thomas McGuane, *The Sporting Club* (Doubleday, 1969; Penguin, 1979)

Leonard Michaels, *Going Places* (Farrar, Straus and Giroux, 1969; Plume, 1971)
*I Would Have Saved Them If I Could* (Farrar, Straus and Giroux, 1975; Bantam, 1976)

Vladimir Nabokov, *Pale Fire* (Putnam's, 1962; Perigee, 1980)
*Ada* (McGraw Hill, 1969; paperback, 1980)

Flannery O'Connor, *Everything That Rises Must Converge* (Farrar, Straus and Giroux, 1965; Noonday paperback)

Grace Paley, *The Little Disturbances of Man* (Doubleday, 1959; Plume, 1973)
  *Enormous Changes at the Last Minute* (Farrar, Straus and Giroux, 1974; Noonday paperback, 1979)
Walker Percy, *The Movie-Goer* (Knopf, 1961; Avon, 1980)
  *The Last Gentleman* (Farrar, Straus and Giroux, 1966; Avon, 1978)
Thomas Pynchon, *V.*(Lippincott, 1961; Bantam, 1968)
  *The Crying of Lot 49* (Lippincott, 1966; Bantam, 1967)
  *Gravity's Rainbow* (Viking hardcover and trade paperback, 1973; Bantam, 1974)
Ishmael Reed, *The Free-lance Pallbearers* (Doubleday, 1967; Avon, 1976)
  *Yellow Back Radio Broke Down* (Doubleday, 1969; Avon, 1977)
Philip Roth, *Goodbye, Columbus* (Houghton Mifflin, 1959; Bantam, 1970)
  *Letting Go* (Random House, 1962; Bantam, 1963)
  *When She Was Good* (Random House, 1967; Bantam, 1968)
  *Portnoy's Complaint* (Random House, 1969; Bantam, 1972)
Hubert Selby, Jr., *Last Exit to Brooklyn* (Grove Press, 1964)
Susan Sontag, *The Benefactor* (Farrar, Straus and Giroux, 1963; Dell, 1978)
  *Death Kit* (Farrar, Straus and Giroux, 1967; Noonday paperback)
Terry Southern, *The Magic Christian* (Random House, 1960; Bantam, 1964)
  *Candy* (with Mason Hoffenberg) (Putnam's, 1964; Dell, 1965)
  *Red-Dirt Marijuana* (Signet, 1971)
Robert Stone, *A Hall of Mirrors* (Houghton Mifflin, 1966; Ballantine, 1975)
  *Dog Soldiers* (Houghton Mifflin, 1974; Ballantine, 1975)
William Styron, *Confessions of Nat Turner* (Random House, 1967; Signet, 1968)
Ronald Sukenick, *Up* (Dial, 1968; Delta, 1970)

*The Death of the Novel and Other Stories* (Dial, 1969)
*98.6* (Fiction Collective, 1975)

John Updike, *Rabbit, Run* (Knopf, 1960; Fawcett, 1978)
 *The Centaur* (Knopf, 1963; Fawcett, 1978)
 *Of the Farm* (Knopf, 1965; Fawcett, 1977)
 *Couples* (Knopf, 1968; Fawcett, 1975)
 *Bech: A Book* (Knopf, 1970; Vintage, 1980)
 *Rabbit Redux* (Knopf, 1970; Fawcett, 1977)

Kurt Vonnegut, Jr., *Player Piano* (Holt, 1952; Avon, 1967)
 *Sirens of Titan* (Houghton Mifflin, 1959; Dell, 1974)
 *Mother Night* (Harper and Row, 1961; Dell, 1974)
 *Cat's Cradle* (Holt, 1963; Delta, 1974)
 *God Bless You, Mr. Rosewater* (Holt, 1964; Dell, 1974)
 *Slaughterhouse-Five* (Delacorte, 1969; Delta, 1970)

## Theater, Music and the Visual Arts

Jerome Agel, *The Making of Kubrick's 2001* (Signet, 1970)

Gregory Battcock, *The New Art*, revised edition (Dutton, 1973)
 *Minimal Art* (Dutton, 1968)

Lenny Bruce, *The Essential Lenny Bruce*, John Cohen, editor (Ballantine, 1967)
 *How to Talk Dirty and Influence People* (Trident Press, 1967; Playboy Books, 1978)

Robert Brustein, *The Third Theatre* (Knopf, 1969; Touchstone, 1970)
 *Revolution as Theatre: Essays on Radical Style* (Liveright, 1970)

Nicolas Calas and Elena Calas, *Icons and Images of the Sixties* (Dutton, 1971)

Robert Christgau, *Any Old Way You Choose It* (Penguin, 1973)

Nik Cohn, *Rock from the Beginning* (Stein and Day, 1969; Pocket, 1970)

Hunter Davies, *The Beatles*, revised edition (McGraw Hill, 1978)

Pierre Diner, *The Living Theatre* (Horizon Press, 1972)

Jonathan Eisen, editor, *The Age of Rock: Sounds of the American Cultural Revolution* (Vintage, 1970)

Albert Goldman and Lawrence Schiller, *Ladies and Gentlemen, Lenny Bruce!!!* (Random House, 1974; Ballantine, 1975)

Richard Goldstein, *Goldstein's Greatest Hits* (Prentice Hall, 1970)

Pauline Kael, *I Lost It at the Movies* (Atlantic Monthly Press, 1965; also in paperback)
*Kiss Kiss Bang Bang* (Atlantic Monthly Press, 1968; also in paperback)
*Going Steady* (Atlantic Monthly Press, 1970; also in paperback)
*Deeper Into Movies* (Atlantic Monthly Press, 1973; also in paperback)

Stanley Kauffman, *A World on Film* (Harper and Row, 1966; Delta, 1967)

Michael Kirby, *Happenings: An Illustrated Anthology* (Dutton, 1965)

Judith Malina, *The Enormous Despair* (Random House, 1972)

Wilfrid Mellers, *Twilight of the Gods: The Music of the Beatles* (Viking, 1973)

Harold Rosenberg, *The De-Definition of Art* (Macmillan, 1972; paperback, 1973)
*Discovering the Present: Three Decades in Art, Culture, and Politics* (University of Chicago Press, 1973, hardcover and paperback)

Anthony Scaduto, *Bob Dylan* (Signet, 1973)

John Simon, *Singularities: Essays on the Theatre, 1964–1975* (Random House, 1975)

Calvin Tomkins, *The Bride and the Bachelors: Five Masters of the Avant-Garde* (Viking, 1965; Penguin, 1975, with expanded text)
*The Scene: Reports on Post-Modern Art* (Viking, 1976)
*Off the Wall: Robert Rauschenberg and the Art World of Our Time* (Doubleday, 1980; Penguin, 1981)

Parker Tyler, *Underground Film: A Critical History* (Grove Press, 1969)

Alexander Walker, *Stanley Kubrick Directs*, expanded edition (Harvest, 1972)

Andy Warhol, *The Philosophy of Andy Warhol, From A to B*

*and Back Again* (Harcourt Brace Jovanovich, 1975; Harvest, 1977)

with Pat Hackett, *POPism: The Warhol '60s* (Harcourt Brace Jovanovich, 1980)

Tom Wolfe, *The Painted Word* (Farrar, Straus and Giroux, 1975; Bantam, 1976)

## Media

Robert Sam Anson, *Gone Crazy and Back Again: The Rise and Fall of the* Rolling Stone *Generation* (Doubleday, 1981)

Michael Arlen, *Living Room War* (Viking, 1969)

Todd Gitlin, *The Whole World Is Watching: Mass Media in the Making and Unmaking of the New Left* (University of California Press, 1980; paperback, 1981)

David Halberstam, *The Powers That Be* (Knopf, 1979; Dell, 1980)

Michael Herr, *Dispatches* (Knopf, 1977; Avon, 1978)

Warren Hinckle, *If You Have a Lemon, Make Lemonade* (Putnam's, 1974)

George Lois with Bill Pitts, *George, Be Careful* (Saturday Review Press, 1972)

Joe McGinniss, *The Selling of the President 1968* (Trident Press, 1969; Pocket, 1970)

Marshall McLuhan, *The Mechanical Bride: Folklore of Industrial Man* (Vanguard Press, 1951; Beacon, 1967)
*Gutenberg Galaxy: The Making of Typographic Man* (University of Toronto Press, 1962)
*Understanding Media: The Extensions of Man* (McGraw Hill, 1964; Mentor, 1965)
*The Medium Is the Massage* (Bantam, 1967)
*Counterblast* (Harcourt Brace Jovanovich, 1969; Harvest, 1970)
*Culture Is Our Business* (McGraw Hill, 1970)

Raymond Mungo, *Famous Long Ago: My Life and Hard Times with Liberation News Service* (Beacon Press, 1970; available in Avon collection, *Mungobus)*

Raymond Rosenthal, editor, *McLuhan Pro and Con* (Funk and Wagnalls, 1968; Pelican, 1969)

Gerald Stearns, editor, *McLuhan Hot and Cold* (Dial, 1967; Mentor, 1968)

Gay Talese, *The Kingdom and the Power* (World, 1969; Anchor, 1978)

Tom Wolfe and E. W. Johnson, editors, *The New Journalism* (Harper and Row, 1973)

**Miscellaneous**

Truman Capote, *In Cold Blood* (Random House, 1965; Signet, 1966)

Frank Conroy, *Stop-Time* (Viking, 1967; Penguin, 1977)

Fred Exley, *A Fan's Notes* (Harper and Row, 1968; Washington Square Press, 1980)